The Bible, Homer, and the
for Meaning in Ancient Myths

MW00785286

The Bible, Homer, and the Search for Meaning in Ancient Myths explores and compares the most influential sets of divine myths in Western culture: the Homeric pantheon and Yahweh, the God of the Old Testament. Heath argues not only that the God of the Old Testament bears a striking resemblance to the Olympians, but also that the Homeric system rejected by the Judeo-Christian tradition offers a better model for the human condition. The universe depicted by Homer and populated by his gods is one that creates a unique and powerful responsibility – almost directly counter to that evoked by the Bible – for humans to discover ethical norms, accept death as a necessary human limit, develop compassion to mitigate a tragic existence, appreciate frankly both the glory and dangers of sex, and embrace and respond courageously to an indifferent universe that was clearly not designed for human dominion.

Heath builds on recent work in biblical and classical studies to examine the contemporary value of mythical deities. Judeo-Christian theologians over the millennia have tried to explain away Yahweh's Olympian nature while dismissing the Homeric deities for the same reason Greek philosophers abandoned them: They don't live up to preconceptions of what a deity should be. In particular, the Homeric gods are disappointingly plural, anthropomorphic, and amoral (at best). But Heath argues that Homer's polytheistic apparatus challenges us to live meaningfully *without any help from the divine*. In other words, to live well in Homer's tragic world – an insight gleaned by Achilles, the hero of the *Iliad* – *one must live as if there were no gods at all*.

The Bible, Homer, and the Search for Meaning in Ancient Myths should change the conversation academics in classics, biblical studies, theology, and philosophy have – especially between disciplines – about the gods of early Greek epic, while reframing on a more popular level the discussion of the role of ancient myth in shaping a thoughtful life.

John Heath is Professor of Classics at Santa Clara University, USA. His previous books include a study of the literary adaptations of classical myth (*Actaeon, the Unmannerly Intruder*, 1992), a popular defense of the study of classics (*Who Killed Homer?* coauthored with Victor Davis Hanson, 1998), an examination of the links between speech, animalization, and status in Greek literature and society (*The Talking Greeks*, 2005), and an exploration of the common themes underlying American bestselling books (*Why We Read What We Read*, coauthored with Lisa Adams, 2007).

Routledge Monographs in Classical Studies

For more information on this series, visit: www.routledge.com/classicalstudies/
series/RMCS

The Bible, Homer, and the Search for Meaning in Ancient Myths

Why We Would Be Better Off
With Homer's Gods

John Heath

Routledge
Taylor & Francis Group

LONDON AND NEW YORK

First published 2019
by Routledge
2 Park Square, Milton Park, Abingdon, Oxon OX14 4RN

and by Routledge
605 Third Avenue, New York, NY 10017

First issued in paperback 2020

Routledge is an imprint of the Taylor & Francis Group, an informa business

British Library Cataloguing-in-Publication Data
A catalogue record for this book is available from the British Library

Library of Congress Cataloging-in-Publication Data
Names: Heath, John, 1955– author.
Title: The Bible, Homer, and the search for meaning in ancient myths :
    why we would be better off with Homer's gods / John Heath.
Description: 1 [edition]. | New York : Routledge, 2019. | Series: Routledge
    monographs in classical studies | Includes bibliographical references
    and index.
Identifiers: LCCN 2018060248 (print) | LCCN 2019011222 (ebook) |
    ISBN 9780429022340 (ebook) | ISBN 9780429666469 (web pdf) |
    ISBN 9780429661020 (mobi/kindle) | ISBN 9780429663741 (epub) |
    ISBN 9780367077204 (hardback : alk. paper)
Subjects: LCSH: God. | Homer. | Gods, Greek. | God—Biblical teaching. |
    Bible. Old Testament—Criticism, interpretation, etc.
Classification: LCC BL473 (ebook) | LCC BL473 .H43 2019 (print) |
    DDC 292.2/11—dc23
LC record available at https://lccn.loc.gov/2018060248

ISBN 13: 978-0-367-72992-9 (pbk)
ISBN 13: 978-0-367-07720-4 (hbk)

Typeset in Times New Roman
by Apex CoVantage, LLC

For Lisa, without whom, nothing.

Contents

Preface

A man said to the universe:
"Sir, I exist!"
"However," replied the universe,
"The fact has not created in me
A sense of obligation."
                    — Stephen Crane

My mother was a failed Episcopalian, and my father a successful agnostic, so I had the good fortune to be raised a "none," as the pollsters would now label it. If we had a "higher power" to venerate, it was perhaps the ocean. We spent hours contemplating the grand indifference of the Pacific from the cliffs behind the southern California beach where we spent my childhood summers. It wasn't reverence, but more a deference to the inscrutable expanse of the water and tireless variety of the waves. (My father, an amateur astronomer, felt the same way about outer space, his study plastered with photos from the Hubble telescope.) But as for belief in a divine being of some sort, most of my family seems to have missed out on the "god" gene. (Yes, I know there is no literal "god" gene. Settle down.) So while my professional life has often focused on the very secular task of analyzing ancient literary depictions of the gods, it has always puzzled me personally why so many Americans put so much value in one particular textual divinity over another. They all looked pretty much alike to me, and where they differed, it seemed obvious (but to me alone?) that the Homeric gods had far more to offer. This book is my effort to suggest that my perplexity was well-founded.

Just a couple notes here on choices I have made in writing *The Bible, Homer, and the Search for Meaning in Ancient Myths*. I hope this book will change the conversation academics (classicists, Homerists, biblical scholars, theologians, philosophers) have – especially between disciplines – about the gods of early Greek epic while reframing on a more popular level the discussion of the role of ancient myth in shaping a thoughtful life. It is aimed at readers interested in comparative religion, Greek mythology, Homer's epics, the Bible, or a humanistic approach to living. I have explained concepts and terms and supplied the necessary background as we go along and have included appendices that outline the epics and the characteristics of the Homeric gods. I provide translations for all non-English texts. Translations from Homeric and Classical Greek (and occasional Latin or German) are mine. I have tried to capture the basic sense of the Homeric passages – I make no claims to any elegance. I read the New Testament in the original Greek, but here I have presented the translations for both the New Testament and the Tanakh from the NRSV (*New Revised Standard Version*) unless otherwise noted. My study of the Hebrew Bible has been a combination of a careful reading in translation (using several), the use of numerous commentaries, and the consultation of many scholarly books and articles. I have supported my discussion of Yahweh in particular with constant reference to these secondary sources. It has been my experience when teaching this material that we will happily believe just about anything about the Homeric gods, but we need to be slightly overwhelmed with evidence before our personal religious assumptions (if not our beliefs) can be nudged out of our comfort zone. I have nevertheless tried not to let citations of secondary material overwhelm my argument, and I refer almost entirely to scholarship in English, as I hope general readers and students will turn to some of this material for further reading.

It will be noted that I am using Tanakh and Hebrew Bible (and even Bible when the context is unambiguous) to refer to what most readers will consider to be the Old Testament. The label "Old Testament" is a Christian invention, not intended as a compliment. While some scholars insist "old" means "venerable," this argument is at least partially insincere. The "New" Testament itself insists that Jesus has a "*more excellent* ministry" and is "the mediator of a *better* covenant, which has been enacted through *better* promises. For if that first covenant had been faultless, there would have been no need to look for a second one. . . . In speaking of a 'new covenant,' he has *made the first one obsolete. And what is obsolete and growing old will soon disappear*" (Heb 8:6–7,13, my emphasis; cf. 10:9). There have been sporadic efforts to use terms with less historical baggage, such as "First Testament" and "Second Testament," but besides the ungainliness, the connotations of priority and quality remain (only reversed).

For that matter, the term "Hebrew Bible" is redundant from a Jewish perspective, since in that tradition there is no other Bible. It is also true that the two terms Hebrew Bible and Old Testament are not synonymous. The Hebrew Bible has a different arrangement and division of books than Protestant Bibles (24 in the former, 39 in the latter), but their content is the same. Catholic Bibles include additional material (46 books), the Eastern Orthodox even more (51). Tanakh is a later Hebrew acronym for the three divisions of their Bible: Torah (Teaching), Nevi'im (Prophets), and Ketuvim (Writings). This contrasts with the four or five divisions (same material, different arrangement: Pentateuch, Historical, Poetical, Prophets, both major and minor) of the Protestant Bible I will be quoting from throughout this book. So by using the NRSV – an "ecumenical" translation but one that derives ultimately from the Protestant tradition of the King James Bible – I'm being a bit disingenuous by referring to it as the Tanakh or Hebrew Bible. But I hope we can agree to live with that. The New Testament remains the New Testament, since Christians can call the collection of their own stories of the divine whatever they wish.

Acknowledgments

I might as well get this out there right away – the fact that the following people helped me in all sorts of ways does not mean that they are at all responsible for me or the content of this book. And this includes the hundreds of scholars whose nuanced interpretations I have put to use in less subtle fashion to support arguments they may want no part of.

My colleague Dan Turkeltaub read a draft of the entire manuscript; Eliot Wirshbo slogged through an even earlier version. They both made many valuable suggestions, especially about the Homeric epics. Bill Greenwalt and Nora Chapman also provided helpful comments on parts or large chunks of various drafts. Funded by a Dean's grant, Mitchell Hart organized my preliminary and unwieldy bibliography. I owe all of these folks – who oddly remain my friends – a great debt of gratitude.

I especially want to thank those brave students at Santa Clara who took a chance on my Honors seminar, "Living With Zeus," during which we worked through a lot of the ideas that you will find here. I think the students at our Jesuit university provide a fair cross-section of intelligent if poorly informed (religiously) Americans. They are bright, relativistic in general but perhaps a tiny bit more devout than many in their demographic, as nearly 50 percent of them are Catholic and many come from Catholic high schools. This background also pretty much guarantees that their preconceptions are innocent of any direct exposure to the Bible. What they think they know about God (or the gods) comes from their families, teachers, communities, and priests – in other words, usually through a reasonably harmless and often failed inculcation in dogma rather than as the result of any critical reading of texts. The seminars were a delight (for me, at least) and an eye-opener for all of us.

And then there's my family. My two daughters assisted in their own ways. During the years I worked on this project, the elder one went to and graduated from college and is now heading off to become an unemployed journalist. Her flair for nonfiction writing and her positive determination are a constant source of inspiration. My younger daughter has put up with her father's focus on the computer keyboard for most of her life, her (semi-)innocent refrain helping me keep my priorities (semi-)straight: "Whatcha doin', Dad? STILL working on that book?" And to my wife, Lisa, to whom this book is dedicated, I owe pretty much everything. We have spent decades talking about these topics. A Homerophile herself, she read, commented on, and edited every manifestation of the manuscript. Next time it will be easier just to have her write it.

1 Introduction

If the man doesn't believe as we do, we say he is a crank, and that settles it. I mean,
it does nowadays, because now we can't burn him.
                                        – Mark Twain (*Following the Equator*)

The marble building that serves as home for the United States Supreme Court
presents to the attentive visitor numerous artistic representations on the pedi-
ments, friezes, doors, and medallions. Most of these symbolize the historical
development of the Western legal system, a progressive scheme that apparently
culminates in the Supreme Court itself. Scores of individuals are represented,
from ethereal abstractions like Wisdom, Justice, and "Liberty Enthroned" to the
rather more substantial Chief Justice William Howard Taft. On the north and
south friezes, sculptor Adolph A. Weinman created in bas-relief eighteen historically significant lawgivers. Greeks (e.g., Lycurgus, Solon, Plato, Aristotle, Dem-
osthenes) and Romans (e.g., Cicero, Octavian, Gaius – the jurist, not the psychotic
emperor better known as Caligula) predominate, but in the 1930s architect Cass
Gilbert commissioned a remarkably multicultural gallery. The Egyptian King
Menes appears, as do Hammurabi, Solomon, Confucius, and Napoleon. On the
north wall frieze, between Justinian and Charlemagne, stands Muhammad holding the Qur'an.

Let's give that a moment to sink in.

It's fun to try to imagine the cataclysm such inclusivity would engender today.
First – do Muslims know about this? Well, yes. In 1997, a coalition of Muslim
groups petitioned to have the figure sandblasted. The sculpture violated a not-
quite-consistent Islamic prohibition of visual representations of their prophet.
The carved figure of Muhammad also carries a scimitar in his right hand, thus
(according to the complainants) reinforcing "long-held stereotypes of Muslims as
intolerant conquerors."

Chief Justice Rehnquist denied the petition, noting that the depiction was "not
intended as a form of idol worship." Besides, he added, there were lots of other
swords on the friezes. He did have the official building documents and tour-
ist pamphlets change their previous identification of Muhammad as "Founder
of Islam" to "Prophet of Islam," as the petition had requested. These official

publications also added a note of explanation still retained on the official web site of the Supreme Court: "The figure above is a well-intentioned attempt by the sculptor, Adolph Weinman, to honor Muhammad and it bears no resemblance to Muhammad."

And what about Congress, who authorized funding for the building so long ago that this government project actually came in *under* budget? Picture the present-day scandal should it turn out that tax dollars went to an artist who put the Prophet of Islam on an iconic American building! There aren't enough travel bans in the world to deal with this threat to our freedom.

Slipping by completely unnoticed, however, has been the actual affront to the U.S. Constitution. Although Moses with the Ten Commandments appears several times on and in the building, the architect was careful to place him in a secular context with other international lawgivers. The tablets themselves do not display the first four distinctively religious commandments, but portray either the essentially temporal injunctions (e.g., "You shall not steal") in Hebrew, which of course very few visitors can read, or merely the Roman numerals I-X (which some have argued refers to the Bill of Rights!), or nothing at all (Coogan 2014:128–9). Yahweh is not shown on Mt. Sinai handing over the two tablets to Moses – the Jewish leader is the star, not God. I doubt God's absence from this 1930s building has anything to do with congressional concern for *Jewish* sensitivities to the artistic depiction of God. Rather, Yahweh is missing because of course *no* divinities could possibly be displayed on a building designed for a judiciary sworn to uphold the Establishment Clause of the First Amendment.

But wait – what are we to make of the deities depicted on the ornamental metopes in the Great Hall? These gods – each appearing eight times – are classical deities: Minerva ("Goddess of Wisdom," the architect's notes inform us); Juno ("Genius of Womanhood and Guardian of Female Sex"); Mercury ("Herald and Messenger of the Gods"); and Zeus ("Father of Gods and Men; God of Heavens and Fertility"). Sure, a classicist might quibble with a few things. For example, Juno does oversee certain aspects of a woman's social role, but anyone familiar with her vicious treatment of her husband's rape victims will be a bit uncomfortable with the label of "guardian of female sex." And then there's always the pedantic grumble about mixing Greek and Roman gods. But still, inside the Supreme Court lives Zeus, "God of Heavens," bearing his Homeric epithet, "Father of Gods and Men." A god! Of heavens! Publicly funded and governmentally approved. Where's the ACLU when you need it? Doesn't anyone care about this breach of the wall separating Church and State?

It turns out that no one does care. The Hellenic gods are not considered *real* gods, the *true* God, the honest-to-god God. We are assured that they were and are not authentic deities, even if the Greeks mistakenly built a successful civilization around their worship for two millennia. Zeus, Hera, and the gang are obvious mythological figures, completely, historically, *ontologically* different from the Judeo-Christian God. Even theologians of the three Abrahamic religions (Judaism, Christianity, and Islam) and the "New Atheists" can agree on this one thing: The Greek gods cannot be *actual* gods. Atheists refer to the unlikelihood that *any* gods exist, impishly suggesting that the difference between atheists and theists is that the latter – hardened *un*believers when it comes to the Greek gods and all other deities except their own – merely believe in *one more* god than atheists do.[1] Theologians over the millennia have dismissed the Homeric deities for the same reason Greek philosophers abandoned them: They don't live up to preconceptions of what a deity should be. In particular, the Greek gods are disappointingly manifold, anthropomorphic (that is, they look and act like humans), and amoral (at best).

But the rejection of the Homeric gods in favor of the Abrahamic deity has been a serious mistake for Western culture. The polytheistic, humanized, and amoral (at best) gods of Homeric epic provide the basis for a more realistic and useful approach to life than has been offered by Yahweh and his interpreters. The Olympians (the major Greek gods in Homer's epics) are, I will argue, a vast improvement on the God that most contemporary believers are taught to worship, a chimerical deity based extremely loosely – and often not at all – on the God that is presented in the biblical texts.[2]

This book makes two connected arguments. First, we must also look closely at Yahweh the way many biblical scholars and literary critics, *not* theologians, do. Upon close inspection, the God of the Hebrew Bible often turns out to be *very much* like the deities found in the *Iliad* and *Odyssey*. Even after a brutal makeover by the sixth- and fifth-century BCE composers and redactors of the Hebrew Bible, Yahweh remains remarkably Olympian throughout the Tanakh (Old Testament). This deity feels quite familiar to a classicist who studies the Homeric gods. The late biblical compilers and the subsequent exegetical traditions (Jewish and especially Christian) have tried to turn Yahweh into something he generally is not. By focusing on a remarkably small part of his biblical persona and applying the wobbly standards of theological argumentation, they have invented a transcendent, nonanthropomorphic, monotheistic deity possessing divine perfections.

But the biblical Yahweh is rarely any of these things. He's solidly Homeric, and as such he is simply not up to the Herculean task he has been assigned in the Judeo-Christian tradition. A significant reason for the failure of the Abrahamic religions to provide a candid and healthy vision of life in the modern world is that Yahweh, the Ur-deity of all three major Western religions, has been forced into a role for which he was not designed and was poorly equipped. Yahweh has needed 2500 years of theological reconstructive surgery to attempt to turn him into the ideal of his surgeons. He has undergone so many interpretative procedures that what his believers now say about him bears only a tiny resemblance to the character in his officially authorized stories. He is the Michael Jackson of the gods. This composite deity has been at best an impediment to, and not infrequently a disaster for, human flourishing. The first part of this book demonstrates the Olympian nature of Yahweh by comparing him to Homer's gods. To that end, we will look closely at the important deities in the *Iliad, Odyssey*, and Hebrew Bible.

The second and more consequential section of the book builds on the first part to demonstrate why we would be much better off with Homer's fictional Olympians than with the fabricated God that the Judeo-Christian tradition has been championing for so many centuries. While Yahweh may be surprisingly similar to Zeus & Company in general, in those areas where the Hebrew and Greek deities differ the Olympians emerge as a superior concept. We would, in fact, lead more honest and fulfilling lives with Homer's gods. The world that results from the epic poet's divine "apparatus" demands that the gods' human counterparts – and that includes us – live fully, ethically, and meaningfully. The universe depicted by Homer and populated by his gods is one that creates a unique and powerful responsibility for humans to discover ethical norms, accept death as a human limit that creates meaning, develop compassion to mitigate a tragic existence, appreciate frankly both the glory and danger of sex, and courageously respond to an indifferent universe whose nature was clearly *not* designed for human dominion.

Not that Homer's mortal characters respond in a better manner to life's challenges any more often than we do in the modern West. The poet paints a portrait of pious mortals *mistakenly* turning to the gods for assistance in their search for justice and meaning, thus foreshadowing 3000 years of similarly failed efforts. But unlike the theologies that derive from the biblical traditions, Homer's gods account perfectly for the vicissitudes of our lives in a universe that remains unimpressed by our efforts and unresponsive to our demands. Plus, the Olympians can *laugh*. We could use a good deal more of these gods in today's world.

Wait, let me explain . . .

Okay, not really. I didn't mean that. Three issues need to be clarified right up front. First, I am, of course, not arguing for the actual existence of Homer's gods any more than for the reality of the biblical Yahweh. This is not a new-age cry for the rekindled worship of the Hellenic pantheon. (Yes, there is such a thing, called the Hellenismos movement. Oy.) I take it as a given (that is, scholars have convincingly demonstrated) that what we have received from antiquity for all the Western religious traditions are heavily edited selections of self-contradictory, elliptical, and ambiguous man-made stories – what scholars call myths – about the divine and its relation to humanity. That some people choose to believe in the Truth of one of these masterful anthologies instead of another is an accident of birth (family, culture, century) and history (the political ambitions of Constantine or the military success of early Islam, for example), as well as a function of personal psychology and inclination. That's a matter of chance and faith, with which this book is not directly concerned.

Here we will look at *stories* about gods, especially those in Homer's epics and the Hebrew Bible, with an occasional dip into the New Testament. My purpose is to demonstrate that the nature of the anthropomorphic gods depicted by Homer – their powers, personalities, relationships, conflicts, values, actions – not only successfully accounts for the world we live in, but creates a demand on us to live self-critical, fully human lives in a far more powerful way than that offered by the world created by Yahweh and currently dominated, in the United States at least, by Jesus. The Homeric poems are inspired works of fiction that have the potential to help us think, reflect, and, yes, even improve. If the Olympians would force us to adjust our lives to a more genuine and honest (if difficult) vision of human existence, we should reconsider just how we are to go about organizing our lives. And we should certainly reconsider the less helpful depictions of Yahweh, the divine Jesus, and Allah.

My second disclaimer: You will find here neither a defense of polytheism as a "tolerant" religion nor an effort to promote current polytheistic "pagan" practices as models of nonviolence. Monotheism has long been attacked for the mayhem its particularism has evoked – the New Atheists are merely its latest and most acerbic detractors. Christianity has especially been targeted, from enlightenment historians (e.g., Gibbon) and philosophers (e.g., Hume, Voltaire) to contemporary scholars of religion, literary critics, philosophers, journalists, and even clergymen. While I share their dismay at the legacy of human destruction that has regularly accompanied the spread and maintenance of the Abrahamic religions, I don't see monotheism itself as the culprit so much as the human heart. With perhaps a very few exceptions (Jainism comes to mind), *all* religion is prone to violence, even supposedly pacific Buddhism. As I write this, the Buddhist majority in Myanmar is in the process of killing, raping, or expelling close to a million Muslim Rohingya, who some Buddhist monks say are reincarnated from snakes and insects (not a good thing, apparently). Religion scholar Michael Jerryson observes that since "the third century BCE, Buddhists have clashed with opponents of different faiths, Buddhists from different countries, and even Buddhists of different origination lineages within the same country" (2013:42; cf. Hitchens 2007:195–204; Parenti 2010:196–214). Violence has been associated with religions as varied as Zoroastrianism (Choksy 2012) and Hinduism (Patton 2012).

It is true that political violence has rarely been sanctioned by *religious* beliefs in polytheistic communities. Scholar of ancient religion Robert Parker concludes that he knows of "no instance in the ancient Near East or classical worlds of intercommunal violence between polytheist groups based on religious difference" (2017:76). These societies, however, easily found numerous other reasons to kill themselves and their neighbors. The exuberantly polytheistic ancient Greeks were at war constantly, both with others and themselves, and the Romans were spectacularly efficient at organized genocide and innovations in public displays of savagery. Alexander the Great and Julius Caesar nearly wiped out entire cultures. The Aztecs may have killed over a million sacrificial victims in less than a century (White 2012:156–60).

Humans find meaning in identity formation, and the unfortunate companion of that process seems to be our tendency to turn others into The Other – it's a "function of power and capacity to wield it" (Smith 2008:24–8). A fanatical commitment to *any* ideology that claims access to the Truth usually leads to mass murder. Genghis Kahn enforced religious *tolerance* while killing perhaps as many as 40 million people. Mao, Stalin, and Pol Pot were not monotheists. Neither was Hitler, although he was certainly no atheist either, as some defenders of Christianity have suggested.[3] Enforced secularism such as the "scientific atheism" – not the least scientific, as Michael Shermer reminds us (2015:137) – of the Soviet communists is likely to be as barbarous as any religion. The common denominator in mass murder is as often totalitarianism as belief in one supreme god. A recent study of religious violence concludes that obedience to authority – of any kind – is the single greatest contributor to violence (Eller 2010:328).

This is not to deny that monotheism has been a particularly hypocritical and extremely *efficient* mechanism for channeling our hatred of difference. As Will Durant noted, "Certainty is murderous" (1992:784, cited in Harris 2005:86). Religious violence is not a "myth" constructed by the modern secular nation-state, as at least one postmodern theologian has suggested (Cavanaugh 2009). In one of the best of the recent studies of the connections between religion and violence, Jack David Eller (2010) concludes that as social and ideological systems, such religions have had the tendency to lay the foundations for violence by creating a reality in which violence is accepted as necessary, even desirable; attributing the authority for violence to the greatest good; setting leadership, at the human and superhuman level, that cannot be questioned or opposed; totalizing identities in exclusive ways, an absolute "us" against an absolute "them"; raising the stakes, with ultimate rewards and punishments; and establishing an ultimate goal that cannot and must not fail and that can and must be pursued by any means possible. This drawing a boundary around the group is the "tragic flaw in religious moral psychology" (Teehan 2010:206; cf. Schwartz 1997).

But the muddy moral record of monotheism does not mean that we should turn to other kinds of religion as a panacea for the perverse psyche that is our human inheritance. Jan Assmann, for example, supports what he calls Egyptian "cosmotheism," a "religion of an immanent god and a veiled truth that shows and conceals itself in a thousand images" (2010:43; cf. 1997). Page DuBois' fine book (2014) on the history of prejudice against polytheism, while not intending to defend polytheism, holds up contemporary nonmonotheistic religions as counterpoints to the dominance of Judeo-Christian traditions and ultimately aims for tolerance of all religions. To my mind, to replace one set of myths with another in the pursuit of Truth is missing the point. The contemporary movement of "pagan polytheism" errantly sees in ancient polytheism a reflection of its own jubilant spirituality, turning it into "an appreciation of the vitality and sacredness of the universe, pluralist and tolerant, enthusiastic and festive, welcoming and in no way fanatical, non-violent and respectful of differences" (Queiruga 2009:68). New-age polytheistic theology avoids addressing the central and inherent conflicts and ambiguities that an active engagement with life elicits, and ultimately attempts to co-opt an ancient polytheism that never existed.

On the other hand, these defenses of polytheism have been part of an important examination of the history of religious prejudice in the West. The term "polytheism" has been polemical and reductive since its first appearance in English over 400 years ago (Schneider 2008:19–26; DuBois 2014:19–21). "Polytheism" took over the work previously assigned to the word "idolatry" (Scheid 1987:320). "Until the 21st century, indeed," writes biblical scholar Beate Pongratz-Leisten, "prompted by the antagonisms expressed in the Bible, research on the development of monotheism was dominated by a pervasive antagonistic notion" (2011b:12). A historian in the middle of the 20th century was reciting mainstream – and, as we shall see, demonstrably false – dogma in his three-volume *History of the Early Church* when he asserted that "the error of polytheism led the peoples into darkness and moral chaos" (Lietzmann 1953:156–7, cited in Kirsch 2005:7). Perhaps, as one biblical scholar has suggested, for defenders of monotheism, "the survival of an idea whose superiority and persuasive power is far from self-evident is always at stake" (Lang 1983:56). Even when monotheists have seen the superior logic of polytheism, they almost always get snagged on their Judeo-Christian roots. Thus a biblical scholar seems to be conceding a bit to the enemy when he writes:

> Polytheism makes far better moral sense, for it explains that suffering, injustice and inadequacy exist in the universe because the great cosmic forces or the gods are in conflict. Polytheism offers far more dramatic myths to explain reality and more poignant and complex rituals by which people might seek to integrate themselves into the cosmos and control it. Finally, polytheism preserves the feminine aspects of religion quite well.
>
> (Gnuse 1997:215)

He's on the right track – my analysis will support most of Gnuse's observations – yet he can't follow his own intuition. Within ten pages he's back to assuming that "the emergence of Jewish monotheism was part of a *great intellectual advance* occurring in many parts of the world during the Axial age" (224, my emphasis). Laura Schneider observes that the concepts of monotheism and polytheism were "coined in the context of anxious early modern European hegemony and colonial expansion" as markers of "evolutionary progress, a high sign of rationalism, and thereby proof positive of the superiority of those religions and cultures" (2008:22, 23; cf. Sugirtharajah 2008:56). Even classicists who study polytheistic societies have felt the weight of the negative connotations of polytheism, a term that "has tended to be avoided in titles of studies in Greek religion to the present day" (Konaris 2016:31–2; cf. Henrichs 2010:24). Fortunately, that tradition of dodging the term has started to change.

My argument does take advantage of this renewed challenge to an obvious Western bias in favor of monotheism, but I am not trying to defend any current religious belief. I don't expect neo-pagans to like what I have to say any more than evangelical Christians or orthodox Jews or Muslims. I am arguing for the value of one particular ancient fictional depiction of the gods over another. In this book, it is Homer's polytheistic picture of the gods that is up for scrutiny as a potentially useful poetic vision for us as we bounce – or are bounced – through an unappreciative universe.

A final clarification: The deities examined in this book are bound by their texts. We'll be looking at Yahweh in the Tanakh, trying very hard to distinguish him from the Yahweh as seen through the lens of the Rabbinical tradition, the New Testament, Christian exegesis, or contemporary worship and cult. This deity – the Yahweh in the *text* – is very familiar to biblical scholars, but he is mostly unknown outside of those academic circles. Yahweh's character, as well as that of other biblical deities (Hendel 2017), shifts throughout the Tanakh, a reflection of different sources, genres, thematic interests, theological positions, and loci of religious beliefs (urban/rural, elite/popular, Israelite/Judahite, etc.). But there are strong currents that cut across these various streams, and we will focus on the major consistencies of Yahweh's character throughout the Tanakh. The Jesus who occasionally pops up in this book is also the *character* found in the New Testament rather than his theologically enhanced avatar, much less the "real" Jesus.

Similarly, the Olympians we will be exploring are neither the generic gods from Greek mythology many readers may be familiar with nor the specific deities worshipped in Hellenic religious practice. The Greeks developed as many diverse interpretations of their divine world as we find in the Abrahamic religions and perhaps more forms of worship. Although there were probably few genuine atheists in the ancient Greek world (Bremmer 2008a, though Whitmarsh 2015:26–7 is less skeptical), the gods were constantly subjected to broad ranging critiques. The Greeks had no fixed scripture or canon, no priestly caste in charge of controlling "sacred" texts, and therefore no thirst for purging or promoting specific understandings of myth. For the Homeric epics, the poet himself is the "theologian": "Unlike other ancient societies, the theology of the ancient Greeks was developed neither by priests(s) nor holy men, but by the poets. These, in turn, did not expound dogma or religious doctrine, but recounted myths about the gods as well as stories of the famous deeds of the heroes of old" (Clay 2003:1; cf. Pucci 2002:18). Imagine: 2000 years of religious practice with practically no councils, tribunals, papal bulls, excommunications, fatwas, tortures, burnings, or crusades over doctrine. There *was* no doctrine per se.

Thus, although the epics of Homer were extremely influential, all subsequent authors were relatively free to invent, re-create, alter, and manipulate stories about the gods for their own thematic purposes. The tragic playwright Euripides was famous for messing with myth, in the process often depicting the Olympians and heroes in an unfavorable light. He even wrote a play in which Helen did not go to Troy at all – he wasn't the first Greek to make this outlandish suggestion – but she instead spent 17 angelic years in Egypt while a "phantom" Helen was carted off by Paris. If we think we know anything about Greek myth, it is that Helen went to Troy. Xenophanes, the first extant Greek author to mention Homer, is also his first critic. Plato famously rejected Homer's Olympians as well, although most Greek authors retained the gods at least for fodder for their own artistic appetites. A fourth-century Greek writer (all dates in this book are BCE unless otherwise noted), Zoïlus of Amphipolis, composed *Against the Poetry of Homer*, a nine-volume (!) critique of the epics that was so harsh he was nicknamed "The Scourge of Homer."

The Greek deities discussed in this book are primarily the major gods as depicted in the *Iliad* and *Odyssey* (and occasional manifestations of those same Homeric characters in contemporary or slightly later Greek literature). Homer leaves out or was unaware of many aspects of what we find in later sources to be central to popular Greek religion. Major deities like Demeter and Dionysus, the worship of dead mortals (hero cult), family and community gods, mystery religions, inherited guilt, serious concerns about purity and pollution – all of these virtually disappear from Homer's narrative (scholars disagree on just *how* much they disappear). The many local gods, and divergent manifestations of these gods, are absent from Homer as he focuses on a family of deities based on Olympus.

Classical Greek religion of the fifth and fourth centuries was quite different. The polis of Athens, for example, one of over 1000 such Greek city-states, was divided into 139 districts called demes. The annual calendar of just *one* of these in the fourth century (400 years after Homer) lists over 40 deities (counting separate epithets), more than 50 kinds of animal victims, nearly 60 different sacrifices, and a score of sacrificial locations (Zaidman and Pantel 1992:83). One ancient visitor to Olympia counted 65 altars in just one sacred precinct on which the locals made offerings each month (Parker 2017:31). And this doesn't count the gods of private associations or deities with no cult. It has been estimated that there were several thousand gods and heroes worshipped in the Greek world, each with his or her own altar, sanctuary, priest or priestess, and function, if you count all their various manifestations under different epithets (Mikalson 2005:49). A character in Petronius' Roman novel *The Satyricon* (17) claims that a heavily Hellenized city in southern Italy had so many divinities it was easier to stumble upon a god than a mortal.

This multiplicity has become a central question in the study of Greek religion: Do the numerous epithets and cultic identities of a god represent different manifestations of the same god, or are they different (but homonymous) gods? In one late author, Pausanias, there are 59 epithets of Athena alone (Versnel 2011:61n144). Do we find here one singular Athena with a lot of different aspects and responsibilities, or actually different deities, or perhaps either, depending upon the context? With Homer, we don't have to worry about this consideration. The gods are characters in an epic and, as such, have just one primary manifestation. Apollo, no matter what his epithet or nickname, is the same character throughout the poem. This does not mean that the Zeus of the *Iliad* must be the exact same Zeus found in the *Odyssey*, however – different texts and thematic needs may call for different aspects of the deity to come to the surface or be pushed into the background. And the *Iliad* and *Odyssey*, while both epics, have different generic bases that can bring out different elements of the gods. But we will focus for the most part on their common characterizations across both texts.

The most insightful attempt I have read to advocate soberly for the Greek gods is that of classicist Mary Lefkowitz, who writes:

> Unlike some modern writers, I am also going to suggest that there is much we still can learn from the religion depicted in the myths, because it describes the world as it is, not as we would like it to be. The gods of traditional Greek and Roman religion do not exist for the benefit of humankind, and they do not always take an interest in what mortals are doing. The gods do not always agree with one another about what should happen in the future, and innocent human beings who are caught up in the conflict suffer or die and are not always avenged. Justice is done in the long run, but often not to the

satisfaction of the mortals who are directly involved. It is a religion from which it is possible to derive little comfort, other than the satisfaction that comes from understanding what it is to be human.

(2003:12)

My one objection to her conclusions – besides her overconfidence in the gods' connection with justice, as we will see – is that she is really talking about *Homer's* gods, which her book's emphasis on the divinities in epic bears out. Not all of the various forms of deities that appear in Greek and Roman religion fit into this picture. After Homer (and perhaps even before) there were many attempts to tame the "traditional" gods, to give them roles in mitigating the meaninglessness of death, for example, or in nurturing important transitional stages in human life. The Homeric gods are only *partially* the same gods of later Greek cult and myth, and some scholars would argue that the differences outweigh the similarities. And the local gods and heroes worshipped throughout Greece far outnumbered the Panhellenic deities housed on Olympus.[4]

This book, then, is about the value of the gods *as presented in Homer's epics* and offers an examination of the ramifications of this divine portrait for real-life decision-making by us mere mortals. It quite intentionally focuses on only one of many Hellenic visions of the gods, albeit the earliest and most influential. I am *not* making an argument about Greek deities in general or Greek or even Homeric religion, just about the stories of the divine as are attributed to one composer of two early epics. We will compare these Homeric gods to Yahweh in the Tanakh, discovering that in his biblical incarnation he is remarkably Olympian. Left to his textual existence, he could have been, at least in part, a useful fiction for Western culture along with the deities of Homer. But after centuries of remodeling by Judeo-Christian believers, his fragmented persona has ultimately left theists (and the world they have created) with a Rorschach deity who has both way too much and way too little to offer those seeking a meaningful life. Homer's gods, on the other hand, are just what they appear to be, and as such they remain a potent backdrop for living an engaged and fully human life.

Myth and "sacred" stories

In other words, we'll be judging the usefulness of two extremely influential sets of ancient divine myths. The word "myth" in this book, and in most academic treatments, means "story." A myth is a "traditional" story, in our case a socially important narrative about the gods and their relations with mortals that continues to have significance for the tellers and listeners. Myths say something important about the world to their audience, explaining while entertaining, providing a sense of identity to the community. And they are not usually innocent: "Myths are particularly useful for ideology production, that is, for presenting culturally constructed phenomena as if they were given, universal, and organic phenomena, because they focus on foundational moments and primarily, though not exclusively, superhuman characters" (Ballentine 2015:4). Myths attempt to justify and validate – and occasionally critique – the status quo, the prevailing social and political institutions and ideas, by grounding them in the supernatural past.

Labeling something a myth does not mean, then, that it is false. The Christian myth, for example, is the story of Jesus – his birth, miracles, mission, death, and resurrection. As applied in this context, the word "myth" says nothing about the veracity of the narratives, even if the "word 'myth' can still act as a red flag to a bull in Christian circles" (Pyper 2000b:463).

There has been a long history of avoiding the word "myth" when discussing the Hebrew Bible as well. Debra Scoggins Ballentine has recently shown how the "negative effects of this bias still linger within biblical scholarship" (2015:8–13). The obviously mythic elements of the Tanakh have been euphemized as "historicized," "legend," or "Hebrew epic." Even more commonly biblical myths have been falsely dismissed as part of a foreign, non-Israelite tradition, labeled "Canaanite" or "Canaanizing" (after the "wicked" natives of the Levant that the Israelites decimate and supplant at Yahweh's command). Elements of early Israelite religion that the final editors of the Tanakh found offensive – cultic acts like worshiping a goddess or sacrificing children, rites that we now know were part of some strands of the polytheistic Yahwism[5] practiced by many Israelites – were similarly dismissed by scholars as "foreign."

This dichotomy of "Israelite-good/Canaanite-bad," or "Israelite-historical/Canaanite-mythical" is a theological prejudice embedded in the Bible rather than a conclusion based on historical analysis or archaeological data (Stavrakopoulou 2010:39). As author Robert Wright observes, historians of early Israelite religion now agree that the "ancient Israelites, notwithstanding the Bible's protestations, were finely intertwined with those polytheistic Canaanites – to the point of being, well, polytheistic Canaanites" (2009:373–4). The Bible is, in the words of another scholar, "a great ancient text of mythology" (Price 2005:16).

Most people learn about the divine through myths. There are mystics, and the few special individuals who are guided to a religious conversion through personal revelation. Believing that you have met God on the road, for example, can significantly alter your perspective. And for many Jews, Catholics, and Muslims, the interpretative tradition can overshadow the texts themselves at times. But for a majority of theists the "choice" of religion remains a matter of which set of divine tales (and set of interpretations of those tales) is preferred, what narrative is going to supply *meaning* to the chaos of daily experience.

I put the word "choice" in the previous sentence in scare quotes because, as commentators have long pointed out, most religious education is directed at the very young. Children are indoctrinated into their parents' favorite set of myths in circumstances that are hardly favorable to an independent decision. "Religions are of course aware of this," philosopher A.C. Grayling observes. "Accordingly they exploit the fact that, for good evolutionary reasons, children are highly credulous, and believe anything that the adults in their immediate circle tell them" (2013:39). The ancient Greeks themselves were raised on the rowdy stories of Homer's gods, something philosophers like Plato found deplorable. Several neo-atheists have referred to this process of mythical inculcation as a form of child abuse. Religious conditioning can stunt (or attempt to stunt – the efforts can fail or backfire) the formation of the ability to think critically about important issues (e.g., Dawkins 2006:311–44; Hitchens 2007:217–28). Philosophers Peter Caws and Stefani Jones (2010) have edited a collection of essays by contemporary academics who detail the cruelty, however unintended, of their own childhood theological programing. We all know adults who are still struggling to recover from the trauma of their religious upbringing.

If we wanted to be fair about these things, we would set up an online quiz for young children, like the ones that tell you which house would best suit you at Hogwarts. For example, after brief paragraphs summarizing various tales of heavenly ascents, children would be asked the following:

1)   Which of the stories about a journey towards heaven would you like to learn more about?

    a)   Elijah
    b)   Jesus
    c)   Muhammad
    d)   Otus and Ephialtes
    e)   Apollo 11

Whichever story is chosen determines our children's spiritual orientation, and they are whisked off to the appropriate institution faster than a limber six-year old is shanghaied to a Chinese gymnastics academy.

There are literally billions of adult humans who believe that one or two of these stories is true. I mean, besides the one about Apollo 11, which was obviously faked. Millions would also be seriously offended by my whimsical proposition. (Did the Chinese gymnastics thing go too far?) Individual religious traditions take the stories and run, often in very different directions. The Talmud comments on twenty-four Jewish antagonistic factions in the early centuries of the common era; only two centuries after the death of Jesus a theologian could list 50 heretical Christian groups (Stark 2001:117). The Church of Jesus Christ of Latter-day Saints (Mormons) alone has engendered some 200 schismatic sects, which is more than one for each year of the religion's existence. Catholics and Protestants still disagree and have often killed each over these narrative differences. Protestants differ widely among themselves on the meaning of their stories, from Baptists to Snake Handlers to Episcopalians. The Sunni/Shia disaster in Islam is but one of the more recent and obvious instances. Religionists can share stories and still want to destroy each other over the interpretation, over who owns the rights to explicate them and impose their reading upon others.

And yet here is something on which they can all agree. Although there will be grave dissension over which story and which interpretation should be the winner, there will also be a quick consensus about the *least* likely of the options. The one story that can be discounted without further reflection is Otus and Ephialtes, a Homeric tale about a couple of gigantic nine-year-olds who pile mountains on top of each other in order to scale heaven. Apparently there are degrees of the ridiculously impossible, and the Homeric tale crosses some invisible line from "stunningly miraculous but true" into "obviously preposterous."

Polytheism is at a disadvantage in promoting its divine stories, mostly because it has no *interest* in promoting its divine stories. Monotheistic religions find strength in their particularism, the belief that their religion is the true religion, that their stories are the *only* true stories. Polytheism by its very nature cannot be so demanding, so exclusivist. When a polytheist meets a foreign god in a new myth, it's usually not an issue. Maybe this novel deity is just another name for one of their own gods, or a different god but functionally similar to one of their own. Scholars call this kind of cross-cultural identification *interpretatio* or translation – a deity from one culture can be equated with a god from another. (This is what the Romans often did so famously with the Greek deities, and how the Greeks often accommodated Egyptian gods; Parker 2017:33–76; Bettini 2016:91–8.) Or maybe it's just one more god to add to the mix, one more interesting story. And so polytheistic cultures usually lack the necessary desire, much less the fervor, to insist on only one understanding of the divine. Sociologist of religion Rodney Stark has argued that monotheism uniquely has the capacity to unite and convert as well as to inspire bitter religious conflicts. But when it comes to polytheism, "lacking the powerful religious justification of doing God's will," we find "no massive mobilizations on behalf of *the Gods*" (2001:35, emphasis in original). Polytheism almost by definition lacks proselytes.

Another all-too-obvious reason for the blanket dismissal of Homer's story of divine ascent is that Otus and Ephialtes are part of a set of tales that no longer nourishes a vibrant – okay, even a living – culture. There are no extant worshipers (save the few hold-outs for Hellenismos), no *faithful* around to vote for Homer's precocious miscreants. "Hellenic and Roman polytheistic deities can be dealt with in modern Western schools as the subject of desacralized stories because they are understood to be safely in the distant past and irrelevant to real religion" (Paper 2005:107–8). Thus their appearance on the Supreme Court building. The same argument could be made about any historically frozen body of myths. I doubt Valhalla would garner much support in our poll as the destination of choice (although it seems you don't have to ascend to get there).

Biblical myths, on the other hand – even the contradictory creation stories in Genesis – have more validity because they are still repeated by the faithful; indeed, many are *still believed to be true*. British theologian R.W.L. Moberly notes that the biblical texts "are privileged because Jews and Christians have privileged, and continue to privilege, them; and they have been formative in Western culture because Christian faith has been formative in Western culture. . . . It is unclear how one can privilege the content of the OT, other than as a cultural artifact, without appeal to the perspectives of Christian or Jewish faith" (2016:485). It's not just that the biblical stories are embedded in Western culture – Odysseus' adventures are as familiar as David's – but that they have a link to contemporary belief. Without *faith* – in the Truth of the story or in its importance in the living religious tradition – the Hebrew Bible would be just another "cultural artifact" – like the *Iliad*.

This may seem self-evident, but I find it puzzling. The ultimate *value* of a story doesn't derive from the number of people who continue to believe it to be literally true. If numbers for religious myth mattered, we would simply count adherents to a faith and award the victory to the majority: Christians 2 billion; Muslims 1.5 billion; Hindus 1 billion; Jews 14 million, etc. Christians win![6] That is, if we lump together Catholics and Protestants, or for that matter the 40,000 denominations with hundreds of different belief systems. But we'd need to poll everyone in the world each year. And we'd have to decide if the vote was worldwide or by region. Even in the West, Christians haven't been in the lead for that long in human history, and they may not be in the future. There could be a sudden surge of some offshoot like, say, the Rastafarians (currently mellowing out at about 600,000). Can we be *sure* that a dead emperor of Ethiopia was *not* Jesus, just because that story was outvoted? How many times in history have the masses been wrong? Think slavery, for example. Or McDonald's.[7]

No one wants to argue that the earlier the religion the better, otherwise we'd all be worshiping Shamash or Nun, and both Christianity (Catholicism as well as its toddler brother, Protestantism) and Islam would have to yield to Judaism and Hinduism. And we don't wish to rely on longevity either, or the 2000-year run of the Olympians would put it in a tight race with Christianity, not to mention Judaism and Hinduism or the religion of the ancient Egyptians, which lasted over three millennia.

We can no longer fall back on the fiction of historical development favored by the early Christian fathers and promoted in the 19th century under the influence of a misapplied Darwinism, an evolutionary progressivism revealed in history's march towards the Truth (Schneider 2008:20–4; Gnuse 1997:62–128; Bowie 2000:13–15): At first there were dumb fetishists or animists (check out those silly natives pretty much anywhere), then foolish polytheists with crude anthropomorphism (e.g., the Greeks) with a possible previous detour to totemism, then primitive monotheists (e.g., the Jews) to be supplanted at last by a morally enlightened monotheism "under the catalytic action of Christianity" (Athanassiadi and Frede 1999:7, cited in Lanzillotta 2010:442).

To be consistent, such an approach would also require that each successive wave of "revelation" be accepted as an improvement over what came before. Islam is better than Christianity, Protestantism an upgrade on Catholicism, with the most recent variant claiming the lead: Mormonism gives way to Seventh-day Adventists and then to Christian Science, all religions finally climaxing in an apocalyptic battle for supremacy between Scientology and the Moonies. No one wants to accept this logical extension of "religious triumphalism." Robert Bellah, then the dean of American sociologists of religion, introduced his lengthy examination of *Religion in Human Evolution* by shutting down this entire line of thought: "But that religious evolution is simply the rise, onward and upward, of ever more compassionate, more righteous, more enlightened religions could hardly be farther from the truth" (2011:xxiv).[8]

And, unfortunately, the answer can't be determined by which of these stories of heroic travel is actually True. They're *all* unbelievable, dependent upon supernatural "evidence" without corroboration, each one incredible to anyone outside the faith. Even the moon landing, which actually *did* happen and *can* be verified, remains incredible to some (in 2013 seven percent of Americans still believed it was faked). Former minister John Loftus has proposed the "outsider test for faith": Since religious faith is causally dependent on the cultural background in which one is raised, and it is inevitable that at best all religious faiths but one are untrue – and it's highly unlikely any has it right – the "best and probably only way to test one's adopted religious faith is from the perspective of an outsider with the same level of skepticism one uses to evaluate other religious faiths" (2012:64–78, 2013). None would emerge from such scrutiny intact.

Yet each group continues to support quite vehemently its own set of fantastic tales. According to the Book of Mormon, shortly after his resurrection Jesus visited his faithful followers in America (3 Nephi 11:8). After all, the New Testament tells us that Jesus visits his disciples after his death, although admittedly to different people for different amounts of time and in different places, depending upon which text you look at. If the canonical sources can't agree on his postmortem itinerary, why can't Jesus take an additional detour to Missouri?[9]

The stories of the Homeric gods and heroes are not less *credible* by any objective standard than the bizarre tales in current religious circulation. Muhammad rode a white animal named Barak – half mule, half donkey – from Mecca to Jerusalem (or so the tale is generally interpreted) and thence to heaven where he chatted with such religious luminaries as Abraham, Moses, John the Baptist, and Jesus. If you have any doubts, in the Dome of the Rock on the temple mount in Jerusalem one can still visit the exact spot of Muhammad's ascent. On one corner of the rock – the same spot Abraham tried to sacrifice his son and where the ark of the covenant resided in first temple days, we are told – can still be seen the prophet's footprints where he stepped to mount Barak. Further evidence is found on another part of the rock, where one is shown the handprint of the angel Gabriel, who grabbed the rock and held it down with all his force as it was attempting to rise and follow Muhammad into the sky.

The value in the various depictions of the divine in world religions can't be found in the Truth, number of believers, or the antiquity (or novelty) of the faith. *All* of these myths about the divine are fascinating fables created by scientifically and culturally primitive people trying to come to grips with the harsh realities of their lives. The composers and editors were poetically talented and reflective but were still people who thought it was a good day if they didn't die from a tooth infection or have their babies eaten by a dingo.

So the honest question becomes, which vision of the divine is most *helpful* in our search for meaning and human flourishing? Which set of divine myths should demand one's attention, not because it supposedly reveals the Truth about the gods or because our parents dumped it on us, but because it is true to our experience and provides sustenance for our continuing wrestling match with life for meaning? The Vedas? The Hebrew Bible? The Qur'an? New Testament? The Book of Mormon? *Dianetics*? The strange challenge I have set for myself in this book is to demonstrate that the picture of the gods found in Homer's epics provides a better, more honest answer than the one standardly presented in the Judeo-Christian interpretive tradition. "The hope is that better stories will prevail," writes philosopher Austin Dacey. We need not just a "receptivity to reason, but an appreciation for which stories are better, and that is perhaps a more subtle art to master" (2009:186).

Outline of the book

Section I of the first part of the book lays out some of the similarities in the method of composition, authorial claims, and historicity of the Tanakh and Homeric epics. We begin to explore parallels between Yahweh and the Olympians by examining their homologous roles in three literary subgenres – besieging cities, bringing plagues, and heading divine councils. We look carefully at the divine assembly scenes at the beginning of the *Odyssey* and the book of Job – it's hard to say whether Zeus or Yahweh is more Homeric.

The next Section, "Yahweh and the other Olympians," introduces the major characteristics of and similarities between the Homeric and Israelite gods. These four chapters examine the polytheistic background of the deities and their thorough anthropomorphism, defined by biblical scholar Anne Knafl as "any description that applies human characteristics, action, abilities, or feelings to a deity" (2014:35). Since everyone concedes that Homer's gods (plural) act much like humans (anthropomorphically), the focus of the first chapter is on the exact nature of the Olympians in the epics as opposed to Greek mythology in general.

The remaining three chapters are devoted to Yahweh. He's worth it. Here we survey Yahweh as a character in the Hebrew Bible, focusing on his Olympian qualities as an anthropomorphic deity living among and competing with other gods. As we'll see in detail, Yahweh has nothing on Homer's petty, backbiting, dramatic, ageless teenagers. If looked at objectively, most of the Tanakh depicts a fairly typical Near Eastern, national, anthropomorphic deity struggling with mixed success to emerge from his polytheistic upbringing. These elements of Yahweh's character and cult were later rewritten as "deviations from orthodoxy" when Yahwistic monotheism emerged victorious as the religion of ancient Israel.

Part Two of the book presents a series of comparisons between Yahweh and Homer's unruly deities that reveal the superiority of the latter for organizing an honest and fully human life. The world represented by Homer's gods is constructive for all of us in coming to grips with the finite and potentially heroic dimensions of human efforts to live a meaningful life. The gods of the *Iliad* and *Odyssey* uniquely transcend their original context.

We first review some of the efforts that Abrahamic theists have made to transform Yahweh from his Olympian presentation in the text to an unrecognizably transcendent deity. The interpretive traditions found the God in the text disturbingly Olympian. What was to be done to suppress his Homeric nature? The winning strategy was bold – ignore what the text clearly reveals. Theology is often little more than literary criticism gone horribly wrong. A metaphysically perfect deity was invented and then projected back onto the Bible. God, it turns out, is not the anthropomorphic (i.e., jealous, proud, angry, rib-resecting, hail-stone throwing – that is, Olympian) character we meet in the Tanakh. Instead, we are told that he possesses "divine attributes" conjured up like a rabbit out of a burning bush: God is now a model of and guarantor of justice, benevolent, loving, perfect, free, omnipotent, omniscient, omnipresent, one, transcendent, eternal, impassive, and immutable.

Yahweh, however, very rarely demonstrates *any* of these characteristics. Consequently, this act of theological legerdemain is often compounded by another, which is to insist that those Olympian traits on such vivid display in the text don't *really* describe God at all. We mortals simply have no choice but to use human (that is, anthropomorphic) language to describe an indescribable God. All biblical accounts of Yahweh are *metaphorical*. The insurmountable challenges to this approach are that it tacitly admits that the Bible can tell us nothing reliable about any "real" God and that we can never actually know or say anything about the divine. Few theists want to accept either of these conclusions. These strained efforts to give Yahweh a makeover have ultimately become the source of much unnecessary foundering and confusion.

Homer, on the other hand, makes no effort at all to rehabilitate his wayward deities. Their delinquency is often exactly his point. We explore in detail the *advantages* of the limitations of the Olympians, the importance of what they do *not* and can*not* do. Close attention is paid especially to the gap between what the characters think the gods know and can do and what Homer reveals about the gods' abilities, actions, and motivations. The Greek deities' extremely imperfect nature – their competition, rivalries, favoritism, and reluctantly shared offices – affects humans unpredictably, both positively and adversely. Homeric polytheism and thorough anthropomorphism account for the indifferent and mercurial universe we seem to inhabit. Anthropomorphism is not an insult to an ineffable god, but an unavoidable and powerful tool for creating meaningful stories. The Homeric gods are what they are, no more and no less, and that paradoxically forces us mortals to negotiate life without a roadmap supplied from any ancient myths. We are thus asked to think for ourselves, to make our actions match our ideas in a more courageous fashion, to be more authentically *heroic* in a capricious world.

The next Section examines the importance of the complete separation between creation and the Olympians in early Greek thought. Although Homer is our first extant Greek author, he was drawing on hundreds of years of oral tradition and often refers casually to events and figures outside of the narrative. We look at the Succession Myth, the narrative of a sequence of intrafamily generational battles between gods for control of the universe. Under scrutiny here are the numerous allusions to the Olympians' struggles both with their parents (Titans) and among themselves for power. What is most important in the case of the Greek variants of this myth – similar to many Near Eastern sacred narratives but crucially different from Genesis – is that the creator god is *not* the deity who presently sits in power. Zeus did not create the universe; rather, he was born, fought to take control, and continues to guard his throne with some justified paranoia. This mythical background again makes sense of what appears to be the random nature of the world we inhabit. And most importantly, humans are not the centerpiece or culmination of creation. Our origins aren't even mentioned. The universe, it turns out, was not made for our benefit nor for us to rule. Surprise!

In complete contrast is Yahweh the creator God. Although a Near Eastern creation myth is also hinted at throughout the Hebrew Bible with Yahweh's battles against the sea to establish or maintain his control, the comparatively late writers of Genesis 1 have tried to "clean up" his ragged, Olympian edges by eliminating his competition. This unfortunate theological step has made it impossible for subsequent believers to provide an adequate explanation of God's relationship to an often-inhospitable world steeped in both moral and nonmoral evil: Why would a "perfect" deity have created such a messy, rebarbative world? The search for the True origins of the universe in an ancient religious myth bound to an omnipotent and benevolent creator has led to an irresolvable theological debate that is unnecessary to apply to Homer's world. The epics provide no grounds for the curious non-Greek assumption that our lives simply *must* be divinely "purpose driven." By separating creation from the god who is currently on the throne, Homer eliminates the doomed efforts necessitated in Abrahamic religions to account for the patently imperfect nature of God's creation under the eternal administration of a theologically manufactured, just, omnipotent, loving, (etc.) deity. "For atheism and polytheism there is no special problem of suffering, nor need there be for every kind of monotheism. The problem arises when monotheism is enriched with – or impoverished by – two assumptions: that God is omnipotent and that God is just" (Kaufmann 1963:139). Homer's tragic vision forces us to focus on our *own* creation of meaning in a universe that just *is*.

Section III argues that the Homeric vision of the finality of death reveals a crucial reality for humans that demands we live our lives with constant self-critique. The essential difference between gods and humans in Homer is that we die and they don't. This constant reminder of our limits creates a world in which we can actually be superior to the gods in our quest to discover what is valuable in *this* life. We investigate how death and the dead are portrayed in the epics and the ways in which the acceptance of this insight compels us to focus on how to live our lives well *now*. While the Tanakh's picture of the finality of death is similar to Homer's, this unidealized vision stands in stark contrast to the anti-tragic eschatology of the New Testament. So here we contrast the virtue of finitude found in the Greek epics with the visions of the afterlife embedded in Christian belief. At best, heaven and hell – concepts about which theists have no agreement – are distractions; at worse, they are dead ends that lead only to an attenuated existence of anticipation. For Homer, human limitations demand courage, critical critique, empathy, and genuine compassion for the human condition. The poet will not allow his hero, Achilles, to dismiss the consequences of his own actions with an unthinking confidence that "everything happens for a reason" or "for the best." It doesn't. Homer asks him – and us – to figure out how to become human without providing any divine footprints to follow and with no promise of a happy eternity just for trying. Achilles looks into that emptiness and stares it down. That is what, in the end, makes him heroic.

The next Section explores the ethical consequences of Homer's penetrating vision of human limitations. Here I argue against some of my fellow classicists who have tried to "salvage" Homer gods in the *Iliad* by turning them into guardians of human justice. We come to see that despite what the heroes believe, the Olympians do not act out of any useful definition of justice, but are always motivated by some personal, amoral agenda. There is a reason the Greeks invented ethics as a human, rational endeavor – their Homeric gods were not up to the task, either as models or as guides. Law and justice for most ancient Greeks were acknowledged to be human inventions, as they still are in Western societies (despite the rhetoric of the politicized evangelicals). As biblical scholar Tikva Frymer-Kensky observes: "The discovery of [ethically] advanced polytheism poses a central theological issue: if polytheism can have such positive attributes, what is the purpose of monotheism?" (1992:3).

But isn't this lack of divine justice an indictment of Homer's pantheon? If we have no god(s)-given meaning, no theistic creation, no divinely sanctioned justice, and humans simply perish, how are we to behave? How can a community thrive without divine guidance? One of the more prevalent assumptions among theists is that without a God of their particular theological preference (just, eternal, punishing, etc.), our lives can flourish neither psychologically nor morally. The angst of well-known Christian apologist William Lane Craig is archetypal:

> If each individual person passes out of existence when he dies, then what ultimate meaning can be given to his life? . . . If life ends at the grave, then it makes no difference whether one has lived as a Stalin or as a saint. . . . For in a universe without God, good and evil do not exist – there is only the bare valueless fact of existence, and there is no one to say that you are right and I am wrong. . . . If there is no God, then our life is not fundamentally different from that of a dog. . . . So if God does not exist, that means that man and the universe exist to no purpose – since the end of everything is death – and that they came to be for no purpose, since they are only blind products of chance. In short, life is utterly without reason. Do you understand the gravity of the alternatives before us? For if God exists, then there is hope for man. But if God does not exist, then all we are left with is despair.
>
> (2008:72, 74–77)

All the evidence, however, points in the *opposite* direction. The *least* religious nations in the world are not overwhelmed with despair or floundering in moral chaos but now have the *highest* standards of living, the best "quality of life," by virtually every measure – the healthiest democracies and per capita income, best educational systems, most affordable health care, longest life expectancies along with the lowest levels of corruption, incarceration, violent crime, alcohol consumption, and unemployment (Zuckerman 2008). As a typically supercilious Californian, I enjoy any statistics that reveal the contrast between the states on the coasts and the Bible belt: "When it comes to nearly all standard measures of society health, such as homicide rates, violent crime rates, poverty rates, domestic abuse rates, obesity rates, educational attainment, funding for schools and hospitals, teen pregnancy rates, rates of sexually transmitted diseases, unemployment rates, domestic violence, the correlation is robust: the least theistic states in American tend to fare much, much better than the most theistic" (Zuckerman 2014:50). The evidence concerning individual psychological health also reveals that atheists and agnostics (as well as the billions of religious people who share little with Abrahamic theology) are as happy, productive, and moral as their theistic neighbors.

More controversially, it turns out that the God of the Bible offers no practical help either as a model or as a divine law-giver in guiding us to live ethically. Yahweh's behavior is no more worth imitating than Hera's, and Jesus himself is hardly a paragon of virtue. Moreover, the divine commands found in the biblical texts are almost entirely mundane bits of folk wisdom, impractically vague, or criminally anachronistic. The Bible – and the entire concept of an absolute morality based on the divine – only becomes ethically useful if we apply a secular template to it, using our nontheistic moral sense to pick and choose what tidbits of scripture can be redeemed for contemporary consumption.

The Olympians' amoral selfishness and capriciousness turn out to be another strength in Homer's divine portrait, not a weakness for which we need apologize. To live honestly and authentically, we must figure how to live together, how to live *good* lives, without divine guidance or fear of supernatural adjudication. That *pursuit* of the examined life, a *meaningful* existence, here and now for the here and now, is perhaps the very definition of a fully human life. It makes life worth living. Someone wise said something like that once. It must have been in the Bible.

And finally, the last Section explores the nature of sex in light of Homer's libidinous gods. The epics present sex in an honest fashion, both its joys and its dangers. Sex is such a central part of human nature in Homer's world that there is even a goddess who embodies and oversees its powers. The Tanakh, however, in its final shape has removed all aspects of sexuality from Yahweh. That leaves the Hebrew God oddly celibate, with nothing insightful to say about this vital area of human activity other than that we should multiply. Well, that's not quite true. The prophetic tradition turns Yahweh into a metaphorical wife beater, presenting in its details of physical and psychological abuse one of the most unsettling (and least familiar) aspects of God's textual persona. Nothing good can come of this, and nothing has, although of course it took Christianity to find a way to make sex truly abhorrent. The Homeric presentation of the relation between the divine and sex can yet bequeath to us a more realistic and useful vision of both the wonders and perils of sex. Just as importantly, the world of the Olympians provides the space for continued (and still desperately needed) improvement in attitudes about gender and sexuality.

The conclusion from this extended comparison of Western deities is that we need *no* gods to flourish. The theologically reconditioned God of the Judeo-Christian tradition has been an impediment to an honest, tragic, meaningful, ultimately dignified, and genuinely joyful manner of living. The triumph of the Bible over the *Iliad* and *Odyssey* is not a victory of Truth over lies, of the "real" god over "demons," but of a debilitating (if beguiling) fiction over a useful (but discomfiting) one. A world with Homer's gods would, in effect, be indistinguishable from a world that offered no evidence of any gods at all, something like, well, the world we live in. If Homer "created" a divine edifice of amoral, anthropomorphic, irresponsible, limited, and ultimately dispensable deities – one that we can all agree never really existed – that helped the Greeks to make profound explorations of the meaning of life, create great art, lead stable lives (at least as stable as those in the modern world!) that embraced compassion and hope and fostered a climate of self-critique that ultimately guided them to create philosophical ethics, invent egalitarian political structures, make scientific discoveries, challenge their own divine mythology, postulate natural origins of the universe, and engage in open reflections about sexuality, then certainly we can flourish in a world without the prophets and divinities that prop up the contemporary religious superstructure.

A final introductory word

The arguments I make in this book align in some important ways with neo-atheistic critiques of the Abrahamic religions, but more often I am giving my own slant on Yahweh supported by well-established readings by biblical scholars. Still, many of these academic interpretations are unfamiliar to most theists, and they may need to sit down while reading. My analysis of the Homeric gods, while mostly situated firmly within mainstream Homeric scholarship as well, occasionally ventures into original territory (as in my discussion of death and fate in the epics). And my examination of certain contentious topics, such as the (non-) existence of divine justice in the epics, will land me in hot water with at least half of my fellow classicists. Indeed, one of the conclusions my research has led me to is that classical scholars reading Homer through the ages may sometimes have been unwittingly influenced by religious preconceptions in ways that prevent them from appreciating the genuine potency of the ancient epic portrayal of the divine. Take the following quote, a reference to the very human behavior of Homer's dysfunctional family of gods:

> The squabbling [of the gods] in Book 21, like the scene of Hera and Zeus in 12, and indeed all instances of ungodlike Olympian conduct in the *Iliad* formed part of the Trojan legend, that is they directly belonged to the plot of that epic.
>
> (Dietrich 1979:132)

Now what could this internationally renowned scholar of Greek religion have meant by the "ungodlike" behavior of the Olympian gods? One would think that anything a deity does would have to be "godlike" by definition. *We* may not like the Olympians' "squabbling," their constant meddling, partisanship, amoral motivation, and generally selfish behavior. The poet may not *want* us to like it. But Homer's gods are certainly acting like gods. Just not the "right" gods.

We all know what Dietrich means, of course. The very meaning of the adjective "godlike," as defined for example by the *OED*, is now thoroughly embedded in a Judeo-Christian theological tradition: "Resembling God or a god in qualities such as power, beauty, or benevolence." It's that supposed "benevolence" that can misdirect critics of the Homeric deities down the slippery road that dead-ends in the divine perfections of theologians' dreams. An adjective like "godlike" and its negation must be used very carefully when examining different religious traditions. There are nearly a dozen adjectives and phrases in Homer that mean "godlike," but they say nothing about the moral character (as we would define it) or kindly intentions or extended lifespan of the hero so described. In fact, such a comparison more often than not draws attention to the *disparity* between mortals and gods, not their similarity. Classicist Laura Slatkin has observed that "when a warrior is designated with the explicit formula 'equal to a god,' it signals his imminent defeat" (2011:319). And defeat in the epics usually means death, a very "ungodlike" state.

Dietrich is telling us that Homer's gods frequently don't act like a "real" god. A "real" god – *the* real god – lurking behind such statements is the God of the Bible. This assumption can still be found in contemporary scholarship, even if in a significantly less severe fashion than in the past. We could once expect scholars of religion thoroughly ensconced in their own faith to make claims like only "the ignorant or moronic" were polytheists or henotheists in an age of monotheism (Albright 1957:288).[10] We are generally much more tactful these days, but old habits, like gods, die hard. A well-respected sociologist of religion in the twenty-first century can still write, "It may have been worthwhile to periodically offer such Gods [as the Olympians] a sacrificial animal or two . . . but they were not worth more" (Stark 2001:22).

It is usually inappropriate in academic writing to speculate about scholars' motives or influences, and I don't mean to suggest that Homerists who disagree with me are cryptic theists trying intentionally to impose a Judeo-Christian theology onto the epics. But we classicists, like everyone else, remain intertwined in contemporary cultural and religious contexts. From his study of the interpretation of Greek gods in classical scholarship, Michael Konaris concludes that the "Christian and Christianizing lenses of scholars are a crucial factor in the history of the study of Greek religion affecting its interpretation in diverse ways *to the present day*" (2016:23, my emphasis). Thus even excellent contemporary classicists sensitive to the thematic power of the Homeric gods as "a way of saying something about the world that humans inhabit" can find that the poems themselves "pursue their vision of human heroism, glory and suffering *at the expense of a plausible and satisfying treatment of the divine*" (Kearns 2004:71, my emphasis). The unstated argument again seems to be that the Homeric vision of the gods does not live up to what we in the Judeo-Christian West think a deity should be. "In Homer, a way of speaking about the Gods which is properly metaphorical has been made literal, elaborated on and pushed to its limit" (Kearns 2004:73). Where does that "properly" come from? It just sort of sneaks in there. The assumptions behind such conclusions – and Kearns is one of the best scholars writing on Greek religion – derive from non-Homeric religious traditions so deeply embedded in our way of thinking that they can pop up without warning at any moment: (1) a "proper" god must be like the one everyone knows about, such as, well, the one in the Bible; (2) the God of the Bible is somehow the same one found in the thousands of disparate theological traditions that often derive, however tenuously, from the biblical texts; (3) the gods in Homer, not being proper (whatever that is), cannot "reasonably be the object of relationship and belief" (Kearns 2004:71 n22). And, of course, the big one: There is such a thing as a *real* god to serve as a model of a proper god with which Homer's unreal gods can be unfavorably compared.

Each of these assumptions will be challenged in this book. The gods in Homer provide a superior vision of the divine for humans struggling to find meaning in our muddled world. So my argument is occasionally not only with the theological facelift given to Yahweh over the centuries, but with some mainstream classicists' negative assessment of Homer's gods (especially in the *Iliad*) that I believe may on occasion derive in part from this theological tradition.

Stop hitting yourself

I'm not fooling myself about the bigger picture here. Belief in the Abrahamic God is not based on evidence and as such cannot usually be countered by evidence. According to one recent poll, 64 percent of Americans would "retain a religious belief even if science disproved it" (Coyne 2015:59). But neither is faith necessarily irrational or hypocritical in the way often depicted by the New Atheists. Given the prevalence of this confidence in the existence of a deity, it is hard to reject the idea that it is a product – or by-product (there is a great deal of debate about which) – of evolutionary forces, what Michael Shermer calls a "Belief Engine" (2000:32–58). It may be more accurate to say that belief in the *supernatural* seems to be a human universal, rather than the acceptance of a supreme deity (Bloom 2010:127).

But belief in the Abrahamic God in spite of no reliable supporting evidence and in the face of substantial counterarguments is *now* often driven, I have come to believe, by what has been termed "identity-protective cognition," "a tendency to selectively credit or discredit evidence in patterns that reflect people's commitments to competing cultural groups" (Kahan 2017:1). It's understandable that people in an indifferent world work very hard, usually subconsciously, to maintain a worldview that connects them to a traditional source of self-identity and meaning. Dan Kahan, a professor of both law and psychology at Yale Law School, has shown how people use this "motivated reasoning" in forming perceptions of scientific evidence. This is especially true of issues that are linked to a particular identity-defining group. It is not so much an irrational rejection of data as a partisan sampling, a form of confirmation bias, "counting as 'experts' only those scientists who agree with their group's position." Most interestingly, corrective, accurate information on vaccine safety or global warming, for example, often drives people *deeper* into their commitment to false beliefs. "When individuals apprehend – largely unconsciously – that holding one or another position is critical to conveying *who they are* and *whose side they are on*, they engage information in a manner geared to generating identity-consistent rather than factually accurate beliefs" (2017:6).

Kahan is examining misconceptions that pertain to scientific knowledge and policy, but the process applies to everything from the blogs we share to news we watch to the books we read (Adams and Heath 2007). Neuroscientist Tali Sharot notes that this process is found in all areas of human decision-making: "In fact, presenting people with information that contradicts their opinion can cause them to come up with altogether new counterarguments that further strengthen their original view; this is known as the 'boomerang effect'" (2017:17). Even worse, experiments reveal that when we receive information that does not fit our prior beliefs, our brains "metaphorically speaking – 'shut off'" (2017:29)! Neurologist Robert A. Burton refers to this false sense of certainty about our beliefs as the "myth of the autonomous mind" (2008).

It seems to me that this informational sifting for what feels like self-preservation applies even more conspicuously to belief in a community's deity, a being who has prominently shaped and maintained the self-conception of all theists. Identity-protective cognition is rational, in the sense that it serves a useful purpose in affirming one's identity and warding off threatening challenges to one's self-conception. And, alas, as Kahan concludes, "Of course, these individually rational stance-takings are disastrous for society at large" (2017:7).

Study after study reveals that our beliefs come first and only then do we apply a rational system that explains and rationalizes what we already believe: "Intuitions come first, strategic reasoning second," and what we call "strategic reasoning" is more accurately labeled "slow and sometimes tortuous justifications" (Haidt 2012:70, 43). Nobel Prize winner Daniel Kahneman has produced a massive indictment of human rationality (this is probably not exactly how he would put it) in his book *Thinking, Fast and Slow* (2011). He examines in detail the "systematic errors" that occur in our decision-making about virtually everything. Our swift, intuitive, automatic, involuntary mental system creates impressions and feelings that are often useful but are rife with "cognitive allusions." These allusions are biases and flaws built into our "heuristics," those basic procedures that allow us to find quick but "often imperfect" answers to the challenges we face. We have a second mental system, our conscious, calculating, reasoning self that is supposed to monitor our intuitive responses, but it is extremely lazy, "more of an apologist for the emotions of [the intuitive system] than a critic of those emotions – an endorser rather than enforcer" (2011:103). Our illusions are very difficult to dispel. They "are comforting," Kahneman concludes, since they "reduce anxiety that we would experience if we allowed ourselves to fully acknowledge the uncertainties of existence" (2011:205).

Although much of Kahneman's interest lies in the economic consequences of our reliance on unregulated impressions, feelings, and inclinations, his model clearly has implications for religious belief. There are many different forms of cognitive heuristics that function to confirm our faith in a deity rather than compel us to examine it closely. Michael Shermer provides a distressing list of over three dozen ways our minds work to corroborate what we already want to believe is true (2011:256–79). "We form our beliefs for a variety of subjective, personal, emotional, and psychological reasons in the context of environments created by family, friends, colleagues, cultures, and society at large; after forming our beliefs we then defend, justify, and rationalize them with a host of intellectual reasons, cogent arguments, and rational explanations" (2011:5). This strikes me as a remarkably accurate description of theology, both the day-to-day justifications of the faithful and the elaborate *apologiae* of the professionals.

Can an argument make a difference to religious belief? If the Enlightenment, Darwin, cognitive ethology, genetics, philosophical ethics, and modern physics, astronomy, biology, chemistry, paleontology, psychology, sociology, biblical history, comparative mythology – as well as the devastating critiques of theism from philosophers as brilliantly diverse as David Hume and Bertrand Russell, along with the delightfully cranky exposure of the failure of Abrahamic religions by the New Atheists and the more painstaking dismantling of the "inerrancy" of the Bible by scholars of religion such as Bart Ehrman and Hector Avalos – have made only a slight dent in the belief in the Judeo-Christian deity in the United States, what are the chances that a book on the Olympians – and this includes Yahweh, of course – is going to send the flock streaming into the bright ether?

Well, miracles happen, right? Besides, it's important – and a good deal of fun – to try.

Notes

1 Etymologically, a theist should be anyone who accepts the reality of a deity (*theos*), and so Homer's heroes would qualify. In fact, there was a definitional fluidity between "theism," "deism," and "monotheism" until the early 19th century (MacDonald 2012:16 and n54). In contemporary discussions, however, the word is commonly limited to those who believe in the Abrahamic God found in scripture, a transcendent deity who also possesses the theologically crafted divine perfections (omnipotence, benevolence, etc.). Since the contemporary use of the word conveniently distinguishes between this set of beliefs and those of deists, pantheists, atheists, and polytheists (like the characters in Homer's epics), I have adopted it throughout the book.

2 Western culture has privileged the God of the Bible, and thus this particular literary fiction earns a majuscule and other gods do not. "The assumption of this usage, however, is that this 'God' is extratextual, that the term refers to a metaphysical entity whose existence and attributes are conceded and known by the critics as well as the authors of the scriptures. Or at least it accords some privilege to this deity over deities that other humans have worshipped and still do" (Davies 1995:14). It's a theological decision. God is capitalized because in a monotheistic world he's the one and only, the true God. Many scholars also tell us is that this is actually the deity's proper name, so the capitalization of the Hebrew God is no different than writing Apollo instead of apollo. It's not theological, it's grammatical. (This use does not derive from the original Hebrew or Greek, however, which did not have both upper- and lower-case letters.)

I don't want to offend readers gratuitously before I have a chance to offend them intentionally, and I'm all for grammar, so in this book I will adopt the conventional capitalization when the word is applied to what *could* be the proper name of the biblical deity. But to be honest, I don't buy it. Confessional authors often capitalize God's pronouns (so-called reverential capitalization). Why is it "He" and "His" rather than "he" and "his"? That's not grammatical. We capitalize Athena but not Her pronouns. Some biblical scholars see the word *elohim* – frequently translated as the capitalized "God" – as denoting a type or a shorthand description or a category (Humphreys 2001:20–1). *Elohim* properly means "gods" and often means a generic god or gods (the word is grammatically plural and the exact meaning must be determined by context; Propp 2006:759 suggests that it is a "plural of abstraction" meaning "divinity"). Uncapitalized "deity" or "the deity" would be less misleading than "God." *Elohim* is often applied to other deities in the text.

It is commonly argued that *elohim* may be used as a title elsewhere, but it is always a proper name in the strand of biblical text called the Priestly Code (e.g., Schmid 2011:283–7). True, God admits that he appeared to the patriarchs as God (El) Almighty, but he frequently makes clear what his *proper name* really is, the one he wants to be known by. He tells Moses his name is Yahweh (customarily translated in Bibles as "the Lord" or LORD set out in small caps): "This is my name forever, and this my title for all generations" (Ex 3:13–15). "Say therefore to the Israelites, 'I am Yahweh'" (Ex 6:2–8). Though in this tradition Moses is the first to learn his real name, in what is usually considered the earliest tradition of the Tanakh it's clear that this was his name from the days of Adam and Eve (cf. Gen 4:3; 28:13; Dijkstra 2001b:83). "I am Yahweh, your God," (or "I, Yahweh, am your deity") he insists as he introduces himself and his commandments (Ex 20:1–2; cf. Ex 15:1–3; Deut 6:4; Miller 2009:72–80). God is his role, at best a title, more likely his job. His résumé reads, "Name: Yahweh. Occupation: god."

3 "The bulk of the evidence indicates that Nazism was indeed a synthesis of Christian anti-Judaism, Israelite ethnocentrism, anti-Christian paganism, and pseudoscientific thinking" (Avalos 2005:319). Hitler saw in Jesus a reflection of himself, "a brave and persecuted struggler against the Jews" (Watson 2014:310).

4 Even some of the most popular Olympians in later Greek cult are hardly recognizable in Homer's epics. Take Artemis. In her sole significant narrative moment in the epics (21.470–513), she gets humiliatingly bitch-slapped by Hera. Yet in Greek cult as we know it from post-Homeric times, Artemis is a much venerated deity. Ivana Petrovic has demonstrated this disjunction, concluding:

> If we were to use early Greek epic as our sole source for the history of Greek religion, we could easily have concluded that Artemis was a marginal goddess. . . . However, Artemis was in fact the goddess with the most widespread cults of all Greek female deities; only Apollo had more shrines and temples than she did.
> (2010:215)

5 Yahwism is a slightly confusing term, used in two conflicting ways. Occasionally it is virtually a synonym for monotheism, but it more commonly refers to any religious praxis of ancient Israel that included the (not necessarily exclusive) worship of Yahweh.

6 It has been estimated that there are between 500 and 750 million nonbelievers in the world – twice the number of Buddhists, for example – which would put them in fourth place. There are nearly 60 times as many nonbelievers as Latter-day Saints, for that matter (Zuckerman 2008:96, 2010a:ix). But at least for now *some* sacred story would have to be victorious.

7 Michael Shermer (2011:178) makes a similar point even more poignantly by citing Scientologist doctrine (which, it must be admitted, is low-hanging fruit on the tree of absurd religious beliefs): "Millions of Scientologists believe that eons ago a galactic warlord named Xenu brought alien beings from another solar system to Earth, placed them in select volcanoes around the world, and then vaporized them with hydrogen bombs, scattering to the winds their thetans (souls), which attach themselves to people

today, leading to drug and alchohol abuse, addiction, depression, and other psychological ailments that only Scientology can cure. Clearly the veracity of a proposition is independent of the number of people who believe it."

8 There has been a long debate in theological circles whether religion has evolved or "degenerated," that is, whether monotheism or polytheism was the original religion of humankind (Schmidt 1987b). This issue was at the heart of 18th-, 19th-, and early 20th-century scholarship on Greek religion and the nature and origin of the Hellenic gods. As most classical scholars were Christian, monotheism was almost universally considered to be the acme of religious insight, so the key questions became how much monotheism could be detected and was it there originally or did the religion "progress" towards it. Despite the fact that no actual development or regress occurred in either direction – "the Greeks were not crypto-monotheists" (Parker 2011:66) – in most of the scholarship of this period "Christianity retains a privileged role as the religion in relation to which Greek religion is positioned" (Konaris 2016:287), what Miriam Leonard refers to as the "stubborn persistence of a Christianized account of Hellenism" (Leonard 2012:9). We will see that a Judeo-Christian perspective on what a god should be continues to play a role in the interpretation of Homer's deities.

9 Latter-day Saints (Mormons) don't actually know just where Jesus touched down in the Americas the first time – LDS archaeologists have not yet been able to find the ruins of the Nephite New World temple "in the land Bountiful" (3 Nephi 11:1). But upon his second coming Jesus will definitely head to Missouri after a stopover in Jerusalem. Biblical scholar Lester L. Grabbe has made a brilliant comparison of a maximalist approach to the history of Israel – one that primarily paraphrases the Bible as if it were history – to what a Book of Mormon history of pre-Columbian America would look like (2011b:224–32).

10 Albright was an equal-opportunity disparager. He goes on to say that many "backward Catholics are polytheists, many ignorant Protestants are tritheists, and unthinking Jews express henotheistic ideas."

Part One

Brothers (and sisters) from a different mother

Section I

Texts with a history

2 Assembling resemblances

Orthodox Jews and more than a few Christian evangelicals still believe that Yahweh dictated the Torah (the first five books of the Tanakh, also known as the Pentateuch) to Moses on a mountain. This ascription of authorship to Yahweh via Moses appeared late in the development of the Hebrew Bible. We first find this claim over 1000 years after these same believers place the exodus from Egypt. Biblical scholar David M. Carr observes that "Judaism had been influenced by Greek culture, where authorship was important and the writings of Homer enjoyed the highest prestige. In response, the Jewish authors of texts such as Jubilees (second century BCE) claimed that their Pentateuch had an ancient author as well – Moses" (1989:7).

All sorts of well-known and curious issues arise from this insistence on Mosaic composition. Moses is dead before the end of the text, for example, making him the author of the story of his own mysterious burial. Especially troubling are the anachronisms and numerous conflicting doublets (stories told twice that often contradict each other). You literally can't get two chapters into the Bible before realizing that if a single voice like that of Yahweh or Moses had composed the Torah, it was the voice of someone on drugs.

To take an obvious example, we immediately encounter two irreconcilable accounts of creation. The most familiar problem derives from divergent accounts of human origins: Are man and woman created simultaneously on the sixth day as the culmination of creation as in Genesis 1, or is man created long before God resected his rib to create Eve as in Genesis 2? The myths are so painfully at odds that some Christian scholars argued that there must have been *two completely separate creations*. The first creation in Genesis 1 was for non-Jews, the second for Jews. Theological discussion quickly turned to which creation was better, and you can imagine where the Jews ended up in that debate in Christian Europe (Fox 1992:20–1).

Later Jewish tradition was particularly bothered by the two separate creations of woman. We all know what became of Eve in the second account, but what about the woman created in God's image at the same time as man in Genesis 1? Did Adam have *two* wives? One influential answer was found in the development of the figure of Lilith (Patai 1990:221–54; Blair 2009:24–30, 63–95). Mentioned briefly in the Bible (Isaiah 34:14) and associated with demons in the Dead Sea

Scrolls (third century BCE – first century CE), by the tenth century CE Lilith had multiple stories attached to her as Adam's "first wife," that is, the woman of Genesis 1. My favorite variant is one in which she defiantly insists that since she was created concomitantly with Adam she should not always have to be in the bottom position during sex. Adam refused to let her hop on top, however, and after the ensuing quarrel she cursed him (mentioning God's unmentionable name) and flew out to the Red Sea to have orgiastic sex with demons, producing over 100 little demon babies every day. She rebuffed the angels sent to fetch her back, eventually focusing her energies on strangling infants and seducing sleeping men – in case you were wondering where wet dreams came from, which you probably weren't.

The Bible, as a narrative, is a hot mess. Biblical scholar Jacques Berlinerblau wryly defines a biblical scholar as "a person who has devoted his or her life to reasoning with a madman" (2005:22). Today *virtually all serious scholars* – of all faiths and backgrounds – understand that the Tanakh shares with the epics of Homer a gestation of many centuries. These ancient texts evolved in an oral culture and through the talents of many generations of composers, editors, and compilers. As with human evolution, the experts disagree on many of the details of this process, but the big picture is beyond debate. Of course, many branches of the Abrahamic religions reject or ignore this scholarly consensus and retain a belief in the perfect revelation and infallibility of the text. A 2017 Gallup poll revealed that a quarter of Americans (24 percent) believe the Bible is the literal word of God.

Homer claims to have divine help in his composition of the epics, but for some reason contemporary readers are not as predisposed to believe him. While appeals to the Muses "are uniquely Greek" (Ford 1992:31–2) in heroic poetry, they function similarly to the avowal that the Bible is divinely inspired. The poet summons the Muses at several crucial moments in the epics – especially but not only in the opening lines – to sharpen his vision, validate his talent, and provide him the necessary information to compose his epics. The successful bards who are depicted within the epics, Homer's doublets (e.g., Demodocus, *Od.* 8.62–73,499),[1] are specifically said to have acquired their ability from the Muses. The poet wants us to have no doubt that he's the kind of guy who has "connections." The sheer existence of the poems is proof of the goddesses' favor, that his work has been divinely authorized.

In this opening section we will briefly look at the similar origins of these texts, and then examine three of the many literary subgenres they share. This survey will provide our first glimpse of the characteristics common to Yahweh and Homer's Olympians and will set up a more careful exploration of these divine cousins in the following section.

Homer (and friends)

We have had conclusive arguments for almost a century that the epics are the products of a long oral tradition. The poems never mention poets or writers but consistently refer to singers and songs. The epics were composed in an artificial mixture of early Greek dialects, a poetic amalgam that was never spoken by any

Greek community and which developed to recall what classicist Andrew Ford refers to as the "poetry of the past," a "presentation of ancient but ever real and valid stories about gods and early mortals" (1992:47). The fates of Thebes and Heracles and Troy had been sung throughout the Greek world for hundreds of years by countless bards (probably accompanied by a stringed instrument as are singers in the poems; West 1988:165) before the *Iliad* and the *Odyssey* reached something like their present shape.

There were many different poetic traditions about the Trojan War – the two extant epics cover only a small fraction of the saga. Many poems dealing with the subject were originally attributed to Homer, but the Greeks later assigned these much shorter epics to other poets in what was eventually called the Epic Cycle. The basis for ascription of authorship seems to have been "a combination of guesswork and befuddlement" (Burgess 2015b:50), and ultimately the cyclic poems were quoted as anonymous. There were as many as a dozen different poems arranged chronologically in this cycle, the last six (along with the Homeric epics) covering the Trojan Saga from the Apple of Discord through the death of Odysseus and the immortality of his son. We have only testimonies, fragments, and (sometimes contradictory) summaries of these poems that now serve to "fill in" the mythological material before, in between, and after the action covered by the two Homeric texts.

The origins of Homer's epics in the ad hoc regeneration of the stories for each singing performance have been deduced from the intricate system of such conventional elements of oral poetics as meter (dactylic hexameter), formulae (adjective and noun combinations attached to nouns, e.g., "swift-footed Achilles," "dark-prowed ships"), and typical scenes (similarly structured descriptions of arming, greeting guests, etc.). The repetitions that encourage students to skim pages at a time are the very stuff of Homeric production.

Homer also mentions places, practices, and artifacts (e.g., body shields, silver-studded swords) that disappeared long before any historical Trojan War could have taken place, so we know that some of the poetic material goes back far into the Greek past and was later incorporated into a saga of Troy. On the other hand, there are elements (e.g., cremation, iron, massed warfare) that refer to post-Bronze Age developments, some from the seventh century or perhaps even later.

Just how this orally transmitted Troy story got mythologically trimmed, thematically focused, and ultimately expanded into two great and complementary epics, and when they took something like their final shape, have been the subject of intense debate termed the "Homeric Question." Was it by Greeks, Anatolians, or some collaborative effort? Was it in the late eighth century? Sixth? There is some consensus that it was not later than the seventh century, but one leading school of thought argues that the tradition, like that of the Tanakh, remained fluid for many centuries, perhaps given shape in the sixth century but not solidified until the Hellenistic world (third and second centuries BCE). Equally abundant are the theories about how and when these particular oral tales became authoritative and were written down. Did a bard (or different bards) dictate the text at some point? Did the poets themselves start writing down their own compositions?

Some scholars even think that the impetus for the reinvention of Greek writing in the eighth century was the desire to record Homer's poems.

None of this speculation is important for this book. As a Stanford Homerist once told me, "I'm not sure when the poems were written down or by whom, but I am fully prepared to accept that they were." That's good enough for us. We can safely follow what is now standard practice by using the name Homer, as did the Greeks, for the creative genius behind the two epics. I will use language throughout this book that assumes a single author creatively adapting and supplementing inherited stories, episodes, and motifs for specific thematic purposes. Since we are focusing on the gods as they are presented in the texts, it usually is of no consequence exactly how they got onto the page we are reading.

The authors of the Tanakh

The development of the Bible is remarkably similar to that of the *Iliad* and *Odyssey*, with homologous scholarly debates. The Tanakh, like the *Iliad*, is the result of many centuries of evolution, although the seams of its various traditions are often more visible and the strands of disparate theologies much more striking. Biblical scholars agree that the text is a composite of the efforts of widely divergent oral traditions, scribes, composers, schools, collectors, and editors ("redactors") over nearly a millennium. Each "source" has its own (often disputed) theological bias; linguistic character; compositional style; themes, political, social, and religious agenda; as well as historical context(s) – and most of them pop up in a variety of places throughout the text. Unlike Homer's poetic epics, the Tanakh contains numerous genres in both prose and poetry – narrative (heroic, epic, tragic), wisdom literature, prophecy, law of various kinds, genealogy, psalms, etc. The earliest layers derive from *perhaps* the tenth century, although some scholars push the oral tradition back in time still further, and most experts place much of the original composition and editing not earlier than the eighth century. The various strands were edited and reworked – with new material added – in exilic (middle of the sixth century) and postexilic or "Persian" period (late sixth century and after). The apocalyptic book of Daniel, a few chapters of which are written in Aramaic (the spoken language of the time) rather than Hebrew, refers to events occurring in the middle of the second century BCE. The book of Isaiah alone – supposedly the work of one prophet – probably has origins extending over half a millennium (Baumann 2003:175).

Exactly when the entire Tanakh was solidified into the "canon" we have today is also contested, but it seems unlikely to have occurred before the early centuries of the common era. A once-popular theory, that the books of the Tanakh were set by a rabbinic council at Jamnia/Yevne towards the end of the first century BCE, is no longer accepted by most scholars. Judaism, unlike Christianity, does not seem to have determined its theology or canon through a series of votes at cutthroat councils.

In general, with each generation of scholarship, the components of the Hebrew Bible get "younger," as the sources are now often dated later than was once postulated. As with the "text" of Homer's epics, numerous variants of the books of the Bible must have been in existence for hundreds of years. The Dead Sea Scrolls found in Qumran, for example, dating from third century BCE through the first century CE, make clear that there was no unified or unchanging "Tanakh" in pre-Christian times. These texts, discovered in the middle of the 20th century, include fragments from every book of the Tanakh except Esther, making them among the earliest extant biblical texts. Some of these ancient texts are nearly identical to the "official" Masoretic version from many centuries later (De Hamel 2001:329). But the language and content of others can differ from what eventually became the accepted text. We find among the scrolls, for example, a Hebrew version of the book of Jeremiah that coincides with the Greek texts of the Septuagint, both of which are one-sixth shorter than the traditional Jewish version and have certain sections in a different order.[2] Inconsistencies such as these reveal a high level of what scholars call the "pre-canonical textual fluidity" of the Tanakh.

One approach to understanding the origins of the Tanakh, especially the Torah, is to attribute different passages to different "original" sources that were eventually combined, sometimes quite complexly but with relatively little alteration, by an editor or editors (redactors). This is called the "Documentary Hypothesis," and it's a complicated business not for the faint of heart. The source for the first creation story, for example, has for hundreds of years been commonly known as P (for Priestly). Differing from P in style, content, the nature and even name of God is the J source – called after the Germanic word for Yahweh, the name used in this source for God – which is responsible for the Adam and Eve version. (Note that this means not every tradition in the Tanakh uses the name of Yahweh, although I have chosen for convenience to apply that name to the Hebrew God throughout the text.) Suggested dates for J range wildly from the tenth all the way to the sixth century. There once was a firmly established E source as well, but today it sometimes becomes a mysterious hybrid labeled something like JE or R^{JE}. Sometimes both J and E disappear altogether and become non-P. Or L. (Römer 2006; Arnold 2009:13; Carr and Conway 2010:165). This digging through the stratigraphy of literary sources has aptly been likened to archaeological fieldwork (Frendo 2011:61–7).

Those who seriously play this Documentary game find multiple strands woven through the biblical texts. Randall Garr introduces his book-length study of a single verse of the Bible – Genesis 1:26 – by dizzyingly suggesting that the P source "probably knew and utilized a combined JE tradition," and that P itself comprises an early source (P), a later "holiness stratum" (H), and a "subsequent, Priestly redactive hand (R^P) can also be detected where Priestly and non-Priestly texts meet" (2003:11–12). Or, in the words of another scholar, what about our apparent need to reconceive the "redaction-critical evidence that points to J redaction of earlier E material, D redaction of earlier E and J material, P redaction of earlier JED material and differentiation within the P material itself" (Sweeney 2012:52)? There's also a T source that some scholars see popping its head out in Numbers, and an H source floating through Leviticus as well, a "Holiness Code" that metastasizes on occasion into Pre-H_1, Pre-H_2, H, and H_R. Holy alphabet, Batman!

There are now many experts who reject either partially or entirely the Documentary Hypothesis, seeing the Bible as growing blob-like over the centuries, with new material added and adapted by various creative editors.[3] Others have adjusted (slightly), calling themselves "Neo-Documentarians." The general theory of edited accretions to the text is very similar to what early Homeric critics did with the epics. Friedrich Wolf, in his *Prolegomena ad Homerum* (1795), argued that "various blocks of tradition and songs in the *Iliad* and the *Odyssey* were put together by editors in the sixth century B.C.E. and . . . continued to be modified by editors until their 'final form' was reached by the greatest editor of all, Aristarchus, in the second century B.C.E." (Van Seters 2006:146; cf. Turner 1997:125–31). Critics of the Homeric texts (called Analysts) undertook to excavate and label the layers of earlier oral tales that Homer had in theory combined to produce his epics (Finkelberg and Stroumsa 2003:2; J. Taylor 2007:5). One 19th-century classicist uncovered *eighteen* separate tales that Homer had allegedly stitched together to create the *Iliad*! (No one believes this specific theory anymore, I hasten to add.)

In any case, no serious scholar of the Bible denies that many voices and hands over many hundreds of years contributed to its final form. The result of this long and labored compositional history is a hodgepodge of ambiguities, ellipses, and contradictions, with conflicting details (who killed Goliath?), competing accounts (how easily did the Jews conquer Canaan?), awkward doublets (how many times does Saul have to throw a spear at David before he starts to suspect the king's hostility?), clashing theologies (how was humankind created?), contrasting variants (was there a single pair of every animal on Noah's ark, or one pair of non-kosher animals and seven pairs of kosher animals?), editorial gaffes (how often can the Amalekites be exterminated?), confusing repetitions (why does Abraham keep trying to pass his wife off as his sister – is there no learning curve here?), divergent traditions (what's the name of Moses' father-in-law or the Mountain of Lawgiving?), amusing redundancies (how does the tenth plague kill the firstborn of the Egyptians' livestock when all their animals have already been killed in previous plagues – twice?!), incoherent composition (how does Joshua dismiss an assembly when he's been dead for an entire chapter?), inconsistent exposition (does God favor the creation of the kingship or not?), and slipshod accounting (did the flood last over a year or just a couple months, was Ahaziah 22 or 42 when he began to rule, were there 40,000 stalls or 4000, 2000 baths or 3000, 700 horsemen or 7000, etc.?).

In other words, the Tanakh shows its origins even more clearly than Homer's epics, which are also the products of many – but far less contentious – strands of composition and contain similar marks of their long gestational history. How many Greeks visit Achilles to persuade him to return to battle, two (as the Greek sometimes suggests) or three (as the scene itself reveals)? How many times can Hector slay Schedius, the leader of the Phocians? (At least twice, apparently.) How, exactly, does Pylaimenes weep for his slain son when he himself was killed by Menelaus eight books before? Is Odysseus an unwilling sexual partner with Calypso or does he "delight" in it? Or both? (And what would *that* say about

Odysseus, the kinky devil?) Do you need to be buried to enter the underworld or not? Are the Phaeacians hospitable as the story suggests, or inhospitable as Athena insists? And if Ocean is a body of water at the edge of the world, encircling the earth, how does Odysseus sail beyond it?[4]

No one really cares much about Homer's "slips," but those in the Hebrew Bible put the kibosh on any theory of divine authorship. The interesting question is how the editors of the Tanakh – pious Yahwists – could bring together such conflicting and contradictory tales into one text that supposedly reveals the Truth about their God. They certainly must have noticed the problems – the subsequent Jewish interpretive tradition is consumed by trying to explain the inconsistencies. Biblical scholar Philip Davies suggests that the ancient reader may have "understood that there was no way of knowing 'what had happened' and that two versions conveyed a fuller understanding than one" (2015:56). Ultimately, we are reminded that the compilers of the final version of the Tanakh were not trying to write history as we understand the term, and "at the expense of coherence and consistency, the Torah has achieved richness, mystery and an appeal to multiple sensibilities" (Propp 1998:53).

Biblical scholar William Propp warns us that "only a pedant would carp at such contradictions [in the Tanakh.] . . . We must not hold the Bible to anachronistic standards of journalistic accuracy" (1998:347). He is right, except that Western culture has been dominated by a belief in the Truth of the Bible, and the study of the Tanakh has not been merely a fascinating academic pursuit as is the study of Homer for classicists. The vast majority of Old Testament theologies have been developed by Christians, "almost exclusively Protestants" (Goldingjay 2016:476). The "field of biblical theology is a Christian field that addresses Christian concerns," affirms the author of an extensive study of the theology of the Tanakh, and "has been a Christian theological discipline throughout its history" (Sweeney 2012:11). Christian scholars have eternal damnation to worry about. They are trying to negotiate their own salvation, and they search for the seeds of it in the older testament. Mess up biblical interpretation, writes the Plummer Professor of Christian Morals at Harvard Divinity School, and you "will be held to a strict account at the final judgment." Yikes! And I thought tenure committees could be tough. "Since discerning what God, in the Bible, means for us to hear and to do is a matter of life and death, we must approach the interpretation of scripture as we do our own salvation, working it out with fear and trembling" (Gomes 1996:52).

The resulting confessional (that is, embedded in and aimed at supporting a particular religious perspective) approach has often resulted in distorted readings of Yahweh and has led some scholars to feel that they must defend the Tanakh's "inerrancy." As one Christian writer admits in his *Survey of the Old Testament*:

> If this written revelation contains mistakes, then it can hardly fulfill its intended purpose, that is, to convey to man in a reliable way the will of God for his salvation. Why is this so? Because a demonstrated mistake in one part gives rise to the possibility that there may be mistakes in other parts of the

Bible. If the Bible turns out to be a mixture of truth and error, then it becomes a book like any other book.

(Archer 1985:22, cited in McKinsey 1995:14)

But a really *cool* book. You know, like the *Iliad*.

Historicity

The Greeks always believed that the Trojan War was a historical reality. And there *was* a city of Troy on the Hellespont (as Homer refers to the Dardanelles in modern Turkey). It was a large and flourishing city off and on in northwest Anatolia for over three millennia. (The Emperor Constantine even considered building his new capital there.) Its walls collapsed in both the 13th and 12th centuries BCE, a reasonable time to set a possible Trojan War. It's not clear if the city was attacked or if an earthquake caused the damage; perhaps both.

We have archaeological evidence that the Late Bronze Age Greeks (called Mycenaeans) were active in the area at that time. Letters from Hittite archives contain over two dozen references to the Ahhiyawa, a group most scholars identify with the "Achaeans," Homer's favorite word for Greeks.[5] In this record of regal correspondence, dating from the 15th to the 13th century, we learn of numerous disputes between Hittites and Ahhiyawans, including a conflict over Wilussa, a toponym that likely refers to Troy (called Ilios or Ilion on occasion by Homer – hence, the *Iliad*). Wilussa in turn is ruled by an Alaksandu, which again generally is said to stand for Alexandros, the name most often given to the Trojan prince Paris in the epics. Clearly there were Late Bronze Age conflicts between Western Anatolians and some sea power in the Aegean – we even have images of Aegean-like warriors in the dedications found in the Hittite capital. Whether the Ahhiyawa are a local Mycenaean power or the mainland Mycenaeans remains a matter of speculation, but most scholars agree that they form at least part of the Greek world. And the *Odyssey* paints a picture of societal disruption and movement around the Mediterranean that is also matched by archaeological and external epigraphic evidence of the fall of the Hittite Empire, attacks on Egypt, and the collapse of Bronze Age Greece.

But we now also know from early Greek records inscribed in Linear B, the Late Bronze Age writing deciphered in the 1950s, that the structure of Mycenaean society bore little resemblance to that depicted in the Homeric epics. Homer does not present a reliable picture of historical Mycenaean life. If anything, the society he pictures may represent in some fashion the world of Dark Age Greece (11th–9th centuries) or, more likely, a period closely contemporary to the composition of the poems, the late ninth through the seventh centuries (Raaflaub 1997; Morris 2001).

The epics offer a poetic mash-up of some fact and a lot of fiction. There is no evidence to suggest that the Mycenaean Greeks put together an armada and sailed to Asia Minor to sack the city, much less to retrieve a valuable prize in the form of a runaway queen. Even classical Greek historians who accepted the historicity of the war rejected the mythical causes of the conflict. Ultimately, there is no material evidence that Greeks had anything to do with the collapse of Troy's walls. So it remains unclear how the legend of a ten-year siege began, and why it developed into such a foundational tale for all of subsequent Greek history. And I mean *all* of Greek history. Nearly a millennium after the traditional date of the Trojan War, Alexander the Great, a fanatical Homerophile, claimed descent from Achilles and was said to keep a copy of the *Iliad* under his pillow (next to a dagger – he may have loved Homer, but he lived among thuggish Macedonians and was no fool).

The Hebrew Bible is not history in any post-Herodotean sense either, but rather religious and ideological literature, or, as archaeologist William Dever labels it, "historicized fiction . . . what is essentially propaganda . . . that . . . does reflect *some* actual events," a "self-conscious attempt to legitimate and enforce the authors' orthodox theological views" (Dever 2005:64–72, emphasis in the original; 2017:5).[6] Real events and authentic references no doubt abound, but determining exactly what parts may contain reliable information – that is, reliable information about the period covered in the biblical narrative as opposed to the (usually) much later period of the production of the texts – remains the major challenge for all historians writing about ancient Israel. A very few mainstream scholars still trust the outline of the entire biblical narrative. These "maximalists" tend to be conservative evangelicals like the authors of *A Biblical History of Israel* (2003), a textbook which one leading biblical scholar referred to in a review as "an exercise in futility – indeed, it could even be considered a con" (Grabbe 2011b:232). There are also "minimalist" scholars who accept claims for the historicity of the biblical text only when they can be confirmed by other sources. Although we know that there was certainly a group of people called "Israel" by 1200 BCE, it's not clear where or what Palestinian entity this refers to. There is no archaeological or extrabiblical support for a mass exodus from Egypt – the earliest textual evidence from the Bible probably dates from at least 700 years after the traditional dating of the event (Berner 2017:206) – although some scholars hold onto the idea that a small portion of the first Israelites must have been formed from stragglers from Egypt.[7] No evidence exists for an escape across a Sea of Reeds (wherever that may be) or a 40-year sojourn in the desert. The story of the battles for the Promised Land provided in such detail in Joshua does not line up with the archaeological data; in fact, the material remains often contradict the story told in the Tanakh. For that matter, there are two very different accounts of Israelite manifest destiny, one represented in Joshua and the other in Judges.

Literary critic Eric Auerbach was echoing the critical consensus in the middle of the 20th century when he contrasted Homer's "legendary" material with the "predominately" historical narrative of David: "Much [of David's story] – and the most essential – consists in things which the narrators knew from their own experience or from firsthand testimony. . . . [It is] impossible to doubt the historicity of the information conveyed" (1953:15–17). And some archaeologists have recently argued that the site of Khirbet Qeiyafa, 20 miles from Jerusalem, is an Iron Age (early tenth-century) military outpost signifying some sort of significant political structure in Israel at that time (Schama 2013:77–87). But other scholars are skeptical, and most doubt the reality of a united monarchy that even vaguely resembles the impressive polity described in the Tanakh: "The problems with a history of the 'united monarchy' are very similar to those of a history of the Trojan War" (Grabbe 2007:223). Neither Saul nor Solomon makes an appearance in any extrabiblical source. King David exists outside the Bible in a single (debated) reference in a ninth-century Aramaic inscription mentioning the "city/ house of David." (Subsequent efforts to read David's name back into two other early inscriptions do not seem to have been persuasive.) But this dynastic phrase "House of David," so central to the Tanakh's story, is otherwise unknown outside the Bible (Lemche 1998:62) for *any* period. At best, David is "only at the threshold of history" (Becking 2011) – biblical scholar Hector Avalos is not alone in comparing him with King Arthur (2007:154–64).

The Deuteronomistic History – the portion of the Tanakh that relates the history of the Israelites in Canaan through the exile – was most likely not composed until the seventh century at the earliest and then was drastically revised after the destruction of the temple, hundreds of years after many of the events it details. Still, it does contain some information verified by archaeology and epigraphy. Israel (usually referred to as Samaria or the House of Omri) and Judah, as well as the names of numerous kings, eventually show up in contemporary records among neighboring nations, although the accounts often contradict the story as found in the Tanakh. Omri, for example, was clearly such an important king of Israel that the entire northern state is often referred to in Assyrian annals as the House of Omri. The "archaeological data . . . would allow us to write a substantial volume on the reign of Omri and its significance on the larger state of ancient New Eastern geopolitics" (Dever 2017:14). Yet the Tanakh covers his reign in four verses (1 Kgs 16:23–6), concluding merely with "he did what was evil in the sight of the LORD."

We can trust the basic narrative of Israel's defeat, exile, and destruction: Samaria was attacked by Sargon in 722 and became of province of Assyria. Many Israelites were deported and non-Israelites brought in, thus bringing an end to Samaria as an independent entity. Some of the surviving Israelites fled south to Judah. The Assyrian kingdom in turn fell at the end of the seventh century to the Neo-Babylonian empire. Judah, with its capital of Jerusalem, twice tried and failed to reject Babylonian dominance. In 597 Nebuchadnezzar pillaged Jerusalem and its temple, deporting thousands of Judahites to Babylon and taking off with the temple treasures. He returned to finish the job in 586, shipping off more Israelites and destroying the temple. In 538 the Persians conquered the Babylonians and Cyrus allowed the Jews to return and rebuild their temple. As we will see, the experience of exile radically altered Israelite (and ultimately Western) religion forever. But beyond this general outline, "there is little consensus" among biblical scholars about the historicity of the biblical accounts (Stavrakopoulou 2016:44).

The Homeric epics and the Tanakh thus share a similar legendary background that was taken as history within their own cultures. No one today *cares* that much if Homer's epics are "true," although apparently one can take a ten-day cruise that follows Odysseus' mythical journey around the Mediterranean. But the stakes are immeasurably higher for the biblical material. Even though the historicity of its early players – the patriarchs, Moses, Solomon, and, of course, Yahweh – is no more secure than that of Agamemnon, Achilles, Hera, and Zeus, billions of 21st-century humans and most Old Testament theologians nevertheless hang their understanding of the meaning of life at least partially on its veracity. In theory there are two distinct approaches one can take to these biblical texts: They can be seen as accounts of what people did believe or of what people *should* believe. In practice, however, biblical scholars can slip into prescriptive analysis, into the domain of theology: "Most [biblical scholars] have been religious believers, often ordained ministers; and description cannot be so easily separated from evaluation in some form" (Moberly 2016:481). Philip R. Davies notes that although confessional (that is, faith-based) and nonconfessional discourse should be separated, "theology has a vested interest in wearing the cloak of academic colours and thus in confusing the two discourses" (1995:27, 44). This blurring of intentions can result in what in most other academic fields would be startling confessions of bias by scholars:

> I do not come to the Old Testament to learn about someone else's God, but about the God we confess, who made himself known to Israel, to Abraham, Isaac and to Jacob. I do not approach some ancient concept, some mythological construct akin to Zeus or Moloch, but our God, our Father. The Old Testament bears witness that God revealed himself to Abraham, and we confess that he has also broken into our lives. . . . I stand in a community of faith which confesses to know God, or rather to be known by God. . . . I belong to a community of faith which has received a sacred tradition in the form of an authoritative canon of scripture.
>
> (Childs 1985:28)

As I said, the stakes are high.

Getting down to business

Given the similarities of the texts in terms of manner, time, Mediterranean and Near Eastern connections, thematic explorations, divine biographies, and influence on Western culture, it is surprising that there has been so little scholarly effort spent over the past few centuries in seriously comparing and contrasting the gods in these two cultures. An exception is classicist Bruce Louden, who wonders, "If I am correct that OT [Old Testament] myth offers the most relevant comparanda for the *Iliad*, why has previous scholarship not engaged in the two traditions more closely?" His speculation is illuminating:

> Perhaps largely because of reasons of faith, a wall exists between the study of Greek and OT myth, resulting in almost complete segregation of the two disciplines. Since polytheistic Greek religion is no longer practiced, whereas Judaism and Christianity are dominant religions, the sacred narratives of

the Bible are held to be 'real' and to provide ethical models, whereas Greek myths are seen, by comparison, as false and even immoral. But however modern audiences may feel about them, Greek myths *are* sacred narratives, were thought to be the word of god, and were written in most of the same specific mythic subgenres as was the OT.

(Louden 2006:8–9)

The parallels, if not their ramifications, between early Greek myth and sacred stories of the ancient Near East have long been registered and more recently cata-logued in detail by noted classicists like Walter Burkert (1992, 2004), Charles Penglase (1994), M.L. West (1997, 2007), and Jan N. Bremmer (2008b), although there has been a reasonable pushback against some of the more expansive claims (e.g., Kelly 2008). Mary Bachvarova (2016) has published a monumental argu-ment for the Anatolian background to the Homeric epics. These and other schol-ars (cf. López-Ruiz 2010:8–22; Haubold 2013) have occasionally noted parallels between Homer and the Tanakh as well, especially in the three-volume compila-tion by theologically trained John Brown (1995, 2000, 2001, cf. 2003). As Brown observes, "Commentaries on the Hebrew Bible emphasize its connections with the ancient Near East. . . . And Greek literature is regularly compared in turn with each of the ancient Near Eastern literatures except the one that it most resembles – Hebrew" (1995:5).

There is thus an odd gap in the scholarship. Scholars over the past century have successfully documented the parallels between the biblical narratives and those unearthed in Mesopotamian, Egyptian, and Ugaritic texts. Biblical archaeologists have also revealed a common religious culture, demonstrating that the people of ancient Israel lived religious lives very similar – in fact, often identical – to those of their neighbors.[8] The similarities between Israelite and nearby cultures have been explored in detail, although the significance of these connections for our understanding of the Bible and early Israelite religion remains the highly debated subject of much contemporary biblical scholarship.

Classicists, both philologists and experts in material culture, have done the same for Greek gods and the Near East with the purpose of understanding early Greece and the Homeric texts in their Mediterranean context. But rarely if ever have we looked at Yahweh through the prism of the Homeric gods. After all, there is usually no question of any direct influence in that direction, so what can we learn?[9] Scholars of religion (other than classicists) are almost never interested in Homer's gods, choosing instead – when they bother at all with the Greeks – to sur-vey either classical Athens or, more commonly, the Greek philosophical tradition and its influence on Christianity. Robert Bellah's masterful 700-page book on the "evolution" of religion from the Paleolithic to the axial age, for example, contains 75 pages on the ancient Greeks but not more than a paragraph on Homer's gods.[10]

Louden is one of very few scholars to bring the Hebrew Bible explicitly into an examination of the themes of the Homeric epics (2006, 2011), even arguing that the Hebrew Bible – especially Genesis – has closer links to the *Odyssey* than any Near Eastern text.[11] His approach is primarily literary and literary-historical, not theological (his works do not focus on the gods). He hopes such comparisons will enrich both our appreciation of the debts that early Greek oral tradition owed to its neighbors and also our understanding of the Homeric epics and the parallel Near Eastern passages. I wish to head in the opposite direction by pursuing some of the implications of these parallels as a comment on *Yahweh's* character.

Louden is no doubt right that the reason for avoiding drawing parallels between the Tanakh and the *Iliad* has often been faith. (It is also virtually impossible these days to have a professional competency in both Homeric Greek and biblical Hebrew while also mastering the immense secondary material in both fields.) But Yahweh shares many obvious characteristics with Homer's gods. And we shouldn't be surprised. After all, Yahweh developed as an ancient Near Eastern deity just as did El, Baal, Dagon, and a variety of goddesses (e.g., Astarte and Asherah) whose vestiges can still be detected throughout the Hebrew Bible (Krebernik 2017:48–54). Zeus, too, shares many Near Eastern and Indo-European mythical motifs. My initial point here is that the God of the Hebrew Bible is described and behaves much like his geographical contemporaries, *especially* the Homeric gods, a point that is rarely noted and even more rarely explored. Amidst numerous similarities on the human/heroic level that Louden (2006) has demonstrated between the Tanakh and the *Iliad* (he identifies 14 "subgenres" of myth found in both texts), he examines some direct links between Iliadic gods and Yahweh. As an introduction to the similarities of (and some of the important differences between) the divine as depicted in Homer's epics and the Tanakh, it will be fruitful to expand on three of Louden's mythical subgenres that involve the gods: Siege myths, "the plague bringer," and the divine council. I should note that this is my own examination of these topics and that Louden himself does not draw (and would probably shudder at) the kinds of conclusions that I draw from my expansion of the evidence.[12]

Trapped behind walls

You don't want to be in *any* besieged city. Ever. It was clearly a common and potentially horrific fate in the ancient Near East. In one Assyrian cuneiform text, the victorious king claims that he built a celebratory pillar after blockading and finally conquering a city – and then he flayed all the chief men who revolted, covering the pillar with their skins (Smith 1989:28). It has even been argued that the story of the Trojan horse itself – in some accounts the Trojans tore down a section of their walls to drag the horse inside the city – contains a memory of a siege engine's assault. The mythological cycle surrounding Thebes involved two separate attacks on the city, both mentioned in passing in the *Iliad*, and the reluctance of the hero Meleager to break a siege is told in the epic as an explicit parallel to Achilles' actions at Troy (9.529–99). Meleager's wife details "all the sorrows that happen to men whose city is captured; they kill the men and fire reduces the city to ash. And strangers lead off the children and deep-girdled women."

The Homeric epics don't supply an account of the fall of Troy itself. The *Iliad* makes several references to a previous sack of Troy by Heracles (5.638–51;

8.282–5; 14.250–6). And the *Odyssey*, in addition to Menelaus' short account of the Greeks' difficult experience waiting within the Trojan Horse, recapitulates the destruction in brief when Odysseus relates his very first venture after sailing from Troy – he attacks a city. "There I sacked the city and destroyed the men; and we took the wives and many of their belongings from the city and divided them up" (*Od.* 9.40–42; cf. *Od.* 14.257–65).

In the *Iliad*, Agamemnon, the leader of the expedition, expresses typical extremes of Near Eastern martial rhetoric when he hopes that not a single Trojan will "escape utter destruction at our hands, not even the one, a son, whom a mother carries in her womb" (6.57–59). Homer, who "normally condemns excessive cruelty and violence" (Kirk 1990:161), calls Agamemnon's gruesome injunction "fitting." We might expect this sort of malevolence from Agamemnon, but Nestor, the geriatric voice of cultural wisdom in the epic, advocates the rape of female captives (2.354–6). All of the women we encounter in the Greek camp are surviving victims of Greek attacks, prizes for the victorious warriors.

Such pitiless treatment was anticipated by those in a besieged city. Andromache, the wife of the Trojan military leader Hector, saw her father and seven brothers all slaughtered when Achilles laid waste to her native city (6.413–28). Her mother was ransomed off for more "prize" money. After Achilles kills Hector, Andromache envisions her slavery and that of her young son, or an even worse fate for him: "Or one of the Achaeans, angry because Hector killed his brother perhaps, or his father, or his son, will grab you by the arm and hurl you from the wall, a miserable death," (24.734–7; cf. Priam's grim vision of his own fate, and that of Troy, at 22.59–76). Her apprehension foreshadows the subsequent fate of the child, Astyanax, who we learn from other sources will be thrown from the walls to prevent his maturing into a future threat to the Greeks.

This behavior is, unfortunately, typical in the ancient Near East, and the Tanakh is also replete with vividly grisly treatments of the defeated. A victor, whether Israelite or an enemy, will not spare the conquered, but will "set their fortresses on fire, you will kill their young men with the sword, dash in pieces their little ones, and rip up their pregnant women" (2 Kings 8:12; cf. 2 Kings 15:16; Isa. 13:15–16; Hos 13:16; Amos 1:13). The psalms are filled with pleas for God to retaliate brutally on "enemies" or "evildoers," the "most troublesome aspect" of the hymns (Davies 2010:9; e.g., Pss 58:8–10; 109:6–19; 140:1–11; 143:12). The psalmist can't wait for vengeance upon the Edomites for aiding Babylon in the capture of Jerusalem: "Happy shall they be who take your little ones and dash them against the rock" (137:7–9). These strangely joyous words conclude the famous psalm which begins with "By the rivers of Babylon . . . ," "one of the most vicious poems found in the Hebrew Bible" (Avalos 2007:239). No wonder conservative and liberal Jews (although not orthodox Ashkenazi) have removed these three lines from their recitation, as have the Catholics when the hymn is used in the Liturgy of the Hours (Römer 2013:117–18).

The gods in their respective texts share the same visceral response. Homeric gods can be vicious. Hera says she would be willing to see her three favorite cities crushed if she can wipe the besieged Troy off the map. Zeus claims that the only way she could quell her rage would be to "devour Priam raw and the sons of Priam and the other Trojans" (4.30–36). Athena, along with Hera, Poseidon, and Apollo, aids warriors in combat, and even helps guide spears on occasion into the enemy (including her brother Ares). The only god to kill a mortal personally (that is, not in assistance of a mortal) in battle, however, is Ares (5.846–8).

Zeus himself is responsible for the renewed slaughter in the battles that comprise the *Iliad*. When the war could have come to an "early" end (with 20 more books to go!), the gods step in at his orders to make sure a truce is broken and the war reengaged. Poseidon has no thought for the Trojans penned up in the city, even the women and children like Andromache and Astyanax, for whom the poet has encouraged the reader to have pity. The god works tirelessly, he insists, so that "the insolent Trojans may be utterly and wretchedly destroyed with their children and honored wives" (21.459–60).

We may not be surprised at such attitudes from Homer's gods, but Yahweh's actions in war are similar, although he's a bit less physically intrusive than some of the Olympians and even more punitive. He literally throws (hail)stones at the enemy of the Israelites (Joshua 10:11), marches into battle (Judg 5:4–5), fights with a (metaphorical?) right hand and arm (Ps 44:3; cf. Ex 15:6, where he may hold a weapon, Propp 1998:519), and defeats Israel's enemies with a "blast" of his nostrils (Ex 15:8). The Hebrew God returns from battle with his garments spattered red with blood "like theirs who tread the wine press" (Isa 63:2–6). Yahweh revels in the blood of his enemies (which often include his own wayward people): The mountains will flow in it (Isa 34:3), his arrows will be drunk with it (Deut 32:42), the victorious "righteous" will bathe their feet in it (or clean their feet of it, Ps 58:10), and the sword will drink its fill of it (Jer 46:10; cf. Ps 68:22–23; Ezek 39:17–20). Indeed, Yahweh loves a good battle as much as Athena and Ares – the Tanakh even retains a reference to an ancient epic entitled the *Book of the Wars of the Lord* (Num 21:14; Korpel 1990:506–22).

Yahweh frequently demands a holy war, or sacred "ban" (*herem*), against an enemy city. Scholars have uncovered different nuances in the concept, but Susan Niditch (1993) has identified three general categories of this ban. (1) *Herem* is considered to be "God's portion," with everything belonging to the enemy "consecrated for total destruction." This requires the elimination of all traces of the besieged inhabitants of Canaan and its surrounding area (Asen 2012:58–65). And by "demands," I mean that one of the canonical laws in Deuteronomy is to "utterly destroy them" and "show no mercy" (7:1–2). And by "inhabitants" I mean not just the men but often the women, children, and livestock who are in the way of Yahweh's rezoning plan for the Levant. (2) Sometimes *herem* is viewed as a sacrifice to Yahweh. Although some defenders of Yahweh want to see this as metaphorical, Niditch has little patience for this dodge: "One cannot but conclude that many scholars are simply incapable of seeing their God as one who demands and receives humans in exchange for victory, because of world-views shaped by the normative theological expectations of their own religious traditions. But some Israelites thought that God desired human beings as offerings" (1993:41). Scholar John J. Collins dryly observes that the enemy is thus deemed "worthy" of being offered: "One hopes that the Canaanites appreciated the honor" (2003:6). (3) *Herem* can also be viewed as divine justice, which means it becomes a necessary act to root out the non-Yahwistic (i.e., the "impure" and "sinful" forces). Yahweh *encourages* wars of annihilation. In the book of Joshua, where the word *herem* appears more than in any other biblical book (27 times), the "ideology of the ban means that the war is not for the purpose of conquest, but of extermination" (Dozeman 2015:54–9). More likely, it's both.

Although some apologists argue that these "urbicides" never really occurred – thus admitting that the Tanakh is not reliable history – it turns out in this case that such genocidal passages are likely to reflect reality. One famous bit of epigraphic evidence, the ninth-century Mesha Inscription, reveals that a king of Moab committed *herem* against a city of Israel: "I took it and slew it all, seven thousand men and infant boys, women and infant girls, and pregnant females, for I performed *herem* against it for Ashtar-Kemosh" (cited in Lemos 2015:30). Biblical scholar Sa-Moon Kang has pointed out numerous parallels between the inscription and Israelite practice as presented in the Tanakh (1989:83–4), and cross-cultural similarities "enhance the historical plausibility of the biblical accounts which picture the *herem* as an actuality of Israel's warfare" (Stern 1991:65; cf. Crouch 2009:174–89; Van Wees 2010:242). In fact, the accounts of the conquest of the Promised Land in Joshua have strong parallels with the military narratives of victorious Assyrian kings (Dozeman 2015:67–74; Römer 2016:119).

Yahweh sets out very specific rules of engagement for when his chosen people are besieging a city (Deut 20:10–20). The Israelites are first to offer peace. If this works out, then the entire population is merely consigned to slavery. However, if the city resists and must be besieged, "when the Lord your God gives it into your hand, you shall put all its males to the sword," and everything else is to be taken as "booty" to enjoy. So far, we're still in the Homeric realm, including the fact that Yahweh not only sanctions but in fact mandates the institution of slavery (cf. Ex 21:20–1; Lev 25:44–62; Deut 15:12,17; Chron 12:7–8; Joel 3:8). But this relatively mild action is only to be taken against cities that are "very far from you." "But in the cities of these peoples that the Lord your God gives you for an inheritance, *you shall save alive nothing that breathes*, but you shall utterly destroy them, the Hittites and the Amorites, the Canaanites and the Perizzites, the Hivites and the Jebusites, as the Lord your God has commanded" (my emphasis).

While some sympathetic scholars have understandably attempted to soften Yahweh's hyper-Olympian portrait (e.g., Miller 2009:235–8), others have argued Yahweh's genocidal commands were completely justified. William Foxwell Albright, one of the most celebrated biblical scholars of the 20th century, was quite clear about the nature of the natives of the Promised Land: "From the impartial standpoint of a philosopher of history, it often seems necessary that a people of markedly inferior type should vanish before a people of superior potentialities, since there is a point beyond which racial mixture cannot go without disaster" (1957:280). His supporting evidence is supplied by parallels to the extermination of "scores of thousands" of Native Americans in America (which he does not admire but thinks "was probably inevitable"). Contemporary Christian theologians like Paul Copan continue to repeat these same charges: "[T]he evidence for profound moral corruption [of the Canaanites] was abundant. God considered them ripe for divine judgment, which would be carried out in keeping with God's saving purposes in history" (2010:160). God's "saving purposes" in this case include killing every man, woman, child, and animal in those towns that don't surrender to the invading Israelites. After all, as Seventh-Day Adventist theologian Richard Davidson reminds us, "these Canaanites, with their abominable practices, were given four hundred years of probation (Gen 15:16), with many opportunities to learn of the true God and the universal standards of morality" (2007:175).

These theistic scholars are repeating what we now know are the errant biblical slanders of the indigenous inhabitants invented by the biblical authors, and they are ignoring the extrabiblical and archaeological evidence. The Canaanites of the Bible are falsely presented as entirely different ethnically, politically, ethically, and religiously from the Israelites, a constructed "Other" created by the authors as the "counter-image of what Israel claimed to be – a precise antithesis of Israelite society" (Niehr 2010:26; cf. Lemche 1999). But the historical reality is quite different. The Israelites were virtually Canaanites themselves: "Israelite and Judaean traditions should be included among Canaanite traditions, not portrayed as being opposed to, completely other than, or superior to Canaanite traditions" (Ballentine 2015:6; cf. Coogan 2010:187–8). Yahweh himself admits that the usurpation of Canaanite land for the Israelites was a matter of good old-fashioned land-grabbing, not punishment for immorality or a failed "probation": "I gave you a land on which you had not labored," he boasts, "and towns that you had not built, and you live in them; you eat the fruit of vineyards and oliveyards that you did not plant" (Josh 24:13).

There are times when Yahweh lets the Israelites keep a little from the sacked city for themselves. On divine orders, Moses eradicates *60* towns, "utterly destroying men, women, and children. But all the livestock and the plunder of the towns we kept as spoil for ourselves" (Deut 3:3–7; cf. Deut 2:31–36). Similarly, the Hebrew God tells Joshua to do to the city of Ai what he did to Jericho (level it), but this time he can keep the spoils and livestock (Josh 8:1–2). Joshua duly obeys, killing 12,000 men and women, "all the people of Ai," taking the livestock and spoils. Finally getting the hang of his God's temperament and demands, Joshua kills "every person" in Makkedah, Libnah, Lachish, Gezer, Eglon, Hebron, Debir, and Hazor but keeps the spoil and the livestock (Josh 10:28–11:15).

Yahweh is, as ever, equally tough on his own people. When the walls of Jericho were about to come a-tumblin' down, Joshua informs them that the city and all within "shall be devoted to the Lord for destruction." The army "utterly destroyed all in the city, both men and women, young and old, oxen, sheep, and asses, with the edge of the sword." But one soldier (Achan) violated the command and took some souvenirs, resulting (through Yahweh's invisible hand) in the defeat of Israel and the death of many Israelites in their next battle. Joshua is informed that this military reverse has been Yahweh's punishment. The guilty man – along with the illegal booty, his sons, daughters, oxen, asses, and even his tent – is quickly stoned and burned (Josh 6.17–7.26), thereby projecting "a portrait of a deity who is cruel, petty, and vengeful" (Clements 2000:114). Disobeying God's demand for total annihilation, for whatever reason, is lethal, even for kings, as Saul famously discovers (1 Sam 15). Joshua is consequently rewarded by Yahweh for cleaning up after the sinners with a victory over the previously successful enemy, slaughtering "all the inhabitants," hanging the king, and burning the city to the ground, making it "a heap of ruins, as it is to this day" (Josh 8:1–29).[13]

The point of this catalogue of divine ruthlessness is that Yahweh's morality towards his human enemies trapped inside a town is similar to that of the Homeric gods, if not in fact even more barbaric.[14] All counting – by those who count such things – there are 1,670,000 mass killings enumerated in the Bible (White 2012:109–11). Military historian Hans Van Wees concludes in his study of genocide in the ancient world that "they [the Israelites] pushed common ancient attitudes to their more-or-less logical and most brutal extreme" (2010:256). The Jesuit scholar of religion Raymund Schwager estimates that the Tanakh contains "over *six hundred* passages that explicitly talk about nations, kings, or individuals attacking, destroying and killing others" (Schwager 1987:47, emphasis in original). In one passage, Yahweh is gleefully given credit for giving a victory to Judah over the Ethiopians (Cushites) that resulted in the deaths of *one million* enemy soldiers (2 Chron 14:8–13).

Yahweh is a Near Eastern deity along the lines of the Olympians. Sitting around some heavenly campfire, they would all have similar yarns to share of crushing despised cities. Yahweh would probably win the boasting contest, but all these deities share an appetite for vengeance. There are, however, two significant differences in the role of the gods in siege stories that are worth noting in this initial comparison.

First, Homer is not interested in justifying the gods' violent passion for revenge. On the contrary, he holds it up for critique. Even Zeus is stunned by the ugliness of Hera's hatred of Troy. The actual destruction of the besieged city is excluded from both poems. Homer does not demonize the Trojans or design the narrative so the audience of the epics roots for their extinction. Most readers find Hector more sympathetic than any major Greek warrior (perhaps excepting Achilles' closest friend, Patroclus) and Trojans Hecuba and Andromache more appealing than Helen. Homer is not playing favorites. While the *Iliad* is filled with vivid details of battle gore that the audience must have enjoyed – the poet knows five dozen ways to say that somebody died (Lateiner 2004:12) – Homer rarely lets a body drop in battle without telling us something about the victim. The poet has sympathy for the human condition, as do even his gods on occasion. The entire point of the Israelites' urbicides, on the other hand, is to emphasize Yahweh's *righteous* liquidation of the "abominable" indigenous population of the Promised Land. We're invited to celebrate the obliteration of the men, women, children, and animals (but not the trees, Deut 20:19–20) of the Canaanites.

Secondly, for Homer's warriors, it's not primarily about religion. The two sides have the same gods. Athena, the great battlefield supporter of the Greeks, has a temple on the acropolis of Troy (6.88,269,297), near one of Apollo, the adamantine defender of the Trojans (5.446), and the Trojans and Greeks pray to both. Zeus admits that Troy, doomed for demolition, is his favorite city (4.44–49). There can be no such thing as holy war for Homer's gods – they are not "national" gods like Yahweh. Hera comes closest to Yahweh in her unremitting hatred, not just for Troy but often for the gods supporting the city (e.g., 21.331–41,412–14,479–92; 24.55–63). But this animus does not derive from any Trojan cultic failures. Yahweh's motives are *all* about religion. He's made a deal (covenant) with his chosen people to give them a homeland and a great nation *provided that they worship him alone of all the gods*. The primary reason that everyone must be killed in a conquered city is so that the Israelites will not "consort" with the natives – something that happens with great frequency – and start worshiping "foreign" gods.

A plague of evils

Ancient Near Eastern gods can be equally lethal when it comes to god-sent disease, but Yahweh is also more impressively murderous in this arena than any Homeric deity. Apollo brings a plague upon the Greeks in the first book of the *Iliad* at the request of one his priests. He sits near the Greek ships and takes aim: "Terrible was the twang of his silver bow. He first attacked the mules and the swift dogs, but then letting fly his sharp arrows at the men themselves, he struck them down; and the dense pyres of the dead burned without end" (1.49–52). The disease lasts for over a week, causing Hera finally to inspire Achilles to call an assembly to determine the cause. Apollo, the most fervent supporter of the Trojans among the Olympians, was no doubt happy to undermine his opponents as well as punish mortals for their lack of respect for his priest. He relents when the Greeks placate the priest and appease the god himself with a hefty sacrifice.

Yahweh also sends plagues upon humans, sometimes delivering the pestilence himself and sometimes through a divine messenger. Dan Barker has catalogued over 50 instances of plagues and pestilence sent or threatened by Yahweh, mostly against his own people (2016:151–65). Several Canaanite gods may have been downgraded and demonized in the Tanakh as vehicles of pestilence under Yahweh's control (Xella 1999:702–3), although this interpretation has been challenged (Blair 2009). Individual Israelites, especially those speaking in the psalms, frequently express the hope that God's arrows and disease fall on their enemies and not on them (e.g., Pss 18:14; 38:2; 64:7; 144:6; cf. 2 Sam 22:15). The most spectacular fulfillment of this wish – after the ten Egyptian scourges – is the plague that sends King Sennacherib scurrying back to Nineveh. Jerusalem is being besieged by the powerful Assyrian ruler, with no hope in sight. Well, none except the Angel of the Lord, who "went forth, and slew a hundred and eighty-five thousand in the camp of the Assyrians" with what many scholars have understood as a virulent disease (2 Kgs 19:35; cf. Isa 37:36).

But Yahweh is just as likely to target his own obdurate people as the enemy. His usual *modus operandi* is to allow a neighboring group to kill hundreds if not thousands of his followers in battle as a punishment for their worshiping additional gods. But disease is an equally effective weapon for displaying his disapproval. Yahweh promises that if the people do not obey all his commandments, the "Lord will make the pestilence cling to you until it has consumed you off the land that you are entering to possess. The Lord will afflict you with consumption, fever, inflammation, with fiery heat and drought, and with blight and mildew; they shall pursue you until you perish" (Deut 28:21–2; cf. Deut 32:20–24; Ps 106:28–9).

Even at the very beginning of his people's 40-year sojourn in the desert, Yahweh had already grown weary of their complaints and misbehavior and wanted to destroy them all. "How long will they despise me?" he asks Moses, if only for rhetorical effect. A little over a year into the journey, Yahweh decides to strike them all with a pestilence and find a "greater and mightier" nation for Moses to lead to the Promised Land. (This passage and similar ones at Ex 32:7–14 and Deut 9:14 have always suggested to me that Yahweh is more interested in a promotion to national god than in Abraham's descendants. He primarily wants loyal followers for some property he's picked out, and he's willing to start over with a new batch of more obedient acolytes.) Moses intervenes, and God changes his mind, instead angrily vowing that only one loyal soul currently over 20 years old will enter Canaan (Num 14:10–24). (In his wrath, Yahweh forgets to include Joshua, Moses' eventual replacement as leader of the Israelites; Yahweh remembers after he has calmed down a little; Num 14:30, 38.) A short time later a Yahweh-sent plague kills another 14,700 of his chosen people (Num 16).

But Yahweh is just warming up. He takes out 24,000 Israelites for consorting with non-Israelite women and worshiping their gods. That plague is only averted after Phinehas, a grandson of Aaron, finishes off one of the couples as they are having sex: "Taking a spear in this hand, he went after the Israelite man into the tent, and pierced the two of them, the Israelite and the woman, through the belly" (Num 25:1–9).

Particularly odd is the story of David's culminating error (2 Sam 24). For no stated reason, "Again the anger of the Lord was kindled against Israel, and he incited David against them, saying, 'Go, count the people of Israel and Judah.'" Apparently taking a census was an actionable crime in this case. (Scholars have noted connections between censuses and plagues, but no convincing solution has been offered to this particular puzzle or other "inconcinnities that the reader of chap. 24 will observe"; McCarter 1984:514.) Divine command or not, David has been bad, and from the three options for punishment offered by Yahweh, David chooses "three days' pestilence." Immediately "seventy thousand of the people died, from Dan to Beer-sheba." That's a lot of dead Israelites for no stated reason beyond God's unspecified displeasure. The angel who was dispatched to do the deed then "stretched out his hand toward Jerusalem to destroy it." Yahweh has second thoughts, "repented concerning the evil," and stops the destruction of the entire city. David is told to build an altar to God, which he does, thereby strangely stopping the plague a second time.

All in all, Yahweh appears in this story as capricious, deceptive, and intemperate as – and a good deal more bloodthirsty than – the Olympians. This act of unwarranted divine (in)justice was acceptable to the composers of Samuel, but by the time the Chronicler was retelling the same story several hundred years later, Yahweh's act needed to be cleaned up. So although the two versions are nearly identical, an important change was introduced at the very beginning of the story. Rather than the unmotivated "anger of the Lord" playing the lead role, we read in 1 Chronicles 21:1 that "Satan stood up against Israel, and incited David to count the people of Israel." When in doubt, there's always Satan, although it's still not clear why this particular census is satanic.

It should be hard, I think, even at this preliminary point in our study, for any objective reader of the Tanakh to insist that Yahweh is a more ethical, reasonable, or transcendent deity than Homer's gods on many occasions. He would be quite comfortable on Zeus's throne, although he would spend far more of his time judging and punishing humans for various personal affronts (cf. Job 7:16,19).[15] Yahweh looks patently Olympian. As Louden observes, "Yahweh's destruction of all the inhabitants of Sodom and Gomorrah, or having the Israelites slay each other in Exodus 32 until over 3,000 die, are at least as problematic as Poseidon's destruction of the Phaeacian crew in *Odyssey* 13" (2011:15). At *least*.

Zeus and Yahweh: Presiding over a family of gods

Okay. Picture this famous scene from an ancient text. We're at a divine assembly, with the chief god surrounded by family members. The conversation turns to the linkage between human behavior and suffering, with the focus on the fate of a particular virtuous man. A subordinate deity, perhaps even one of the chief god's children (with no other parent, it seems), confronts the supreme ruler: Let me intervene in the life of this exemplary human. The supreme god quickly agrees: Go ahead, do what you wish. The matter seems to have run its course, but the subordinate returns later for a second meeting. Again they discuss the actions and fate of this righteous mortal. And again the chief god gives his subordinate permission to take care of matters as necessary. At this point the real story begins, a poetic account of heroic suffering and the tangible reward of the return of everything once lost by the long-suffering hero – possessions, status, and family.

On the one hand, we're talking about the beginning of the *Odyssey*. At a divine assembly of the Olympians, Zeus draws attention to the behavior of a nefarious man (Aegisthus) who ignored divine warnings and has met the anticipated punishment. Nevertheless, Zeus complains, humans blame the gods. True enough, his daughter Athena cuts in, but what about Odysseus, a just man who has been struggling to get home from the Trojan War for ten years? Zeus tells Athena to go ahead and do what she needs to get Odysseus home. She takes some action, but four books later Odysseus is still stuck on an island with no escape in sight. Athena returns to the council and again complains about her favorite's fate, and Zeus, understandably a bit perplexed, tells her again to take care of it. This time Zeus also sends one of his other children, Hermes, to see to Odysseus' release, and the wandering hero is soon on his final leg to recover his kingdom, wife, and son.

But on the other hand, we've also just described the tale of Job. The book of Job is a marvelous bit of the "wisdom tradition," ostensibly the tale of a righteous man who is "tested." Will he curse God if all the goods in his life (livestock, servants, children, health, reputation) are taken from him for no apparent reason? The book is a testament of self-dignity in the face of iniquitous divine actions and lousy friendships rather than in any real sense the exploration of the nature of suffering, as is often claimed.

Stationed before the poetry are two chapters of a dramatic prose prologue setting up the following 40 chapters. For those of you who have not looked at this introduction for a while, you may be surprised to recall the details. A flourishing seminomadic sheik, Job is described in the second verse as "blameless and upright, one who feared God, and turned away from evil." Job is blessed with a wife, ten children, and so many sheep, camels, oxen, donkeys and servants that he "was the greatest of all the people of the east."

More significant to the themes of the book, Job does all that is right in the sight of God. But his pleasant life is about to take an unfortunate turn: "One day the heavenly beings [sons of God] came to present themselves before the Lord, and Satan also came among them" (1:6). Satan is not a proper name here. It should be "the satan," a (temporary?) title indicating his role in this particular story. It is not until many hundreds of years after the composition of Job that the satan becomes Satan, the fallen, demonic angel who tempts us into having premarital sex or coveting our neighbor's ox, and rules over a Kingdom of Darkness (Breytenbach and Day 1999; Kelly 2006). In Job, he's merely another divine being in Yahweh's council playing an oppositional role, an "adversary" or "accuser."

My immediate point is the Olympian council itself. Yahweh is surrounded by his fellow deities, the "sons of God" (or "sons of *gods*"), of whom (the) Satan is probably one (Clines 1989:19). As we will see in a later chapter, this council of gods is referred to numerous times in the Tanakh. It's part of a common Near Eastern image of the divine pantheon, with one patriarchal deity holding royal court in the midst of his subordinates. It's a "mythical subgenre" that is shared by the Homeric epics and the Tanakh.

But we shouldn't stop there. The two texts share not just similar literary topoi revealing a polytheistic background, but they also introduce similarly anthropomorphic deities. Yahweh, with an unmistakable tone of pride, asks Satan if he had noticed Job, the most blameless and upright man on earth "who fears God and turns away from evil" (1:8). Satan insidiously connects Job's piety with his enviable circumstances. Take away his good fortune, Satan insists, and Job "will curse you to your face" (v. 11). God is not going to back down from this challenge, so he tells Satan to do whatever he wishes to Job's "possessions"; his only restriction is not to touch Job directly. Satan enthusiastically accepts the offer, immediately causing (in quick succession): (1) the theft of oxen and asses, and the murder of servants; (2) the conflagration ("fire of God") of the sheep (and more servants); (3) more livestock rustling, this time of the camels (and the murder of even more servants); and (4) the death of all ten children when a divine wind blows the house down upon them. Job formally indicates his grief by tearing his robe and shaving his head, but his most pronounced reaction to losing everything but his wife in one day is to fall upon the ground and worship Yahweh: "In all this Job did not sin or charge God with wrongdoing" (v. 22).

So far, it's God one and Satan zero. In the second chapter of the book, the initial scenario is repeated with a twist. Satan returns with the sons of God for another council meeting, and Yahweh boasts to Satan again of Job's fidelity, even though "you incited me against him, to destroy him for no reason" (v. 3). Satan can't let it go, noting that Job may have lost everything external, but he still has his health. "But stretch out your hand now and touch his bone and his flesh, and he will curse you to your face" (v. 5). God, confident as ever, tells Satan *to do whatever he wishes to Job short of killing him*! Satan again jumps at the opportunity, afflicting Job with such torturous sores "from the sole of his foot to the crown of his head" that his wife's only advice is to "curse God, and die" (v. 9). Job doesn't. Four "friends" try in vain to convince him that his affliction must be in some way deserved – God doesn't inflict such torments on the innocent. And thus begins the tension between suffering, sin, innocence, pride, piety, prosperity, conventional understandings of how God works, and God's arrogance and incomprehensibility that has earned the book such a warranted reputation.

One of the major revelations that comes late in the text is the inscrutability, the power, the distant nature of Job's creator God. Yahweh's self-avowed isolation from humanity is especially painful since the innocent Job primarily wants to confront his irresponsible accuser (Yahweh) face to face to learn what he has done to deserve his terrible afflictions. (The answer, as we are all informed up front, is nothing.) And he gets half of his wish. His accuser does appear in some fashion – and that's important: God *does* exist, even if he is nasty. But what Job gets from Yahweh the storm-god is a whirlwind of bravado, speeches of such arrogant misdirection and pompous posturing – "sublime irrelevance," James Crenshaw labels them (1992:76) – that even the unrelenting Job can do nothing but concede to God's very different point. Job's last words are ambiguous according to specialists in biblical Hebrew. It is not clear if he "recants" or "despises" or "regrets" or "yields" – or simply shudders for the human condition, not conceding anything to Yahweh at all (Miles 1995:317–27 with 425–30).[16] The tale, ultimately, is "replete with ambiguity" (Cooper 1990:74).

Yahweh's poetry is brilliant, the fulminations of a hectoring despot in a "nightmare world of divine tyranny in which unsubstantiated suspicions of disloyalty may lead to death of the innocents and to unbelievable personal suffering even by those renowned for their wisdom, devotion, and moral virtue" (Perdue 1994:131). He recites his résumé, conjuring up his strength and backing it up with threats of his thunderbolts: "Who shut in the sea with doors? . . . Can you bind the chains of the Pleiades, or loose the cords of Orion? . . . Can you send forth lightnings . . . ?" (Job 38:8,31,35). The Hebrew God sounds a lot like the father in Roald Dahl's *Matilda*, who (in the movie version) protests his superiority over his daughter in similarly blustering language: "Listen, you little wiseacre: I'm smart, you're dumb; I'm big, you're little; I'm right, you're wrong, and there's nothing you can do about it." And he sounds very similar to Zeus threatening his fellow gods with his own thunderbolt: "Whichever one of you I notice choosing, apart from the gods, to go to aid Trojans or Danaans, struck by lightning will he come back to Olympus in no pretty fashion. . . .

Whenever I really wanted to, I could drag [you] up with the earth itself and the sea as well" (8.10–12, 23–4).

Job is heroic in his relentless self-assertion, his patient subservience to God in the prologue shifting to an angry protest of his innocence and a demand to meet his accuser. The text forces the reader to reflect not just upon the nature and strange unintelligibility of God but on the apparent randomness of existence, the (im)possibility of moral order, and the human struggle of living in an imperfect world. It's the closest the Bible comes to tragedy in the real Greek sense (Exum 1992:8).[17] Even the disappointing ending of Job – Job turns out to be "right" and gets all his "stuff" back – offers a Greek *deus-ex-machina* kind of tragic resolution that recalls Sophocles' *Philoctetes* (or vice versa).

Here's the rub: If this had been a story about Zeus, we would be lectured by Abrahamic theologians about his selfish pride and inexcusable cruelty. These theologians would highlight the moral weakness inherent in a polytheistic religion, as Yahweh's primary motivation is to defeat a verbal challenge from a divine adversary sitting in some sort of heavenly meeting. The deity's indifference to human life – afflictions brought "for no reason," Yahweh admits – would be labeled "typical" if not "demonic," as he is willing to be the cause of the deaths of ten guiltless children and a lot of guiltless servants as part of his self-promoting experiment. And that's not counting the guiltless livestock. (There were 11,500 of them – I counted – a good portion of them innocent, self-combusting sheep.) More than one biblical scholar has concluded that the book of Job portrays Yahweh as an "omnipotent sadist" (Levenson 1988:154; cf. "devilish sadistic," Pope 1965:lxix). "If the incident is an example of the way in which Yahweh decides about the treatment to be meted out to his human creatures – and there is nothing in the text to suggest that it is untypical – it presents a picture of an immoral, unjust and uncaring God" (Whybray 1996:106). David Clines, trying to limit the damage, suggests that Yahweh, "like everyone else, does not know what the outcome will be." That is, he is not entirely omniscient here, confident but unsure just how Job will respond. Otherwise, Clines worries, we're left with a "worse" alternate reading: "Affirm that Yahweh is infinitely omniscient, and you assert that Job's suffering serves only to prove God right in the eyes of one of his subordinates" (1989:28–9). Exactly.

And what of God's refusal to take responsibility? While acknowledging the complete unfairness of their test which he himself had set up, Yahweh puts all the blame on his adversary: "*You* incited me against him, to destroy him for no reason" (2:3, my emphasis). Yahweh here sounds a lot like Adam, who, when confronted by God about eating the illicit fruit, blames *both* Eve *and* Yahweh! "The woman whom *you* gave to be with me, *she* gave me fruit from the tree, and I ate" (Gen 3:12, my emphasis). Adam may not be genetically linked to God, but he certainly was created in his image. Similarly, Zeus points back to Athena's own responsibility for the delay in Odysseus' return: "For didn't *you yourself* devise this plan that Odysseus avenge himself on these men when he returned?" (*Od.* 5.23–4, my emphasis). (Zeus at one point blames his son Ares' "unbearable spirit" on . . . Ares' mother!)

The entire setting is Homeric. Clines summarizes the picture well: "The freedom with which he [Satan] can address his lord, the influence he can have upon him, and the plenipotentiary powers granted him all seem more at home in a polytheistic culture than in the world of the OT. . . . The scene echoes in spirit the assembly of the gods, whether in the Mesopotamian heaven, in the Canaanite 'heights of the north,' or on the Hellenic Olympus" (1989:21). The answer to Cline's implied question, as we will soon discover, is that the "world of the OT" *is* polytheistic. Moreover, the dramatic irony created by revealing God's will to the audience but leaving the mortal characters out of the loop is, as we will see, downright Homeric.

The *Odyssey*, with its happy ending and restoration of everything to its hero, also neatly parallels Job's infelicitous epilogue that seems to undermine the very mystery of God so central to the story. Job is rewarded for his "good" behavior: "Job's rehabilitation, in which he receives a bonus for his pains, appears to confirm the very doctrine of retribution which Job had so effectively refuted in the Dialogue" (Pope 1965:xxviii). Yahweh restores Job's "fortunes," giving him seven more sons, three more daughters (this time with an inheritance), money, and, of course, lots of livestock. Does Yahweh do it out of guilt? Does he know he blew it, prodded into unjust behavior by a clever member of his own divine council?

There is no closure to the initial wager. Yahweh never gets to do his victory dance over Satan. Meanwhile he has managed to avoid answering Job's criticisms about the goodness or justice of God's world. The text, then, may offer a skeptical view of God and the world, and perhaps even deliver an indictment of God's mysterious indifference to human suffering, the same conclusion Achilles reaches at the end of the *Iliad*. At best, "the complete evasion of the issue as Job had posed it must be the poet's oblique way of admitting that there is no satisfactory answer available to man, apart from faith" (Pope 1965:lxxv; cf. Sawyer 2011:35). Or at least to theistic man, whose theism causes the conundrum of theodicy in the first place.

My larger point here is simple: An objective reading of the Hebrew Bible often reveals a God who would in many ways fit comfortably on Olympus. The entire polytheistic council scene in the prologue could come out of Homer. Yahweh is surrounded by divine beings known variously in the Bible as servants, messengers (angels), holy ones, exalted ones, sons of gods, heavenly bodies, and even troops. And Yahweh's behavior towards Job "can only be described as immoral" (Whybray 1996:111); minimally it's Homerically anthropomorphic. True, Yahweh does not manifest himself directly to Job; he's a force of nature rather than corporeal. The "Lord answered Job out of the whirlwind" (38:1), or, as scholars note, out of a "storm" or "tempest." Homeric deities like to work with and from within clouds and storms as well, occasionally even cloaking themselves in a cloud like Yahweh, an image that is usually meant to imply invisibility rather than an actual darkness (e.g., 16.788–804, although one cloud protecting the gods is called "impenetrable," 20.150; Bettini 2017:31–5). But even in/as a force of nature, Yahweh acts and speaks in a very human fashion.

For anyone raised on Homer, this is quite comfortable ground. Yahweh and the Olympians share numerous literary topoi or "mythological subgenres," but they are subsets of the two overarching areas of interest for our comparison of these deities in the Tanakh, namely anthropomorphism and polytheism. Christian theology can almost be defined as a history of unconvincing efforts to rescue God from his textual reality in the Tanakh and to disentangle the knotty anthropomorphism in the New Testament (as well as the impenetrable polytheism of the theologically crafted Trinity). But Jewish Professor of the Bible Yochanan Muffs, for example, also takes it for granted that "pagan" anthropomorphism results in "embarrassing" deities. But, he insists, "the humanness of the biblical God is, by contrast, a sign of His superiority. In spite of some godlike excesses (most unbecoming a bourgeois divinity), this anthropomorphic deity is, on the whole, a paragon of human virtue, a kind of *Übermensch*, in comparison with the *urmensch* represented by . . . pagan anthropomorphism" (2005:30).

One final word here before we explore the similarity of these ancient fictions in more detail. Yahweh is the Ur-Deity of the Western Big Three contemporary religious traditions, all of which must in some form embrace his textual persona. His presence towers over the three Western religions. Take him on and you take them all on. To critique and criticize Western interpretations of Yahweh is thus not to question Jewish religion more than Christian or Islamic beliefs. There is a long and ignoble history, going back to the early Christians and reaching a new peak in the Enlightenment, of anti-Semitic attacks on Yahweh. Nazi ideology was supported by such anti-Semitic works as Theodor Fritsch's *Der faslche Gott: Beweismaterial gegen Jahwe* (*The False God: Evidence against Yahweh*), which went through 11 editions between 1911 and 1933 (Römer 2013:4). As will be clear by the end of the next section of the book, my objective is not to censure Yahweh, much less Judaism, but to expose him as the Olympian deity he is. I have no personal quarrel with the textual Yahweh, any more than I do with Zeus. They are characters in texts. Both of them are fascinating; neither is very amiable. Both can be petty and homicidal, as well as magnanimous and full of pity. My disagreement is with the errant interpretations that have been forced upon Yahweh – and Homer's Olympians on occasion – and especially with the subsequent unhelpful conclusions about the nature of life that these mistakes have foisted on Western culture. We'll get to those soon enough.

Now we must explore the characters of the gods in our texts, the natures of Yahweh and the Olympians. In the next section we will thoroughly vet the Homeric and Hebrew gods and discover just how closely related they really are.

Notes

1 When verses from the *Odyssey* are cited, *Od.* will be placed before the book and verse numbers. If there is no *Od.* supplied, then the reference is to the *Iliad*.

2 The Septuagint is an early (probably begun in the third century BCE) translation and expansion of the Hebrew Bible into Greek. It eventually contained some books that are not considered canonical by Jews, and we know that some passages reflect theological differences from the original. But the Septuagint supplies some of the earliest

evidence for the Hebrew Bible and can be an invaluable resource (along with other non-Masoretic traditions such as the Samaritan Pentateuch) in trying to reconstruct the earliest possible Hebrew text.

3 Jewish scholars often note the inherent anti-Semitic strain in the original Documentary (Graf-Wellhausen) Hypothesis, which postulated that Israel's religion devolved from the prophets' emphasis on ethical teaching to a religion dominated by ritual and legalism.

4 The Qur'an and New Testament have just as many contradictions, of course – try to provide a coherent account of Jesus' death and resurrection using all of the details of the Gospels, for example.

5 Homer never uses the term "Greek," a word that derives from Italic contact with one Hellenic tribe of that name. Later Greeks called themselves Hellenes once they had developed a more complete sense of cultural identity. But Homer uses neither Hellenes nor Hellas as a national label, instead applying the more specific terms Danaans, Argives, or Achaeans to those trying to conquer Troy. I will occasionally use one of these three terms when referring to the characters in his epics, but to keep things as clear as possible, I will generally refer to them as Greeks.

6 Some biblical scholars argue that the Tanakh is not categorically different from the historical inquiries of Greek historians. But most recent critics, even those who reject the "conventional genre demarcations" that mark Greek historiography (e.g., Kofoed 2005), acknowledge that the authors of the Tanakh were not critically weighing sources, had no firsthand knowledge of the events, make no clear expressions of any historical intent, make no serious effort at objective inquiry, and were consciously composing theological and religious texts. There is nothing in the Deuteronomistic history or the narrative of Chronicles, writes Ehud Ben Zvi, "to encourage or allow the writing of works such as those of Herodotus, Thucydides, or Xenophon, or for that matter, Josephus" (2011:24).

7 The term "Israelites," or "ancient Israelites," should in theory only apply to this group after they have established a place called Israel (thus, for example, *not* when they are slaves in Egypt). The word that becomes "Hebrew" is an early appellation, but it is often applied in a negative sense by outsiders to mean something like "foreigners." And the term "Jew" is rather late. I have usually opted for Israelite, but for variety the other terms appear here and there. There is also the customary awkwardness that the term "Israel" itself can evoke, for it can apply to a person (Jacob), a people, the land, the united kingdom of David and Solomon, or to just the northern half after the post-Solomonic division of the kingdoms (Pyper 2000a:332). Adding to the confusion, in later texts it can even refer to just the *southern* kingdom (Judah) or those who live there (Judahites)! I hope the context will make my intentions clear.

8 Archaeologists working in the Levant often prefer the discipline to be called Syrio-Palestinain Archaeology. The adjective "biblical" recalls the origins and long history of the field that was primarily dedicated to finding supporting evidence for the biblical narrative.

9 The final redaction of the Tanakh *may* have been late enough to allow for Greek influence on some texts, like that of Jonah; see Louden 2011:318–27. And a thousand years earlier there was a close affinity between the Mycenaean world and Western Asia. The Philistines were an amalgam of cultures from the "Minoan and Mycenaean world, mediated to the Levant via Cypriot and Anatolian adaptions" (Dever 2017:140). In an important sense, then, the Philistines were "assimilated Achaeans" (Finkelberg 2005:152–60).

10 Karen Armstrong's popular *A History of God* (1993) – admittedly a search for the Abrahamic deity – offers the reader one page out of 400 on the Greeks, and one mention of the *Iliad*. Reza Aslan's excellent survey, *God: A Human History* (2017), even though specifically about *humanized* depictions of the divine in the Western tradition, can squeeze in only six pages on the Greeks, half of which examine philosophical critiques of the Olympians.

11 One book recently appeared (2015) that by its title, *Homer und die Bibel: Studien zur Intepretation der Ilias und ausgewählter alttestamentlicher Texte* (*Homer and the Bible: Studies on the Interpretation of the Iliad and Selected Old Testament Texts*) seemed to be trying to fill this gap. But the author, Meik Gerhards, is an Old Testament scholar at an institute for Evangelical Theology and naturally is more comfortable with the biblical material. Moreover, as the "ausgewälter" ("selected") suggests, there is no overall thesis to this study, which comprises a series of explorations of isolated texts and concepts. He does value Homer's epics as powerful fiction, even concluding that they are "better literature than the Bible!" But as a Christian scholar in a theological setting, he eventually falls back on the power of revelation: "But if the basic Christian understanding of the Bible is warranted as the medium of the experience of God, then the Bible can enrich life in a much different way than can literature and art" (416).

12 I try throughout the book to provide the necessary context when discussing particular passages in the texts. I have put a brief outline of the *Iliad* and *Odyssey* in Appendix 1 for those whose memory of the texts is hazy or has been occluded by watching the movie *Troy*.

13 Moses grows furious that the officers of his army "killed every male" of the Midianites – that was fine, to be sure – but "took the women of Midian and their little ones captive; and they took all their cattle, their flocks, and all their goods as booty." "Kill every male among the little ones and kill every woman who has known a man by sleeping with him," he tells his men. "But all the young girls who have not known a man by sleeping with him, keep alive for yourselves" (Num 31:1–18; cf. Judg 21:11–12, part of the ugly episode in which the Israelites almost wipe out their own tribe of Benjamin). Makes you glad you took that virginity pledge, doesn't it? Agamemnon similarly becomes incensed when Menelaus is about to take a Trojan alive as a war prize. Menelaus follows his brother's advice and butchers the suppliant. The difference between the two texts, as so often, is in the breadth of the carnage demanded by Moses. Moreover, the Greeks do not wreak mass destruction on their own people as Moses and other Israelite leaders frequently do at Yahweh's behest.

14 Harris (2005:117–23) offers a startling list of statements from the Qu'ran that match anything the Tanakh has to offer on vilifying, punishing, and destroying the "infidels" and "unbelievers"; cf. McKinsey (1995:476–80).

15 On the other hand, God punishes, or threatens to punish, the Israelites at least two dozen times by *withdrawing* his presence or "hiding his face" (Travis 2009:22–3) – they really can't win either way.

16 Many possible meanings have been proposed for Job's response at 42:1–6 (Clines 2011:1218–24; Crenshaw 2005:189). It is not at all clear just what Job comes to understand, if anything, as a result of his suffering and divine visitation. Clines concludes his three-volume, 1300-page commentary on this anticlimactic note: "Job is neither triumphant nor defeated. The divine speeches have in the end neither satisfied nor humiliated him. It is almost as if Yahweh had not spoken from the tempest. . . . He has learned nothing except to have his worst fears confirmed, that he will not get justice from God" (2011:1224).

17 Some scholars have seen Saul as a tragic figure, but God's hand is too heavy for the story to be read that way (Williams 2007).

Section II

Yahweh and the other Olympians

3   Homer's gods

Homer deserves to be thrown out of the contests and flogged.

– Heraclitus

In a famous passage from his *History of the Persian Wars*, the fifth-century historian Herodotus – called "most like Homer" by a later Greek literary critic – argues that Homer (and his near-contemporary epic "rival," Hesiod) virtually invented the basic characteristics of the Greek gods:

> But from where each of the gods came to be, or whether all of them were always in existence, and in what sort of form, no one knew until yesterday or the day before, so to speak; for it seems to me that the prime of Hesiod and Homer was four hundred years before me and no more; and these are the ones who created the genealogy of the gods for the Greeks, and gave the gods their names, and distributed their spheres of interest and functions, and put a stamp on their forms.
>
> (2.53)

While the influence of these epic depictions of the Olympians cannot be overestimated, Homer was not creating the gods ex nihilo. We know from the conventions of oral poetry (the divine epithets, for example) and Late Bronze Age writing (Linear B) that many of the gods mentioned by Homer had been objects of worship and characters in songs for numerous generations. More than three dozen names of divinities are found on Linear B tablets, baked into clay over 400 years before Homer. At least a third of these gods survived in some form in later Greek myths and cult (Bremmer 2010:3). Any reader picking up the *Iliad* for the first time is immediately aware that Homer expects him or her to know the outlines of the various relationships among the deities without his having to spell them out. The consequent gaps in background explication can be frustrating even for the scholar, since there are occasions when the poet seems to be drawing on or inventing details that differ from what were later considered "standard" accounts. Homer's epics crystalized the nature of the gods in such a memorable fashion that no subsequent Greek could ignore his characterizations, but there remained plenty of room for creative tinkering.

As for their "Olympian" nature, Olympus is both topographic (a mountain) and conceptual (the heaven or sky), the two ideas often conflated. A number of mountains in Greece were named Olympus, but one in particular on the northern boundary, the highest mountain on the peninsula, was considered to be the home and meeting place of the primary group of Homeric gods. Zeus's brothers live elsewhere: Poseidon controls the sea (although he spends a lot of time on Olympus), and Hades resides in the underworld. The other major Homeric divinities have actual houses built by Hephaestus on the peaks of Olympus, the "seat of the gods." While Zeus is the only individual god to be known as "the Olympian," the poet frequently refers to the gods as "the heavenly ones," "in heaven," "holding Olympian homes," "the Olympians," "the gods who hold Olympus," and those "who hold wide heaven." Although commonly described by epithets like "many-peaked" and "snow-capped," Olympus often seems to be located somewhere high up in the sky (the heavens) rather than to rear up towards the skies as a mountain. On one occasion (8.23–7) Zeus says he can pull earth and hang it from Olympus, an impressive feat that clearly suggests Olympus could not be part of earth itself. Homer describes Olympus as a paradise unlike any earthly mountain, especially one that towers 10,000 feet into the Macedonian sky: "It is not shaken by winds nor ever dampened by rain, nor does snow come close, but the clear sky spreads out without clouds, and a white radiance runs over all of it. In this place the blessed gods enjoy themselves all their days" (*Od.* 6.43–6). Like so much of Homer's divine machinery, Olympus is whatever the poet needs it to be at any given moment. But whether mountain or heavenly abode, it serves as a brilliant poetic vehicle for bringing what must have been diverse local deities into a relatively unified and extremely influential "Panhellenic" pantheon.

This chapter will survey these Homeric deities in light of their polytheistic and anthropomorphic natures. My intent is to recall the major aspects of the important Olympians. For those of you interested in more detailed biographies, Appendix 2 provides an overview of all the major divine characters in the epics. The poet can emphasize different aspects of any particular god in each epic (and most of the Olympians play a much smaller role in the *Odyssey* overall). I will discuss these varying characteristics when relevant. But for the most part I have tried to capture the basic nature of the Homeric gods across both poems. The focus here and in the next few chapters is on two aspects of the divine that, according to theologians, clearly distinguish the Homeric deities from the Judeo-Christian God: Life on Olympus is unabashedly polytheistic and anthropomorphic.

Homeric polytheism

The belief that multiple competing deities intrude into our world is the most sensible form of supernatural belief. Much of the rest of this book seeks to demonstrate that simple reality. At this point, however, we can uncontroversially note the polytheistic setting of the Homeric gods and move on. All you have to do is count. Put simply, life on Homer's Olympus is a family affair. An incestuous, dysfunctional family of extremely powerful, immortal, and overgrown adolescents, to be sure.

The first book of *Iliad* ends, and the first book of the *Odyssey* begins (as we have seen), with a divine council. In each, the patriarch Zeus is accosted by a fellow deity, and in each the decision made or confirmed by the "father of gods and men" drives the rest of the plot. By the end of these opening books, we will already have met in person or heard about Apollo, Athena, Atlas, Briareus, Calypso, Cronus, the Harpies, Helius, Hephaestus, Hera, Hermes, Leto, the Muses, Nereus ("the old man in the sea"), Phorcys, Poseidon, Thetis, Thoösa, and Zeus. These are just the appetizer – there are a *lot* of gods flitting about Homer's universe. In the *Iliad* alone, 19 gods have speaking parts – not counting an immortal horse – and scores of other deities have some sort of role. Here's a genealogical chart of the most important Olympians in the epics, with brief descriptions of each. You will note that Zeus gets around. All of the major Olympians are either his siblings or children. (We'll examine in detail the myths surrounding the origins of the gods in the chapter on Homeric creation.)

The major Homeric gods

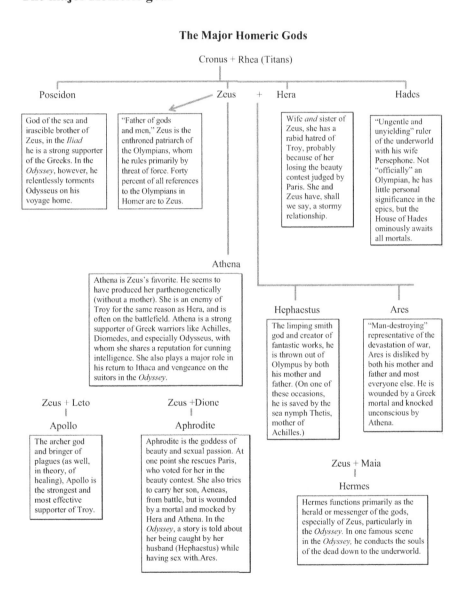

The Major Homeric Gods

Figure 3.1

Homeric anthropomorphism: Looking like a god

Most of us today know what Homer's "immortal and ageless" gods must have looked like because we've seen their faces in museums, coffee-table books, or darkened classrooms. Or maybe you've watched Disney's *Hercules* (very catchy songs) or caught the FTD logo. Perhaps even now you're finding it hard to purge the vision of a sexagenarian Sir Laurence Olivier hamming it up as Zeus in the original *Clash of the Titans*. (So much for immortal and ageless.) The Olympians look and act like humans. They are, as one classicist has put it, "unashamedly anthropomorphic" (Versnel 2011:239). Homer's deities are more powerful, often more prescient, almost always more attractive versions of human beings. They appear as immortal anthropoids frozen in various manifestations of their "prime": Zeus and Poseidon macho males at their peak of potency; the virginal Artemis and supremely nonvirginal Aphrodite women at the acme of their sexual attractiveness; Hermes and Apollo young men in distinct stages of youthful perfection; Athena an Amazonian beauty; Hera the arresting queen.

In general, the gods' ageless immortality does not affect their quotidian manifestation. Rarely, it is true, they can emit a numinous aura. Unaware of Athena's presence, Telemachus tells Odysseus that the walls of the house and the pillars seem to glow as if from fire, and his father informs him that, "be assured, this is the custom of the gods who hold Olympus" (*Od.*19.43). When guard dogs see Athena, they whimper and slink away in fear (*Od.* 16.162–3). (Strangely, I have a colleague who has the same effect on his students.)

The poet is selective in his description of his gods. No doubt he expected his audience already to have a solid picture of them in their minds, just as he worked on the premise that his listeners knew the basic outline of the Trojan War. On the other hand, the lack of specific details may be embedded in early epic style. Homer's portraits of mortals are often equally fuzzy, especially in the *Iliad* (Pucci 1998:80). What, exactly – or even approximately – are Helen's notable features? (Her beauty is emphasized generically but unhelpfully as "terribly like immortal goddesses to look at," 3.158.) Even in the much-delayed teichoscopy ("viewing from the walls") in Book 3 of the *Iliad*, where King Priam finally (after nine years!) works up the curiosity to ask Helen to identify the Greek warriors who have gathered outside the walls of Troy, we learn little more than that Agamemnon is "royal-looking," Odysseus shorter but broader than Agamemnon, and Ajax tall. (One great exception to Homer's taciturnity is his depiction of the misshapen troublemaker Thersites, in the details of whose disfigurement – and thus by ancient convention, his questionable character – the poet seems to revel; 2.216–19.)

Nevertheless, certain features of the Olympians as a whole can be gleaned from Homer's comments. With the exception of the limping Hephaestus, they look like humans on our impossibly best day. When Odysseus emerges from a bath, the physical upgrade from Athena gives him "much beauty, making him taller to look upon and more powerful," with "grace on his head and shoulders ... *just like the immortals in form*" (*Od.* 23.156–63, my emphasis; cf. *Od.* 6.243). Similarly, when Odysseus first appears in his undisguised and slightly enhanced form to his son, Telemachus thinks he is a god (*Od.* 16.181–5). The gods have beautiful (and gendered) human bodies, with appropriately impressive hair, heads, eyes, mouths, chins, beards, necks, chests, bosoms, arms, hands, bellies, legs, knees, and feet. Their epithets occasionally help paint a better picture. Athena has gray or green (or bright or darting or possibly even "owlish") eyes, while Hera is frequently called "ox-eyed," which may refer to large, dark eyes. (At least one critic has suggested that her visage is "placid," but it is hard to imagine a less bovine character.) Her "white arms" are another mark of her feminine beauty. Poseidon has dark hair. Apollo's is "unshorn," and when Zeus nods his head, his "ambrosial locks" shake. Aphrodite and Artemis are credited with a beautiful crown or headband.

Homer's gods wear clothing, including sandals, perfume, and jewelry. Hera even has "nicely pierced ears." They don armor usually described in identical functional terms to that worn by mortals. Hera sports a veil, as do the minor goddesses Ino, Circe, and Caylpso; Thetis, mother of the doomed Achilles, wears a black one by the end of the *Iliad*. Again, the divine epithets can be helpful. Ares is "helmet-shaking" and "with a glancing helm." Apollo is called the god "of the silver bow," his penchant for archery marked nearly 60 times with nine different epithets. Hermes has a "golden wand," Hera "golden sandals." More than 50 times Zeus is said to "bear the aegis," although, as so often in Homer, the epithet conjures up a general truth about a character rather than an accurate description at any particular moment.[1] Not surprisingly, Zeus is frequently associated with his thunderbolt by six different epithets.

The gods are fully physical, at least in their natural state and on earth when they choose to be. They sit on thrones, drive chariots, live in houses (some with locks!), lie in beds, and ply weapons in the same fashion as humans. The construction material of their physical world mostly overlaps with that of humans, although the Olympians must either like or be unaware of elephants, since only mortals seem to make use of ivory. But the gods *love* gold even more than humans do. The divine world is afloat with the stuff, a "golden haze," as one critic puts it.

There appears to have been enough direct interchange with the gods that often "mortals both perceive gods and recognize their divinity" (Turkeltaub 2007:51n3), an event called an epiphany. When Athena rushes to Diomedes' side to chastise his laxity, the warrior's first words in response are "I recognize you, daughter of Zeus who wields the aegis" (5.815). The Olympians appear to mortals in their full divinity relatively rarely, however, and only to a few privileged individuals or groups. When they do, we have to look quickly – and carefully – to catch a glimpse of their "true" natures. Hera herself observes to her fellow Olympians that "the gods are dangerous when they appear in their true form" (20.131; cf. 24.463–4).

For reasons that are rarely made explicit in the epics, the Homeric gods enjoy disguising themselves in some fashion when mixing with mortals. Athena in the two epics takes the likeness of heralds, Trojan warriors, Achilles' old mentor Phoenix, unidentified "mortal" men, old family friends of Odysseus (Mentes and Mentor), young women, a shepherd, Telemachus(!), and perhaps also a vulture, sea eagle, and swallow. Apollo, among many other impersonations, takes on the form of both the Trojan Asius *and* Asius' son Phaenops. Poseidon is even said to have taken on the appearance of another god in order to have sex with a woman (*Od.* 11.235–52), a tactic more commonly associated in Greek myth – but *not* in the Homeric epics – with his brother, the ever-concupiscent Zeus.

To be honest, it is often difficult if not impossible to determine if a particular god is visible in a natural state, in disguise, or heard only through his or her voice. Much of the time the distinction just doesn't seem to be of much importance to the poet. Humans often, but not always, find it difficult to see through the gods' disguises. As Odysseus observes, "Who with his eyes could look at a god if the god didn't wish it, whether going here or there?" (*Od.* 10.573–4). Yet the Olympians can emanate divinity so strongly that they fail to disguise themselves completely. Helen recognizes Aphrodite in the guise of an old wool-comber by her beautiful neck, lovely bosom, and flashing eyes (3.396–7). Poseidon's feet (footprints?) and shins give his divinity away to Ajax the Lesser (13.71–2), although the Greek hero's subsequent boast that he recognized the disguise "easily" because "even the gods are easy to recognize" reveals an arrogance that foreshadows his ugly post-Iliadic actions and fate.[2]

The Olympian gods can be louder in their natural state than humans, and occasionally much bigger, but in the epic action itself, the gods seem to inflate or shrink to fit their – and thus the narrative's – immediate needs. Most of the time, we can safely imagine a deity as basically human-sized, if perhaps on the impressively large (and shiny) end of the spectrum. And logic – if one must use such a crude tool – also suggests that the gods in their normal state are not always giants. The minor goddess Calypso, for example, recognizes Hermes in what must be his natural form – he has no reason to metamorphose – when he suddenly confronts her "face to face" at her doorstep, "for the immortal gods are not unrecognized by each other, not even if one dwells in a home far away" (*Od.* 5.79–80). Hermes is apparently the same approximate size as Calypso, since he sits down on a chair and at her table without any need to shrink and with no reference to a special "gods' table" in the kitchen. Later, Odysseus sits down "upon the chair from which Hermes had gotten up" (*Od.* 5.195–6). Odysseus and Hermes then are about the same size, and one thing we know about Odysseus is that he is not especially tall. But sometimes the narrative demands a more imposing physical presence, and so a god can get bigger. Immense, even. When Athena knocks out Ares with a rock, the unconscious deity is stretched out "over seven plethra" (21.407; cf. *Od.* 11.576–7; a plethron was later said to be equivalent to 100 square feet).

Questions such as this – how big were the Olympian gods? – smack of medieval quagmires like "how many angels can dance on the head of a pin?" But they reveal an important reality for all tales about gods: They are shaped for a thematic purpose. Homer's gods are fully anthropomorphic in their usual depictions. The differences are almost always a matter of degree rather than quality and are adjusted to the context.

Homeric anthropomorphism: Acting like a god?

The Olympians not only possess human physical features, they sing, laugh, sleep, drink, toast, eat, fear, mock, quarrel, weep, whine, bleed (well, drip ichor), feel pain (both emotional and physical), make alliances, put together chariots, and have favorite animals and heroes. Their "obsession with honor (*timê*) [is] identical to [that] of humans" (Schein 1984:53). Most of them have sex, although not Athena or Artemis. Some of them have a *lot* of sex. They have parents, and many have children as well as spouses and siblings. Occasionally their spouses *are* siblings. Their primary function in the epics is to interact with humans, or perhaps more accurately, to intervene in – or complain about and threaten to affect and sometimes just plain watch – what's happening on earth. Poetically, they – along with the mythical tradition itself – are vehicles that help shape the principal movements of the plot, while occasionally providing a bit of (thematically relevant) comic relief.

Perhaps most notoriously, as far as critics of Homer's gods have been concerned, their psychological range and violent responses could give even one of the nuttier Roman emperors a run for his money. They lie, cheat, act on the basest of human emotions, and are "utterly capricious" (Versnel 2011:388). The Homeric deities are not models for human behavior in any fashion. Most of their decisions and actions are driven by their loves and hates, as they support personal favorites and act on private animosities. As one scholar concludes, "the Olympians resemble nothing so much as a delinquent band of production assistants only sporadically controlled by director-Zeus, who himself sometimes seems to have only a rather shaky hold on the plot" (Emlyn-Jones 1992:95). Men live by the hope of reciprocal favor from the gods, what the Greeks called *charis*, but because of the nature of these deities "it is never possible to count on this with certainty" (Burkert 1985:189).

In their irresponsibility, capriciousness, inflated human passions, petty bickering, domestic squabbling, and sibling rivalries, Homer's gods are often an uncomfortable combination of Roger Rabbit and the British royal family. They are "terrifying, unpredictable, cruel and occasionally ludicrous" (Lateiner 2004:21). The Olympians act on the same human emotions as the mortal heroes, usually at an exaggerated level. Poseidon, Hera, Athena, and Apollo – even "ungentle and unyielding Hades" – all pity and fear for mortals. Thetis weeps for the fate of her son Achilles; Achilles' immortal horses grieve for their dead charioteer. Zeus sheds bloody raindrops as he awaits the death of one of his mortal sons. The gods experience shame, regret, jealousy, and pride – Athena gloats that her disguise has been clever enough to fool the cunning Odysseus.

The most frequent emotion on display is anger, a violent passion that drives much of the action in both epics: Hera, Athena, and Poseidon won't rest until Troy is razed; Zeus's anger is a dominant motif in the *Iliad*; Poseidon's ire drags Odysseus across the Mediterranean, and Athena and her wrath have been shown to shape the structure and plot of the *Odyssey* (Clay 1983). A river even grows so vexed at the corpses filling up his waters that he tries to drown Achilles. Indeed, "wrath constitutes one of the central themes of archaic Greek epic at large" (Tsagalis 2016:95).

As we will see, Yahweh also feels all these emotions. But unlike the Olympians, he doesn't smile or laugh or experience joy at anything positive. For that matter, Jesus never laughs at all. The Olympians cackle at others' misfortunes, but they can also enjoy the moment. Helius, the sun god, for example, takes delight in simply watching his cattle. And Homer's gods on occasion are said by both the poet and the characters to love mortals: Hera loves and cares for both Achilles and Agamemnon; Zeus loves the people of Rhodes. After the war, the senescent Greek counselor Nestor says that he has "never yet seen the gods so openly loving" as Athena was to Odysseus (*Od.* 3.221–2).

Homeric superpowers

Some modern scholars, perhaps influenced by later Greek (and Judeo-Christian) ideas about the divine, emphasize the numinous nature of the Homeric gods, their ultimate "otherness." And it is true that while the gods may look like us and act like us, they are gods after all and have powers neither we nor the epic heroes possess. (As we have seen, they can transform themselves to look like any human or god, and even shape-shift into animals.) Perhaps the most benevolent superpower of the gods is what I call "the glow," the supernatural corporeal upgrade Athena gives in the *Odyssey* at one time or another to every member of Odysseus' family. Captain Kirk in the original *Star Trek* television series used to get the glow when he met a hot alien babe, as the camera gave him a fuzzy, mellow aura indicating that he was suddenly stronger, taller, and more handsome. Odysseus receives the most impressive divine makeovers, but Telemachus also gets the glow, a "divine grace" shed by Athena, and "all the people looked at him admiringly as he came" (*Od.* 2.12–13; 17.63–4). Penelope, too, receives these "immortal gifts" in her sleep – she seems to spend half the epic knocked out by divine tranquilizers – awaking "taller, stronger, and whiter than sawn ivory" (*Od.* 18.187–96). Even Laertes, Odysseus' doddering father, has one final moment of glory when Athena "fills out" his limbs and makes him "taller than before and stronger . . . like the immortal gods to behold" (*Od.* 24.367–71).

These heavenly upgrades show up only in the *Odyssey*, a text replete with disguises, recognitions, and challenges to identity. The Iliadic gods find no need – or time – to exercise this particular divine superpower. Homeric gods are part of a humanly constructed narrative and their "existence" is shaped by human needs, those both of the characters and of the poet. They have the powers the plot twists demand and are denied those powers as well when thematically necessary. Their means of movement is a good example. Sometimes they take a chariot; sometimes they fly; most often Homer merely says that they "go." On occasion they leap across mountains or skip across the sea; frequently they just are there without further explanation. When Aphrodite is slightly wounded trying to rescue her injured son Aeneas, she requires a divine ambulance. She barely manages to stagger over to Ares' chariot, in which she is driven to Olympus by a suddenly materializing Iris (the primary messenger of the gods in the *Iliad*). The passage emphasizes Aphrodite's weakness and vulnerability – she has no place on the battlefield. Yet just minutes later Ares himself is stabbed in the stomach, and he somehow stumbles back to Olympus without any transportation whatsoever.

But when the divine travel *means* something, it can take both time and effort. Ogygia, the island of Calypso where Odysseus languishes (if having sex with a goddess each night can fairly be labeled "languishing") for seven years, lies in a remote part of the world, somewhere in the far west. Athena says it is positioned at the "navel of the sea" (*Od.* 1.50), which emphasizes not its central location but its isolation. Zeus sends Hermes to Ogygia to command the goddess to release Odysseus. Even with his "beautiful sandals, immortal, golden, which carried him both over the waters and also the boundless land as swift as the blasts of the wind" (*Od.* 5.44–6), Hermes complains to Calypso of the length of the journey: "Zeus commanded me come here against my will. For who would willingly race over so great an expanse of salt water, vast as it is? And nearby there is no city of mortals who offer sacrifices and choice hecatombs to the gods" (*Od.* 5.99–102). Hermes' grouse tells us nothing about his air speed but rather emphasizes the great distance Odysseus is removed from Olympus, civilization, and especially his home. The god's long and laborious journey – and this for a messenger god known for his swiftness – provides a poignant introduction to Odysseus' isolation. The powers of the gods are contextually bound.

Most of the superpowers of the Homeric gods can be gathered under two kinds of interventions – physical and psychological. They participate bodily or by providing advice or even manipulating psyches. There have been injudicious attempts in the past (starting with some ancient Greeks themselves) to reduce most or even all divine activity in the epics to the level of metaphor: The gods represent the human mind or heart at work. The classic example of this kind of misunderstanding is Athena's effort to stop Achilles from attacking Agamemnon in Book 1 of the *Iliad*. Surely a real god wouldn't grab a hero's hair and explain the benefits of changing his mind. Her appearance must be *symbolic* of Achilles' own change of heart, his better second thoughts. But . . . Athena stands behind him and *grabs his hair* – that's what the Greek clearly says. Achilles spins around, recognizes her, converses with her, and then the goddess bribes him with promises of future recompense. This would be one heck of a personal insight.

Gods physically intervene to aid a favorite or support a cause or defend their own honor. Likewise, they do everything they can to undermine those who oppose their chosen heroes or resist their causes or insult their honor. Sometimes their actions are synonymous with – that is, explanatory of – everyday chance events (a broken bow string, a missed spear toss, an accident in a chariot race). There are few "random" events in Homer. Chance and luck have other causes in the epics, and the gods function as excellent *ex post facto* explanations (Schein 1984:57). The imagery can be striking: Athena sweeps away an arrow headed towards Menelaus like a mother swatting a fly (4.130–1; cf. 5.853–4). Patroclus' uncanny death results when Apollo, "covered in great cloud," comes up unseen behind the overmatched mortal and hits him so hard on the back with his hand that Patroclus' helmet, corselet, and shield fly across the battlefield and his spear shatters. He is left unprotected and dazed, easy pickings for the Trojans (16.786–828). These are real, physical beings, and potentially nasty ones at that. Even *bad* metaphors don't knock off your helmet.

The gods often intervene in less physical fashion. They pop into the action to give advice or warnings to their favorites. Sometimes all Homer tells us is that a god "urged on" his favorites, as in the *Iliad* when one god (e.g., Apollo or Ares) "encourages" the Trojans, while another god (e.g., Athena or Poseidon) "rouses" the Greeks (e.g., 4.439,509–13; 14.361–78). Sometimes the god inspires the warriors with a shout. On occasion, when a god so desires, a hero runs faster on lighter limbs (e.g., 5.122; 22.204). The gods regularly give, put, rouse, or breathe strength, fight, force, or courage into a flagging hero. The other side of this inspirational coin is the fear and panic the gods spread through the troops. Apollo casts "wondrous fear" upon the Greeks (17.118), and Poseidon "ensnares" a Trojan's limbs so he cannot flee or avoid a Greek spear (13.434–6). The gods don't need to play fair.

Perhaps the most interesting category, and one that comes closest to satisfying those who wish the Homeric gods to be explanatory metaphors, is a sort of divine telepathy that appears sporadically in the epics. Homer occasionally tells us that a god "put an idea in" or "planted a thought in" or "put it into the mind of" a character to do something. This is especially common in the *Odyssey*, as Athena smooths the way for Odysseus' return, revenge, and reunion: She plants thoughts of marriage in Nausicaa as she sleeps (*Od.* 6.25–40); she turns Eurycleia's thoughts "aside" when she recognizes Odysseus' scar and in her excitement tries to catch Penelope's attention (19.478); she puts it into Penelope's heart to show herself to the suitors (18.158) and set up the contest of the bow (21.1).

But Homeric characters hedge their bets with what is known as "double motivation" (or "over-determination"), as they often credit decisions or actions to both a divine *and* a human source. For example, in the passage above where Eurycleia discovers Odysseus' scar, Athena may turn her thoughts aside, but Odysseus also grabs her by the throat and threatens to kill her if she reveals his identity. After the embassy to Achilles fails to bring him back into battle, Diomedes states, "Then Achilles will fight again when his heart commands him and a god rouses him" (9.702–3). The poet and his characters often see the origins of human initiative in overlapping or parallel forces, both from within and without.

This would be a good time to correct an easy misconception – getting help from a deity is *heroic* in Homer's world. My students invariably complain that *anyone* could be a successful warrior if a deity swats away arrows and fetches extra weapons. Maybe you, too, were thinking, "Hey, *I* could be a Homeric hero with that kind of ally." Alas, no. The gods would not bother helping you. Or me. Especially me. Heroes are naturally *worthy* of divine aid – that's one of the things that marks a hero. And so they get divine support (whether the character realizes it or not). The gods accentuate a hero's innate ability, thereby increasing, not diminishing, his status. They back a potential winner, glorifying the heroic action. A god's assistance calls attention to the victor and his success.

Homeric gods are known to nudge favorites into certain actions not just by direct intervention, but through oracles, prophecies, dreams, and omens. Omens are signs from the gods, usually unexpected but on occasion requested, that confirm (or, more rarely, discourage) a particular statement, hope, or intended action.

They almost always foreshadow central elements of the plot. With expert exegesis, they can also reveal important information about the future, such as Odysseus' imminent return. In fact, it can seem that just about everything in the *Odyssey* – a bird flying on the right, some random words, thunder, a sneeze, a seemingly misplaced laugh – is construed (correctly!) by someone as an indication that the hero is close by and that the suitors will soon get what they have coming. The suitors miss every sign, and for sheer doltishness alone deserve to die.

After all, Homeric omens can be hard to miss. Odysseus reminds the restless Greek troops of the omen at Aulis – the Greek port where the fleet gathered to sail to Troy – when a snake slithered up a tree, devoured eight sparrow nestlings and their mother, and then metamorphosed into stone (2.301–32). The prophet Calchas interprets this as a message from Zeus that they will sack Troy in the tenth year. Things like animal petrifaction and dewdrops of blood (11.53–5) are prodigies likely to grab anyone's attention. More commonly Zeus relies upon less startling signals like lightning, thunder, birds (particularly eagles, "the surest omen of birds in flight," 8.247), or a rainbow to communicate with mortals. Apollo sends a hawk; Poseidon shakes the earth; Athena and Hera even steal Zeus's thunder once by thundering (11.45–6). There is a wide range of professional interpreters of divine messages in Homer's world whose abilities overlap – diviner, prophet, priest, dream-interpreter, bird-specialist (augur). It's a good job, a gift from Apollo that often runs in families. Several nonspecialists are also "inspired" to prophesy (12.195–229; *Od.* 15.172–8), and the dead and dying can suddenly possess the gift of clairvoyance as well (16.851–4; 22.356–60; 23.80–1; *Od.* 11.444–51). Teiresias as both prophet *and* ghost is well positioned to forecast the future for Odysseus (*Od.* 11.100–137).

But it's not a perfect system, because neither the gods nor humans are perfect. Omens and prophecies can be missed, ignored, misinterpreted, or forgotten. Agamemnon appears to misinterpret the only prophecy from the Delphic oracle mentioned in the epics (*Od.* 8.73–82; Hainsworth 1988:352; cf. Gould 1985:23). Meat moving and lowing on the spit would convince anyone but Odysseus' beef-starved and mutinous men to skip the meal. They chow down and are all shortly drowned at sea by Zeus. It does not pay in Homer's world to shun potential omens, especially avian messages – bird signs *always* come true if correctly interpreted (there's always that snag) – but even Hector rejects the entire process when the results are inconvenient (12.237–43), much to his and his comrades' ultimate regret (cf. 13.821–32; 16.859–61). And of course, humans forget. Several times in the *Odyssey* characters realize too late that an unfortunate turn of events had been predicted long before (e.g., *Od.* 9.507–16; 10.330–2; 13.172–8).

Zeus

In most ways, Zeus is different from the other Olympians only in degree – chiefly he's just plain *stronger* than the rest of his family. Some scholars have argued that his interest in justice is greatly expanded (if not radically altered) in the *Odyssey*. While it is true that the two epics can present different facets of a god – Hermes has only one minor scene in the *Iliad* but in the *Odyssey* becomes Zeus's main emissary – I think Zeus is equally disinterested in human morality in both poems. (We will return to this issue in a later chapter on justice.) Zeus is different in one important way from his fellow gods. Distinguishing him in the Homeric epics is his apparent refusal to intervene in events on earth *in person*. Zeus never shows up on the battlefield, or anywhere else on earth. It's not that he is above mortal affairs. (Speaking of which, we know he has visited earth in the past because he lists some of the mortal women he seduced or raped.) Well, literally he is above all that, for he likes to sit on Olympus or on the highest peak of Mt. Ida in Troy and watch the battle unfold beneath him. Apollo, too, likes to look down on the war from the acropolis of Troy, and Poseidon spots the escaping Odysseus from the mountains of the Solymi. Classicist Jasper Griffin (1980:179–204) has shown how one of the major functions of the Iliadic deities is to serve as a divine audience for the human suffering below. While other deities leave their seats to enter the fray, Zeus doesn't get his hands dirty with terrestrial soil. He is very invested in the plots of both epics, especially the *Iliad*, but works his will rather indirectly. Note his physically distant but tight control of the plot in this passage:

> The Trojans, like flesh-eating lions, charged at the ships, fulfilling the commands of Zeus, who was constantly rousing great might in them; but he was beguiling the hearts of the Argives and he took away their glory, while he stirred on the others. For Zeus in his heart wanted to give glory to Hector, son of Priam, so that he would cast fiercely blazing, tireless fire on the curved ships, and bring to fulfillment the entire outrageous prayer of Thetis. For all-wise Zeus was waiting for this, to see with his eyes the gleam of a ship on fire; for from that time on he intended to bring about a retreat of the Trojans from the ships, and to extend glory to the Danaans . . .
>
> (15.592–602)

Homer does not explain how Zeus brings any of this about. Even when he throws one of his famous thunderbolts (8.133–5; *Od.* 24.539–40) or stirs up a gust of wind against the Greek ships that "beguiled the minds of the Achaeans" (12.252–5), he works from afar.

Zeus uses intermediaries like Iris and Hermes to deliver messages, and he also dispatches Apollo and Athena, as well as personified abstractions like Strife and Dream, to fulfill his commands. Most of his many interactions, however, seem to be the results of his will alone. All of the gods on occasion affect the outcome of events without any explicit reference to their physical intrusion. But the other gods are usually there on the battlefield or standing next to a favorite as they support or hinder mortals. Zeus, on the other hand, *always* stands aside. He "stretches" battle lines, "brings together" soldiers in combat, "draws the evil toil of men and horses," "wards off" fate from his son, "grants" glory, "drives" Greeks in rout, and frequently "rouses might" (he even "puts force" into Achilles' horses) without a word from the poet on how this is accomplished. And Zeus shares in the Olympian fondness for spreading and removing "darkness" (e.g., 17.269–70,648–50).

On the other hand, Zeus is specifically credited with certain telepathic and telekinetic powers. Homer tells us that it is Zeus who steals Glaucus' wits when he trades away his golden armor (6.234; cf. 9.377; *Od.* 21.102). And he on occasion controls people and events with his *mind.* Achilles allows Patroclus to enter battle in his armor but warns him not to attack Troy. Patroclus forgets the admonition, because of Zeus's machinations: "The *mind of Zeus* is always stronger than the mind of men" (16.686–91, my emphasis; cf. 17.176–8). The "mind of Zeus" also revives the injured Hector (15.242), and, as if to focus our attention on the superiority of Zeus, Homer tells us that immediately Apollo – who in this case bears the ironic epithet "who works from afar" – is sent by Zeus to tend to the Trojan hero personally. The "mind of Zeus" actually subdues Ajax, along with the missiles of the Trojans (a nice bit of "over-determination," 16.102–4; cf. *Od.* 24.164–6).

Two crucial things to know about Homer's gods

Throughout much of this book I will be emphasizing how similar the Homeric gods are to mortals, and how their essentially human nature makes sense of the world the Greeks – and we – experience. There are, of course, important differences as well. As we've seen, the Olympians have more power and more beauty and more knowledge; power is a defining characteristic of all gods (Henrichs 2010:35–7). As Apollo reminds a Greek hero at the height of his success, "Do not seek to think on a par with the gods, since never equal is the race of immortal gods and the race of humans who walk upon the ground" (5.440–2). But upon close inspection much of the difference in those realms, even if substantial, is a matter of degree. The gods are not mere hypostases of power but personalities as well, "powers that were treated as if they were persons" (Parker 2011:95; cf. Bremmer 2010:16–17). They are just what they seem to be, that is, humanoid characters who sometimes (at the poet's whim) have some superhuman powers. In his monumental study of ancient Greek theology, H.S. Versnel concludes that "it is my unfashionable impression that in everyday religious practice individual Greek gods were practically never conceived of as powers, let alone as cultural products, but were in the first place envisaged as *persons* with individual characters and personalities" (2011:317).

The two insuperable chasms between mortals and anthropomorphic immortals are more obvious, and more profound: The gods do not age after quickly reaching their particular peak, and they do not die. The epic mortals, like all of us, do. (There are a few apparent exceptions that we will examine in a later chapter.) Qualitatively these two simple facts are the primary definitions of the divine. The gods don't get old and die.

Mortality is the Homeric definition of humanity. We are ephemeral, a Greek word that means "for the day." While that is a self-evident if painful truth of all life everywhere and at all times, most religions promote numerous other significant distinctions between gods and humans, and the most popular contemporary Western religions thrive on the promised negation of the tragedy of human finality. But for Homer's world death is the ultimate dividing line. One of the most common words for the gods (over 160 times) is a negative formation of our own limitations – *athanatoi*, the "deathless ones" – in contrast to us, for whom death is inevitable as mortals, "ones who die" (*thnêtoi*). The gods have two common epithets that suggest they "are forever" (*aieigenetai, aien eontes*), the emphasis understood to be on their future existence rather than their past.

This basic definition underlies all the other differences between the gods and humans (Heath 2005c:51–7). The gods live on Olympus, holding "wide heaven," while men live on the earth – and are buried in it. The Olympians consume nectar and ambrosia, while mortals eat the fruit of the fields, especially bread and cooked meat, and drink wine. Both the poet and the gods themselves tie human mortality to the agricultural cycle of life and death (Kitts 1994). Homer notes in passing that "great Telemonian Ajax will give way to no man who is mortal and eats the grain of Demeter and is vulnerable to bronze or great stones" (13.321–3). Apollo is even more direct, referring to humans as "miserable mortals, who are now like leaves full of the fire of life, eating the fruit of the field, but now waste away to death" (21.464–6).

Linked with the gods' divine diet is the ichor flowing in their veins. When Aphrodite is wounded by the mortal Diomedes, "the immortal [literally 'ambrosial'] blood of the deity flowed, ichor, that which flows in the immortal gods. For they do not eat bread, nor do they drink fiery wine, and so they are bloodless and are called immortals" (5.339–42). The poet, or the poetic tradition he adopts and adapts, had connected a word for mortals, *brotos*, with a rare word for blood (*brotos* as well, but with a different accent). Gods are "not-mortals"; the adjectives *ambrotos* and *ambrosios* mean not-mortal and thus divine. And anything immortal (not-*brotos*) must therefore not eat human food or have human blood. Twice Homer labels this not-mortal nonblood *ichor*.

The gods imbibe nectar (whatever it is, it is the not-wine of Olympus) and literally eat "nonmortal" stuff. Ambrosia is just the adjectival form used as a noun. The Ethiopians and Phaeacians are said to share in divine-mortal feasts (23.205–7; *Od.* 1.22–6; *Od.* 7.201–3; cf. 1.423–4), which *may* suggest a common meal, and in the past the gods came to at least one mortal wedding feast (24.62–3). This is probably a reflection of an earlier tradition in which the gods actually shared in the sacrificial feast provided by mortals, but in Homer's epics this feasting has been mostly "de-carnalized" (Kirk 1990:9–13; Bremmer 2007:139–40; Hitch 2009:109). In fact, the gods are said to enjoy the savor of a burnt offering (*knisê*) only twice in the epics, where it is called the "entitlement" (*geras*) of the gods (4.48–9 = 24.69–70). (The best cut of meat is also a *geras* for triumphant warriors, guests, and kings; 7.321–22; *Od.* 4.65–6; 14.437–8.) Just once is the savor even said to rise to the sky towards the gods (1.317), and we never hear that "the god sniffed or even relished the savour, let alone that his hunger was allayed by it" (Kirk 1990:11). The gods demand sacrifice and libations as evidence of mortal piety, a source of their honor (Ekroth 2011:36). These cultic acts are believed by characters to be an important source of a binding reciprocal relationship but turn out to be very unreliable claims on divine favor.

As for ambrosia, the noun most often appears as a liquid, a fragrant fluid that is used to cleanse and perfume divine bodies and hair, block out foul odors, and prevent the corpses of Sarpedon, Patroclus, and Hector from decaying. This is potent stuff, nothing like its horrifying contemporary American dessert doublet. Classicist Jenny Straus Clay (1981–2:114–17) has shown that in Homer ambrosia is associated with the prevention of decay – the deities' agelessness – more than with the resistance to death. Athena puts ambrosia and nectar into Achilles' breast to maintain the fasting hero's strength, not to make him immortal, which he certainly is not (19.352–4).[3]

And we don't want to ignore the importance of the "ageless" half of the formula "immortal and ageless for all time." The classic Greek example, the fate of Tithonus, is not mentioned directly by Homer, although the poet does know something about the story. Tithonus was a mortal Trojan, the brother (probably half-brother) of King Priam (20.237), who became the consort of Eos, the goddess of dawn. Twice in the epics Eos is said to rise "from her bed next to illustrious Tithonus, to bring light to immortals and mortal men" (11.1–2; *Od.* 5.1–2). That's all Homer reveals. In an early and anonymous poem, a *Homeric Hymn* to the goddess Aphrodite (5.218–38), we learn that Eos was erotically smitten with the Trojan and asked Zeus to make him immortal and "to live" for all time. In other words, the "fool" made a redundant wish and mistakenly replaced "ageless" for all time with "to live" for all time. As long as Tithonus retained his handsome youth, they enjoyed each other, but, as you can imagine, when he started to age, a serious rift developed. Talk about your May-December relationships. At first Eos merely avoided his bed, providing him with ambrosia and nice clothes. But since he was immortal, he just kept getting older, until she stuffed him in a chamber and closed the doors. (My wife and I have a similar agreement for whoever goes senile first.) Again, this tale is not in Homer's epics, but it is illustrative of the significance of keeping in mind the entire package of eternal, unaging deities.

Consequences

As commentators frequently note, this imperviousness to death and aging forms the crucial foil to the human search for meaning in Homer's tragically limited world. The gods' irresponsibility and ultimate inconsequential eternity derive from the lack of personal repercussions for their actions. Easily healed and living "at ease," the Olympians witness life but are excluded from change, maturation, and genuine suffering. "So in some ways the audience is given a privileged insight into athanatology by the poet, an eavesdropping on divine behavior, motivation and relationships. In other ways the narrative alienates the gods from the human perspective, since in their immortality, they cannot live through the pressures and agonies of human life" (Taplin 1992:143). Achilles comes to believe that the gods have decreed that "wretched mortals" live among sorrows, while the gods themselves "are without cares" (24.525–6). This is only mostly true, since the Olympians at times are momentarily affected by human suffering, and Thetis, Achilles' divine mother, will be cursed with eternal mourning for her son. But overall, because the gods usually pay little immediately and nothing in the long run for their ill-conceived actions, they have little chance at a significant existence.

The gods' immunity to the definitive human experiences removes any possibility that they can serve as models for humans on any level. Zeus may marry his sister, but that provides no warrant for the Greeks to do the same. Vengeance may be a simple and satisfying basis for Hera's morality, but Achilles learns otherwise. Ultimately, the Homeric gods are contrasting foils for mortals. It is *because* the odds are eternally stacked against us humans – our actions and decisions count, no one gets out alive, the gods are unreliable at best, and death offers no comforts – that our human struggles make a difference, the "blessings of mortality" as Peter Ahrensdorf labels it in his overview of Homeric theology (2014:64–72). Homer's tragic vision requires not the passive acceptance of an uncaring cosmos but a heroic response to that realization. The great whiners of the Greek world are the gods, who never grow up because, ultimately, they have nothing to risk, nothing to lose, no way to learn.

Homer did not invent the tragic dilemma, the understanding of the world as an indifferent place in which flawed humans must confront their own and the gods' limitations to create any real meaning, to live a life worth living. Gilgamesh and Job both find themselves staring into unexpected and unexplained chasms in their roads of life. At the end of the classical period, Augustine also tried to accommodate the tragic vision to the Christian dilemma of what he believed was a sinful humanity and an ever-loving God. But it was Homer who began to examine, shape, and perfect this stark view of human nature and the crucial role the fickle gods play in our destinies. Gilgamesh, after all, still had his walls; Job got his sheep back (with interest); and Augustine generously, if ultimately to our great disadvantage, promoted God's grace as the ultimate escape clause. Most non-Greek authors thus blink at the last moment – just when it gets really interesting – unable to stare for long at the abyss. Homer may nod now and then, but he never blinks.

We will return to Homer's tragic vision in later chapters, but now we must look closely at Yahweh. Just how different is the creator God of the Abrahamic religions from Homer's anthropomorphic gods? And if Yahweh in the Tanakh is different in some ways, is that an improvement, as the theologians universally insist and a vast majority of Westerners still believe? The God of the Hebrew Bible may not quite be "The Most Unpleasant Character in All Fiction," the title of Dan Baker's case against Yahweh (2016), but he's definitely an Olympian. Yet we should not blame Yahweh. He's a character in a collection of ancient stories, an incoherent, composite creation who reveals his historical development at every turn. Like a third-world high-rise building, Yahweh was not designed to support the tumultuous weight that has accumulated over the years. Yahweh was initially a god very similar to the gods in Homer's epics; he still looks like a close cousin. The Hebrew God is pretty much exactly what we would expect from a

Near Eastern deity created at least three millennia ago – anthropomorphic, despotic, obsessed with honor, and hanging out with other gods. And so to a detailed exposé of Yahweh the Olympian we now turn.

Notes

1 The aegis is a divine apparatus that belongs to Zeus but is borrowed by Apollo and Athena. Or maybe just by Apollo. Some scholars have argued that Athena has a different aegis, since they are given different descriptions and provenances. Zeus's seems to be a metallic shield (or corselet), held in the hand and manufactured by Hephaestus, while Athena's is more like a shawl that can be wrapped around the shoulders. Each aegis, however, functions the same way, primarily stirring up fear and confusion among mortals.

2 This Ajax is not to be confused with the more famous Ajax, son of Telemon, who carries a huge shield and is one of the best Greek warriors in the *Iliad*. Ajax the Lesser (also called "Locrian" or son of Oileus) notoriously rips the Trojan princess Cassandra away from her refuge at the statue of Athena as Troy falls. Nearly drowned by the angry goddess as he starts to sail home after the war, Ajax saves himself but is ultimately killed by Poseidon for boasting that he had escaped "against the will of the gods" (*Od.* 4.499–511).

3 Oddly enough, although there seems to be plenty of nectar on Olympus (e.g., 1.598; 4.3), ambrosia is depicted unambiguously as sustenance for the gods only in one scene, on Calypso's island, where nectar and ambrosia are served both to her and Hermes (*Od.* 5.93, 199). Here ambrosia must be a solid, the equivalent of meat or grain, since nectar stands in for wine. Homer's gods are never shown eating on Olympus, which may be part of the poet's effort to separate his gods from the hungry deities found in some Near Eastern tales. In *Gilgamesh*, for example, the gods are said to swarm on a sacrifice "like flies" (*ANET* 94f.).

4 Biblical polytheism I

Yahweh's divine competition

Who is like you, O Lord, among the gods?

– Moses (Ex 15:11)

Homer doesn't seem to like Ares very much. The war-god is wounded twice in the *Iliad*. Once by a *mortal*. The Greek Diomedes stabs Ares in the stomach with Athena's help, Hera's approval, and Zeus's explicit permission – and Zeus and Hera are his parents! Later in the epic, Zeus arranges for the gods to line up according to which side they support in the war and to duke it out amongst themselves. Zeus will get a kick out of watching this "theomachy" (a battle between gods, 20.2–75; 21.328–520). Although most of the Olympians successfully avoid their prospective duels, bellicose siblings Athena and Ares are only too happy to oblige. The face-off doesn't last long. Ares is knocked stone-cold by Athena with – you guessed it – a stone, much to his own mother's delight (21.391–414). When Aphrodite tries to help the semiconscious Ares leave the field of battle, Hera tells Athena to go after "the dog fly" as well. Athena "rejoicing in her heart" proceeds to smack Aphrodite on the breast so violently that the goddess is knocked to the "bounteous earth" (21.415–34). The animus of Athena and Hera is real. Ares apparently once supported (or promised to support) the Greeks but has been fighting for the Trojans. Aphrodite is a love child of Zeus who not only favors Troy but defeated Hera and Athena in their contest for the apple of Discord, the prize in the divine beauty contest decided by the Trojan Paris.

Readers expect this kind of behavior from Homer's polytheistic deities. If you have more than one god, there are going to be issues. Theomachies are found throughout Near Eastern polytheism both on the cosmological and personal level. Yahweh also goes head to head on at least one occasion in his own theomachy, or as I like to call it, "Theistic Thunderdome": Two gods enter, one god leaves. At perhaps the nadir of the Israelites' efforts to seize the Promised Land, the Philistines (the Israelites' most persistent enemy) capture the ark, the sacred chest containing the tablets of the Ten Commandments. They place it in the temple of Dagon, their primary deity, next to his cult statue. When the people enter the temple the next day, they find "Dagon . . . fallen on his face to the ground before the ark of the Lord." This theomachy is all the more vivid because the author refers to the statue as if it were Dagon himself. The Philistines "took Dagon and put him back in his place. But when they rose early on the next morning, Dagon had fallen on his face to the ground before the ark of the Lord, and the head of Dagon and both his hands were lying cut off upon the threshold; only the trunk of Dagon was left to him" (1 Sam 5:1–4). Yahweh 2; Dagon 0.

The Hebrew Bible is nearly as saturated with deities as the Homeric epics. To be sure, Yahweh is usually depicted as in control of and superior to the other gods. Zeus can only *dream* of having it so good. But Yahweh still must share divine space with a myriad of divine characters. My students are startled by this fact. They think that the Bible, in complete contrast to the Homeric epics, offers an unsullied monotheism. And they are not alone: "The average layman, whether Jew or Gentile, still believes that the official Hebrew religion was a strict monotheism beginning with God's revelation of Himself to Abraham" (Patai 1990:27). We have been *told* that the Bible is monotheistic – that is foundational dogma. What is odd is that it's just about completely wrong. The *eventual* emergence of monotheism and its *subsequent* success are highlights in the history of religions derived from the Bible. But radical or absolute monotheism, a belief that there is one and only one god in the universe, plays an extremely minor and relatively late role in this ancient text. What we actually find in the Bible is a polytheistic world, although there are special terms (e.g., monolatry and henotheism) that scholars have devised to distinguish the biblical versions from other Near Eastern polytheisms such as that found in Homer's epics. To place Yahweh in this Homeric, specifically polytheistic context, we must now introduce some of those other deities. In this chapter we will look briefly at the foreign competition, gods like the Philistine Dagon, and consider what we now know about the transformation of ancient Israelite polytheism to monotheism. The next chapter will highlight the divine multitudes that do Yahweh's bidding.

Yahweh, polytheism, and the Bible

You might be surprised to learn that the dominant form of *ideal* worship on display in the Hebrew Bible – the cultic behavior the Israelites are *supposed* to engage in – is not monotheism, the belief that only one divine being exists. Rather it is monolatry, the acceptance of the existence (or the absence of explicit rejection) of other gods while simultaneously worshiping one god exclusively. Most of the scholars who push back against this realization, instead arguing for a monotheistic Tanakh, usually are simply redefining the word. For example, Benjamin Sommer, following the work of Yehezkel Kaufmann, argues that the Bible "is rightly regarded as a monotheistic work" but acknowledges that this requires a new definition, "diffused monotheism," in which "people pray to various heavenly beings to intercede on their behalf with the one God in whom all power ultimately resides" (Sommer 2009:145–74; cf. 2016:240–2; cf. Albright 1957; Halpern 1987; Penchansky 2005:xi). Thus the real difference between Zeus and Yahweh is that the biblical authors are far more attached to the idea that Yahweh is, and always has been, the sovereign ruler of a divine pantheon – nothing gets done without his approval. Monotheism is a misleading term, however, whether labeled "diffused" or "affective" or "de facto" or "virtual" or "practical" or "positive and negative," because it implies to most people that only one divine being exists. And that is plainly not the case.

Monolatry ultimately became the authorized ideology of the Bible, but the principal religious *belief system* of the Israelites as depicted through their actions in the Tanakh is closer to "henotheism" – the "privileged devotion" to one primary deity, "who is regarded as uniquely superior, while other gods are neither depreciated nor rejected and continue receiving due cultic observances" (Versnel 2000:85–6; cf. Ehrman 2014:53; Smith 2008:168–9 dubs this "summodeism"; DuBois 2014:156 reminds us of "kathenotheism," the shifting, intermittent, and temporary centering on one of many gods that has been applied to Hinduism). Given the number of times the Israelites seem to "slip" and worship Yahweh alongside other Canaanite deities, however, it seems to me that many passages reveal a good old-fashioned polytheism. Yahweh is often depicted (much to his indignation) as merely one of many deities worshipped *equally* by the Israelites. "Gods other than YHWH were worshipped in ancient Israel, and the Old Testament itself is the principal witness to this pluriformity within pre-exilic Israelite religion" (Gordon 2007b:3).[1] We will see that the archaeological evidence from ancient Israel supports this polytheistic reading of much of ancient Israelite religious practice.

The fine terminological distinctions are important here, but the basic idea is simple enough: The Bible does not promote a monotheistic perspective except in a very few later passages, primarily in Deuteronomy (e.g., 4:35,39; 32:39; cf. 1 Kgs 8:60, 2 Kgs 5:15) and especially Deutero-Isaiah (e.g., 43:10–11; 44:6,8; 45:5–6,14,18,21,22; 46:9), which has been labeled the supreme or "parade" example of biblical monotheism. But if the concept underlying polytheism is the belief that there is more than one god, the Bible is polytheistic, a label which some scholars do not shy away from: "In earlier times Israelites and Judahites were polytheists like any other Canaanites and worshipped Yhwh as a god of weather and of fertility" (Stavrakopoulou and Barton 2010b:3; cf. Koch 2007:206; Lang 2002:24, 185). We can use the more exacting terms, even if scholars don't see eye to eye on their precise nuances – the definitions of monolatry and henotheism are the subject of some debate. (Some scholars use the term "monolatry" to describe the cultic practice of henotheism, for example, thus rendering the two terms for all practical purposes identical.) But the Bible is closer to polytheism than it is to monotheism on almost every page. Even the monotheistic-leaning Second Isaiah refers to divine monsters and heavenly beings (Hendel 2017:266n62). "Astonishing as it might seem, then, the religions of Judah and Israel were not monotheistic right from their beginnings, but were as polytheistic as the Canaanite religions of the Late Bronze and Iron Ages. Monotheism is best seen as a late-comer onto the stage of religious history in the ancient Near East" (Niehr 2010:30–1).

The competition

The Tanakh is a text that accepts the reality of hundreds of divine beings (often called *elohim*, the basic Hebrew word for god or gods) other than Yahweh. The scholarly compendium entitled *Dictionary of Deities and Demons in the Bible* (both testaments) runs to nearly 1000 pages and has over 500 entries. Those local, sometimes national deities featured prominently in the Tanakh as competitors to Yahweh include Baal, Chemosh, Moloch, Tammuz, and various astral bodies, as well as the goddesses Astarte, Asherah, and The Queen of Heaven (who may actually be Astarte or Ishtar or Asherah or some combination thereof). The Israelites shared many of the polytheistic practices, and actual deities, with their close Semitic neighbors. Ellen White observes that the personal name of God appears 6551 times in the Tanakh, 39 times next to the names of *other deities* (2014:50). And that's not to mention the major national gods who whip Yahweh in international warfare, such as Ashur of Assyria and the Babylonian Marduk.

Here's a shocker: Yahweh himself is not a monotheist. Yahweh knows that there are other gods – he just doesn't like them or the people who worship them, like the Egyptians: "On all the gods of Egypt I will execute judgments" (Ex 12:12). Even in the second commandment – second in the Jewish tradition, first in the Christian tradition (the Abrahamic religions don't even count to ten in unison) – Yahweh acknowledges his competition: "You shall have no other gods before me/besides me/except for me/before my face" (Ex 20:3; cf. Deut 5:7). He doesn't insist that there *are* no other gods, just that the Israelites are to work with him alone. In fact, he explicitly accepts the existence of other deities: "You shall not bow down to them or worship them; for I the Lord your God am a jealous God . . ." (Ex 20:5–6; cf. Ex 34:14; Deut 4:24; 5:9; 6:15). He is jealous of *other gods*.

Almost everyone in the Tanakh agrees with Yahweh that there are other, *real* gods out there. In his song of praise of Yahweh, Moses can legitimately (that is, not merely rhetorically) and without giving offense, wonder, "Who is like you, O Lord, among the gods?" (Ex 15:11, where "gods" probably refers to both his own divine entourage and gods of other nations; Propp 1998:527). And Job's "friend" Eliphaz, who would no doubt claim to be the most rigorous of Yahwists, asks, "to which of the holy ones will you turn?" (Job 5:1). Similar statements abound in the Tanakh. A few examples:

Ex 18:11: Now I know that the Lord is greater than all gods . . .

Ex 23:13: Do not invoke the names of other gods; do not let them be heard on your lips.

1 Kgs 8:23: O Lord, God of Israel, there is no God like you in heaven above or earth beneath . . .

Ps 77:13: What god is so great as our God?

Ps 86:8: There is none like you among the gods, O Lord, nor are there any works like yours . . .

Ps 95:3: For the Lord is a great God, a great king above all gods . . .

Ps 96:4 (= 1 Chron 16:25): For great is the Lord, and greatly to be praised; he is to be revered above all gods . . .

Ps 97:7, 9: . . . all gods bow down before him . . . you are exalted far above all gods.

Ps 135:5: For I know that the Lord is great; our Lord is above all gods . . .

Ps 138:1: I give thanks, O Lord, with my whole heart; before the gods I sing your praise . . .

The prophet Micah notes that "all the peoples walk, each in the name of its god, but we will walk in the name of the Lord our God forever and ever" (Mic 4:5). Some of these passages, like those above, simply acknowledge the necessary precedence of Yahweh over other deities (cf. Josh 23:7; Judg 6:10), examples of a comparatively "tolerant" monolatry.[2] But far more carry the threat of nasty consequences should the Israelites fail in their monolatry and become (as they often do) true polytheists. Biblical scholar Juha Pakkala (1999) has analyzed scores of passages just in the so-called Deuteronomistic history (Joshua through 2 Kings, with Deuteronomy as its theological introduction) that combine this insistence that Yahweh be worshipped to the exclusion of all other deities with noxious ultimata. Pakkala calls this "intolerant monolatry" – the Israelites accept the existence of other gods while simultaneously worshiping one god exclusively, but also severely punish anyone who venerates another god. Pakkala argues that this intolerant monolatry did not develop until the exile. Before that the Israelites would have been tolerant monolatrists or true polytheists. Ronald E. Clements (2007:55) characterizes this form of late Israelite religion "as an aggressive, cruel and intolerant monolatry." Should the Israelites slip up – and you know they will – they will perish (Josh 23:16), be harmed and consumed (Josh 24:20), be abandoned to their enemies and "sold" for plunder (Judg 2:3,11–18; 3:5–8; 10:6–16), be "cut off from the land" (1 Kgs 9:3–9), and ultimately be carried away to Assyria (2 Kgs 17) and Babylon (e.g., 2 Kgs 21:2–15). The people of Israel suffer for their disobedient devotion to other rival gods, *not* for their worship of imaginary deities. *Exclusion* is the point, not oneness (Assmann 2010:39–43). The monolatrists – "Yahweh-aloneists" some scholars call them – share the zeal of the later monotheists, just not the complete denial of the competition (Gnuse 1997:83).

We read in the Tanakh of precious teraphim (mentioned 15 times) owned by important biblical figures, including David. This term (always in the plural, even when referring to a singular object) is usually interpreted as images of household gods or, more specifically, of deceased ancestors. There is no consensus, however, on just what these were (Lewis 1999). Michal, David's first wife, uses one as a dummy for David (she adds clothes and hair and sticks it in bed! 1 Sam 19:13–16), but Rachel, Jacob's favorite wife, can hide these objects – which Jacob refers to as "gods" – in a saddlebag on her camel (Gen 31:34; cf. Judg 18:16–20, where they are called "teraphim" but are later referred to as "gods," v. 24). Nevertheless, it is clear that the teraphim are linked to non-Yahwistic divine powers.

Several other terms are used repeatedly throughout the Bible to refer to the "idols" (more accurately translated "images") of the gods. Archaeologists have uncovered numerous female figurines, "the most common religious artifact encountered in the archaeological excavations in Palestine" (Davies 2010:111). While these may not be the teraphim mentioned by biblical authors, most scholars identify some of them with goddesses such as Astarte or Asherah worshiped by Israelites (Hadley 2000:205; Miller 2000:36; Vriezen 2001; Stern 2010:401). These figurines "suggest that a number of female deities were part of Israelite religion" (Zevit 2001:346).[3]

Yahweh's pervasive fear that the Israelites will "serve other gods" is thus well-founded: "The cultic reality was polytheistic (Baal, Asherah, Bes, and Horus) and poly-Yahwistic and included a wide variety of local manifestations" (Berlejung 2017:70). These gods actually exist (at least as much as Yahweh "exists"), and God's people frequently choose and serve them, much to his disgust. As we saw at the beginning of this chapter with Yahweh's confrontation with the Philistines' god Dagon, the Hebrew God can fight his own fights. But these divine duels are more often fought by proxy, as in Moses' first meeting with Pharaoh (Ex 7:8–12). Aaron, Moses' brother, is commanded by God to throw down his divine rod before the king, whereupon it immediately becomes a serpent. The Egyptian wise men, sorcerers, and magicians do the same "by their secret arts," and their rods also become serpents. It looks like a draw until Aaron's rod "swallowed up their rods." The text assumes that the Egyptians have genuine religious potency – thus the successful metamorphosis – but that Yahweh's power is greater. For that matter, the biblical authors acknowledge the efficacy of a Moabite (non-Israelite) king's sacrifice of his son to his own national god (2 Kgs 3:27; Smith 2011:251–4).

Even more impressive is the prophet Elijah, who challenges 850 prophets (450 of Baal and 400 of Asherah) to the great "Miracle-Off on Mount Carmel" (1 Kgs 18:17–39). He wins when God performs some spectacular fire magic, and in good Yahwistic fashion the prophet takes advantage of the religious pendulum swinging his way by immediately ordering the people to kill all 450 prophets of Baal. The point – beyond the murderous propensities of the monolatrists (who, to be fair, were just getting even with Jezebel for "killing off the prophets of the Lord") – is that the text casually insists that there were nearly 1000 prophets of a rival god and goddess other than Yahweh flourishing among the Israelites.

The evolution of monotheism

During most of its history ancient Israel was characterized by a religious pluralism, not monotheism. Even the "wicked" King Ahab who "did evil in the sight of the Lord more than all were before him" (1 Kgs 16:30) had sons and a chief minister with Yahwistic names, "which would seem to indicate that Ahab worshipped Yahweh, perhaps as well as Asherah or even Baal" (Hadley 2000:67). The exilic and postexilic composers and editors of much of the Hebrew Bible came into the picture perhaps as long as half a millennium after the creation of its first stories, gaining authority only towards the end of the long development of the text. "Yahwistic monotheism was the *ideal* of most of the orthodox, nationalist parties who wrote and edited the Hebrew Bible, but for the majority it had not been the *reality* throughout most of ancient Israelites' history" (Dever 2005:252). These late redactors got the last say – shifting, changing, and adding new texts and passages to fit their religious vision and promote their theology while eliminating, altering, or burying references to the earlier religion(s) of the Israelites. The editors have "amended and aligned, embellished and erased, melded and moved the received documents according to the theological, political, and aesthetic demands of their day" (Berlinerblau 2005:33). Or, as two professors of Jewish and Bible Studies at Hebrew University of Jerusalem subtitle their book (*From Gods to God*): *How the Bible Debunked, Suppressed, or Changed Ancient Myths & Legends* (Shinan and Zakovitch 2012). Although these late biblical compilers had a distinct vision of Yahweh and Israel's religious history, they did not eradicate completely the earlier competing traditions, and clear vestiges still lie scattered throughout the Tanakh.

So when did monolatry emerge from a more extensive polytheistic background? As usual, it depends upon whom you ask. Some scholars argue that monolatry was there from the start. Bernhard Lang (1983) suggests that there were five different manifestations (one is tempted to say "outbreaks") of monolatry – what has been called the Yahweh-Alone Party – from the eighth century until exile. Robert Gnuse (1997:321–45) even terms this theological vacillation "punctuated equilibrium," equating the jumps and plateaus along the route to monotheism with those in some theories of human evolution. Josiah's reforms at the end of the seventh century "against the native Israelite and Judean noncomformist religions which had always been polytheistic" are often cited as a turning point towards monolatry, but both the biblical texts and archaeology strongly suggest that they did not succeed (Dever 2017:614). Juha Pakkala even argues that Josiah's religious reforms as presented in the Tanakh were invented by the postmonarchic authors (2017:273). He concludes that, although Israel remained essentially polytheistic, there was a "tendency towards YWHW-monolatry" in Judah by the seventh century (2017:273) and that the familiar "intolerant monolatry" – the acceptance of the existence but vehemently aggressive indictment of other gods – was an invention of the exiled Jews in the sixth century (1999).

Biblical scholars even more vigorously debate the nitty-gritty details of Israel's shift to radical monotheism. Some scholars argue that there had always been at least a strain of monotheism in Jewish life (e.g., Sommer 2009). A few serious scholars, often citing the possible influence of two failed efforts to develop monotheism in Egypt (Akhenaten) and Iran (Zarathustra), still insist that it emerged as a dominant tradition suddenly and very early among the Israelites (e.g., Propp 2006:762–94; these influences, however, are now rejected by many scholars; Skjærvø 2011; Baines 2011). Others believe that it first appeared at some point in the monarchy but "certainly not prior to the eighth century" (Smith 2011:268). Many biblical scholars and archaeologists nowadays, however, think that absolute monotheism really did not materialize as a force until after the exile in the sixth century, and when it did, it was pugnaciously exclusive. Why? What happened?

What happened was the devastation of the northern half of the kingdom by the Assyrians, followed by the destruction of Jerusalem and the exile of the Judahites to Babylon. This crucial deportation was the result of two punitive expeditions in 597 and 586 against Israel by the King of Babylon. The temple in Jerusalem was ransacked and destroyed. A second temple was built at the end of the sixth century, a couple of decades after the exiles were allowed to return to Israel in 539 by Cyrus, the Persian conqueror of Babylon. To explain Israel's crushing defeats, history was revised. The new version of history was that Yahweh had used the Israelites' polytheistic neighbors to punish his people not just for worshiping other gods (as depicted in most of the Tanakh) but for accepting and worshiping *false* gods – Yahweh became the one and only God in the latest parts of the text. "The Israelite elite . . . did not arrive at a doctrine of monotheism by rejecting the gods of other peoples. Rather, it arrived at this pass by rejecting the gods that traditional culture, and earlier elite culture, had inherited from the fathers from the remotest bounds of the collective memory" (Halpern 2009:96). The editors projected this new, alternative, religiously exclusive perspective back onto the early history of Israel. "The introduction of monotheism among the Jews was, in other words, a means of rationalizing Israel's catastrophic defeat at the hands of the Babylonians" (Aslan 2017:126–7).

Regardless of exactly when and how monolatry and monotheism developed in the Jewish world, many scholars of early Israelite religion and Levantine archaeologists agree that numerous early Israelites were polytheistic, and traces of these beliefs and practices remain in the Tanakh and have been unearthed in the ancient material culture. The Israelites worshipped a number of deities who gathered at a divine council or assembly in a generational system very similar to that of the gods of their neighbors in the Levant and wider Near East (including Greece). No one knows exactly where or when Yahweh emerged on the scene or how he became the national god of Israel. His name is not attested in the area before the ninth century. The various biblical traditions of a period before Yahweh's name was known suggest a "memory of a time when Yhwh was not known to the Israelites but was introduced for the first time" (Grabbe 2007:153). A common theory is that Yahweh was initially a warrior-god (the "God of Hosts") imported from the southeast (Leuenberger 2017; though cf. Pfeiffer 2017).

The name of the chief patriarchal god for the Israelites was originally El (as in Isra-el), a great Canaanite/Ugaritic god depicted as an elderly figure enthroned. The Bible has more than 230 references to El as both the Israelite deity and a foreign god (even using it in the plural), and many of these are found in the oldest literary strands of the text (Dever 2005:257–63). "Because the Yahveh [Yahweh] cult appropriated the name of El to its own object of worship, we cannot always tell whether an *el* reference in a biblical text is to the Canaanite El, to Yahveh, to a blend of both, or to another divinity entirely" (Sperling 2014:3538). The lack of any polemic in the Tanakh against El suggests the great comfort early Israel once had with El as their primary deity. Yahweh may have originally been a cultic name of El as worshipped in the south (Miller 2000:24–5) or a second-tier deity in the pantheon who worked his way up to converging with El. Yahweh is referred to in the Tanakh under various "El" names such as El Elyon, El Olam, El Roi, El Berith, perhaps each representing a variant of the god worshipped in different areas (Bellinzoni 2009:71), not dissimilar to the way Greek gods eventually take on distinct "personalities" with different cults in various locations.[4] In the process of this assimilation (sometimes labeled "convergence" or "inclusive monotheism"), Yahweh came to share much of El's personality and gained many of his elder mentor's accoutrements, including a cherubim throne, a court of divine beings, and a consort Asherah.

But even Baal, El's son who becomes Yahweh's bête noire and his primary competitor for worship in Canaan, may at one time have been part of the divine pantheon who merged with Yahweh. One important aspect of Yahweh's character that is found in what many believe to be the oldest parts of the Tanakh reveal his similarities with Baal as a weather or storm god (Müller 2017:211–18; Pfeiffer 2017), a "divine warrior providing precipitation" (Smith 2017:37).[5] Baruch Halpern has argued that "Baal functioned to designate Yahweh's male underlings whether in the singular or the plural," and that Yahweh was "probably 'the baal' par excellence in the Israelite pantheon of baals" (2009:57–97). Scholars are divided about which is the more important, but both El and Baal clearly have been incorporated into Yahweh in some serious fashion (Berlejung 2017:74–5).

We have remarkable inscriptions attesting to eighth-century Jewish worship of "Yahweh and his Asherah," that is, Yahweh and his female consort. Asherah is the name given to Athirat, a northwest Semitic deity adopted and adapted by the Israelites. Scholars debate the nature of these references – is the Asherah here a goddess or a wooden icon or tree representing a goddess? Although there are some grammatical difficulties (though see now Tropper 2017:19–20), "the general consensus seems to have been moving toward reading the term [asherah] not as a pole or tree-like symbol but rather as the personal name of the deity" (Dever 2017:596; cf. Grabbe 2007:157; Dijkstra 2001a:44). In any case, that distinction makes little difference to the argument for the existence, rather than about the nature, of early Israelite polytheism. There are 40 references to Asherah (or asherah) in the Hebrew Bible. While some scholars believe they all refer to a cultic object, it is more likely that at least a handful designate the goddess who was worshipped along with Yahweh by early Israelites (Hadley 2000; Wiggins 2007:105–50). A tenth-century cult stand unearthed in Tanaach seems to depict "the clearest picture so far discovered of the worship of both Yahweh and Asherah together" (Hadley 2000:169–79).[6] The asherah said to be in the Jerusalem temple was the symbol of the goddess herself (2 Kgs 21:7; 23:6–7; cf. 1 Kgs 15:12; 2 Kgs 17:16; 23:4) – there were certainly "high status" female worshipers of Asherah in Jerusalem (1 Kgs 15:13; perhaps Jer 7:16–18; 44:24–5; Stavrakopoulou 2010:42; Zevit 2001:652). Thus, Asherah may have had an important place at times in the official cult, and in some places worship of a goddess continued for centuries. We know from epigraphical evidence that at Elephantine (an island on the Nile) in the fifth century BCE, for example, as Jerusalem was becoming a vassal state and monotheistic theocracy, Yahweh was still worshipped by the Jewish inhabitants along with several other deities, including a goddess. God may have been viewed there as "an apparent androgynous blend of Yahveh with the ancient Canaanite goddess Anat" (Sperling 2014:3541).

As the nature of Yahweh changed, especially with the eventual triumph of the monotheistic Yahwists, much of the textual material referring to the early, polytheistic version of Israelite religion had to be removed (e.g., Asherah) or severely altered (e.g., Baal). Good kings, according to this later theological perspective, do "what is right in the eyes of the Lord" by trying to eradicate all non-Yahweh worship (e.g., 2 Kings 18–20). Baal-worship was often the primary target. Jehu, King of Israel (that is, the northern part of the kingdom), "wiped Baal from Israel," luring all the worshipers, priests, and prophets of Baal into a temple under the pretense of "sanctifying a solemn assembly" for the god. (Although in earlier times, as you will recall, there were 450 prophets of Baal, in this story it is more convenient to be able to squeeze all Baal worshipers into a single temple.) He then sent in his guards to slaughter them all. Yahweh, pleased with a tactic reminiscent of Viking or Rwandan church massacres – "you have done well in carrying out what I consider right, and in accordance with all that was in my heart" – promises that "your sons of the fourth generation shall sit on the throne of Israel" (2 Kgs 10:18–30).

Scholars note that the later editors of the Tanakh did their best to eliminate traces of the importance of Baal in early Israelite culture. Jewish names like Eshbaal (or Ishbaal, 1 Chron 8:33; 9:39) and Meribbaal (1 Chron 8:34; 9:40), which originally contained the (eventually) ostracized deity's name (-baal), understandably made some biblical editors uncomfortable. The damaging "theophoric" (god-bearing) element was removed and replaced with a less offensive component – Ishbaal changed to Ishbosheth in 2 Sam 2:8, Meribbaal to Mephibosheth in 2 Sam 4:4 (although Hutton suggests that the original "-baal" names may not have referred to the deity; 2010:154–5).

The goddess Asherah, once Yahweh's consort for some Israelites, also fell victim to the editorial axe. She is only mentioned as a divine female figure a handful of times in the final redaction of the Tanakh, worshipped solely by "bad" Israelites and foreigners. In these contexts, she is linked with the evil Baal rather than the benign El, an association never attested outside the Tanakh, thus revealing the polemical move by later authors to discredit a goddess probably still worshipped by many Israelites (J. Day 2000:48). Asherah "was sufficiently important that she terrified the biblical authors," Lowell Handy observes, "and the inscriptions that link Yahweh and Asherah suggest, if not prove, that this was the divine couple of highest authority in the area" (1996:39).

The Israelites worshiped their many gods in a variety of cultic acts and places. But in shaping the Bible, the late editors also repurposed some of these legitimate religious *practices*, turning them into cautionary tales of idolatry and apostasy that served to "explain" Israelites' past political disasters. The Bible paints these "idolatrous" activities as the cause of God's wrath and thus Israel's various humiliating military defeats.

So what were these acceptable practices that are later transformed into "abominations," the purview of "bad" judges and kings who allow the Israelites to worship additional gods? In particular, they build statues, set up stone steles, pillars, and asherim (wooden poles), use divination, and burn incense on high places. "Good" kings keep removing the signs and destroying these sites of polytheistic worship, but to no real avail. "In mentioning so often the destruction of these places of worship by the kings of Judah," observes Mario Liverani, "the compilers (both the Deuteronomist of Kings and the later Chronicler) actually confirm the inefficacy of such efforts in erasing a deep-seated religious loyalty" (2003:139). Traces of the legitimacy of these rituals can still be found in the Bible, for they are often directed towards Yahweh himself! Jacob twice sets up a stone as a pillar, pouring oil on it, taking a vow and claiming that this "shall be God's house" (Gen 28:18–22; 35:14–15). Although stone or pillar worship was *verboten* by the reforming monotheists, Moses also built an altar at the foot of a mountain and set up 12 pillars (Ex 24:4), one for each tribe – a "classic Semitic shrine" (Propp 2006:294; cf. Gen 31:13,45; Ex 24:4; Josh 24:26). Solomon sacrificed at an open altar on a high place (later associated with non-Yahwistic cult) without damage to his reputation (1Kgs 3:2–5; cf. Gen 12:7; 13:18; 26:25; 33:20; 35:1,3,7). Sacred trees were chopped down by later "reforming" kings, but Abraham (Gen 12:6; 13:18; 14:13; 18:1; 21:33), Jacob (Gen 35:4; cf. 35:8), and Joshua (Josh 24:26) all have close cultic links with them (cf. Deut 11:30). Most scholars see in the "sin of Jeroboam" – the two theologically detested statues of calves erected at cult sights in the north – objects that were originally a legitimate form of Yahwistic worship. Jeroboam's real "sin" was more likely in establishing a rival to the central sanctuary for Yahweh in Jerusalem, not in the introduction of a foreign idol (Cross 1973:75). "The texts [rejecting the calves] reflect the hindsight practice of a single central temple and wish to present that as a norm throughout the monarchic period" and even earlier (Edelman 2010:83–4; cf. the later rejection of a bronze serpent (2 Kgs 18:4) Moses had made on Yahweh's explicit orders (Num 21:4–9); Hendel 1999:746).

Besides worshiping other gods in heterodoxical ways, the early Israelites engaged in some behaviors that might truly be called "abominable." One practice in particular that they shared with neighbors became a source of humiliation and ultimate denial – they burned up their children. The late editors tell us that it is a mark of the worst kings in both Judah and Israel (e.g., 2 Kgs 23:10) that they "made their sons and their daughters pass through fire," the biblical euphemism for human sacrifice. Numerous biblical texts recoil against child sacrifice, considering it a cultic act of barbarism directed to a foreign deity (e.g., Deut 12:31; 18:10; Jer 7:31; 19:5; 32:35; 2 Kgs 23:10; Ps 106:37–38). It's just this kind of rite that forces Yahweh to remove "them [the Israelites] out his sight," that is, to call in the Assyrians to wipe out Israel (e.g., 2 Kgs 17:17).

Yet many scholars have concluded that these Israelite sacrifices originally were just as often made to *Yahweh* (e.g., Levenson 1993; Gnuse 1997:118, 188–91; Dever 2005:217–19; Stavrakopoulou 2004). At least one passage clearly implies that Yahweh found the sacrifice of a young girl, the daughter of Jephthah, to be a perfectly acceptable offering (albeit a stunningly stupid vow, Judg 11:34–40). Elsewhere Yahweh demands that *all* firstborn males (oxen, sheep, *boys* – the so-called law of first born) be given to him on the eighth day, and not always with the expressed possibility of "redeeming" the son through a substitute offering (e.g., Ex 22:29; cf. Ex 13:1–2). And the prophet Micah (6:6–7) lists year-old calves, rams, oil, and "my firstborn . . . the fruit of my body" as acceptable offerings to Yahweh. "From the heated denials of Jeremiah . . . that YHWH ever commanded it, it can be inferred that in the seventh century B.C., it was part of the worship of YHWH" (Greenberg 1983:281; cf. Hutton 2010:164).

According to Ezekiel, Yahweh intentionally insisted on child sacrifice – "bad statutes" – in order to punish his own intractable people as they wandered in the desert! "I gave them statutes that were not good and ordinances by which they could not live. I defiled them through their very gifts, in their offering up all their firstborn, in order that I might horrify them, so they might know that I am Lord" (Ezek 20:25–6). Yahweh's explanation looks like a drastic editorial effort to justify an early Israelite religious act no longer found acceptable. Yahweh gave his people horrific instructions as an excuse to punish them and explain away his own incompetence as their defender: "The law itself was evil, given by Yahweh as punishment for their sinfulness in the wilderness, in order to guarantee their ultimate destruction, while preserving Yahweh's righteousness in the face of this disaster" (Patton 1996:79). Indeed, the Hebrew deity's brand of justice finds no moral ambiguity in killing all of the firstborn of the Egyptians, even though it is clearly Pharaoh – whose heart Yahweh has intentionally hardened so as to insti-gate infanticide – who bears complete responsibility (Ex 12:21–31).[7] Even the texts that outlaw the practice condemn it "not because it is ethically untenable, but because it is foreign" (Stavrakopoulou 2004:149). Altogether, despite some residual modern efforts to squirm out of this unpleasant conclusion (e.g., Propp 2006:264–71), the evidence leads to the verdict that child sacrifice was at one point a legitimate element of Yahweh-worship.

Athena, like Yahweh, sees to it that no suitor in the *Odyssey* will change his mind or soften his heart – she wants them all to be punished. The suitors, like Pha-raoh, have messed with the wrong divinely aided hero. But in Homer no Olym-pian ever demands a human sacrifice. In later sources, Agamemnon sacrifices his daughter Iphigenia to appease Artemis, but an explicit reference to this infamous slaughter is absent from Homer's two epics.[8] And when this terrible act is brought up by post-Homeric Greek authors, it is almost always to critique the gods unfa-vorably and paint yet another disparaging portrait of Agamemnon or Menelaus (or of a cynically demagogic Odysseus). In the *Iliad*, Achilles sacrifices a dozen young Trojans on the funeral pyre of Patroclus (23.175–6), but this deed is part of a series of monstrous actions culminating in Achilles' attempt to desecrate Hec-tor's body: "Wicked were the deeds Achilles designed in his mind" (23.176), the poet remarks. "Clearly attention is being drawn to the exceptional savagery of this action" (Richardson 1993:189). Homer's *point* is Achilles' loss of humanity; we are not meant to admire him. No god demanded, or even *wanted*, much less accepted this sacrifice, as far as Homer tells us. The entire "wicked" idea derives from Achilles' guilt and anger over Patroclus' death. Is it coincidental that the funeral pyre won't light?

Consequences

As a result of this transformation of Yahweh from one important god among many to a self-admitted "jealous" God surrounded by competing and forbidden deities, he came to be depicted as especially vicious to his own people. Every defeat they suffered was reinterpreted in this new theological light, transformed from a military failure into a morality tale of Yahweh's "justified" wrath at the Isra-elites' failure to worship him alone. They had "slipped" from their monolatry (and eventually their monotheism) and were deservedly punished by their own God. This theme dominates the final version of the Tanakh. The northern state

(Israel) became notorious (in the eyes of the southern editors of the Tanakh) for its idolatrous behavior. The two halves even fought each other, and Yahweh happily "defeated Jeroboam and all Israel," that is, granted victory to the southern Israelites from Judah over the theologically corrupt northern Israelites: "Five hundred thousand picked men of Israel fell slain" (2 Chron 13:13–18). That's half a million of his own people.

As a result of this ahistorical revisionism, Yahweh now lives in perpetual suspicion that his chosen people will worship other gods, and he acts quickly to punish and make examples of defectors. Apostasy is catching and penalized by immediate destruction, and guilt is collectively punished. One of Yahweh's laws (Deut 13:12–18) requires that if "scoundrels" should try to introduce a competing deity, "you shall put the inhabitants of that town to the sword, utterly destroying it, and everything in it – even putting its livestock to the sword." The spoils are to be piled up and the city burned "as a whole burnt offering to the Lord your God: it shall remain a perpetual ruin, never to be rebuilt." He's talking about Israelites killing fellow Israelites. Right before this, Yahweh had commanded that anyone – even "your father's son or your mother's son, or your own son or daughter, or the wife you embrace, or your most intimate friend" – who tries to entice you to "worship other gods," you "shall stone them to death" with your own hand. This may sound like the fate of the latest community overrun by a jihadist Islamic group, and their actions have good biblical precedent.

Yahweh's vindictiveness, especially towards his own people, suggests another disquieting difference from Homer's gods that is worth noting. As we have already seen, the Olympians are accustomed to their polytheistic existence and would never think of demanding cultic fidelity to one god alone. These fickle gods may play favorites, but only the despised Ares is accused of switching sides. They do not often turn on their own "chosen" heroes. In the story of his homecoming Odysseus has run afoul of Poseidon, who had been an ardent supporter of the Greeks in the *Iliad*. But such mythological animosities – similar is Athena's post-Iliadic pursuit of Ajax the Lesser (and consequently all the Greek ships, *Od.* 4.499–511; 5.106–9) after he drags Cassandra from the goddess's temple during the sack of Troy – are individual disputes. The Homeric gods do not generally destroy entire families, houses, armies, and cities of their previous favorites; they rarely go after anyone but particular offenders. Poseidon doesn't try to drown Penelope or sink Telemachus' ship. Achilles tells the story of how Artemis and Apollo kill all 12 of Niobe's children, but she was never one of their "chosen" followers, and she has directly insulted the twin deities' mother. Hera's consummate anger comes close to that of Yahweh. The goddess says she is willing to let her favorite cities be demolished in return for Troy's annihilation, although that swap never actually happens. The best parallel to Yahweh's vindictiveness occurs when Poseidon grows angry at the Phaeacians, a race "of his own lineage," for conveying Odysseus safely home. The god transforms the returning ship with its rowers into stone with "the flat of his hand" (*Od.* 13.162–4). He also threatens to "cover their city with a towering mountain" (*Od.* 13.152). The Phaeacians try to forestall this disaster through prayer and an elaborate sacrifice; we never learn if their efforts succeed. Still, the god is not motivated by jealousy of another deity. Yahweh is the insecure god, resisting his polytheistic nature by decimating his own disappointing followers.

The conclusion of this survey is clear and one accepted by most scholars of the Tanakh: Yahweh had lots of competing deities, gods to whom both the surrounding communities and many Israelites often turned as well. But Yahweh *also* had divine beings at his command, an immortal crew to do his bidding. No wonder he's not a monotheist – otherwise he'd have to do all that work on his own. Let's take a look at Yahweh's divine staff.

Notes

1 A word about YHWH. Hebrew text of the Tanakh did not write out the word "Yahweh" but instead produced the tetragrammaton, the four consonants YHWH. Next to the consonants YHWH the vowels of a different Hebrew word for "Lord" (usually *Adonai*) were eventually attached as a reminder not to say the actual name when reading aloud. (Thus arise both the convention of writing LORD in small caps – a nod to saying Adonai instead of Yahweh – and the nonsensical "Jehova" – "a morphological monstrosity with no claim to legitimacy" (Pope 1965:xiv n1) that results when one combines the consonants of God's name (YHWH) with the vowels from a completely different word.) This effort to refrain from using God's name was a late (Hellenistic), extrabiblical decision. In fact, preexilic "literature and Hebrew inscriptions often tend to invoke YHWH by pronouncing his name, a phenomenon also attested in the fifth-century BCE" (Lemaire 2007:128). So we are not stepping on the toes of the original authors when we use the full name. Admittedly, the original vowels in his name remain a bit of a guess. There are at least three possible pronunciations (Lemaire 2007:135–8), but the vast majority of scholars writing in English have settled on Yahweh. Some modern biblical scholars still write the tetragrammaton, YHWH, either honoring postbiblical sensitivities or simply acknowledging the missing vowels.
2 In one interesting passage, Jephthah the Israelite judge tries to avoid direct conflict with the Ammonites. His argument is remarkably polytheistic, as he asks the Ammonite king: "Should you not possess what your god Chemosh gives you to possess? And should we not be the ones to possess everything that the Lord our God has conquered for our benefit?" (Judg 11:24). This is a surprisingly "pacific theology, implying that one should accept the will of both one's god and the god of one's foe (and that their wills are reconcilable)" (Stern 1991:49). Sasson (2014:429) argues that Jephthah may be sarcastic here, which strikes me as extremely unlikely.
3 Eventually it was forbidden to try to represent God iconographically. The reasons (and exact date) for this restriction are still debated, but clearly one of the major issues was potential confusion with the "idols" of other gods. Both Jewish and Muslim traditions still reject efforts to depict God, although the commandment upon which this idea is based probably developed relatively late and perhaps did not always apply to images of Yahweh (Bevan 1940:46–7; Mettinger 1997; Besançon 2000:74). As late as the fourth century CE, the second commandment was still often considered to be a ban only on three-dimensional objects that were likely to lead to idolatry. Many early synagogues were "profusely decorated" with paintings and mosaics of biblical passages, and medieval Hebrew manuscripts overflowed with illustrations (Schama 2013:176–201, 367–73). In ancient Israel, "Yahweh was sometimes represented zoomorphically [that is, as an animal, as in the case of the golden calves]" (Weeks 2007:14). Not only did the early Jews make idols but crafted and treasured images of other gods. Some historians have argued that there was an anthropomorphic cult image of Yahweh in the Samarian temple

that was hauled off by Sargon II (the Assyrian king makes a reference to "carrying off the gods" in one of his Nimrud Prism inscriptions, Becking 1997:158–67; Uehlinger 1997:125–8) or even in the temple in Jerusalem (Niehr 1997; Pakkala 2017:274n26). Minimally this reference points to polytheistic worship in Samaria in the eighth century. Although no agreed-upon representations of Yahweh are extant (Niehr 1997), Hendel (1997:212–18) lists over half a dozen representations of male deities from Iron Age Palestine that could be "legitimate candidates for images of Yahweh." Since most male deities from ancient Israel/Palestine are lumped into one of only two types of figures – the Baal or El types, both of which influenced the development of Yahweh – we can't tell if any of these could be an image of the Israelite God (Berlejung 2017). So it remains a possibility that in cult Yahweh may have been treated at some points and by some Israelites in very similar fashion to Zeus and the rest of the Olympians.

4 Some biblical scholars suggest that Israelite religion, even when focused on one God, might be better labeled "poly-Yahwistic." That is, much like in the post-Homeric worship of the Greek gods, different places focused on different aspects or natures of Yahweh with distinct forms of worship. These local manifestations of a national god might be better called Yahweh-in-Hebron, Yahweh-in-Zion, Yahweh of Samaria, Yahweh of Teman, etc. (McCarter 1987).

5 Like Zeus, Yahweh is a weather-god who manifests himself in thunder and lightning; provides rain, hail, and snow; controls winds; and even wraps himself frequently in a cloud like that notorious fog of the Olympians. Both deities are manifestations to some degree of the Storm-God in the ancient Near East (Korpel 1990:599–613; Green 2003:253–75). Both Zeus and Yahweh can be the subject of meteorological actions. They "rain" and "thunder" (Brown 2000:61). Some scholars have even suggested that etymologically Yahweh's name is not so much derived from a meaning "to be" as "to blow" (Römer 2013:23).

6 There is also one slightly possible reference in the Tanakh to Yahweh and his Asherah at Deuteronomy 33:2, although this involves a minor emendation of a text of uncertain meaning (Dijkstra 2001b:113).

7 This is, after all, the same God who famously demands the sacrifice of Abraham's only son, Isaac – a "monstrous test" (Crenshaw 1984:13) – and then blesses the father for his willingness to carry out the deed (Gen 22:1–19). As Philip Davies concludes, "Abraham is certainly no model father or husband, and Yhwh no model god" (Davies 1995:113). Many early Jewish commentators were so upset (and rightly so) by the passage that they argued the command must have come from Satan, not Yahweh. (They were also concerned that there is no mention of Isaac on the return trip and therefore speculated that Isaac had actually been slaughtered – and revived!) Some of these same interpreters argued that the story is meant to mark the *end* of child sacrifice, but the passage celebrates Abraham's heartless faith. It is his very "*willingness* to do it that makes him the Father of Faith, not the fact the God put an end to the practice" (Delaney 1998:101, emphasis in the original; cf. Thatcher 2008:89). Still, contemporary Christian scholars can conclude that Yahweh's test was perfectly reasonable, that "Isaac belongs to God, and Abraham must acknowledge God's prior claim to his life" (McKeown 2008:117) or that "God is more important than life itself, whether one's own life or that of those who may be dearer than one's own life" (Ford 2007:231, cited in Thatcher 2008:89) or that, simply, "what God asks of him must be right" (Hayes 1989:20). Christian theologian Paul Copan goes so far in his projection of Christian doctrine onto the passage that he cites the New Testament (Hebrews 11:17–19) to argue that Abraham wasn't really all that worried about his son's fate, since he "believed God could even raise Isaac from the dead" (2010:48)! Both contemporary Jews and Muslims still feature the Abrahamic story of the binding as a *good* thing at key religious festivals (Rosh Hashanah and the *Hajj*).

8 Classicists debate whether Homer hints at the story when Agamemnon admits that he has a grudge against the prophet Calchas: "Prophet of evil, never yet have you said

anything helpful to me; it is always dear to your heart to prophesy evil. You have never yet spoken or fulfilled any good word" (1.106–108). In post-Homeric accounts, Calchas is often assigned the role of announcing the necessity of the sacrifice if the Greeks are to sail to Troy, much to Agamemnon's horror. In the *Iliad*, Agamemnon has a daughter named Iphianassa, whom some scholars equate with Iphigenia (Lyons 1997:139–43), but she is still very much alive when the war begins.

5 Biblical polytheism II
Yahweh's little helpers

One of the most memorably weird tales in the Tanakh is the story of the non-Israelite seer Balaam (Num 22:1–35), whose character may have been based on a prophetic figure in a rival cult (Hackett 1987:127–8; Puech 2005). The king of Moab (a kingdom bordering the Dead Sea) tries to hire Balaam to curse the Israelites, but Yahweh himself comes to Balaam and tells him not to go and definitely not to curse Israel, "for they are blessed." Balaam obeys. It's not clear why a non-Israelite should be listening to someone else's national god, but that's merely the tiny tip of the iceberg of chaos floating through this story.[1]

After Balaam receives a second request from the king, Yahweh changes his mind and tells Balaam to "get up and go" with the king's officials and "do only what I tell you to do." "So Balaam got up in the morning, saddled his donkey, and went with the officials of Moab." The narrative is already a little strange, with God altering his plans for no apparent reason. But now the story takes an especially unexpected turn: "God's anger was kindled because he [Balaam] was going, and the angel of the Lord took his stand in the road as his adversary (*satan*)." Whoa! What's a seer to do? God is mad because . . . Balaam did exactly what he was told by God! The story seems designed to mock Balaam. In fact, although Balaam ends up blessing Israel and eulogizing Yahweh, just a few chapters later (Num 31) Yahweh has the Israelites kill every male Midianite, including Balaam (cf. Josh 13:22). In other references to Balaam in the Tanakh, he is presented in an increasingly negative light until he finally tries to curse Israel and gives advice on how the Moabite women can seduce Israelite men (Noort 2005). In the rabbinic tradition and the New Testament, Balaam is interpreted as the "typical gentile sorcerer and evil, greedy person" (Hackett 1987:127–8).

It gets funkier. The "angel of the Lord" – a shadowy doublet of Yahweh on occasion, as we will soon see – blocks Balaam's path, but only the donkey can see the sword-wielding "adversary." The startled creature naturally swerves off the road. Balaam, puzzled and annoyed at his donkey's behavior, beats him. Two more times the angel of Yahweh confronts the donkey; two more times it reacts, first moving aside and finally lying down in desperation. Just when you think the tale can't get much quirkier, "the Lord opened the mouth of the donkey," and Balaam and his loyal steed have a heated conversation about the latter's reliability. Then – finally – "the Lord opened the eyes of Balaam, and he saw the angel of the Lord standing in the road, with his drawn sword in his hand." Oh, *that* scary blade-wielding adversary!

The narrative is a mishmash of mythological motifs that are handled more elegantly in Homer – the talking equid (Achilles' horse), the animal awareness of a numinous being and the obliviousness of the master (Telemachus' dogs), the bestowing of the magical ability to see the divine (Athena for Diomedes). And Balaam's tale concludes in more confusion. The angel informs Balaam that the donkey saved his ass (so to speak), for "if it had not turned away from me, surely just now I would have killed you and let it live." Balaam confesses his sin – whatever that could possibly have been – and quickly adds that "if it is displeasing to you, I will return home." How, exactly, it could be displeasing to the angel of God that Balaam was doing precisely what God had commanded him to do is left a mystery, an oddity that climaxes in the angel's final command: "Go with the men."

This is Homeric ring composition cobbled together by a lunatic. The angel of Yahweh repeats Yahweh's initial words. And he was prepared to kill, something he does very well. It is the angel of the Lord who destroys the 185,000 Assyrians besieging Jerusalem and sends King Sennacherub racing home (2 Kgs 19:35–6; Isa 37:36–7). This same murderous functionary wipes out 70,000 *Israelites* "from Dan to Beer-sheba" after Yahweh inexplicably takes offense at David's census-taking (2 Sam 24:15–17).

Balaam's story takes for granted that Yahweh has lackeys to do his bidding – divine lackeys, and unpleasantly obedient ones at that. Ancient Israel was afloat with gods *and goddesses* worshipped by many Israelites. "You have as many gods as you have towns, O Judah," Jeremiah snipes in disapproval (2:28). In this chapter we'll take a look at some of Yahweh's divine entourage, once again discovering the Olympian nature of the Hebrew God.[2]

Yahweh's crew

There are many species of supernatural powers that serve Yahweh. The old Israelite "host of heaven" peek their polytheistic heads out from behind the monotheists' efforts to sanitize or eliminate them, as we will discover in the efforts in Genesis 1 to reduce the sun, moon, and stars to mere astronomical entities. We saw in Job how Satan started his doomed career merely as "the satan," an adversarial divine being among the "sons of God" (Job 1.6; 2.1). What about those innumerable angels? The Talmud says that there are many billions of them, and the Church Fathers debated the number of angelic choruses: five? eight? nine? (Ranke-Heinemann 1994:55). Alas, a Roman Synod in 745 forbade expanding angelic personal names beyond Gabriel, Michael, and Raphael. (The first two names alone appear in the Tanakh, and only in the late book of Daniel, although rabbinic tradition read Raphael back into some of the texts.) There are various categories of angels, including cherubim (four-faced, winged sphinxish humanoids in Ezekiel who also guard the gate of Eden in Genesis, 3:24; cf. Ex 25:18–22) and the winged, fiery serpentine things known as seraphim in Isaiah (Isa 6:2–6; cf. 14:29, 30:6). There were clearly numerous Israelites who actually worshipped some of these angelic figures as well or we would not find the insistence that such devotion be stopped (Ehrman 2014:55; see below). The later editors tried to remove as much of that as possible. Yahweh alone is to benefit from cultic actions in the final revision of the text we now possess, and the rest of his divine crew is to do his bidding. As one of the psalmists notes, "The Lord has established his throne in the heavens. . . . Bless the Lord, O you his angels, you mighty ones who do his bidding, obedient to his spoken word. Bless the Lord, all his hosts, his ministers that do his will" (Ps 103:19–21).

Although it is sometimes difficult to determine the exact species of any particular heavenly being – it's all a bit like keeping track of the various critters in Tolkien's Middle-earth – for our purposes it doesn't much matter. The point is that Yahweh has countless divine agents: messengers, stewards, hosts, spirits, a divine council, hit men, etc. Yahweh is by no means the only divinity. True, he lacks a social life among the other gods (Miles 1995:86–8), focused as he is solely upon his creation in a way even the Olympians would find tedious. But this so-called monotheism looks more like a crowded divine royal court or, given the numbers, a supernatural army. You can't dismiss Zeus because of his divine entourage without abandoning Yahweh as well. And the one major distinction – that Yahweh is always, always, *always* in complete control of his fellow deities – has been a lead weight in the theology of the Abrahamic religions. If Yahweh has absolute control of his fellow divinities and the cosmos, how can we account for the patent natural evil in a world governed by his unwavering agents? Homer's feuding adolescents will emerge as the more insightful and realistic option.

Yahweh's council

Bruce Louden has pointed out numerous close parallels between individual divine councils in the Tanakh and the Homeric epics and parsed the different types of assembly (Louden 2006:207–11, 2011:16–29). Earlier we examined the similarity between the divine meetings in Job and those at the beginning of the *Odyssey*. For our purposes, the important point is that Yahweh in his heavenly council is depicted in strikingly similar fashion to Zeus and his divine assembly on Olympus, of which there are 15 primary examples (West 1997:177–80; Bonnet 2017:91–100). Biblical councils derive from the earlier depictions of Near Eastern assemblies, especially El presiding over the Canaanite/Ugaritic pantheon. Isaiah sees God sitting high and lofty on a throne, with singing seraphim in attendance (Isa 6). Daniel actually witnesses God take his place on a fiery throne in what must have been a packed council meeting: "A thousand thousands served him, and ten thousand times ten thousand stood attending him" (Dan 7:10). Yahweh one-ups his Mesopotamian competition, where a full council apparently included only 57 gods (Mullen 1980:175). At one point Olympus also seems to be similarly teeming with divinities: "Zeus commanded Themis to summon the gods to the assembly from the peak of many-ridged Olympus; and she hurried in all directions and commanded them to return to the house of Zeus. None of the rivers was absent, except for Oceanus, nor any of the nymphs who inhabit the fair groves and source of rivers and the grassy meadows" (20.4–9). Somehow they all manage to wedge themselves within "the polished corridors" of Zeus's house.

Unlike the Olympian councils, however, which are restricted to divine members, it becomes the mark of a genuine (human) prophet to have sat in on Yahweh's crowded assembly. This addition seems unique to Israel in the Near East (Mullen 1980:218). Jeremiah challenges false prophets by asking which of them "has stood in the council of the Lord so as to see and hear his word" (Jer 23:18, 22; cf. Job 15:8). In the fourth vision of the slightly zany Zechariah (3:1–10), he witnesses the trial of the high priest in Yahweh's courtroom/council. The angel of the Lord provides the defense while Satan (still just an adversary) is the prosecutor. Before the charges can even be read, "the Lord said to Satan, 'The Lord rebuke you, O Satan.'" God's tolerance for evidence can only be pushed so far. The case is quickly resolved, and the high priest is promised "the right of access among those who are standing here" – that is, to Yahweh's council – should he behave appropriately. The whole passage has a decidedly political flavor, perhaps reflecting the authors' belief, amidst postexilic political turmoil, that the high priest should have the highest authority. But the most distinctive part of the trial scene for me is when the angels, serving now as personal shoppers, give the priest new clothes and a turban.

Biblical scholars have analyzed the makeup and nature of Yahweh's council, even divining the various functions of its members while noting its many similarities to Canaanite (Ugaritic) and Phoenician divine assemblies (e.g., Mullen 1980; Handy 1994; Smith 2001:47–53; White 2014:105–37). Yahweh's assembly fulfills many of the same tasks as other Near Eastern polytheistic councils: "It serves him, gives him advice, glorifies him, mediates between God and humans, protects peoples and human beings, and hears the prayers of humanity" (Niehr 1996:62). But the key point for the Israelite version is that Yahweh is said to be in complete control of the proceedings and the attendees. There may be thousands of divine beings hanging around Yahweh, but there is never a moment when his authority is directly challenged: "A heavenly bureaucracy could have diminished God's sovereignty by suggesting that he is not in full control" (Brettler 1989:104). "For who in the skies can be compared to the Lord?" asks the psalmist. "Who among the heavenly beings [i.e., sons of God] is like the Lord, a God feared in the council of the holy ones, great and awesome above all that are around about him?" (Ps 89:6–7; cf. Ps 29). As Ellen White concludes in her recent study of Yahweh's council, "It seems that perhaps the importance of monotheism in relation to the council is not the denial of other divine beings, but that Yahweh be held in complete and absolute control of the cosmos" (2014:41; cf. Dahood 1968:313). The divine host's primary function is to praise, celebrate, support, and take orders from Yahweh. Occasionally there is a bit of give and take (e.g., 1 Kgs 22:19–23), but inevitably Yahweh's will emerges uncontested and his power is extolled by the assembly. There is no Hera to register a complaint, no Poseidon to try to put his foot down, no Thetis calling in favors – and thus no one to blame but Yahweh for the state of the world.

But as so often is the case with the many-layered nature of the Tanakh, Yahweh's true mythological background still sneaks out. Biblical scholars have pointed out that two council scenes are best read as revealing a time when Yahweh was not *yet* in complete control, but merely one member of the divine assembly, perhaps even the son of El, the presiding deity (White 2014:33). Deuteronomy 32 has made monotheists uncomfortable for over 2500 years, despite the fact that it contains one of the few direct claims that "there is no god but me" (v. 39), a "monotheistic foundation narrative" (Smith 2011:260). I quote here the NRSV translation, which tries to compromise:

> Remember the days of old, consider the years long past; ask your father, and he will inform you; your elders, and they will tell you. When the Most High apportioned the nations, when he divided humankind, he fixed the boundaries of the peoples according to the number of the gods; the Lord's own portion was his people, Jacob his allotted share.
>
> (Deut 32:7–9)

We are at a meeting of the divine council, at which the god El Elyon (translated here as "Most High") presides. El was the name of the senior Canaanite god with whom, as we saw earlier, Yahweh's character merged. But in this passage, El Elyon ("Most High") is not (yet) the same god as Yahweh (translated "the Lord") – they are in fact two distinct deities. At this divine assembly, Yahweh is merely one of the many junior gods "among the number of gods" receiving his allotted people (Israel in his case) from the senior deity.

But this scene would naturally be upsetting to monolatristic redactors – Yahweh must *always* have been the senior god, right? So they wanted to read this as a council setting in which Yahweh is (awkwardly) named first Elyon and then assigns Israel to *himself*, identified in this second instance as Yahweh. Elyon and Yahweh must be the same god so that Yahweh is not *ever* subordinate. But even that interpretation would still leave the troubling polytheistic overtones – Yahweh has colleagues! The compilers of the Hebrew (Masoretic) text tried to avoid the polytheism by substituting "according to the number of the *Israelites*" for "according to the number of the *gods*" (Smith 2001:49, citing E. Tov, calls it an "anti-polytheistic alteration"; cf. Block 2000:25–32). But "gods" belongs to the earlier textual tradition, and a fragment of Deuteronomy 32:8 discovered at Qumran reveals that the polytheistic reading "represents the more original version of the book" (Dozeman 2015:63; there are in fact at least four different readings in different textual traditions, Smith 2011:259–66). But note that the translators of the NRSV, even though they leave the reference to the plural "gods," still want to suggest that Yahweh is in control. And so they have added the word "own" – the Lord's *own* portion – a reflexive possessive that, as the New Oxford Annotated commentary observes, has been invented by the NRSV "in order to identify Yahweh with Elyon and avoid the impression that Yahweh is merely a member of the pantheon." Yet that is exactly what is being portrayed here. Yahweh has not yet worked his way up the bureaucratic ladder to separate himself from all the other divine underlings and take over El's role as primary deity. "The passage presupposes," Mark Smith concludes, "even as it disputes, an older world view of the nations each headed by its own national god" (2011:259).

Of course, in most of the Tanakh Yahweh is already functioning as CEO. Scholars have even detected that crucial moment when Yahweh steps forth and establishes himself as the head honcho. Outraged that his fellow gods, the "children of El Elyon," have not taken their duties seriously and are falling woefully short on social justice, "God has taken his place in the divine council; in the midst of the gods he holds judgment: 'How long will you judge unjustly and show partiality to the wicked?' . . . I say, 'You are gods, children of the Most High [El Elyon], all of you; nevertheless, you shall die like mortals, and fall like any prince'" (Ps 82:1–2, 6–7; cf. Ps 58:1–2). The other immortal beings are condemned to die (that is, become defunct), an event that can actually happen in Near Eastern mythology (Machinist 2011). El may be the convener of the assembly in this scenario as well, although the exact setting is unclear. Yahweh takes this moment to step out from the divine pack and seize the ethical high ground – and political authority – accusing his fellow gods (siblings?) of moral weakness. The other gods may not actually die, but they suffer such a severe demotion throughout the rest of the text that most readers of the Bible aren't even aware they are still hanging around.

The divine council also survives in the startling use of the first-person plural by Yahweh on occasion, especially in the first books of Genesis: "Let us make . . ." (Gen 1:26); "like one of us . . ." (Gen 3:22); "let us go down . . ." (Gen 11:7; cf. "Who will go for us?" Isa 6:8). For that matter, to whom is God speaking when he says things like "It is not good that man should be alone" (Fretheim 2010:28)? Christian tradition has often insisted that in these moments we find a reference to the coeternal and preexistent Jesus, or even to the triune nature of God: Yahweh, the Hebrew deity, was apparently chatting at the time of creation with Jesus and the Holy Spirit. Other implausible explanations include the following: God speaks to the earth, dust, or the other elements he has created, or God uses a weird grammatical plural (of "majesty" or "exhortation" or "deliberation" or "fullness") none of which make sense here and some of which don't exist anywhere else in the Bible! Or perhaps it's not a plural form at all but a use of the "dual," a form found only with two subjects, thus referring to . . . God and his consort? God and some other divine figure who shares God's throne (Segal 1977)? The two different genders embedded within the godhead (cited in Garr 2003:17–21)? Or maybe it's simply what it appears to be – an indirect command to Yahweh's divine helpers.

The important difference between Israel's divine council and that in other Near East cultures, including Homer's, is that Yahweh is the absolute ruler. The rest of the council remain nebulous and indistinct; they are there to obey and praise. There is no "primitive democracy," to use Jacobsen's phrase (cited in Miller 1973:73), as found in Mesopotamia and Canaan, and on Olympus as well. Zeus is in charge, no doubt, but others have distinct personalities, disagree, grumble, push back, disobey, even if they are always ultimately brought back in line (for the moment) by his threats.

God's fellow gods

We need to take a census – yikes! – of the divine comrades of the not-so-lone God in heaven. If Yahweh's swarming heaven is unobjectionable, Olympus should not present any *a priori* problems as a home of the divine. And if Yahweh is completely in charge of the universe – and you see what our mortal share of the universe looks like – what are we to say about his competence or benevolence?

Interestingly, many scholars and translators often appear reluctant to call the group known as "sons of (the) god(s)" – the definite article and plural come and go (Parker 1999b:794–5) – what they clearly must be, or have been: gods. They are labeled "heavenly ones" or "divine beings" or "heavenly beings." We've already met this group in Job, where Satan twice shows up to the council meeting along with them (Job 1:6; 2:1; cf. 38:7), translated as "heavenly beings" in the NRSV. "Most Israelites, Yahwists in the main, knew their patron to whom they called by name, knew his consort Asherah, and knew other deities as well to whom they referred by the general idiom 'sons of gods' and 'other gods'" (Zevit 2001:652). Refreshingly, biblical scholar Ronald Hendel admits that in Genesis 6 these beings "are simply randy gods, subservient to YHWH, who overstep their bounds in the chaotic times before the flood" (2017:251–2). In order to avoid pagan (especially Greek) connotations – these could actually be *sons* of God – in a number of places the Septuagint replaces the phrase "sons of God" with "angels of God" (Mussies 1999:344). But some scholars concede that this familial relation is very likely the provenance of the term "*sons* of god," its original significance having been removed just as the once-legitimate goddesses and a possible wife for Yahweh have been expunged or demoted (Korpel 1990:54–9; Ehrman 2014:58).

Conservative Christian scholars often will go to great lengths to deny divine status to anyone but Yahweh (and Jesus, ultimately). Iain Provan, for example, tries to sidestep the issue by creating his own label and citing Christian dogma: "These messengers are indeed creatures, and not divinities. God is not many but One" (2014:53). (Provan also denies that the many foreign deities that even Yahweh acknowledges as divine competition are gods.) Now if you're a son (or the children) of a god (e.g., Gen 6:2; Pss 29:1; 89:7) and you live in heaven and you seem to be eternal, you are a divinity in any other context. The author of Psalm 82 has Yahweh say directly of his fellow council members, "You are gods, children of the Most High, all of you" (v. 6; cf. v. 1). John Day suggests that "Originally, these were gods, but as monotheism became absolute, so these were demoted to the status of angels" (J. Day 2000:22; cf. Smith 2001:49–50; Dahood 1966:175). The angels are thus often tossed into theological limbo, considered divine but somehow not gods because they were "created." This is special pleading, as well as ill-informed – at no point in the Hebrew Bible do we hear of their creation. Moreover, in both creation accounts in Genesis, God already addresses his fellow divinities ("let us . . .") with comfortable familiarity. *Someone* must have been there from the beginning.

Hermes is the son of god and lives on Olympus and is eternal and serves as Zeus's messenger and herald and attends his assemblies. Many of the Homeric gods fulfill these roles at one point or another in the text. They, too, are called "heavenly ones" and "divine beings" and "heavenly beings" – and *gods*. The same is true in all other Near Eastern mythologies, where messengers of the gods are gods themselves. Yahweh hangs out with fellow, lesser divinities, no matter how unsettling that is to later theological speculation: "Even within Judaism there was understood to be a continuum of divine beings and divine power, comparable in many ways to that which could be found in paganism" (Ehrman 2014:54).

The difference between the Homeric and biblical subordinate divinities may be ontological, I suppose, if you want to *believe* that. But their extratextual reality is not a topic that can be honestly examined, although it has often been the subject of much heated debate among the church fathers and in the rabbinical tradition. But the interpretative hesitation to call these divine folks of the Bible "gods" derives primarily from a theological discomfort with the textual reality of multiple divinities. Another source of this reluctance to call a duck a duck is the other divinities' inherent blandness, a generic dullness that derives from the unfortunate sycophancy required of Yahweh's subordinate gods. They have no independent wills, no distinct personalities, no opinions. They are extensions of the supreme authority whose task is usually no more than to "ascribe to the Lord glory and strength" (Ps 96:7) and do exactly what he commands. This is quite different from the squabbling and competitive Olympian deities variously obeying, chafing under, and attempting to undermine Zeus's will.

Well, Satan has a bit of flair. He, too, is mostly under Yahweh's control in his four appearances in the Tanakh as a divine being (the noun occurs five times to describe a human opponent). Only the late Chronicler finally gives him a little freedom, a single moment when he seems to (but probably does not) act independently of Yahweh in inducing David to conduct the census (1 Chron 21:1).

On the other hand, in one scandalous scene the sons of God go completely AWOL. In that notorious passage, these divinities are caught behaving more like Ovidian reprobates than biblical paragons, as the "sons of God" have sex with the fair "daughters of humans" and create a race of "heroes" (Gen 6:1–4):

> When people began to multiply on the face of the ground, and daughters were born to them, the sons of God saw that they were fair; and they took wives for themselves of all that they chose. Then the Lord said, "My spirit shall not abide in mortals forever, for they are flesh; their days shall be one hundred twenty years." The Nephilim were on earth in those days – and also afterward – when the sons of God went in to the daughters of humans, who bore children to them. These were the heroes that were of old, warriors of renown.
>
> (Gen 6:1–4)

This whole episode could come right out of the mythology of the Greeks (or any other Near Eastern culture). At least one early Christian insisted that the children of the angels and their mortal wives were the gods of the Greeks and Romans (Knust 2011:182–3)! Multiple divine beings related to the chief god come to earth to have sex with mortal women, the offspring of which union form a race of heroes "of old, warriors of renown." Sounds Greek to me.

Yahweh responds to his wayward staff (family?) by taking out his frustration on the humans and their illegitimate offspring rather than on the "sons of God." Hera is also famous for going after Zeus's lovers and their offspring rather than Zeus himself, a characteristic Homer alludes to numerous times when referring to problems she caused Heracles, the product of one of Zeus's many infidelities. Yahweh cranks this misdirected retaliation to a whole new genocidal level, the first example in the Tanakh of Yahweh's "bloody orgy," in which he ignores the difference between the guilty and the innocent (Schwager 1987:54):

> The Lord saw that the wickedness of humankind was great in the earth, and that every inclination of the thoughts of their hearts was only evil continually. And the Lord was sorry that he had made humankind on the earth, and it grieved him to his heart. So the Lord said, "I will blot out from the earth the human beings I have created – people together with animals and creeping things and birds of the air, for I am sorry that I have made them." But Noah found favor in the sight of the Lord.
>
> (Gen 6:5–8)

While similar flood stories have now emerged from texts unearthed throughout the ancient Near East, the flood is not mentioned in the Homeric poems. Homer's Zeus is not presented as a primeval power, as we will see, and the poet wanted his audience to feel a continuity with the heroic past (Finkelberg 2005:161–3, 175). But another early Greek epic, the *Catalogue of Women*, seems to begin with a near exact parallel to Genesis 6 as mortal women, mingling with the gods, produce a race of heroes, whom, according to at least one reconstruction of a fragmentary papyrus (204.95–119), we learn Zeus plans to destroy (but see Koenen 1994:26–33). Early Greek myths also related how Zeus instigated the Trojan War to separate men from gods, or to punish human impiety, or to reduce the human population. These are variants of the Near Eastern deluge narratives, familiar from *Gilgamesh*, the *Atrahasis*, and especially Yahweh's own war again his creation.

But Homer wants nothing to do with any tradition of Zeus's annihilation of mankind. The Greek poet suppressed or ignored that version of the origins of the war – assuming he knew of it – instead focusing on a few months of battle and shifting the responsibility for the death and destruction of the *Iliad* onto the wrath of Achilles. The will or plan of Zeus (1.5) that is accomplished in the epic is probably limited to the fulfillment of his promise to Thetis to support the Trojans until the Greeks repair Achilles' honor. When Zeus is said to "be about to hurl to Hades many mighty souls [literally 'heads']" (e.g., 11.54–5), it is to bring to fruition a vow to Achilles' divine mother, not to wipe out all of the Greeks or Trojans, much less mankind and the earth itself, as Yahweh does in the Tanakh.[3]

This is the only passage in the entire Bible, in either testament, where Yahweh or his assistants are directly credited with any sexual appetite. St. Paul, however, advises women to wear veils "because of the angels" (1 Cor 11:10), apparently fearing "that the angels will be aroused to lust by the sight of exposed women" (NOAB). But mostly angels in the Bible are, well, angelic. Jesus, the most famous abstinent Jew, insisted on the abstinence of angels. He told the Sadducees that in the resurrection there is no sex, but the revivified are "like angels in heaven" (Matt 22:30). (The New Testament of course leaves to the fertile theological imagination just how the Holy Spirit impregnated the virginal Mary.)

Heavenly angels are divine humanoids who for the most part seem to be at the bottom of Yahweh's civil service. They are the ultimate lackeys, doing whatever God requires (Garr 2003:51–83). They talk to prophets (and each other) and reveal visions; they deliver messages; they patrol the earth; they guard the faithful and guide the chosen; they supply food and water to God's favorites; they can act as a mediator for the condemned; at least one serves, sword in hand, as the commander of the "army of the Lord." And anyone who has read Genesis knows that they can climb and descend ladders. Really long ladders. The primary function of these supernatural emissaries – like just about every being in the Bible – is to praise and obey Yahweh. "Praise him, all his angels; praise him, all his host!" (Ps 148:2). On the other hand, they also act like humans: "They look like men, they talk like men, they can sit down and walk around and maybe even eat like men" (Kugel 2004:23).

But there is one special activity at which certain angels – or a specific branch of angelhood – excel. These divine special forces serve as Yahweh's assassins. One of his hit men was known only as "The Destroyer," a sobriquet worthy of a professional wrestler, if it weren't so horrifically literal. Like (the) Satan, it's not clear whether this is the name of the agent or his office. The Destroyer is responsible in one tradition for the killing of the firstborn in Egypt in the tenth "plague" (Ex 12:23; though cf. Ps 78:49). In an especially unappealing story, Ezekiel relates a vision in which Yahweh sends a divine hit squad through Jerusalem to kill wayward Israelites. In this inversion of the Exodus butchery, six angelic "executioners" (as Yahweh calls them), "each with his weapon for slaughter in his hand," are to kill God's *own people*. A divine scribe is sent ahead to put a mark on the foreheads of those loyal Yahwists who "groan over all the abominations that are committed in it [Jerusalem]." The hired guns are then to "pass through the city after him, and kill; your eye shall not spare, and you shall show no pity. Cut down old men, young men and young women, little children and women, but touch no one who has the mark" (Ezek 9:1–6).

Apollo guns down Greeks with a plague as the first divine action of the *Iliad*. Ares actually fights on the battlefield, and a handful of gods guide their favorite warriors in lethal combat. Zeus can be callous, to be sure, willing to allow the Greeks to lose battles and die if it will fulfill a debt to a minor deity. He is happy to watch the human butchery he has arranged from afar and to set the gods at each other's throats. And he bitterly relishes the coming death of Patroclus, the killer of his own son Sarpedon. But even then he did not act directly but "debated much about the slaying of Patroclus" (16.646–51), allowing him to continue his victorious run before perishing at the hands of Hector as fate would have it. Zeus himself may disapprove of Aegisthus' plan to seduce Clytemnestra and kill Agamemnon, but he merely dispatches Hermes to warn him not to do it and lets events take their course (*Od.* 1.32–43). Homer's Zeus never dispatches a god to kill children, much less children whose sole crime would appear to be following their parents' religion.

The Nardelli deity: God gets a promotion

In December of 2000, after 29 successful years at General Electric, Robert Nardelli was passed over to become head of the giant conglomerate. Rumor has it that he received a job offer to become CEO of Home Depot only ten minutes after resigning from GE. By the time he departed from that position in 2006, his total *yearly* compensation was somewhere between $131 and $200 million (I've seen both figures). He knew nothing about retail. His attempts to implement the management system he had learned at GE frustrated employees, and he ended up firing many of the most experienced workers and replacing them with novices who earned less money. The resulting poor service drove away customers in droves. The stagnant stock prices and declining market share displeased shareholders, and pretty much everyone was annoyed at his enormous salary. When the board asked him to tie his pay more closely to shareholder gains, he and they "agreed to a mutual separation." His golden parachute – divinely golden, indeed – was worth over $200 million.

Eight months later, in August 2007, Nardelli was hired by Cerberus Capital Management to take over ailing Chrysler. He had no experience in the automobile industry. Nardelli tangled with and fired managers and engineers. When the big three automakers went to Washington in November of 2008 to ask for a $25 billion bailout with taxpayer money, Nardelli was one of the notorious CEOs caught taking a private jet (estimated at $20,000 per trip). He failed to save Chrysler, ending his position as CEO when the company filed for bankruptcy just two years into his tenure. Despite his consistent failure, he remained in a top role at Cerberus, including serving as interim CEO of Freedom Group, a holding company for a dozen different firearms manufacturers. In 2012 Nardelli founded XLR-8 LLC, an "investment and advisory company" that boasts – and this is apparently said without humor – of its "unparalleled skills in fixing and growing companies."

The failures of Yahweh similarly led to infelicitous promotions. A warrior- and weather-god eventually finding himself a supreme divinity of an expanding Levantine people, he could take credit for its political and economic success in the time of the early monarchy (exaggerated and anachronistic though this triumph undoubtedly is in the biblical tales). Promoted from tribal to national god, he was doing his job. As Daniel Block concludes in his study of the national gods in the Bible, "the role of patron deities was to maintain the welfare and prosperity of their subjects. . . . The reputation of divine patron depended on the fate or fortune of the nation. Failure to provide for their well-being constituted a public demonstration of incompetence and impotence" (2000:151). Yahweh knows that defeated gods could be banished (Jer 48:7; 51:44).

But Yahweh's people were soon in trouble. Deep trouble. Internecine squabbles among the elite resulted in the splitting of his nation in two (if it had ever been united). A string of assassinations, internal political struggles, and risky alliances weakened his people further. And Israel could ill afford to be weakened, caught as it was between the alternating empires of Mesopotamia and Egypt (not to mention the many lesser powers in the area like Syria). When Israel (the Northern Kingdom) was destroyed and many of its inhabitants carried off for good to Assyria, the remaining Judahites could assign the blame to a variety of causes. After all, Jerusalem and the temple still thrived. It's likely that the Yahweh-Alone movement gained some momentum at this point (Zevit 2001:688–9). The prophet Hosea interpreted the disaster as God's punishment for Israel's unfaithfulness, for worshiping "idols of silver" and "kissing calves" (13:2). As David Carr observes, "to a typical polytheistic Israelite, such words [that is, the suggestion that it was wrong to worship other gods than Yahweh] must have sounded nothing short of blasphemy" (2014:25–39).

The crushing defeat of Jerusalem, however, changed everything. With the destruction of the temple, and the subsequent exile to and captivity in Babylon, Israelites faced a crucial turning point. Their national God had not saved them; Marduk was victorious. Marduk! The Israelites were "Israelites" no longer; they had no nation, no temple (and thus no place for cultic rituals), no real identity of their own. Their king had been dragged before the triumphant Nebuchadnezzar, where his sons were butchered in his presence and his own eyes put out. The theology based on king and temple could no longer be sustained. What now, exactly, was Yahweh supposed to protect? All those *other* gods had been triumphant. Yahweh had been worthless or, perhaps worse, had abandoned them: "But Zion said, 'The Lord has forsaken me, my Lord has forgotten me'" (Isa 49:14; cf. Ps 74:18, 22–3).

Yahweh himself is conscious of how it looked. He had thought to "blot out the memory of them [his ever-disappointing Israelites] from humankind," but he feared that the enemy "might misunderstand and say, 'Our hand is triumphant; it was not the Lord who did all this'" (Deut 32:26–7). And here comes the brilliant theological twist that turns national lemons into cosmic lemonade: It wasn't *Yahweh's* failure that caused the defeat of Israel. Things were never out of his control. All that humiliating trouncing of his people? It was *their* fault and *his* will! And thus the familiar schoolyard bravado after a potentially mortifying debacle: "I *meant* to do that!" William Dever aptly summarizes this surprising turn of events, how the exiled and postexilic authors snatched a divine victory from terrestrial defeat:

> The supreme irony of Israelite and Jewish history is that the first edited version of the Hebrew Bible was not a product of the Jerusalem Temple and court in their heyday, but of the experience of slavery, destitution, and despair in a foreign land. There the faith that we think of as "biblical" was born, after Israel's history was over. . . . Yet herein lies a mystery: *why* did tragedy issue in what many regard as the sublime achievement of ancient Israel and the biblical tradition, monotheism? Shouldn't this tragedy have meant not only the death of all the other gods, but also of *Yahweh*, who seemed to have deserted his people? . . . Virtually all mainstream scholars (and even a few

conservatives) acknowledge that true monotheism emerged only in the period of the exile in Babylon in the 6th century B.C., as the canon of the Hebrew Bible was taking shape. . . . Monotheism did not arise out of folk religion, out of a common *practice*, but rather out of theological reflection *after* the fact. This reflection on experience, including disaster, is what informs the Hebrew Bible. The Bible is thus "revisionist history," revised on the basis of the lessons that the authors presumed to have drawn from their own stormy history. The fundamental lesson for them was that Yahweh was indeed a "jealous god," punishing those who flirted with other gods. The conclusion? Don't do this again!

(Dever 2005:294–5)

The Israelites – a defeated people in a foreign land surrounded by Otherness, more susceptible than ever to outside influences and the temptations of Babylon – had to redefine who they were and who their God was. Daniel Smith (1989:especially 50–65) has laid out the sociological mechanisms of minorities when confronted with exile and a "culture of power," what can be called "boundary maintenance." But theologically it seems to me that the exiles had several options. Monotheism wasn't inevitable. They could have fired Yahweh. To any objective observer he clearly was not cut out to be a major actor in the region, and there were plenty of other eligible candidates – too many – for the position. Cultures can do that. Much of the Roman empire eventually rejected the pagan gods and rituals that had worked for them for many centuries.[4] Or the Jews could bring in some executive help, going back to an earlier time when Yahweh shared his leadership position with other powerful corporate players. Again, the Romans often imported additional deities and rites when they met with a national disaster.

But the Israelites did something completely different, something in fact more predictable, something that religious people often do – they doubled down. Yahweh got a fantastic promotion! They created a brand new position for Yahweh, the biggest any society had yet conceived (with the possible exception of Akhenaten's brief and failed Egyptian experiment), as sole universal god, creator and CEO of the universe.[5] "As Judah's situation on the mundane level deteriorated in history the cosmic status of its deity soared in its literature" (Smith 2001:165). Their history was reconfigured as a trajectory towards their *warranted* fate (and eventual return). Assyria and Babylon were merely Yahweh's tools to punish a wayward Israel (e.g., Isa 10:5; Jer 25:9, 27:6–8) and would, in turn, be punished for doing exactly what God had commanded (Isa 10:12–19; 47; Jer 25:12–14, 27:7).

The exiles could now find Yahweh outside of Israel, as he became a universal God who transcended his former national limitations: "By grafting in ideas of the one Creator of the Universe, and of a universal rule of justice and morality for all mankind, Israel's monotheism became a meaningful expression of truth" (Clements 2007:59; cf. Koch 2007:219). Or at least a way of transcending an inconvenient truth.

Ironically, with the destruction of Jerusalem, polytheistic Israel had to die as well, and "out of its ashes arises Judaism, being firmly based on the teaching of the aloneist movement" (Lang 1983:41). Its extreme version, a national monotheism, returns to Jerusalem from exile in the hands of its new leaders, and thus to the final significant redaction of the Bible, and ultimately to us.

> "I venture to claim that without the experience of the exile, Israel would never have made the discovery of monotheism in the strict sense; without it, Israel would never have transcended the limits of its national religion; without it, the idea of a worldwide mission would never have emerged within Israel. In short, without the exile of Israel, there would be no Judaism, Christianity, or even Islam in the distinctive form we know these three world religions"
> (Albertz 2003:435–6).

When Cyrus of Persia defeated the Neo-Babylonians and sent the Israelites back to Judah, the exiles came home with a new vision. They soon erected a second temple, the symbol of their trajectory towards Judaism and a theocratic state. "Seized by the self-blame endemic to trauma, the exiles took to heart such previously marginalized judgment prophets and saw the exile as God's promised judgment for their sins" (Carr 2014:76). Exile became the "incubator" for their new, dominant theology and reconfiguration of their history, what eventually becomes the legacy of the Tanakh.

This psychological reaction to complete disaster is reminiscent of the rationalization and cognitive dissonance redirection found in doomsday cults. After the anticipated cataclysmic "end-days" fail to materialize, many members of the failed sect actually feel a strengthened commitment to the group. Jesus is similar to Yahweh in this respect. As Bart Ehrman has emphasized (2014), the earliest sources of the New Testament agree that Jesus was originally an apocalyptic Jewish preacher who proclaimed the imminent arrival of the Son of Man – a "cosmic judge of the earth who will judge people according to whether they accept the teachings of Jesus" (Ehrman 2009:78–82) – and the final judgment. The end, according to Jesus and other similar figures at the time, was coming very, very soon: "Truly I tell you, there are some standing here who will not taste death until they see that the kingdom of God has come with power" (Mark 9:1); "Truly I tell you, this generation will not pass away until all these things have taken place" (Mark 13:30). The same idea is repeated in other gospels (Matt 16:28; Luke 9:27; cf. Matt 10:23; 16:27–8; Mark 8:38–9:1)! But the cruel, temporal world did not disappear. We're still waiting.[6] Jesus also failed as the *worldly* messiah who would "reign as king in the coming kingdom of God to be brought by the Son of Man, as Jesus himself had taught" (Erhman 2104:228). As in the case of Yahweh, Jesus' failures were masked by a rewriting, this time not by a reworking of the earliest texts so much as by the accretion of later texts that ignore or reinterpret Jesus' fallacious apocalyptic message. And Jesus consequently got his own series of really nice promotions, from human preacher to earthly king manqué to resurrected messiah to elevated co-regent at the side of God to preexistent and everlasting divinity.

Rather than find fault with Yahweh for their national disasters, the Israelites blamed themselves. Robert Lane Fox titles his chapter on the exile "In Defiance of the Facts" (1992:71–89). Another scholar has compared this Israelite response in exile to a form of PTSD, as Isaiah attempts to get the discouraged community to overcome its "learned helplessness," their "psychological and theological impasse" (Morrow 2004). But I think we can be even more specific and call it something like "Battered Culture Syndrome."

Or, if you're uncomfortable with analogies drawn from psychological distress (though it's probably too late now – where are those trigger warnings when you need them?), let's go back to the Wall Street imagery: It was the investors' fault. And not because they had bet on the wrong political alliance or backed the wrong god or performed the wrong rites for the right god (this last was a favorite explanation of military disaster among the Romans). Like CEOs who put the blame for the 2008 economic meltdown on the financially unsophisticated individuals wanting to buy homes, the Israelite theologians turned on the consumer, their own people.[7] The Israelites were told that they hadn't worshipped Yahweh *thoroughly* enough. So they edited their record books to reflect this belief, now viewing their entire history in light of their, not Yahweh's, failures. Monotheism wins as "the poetry of Second Isaiah brilliantly turns the rhetoric of political defeat into cosmic victory" (Schneider 2008:32).

Well, of course it didn't actually happen that fast or that easily. There probably had been many people on the board of directors who had been pushing for this kind of absolutist Yahweh-alone movement for some time, and no doubt there were some (soon sent packing) who opposed the developments. The development of monotheism was probably just as much the result of a series of "microprocesses" as it was a "revolutionary rupture" (Pongratz-Leisten 2011b:40). The late Deuteronomists who authored the new intolerant monolatry were still a small group whose ideas were adopted slowly, so the worship of other divinities probably "continued in many Yahwistic contexts much after these texts were written" (Pakkala 2017:277). Historian Simon Schama concludes that even after the Babylonian destruction there were Israelites who clung for comfort and hope "not just to YHWH, but to the household and local gods and cults of their own ancient traditions" (2013:35). And just as there were Roman "pagans" who blamed Christianity for the fall of the Western Roman empire, there were exiled Israelites who found the cause of their dismal fate not in their failure to focus on Yahweh but in the new monotheistic restrictions. Here are the former Israelites, now forced to live in Egypt, rejecting the prophet Jeremiah's demand for strict worship of Yahweh alone:

> As for the word that you [Jeremiah] have spoken to us in the name of the Lord, we are not going to listen to you. Instead, we will do everything that we have vowed, make offerings to the queen of heaven and pour out libations to her, just as we and our ancestors, our kings and our officials, used to do in the towns of Judah and in the streets of Jerusalem. We used to have plenty of food, and prospered, and saw no misfortune. But from the time we stopped making offerings to the queen of heaven and pouring out libations to her, we have lacked everything and have perished by the sword and by famine.
>
> (Jer 44:16–18)

Robert Goldenberg (1998:13) aptly concludes that in this passage we see the "plea of individuals as terrified of the other gods and their wrath as Jeremiah is of YHWH and his." Both the polytheists and the Yahwists agree that Jerusalem was destroyed by irate gods – Jeremiah thinks it's Yahweh, and the Israelite exiles note that the disaster followed soon upon the "good" king Josiah's attempted abolition of the worship of their own deities. In either case, "this explanation is an ex post facto rationalization of the catastrophe that had happened and at the same time a theological interpretation of the historical facts" (Kratz 2016:137).

The Tanakh as we have it, then, still reveals Yahweh's origins and nature as one of many gods. It's a polytheistic text with a (very) few nods to the triumphant postexilic efforts to enforce an absolute monotheism. Yahweh handles his fellow divinities with more success than Zeus can consistently manage, to be sure, but struggles endlessly to corral his Israelites into acknowledging him alone. Both deities face Olympian challenges to maintain their authority. But even more Homeric is Yahweh's character, as an investigation into biblical anthropomorphism will make abundantly clear.

Notes

1 Baruch Levine suggests that Balaam's chief god is El, Israel's original deity, and that the episode was composed by "a circle of biblical authors who had not yet synthesized El with YHWH, and had not deprived El of his individual identity" (2000:225).

2 The gods of other nations may *also* sometimes be conceived as part of Yahweh's retinue (e.g., the sons of God; Hendel 2017:251–2; Propp 2006:762), but generally Yahweh's divine subordinates exist to serve God alone.

3 Some scholars find it significant that the phrase "plan/will of Zeus" is used in the *Cypria*, a poem in the Greek epic cycle, to describe Zeus's efforts to use the Trojan War to reduce the population on earth. But this myth is never mentioned by Homer. Several classicists (e.g., Scodel 1982; Slatkin 1991:118–22) have suggested that Homer "reconfigures" the extermination of humans by the war and the flood in a strange episode in the *Iliad* involving the destruction of a defensive wall (7.433–66; 12.3–35). The exact meaning of "Zeus's plan" remains elusive – at least five different interpretations of the phrase have been offered. Perhaps David Elmer is correct in suggesting that these "opening lines seem deliberately constructed so as to frustrate any precise determination of the scope of Zeus' will" (2013:157; cf. Allan 2008:214).

4 This is what sometimes happened in the early 17th century when smallpox epidemics wiped out 90 percent of the Native Americans in coastal New England but spared most of the European Americans. James Loewen (2007:76) points out that many Natives "inferred that their god had abandoned them." The Cherokee at one point "despaired so much that they lost confidence in their gods and the priests destroyed the sacred objects of the tribe," wrote one eye-witness. Many survivors converted to Christianity – or turned to alcohol or "simply killed themselves." We know that many of the Israelite exiles took up Babylonian customs, some even giving their children names with the theophoric elements of Mesopotamian gods (Lemaire 2007:109).

5 The efforts of a few scholars to prove that the Assyrians were essentially monotheistic, even though the Great God list contains nearly two thousand divine names and epithets and assigns them to hundreds of different deities, have not been convincing (Porter 2000b; Rochberg 2011). As for the Egyptians, Akhenaten insisted that he was a god as well as the Aten, so there may have been two gods (ditheism) (Hendel 2017:266n62), and it is very unlikely that doomed experiment had any influence on Israel (Baines 2011).

6 Medieval theologians, horrified at Jesus' miscalculation, invented the tale of the "Wandering Jew" to save Jesus' infallibility. It turns out there was a Jew alive in Jesus' day who has been cursed to wander the earth ever since, and is unable to die until Jesus actually *does* reappear (Gardiner 2000:274–86)! Christian Preterism is an eschatological doctrine specifically designed to salvage biblical prophecy by arguing that the predicted events have already occurred. Thus Jesus' prophecy of the coming *eschaton*, for example, was fulfilled by the destruction of Jerusalem and the temple by the Romans in 70 CE.

7 One of the major hedge fund managers responsible for the financial disaster, commenting to *Money* magazine (shortly before everything collapsed) on the absurd adjustable rate mortgages he backed, boasted that "the consumer has to be an idiot to take on one of those loans, but it has been one of our best-performing investments."

6 Biblical anthropomorphism

Yahweh's da man

Yahweh is a guy. Well, a guy god. Like Zeus, I mean, rather than Hera. This conclusion should hardly be surprising – the Tanakh is a typically Near Eastern text born, raised, and lodged in a patriarchal culture. Chances are, unless you're a theologian or theistic feminist, it may never have crossed your mind that Yahweh isn't male. According to a Harris Poll in 2013, more Americans conceived of God as a male than as genderless; one percent believe she is a female. You've seen the painting on the ceiling of the Sistine Chapel.

But there are obvious theological difficulties and gender sensitivities that this conclusion evokes. The Catholic Catechism, as well as most strands of Protestant theology and Judaic commentary, insists that God "transcends" sexual identity – "the Hebrew deity is above the polarity of sexuality" (Davidson 2007:127). God is *pictured* as a male, but that's just how the language must work: It's a necessarily inept attempt by mortals to talk about an ineffable deity. The text doesn't mean what it says. Apologists insist that in *this single* case we must be careful *not* to take the text seriously. We need to read it through the eyes of our religious tradition, or at best, to remember that this is an old text embedded in a particular historical setting: "The cultural context of the ancient world means that there are many more references to paternal role models than to maternal" (McGrath 2015:69). Yahweh's origin as a Near Eastern, anthropomorphic, patriarchal deity in a polytheistic setting is admitted in this one instance to explain (away) his obviously gendered portrait.

But that's all theological moonshine. The Tanakh itself is clear about Yahweh's gender: "Through all of the biblical texts – poetry, prose, and the law – the visible, unignorable fact is that God is pictured as a male . . . all of the signs indicate that biblical Israel conceived of God as male" (Friedman and Dolansky 2011:115). Masculine singular verb forms and masculine pronouns are used for the Hebrew God – his *name* is masculine. When Yahweh speaks to Moses face to face, it is as "one man speaks to another" (Ex 33:11, NJPS translation). Almost every image and metaphor applied to Yahweh is used only of males in ancient Israel. Yahweh is a warrior, a male commander who leads armies of both heaven and earth into battle (e.g., Ex 15:3–12; Judg 5:4–5; Ps 44:3; Miller 1973). The actual Hebrew word for "man" is applied to him as a "man of war" (Ex 15:3; cf. Isa 42:13). Often equipped like the Olympians with horses, chariot, spears, bow, and arrows, he hurls lightning to panic the enemy just as Zeus does (Louden 2006:225–6). As the aegis is a symbol of Zeus's power and strength that he can loan to others, so the ark was the "battle station from which Yahweh, the divine warrior, the creator of divine armies, fought for Israel" (Miller 1973:158). Yahweh's original nature was at least partially a male warrior-god, his military characteristics depicted in some of the earliest material in the Bible (Smith 2014:262–6).

Yahweh is also a metaphorical farmer (and he plants a real garden, of course; Batto 1992:28), shepherd, merchant, and smith – all masculine professions. The word "king" is applied directly to the Hebrew God 47 times in the Tanakh (Lipton 2007:74), and the royal imagery is far more pervasive than that, as he is in general portrayed as a Near Eastern emperor making a treaty (covenant) with vassals (Geller 2000:281). Other dominant images are all masculine – master, judge, father, husband. Many Israelites acknowledged and even worshipped female deities like Astarte and Asherah, and the latter at least was considered Yahweh's wife (not husband) at some times and places. When goddesses and spousal connections were no longer acceptable – when God ceased to be sexual – Wisdom becomes Yahweh's figurative *bride* (e.g., Wisdom 8:3; 9:4, 9).[1] Yahweh is described as the husband or groom of Israel; Jerusalem is his whorish wife. He is called "father" 21 times, which admittedly pales in comparison to the 255 such references in the New Testament (Korpel 1990:237). Jesus and the other Jewish creators of early Christianity were certainly convinced about God's gender. Some aspect of the divine impregnated a *woman*, after all. There are no obvious references to his genitalia, although at least one rabbi argued that Adam was like God because both were circumcised (Mo. Smith 1968:323–4). God is male – he just isn't imagined below the waist (Frymer-Kensky 1992:188). Descriptions of genitalia are absent from Homer as well, but there is an amusing passage about the size of El's penis in Ugaritic texts (Eilberg-Schwartz 1994:105–8), and Yahweh is apparently jealous of the size of the personified Egypt's member (Ezek 23:20).

An occasional female metaphor or simile slips into Yahweh's masculine characterization (Mollenkott 1983). He is reported to say to the king that "You are my son; today I have begotten you" (Ps 2:7; but this could be by adoption, Dahood 1966:11), and a series of images (especially in Isaiah) portrays Yahweh's relationship with Israel as having given birth to the people, or as a nursing mother (e.g., Num 11:12; Deut 32:18; Job 38:28–9; Isa 42:14; 45:10; 46:3; 49:15; 66:13), or even as midwife (Pss 22:9; 71:6; Isa 66:9). But these *are* merely useful analogies to describe the closeness of the covenantal relationship (and appropriate subordination). The maternal imagery doesn't mean Yahweh actually has a womb or a lactating breast. The celibate Yahweh is also a *father* only by analogy, at least as far as the eventual text of the Tanakh reveals. Yahweh is not an eagle (vulture?) either, although his protection of Jacob is compared to the bird's watchful guardianship of its young in the nest (Deut 32:11–12; cf. Ex 19:4). Female imagery was used for other male deities in the Near East (Smith 2002:137–40): "In the ancient Near East it was not unusual for gods to be called both Father and Mother, just as the human king Kilamuwa called himself both father and mother of his people" (Korpel 1990:239).

But what does it mean, we are asked by piqued readers, that Yahweh created humans, man and woman, "in his image"? Doesn't it suggest that the first creation was androgynous or sexless, an "earth creature" . . . like their (its?) creator? Like God, Adam was genderless, or some sort of composite of both genders, until Eve appeared. This was suggested by some early Jewish commentators (Kugel 1998:84; Knust 2011:51) and has been developed by a few contemporary feminist theologians (especially Trible 1978:79–82). God needed no consort because "in a sense, he could self-fertilize" (Penchansky 2005:49–50). Yikes! He created humans with one sex and two faces, and then split them in two, say the late-antique rabbis, borrowing (intentionally?) from Aristophanes' brilliant account of the nature of *eros* in Plato's *Symposium*.

Yahweh for the Israelites of the Bible was not neutered or androgynous – "he is an otherwise male being who has no parents, wife, or children, and no sexual relations of any kind" (Miles 1995:266). Despite the reluctance among some sympathetic theologians and concerned feminists to accept Yahweh for what he is, he's a guy. Jesus is sure that he and "the *Father*" are one – and he ought to know. The New Testament insists that the Church is the "bride of Christ," an image Catholics take so seriously that it still provides a cornerstone for justifying the exclusion of women from the priesthood. The conclusion that the deity of the Tanakh is a male is understandably offensive to some who want to extend Yahweh's existence beyond an ancient myth, but this emotional umbrage does not give permission for interpretative skullduggery. Perhaps a mythological figure of dubious character in a 3000-year-old patriarchal tradition should not be accorded such a definitional role in one's life. It's a thought.

Anthropomorphism: That immaterial guy with a beard

The discussion over the next few pages about Yahweh's physical nature is likely to be considered by many theists to be obvious and unnecessary, and at the same time to be found completely wrong-headed by theologians. For many (I would guess most) contemporary believers, God is a combination of an anthropomorphic, fuzzy father-figure with an incorporeal being of divine perfections. Everyday churchgoers are perfectly comfortable with a mature, paternal deity sitting on a heavenly throne who is *also* an omnipotent, spectral power who can be everywhere at all times and hears everyone's prayers. Theologians, however, nearly universally object that there is no logically successful way to stuff an unchanging, atemporal, transcendent deity of divine perfections into a physical body. "[T]he core of classical theism includes the doctrine that God is immaterial and the doctrine that God is immutable (thus not embodied, and cannot become embodied), and includes the idea that the prevailing model of all language about God is necessarily analogical" (Hamori 2008:46). That is, *all* the descriptions God's physical nature – both those in the Bible and any we may choose to use in trying to understand the divine – are figures of speech. God has only a metaphorical body. Despite Yahweh's obvious human qualities – a fact of the text that many ancient Jewish interpreters accepted (Kugel 1998:80) and which we will see in some detail below – theologians have insisted over the past 2000 years that God simply can*not* possess human, carnal characteristics.

In the next chapter we will look more closely at the challenge of anthropomorphism to the theologian, what has been called "a central problem in the history of religions, theology, and religious philosophy," as well as "one of the major unresolved puzzles in the study of religion" (Werblowsky 1987:317; Penner 1989:11, cited in Hamori 2008:26 n.2). That this is a "central problem" or "major unresolved puzzle" will be a surprise to the average theist, I think. So this next section on Yahweh's Olympian, that is, anthropomorphically corporeal presence in the Tanakh, presents the case for the weekend theists. "The God of the Hebrew Bible has a body," professor of the Bible Benjamin Sommer boldly and correctly claims at the very beginning of his lengthy study of the "bodies of God." "This must be stated at the outset, because so many people, including many scholars, assume otherwise" (Sommer 2009:1; see Knafl 2014:1–33). So let's get Yahweh's body on the examining table. After that inspection, we will turn to his even more Olympian personality.

Let's get physical: God's back

Yahweh's gender is merely one of the most obvious elements of his physical anthropomorphism. These very human, very Homeric images of the divine permeate the Hebrew Bible, although the many traditions and genres use anthropomorphic language differently and with varying intensity. Still, theologians have been insisting for thousands of years that Yahweh is above all that Olympian nonsense. They quote certain carefully chosen passages from the Bible, ignoring the rest of the evidence and trying to wriggle out of the patent depiction of a very corporeal god. In Exodus (33:20–23), for example, Yahweh responds to Moses' request to "show me your glory" with the admonition that "you cannot see my face; for no one shall see me and live." If we stop right there and simply quote the passage, we may expound upon the power of a transcendent deity who cannot be seen. (Although isn't God admitting that he *has* a face? And he certainly can talk!) But Yahweh is bluffing. Lots of people in fact see the Hebrew God and live, and several of them look him right in the face. One even wrestles with him all night – and sort of wins!

Nevertheless, Yahweh's general point is solid. Most people don't get a very close look at him, and it's probably a good idea to take his admonition seriously. After all, this is a God who will kill instantly a man who simply tries to keep the ark from toppling over (2 Sam 6:6–7). (Yahweh once killed 70 Israelites for looking into the ark, although the Hebrew text seems to suggest it was 50,070! 1 Sam 6:19.)

Fortunately for Moses, Yahweh isn't serious this time. For some reason he really wants Moses to get a glimpse of him. So he tells Moses that he will cover him "with my hand until I have passed by; then I will take away my hand, and you shall see my back; but my face shall not be seen." Yahweh does not say that he has no face or suggest that his hand and back are manufactured artificially and only momentarily for the convenience of the poor shepherd. It's a *big* hand, to be sure, if it can cover all of Moses, but a hand it is. The New Oxford Annotated Bible tells us that "*Back* (like arm, hand, and face) refers to God in anthropomorphic, metaphorical terms." The editors do not explain how they know this anthropomorphism is purely metaphorical, although the answer surely derives from various theological assumptions. The particular word for "back" or "backside" here "is used elsewhere to describe the backsides of both oxen and men" (Eilberg-Schwartz 1994:70). Besides, what could a "metaphorical" interpretation mean here? The Tanakh is filled with aniconic representations of God – a cloud, some fire, a whirlwind. The creators of the Bible were not hesitant to paint Yahweh in nonhuman imagery if they wanted, although the exact relationship between Yahweh and the natural phenomenon is not always clear (Propp 1998:549–50). The expression "hand" or "arm of god" in both Greek and Hebrew can be figurative for the unseen power of the deity. But that doesn't mean it is *never* literally a hand. Amos sees Yahweh "standing beside a wall built with a plumb line, with a plumb line in his hand" (Amos 7:7). Do we really want to argue that this is a *figurative* Yahweh with a *metaphorical* hand holding a *symbolic* plumb line next to an *allegorical* wall? In fact, Yahweh himself reveals that this is a literal image, since he subsequently provides his own metaphorical interpretation (Amos 7:8–9). As an isolated image, a hand or face or arm may well be metaphoric. But "in a dramatic or visionary context," observes biblical scholar Michael Fishbane, "these figures function as the active anthropomorphic elements of living myth" (2003:82).

Yahweh's hand has fingers. The Ten Commandments were "tablets of stone, written with the finger of God" (Ex 31:18; cf. Deut 9:10; 10:2,4). They are the "work of God, and the writing was the writing of God, engraved upon the tablets" (Ex 32:16) "which I have written" (Ex 24:12). For any other Near Eastern deity would we insist the image is figurative only? Yahweh himself reveals his compositional process on his second set of tablets (Moses smashes the first set in anger upon discovering the golden calf): "Cut two tables of stone like the former ones, and *I will write on the tablets the words* that were on the former tablets, which you broke" (Ex 34:1, my emphasis). As William Propp concludes in his monumental commentary on Exodus, "one may presume that Yahweh himself has inscribed the tablets. . . . Yahweh has literally engraved the stone with his adamantine digit as easily as a man might write in the dust with his finger" (2006:495).

Yahweh clearly has body parts when the narrative requires them: "There are no theophanies [in the Tanakh] which are incompatible with an appearance in human form" (Fretheim 1984:93). Moses, who glimpsed God's back just as Helen caught a glimpse of Aphrodite's neck in the *Iliad*, is permitted unique access to Yahweh. The two had such intense personal meetings that Moses' own face began to shine with a heavenly luminescence (or became hardened) from God's divine radiation. Moses wore a veil over his incandescent face in order not to frighten his people, but he took it off when whenever he "went in before the Lord to speak with him" (Ex 34:29–35). This is the Bible's version of "the glow" that Athena pours over Odysseus and his family. As the composer of Deuteronomy observes in his eulogy for Moses, "there has not arisen a prophet since in Israel like Moses, whom the

Lord knew face to face" (Deut 34:10). Divine body parts often represent divine attitudes, and "face to face" (used 236 times) can stand for God's presence or access or sanctuary (Smith 2001:92), but "face to face" in this case seems to be literal. As Marjo Korpel notes in her exhaustive study of Ugaritic and Hebrew anthropomorphic descriptions of the divine, "originally, however, the Israelites did believe that God could reveal himself with a human face" (Korpel 1990:102). As he tells Miriam and Aaron, Yahweh usually speaks to his prophets through dreams: "Not so with my servant Moses; he is entrusted with all my house. With him I speak face to face – clearly, not in riddles; and *he beholds the form of the Lord*" (Num 12:6–8, my emphasis). God and Moses were buds: "Thus the Lord used to speak to Moses face to face, as one speaks to a friend" (Ex 33:11). And face to back.

The divine directive about seeing and not seeing God is repeated throughout the Tanakh, several times by Yahweh himself (e.g., Ex 19:21; Deut 4:12,15) but usually by people who have seen God *and lived*. They are always surprised by their survival – they have clearly heard the rumors.[2] Jacob wrestles with what he believes to be God himself and marvels that "I have seen God face to face, and yet my life is preserved" (Gen 32:24–31), an expression biblical scholar Anne Knafl takes to mean that Jacob, like Moses, sees Yahweh in his "true" form (2014:120). Other scholars have noted that the expression "to see face" can mean "to confront" and suggest that the original story told of a prehistoric battle between Jacob and God (Shinan and Zakovitch 2012:73–83). Hagar, Abraham's "mistress" (what do you call your wife's slave-girl whom your wife has told you to have sex with?), wonders if she has "really seen God and remained alive after seeing him" (Gen 16.7–14). The same is true of Gideon (Judg 6:20–3), Manoah and his wife (Judg 13:22–23), and the many prophets who are given a vision of Yahweh and his council (Micaiah in 1 Kgs 22:19–23; Isa 6:1–5; 7:9–10; Ezek 1:26–28; Amos 9:1; Zech 3:1–10). Seeing God isn't as lethal as, say, touching the ark (2 Sam 6:6–7). In fact, it's *never* lethal! The passages suggest that the actual injunction is probably against seeing God without his permission, which should be an impossibility for an omniscient and omnipotent deity unless he just *wants* people to die. Odysseus, we recall, observed a similar rule applied for Homeric deities that is also violated within the text: "Who with his eyes could look at a god if the god didn't wish it, whether going here or there?" (*Od.* 10.573–4).

Just as with Homeric heroes like Achilles and Odysseus, some ancient Jewish heroes are granted an unmediated meeting with the divine, although the Homeric gods don't kill or promise to kill those who spot them in their earthly adventures. Yahweh threatens to destroy anyone trying to approach him on Mt. Sinai (Ex 19:10–15, 21–4; cf. Deut 5:4), but eventually a crowd of 70 Jewish leaders led by Moses and Aaron was allowed to scale the mountain and "saw the God of Israel," and "God did not lay his hand on" them. All 72 actually *see Yahweh's feet* (which some scholars suggest is euphemistic for his genitals!) under which "there was something like a pavement of sapphire stone" (Ex 24:9–11, my emphasis; cf. Ezek 1:26–27 and 8:2 for the prophet's glimpse of "what appeared to be the loins" of God).

Yahweh, like Zeus, prefers to use intermediaries (prophets, kings, angels, dreams) for most of his communicative needs. But, like Zeus, this does not mean he lacks anthropomorphic qualities. And like many of the Olympians, he is willing to appear in person as the occasion warrants. Ronald Clements suggests that "declarations regarding the uniqueness, invisibility, formlessness and unapproachability of God serve to endorse the sense of transcendence that throughout constrains the Bible's portrait of divinity" (Clements 2007:51). But what actual evidence is there for this transcendence? A more accurate interpretation would be that these declarations *attempt to* endorse a transcendence that in fact is *rarely found* in the Bible's portrait of divinity. There is simply a tremendous disjunction between what Yahweh and commentators *say* about him and what he actually *does*. As Harvard scholar James Kugel (2004:98) observes, one of the most significant aspects of God's nature in the Bible is his physical manifestation: "He appears to people." Lots of people. Abraham, Jacob, Moses, Joshua, Manoah's wife, Gideon, David, Solomon, the prophets, and large groups of Israelites. Yahweh is not nearly as bashful as he – and his apologists – claim.

Since Yahweh can chat one-on-one, face-to-face, with humans, he would seem to have a mouth. All of the many references to his mouth are in contexts of speech: He shouts, roars, rebukes, curses, and mocks (Korpel 1990:156–60). The truth is, you can't get him to shut up: "In much of the Hebrew Bible . . . God simply buttonholes people and starts speaking" (Kugel 2004:44). When Jeremiah prophesies that the Lord "will roar from on high" and "utter his voice" and "roar mightily" and "shout," we are told "the clamor will resound to the ends of the earth" (Jer 25:30–31). God's wrath is clearly voiced, especially when heard in its Near Eastern context and the "similar phraseology in Akkadians sources, where one would be hard pressed to deny its mythic valence" (Fishbane 2003:19).

We don't see Yahweh eating and drinking up in heaven as we do Zeus and the Olympians (they drink, at least). But David Penchansky (2005:29–30; cf. Batto 2013a:77) suggests that the two outlawed trees in Eden must supply fruit for the Yahweh and his fellow gods – why else are the trees there in Yahweh's garden, through which he strolls so comfortably, and yet are denied to humans? And it looks like at one time the sacrifices made to Yahweh were considered to be his food, although for later authors of the Bible this became metaphorical. Like the Homeric gods, Yahweh considers sacrifice to him as a primary gesture of appropriate respect. A sign of sin is the Israelite neglect of making sacrificial offerings (or, of course, making them to *another* deity): "You have not brought me your sheep for burnt offerings, or honored me with your sacrifices. I have not burdened you with offerings, or wearied you with frankincense" (Isa 43:23–4). The sacrifices are often called "food offerings" (e.g., Lev 3:11,16) or simply the "food of/for/to God" (e.g., Lev 21:6,8,17 21; 22:25) – he gets bread in his temple (Knafl 2014:91–5), and his sacrifices provide a "feast of rich food" (Isa 25:6; cf. Ezek 44:7), an expression the New Oxford Study Bible states was "conceived of as a meal or banquet shared by people with their god." And he can get quite incensed if the Israelites skimp on his meals, offering blind, lame, or sick animals (Mal 1:7–8; 3:8–10).

When Yahweh's need for sustenance eventually seemed too crude, as it ultimately did for the Olympians, the *scent* of the sacrifice became the essential ingredient. "My offering, the food for my offerings by fire, my pleasing odor, you shall take care to offer to me at its appointed time" (Num 28:2; cf. 28:24; Judg 13:16). Yahweh, like many other Near Eastern deities, loves the smell of the sacrifice, although on occasion he likes it even better with a side of obedience (1 Sam 15:22–23; Isa 1:11–23; cf. Noah's first sacrifice at Gen 8:20–1; Noort 1998). There are nearly three dozen references to a sacrifice – bulls, rams, goats, turtledoves, pigeons, grain, wine – as a "pleasing odor to the Lord" (Milgrom 1991:162). The mere fact that the odor was *pleasing* (or that he can grow "weary" at their absence) renders these passages fully anthropomorphic, regardless of whether Yahweh has nostrils. For scholars who want to diminish Yahweh's anthropomorphism, expressions such as "food" and "pleasing aroma" are termed "linguistic fossils" (Milgrom 1991:59), but the obvious point remains that Yahweh of the text as we have it still likes the smell of food offered to him: "Yahweh is believed to snuff up the vitality of these sacrifices through his nostrils (Gen 8:21; Lev 26:31–2; Num 28:3–24)" (Propp 2006:462).

Although it could be taken as a metaphor, the Hebrew God is comfortable using such idioms as "because you have raged against me and your arrogance has come to my ears . . ." (2 Kgs 19:28). The Bible is filled with references to Yahweh literally hearing the "cry of the victim" (Kugel 2004:109–36). It seems clear that in general the Hebrew God is considered to possess and to use human organs and faculties. Moses predicts that the Jews will become complacent and will serve "other gods made by human hands, objects of wood and stone that neither see, nor hear, nor eat, nor smell" (Deut 4:25–28). The implication is that foreign idols aren't like Yahweh, who *does* see, hear, eat, and smell (cf. Pss 115:5–7; 135:16–17).

The Olympians sleep, although Homer doesn't tell us that they get tired. Hera and Zeus crash together at the end of the first book of the *Iliad* after a night of bickering and drinking nectar. In another famous scene, Zeus falls asleep after having sex with Hera, just like all loutish males (14.352–3; cf. 24.677–8). Yahweh neither drinks nor has sex, but he does need to get some rest. We are told in Genesis 2:2 that "God finished the work that he had done, and he rested on the seventh day" (cf. 2:3). Some scholars note that the verb is better translated as "ceased" or "stopped." But this does not seem to be how the authors of the Ten Commandments interpreted the passage. "But the seventh day is a sabbath to the Lord your God; you shall not do any work. . . . For in six days the Lord made heaven and earth, the sea, and all that is in them, but rested the seventh day; therefore the Lord blessed the sabbath day and consecrated it" (Ex 20:10–11; cf. Ex 16:29–30; Lev 23:3; at Ex 31:17 we learn Yahweh was "refreshed"). The verb takes on its "natural extension" to mean "rest" (Milgrom 2000b:1959) and is contextually tied to the sabbath as a day of rest for humans from work. The Hebrew God wanted (needed?) a day to catch his breath after the heavy lifting required in creation.

Like many of the Olympian gods, Yahweh drives a chariot and rides through the heavens. A Psalmist tells us that he made "the clouds your chariot" (Ps 104:3). This and other similar references (e.g., Deut 33:26; Isa 19:1; Ps 68:33) remind scholars of Baal, the Canaanite storm-god, who was known as The Rider of/on the Clouds and He Who Mounts the Clouds (Herrmann 1999:704; López-Ruiz 2010:110). At other times Yahweh comes on horses and a chariot just like Hera, only with a *lot* of other "mighty" chariots, "twice ten thousand, thousands upon thousands" (Ps 68:17). In Habakkuk he looks more like Poseidon, driving his horses and chariots to victory (3:8), trampling "the sea with your horses, churning the mighty waters" (3:15). Both Athena and Elijah fly off on fiery chariots, and I think it's safe to assume that the Hebrew prophet is borrowing Yahweh's transport (*Il.* 8.389; 2 Kings 2:11). Or Yahweh can skip the chariot completely and hop on a cherub (Ps 18:10 = 2 Sam 22:11) – the Olympians can't do that! And then there's Ezekiel's wondrous description of the moving cherubic throne, seated on which was God, "something that seemed like a human form" (Ezek 1:4–26).

With all these anthropomorphic references, the obvious if heretical question is, what does Yahweh look like? Admittedly, we have even less of the superficial information to go on than is supplied by Homer about the Olympians. The Homeric gods are fairly nebulous, as we have seen, and the authors of the Bible are not much more specific when it comes to characterization in general. "The fact is that the Bible contains no descriptions of goats, rams, bulls or horses; the physical attributes of even the central biblical characters are never conveyed. Basically everything goes undescribed" (Aaron 2002:184). Daniel tells us that God's hair is as white as pure wool (Dan 7:9), although other references to possible senescent imagery are debated (J. Day 2000:17–19; Bembry 2011:91–150). And Yahweh, like the Olympians, wears clothes. Isaiah says that the hem of his robe filled the temple (6:1), and Daniel adds that "his clothing was white as snow" (7:9). Usually, however, Yahweh is dressed metaphorically, clothed in majesty or strength or righteousness, girded with strength or valor, wearing a helmet of salvation (not easy to find – I need one). He may have a knack with needle and thread, since he "made garments of skins for the man [Adam] and for his wife, and clothed them" (Gen 3:21). He's big when he's sitting on his throne, perhaps like Athena in her Trojan temple (6.92,273) or in the later ancient wonder of the world, Phidias' Zeus at Olympia. Yahweh claims that "heaven is my throne and the earth is my footstool" – does he mean it literally? – reminding us of Homer's description of Strife, who "at first rises to a small peak, but then fixed her head in the heavens while walking on the earth" (4.440–43). (And if Yahweh uses a footstool, does he have real or only metaphorical feet? Cf. Propp 2006:519–20.)

But generally Yahweh's body seems to shrink and expand as needed, just like those of the Olympians. His hand can cover Moses, but he can also fit into the *debir* (the inner shrine of the temple) since numerous references indicate that the sculpted cherubim over the ark form a symbolic throne upon which Yahweh "sits," both in the tabernacle and the temple. If he spoke to Moses "face-to-face" inside the tabernacle, he must have been basically human-sized. And some scholars have argued that the theological norm against which the final composers of the Bible were arguing "was the belief that God lived in the ark" (Aaron 2002:164–70). That may be true: I've seen *Raiders of the Lost Ark*, and *something* pretty powerful was in there. Like the Olympians, Yahweh has an abode on a divine mountain,

Mount Zion, on which sits the temple where Yahweh is enthroned. This famous sacred height is frequently identified with Mount Zaphon, the "divine mountain par excellence in northwest Semitic religions" (Niehr 1996:63–5). And like Olympus, the name seems to alternate between a geographical reality and "heaven" (e.g., Job 26:7).

But we've avoided the most obvious evidence of Yahweh's anthropomorphism. The first human creation in Genesis (1:26–27), in which we humans are formed in the "likeness" and "image" of God, is theomorphic; that is, we are shaped in God's likeness and image. Just what these two terms are meant to signify has been a bone of contention among theological hounds for thousands of years. "Then God said, 'Let us make humankind in our image, according to our likeness. . . .' So God created humankind in his image, in the image of God he created them." To what, exactly, does the image of God (*imago dei*) refer? Just about whatever you want it to. There is an entire well-researched tome that surveys the history of interpretations of Genesis 1:26–28 just between 1888 and 1988 (Jonsson 1988). Biblical scholar W. Sibley Towner more recently has examined 11 different categories of interpretation (2005). Walter Brueggeman reminds us that "Christian interpretation will hear this text in terms of Jesus of Nazareth, who is confessed as 'the image of God' (2 Cor 4:4; Col 1:15)" (1982:34). Oh. The ancient Israelites were talking about *Jesus*!

Christian theologians have generally rejected the possibility that this is a reference to a physical resemblance, although biblical scholars have at times been more open to this possibility (Grenz 2001:193–4). Benjamin Sommer (2009:69) observes that the two terms for image and likeness are used of visible, concrete representations of physical objects in Semitic languages, not in metaphorical or abstract contexts. The same word for "image" is used shortly afterwards in Genesis to describe the similarities between Seth and Adam, who "became the father of a son in his likeness, according to his image" (Gen 5:3). This is most naturally taken as a reference to Seth's physical appearance. Theologians have nevertheless argued over the past 2000 years that we humans are shaped in God's image only in our moral, intellectual, or spiritual nature, or in our self-awareness or sense of responsibility, or in some functional or relational rather than substantialist fashion, such as our shared dominion over nature. This last possibility at least fits the context (Garr 2003:117–76; Jonsson 1988), and some find here a polemic against the royal ideology of Israel's neighbors, where the power of the king alone over his people parallels the power of god over creation (e.g., Walton 2011:175; Middleton 2005:55–60; cf. Ps 8:5–6). In Genesis, humans are given the opportunity to share in this dominion.

If context is the major criterion for interpretation, however, the very next words out of God's mouth after his act of human creation are "Be fruitful and multiply." Is *this* in his image as well? Most theologians would be unhappy with the conclusion that we are to have child-yielding sex *just like God*.[3] One other interpretation can be eliminated. The Tanakh does not differentiate corporal and spiritual capacities, as this was Greek philosophy's later contribution to Western religious conceptions. Jewish thought remained unitarian (that is, with no concept of a soul separate from the body) until the first century CE (Bremmer 2002:8). Whatever the Hebrew means here in Genesis, it is not suggesting that we are like God in our *souls* (Barton and Boyarin 2016:15–17).

I think that the priestly authors of Genesis 1 are intentionally vague. We are probably thought to be cast in God's image in a variety of ways, and there is no convincing reason to deny the physical aspects of the "image" and "likeness." The same biblical authors stoop to polytheism as well, as we have seen, by creating a God who turns to his fellow deities for support (or at least historical complicity) in human creation with his indirect command "Let us . . . ." Interestingly, since God says to his divine comrades, "Let *us* make . . . in *our* image," it is logical to conclude that Yahweh, his council members, and humans *all* share in this same "image." The Genesis Rabba, a midrash (rabbinical explication dating from 300 to 500 CE) on the first book of the Torah, includes a story in which the divine beings present at human creation think the first man actually *is* God because of the corporeal similarities (Neusner 1992:14–15).

In whatever way this problematic text is taken, it is ultimately anthropomorphic. The language, just like that in the second creation account in which Yahweh "forms" and "breathes" and performs thoracic surgery, presupposes some sort of humanoid deity, although this inference is dismissed by uneasy theologians if not all those who have called themselves Christians. Those of us who read the text as indicating physical similarities are reviving numerous Christian heresies, including a fourth-century blasphemy labeled Audianism, which was based on a similar understanding of the passage. It was dismissed as "absurd" and "senseless" by the orthodox bishops back then, and many current theologians are equally impatient. But humans most likely look like God as the text actually suggests and as we are led to expect from other Near Eastern creation tales – and Homer. Biblical scholar David Carr sums up the matter boldly: "However startling it may seem to us, this text presupposes that God has a body and that humans were made to resemble it" (2005:22). Later theologians came to understand this anthropomorphic creation in a radically different fashion. But the very concept of *imago Dei* must be anthropomorphic at heart. We are like God in some crucial fashion, which means he is like us in some crucial fashion.

Olympian epiphanies

The most remarkable angel in the Tanakh is one who makes numerous appearances as the Angel of Yahweh (Angel of the Lord, Angel of God). It is difficult to determine if this is the same supernatural being each time he is mentioned or the term for a particular office held by different individuals. (Occasionally the phrase describes a human "messenger of God," either a priest, e.g., Mal 2:7, or prophet, Hag 1:13.) In theory, *all* angels are "angels of Yahweh," of course, and the term is occasionally used in the plural (e.g., Gen 32:1–2). But the phrase usually identifies one special agent. Sometimes this angel acts as any regular ole divine subordinate – leading the Israelite army as a pillar of cloud, pursuing an enemy, saving the faithful, delivering messages. But by the far the most interesting aspect of the angel of

Yahweh is that he is "often perplexingly and inconsistently identified with Yahweh himself" (Meier 1999:55; Barker 1992:31–5). The two characters are frequently synonymous in the minds of the biblical authors as the actions and speeches of one of them suddenly are attributed to the other.

For example, the angel of God speaks to Jacob in a dream but then identifies himself as "the God of Bethel, where you anointed a pillar and made a vow to me" (Gen 31:11–13). Who's talking, the angel or God? In Judges 2, we are told that the angel of the Lord is speaking (2:1) and that he finished speaking (2:4), but the speech in between is from Yahweh in the first person (e.g., "I brought you up from Egypt . . .").[4] One of the best examples of this seesaw game of divine identity, part of what James Kugel labels "The Moment of Confusion" (2004:5–36), is in the story of Gideon's appointment as judge (Judg 6:11–23). The angel of the Lord, explicitly identified twice at the beginning (6:11–12) and four times later (6:21–22), sits down under an oak and addresses Gideon. But the narrator twice tells us that Yahweh himself is speaking with Gideon: "Then the Lord turned to him and said . . ." (6:14–16). The messenger and Yahweh are one and the same (Sasson 2014:331). In Genesis, Abraham's mistress, Hagar, is visited by the angel of the Lord and told she will have a son (Gen 16:7–9). But the angel suddenly switches to first person, promising that "I will so greatly multiply your offspring . . ." (v. 10). And although the next verse insists that the angel of the Lord is still speaking (v. 11), Hagar is convinced that she has seen God himself, and the narrator agrees. "So she named the Lord who spoke to her, 'You are El-roi'; for she said, 'Have I really seen God and remained alive after seeing him?'" (vv. 13–14; cf. Gen 21:17–19).

Even Yahweh's most enduring epiphany, out of the flaming bush, conflates the two divine beings (Ex 3:1–4). On Horeb, "the mountain of God," the "angel of the Lord appeared to Moses in a flame of fire out of a bush" (3:1–2). Yet we are immediately informed that it is not the angel but Yahweh himself: "When the Lord saw that he had turned aside to see, God called to him out of the bush, 'Moses, Moses!'" (vv. 3–4). And the angel completely disappears from the rest of the dialogue. This "anomaly" clearly caused great theological anxiety in antiquity. The Latin vulgate makes no reference at all to the angel of the Lord, for example – it is God alone who appeared to Moses (*apparuitque ei **Dominus** in flamma ignis de medio rubi*). The New Testament goes out of its way to clarify things in the opposite direction: "It was this Moses . . . whom God now sent as both ruler and liberator through the angel who appeared to him in the bush" (Acts 7:35). In this case, it's only the angel. In fact, in many of the passages involving this conflation of Yahweh with his angel there are textual differences between the Hebrew, Septuagint, Vulgate, and Syriac versions, thus confirming the uneasiness felt over time about the fluidity of divine identity (Meier 1999:54–5).

There are various theories about the origins and significance of this conflation. William Propp suggests it could be an example of the avoidance of a direct reference to the physicality of God, or the transfer of identity between messenger and dispatcher, or the absorption of what in other cultures would be a minor deity into the "unique Deity" (1998:198). Some suggest it is a vestige of an older polytheistic tradition, or that the angel of Yahweh has often been added to a text in which Yahweh originally mixed with humans on a direct, personal level: The two figures are identified because the early version of the story starred a human-like Yahweh before the angel was interpolated (Hamori 2008:5–13; Meier 1999:58). The angel of the Lord became a convenient means of diminishing Yahweh's physical presence. Rather than eliminate God entirely from the passages, however, the angel was awkwardly tacked on to the scene, often to the beginning or end, or both, by "someone who was a bit squeamish about direct appearances of the deity" (Aaron 2002:93). This kind of editing, not uncommon in the final version of the Tanakh, has left a narrative mess but provided a crucial (if bungled) theological escape clause for those whose vision of the Hebrew deity did not include his talking from a burning bush or sitting under an oak tree. But there are two passages in Genesis that reveal genuine anthropomorphic theophanies – that is, moments when Yahweh manifests himself directly and intentionally to Jewish patriarchs on earth *in human form* as a man (Hamori 2008:1), just like Apollo or Poseidon (but not, of course, Zeus).

In Chapter 18 of Genesis, the Hebrew God appears to Abraham by the oaks of Mamre. We know it's Yahweh because that's exactly what it says in the first verse. After that, all anthropomorphic hell breaks loose. Abraham sees "three men standing near him." We must eventually assume that the trio are to be identified as Yahweh and two angels, but this is immediately obvious neither to Abraham nor the reader. The patriarch, naturally thinking them human visitors, suggests that water be brought to wash their feet while they rest under a tree. He offers to bring them bread, and they tell him to "do as you have said." Abraham instructs his wife Sarah to make cakes while he himself selects a calf for a servant to prepare. The food is brought, and while the host stands next to them under the tree, "they ate." They ask about Sarah, stating that she will have a son "in due season." Sarah overhears this prediction and chuckles to herself – the couple is much too old, and she has been barren. Suddenly, the narrator sheds light on the identity of at least one of the visitors: "The Lord said to Abraham, 'Why did Sarah laugh? . . . Is anything too wonderful for the Lord?'"

One of these visitors in human guise, then, is Yahweh. As the three visitors depart, Abraham accompanies them "to set them on their way." At this point, the narrator stops playing games and for the next 18 verses Abraham and the visitor, now patently "the Lord" (mentioned ten times), openly discuss the fate of the doomed cities as the two other divine visitors head off toward Sodom. Abraham catches on that he is conversing with God, calling his visitor the "judge of all the earth" and eventually "the Lord" and negotiates the safety of Sodom and Gomorrah if at least ten righteous men can be found there. "And the Lord went his way, when he had finished speaking to Abraham; and Abraham returned to his place. The two angels came to Sodom in the evening. . . ."

What's a theologian to do? Here's the supposed sole deity in the universe, the transcendent, never-anthropomorphic creator God, in fully human form walking with other divine beings, chatting with a human couple, washing his feet, and – did you catch it? – eating cakes, beef, curds, and milk. Even Zeus and the

Olympians aren't shown eating mortal food in the epics, although we do know that they attend feasts with certain human societies at the fringes of the world (the Ethiopians and Phaeacians).

But perhaps you are still holding out. There is an important degree of difference between Yahweh and the Homeric deities, isn't there? The Olympian anthropomorphism is so thorough that the gods frequently have physical exchanges with humans: Apollo slaps Patroclus so hard his armor flies off; Ares strips armor off a corpse; Aphrodite moves a chair for Helen; Athena grabs Achilles by the hair and flings Diomedes' driver out of his chariot; Aphrodite, Apollo, and Poseidon carry warriors away from battle (something not generally found in other Near Eastern mythologies; West 1997:209). Even the major Olympians are not so superior to humans that they can't be wounded by them, as Aphrodite, Ares, Hera, and Hades can all testify. At least Yahweh doesn't stoop that low, right? Right?

Well, he does lose a wrestling match with Jacob, a figure some scholars have associated with the traditional "trickster" figure and who becomes the namesake of Israel. Actually, the match looks like it's more of a draw, but everyone, including Yahweh, agrees that Jacob "strives face to face" with God. As the New Oxford Annotated Bible notes: "Abraham unknowingly hosted divine visitors (Gen 18.1–15); now Jacob unknowingly fights with God." The episode is strange and disjointed. You'll have to read this for yourself (Gen 32:24–30; I will add some explanatory comments):

> Jacob was left alone [at night, after he had sent his family and possessions on ahead]; and a man wrestled with him until daybreak. [I know, you didn't see that coming. No one does. There is no preparation anywhere in the previous text for this brawl, no motive supplied.] When the man saw that he did not prevail against Jacob, he struck him on the hip socket; and Jacob's hip was put out of joint as he wrestled with him. [This is the first sign, at least for me, that the stranger – labeled only a "man" so far – is anything other than a deranged human wrestler.] Then he said, "Let me go, for the day is breaking." [This taboo reveals the wrestler to be supernatural in some form, and since he's probably not a vampire or a werewolf, he is probably an angel, son of god, etc., or Yahweh himself.] But Jacob said, "I will not let you go, unless you bless me." [Jacob knows something we're only suspecting. After all, he's been grappling with the guy for 12 hours. The patriarch thinks his opponent is divine and thus empowered to "bless" him.] So he said to him, "What is your name?" And he said, "Jacob." [God asks a lot of questions to which he should know the answer. This one serves to set up the subsequent and significant renaming.] Then the man said, "You shall no longer be called Jacob, but Israel, for you have striven with God and with humans, and have prevailed." [So according to the divine visitor, he is God. Jacob's new name is interpreted to mean "the one who strives with God," though it probably just means "El rules." This is where the nation gets its name – Jacob's 12 sons, we will remember, are the origins of the 12 tribes of Israel, so it's an important etiology.] Then Jacob asked him, "Please tell me your name?" But he said, "Why

is it that you ask my name?" [This is a power play. Knowing a name, even saying a name, is to have power. Adam names the animals, thereby earning his (and our) dominion over them. This religious scruple is one of the reasons in the later tradition Jews couldn't say God's name but used the tetragrammaton.] And there he blessed him. So Jacob called the place Peniel [meaning "the face of God"], saying, "For I have seen God face to face, and yet my life is preserved." [Jacob is clear about his wrestling opponent – it was God.]

This very corporeal deity, manifesting himself in human shape, bears a striking external likeness to the Homeric gods. And perhaps Yahweh is embarrassed at the whole mess. After this nocturnal struggle he withdraws from the active engagement with humans we have grown comfortable with in the first half of Genesis (Humphreys 2001:256).[5] What's happened here is likely the same thing we found with the blurring of identities of Yahweh and his angel. At one time stories were told about Yahweh and the Israelite heroes that were strikingly similar to those in the Homeric epics. The Hebrew God walked, talked, fought, and even broke bread side by side with his chosen leaders. Eventually this sort of deity no longer matched the needs and expectations of the biblical redactors, and the stories were shifted and emended. Some tales, no doubt, were completely excised, but others still reveal Yahweh's checkered past, his Near Eastern setting, his Olympian nature. What is especially interesting about these two stories, however, is that this kind of divine-human interaction is not common in the mythologies of the surrounding cultures that customarily serve as comparisons. Esther Hamori, whose study of these two theophanies is the most recent and thorough, argues that nowhere else in Near Eastern myth (Sumerian, Akkadian, Ugaritic, Egyptian, or Hurrian) can we find a similar case of such anthropomorphic realism, where gods are indistinguishable from humans (2008:129–49). She notes as an aside that this divine-human interaction is "common" in Greek myth, yet she still insists that the biblical theophany "remains distinct." But in fact the one real similarity with Yahweh's theophanies is to be found in Homer's Olympian gods.

An angry deity (he must be a south pole god)

There can be no reasonable doubt about Yahweh's periodic corporeal, that is, Olympian anthropomorphism. But even more pervasive and extraordinary is his emotional anthropomorphism, what some scholars label anthropopathism. So this section of the chapter will not be a happy one for either the theologians or the weekend theists, since both groups want to believe in a divine benevolence, love, and goodness – the *perfection* of God. (Some theologians try to evade charges of anthropomorphism by assigning these human qualities to God's *divine* attributes, which is simply cheating.) Yahweh reacts in human fashion most of the time, but upon close inspection it turns out that he almost *never* acts with love or benevolence. And one emotion he doesn't share with us and the Olympians at all is joy. Marjo Korpel notes that although many of the same Semitic roots appear in descriptions of Ugaritic gods and Yahweh, "none of the Hebrew equivalents of

the Ugaritic words for 'happiness' is ever used to describe the feeling of YHWH"
(Korpel 1990:167). "It is no exaggeration to say that, to judge from the entire text
of the Bible from Genesis 1 through Isaiah 39, the Lord does not know what love
is. Equally striking, if not more so, God takes no pleasure in anything or anybody"
(Miles 1995:238), although we have noted that he does enjoy the smell of burning animal flesh. The only times he laughs it is with derision and mockery (e.g.,
Ps 2:4). Zeus can laugh mockingly, but he also smiles at his daughters' words
(5.426), and the Olympians can laugh with (as well as at) each other.

On the other hand, words denoting anger are used three times as often in connection with Yahweh as with human beings in the Tanakh – there are some ten
Hebrew terms to denote the idea of wrath (Fretheim 2002:4). By far the most
dominant characteristic of the Hebrew God is anger. If the *Iliad* is about the wrath
of Achilles and its consequences (which include a new-found pity and compassion), the Hebrew Bible is about the wrath of Yahweh and its consequences, not
about his love and benevolence. "Approximately one thousand passages speak of
Yahweh's blazing anger, of his punishments by death and destruction, and how
like a consuming fire he passes judgment, takes revenge, and threatens annihilation. . . . No other topic is as often mentioned as God's bloody works" (Schwager
1987:55). We keep hearing that God is "slow to anger" (literally "long-faced,"
e.g., Ex 34:6), but that patience is almost never on display. The "mercy" and
"grace" theologians talk about are merely brief respites in a predictable sequence
of violent emotions. True, it's not a huge *range* of emotions. Yahweh's very
human passions cycle interminably from covenantal closeness to vindictive punishment through the intermediate stages of support, jealousy, and anger. When his
body parts *are* metaphorical, they usually refer to his wrath: His lips are full of
indignation; his tongue is like a devouring fire; his breath is like an overflowing
stream (Isa 30:27–28). He gnashes his teeth at Job (16:9). He may never be shown
drinking, but if he does take a cup in his hand, it is inevitably a cup of his wrath
(Ps 75:8; Isa 51:17; Jer 25:15; cf. Jer 49:12) or even an entire bowlful (Isa 51:22).
As Diana Lipton slyly notes, "there are surprisingly few explicit cases of divine
anger management" (2007:78).

One of the most common metaphors involving God's schnoz is his "nose-
burning anger" or the "heat of Yahweh's nose." When he gets angry, "smoke
went up from his nostrils, and devouring fire from his mouth; glowing coals
flamed forth from him. . . . The channels of the sea were seen, the foundations
of the world were laid bare at the rebuke of the Lord, at the blast of the breath
of his nostrils" (2 Sam 22:9,16). Anger just oozes from the Lord.

Homer's gods get angry too – it may be Hera's dominant mode. Artemis is
reported to have become incensed at a missing sacrifice, just like Yahweh, when
the king of the Calydonians "did not offer her the first fruits of the harvest" while
"the other gods feasted on hecatombs" (9.533–40). She "rouses" up a great boar
to tear up the orchards from which her sacrificial food should have come. There
is even a word, *mênis*, that is especially associated with the wrath of the gods –
and of Achilles. But Homer, unlike the authors of the Tanakh, explores and critiques this destructive passion in the *Iliad* through the emotional journey of his

major character, who finally checks his anger (for the most part) when his meeting with King Priam evokes a profound pity and compassion for the human tragic condition. Indeed, Achilles' displacement of anger with pity in the finale of the *Iliad* is part of an essential thematic movement of the epic. Over one-third of all the occurrences of words for anger are found in the first five books of the *Iliad*, whereas only nine percent of those for pity are located in those books. But the reverse is true for the end of the epic – just over ten percent of words for anger and half of those for pity are found in the last five books (Most 2003:51).

Yahweh's anger undergoes no such transformation. For a supposedly omnipotent, omniscient, loving, benevolent, *impassive* god, Yahweh spends a surprising amount of his time worked up and ill-temperedly reactive. He insists that he "is not a human being, that he should lie, or a mortal, that he should change his mind" (Num 23:19; cf. 1 Sam 15:29), but he is quickly shown to be dissembling about both. He acts just like a human despot – and Olympian. He frequently changes his mind (or claims that he will change it) (e.g., Gen 18:23–32; Ex 32:14; 2 Sam 24:16; Jer 18:8; 26:3,19; Jonah 3:10), regrets (e.g., Gen 6:6; 1 Sam 15:11,35), pities (Judg 2:18), weeps (Jer 9:10; 48:31–2; cf. Isa 16:11), desires (Ps 68:16; 132:13–14), feels distress (Hos 11:8), and is jealous (Ex 20:5–6; cf. Ex 34:14; Deut 4:24; 5:9; 6:15). There are nearly 40 references to Yahweh's repentance in the Tanakh (Fretheim 1984:17). He is even given a lesson in justice by Abraham (Gen 18:22–32), where he comes off as "a God who does not know his own mind and so cannot be trusted to do what is just" (Whybray 1996:103). Moses more than once has to try to talk him down from a homicidal ledge, usually with only mixed success.

Yahweh is quite pleased with himself on some aesthetic, moral, or intellectual level at his acts of creation, for he sees that "it is was good," even concluding with the superlative "very good" (Gen 1:31). Again, the theologians tell us that these are merely useful and necessary expressions rather than actual depictions of God's psychological state. God *has* no psychological state. He is above human sentiment, they insist. But then what about this divine love and mercy and compassion they keep telling us about? You can't have it both ways. God himself famously cops to his emotions in the second commandment, words he personally inscribed and handed directly to Moses. Twice. There he not only admits that "I the Lord your God am a jealous God," but he also promises to show "steadfast *love* to thousands of those who love me and keep my commandments" (while rather unfairly "visiting the iniquity of the fathers upon the children to the third and fourth generation of those who hate me").[6] This cycle of violence and forgiveness forms the core of Yahweh's actions, and his passions are the driving force behind most of the events recounted in the Hebrew Bible. The entire "history" of the conquest of Canaan as told in Judges and the entire "history" of the kingships in both Judah and Israel are built upon this interminable eruption and remission of Yahweh's pathologies, an "unhealthy cycle of error and terror" (Sasson 2014:205).

Biblical scholar Monica Melanchthon has catalogued 120 different occurrences of this "rejection" motif (2001). Although God's rejection of Israel can be manifested in famine, drought, blight, pestilence, and supernatural firebombs

(Amos 4:6–11), Melanchthon concludes that "military success or the lack of it seemed to be the largest category within which Yahweh's rejection was experienced." One relatively short sequence will have to stand in for them all (Judg 10:1–16). After a relatively calm, no doubt religiously orthodox period under a couple of unremarkable judges (charismatic tribal leaders whom God raises up to guide the Jews), the "Israelites again did what was evil in the sight of the Lord" and "abandoned the Lord." There follows the customary type-scene of worship of foreign gods and the inevitable anger of Yahweh. He sells his chosen people "into the hand of the Ammonites, and they crushed and oppressed the Israelites" for 18 years. The people are brought to their knees. "We have sinned against you, because we have abandoned our God and have worshiped the Baals." Yahweh plays hard to get this time, citing his past deeds on their behalf – he is very much like Nestor in the *Iliad* at times, endlessly recounting his past heroic actions to validate his currently wavering status – and finally telling them to "go and cry to the gods whom you have chosen; let them deliver you in the time of your distress."

That's a lot of resentment bursting forth from this theoretically imperturbable deity. The Israelites crawl back to Yahweh once more, truly contrite for the moment, putting away "the foreign gods from among them" and worshiping the Lord. Yahweh "could no longer bear to see Israel suffer." (Ah, *here's* the love!) A new judge is raised up, Jephthah, who defeats the Ammonites in a "Blitzkrieg triumph" (Sasson 2014:438). Yahweh gets the last (metaphorical) laugh, however, and for no apparent reason in one of the passages in the Tanakh that biblical scholar Phyllis Trible refers to as "texts of terror" (1984:93–116). When the "spirit of the Lord came upon Jephthah" before the war – that is, the authors are telling us that his decision is sanctioned by God himself – he vowed that if Yahweh granted him victory, he would sacrifice to him "whoever comes out of the doors of my house to meet me." It turns out to be his daughter, his only child. She "bewails her virginity" for two months, and then Jephthah fulfills his vow without objection or comment from the God of gods (Judg 11:29–40): "And through it all," Trible notes, "God says nothing" (1984:102).

Yahweh here is analogous to Artemis in Euripides' tale of the sacrifice of Iphigenia in his *Iphigenia among the Taurians*. Agamemnon had sworn to sacrifice to the goddess the most beautiful thing the year had brought forth, which turns out (many years later) to have been his daughter.[7] Homer seems to avoid the tale altogether, and Euripides chooses a variant in this play in which a deer is substituted at the last second for Iphigenia (as a sheep is delivered to take Isaac's place). Even the semibarbaric Artemis is not as heartless as Yahweh in this tale. Perhaps Jephthah had it coming, selfishly willing as he was to sacrifice just about anything in order to gain victory. Or maybe, as Esther Fuchs has recently suggested, his comparison of Yahweh to the god of the Moabites (a deity associated with child sacrifice) earns him Yahweh's wrath (2016:82). Nevertheless, Jephthah is considered a model hero later by both Israelites (1 Sam 12:8–11) and Christians (Heb 11:32–4).[8] He is successful in war, dies a natural death, more insignificant judges are listed, and then the "Israelites again did what was evil in the sight of the Lord, and the Lord gave them into the hand of the Philistines forty years" (Judg 12–13:1) until Samson can grow up to become judge. Stop me if you've heard this one.

Olympian perfections

Intellectually, Yahweh apparently needs a memory prompt at times. He set his bow (that's right, his *bow* as in bow and arrows, the kind Apollo uses) in the sky so when it appears, "I will remember my covenant that is between me and you and every living creature of all flesh; and the waters shall never again become a flood to destroy all flesh" (Gen 9:13–16). Without the rainbow, we can only assume that he may forget and wipe out humanity once again. Zeus uses the rainbow for far more pragmatic purposes, as a portent of a coming storm or war (17.547–50; cf. 11.27–8).

The "omniscient" Hebrew God, like the Olympians, is also either unaware of many events on earth, or is cloyingly prone to asking questions to which he knows the answers. In the first few chapters of Genesis alone he doesn't seem to know what Adam will name the animals (2:19), what kind of helper Adam requires (2:20), where Adam is or what he has eaten (3:9–11), where Abel may be (4:9), or what exactly is going on in Babel (11:5). He has heard rumors about Sodom and Gomorrah, but he needs to go there in person to reconnoiter for himself: "I must go down and see whether they have done altogether according to the outcry that has come to me; and if not I will know" (Gen 18:21).

Yahweh can be as strategically cunning and duplicitous as Zeus. Actually, he just plain lies as deliberately and easily as Athena does in disguise to Odysseus on the beach in Ithaca. Although there is repeated emphasis on Yahweh's truth, "straight" judgments, faithfulness, and righteousness (e.g., Num 23:19; Deut 32:4; 1 Sam 15:29; Pss 19:9; 31:5; 33:4; 92:15; 119:137,151–60; Roberts 1988:211), just as with his supposed love and mercy, his actions do not live up to the PR. Most famously, the very first words spoken by the Hebrew God to a human are manifestly untrue: "And the Lord God commanded the man, 'You may freely eat of every tree of the garden; but of the tree of the knowledge of good and evil you shall not eat, for in the day that you eat of it you shall die'" (Gen 2:16–17). The serpent knows it's a lie and tells Eve so: "You will not die; for God knows that when you eat of it your eyes will be opened, and you will be like God, knowing good and evil" (Gen 3:4–5). God himself later acknowledges that the serpent was right: "Then the Lord God said, 'See, the man has become like one of us, knowing good and evil; and now, he might reach out his hand and take also from the tree of life, and eat, and live forever'" (Gen 3:22). Yahweh is clearly upset, suddenly jealous, and very worried – this is the only sentence in the entire Bible that he leaves unfinished (Humphreys 2001:49).

Even more poignantly, neither Adam nor Eve dies "in that day that you eat of it [the fruit]"; Adam in fact lives to be 930 (Gen 5:5)! And no, a "day" to Yahweh is not 900 years to humans, as if we are talking about "dog" years, as concordist or "Day Age" interpreters suggest (Loftus 2012:321; Hamilton 1990:53–6;

Wilkinson 2009). Many attempts have been made to exculpate Yahweh here, but the threat would be pointless if Yahweh didn't mean that Adam would die soon, instantly even, for his disobedience. "There is no reason to suppose that 'in the day that . . .' is not to be taken literally or that 'die' in 2:17 has anything other than its usual meaning" (Whybray 1996:91; 2000:4–5).

At the beginning of Book 2 of the *Iliad*, Zeus starts the ball rolling in his plan to grant the request of Thetis to give victory to the Trojans. He sends "a destructive Dream" as a nocturnal messenger to Agamemnon that tells him to arm the Greek troops and head into battle, "for now he [Agamemnon] may take the wide-streeted city of the Trojans" (2.1–15). What Zeus actually has in mind is getting the Greeks out on the battlefield so he can inspire their temporary rout at the hands of the Trojans. This kind of lying dream has solid Mesopotamian parallels (Noegel 2007:213). It's just this sort of underhanded action that sends shivers up the spines of monotheistic followers of the Judeo-Christian God. But Zeus has nothing on Yahweh, who wants Ahab, one of the prototypical "evil" kings of Israel (he was married to the notorious Jezebel), to die a humiliating death (1 Kgs 22:1–40). Having asked his 400 prophets if he should go to battle against a neighboring town, Ahab is informed by them all that "the Lord will give it into the hand of the king." Coerced into asking one more prophet, he summons Micaiah, reluctantly, for "I hate him, for he never prophesies anything favorable about me, but only disaster." Micaiah, like Calchas in the *Iliad* (1.106–8), hesitates at first to give a true response to the king, but the king insists. When Micaiah then predicts in typically figurative language Israel's defeat, Ahab is annoyed. This prompts Micaiah to deliver the following vision (quoted in full so the entire picture of Yahweh's maneuvering is clear):

> Then Micaiah said, "Therefore hear the word of the Lord: I saw the Lord sitting on his throne with all the host of heaven standing beside him to the right and to the left of him. And the Lord said, 'Who will entice Ahab, so that he may go up and fall at Ramoth-gilead?' Then one said one thing, and another said another, until a spirit came forward and stood before the Lord, saying, 'I will entice him.' 'How?' the Lord asked him. He replied, 'I will go out and be a lying spirit in the mouth of all his prophets.' Then the Lord said, 'You are to entice him, and you shall succeed; go out and do it.' So you see, the Lord has put a lying spirit in the mouth of all these your prophets; the Lord has decreed disaster for you."
>
> (1 Kings 22:19–23; cf. 2 Chron 18:4–34)

Yahweh listens to his divine advisers, and then chooses the path of chicanery in order to destroy his idolatrous king. "He [Ahab] is defeated by an ingeniously deceptive god," concludes K. L. Noll, "who chooses a false prophet to speak a true message that is articulated in such a way that the king is compelled to reject it as false" (2013:140). The Hebrew God acts like a Homeric deity, and Yahweh's behavior in this counsel scene has been directly compared to that of Zeus in Book 4 of the *Iliad* (Gerhards 2015:210–42). It's not Yahweh's only act of deception (cf. Ezek 14:1–11; Jer 20:7–13) – these passages "have obviously been troubling for theologians" (Bowen 1995:356–7). Yahweh even encourages Samuel to lie (1 Sam 16:2). One would be hard pressed to distinguish his actions from those of Hera or Zeus or even Ares, who once gives strength to Menelaus solely in the hopes of getting him killed (5.563–4).

You only hurt the ones you love . . . and the ones you hate, and some others who were just hanging around

Yahweh's anthropomorphic depiction often reveals an even more cruel, dogmatic, and murderous variant of a Near Eastern anthropomorphic deity than we find on Olympus. No doubt compilers of the Tanakh felt more was at stake. "When God is executing judgement, there is often a scandalous disproportion between desert and punishment," observes biblical scholar John Barton. "Not only are the wrong people punished, but even the real culprits are often punished to an excessive extent" (2007:43). When some "small boys" jeer at the prophet Elisha, yelling "Go away, baldhead" – horrible, I know – the prophet "cursed them in the name of the Lord" and two bears immediately maul 42 of them to death (2 Kings 2:23–24; cf. the peculiar motive for Yahweh's depriving Moses of entering the Promised Land, Num 20:1–13, with Levine 1993:483).

The heroes of the *Iliad* and the *Odyssey* occasionally wonder whether their current plight results from a deity's offense at a missed or botched sacrifice (1.65; 5.177–8), but the actual consequences for such a mistake are usually limited to reparable misfortunes like the appearance of a rampaging boar (9.533–42), a rampart destroyed long after it matters (12.17–35), a loss in an archery contest (23.862–9), or the temporary disappearance of favorable winds (*Od.* 4.351–3). Yahweh is less subtle and his reactions more permanent. When Moses' nephews make what appears to be an honest procedural mistake – "unauthorized coals" (Milgrom 1991:598) – in offering incense "before the Lord," they are instantly incinerated by Yahweh's fire (Lev 10:1–3). Moses supplies Yahweh's justification in what Tod Linafelt (2016:35) refers to as his "extemporaneous theologizing": "Through those who are near me I will show myself holy, and before all the people I will be glorified." Aaron, the boys' father, "was silent." What could he possibly say? It's about Yahweh's power, not his justice, and we should not be any more reluctant to be appalled at Yahweh's actions than we are at Zeus's eagerness to arrange the death of the killer of his son.

How can we not see Yahweh as Zeus's (or Hera's or Athena's) emotional counterpart? Remove his outbursts and reconciliations, his physical interventions and emotional intrusions, and most of the divine narrative disappears. Thomas Jefferson famously produced a book entitled *The Life and Morals of Jesus of Nazareth* (informally known as the "Jefferson Bible"), in which he literally cut out with a razor all references in the gospels to Jesus' miracles, resurrection, and divinity – passages he felt were "contrary to reason." The entire text comprises only 69 pages (large font) in the edition I own and apparently ran to 84 in the original. So try this Jeffersonian experiment on the Hebrew

Bible: Take some scissors and cut out every passage that applies anthropomorphic language or concepts to Yahweh. You'll have virtually a godless Bible.

Indeed, Christian theologians themselves have been eager to hide – and on occasion simply abandon – the Olympian Yahweh. The consequences of this process have proven to be costly to the success of the human spirit, and it is here that Homer's Olympians will begin to show their true usefulness.

Notes

1 Most scholars argue that Wisdom was a divine hypostatis, a challenging idea that an aspect of God can also have a separate divine existence (e.g., Wisdom 8). Michael Coogan, however, suggests that these passages reveal that "the author is not drawing directly on old mythological material but on actual Israelite belief in the consort of the deity" (1987:119–20).

2 Moses must be adlibbing, though, when he asks his followers, "Has any people ever heard the voice of a god speaking out of a fire, as you have heard, and lived?" (Deut 4:33; cf. Ex 20:19). *Hearing* the disembodied voice of a deity never seems to be a deadly concern.

3 Christian Old Testament theologian Richard Davidson, for example, is quick to insist that human procreativity must not be seen as a manifestation of God's image; otherwise, the passage would be similar to the "orgiastic celebration of divine sexual activity" found in competing mythologies (2007:49).

4 The angel may be reproducing God's words in the first person, but it would be unusual for this to happen without any formal indication that someone else's message is now being delivered. There are scores of examples in the Bible when a messenger relays a message, and these are introduced by some sort of clarifying statement. In fact, one of the manuscripts of the Septuagint adds at Judg 2:1 the prefatory "Thus says the Lord" to this passage, an indication of the theological unhappiness with the blending of Yahweh and his angel.

5 This is not the only time Yahweh's unmotivated hostility toward a favored patriarch gets the better of him, however. Shortly after the episode of the burning bush, God tells Moses to "go back to Egypt," an injunction Moses quickly obeys. But that wild and crazy Yahweh likes to keep us guessing (Ex 4:19–26): "On the way, at a place where they [Moses, his wife and sons, and a donkey] spent the night, the Lord met him and tried to kill him." No motivation is supplied for a divine sneak attack at night. Yahweh apparently just goes postal now and then. Why would he try to kill the very person he has chosen to save his people from slavery and to lead them to the Promised Land? And how could a deity who can wipe out the firstborn of an entire nation fail to knock off one lowly shepherd? This passage struck even the ancient Jews as odd. In the late (second-century BCE) book of Jubilees, it is Matema (Satan), not God, who attacks Moses. Modern scholars have concocted all sorts of interesting interpretations, none of which seem to have garnered much approval (Stavrakopoulou 2004:197–8; Propp (1998:233–8; Römer 2013:68).

6 This love is often misunderstood and quoted out of context. Love as envisioned in the Tanakh is not an emotional connection shared by equals, but a basic attitude of loyalty and devotion between entities marked by very different status and power (Carr and Conway 2010:142).

7 Sasson (2014:447) notes that there are three other Greek myths involving human sacrifice that "compare well" (indeed, better than the tale of Iphigenia) to Jephthah's, but all are late (common era).

8 Susanne Scholz aptly labels the literary strategy in Judges that "excuses Jephthah's murder, makes the dilemma of his position palpable, and requires his daughter's

acquiescence" an "ideology of obfuscation" (2012:120). By the Middle Ages some Jewish commentators were uncomfortable enough with the story that they proposed a different ending to Jephthah's tale in which he did *not* sacrifice her. And in fact the text does not present the details of the fate of the daughter. Similarly, by the 14th century one Christian interpretation of the story avoided telling of her death as well. Still, Christian authors "cited Jephthah's daughter as a model for young nuns" (Steward 2012:136).

Part Two
Diverging deities
Where Homer got it right

Section I

Theological (dis)honesty

7 Cleaning up Yahweh

There is one god, the greatest among gods and men, in no way like mortals either in body or in thought.

— Xenophanes (Fr. 23)

The first extant Greek author to mention Homer is also his first extant critic. Isn't that just life. Xenophanes of Colophon, a poet and admirably snarky philosopher of the sixth century BCE, denounced the Homeric deities with many of the same arguments and with a similar mocking tone as early Christian apologists. So what's wrong with anthropomorphic gods in a polytheistic pantheon? Here's Xenophanes' take:

Both Homer and Hesiod attributed to the gods everything that is a disgrace and reproach among men: Stealing, committing adultery, and deceiving each other.

(Fr. 11)

But mortals imagine that gods are born and have clothes like theirs as well as a voice and body.

(Fr. 14)

But if cattle and horses or lions had hands, or could draw with their hands and accomplish the works that men do, horses would draw the forms of gods like horses, and cattle like cattle, and each would make their bodies such as they themselves had.

(Fr. 15)

Ethiopians say that their gods are flat-nosed and black, and Thracians that theirs have blue eyes and red hair.

(Fr. 16)

The Olympians cannot be *real* gods because (a) they look and act like humans, especially and all-too-suspiciously like the humans in the cultures that worship them; (b) they do not possess the kind of moral character a deity ought to possess;

(c) there should be some sort of immaterial, transcendent "oneness" and radical "otherness" in the ideal, cosmic deity, although the exact nature of Xenophanes' "one god" is highly debated – note that even here he says that god is the greatest "among *gods*" (Trépanier 2010:278–81; Versnel 2011:244–68). In short, in the terminology of Greek critics, Homer's Olympians are not "seemly" or "fitting." Plato famously rejects the stories of Homer and Hesiod because they are "ugly lies" (e.g., *Rep.* 2.377c-e). Later Christian theologians built on the Greek critiques. Some of the fragments of Xenophanes are actually preserved in a work of Clement of Alexandria, a second-century church father. Aquinas' censure of anthropomorphism draws on many of the lines of attack initiated by Xenophanes (Schoen 1990:123–5). From a post-Homeric theological point of view, Zeus & Company clearly lack the divine "perfections" that 2500 years of effort have tried to impose on a recalcitrant biblical deity.

But the Tanakh presents many of the same difficulties. As we have just seen in some detail, Yahweh is frequently portrayed in anthropomorphic fashion in a polytheistic setting, an irascible divine monarch enthroned among other heavenly beings. The Bible itself reveals the theological efforts of its eventual redactors to tone down Yahweh's wildness, as they grew increasingly uncomfortable with Yahweh's Homeric nature. Biblical scholar Mark Smith (2002:140–7) has shown how the Tanakh reveals that, over the course of its history, Israelite religion reduced (but did not eliminate) divine anthropomorphism in at least five areas: (1) the new legal and prophetic requirement forbidding images; (2) some biblical sources, such as Ps 50:12–14, play down the notion of Yahweh consuming sacrifices despite indications to the contrary; (3) authors like Ezekiel avoided obvious anthropomorphisms such as "walk" and "abhor" that permeate most biblical texts and are evident in parallel passages; (4) entities personifying divine aspects such as God's name, face, and glory sometimes describe the divine presence in later traditions; (5) the divine council shows a decreasingly anthropomorphic depiction of Yahweh. In addition, the most glaring whitewashing is found in the removal of nearly every connection of Yahweh with the two most significant biological anthropomorphisms, sex and death.

Yahweh may be depicted as slightly less human over the course of biblical composition, but his motives, responses, and actions remain anthropomorphic. Sociologist of religion Rodney Stark is misleading when he suggests that what "the Old Testament reveals is the evolution of Hebrew images of God from a moody and touchy 'Holy Terror' into a virtuous being" (Stark 2001:28). The primary development over course of the Tanakh, read from beginning to end, is not the improvement of Yahweh's character, but the gradual disappearance of Yahweh's personal confrontation with individuals (Friedman 1997). He's pretty much the same disagreeable Olympian whether he's ranting to Moses or speaking through prophets – he just becomes less hands-on: "In all sources, God possesses quasi-human faculties and limitations" (Propp 1998:180). Many of the most flagrant passages describing God's demand for intolerant monolatry are from some of the latest parts of the Tanakh. Although proposed dates for the text range from the eleventh century to the second, most scholars think Job is relatively late (late sixth century at the earliest; Seow 2013:40), and Yahweh's truculence is on full display in that text.

So despite these efforts to clean up Yahweh in the eventual canon, he remained remarkably Homeric in much of the text. Many early Jewish and Christian interpreters of the Tanakh were stunned by Yahweh's manifest and flawed humanity, just as some Greek philosophers were appalled at Homer's pantheon. Numerous strategies have been adopted by concerned theists over the millennia to whitewash Yahweh's Olympian qualities, but three approaches can be singled out: Offended readers could reject the Tanakh as a reliable portrait of God (just as Homer's depiction of the gods was rejected by Plato); the textual Yahweh had to be rehabilitated, that is, transformed through theological exegesis into something completely different than what the text portrays (we will see that some Greek intellectuals tried a similar maneuver with Homer's gods); the biblical language used to describe Yahweh was to be considered a mere *façon de parler*, nothing but an extended metaphor for an ineffably divine something that remains forever hidden to humans. None of these efforts has proved to be convincing.

Bad Tanakh, bad

Marcion of Sinope, a second-century Christian heretic, took the first route. Like some of the Gnostics, he found the Old Testament God so unappealing – so *Olympian* – that he concluded Yahweh "the demiurge" (that is, the Creator-God who established the covenant and gave the law) was a separate and inferior being to the all-loving, merciful, and forgiving God of the New Testament, who in his goodness "accepted the men whom he did not create and who do not belong to him" (May 2004:53–61). Marcion was the first Christian of record to have created a distinct canon of scripture (Ehrman 2011:139–44), an alternative to the jealous, physical God of the Hebrew Bible. His "Bible" was apparently based on ten letters of Paul and the gospel of Luke "carefully edited to remove [what Marcion believed to be] the Judaizing interpolations which incorrectly referred to the God of the Old Testament as Jesus' father" (Hopkins 2000:328). The whole point of Christ's appearance on earth was to "set humanity free from the evil creator God of the Bible" (Aslan 2017:138–9). This interpretation bears a striking resemblance to the generational picture of the gods found in the early Greek epics, where (as we will see) Zeus must deal with a cosmos and mortal race he did not create. Marcion's ideas were extremely popular in Asia Minor and Syria – "in Iraq and foothills of Iran, Marcionites successfully monopolized the term 'Christian' up to the end of the sixth century" (Brown 1988:90).

But here's the problem: Jesus was of course a Jew who repeatedly endorses the Tanakh (he refers to at least two dozen books of the Hebrew Bible). He famously insists that he has not "come to abolish the law or the prophets; I have come not to abolish but to fulfill" (Matt 5:17). The Tanakh was inextricably woven into Christian DNA, so you can imagine how well Marcion's views were received by the Church leaders. I did say he was a heretic. He was expelled from Rome, and his radical ideas (which included appointing women as priests and bishops) were eradicated so thoroughly (Tertullian wrote a five-book diatribe against him) that none of his writings have survived.

Although orthodox Christians have maintained the "identity between God the Creator and God the Father of Jesus Christ" (Pyper 2000c:494), the nature of the link between the two testaments has always been problematic. A few prominent Christian theologians have continued to dismiss the Old Testament as a failure, and it is a mandatory Christian belief (though often softened in public rhetoric by murky rejections of "supercessionism") that the "New" Testament fulfills and in some essential ways supplants the Old.[1] At best, the Tanakh can be retained by reading it with Christological eyes – what is called a "typological exegesis" – as a prophetic text bearing predictions of the arrival of Jesus the Messiah and the need for his act of redemption.[2]

Christian and Islamic theologians often disagree on the exact nature of the relationship of their God with the Hebrew God, although they also do not hesitate to cite the Old Testament when a passage can be read as appropriately prophetic. Muhammad himself explicitly identified Allah with Yahweh – it was Allah/Yahweh who made the covenant with Abraham, appeared to Moses, caused the flood, sent an angel to Mary, and revealed both the Torah and the Gospels (Aslan 2017:154). Still, there are many Christians and Muslims who do not share the confidence that Yahweh, the God of the New Testament, and Allah are exactly one and the same. Then there's the notion of the "son of God / messiah" that gets in between Christians and everybody else (Nogales 2009). The extrabiblical concept of the Trinity – by which Christian theologians have tried to reconcile how they can be monotheists and yet worship three separate entities – has proven to be so incomprehensible even to Christians that some denominations reject it. Latter-Day Saints have been accused of being modern-day Arians, the name of the Christian "heretics" who considered Jesus to be subordinate to God the Father. And the official doctrine of the Jehovah's Witnesses states that members "take Jesus at his word when he said: 'The Father is greater than I am.' (John 14:28) So we do not worship Jesus, as we do not believe that he is Almighty God." Even Aquinas, nearly a thousand years after the Trinity's final formulation, was forced to admit that "there are some truths about God that exceed all ability of human reason, as that God is threefold and one [*trinum et unum*]" (*Contra Gentiles* 1.3 n.2). Despite its inherent absurdity – most of the heresies in the first 400 years of Christianity involve disputes over the relationship of the Father, Son, and Holy Spirit – theistic authorities have taken it murderously seriously for centuries: "Just questioning the doctrine of the Trinity was enough, in England of the 1650s, to incur the death penalty" (Curley 2007:85).

Most contemporary Christians ignore this enigmatic polytheism, and they don't balk at anthropomorphism – that's the entire point of Jesus (Hammes 2009:79). The "two natures of Christ, human and divine, joined together in one person" – accepted as official doctrine by all Catholics, Orthodox, and most Protestants – was the decision of the council of Chalcedon in 451, just two years after a council had been (literally) beaten into rejecting Christ's humanity (Jenkins 2010). The scales of Abrahamic history have come decidedly down on the inseparable link between the two testaments and their two (or three) leading divine characters. In the words of religion scholar Reza Aslan, current Christian dogma (as supported especially in the Gospel of John) is that "the maker of heaven and earth spent thirty years in the backwoods of Galilee, living as a Jewish peasant; that the one and only God entered the womb of a woman and was born from her; that the omniscient Lord of the universe suckled at his mother's breast, ate and slept and shat as a helpless infant while the universe simply proceeded without him; that the creator of men was reared by men and then at the end of his life on earth, was murdered by men" (2017:131). For almost all Abrahamic theists, there is no separating the Olympian Yahweh of the Tanakh from the God currently overseeing his creation.

Theological legerdemain and divine perfections

Rejecting the Tanakh, then, has not turned out to be a viable vehicle for rehabilitating Yahweh's Olympian nature. So what is to be done with biblical texts that either echo or dangerously flirt with a Homeric pantheon? Enter the theologians once again. If only the creativity and energy that have gone into "saving" Yahweh for the past two millennia had been directed at something more universally beneficial – curing cancer, for example, or eliminating the electoral college. Taking pride of place in this feverish effort is the most peculiar approach of all – ignoring most of the text and substituting God's divine perfections.

Believers in the Truth of the Bible (although not all scholars of the Tanakh) will quickly tell you – particularly if you happen to be writing a book on Homer's gods – that their God is nothing like his "pagan" counterparts. When asked to defend this proposition, Yahweh's promoters inevitably and often unwittingly fall back on a theological interpretation of the divine tales, rather than on the actual Olympian stories as related in the Bible that we examined in the previous chapters. If well-schooled, apologists use hazily defined concepts like "transcendence" (the concept of a god who is completely separate from the material universe) and "immanence" (the inverse, when god is conceived of as present and accessible). When pushed for undiluted textual examples of the former, they are hard pressed to provide examples that cannot be paralleled from the Homeric texts except, perhaps, the creation in Genesis 1. (And we will see how biblical creation provides an inferior narrative to the one floating through Homer's poems.) A transcendent God is a late development (Armstrong 1993:242–3).

Many biblical scholars, however, have found these terms increasingly unhelpful in trying to understand Yahweh: "The uses of terms like *immanent* and *transcendent* often serve to obfuscate the problem" (Muffs 2005:3). Richard Friedman rejects the appropriateness of these categories, noting that through the course of the Hebrew Bible the deity appears and speaks less and less to humans: "It does not appear to me to be so much a matter of God's 'transcending' history as simply dis-appearing, becoming more and more hidden" (1997:72). Some defenders of a transcendent God, reluctant to abandon these textually elusive but theologically essential concepts, have done what scholars often do – they invent more misty, equivocating terms like "anthropomorphic transcendence" or "transcendent immanence" to paper over the gaps. But as Anne Knafl concludes in her study of biblical anthropomorphism, "there are few passages in the Bible that even approximate the OED definition of transcendent. . . . The problem though is that these terms necessarily introduce philosophical concepts (that a true deity is totally other than his or her creation and not subject to the same forces as creation) that developed after the composition of the biblical books was completed" (2014:15–16).

I don't envy the theologians, who claim to be exploring the nature of what they believe to be the actual sole deity still operating in this world. They have the unenviable task of attempting to align an interpretation of the textually complex and contradictory God of the Bible with the realities of human existence. To work their way out of what strikes me as an imbroglio of their own creation, theologians of the dominant Western religions have invented a set of constraining assumptions known as "divine attributes" or "perfections." These proposed characteristics of God form the foundation of Judeo-Christian belief and have become articles of faith for most followers of the biblical religions. According to a recent Pew survey, 56 percent of Americans believe in "God as described in the Bible," which they define as an "all-powerful, all-knowing, loving deity who determines most or all of what happens in their lives" (April 5, 2018). Seventy-five percent of Christians believe God is loving, omniscient, and omnipotent. As I hope to have shown, they are not describing the God of the text, but a theological ghost – a deity of divine perfections. There is no universally accepted list of God's attributes, but a glance at the various creeds, confessions, catechisms, and doctrinal gurus yields some combination of the following: God is good, benevolent, loving, perfect, free, just, omnipotent, omniscient, omnipresent, one, transcendent yet personal and accessible, eternal, impassive, immutable. As the creator, he makes possible a meaningful life, provides the foundation for or is the source of human morality, and ultimately will reward the "good" in this life or more likely in the next. Although a few offshoots (e.g., Process Theology) have dropped or severely altered one or more of God's perfections such as omnipotence, and some theologians are willing to limit one or two of God's abilities (to foresee the future, for example), the mainstream Judeo-Christian-Islamic theological traditions insist upon them, as does the average believer.

Read this wish list carefully, because these characteristics are, it seems to me, painfully at odds with most of what we actually discover about Yahweh in the Tanakh. The God of the Tanakh clearly does not possess these attributes with any more consistency than the Homeric gods possess them, which is only when it's convenient for the plot and the themes. It is impossible to take theologians seriously when in their efforts to find the divine perfections *in the biblical deity* they insist that this Yahweh "does not commit crimes or even misdemeanors" or that "God's anger is not quickly or lightly expressed" (Provan 2014:58, 69). Seriously? When people say that they believe in the "God of the Bible" and assign these perfections to him, they are rehearsing theological banter rather than evincing any true familiarity with the deity as presented in the Tanakh.

Even logically these theologians are in trouble, as philosophers have demonstrated that many of these attributes are incompatible either with themselves (e.g., omnipotence and omniscience) or with other perfections. But it's in the application that the whole edifice of "perfection" collapses. Pity the poor theologian (or theistic philosopher) who must fit all or even a handful of these characteristics into an intelligible picture that in any way reflects or explains or aids human experience!

The theologians, eager to overlook or deny Yahweh's Olympian nature, have invented a God they would like to find. And *they*, along with the various teachers, priests, ministers, rabbis, mullahs, etc. mimicking the theologians, have shaped Western religion far more than direct exposure to the texts. Even educated theists read the texts with ideological blinkers, looking for what they want to find and what they have been assured is there (Ehrman 2009:1–18). Many don't read them at all. A 2006 survey by Baylor University's Institute for Studies of Religion revealed that one-third of American Catholics and 22 percent of mainline Protestants "never" read Scripture. Never, as in *never ever*. Religion scholar Stephen Prothero's exposition of American's religious illiteracy collected the various polls and studies that reveal American's unfamiliarity with the Bible as well as virtually every other religious tradition (2007:27–48). Included is the infamous survey that revealed ten percent of Americans – a vast majority of whom are self-identifying Christians – believe that Joan of Arc was Noah's wife. Many devout theists don't know the stories of their own God, and if they have read them, their understanding has been molded by their local religious exposure. They only know what they have been told, and they have been told that God possesses the divine perfections.

Theological legerdemain and divine "metaphors"

So what is an honest Abrahamic apologist to do with Yahweh's Homeric character if the Tanakh cannot be excised from the Bible and the divine perfections are not on obvious display throughout much of that text? A third answer was invented to remove Yahweh the Olympian entirely, leaving room for the extratextual God of perfections to slip into the void. We are told anthropomorphism is inherently unsophisticated, the mark of a "primitive" religiosity, whereas the enlightened vision of the Bible only stoops to such concepts *metaphorically*. Both Christian and rabbinic interpretation acknowledge various hermeneutical principles for interpreting biblical passages – philological, allegorical, homiletical, mystical, moral, anagogic (hidden messages about heaven), etc. (Callahan 1997:44; Greenspahn 2016:382–4). Thus from early on the sacred texts could say what one needed them to say, in addition to – or directly counter to – the "literal" meaning.

We humans may need to use anthropomorphic language to attempt to understand and explore the divine, so goes the story, but God ultimately cannot be described or known, and so our figurative language is never to be taken literally. Maimonides, the most influential medieval Jewish scholar of the Torah, stood in a long line of Jewish interpreters who "attempted to qualify, filter, or otherwise reinterpret the anthropomorphic and anthropopathic depictions of God in the Hebrew

Bible, and thus save Scripture from the merest taint of mythic irrationality" (Fish-bane 2003:3–4). The third of the "Articles of Faith" passed down by Maimonides reads: "I believe with perfect faith that the Creator, Blessed be His Name, has no body, and that He is free from all the properties of matter, and that there can be no (physical) comparison to Him whatsoever." Maimonides spends the first 70 chapters, 175 pages in translation, on the "question of why the Bible speaks so often in corporeal terms of a deity who is incorporeal" (Sommer 2009:4–8). All contemporary Abrahamic religions can at least agree on this one thing.

Theologians insist that the composers of the Bible must "accommodate" us by using human language:

> The justification of this language is found in the fact that truth can be con-veyed to men only through the medium of human ideas and thoughts, and is to be expressed only in language suited to their comprehension. The limi-tations of our conceptual capacity oblige us to represent God to ourselves in ideas that have been originally drawn from our knowledge of self and the objective world. The Scriptures themselves amply warn us against the mistake of interpreting their figurative language in too literal a sense. They teach that God is spiritual, omniscient, invisible, omnipresent, ineffable. Insistence upon the literal interpretation of the metaphorical led to the error of the Anthropomorphites.
>
> (Catholic *Encyclopedia*)

This quotation comes from a Catholic publication from 1907, but over 100 years later theologians are still in denial: "The texts make clear that YHWH is hid-den and inscrutable, beyond domestication into any of Israel's categories. . . . The result is that Israel's characteristic speech concerning YHWH, expressed in song, oracles and narrative, is according to image and metaphor that proceed play-fully and imaginatively without any claim to be descriptive" (W. Brueggemann 2008:89 cited in Knafl 2014:38 n. 13). Or more succinctly, "All God-talk, all the-ology, even ours, is metaphorical" (J.C.L Gibson 1998:22 cited in Knafl 2014:55). One can't use *any* text – or for that matter, *any* words or ideas – to try to under-stand God accurately. But shouldn't that put the theologians out of business? No language can be used to access God, and nothing can be written or said with any reliability. It would certainly signify that the textual presentation of Yahweh in the Tanakh would necessarily be only "analogous" to any real deity, essentially an earnest fiction like, say . . . Homer's Zeus. The natural conclusion would be that these are *all* simply fictional efforts to describe a very humanly constructed vision of the divine. The Bible really is no different from the *Iliad*.

Now I can live with that, but the theologians can't, because they believe that there is a real God out there who bears some resemblance to the picture in their sacred texts. But this picture is routinely anthropomorphic, so they're in a huge predicament.[3] At best, as Christian theologian Terence E. Frethiem argues, one must take a middle (Homeric!) path "between Scylla and Charybdis" by accepting that "the metaphor does in fact describe God, though it is not fully descriptive" in every respect (1984:7). Basically, these God-fearing writers have the impossible task of describing an unknowable God of manufactured divine perfections in humanly accessible terms. "Either we can use human language to speak meaningfully of God (in which case God cannot differ in kind from finite existence)," philosopher George H. Smith keenly observes, "or human language cannot be applied to God at all (in which case the word 'god' becomes meaningless)" (1974:56).

Theologians are compelled to make one concession: The use of anthropomorphic *language* to describe a nonanthropomorphic deity is necessary if there is to be any positive theology, anything that can be said of God other than what he isn't. We just need to be careful to use the *right kind* of anthropomorphism, the *non-Homeric* kind: "It is, however, not vulgar anthropomorphism, attributing obscene or unworthy traits to the divine. On the contrary, it is precisely by the selection of specific traits acknowledged as eminently worthy that (logically) believers may eliminate the unworthy in connection with the Most High" (Ferré and Ferré 1984:207). The divine must be everything we admire, even if what we want is virtually absent from the sole source of evidence, even if Yahweh frequently possesses the same patently *unworthy* traits as Homer's Olympians.

In practice, few contemporary theists reject *everything* in the Bible as mere metaphor. In fact, there are millions of theists who accept every word in the Bible as the literal, not figurative truth. Twenty-eight percent of Americans believe that the Bible is the "actual word of God and is to be taken literally, word for word." The Southern Baptist Convention is paradigmatic, insisting that the Bible "has God for its author, salvation for its end, and truth, without any mixture of error, for its matter. Therefore, all Scripture is totally true and trustworthy." But most believers are more eclectic in practice, their faith ensconced in a tradition that explains to them (with the guidance of professional exegetes) which parts of the Bible should be read literally and which figuratively and which can be safely ignored altogether (death for those caught working on the sabbath, for example). They rely on profession guidance to which is which, which words, phrases, concepts, characters, passages in these self-contradictory texts are the literal ones, which metaphors, and which ones we can we ignore with impunity. My current favorite example of the problems involved in deciding which mythological stories from antiquity are to be read as Truth comes from *Theopedia*, an online evangelical encyclopedia of biblical Christianity. Under its definition of "anthropomorphism" comes a subheading "Literal vs. figurative anthropomorphism," which presents the following clarification:

> It is important to establish what texts in the Bible may be taken literally and what verses we must take figuratively.

Literal

> Jesus said to him, "I am the way, and the truth, and the life; no one comes to the Father but through Me. If you had known Me, you would have known My Father also; from now on you know Him, and have seen Him."
>
> John 14:6–7

Figurative

So Jesus said to them, "Truly, truly, I say to you, unless you eat the flesh of the Son of Man and drink His blood, you have no life in yourselves. He who eats My flesh and drinks My blood has eternal life, and I will raise him up on the last day. For My flesh is true food, and My blood is true drink. He who eats My flesh and drinks My blood abides in Me, and I in him."

John 6:53–56

The previous verse shows errors of incorrectly interpreting Biblical anthropomorphism in those that advocate transubstantiation.

Of course we (evangelical Protestants) must accept as gospel truth the claim of Jesus in the Gospel of John that he is the same as God (a form of what is called "high Christology" that is found in none of the other gospels). *Obviously*, so the evangelicals insist, the suggestion that the magical rite of transubstantiation could really have been Christ's intent and thus ritually efficacious is patently ludicrous. The wine is *symbolic*. It's a *metaphor*, dummy! As skeptic C. Dennis McKinsey observes, "Fundamentalists love to talk about a literal interpretation until they begin to feel the pinch, at which time they immediately opt for a figurative analysis" (1995:33).

Theological denial

In the introduction I referred to this brand of Western theology as "literary criticism gone horribly wrong." I'm not suggesting that it is any less convincing than the "constructs" of many literary theorists in university English departments, but very few people know or are influenced by the ideas of the latter. Ideologically distorted *biblical* criticism, on the other hand, has had a profound influence on the Western world, even if most Abrahamic theists are unaware of it. As John Loftus notes, "Most Christians do not believe in the God of the Bible anyway, despite what they claim. Instead, they believe in the perfect being offered by St. Anselm in the eleventh century after centuries of theological gerrymandering" (2012:102). I would add that this perfect being simultaneously (and incompatibly) comes in the shape of a severe but solicitous man with a beard.

Let's take a current and authoritative example of what strikes me as theological mismanagement. Recall the tale we looked at earlier from Genesis 6, where God's sons have produced a race of "warriors of renown" by having sex with mortal women on earth. Full of anger and regret, Yahweh decides to wipe out mankind for its wickedness. While the only real iniquity explicitly expressed in the text so far is that of the "sons of God," *everything* must perish: "Now I am going to destroy them [all flesh] *along with the earth*" (Gen 6:13, my emphasis). God lets two of each animated species live (or maybe it's seven for the kosher animals – there are two different versions provided). It's a safe assumption that all plant life is wiped out in the ensuing flood. I have argued that any reasonable understanding of this passage would conclude that God is powerful, punitive, and temperamental. Very human, very Olympian. He acts *just like* the other Near Eastern patriarchal deities, many of whom drown humanity for similarly hypermoral reasons in a variety of flood tales.[4]

But that is not how a Christian theologian wants to read it, since he or she approaches the sacred text with thousands of years of assumptions about God, especially that he possesses those lofty divine attributes. And so, for example, the present Pope in his powerful encyclical on the environment (*Laudato Si*), reads the flood story in Genesis as follows: "Although 'the wickedness of man was great in the earth' (*Gen* 6:5) and the Lord 'was sorry that he had made man on the earth' (*Gen* 6:6), nonetheless, through Noah, who remained innocent and just, God decided to open a path of salvation. In this way he gave humanity the chance of a new beginning. All it takes is one good person to restore hope!" (71).

Does it not seem odd that in a papal text whose primary purpose is to sensitize Christians to environmental issues and which frequently lectures us on our responsibilities to the underrepresented, animals, and bio-diversity, the author fails to mention that his God decided to "blot out from the earth the human beings I have created – people together with animals and creeping things and birds of the air, for I am sorry that I have made them" (Gen 6:7)? Now what could the animals and trees have done to deserve God's remorse and violent wrath? What perturbed him about the birds of the air to such a degree that they all had to go? Surely it wasn't that "every inclination of the thoughts of their hearts was only evil continually" (Gen 6:5). After all, the Catholic Church denies that animals and trees have minds or souls, while simultaneously confident that humans have both. And no word at all from the Pope about those sons of God, much less why God doesn't punish them alone, or why a destruction of virtually everything was an omnipotent creator's only solution to a problem an omniscient God had to see coming and a benevolent deity might have prevented. Cultural critic Michael Parenti concludes harshly but not unfairly, "having bungled the Creation, Yahweh did even worse with the Deluge, which might better be called 'the Overkill'" (2010:23).

How is this reading of "history" – the Pope cites the flood narrative as if it were actual historical fact – different from the argument that Hurricane Katrina drowned over 1000 people in New Orleans because God was upset at America's abortion policy, as Pat Robertson declared? Or as popular American evangelist John Hagee opined, the hurricane was designed by God to stop a gay-pride parade scheduled to be held in New Orleans a few days after Katrina made landfall? (Gerhard Maria Wagner was appointed auxiliary bishop of Linz, Austria, by Pope Benedict XVI, despite his insistence that an angry God used Katrina to punish New Orleans for its "sins.")

Although Christian theologians can't bring themselves to see Yahweh in Genesis as vengeful, of limited foresight, and thoroughly Olympian, Yahweh himself later comes to regret his actions, or at least to embrace their senselessness, after smelling the "pleasing odor" of Noah's gargantuan animal sacrifice. God says "in his heart" that he will "never again curse the ground because of humankind, for the inclination of the human heart is evil from youth . . ." (Gen 8.21). In other words, the flood was pointless. Shouldn't Yahweh have known that? Even after wiping out every human on earth except the "righteous" Noah and his immediate family, the human heart remains evil. This new "creation," inherently flawed, is apparently no better than the first. This omniscient God takes a surprisingly long time to understand fully the true nature of what he has done in his omnipotence. Perhaps Yahweh has regrets, which would explain why he doesn't carry through on his initial threat, that he will limit human life to 120 years (6:3) in another of his efforts to separate the human world from the divine. Noah himself lives to be 950; Shem, his eldest son, makes it to 600.

The biblical text is fascinating in its elaborate efforts to explore (and seemingly excuse) the ambivalent nature of God and his relation to creation. It's an influential version of a very common story in the Near East. The Pope's interpretation, however, is falsely consoling and disappointingly jejune. It's an unnecessary effort to link a fickle divine character and nasty ancient myth to a genuinely impressive call for environmental reform and social justice.

Yahweh's human elements are not identical to those of Zeus. The two deities are cousins rather than siblings. But the genetic relationship is obvious. Thus it is hard for a classicist reading the Tanakh to understand the conclusions some biblical scholars and theologians arrive at after spending a life studying Yahweh. What in the text could rouse laudations of the Hebrew God's mercy or compassion, how his "gracious dealings with Israel in particular precisely parallel his gracious dealings with the world in general," the evidence for which is the *flood narrative* (Moberly 2007:100)? We learn from the apologists that Yahweh is "undeniably just" – for destroying everything on the planet after his "sons" have sex with mortal women (Arnold 2009:91)! Or that "the 'weight' of God's character is toward compassion, grace, and love. . . . Love is for thousands; punishment is for 'three and four'" (Wright 2008:78), which somehow helps to explain why God's extermination of the Canaanites is, if looked at correctly, admirable divine judgment and not genocide. Or we are told that Yahweh is superior to his Near Eastern counterparts in just those ways he clearly is the same, or worse: ". . . it is perhaps the gracious nature of his dealings *with his own people* that distinguishes him from all other deities. He is not capricious, egotistical, or self-indulgent, as are his rivals. The history of biblical revelation is a history of merciful condescension" (Block 2000:151, my emphasis). What?!

True, the Bible keeps *telling* us that Yahweh is compassionate and merciful and "slow to anger," a "cliché" so frequent that James Kugel says it deserves the label "axiomatic" (Kugel 2004:129; cf. Avalos 2007:257). And Yahweh *himself* keeps repeating that he is "merciful and gracious, slow to anger, and abounding in steadfast love and faithfulness, keeping steadfast love to the thousandth generation, forgiving iniquity and transgression and sin . . ." (Ex 34:6–7; cf. Ex 20:5–6; Num 14:18; Deut 7:9–10; 5:9–10; Neh 9:17; Pss 86:15; 103:8–9; 145:8; Joel 2:13; Jonah 4:2; Nah 1:3). But that's not what we usually see in the text. Even these passages celebrating God's "steadfast love," "mercy," and "slowness to anger" are often combined with his insistence that he will visit his anger unmercifully and immorally on the innocent third and fourth generations. Confessional scholars and theologians read the Bible through an interpretative lens that only allows favorable comments and the few positive moments – and a sliver of transcendence – to filter through.

Why theological illusions matter

When it comes to sacred tales – that is, myth like that found in the *Iliad*, *Odyssey*, Bible, and Qur'an – once you decide to step outside their comfortable home in oral-turned-literary fiction and enter the random world of religious revelation, anything goes. One person's metaphor is another person's unimpeachable reality: "The religion emerging from the vestiges of uncensored materials demonstrates that one generation's metaphor is another's literal proclamation of faith" (Aaron 2002:57). Anne Knafl, citing David Aaron's work, observes that "scholars will identify the same idiom used outside Israel as literal, but with the Hebrew Bible as metaphorical" (Knafl 2014:38). Marjo Korpel's 700-page book (1990) masterfully gathers the anthropomorphisms applied to both the Ugaritic gods and Yahweh. She identifies scores of verbs of divine action and motion that share the same Semitic verbal roots and appear in both the Tanakh and the Ugaritic texts. Korpel, however, is more likely to take the Ugaritic examples as literal and the identical Hebrew idioms as metaphorical. Six hundred pages into her catalogue of hundreds of correlations between Yahweh and his Near Eastern colleagues, she suddenly concludes that the biblical anthropomorphisms alone are "merely a way of speaking" (1990:627)! But as Aaron demonstrates, the challenge is to those who deny biblical anthropomorphism: "The burden is upon us to demonstrate that the meaning of the imagery applied to Yahweh is different from the meaning of the imagery applied to pagan deities, even though the words used in the imagery are identical in both cultures" (2002:35).

I have found no cogent philological, historical, or theological argument for reading most of the references to Yahweh's human attributes as intentionally metaphorical. The language is too pervasive, the cultural context of early Israelite mythology too familiar, and the historical development of the religion now too well known. "All theism is anthropomorphic," biblical scholar Esther J. Hamori observes, and the theological "rejection of anthropomorphism is a bungled endeavor from the start" (2008:46). Michael Fishbane, a scholar of biblical and rabbinical literature, concludes that the traditional Jewish (and I would add Christian) negation of biblical myth and mythic imagery is simply wrong:

> Equally tendentious is the presumptive dismissal of certain apparently mythic features of biblical language (its unabashed and pervasive depictions of God in anthropomorphic and anthropopathic terms) that blatantly occur in the monotheistic canon of Scripture – as if these were merely due to "the inadequacy of human language" and "limitation of human thought", or to some sort of necessarily "indirect grasp" of "spiritual concepts" by "images . . . that emphasize the sensual". But on what grounds are such assertions made? Surely there is nothing in Scripture itself that would point in this direction, or suggest that the representations of divine form and feeling in human terms are anything

> other than the preferred and characteristic mode of depiction. . . . One can only conclude that the evasions of the direct sense of Scripture that such attitudes represent are attempts to save Scripture from itself – for oneself, and must thus be considered a species of modern apologetics.
>
> (2003:6–7)

There is wonderfully figurative language throughout the Tanakh, to be sure, and it is easy to slip into anthropomorphic expressions that may not involve a truly corporeal meaning. Even Xenophanes, who denounced Homer's gods for having human characteristics, said of his "one" deity that he "sees as a whole, he knows wholly and hears wholly" (Fr. 24), the language indicating at least a metaphorical gender and body. When something is controlled by the "hand of Yahweh," we have good Near Eastern parallels, even in the *Iliad*, for reading this as a metaphor most of the time.

But how are we to read the prologue to Job "metaphorically"? Eliminate the humanized characters of Yahweh and Satan and the meaning of the entire book shifts dramatically.[5] Or is it *all* symbolic in some fashion, just a fictional tale that examines the issue of God's connection to humanity, or to human suffering, in a purely literary or symbolic fashion? Wouldn't that approach just make it all, well, the *Iliad* and *Odyssey*? As Mark Smith concludes, "to regard anthropomorphism as little more than a figurative ornament expressing divine-human communication and interaction diminishes the religious expression and experience of the Israelites and other West Semitic peoples" (2001:93). And of the Greeks.

Yahweh's most important act in the entire Tanakh (after creation itself) is his covenant with Abraham (e.g., Gen 12:1–3; 15:18–21; 17:2–4), the agreement between the Hebrew God and the patriarchs (renewed over the centuries several times) that a great nation will come of their descendants, that a "Promised Land" will be granted them, with obedience, celebration of the sabbath, and male circumcision as the irreversible signs of this arrangement. This contractual transaction is ineluctably human, the violation of which evokes Yahweh's most visceral responses. "Covenant religion was aware that this anthropomorphic God was not the whole, or even the essential, aspect of God. Indeed, it asserted divine transcendence as a basic dogma, but, paradoxically, violated this dogma perpetually . . ." (Geller 2000:308–9). Yahweh is in many ways more humanized than gods in any other Near Eastern tradition except the Greeks, who are very rarely brought into the discussion: "The Old Testament is, in a manner of speaking, his biography, and in it he is anthropomorphized and his character is limned to an extent true of no other god in the ancient Near East" (Gordon 2007b:3). What about Zeus or Athena? Stephan Geller is one of the few biblical scholars to draw the obvious comparison with the Greek vision of the divine, pointing out that "Greek and biblical anthropomorphisms represent a radical reinterpretation of human identity projected onto a deity," and concluding succinctly that "His [Yahweh's] majesty is as perturbed as that of Zeus in Homer" (Geller 2000:280).

This is not a book about religion or belief per se. We don't have to guess why gods so often have human characteristics. That's not to say that credible cultural, psychological, emotional, social, and evolutionary cognitive reasons for the phenomenon of divine anthropomorphism have not been developed. The presentation of the chief god in human terms is common to all ancient Near Eastern religions. "The admitted inability of religious writers, despite their apparent desire, to extricate religion from anthropomorphism suggests there is nothing much to extricate" (Guthrie 1993:179). Writing about the gods in ancient Mesopotamia, Beate Pongratz-Leisten concludes that rather than dismissing the aspects of ancient cultural expressions of religiosity as "primitive," we should "interpret them as an expression of anthropomorphism and animism innate to the human mind" (2011c:141). One of the more credible theories involves our evolutionary need to detect agency, what cognitive theorists refer to as our Hypersensitive Agency Detection Device (HADD – it is "hypersensitive" because its success in detecting danger also led us to a propensity for false positives, to find an agent behind *any* unexplained event). This adaptive neurological impulse merged with a Theory of Mind, the idea that we see ourselves in others, even nonhumans, and thus we are programed to impart agency and intention. "Our Hypersenstive Agency Detection Device makes us susceptible to perceiving agency in natural phenomena," religion scholar Reza Aslan summarizes. "Our Theory of Mind makes us inherently biased toward 'humanizing' whatever phenomena we encounter. So then, how else would we picture the gods except in human form?" (2017:57)

The origin of the presumption of incorporeality and incomprehensibility in the face of Yahweh the Olympian seems to be a pressing need people have for there to be something more to, something better in the universe than, what is available to human senses or cognition or found in their sacred texts. After all, what kind of world would we have if, say, the divine sphere worked as it does in Homer? The answer – not one Western culture has wanted to hear for 2000 years – is just the world we actually experience, an indifferent universe dominated by random events over which we have limited control and from which one day we will all disappear without evidence for compensatory reward or punishment. The disjunction between the manifestly imperfect world we live in and a "perfect" transcendent deity is the unhelpful invention of subsequent theologians abusing the biblical texts. And the tragedy of the whole disaster is that it was unnecessary. The Olympian vision of god as found in the Homeric epics is a far more beneficial vision of the divine than the theological fantasy. The rest of this book sets out to show exactly how and why this is so.

Notes

1 Supercessionism is a common term in biblical criticism used for the "belief that the New Testament covenant supersedes the Mosaic covenant of the Hebrew Bible, and that the Christian Church has displaced Israel as God's chosen people" (*OED*).

2 One Christian apologist claimed that 61 Old Testament prophecies were fulfilled in the life of Jesus. Upon examination, none stand up (Callahan 1997:111; Tobin 2009:580–628). Tim Callahan (1997) subjected all of the biblical prophecies to the following test: (1) Is it true? (2) Was it made before or after the fact? (3) Was it deliberately fulfilled by someone with knowledge of the prophecy? (4) Was it a logical guess? The results

should not be surprising: "I must confess that I know of no prophecy that passes the test by eliminating the non-supernatural alternative explanations."

3 Reza Aslan points out a similar challenge in Islam. Allah is supposedly completely non-anthropomorphic, yet his psychological (e.g., will, intention, preferences) and physical (e.g., hands, eyes, face) characteristics are constantly on display in the Qu'ran. More-over, the "metaphor" escape clause is unavailable to most Islamic exegetes: "Nearly every school of law in Islam insists that God's words in the Quran must be taken liter-ally. . . . So if the Quran happens to mention Allah's hands or eyes or face, it means that Allah must literally have hands and eyes and a face. Never mind the theological twists and turns necessary to make sense of such a view . . ." (2017:157).

4 Academic defenders of Yahweh sometimes erroneously follow the early Christian fathers in contrasting the Hebrew God's supposedly "moral" destruction of the earth in a flood with the Near Eastern variants of the tale *including* the Greek and Roman vari-ants (Benjamins 1998:138). J. David Pleins, for example, writes that "YHWH . . . may be depicted as an Enlil or Zeus but an Enlil or a Zeus who happens to have some moral standards" (2003:127). The only (im)morality visible in the Genesis tale, however, is an unspecified "wickedness" (6:5), corruption, and violence (6:11) of humankind. Noah is spared for being "righteous" and "blameless" (6:9) – the exact quality of this "moral-ity" (as opposed to "fidelity") is up for debate. While in the Mesopotamian flood story the gods attempt to destroy mankind for trivial, nonmoral reasons, that is not always the case with Zeus. Pleins doesn't specify which Zeus: Homer's? Hesiod's? Aeschylus'? Or take Ovid's Jupiter (a favorite target of the Christian apologists). The Roman poet tells two tales of the flood (Deucalion and Pyrrha, *Met.* 1.262–415; Baucis and Phile-mon, *Met.* 8.626–724) in both of which a husband and wife are explicitly spared for their (classical) piety. The Olympian gods are as "moral" in these tales as Yahweh, and a good deal more clear about the reasons behind their actions.

5 Many biblical scholars think the prose prologue and epilogue are part of a different, older tradition than the poetic body of the work. Personally, the book would suit my own preferred vision of life if the epilogue were removed, but that's unfair to the text, like choosing one creation myth in Genesis over the other.

8   Homer's perfectly fallible gods

Prayer doesn't seem to work with any regularity in the modern world. It didn't work for the good citizens of Texas and their governor Rick Perry, a two-time seeker of the Presidency who was not laughed out of politics (as I write, he is the U.S. Secretary of Energy) by his proclamation during a drought:

> I, RICK PERRY, Governor of Texas, under the authority vested in me by the Constitution and Statutes of the State of Texas, do hereby proclaim the three-day period from Friday, April 22, 2011, to Sunday, April 24, 2011, as Days of Prayer for Rain in the State of Texas. I urge Texans of all faiths and traditions to offer prayers on that day for the healing of our land, the rebuilding of our communities and the restoration of our normal way of life.

God only knows what a Republican governor of Texas meant by the restoration of a "normal way of life."

None of the various studies of the efficacy of intercessory prayer has revealed any correlation between bequests from individuals to their god(s) of choice and a positive result. Yes, there have been studies. The Templeton Foundation sponsored a 2.4-million-dollar test, "The Great Prayer Experiment," that revealed no difference in the outcomes for hospitalized patients who received prayers than for those who didn't (Brain 2014:73–4). The Bush Administration alone spent over $2.3 million of taxpayer money on prayer "research" (Parenti 2010:69). Between 2000 and 2012 a branch of the NIH spent $22 million testing the healing power of prayer ("distance healing"). I suppose it's the government's way of providing affordable health care. About $823,000 was given to a "complementary medicine research institute" in San Francisco to study the effectiveness of prayer on glioblastoma, an aggressive form of brain tumor. The results have never been published, although one anecdote is telling: One of awardees died at age 41 while conducting this study, despite the prayers of family, friends, and colleagues – of glioblastoma (Mielczarek and Engler 2012:37).[1]

So here's the age-old problem created by the theologians: If the Abrahamic God possesses all those divine attributes – if he's the all-loving, omnipotent theological version and not the volatile Yahweh we meet throughout the Tanakh – why doesn't he listen more carefully? Why are his benefits so elusive? Why is he so mean-spirited at worst, disinterested at best? Why doesn't he *do* something more often? Why is he so stingy with miracles these days? Why, in the words of a compelling web site, won't God heal amputees? Why – put simply – is there so much unnecessary suffering? Why don't prayers *work*? This dilemma will always tie thoughtful believers into Gordian knots – and keep the religious establishment busy. Although they've been trying for 2000 years, no convincing answer has – or can be – found. An entire library could be filled with these elaborate and futile efforts. The Abrahamic religions are a complete bust at accounting for natural evil.

It's time to play Alexander and cut through that theological tangle with the help of Homer's gods. There is no need to keep manufacturing Byzantine excuses for God's evasiveness. There's a very simple answer: The gods of the universe are *not* all-powerful, all-knowing, all-loving, or all-good. Homer's gods deserve to be taken seriously because the epic world of the divine accords neatly with and "explains" the circumstances of our imperfect existence – and thus makes realistic demands on us. As Achilles comes to see by the end of the *Iliad*, the gods distribute fortune and misfortune just as it appears – randomly – and they never give anyone only good fortune. The poet takes every opportunity to demonstrate that his gods are *not* consistently omniscient, omnipotent, or essentially benevolent, *despite the frequent hopes and beliefs of his characters to the contrary*. Homer offers us a stark and honest vision, a world of competing gods with restricted powers overseeing a theologically deluded humanity.

What kind of world results from this portrait? A chaotic and unpredictable one, no doubt, one that actually matches human experience – unlike a world supposedly created *for* human beings and managed by the perfect god created by Western theologians. The Homeric gods are what they are, no more and no less, and human lives – including ours – reflect those divine limitations. Anthropomorphism and polytheism turn out to be *strengths* of the Homeric presentation of the divine rather than a "primitive" stage of thought dismissed by monotheists. "The emotional actions of the gods allow for a rational explanation of fateful events in human life" (Kullman 1985:5). If we can accept that reality – an existential cry that Homer links directly with Achilles' tragic story – we mortals may be compelled to think about life in a far more refreshingly genuine fashion than the major Western religions have been able to encourage. We are asked to make our actions match our ideas in a more honest fashion, to be more authentically *heroic* in a randomly generated world over which no single, much less flawless, divinity exercises control. Stop pretending, Homer tells us. So far as living a flourishing life goes, you're on your own. Will the gods come through in any reliable or predictable fashion? Prayers? Sacrifices? Connections? "Good" deeds? Fuhgeddaboudit.

In this chapter we will look at the limitations of Homer's gods with an eye to the liberating explanatory power they provide. (We'll examine the specific issues of creation, life-after-death, justice, and sex in later chapters.) Homer's characters, for the most part, are solidly religious in some central ways that modern readers will recognize, looking to the gods for support, guidance, and justification. But Homer, with his ability to peer directly into divine activity and reveal it to his audience, provides a counter-story to the one promulgated by pious mortals. In this disjunction between human expectation and divine "reality," the poet produces a powerful and yet ultimately sympathetic reflection upon human credulity and ignorance of the divine.

The power of convention

After struggling in vain for many years to sail home after the sack of Troy, Menelaus finds his ship becalmed for three weeks on a small island off the coast of Egypt. Eidothea, divine daughter of the sea-god Proteus, takes pity on the near-starving Greeks. (We know they're starving because they're fishing, and Homeric heroes do not like to fish.) She approaches Menelaus to find out why he has not sailed away. The Spartan king suggests that he must have offended the gods in some way, but he doesn't know how or whom. "But tell me – *for the gods know everything* – who of the immortals detains me . . ." (*Od.* 4.379–80, my emphasis). Menelaus is not merely sucking up to the sea nymph but honestly revealing the opinion of Homeric mortals (and contemporary theists): The gods know everything and can do anything. Surely Eidothea can tell him how to appease the correct powers and "how I may cross over the fish-filled sea" to Sparta.

Menelaus' first hint that the cultural belief in divine omniscience may be on shaky ground should have come immediately in Eidothea's response. The goddess can't answer the questions but must refer Menelaus to her father, Proteus, the "old man of the sea." Eidothea is a divine disappointment, apparently *not* knowing all things. But she knows (or can make a good guess at) *something*, that this stranger has had a long and difficult journey. And she can recommend Proteus, who is especially knowledgeable even by divine standards, possessing insight of the past, present, and future, as well as the powers of shape-shifting so often associated with deities of the water (Larson 2007:68). There's a catch, in this case a literal one – Menelaus and his men must physically grab the god and hold onto him as he transforms himself into various shapes (fire, water, lion, serpent, etc.). If they are still in control of the protean god when he turns back into his original shape, he will be compelled to answer the king's questions. Menelaus asks how he can "lie in wait" to catch him, and Eidothea comes up with a low-tech disguise – seal skins and an ambrosial perfume to cut down on the dead-seal smell – for him and three of his comrades.

Menelaus and his men rush from their camouflage, pin Proteus and hold on through his metamorphoses until he returns to his natural form. (His wrestling match with a god is reminiscent of Jacob's bout with Yahweh; Hamori 2008:14–18; Louden 2011:115–16.) Proteus' first words should have been the Spartan king's second hint: "Now who of the gods, son of Atreus, helped you come up with the plan to ambush me and seize me against my will? What do you need?" (*Od.* 4.462–3). The sea-god knows he is talking to Menelaus – one point for his otherworldly wisdom – but apparently he has no clue that his daughter was the informant. It's not a rhetorical question, since Proteus was caught completely off guard and overcome both strategically and physically. And shouldn't he also know exactly "of what" Menelaus has need? At this point perhaps a more skeptical hero would have wondered just how much good advice he was going to get from an "omniscient" god who was deceived by his daughter, mistook Greeks hiding in seal skins for the real things, and was trapped by four undernourished sailors "against his will." But Menelaus' faith is unshaken, as he repeats verbatim his original request of Eidothea: "But tell me – *for the gods know everything* – who of the immortals detains me . . ." (*Od.* 4.468–70 = 4.379–81, my emphasis). Menelaus remains certain that the gods are omniscient against the direct evidence of divine fallibility. His is a truly religious personality, one who in modern times would continue to give money to a scandal-ridden TV minister or send his son off to be an altar boy.

Proteus does reveal some important information regarding the past, present, and future of several Trojan heroes, including Agamemnon, Odysseus, and Menelaus himself. And Menelaus learns what he has done to offend the gods and how to fix it. But the important point for us is the disjunction between what mortals believe about the gods and what the poet reveals to be true. One of the fun things about the epics, especially the *Iliad*, is the irony created by the gap between what the poet knows about the gods and what his characters think they know, "the importance of separating off the words (and actions) of the human characters . . . from what we are told of the attitudes of the gods of whom they speak and in whose name they act" (Winterbottom 1989:36). The epics often reveal that mortals have no or little idea what is really happening on the divine plane. They *think* they do, but they are usually wrong. Proteus knows a lot about the past, not everything about the future, and is quite blind to the threat lying just a few feet in front of him in the present. The poet has divinely sanctioned insight into the "real" workings of the gods, a vision he shares with us, his audience, but not with his characters. Homer manipulates poetic conventions about which characters have access to what information (a feature classicists call Jörgensen's Law) to full thematic effect when it comes to the gods. The epics ultimately provide a humbling paradigm for mortals (including those of the 21st century) who believe they have insight into, access to, and some control over, the mysteries of divine actions and motives. President George W. Bush claimed that God told him, "George, go and end the tyranny in Iraq," which suggests that either Bush should have asked a few follow-up questions or the Christian God has a much darker sense of humor than he is usually given credit for.

Getting it wrong

The characters in the *Iliad* and the *Odyssey* share with most contemporary followers of Western religions a belief that the divine is both omniscient and omnipotent. This is an especially baffling conviction to those of us who have actually read the texts featuring those deities. Homer's characters don't get to read the epics, unfortunately. Menelaus is not alone in his misplaced confidence that "the gods know all things."

Penelope, too, observes that Zeus "knows everything." She includes this optimistic comment on divine omniscience as an aside within a unique tale that in fact highlights the major gods' *lack* of omniscience. Penelope tells us that Aphrodite, Hera, Artemis, and Athena raised three orphaned daughters. The goddesses poured their considerable energies and distinct talents into these girls, providing them with food, beauty, wisdom, stature, and maidenly skills. Then, while Aphrodite was on her way to Olympus to arrange a "blossoming marriage" for each, for incomprehensible reasons (Levaniouk 2008:24) "the powers of the storm-winds snatched up the maidens and handed them over to wait upon the hateful Furies" (*Od.* 20.61–78). Not even the goddesses saw that one coming – and that's my point. The goddesses had no clue that their efforts would be futile; Aphrodite's travel to Olympus takes up enough real human time for the girls to be kidnaped and whisked out of sight; and apparently nothing can be or was done about the crime, since Penelope wishes that the gods on Olympus would blot her from sight as well, the Greek verb suggesting that the girls have disappeared forever (Russo 1992:112).

Homer's invocation of the Muses before he attempts to sing his long list of Greeks who came to Troy (the Catalogue of Ships) is the *only time in the epics* the poet himself vouches for some sort of divine omniscience: "Tell me now, Muses, you who have homes on Olympus – for you are goddesses and are at hand and know all things, but we hear only rumor and do not know anything – who were the leaders and rulers of the Danaans" (2.484–7). But the poet *is* sucking up this time. The Muses never appear in their own person to reveal any knowledge or information – their omniscience is never tested in the narrative.[2]

There are, to be sure, numerous times in the epics when Homer shows us that the gods do know what is going on well beyond their immediate line of sight. Most impressively, several Homeric deities are shown to possess some genuine knowledge of future events, although this insight is sporadic and thematically bound: *Some* gods have *some* knowledge of the fate of *some* individuals and the outcome of *some* events when it suits the purposes of the poet. In particular, Homer's deities often share with the poet an awareness of the basic plot of the epics and the content of some of the Trojan saga, such as the ultimate fate of Hector, Achilles, and Troy.

Homeric mortals, on the other hand, seem to assume that the gods know *everything*, including the future, *all the time*. And in this they are often proven wrong. Neither Zeus nor any other major god knows all – their "omniscience" is severely circumscribed by contextual demands. They know things when it is convenient for the story; they don't when it's important that they don't. As Paris and Menelaus prepare to duel, for example, Priam admits that he can't bear to watch, fearing for his son, and adds in typical Homeric fashion: "But Zeus no doubt knows this, and the other immortal gods, to which certain death is decreed" (3.308–9). As it turns out, the immortal gods don't know. It is only when Paris is about to be killed that Aphrodite rushes in to save him. Apparently she didn't see this coming either.

The entire system of reciprocity – of human communication with, honoring of, and favor from the gods – depends upon faith in the gods' access to what's going to happen and their occasional willingness to share their knowledge with mortals. This connection with the divine, however, is an unreliable system manned by fallible deities. Information from the gods can be annoyingly imprecise. Divine predictions are often inexact or slightly off, something noted by Homer's first commentators. Zeus says it is ordained that there will be great fighting over Patroclus' body at the sterns of the ships (8.474–7), whereas he is in fact killed near the walls of Troy. Not a biggie, to be sure, but you like your divine knowledge to be exact. Tiresias relates all kinds of information to Odysseus, but somehow doesn't ever tell him how to get home or exactly what will happen when he does.

More notorious are the strange "double" fates. Most famous is Thetis' prediction of her son's "twofold fates," either to fight and die at Troy and gain imperishable renown, or live a long life without fame (9.410–16; cf. Euchenor's two possible fates at 13.663–72). After losing his wrestling match, Proteus warns Menelaus to get home as soon as possible, where "either you will find him [Aegisthus] alive, or Orestes will have gotten there first and killed him, and you might get there for the funeral" (*Od.* 4.546–7). Come on, man, take a guess! You're a god! You've got a 50/50 chance. Both Tiresias and Circe know that Odysseus and his men will encounter Helius' cattle, but neither can predict if they will leave the herd "unharmed" and all reach home, or whether the hero will lose all his comrades (*Od.* 11.104–117; 12.137–41). Tiresias also foretells that Odysseus will slay the suitors but doesn't know if it will be "by guile or openly with a sword" (*Od.* 11.119–120). Both, as it turns out.

God-sent omens can be false. Intentionally so. As we saw earlier, in order to instigate his plan to aid the Trojans and thereby "do honor to Achilles," Zeus sends a destructive dream to Agamemnon with a false message: Arm the Greeks and go to battle, for they can now capture Troy (2.1–35). Even in antiquity there were critics who tried to exculpate Zeus by eliminating or smoothing over his outright lie, but we have seen that Yahweh himself is not above sending out false prophetic messages if it suits his purposes. Agamemnon is a "fool" for believing the lie, according to Homer, but of course the king *wants* it to be true, and what else was he to do? As classicist Peter Ahrensdorf says of the episode, by "highlighting not only the deception but also the ineptitude of the gods, and specifically their lack of understanding of how to rule human beings, Homer challenges the [epic characters'] conventional, trusting, pious belief in the wise providence of the gods" (2014:46).

It is understandable, then, that while characters customarily "trust in portents" (e.g., 4.398; 6.183; 12.256), there is no stigma on a person who is cautious about the process of divining the gods' will. Homer leaves room for skepticism and even disrespect towards divination and professional interpreters (2.299–300, 348–9; 24.220–24; *Od.* 1.415–16; 24.450–66; Trampedach 2008:213–14, 225). Personal contact with god, an epiphany, is far more trustworthy than unreliable professional intermediaries, just as it is in the Tanakh (Niditch 2010:14). Dreams, though thought to "come from Zeus" (1.63), are known to be especially unreliable (2.80–1; 5.148–51). Penelope famously dismisses all efforts to read dreams as inherently flawed. She tells the disguised Odysseus that "dreams are inscrutable and enigmatic" and that by no means do they all lead to anything (*Od.* 19.560–7).

In an excellent article on bird signs in early Greek epic, classicist Derek Collins concludes with an important question, namely, "why early epic presents mantic authority in general, and bird divination in particular, as so malleable and subject to criticism" (2002:41). Part of the reason is thematic and an essential element of characterization and plotting. The suitors by nature and necessity will dismiss and miss the signs, for example. But this critique also contributes to Homer's larger picture of the untrustworthiness of the gods and the difficulty of understanding their messages. Even when the gods are trying to be helpful, both divine and mortal mistakes are rampant.

Divine ignorance

The errors in the prophetic "system" pale in comparison to the failures of the *knowledge* of the gods. To be omniscient means to know all things *at all times*, not just the future once in a while. (I correctly predicted that my daughter would not pitch for the Dodgers, even though she was pretty sure she would.) Homer is not at all subtle about the gods' fallibility – his divine characters only know what they need when *he* needs them to. The gods don't even know what's going on around them much of the time. Here are some of the more notorious examples:

- Zeus doesn't know Hera's plans or see through her patent sexual deception that renders him unconscious and her temporarily in charge of the war (14.153–353).
- Agamemnon insists that Zeus was also deceived by Hera's "craftiness" long before when the god was tricked into allowing Heracles to be born into servitude (19.95–97).
- Although Zeus has threatened the gods with every punishment in his divine toolbox should they intervene in the war, Poseidon still "secretly emerged from the gray sea" to aid the Greeks unbeknownst to Zeus (13.351–3). Homer tells us that Zeus "turned his bright eyes away" to study faraway lands and peoples (13.7–9). In this case, what Zeus doesn't see he doesn't know.
- When Zeus returns from the Ethiopians with no apparent knowledge of the quarrel between Achilles and Agamemnon, Thetis quickly approaches to call in a favor, namely support for the Trojan side "until the Achaeans show respect to my son and give him his due honor." Zeus agrees, but asks Thetis to depart quickly "so that Hera not notice anything" (1.493–523). The possibility of doing something on the sly is apparently real. According to Zeus, we recall, he and Hera had sex without their (divine) parents' knowledge. Hera is eternally (and reasonably) suspicious of him, so he "can keep nothing secret" from her (1.561). This isn't "omniscience" but the ordinary snooping, prying, and paranoia embedded in their troubled marriage.
- At one point Hera dispatches Iris, Zeus's own messenger deity, to Achilles "unknown to Zeus and the other gods" (18.165–8).
- After Hera threw Hephaestus off Olympus, he lived for nine years with Thetis and Eurynome (his eventual mother-in-law) in the "stream of Oceanus," and, he adds, "no one else knew, either of gods or mortal men" (18.403–5). (Ocean, at the edge of the world, served as a kind dumping ground for the odd

and untouchable, like the "special room" for rejected prospective pledges of the main fraternity in the movie *Animal House*.)

- In order to aid the Greeks, Athena convinces the Trojan supporter Ares that the two of them should both leave battle. Ares agrees, but Athena then slips back into the fighting without his noticing it (5.29–37,121–33).
- Ares also isn't aware that his mortal son has been killed (13.521–5), yet he cares dearly. When he is finally informed of Ascalaphus' death by Hera, he wails and tries to enter the battle for revenge in suicidal defiance of Zeus's commands (15.110–18).
- The famous story told by the Phaeacian bard Demodocus of the love affair of Aphrodite and Hephaestus (*Od*. 8.266–366) is predicated on the gods' lack of awareness of the facts. First, Hephaestus doesn't know his wife is having sex with Ares. When informed by Helius of the affair, he sets a trap made of bonds so fine that "no one even of the blessed gods could see them." Neither Aphrodite nor Ares figures out that Hephaestus is lying about going away on a business trip. Though a human narrative, Demodocus is "loved by the Muse," and we are given no indication in the epics that his tales of the gods are less authentic than Homer's. The "voices of the narrator and Demodocus seem to merge" (Jong 2001:195–6).
- Helius, we are told by Odysseus, "sees everything and hears everything" (*Od*. 12.323) – his ability to witness all human activity is perhaps his major characteristic and the reason he is called upon in oaths – but he nevertheless does not see Odysseus' men slaughter and eat his beloved cattle. One of the immortal shepherds, his daughter Lampetia, must inform him (*Od*. 12.374–5).
- The land of the Ethiopians seems to isolate the gods from the rest of the world by an information blockade worthy of the most efficient totalitarian government. Thetis doesn't even think of trying to notify Zeus when he goes there for a feast (1.423–27). Athena and Zeus have apparently been waiting seven years for Poseidon to visit this semi-mythical land so they can work to free Odysseus without the sea-god's knowledge (*Od*. 1.22–26,76–9). When Poseidon eventually returns, he is stunned to learn of Odysseus' near escape (*Od*. 5.286–89).

Homer has no problem in presenting gods with limited knowledge when it fits the context. His imperfect gods fit in perfectly with his vision of the way the world works. They intrude when they wish through a system of omens and prophecies, but we have seen that if they really want something done, they can be far more direct and personal. If Homer's gods are not omniscient and are therefore unreliable, their omnipotence is even more suspect.

Doing it all. Just kidding

Mortals in the Homeric world, like contemporary theists, also make unwarranted claims about the power of the divine. Both Odysseus and his loyal swineherd

Eumaeus, for example, claim that the "gods can do everything" (*Od.* 10.306; 14.444–5). As we have seen, each god does have powers well beyond those of mortals. But – and this is a very important "but" – there are severe limitations. Some shortcomings seem rooted in the nature of the universe. Even the proud Athena in the "happy-ending" *Odyssey* admits that "certainly not even the gods can avert death, the great leveler, from a man even if he is dear, whenever the destructive fate of mournful death takes him down" (*Od.* 3.236–8).

The very nature of polytheism also leads to internal struggles for power, to disagreements and altercations that are usually resolved in favor of one god over another. True, on Homer's Olympus the kingly Zeus, father of men and gods, is often acknowledged by his family as mightiest or mightier than other individual deities (e.g., 4.56; 8.31–2,211; 15.107–8; 21.441–5; *Od.* 5.103–4,118,137–8). Even the poet grants that Zeus's "power is greatest" (*Od.* 5.4). Zeus himself is suspiciously insistent upon his supremacy, frequently threatening punishment to those who would disobey his commands. The most impressive example of this imperiousness comes with his decree forbidding the rest of the Olympians to interfere in any way with the course of the battle (8.1–27). He will either strike the offenders with lightning or hurl them into Tartarus:

> Then you will see by how much I am the strongest of all gods. So come on and try it, you gods, so that you all may know. Hang a golden cord from heaven, and grab hold of it, all you gods and all you goddesses; but you could not drag Zeus, the highest counselor, out of heaven to earth, not if you labored with all your might. But whenever I really wanted to, I could drag [you] up with the earth itself and the sea as well. The cord I would then bind around the peak of Olympus and everything would hang in the air. By so much am I superior to gods and humans.
>
> (8.17–27)

The gods are hushed. They clearly believe him, and for portions of the subsequent fighting they try their best (which, admittedly, is often not very good) to confine themselves resentfully to Olympus. Ares has to be talked down from reentering the war by Athena of all deities, who fears not so much for her unlikable sibling as for herself, since Zeus "will come to Olympus to drive us all into confusion, and he will seize one after another, both the guilty and the innocent" (15.136–7).[3]

But even though his divine family fears and respects him, they defy him as well. Zeus is no Yahweh when it comes to managing the divine bureaucracy. Hera, Athena, and Poseidon spend a good deal of their textual time attempting, with some success, to aid the Greeks surreptitiously. The personified Strife pays no attention whatsoever to Zeus. Hera even seduces her husband so that he falls asleep, thus allowing Poseidon to run wild on the battlefield. And Homer wants us to know that these are not the first efforts of the Olympians to thwart Zeus's will – there's some ugly history that the king of gods remembers very well.

One of the primary functions of the Heracles myth in the *Iliad*, for example, is to remind us of past conflicts between Zeus and Hera – conflicts that Hera partially wins. Agamemnon tells the story of how Hera deceived her spouse into allowing Heracles to be born into servitude to another rather than becoming one who would "rule over all those who dwell nearby, one of the race of the men who are from my blood" (19.104–5). A separate tale of Hera's efforts to work against Zeus's favorite love child is told over the course of the *Iliad*. When Hera first tries to bribe Sleep into assisting with her seduction of Zeus, he refuses. He recalls the day that Heracles sailed from Troy after sacking it. Hera had a similar scheme up her sleeve then, commandeering Sleep to "charm the mind of" Zeus while she raised a storm to blast Heracles "away from all his companions" and drive him off course. Zeus awoke and began "hurling the gods about his halls." He would have tossed Sleep from heaven into the deep "to be seen no more . . . if Night, subduer of gods and men, had not saved me. . . . Zeus stopped himself, although he was angry, for he recoiled from doing things displeasing to swift Night" (14.243–62). Note that Zeus is deceived by one god, overpowered by another, and scared of riling a third (for reasons that are never revealed).

When he awakens from his postcoital snooze and finds that Hera has stirred the Greeks to temporary victory against his explicit orders, "with a terrible glance he spoke to Hera." His threats are explicit as he recalls the consequences of her previous deception:

> I think rather that again you may first reap the fruit of your troublesome mischievousness, and I will lash you with lighting-strokes. Or don't you remember when you were hanging aloft, and I let down two anvils from your feet, and I whipped a golden, unbreakable binding around your hands? And you were hanging in heaven and in the clouds, and the gods throughout Olympus were angry, but they could not come near to free you. But laying hold of anyone I could seize I would hurl him from the threshold so that he came to earth with no strength left.
>
> (15.16–24)

Zeus is certainly good at threatening and punishing miscreant deities, but he would have no need to devise torments for them or fling them from Olympus if he were actually omnipotent (or omniscient) in the first place or if he didn't have good reasons for suspecting a genuine challenge to his authority.[4]

God versus god: Live from Vegas

The advantages of polytheism in describing the general chaos of mortal experience are obvious. Even if there are divine powers involved in human life – even if one of them is supposedly "far mightier" than the others – the multiplicity of actors makes it impossible to count on any of them, and extremely difficult even to know which deity (if any), or which of the many aspects of each deity, may be responsible for one's current predicament. Misfortunes and miracles are therefore commonly attributed to "a god" or "some god" or the "gods," generic expressions denoting some "supreme anonymous supernatural steering power" (Versnel

2011:176). The word *daimôn* is used by Homeric mortals who feel something divine has intruded but have no idea whom to blame or celebrate. The archer Teucer, who has more than his share of bad luck in the *Iliad*, has Hector in his sights and the poet tells us Teucer "would have stopped him from battle by the ships of the Achaeans" if Zeus hadn't broken the bow string. Teucer cries out that a *daimôn* has ruined his plans (15.458–70). Ajax thinks some god (*theos*) has destroyed the bow (15.473), and Hector guesses correctly that it's Zeus (15.489–90; Clay 2011:191). The gods often stand in for the secular realization that "shit happens."

Or take something as simple as the wind. Zeus as the weather-god sends wind, lighting, thunder, rain, snows, etc. in the epics. But Athena and Hera also thunder; Hera sends ruinous winds; Poseidon naturally raises fierce storms; Athena, "the gods," Calypso, Aeolus, and Circe send favorable breezes; a *daimôn* lulls the waves to sleep. What's a sailor to do? You can't blame Odysseus for thinking Zeus has "stirred up the sea" against him when in fact we know that the storm is the nasty brainchild of Poseidon alone (*Od.* 5.303–305). And if Zeus is really the most powerful, and heavenly bodies are their own divine characters, how is it that *Hera* has the authority to make the "unwilling" Helius set (18.239–42), or Athena to force night to linger and hold back the horses of golden-throned Dawn so Odysseus and Penelope can enjoy an extra-long reunion night together (*Od.* 23.241–6)?

Homeric heroes are often shown attributing blanket powers and interests to the gods, especially to Zeus, that are then revealed to the reader to be sporadic and restricted. Aeneas, saved by Poseidon from Achilles' attack, is typically myopic: "Zeus both increases and diminishes a man's excellence, however he wishes, for he is the most powerful of all" (20.242–3). Even his cautious awareness of Zeus's inscrutability is overly optimistic and ultimately mistaken. The truth is far more complex, and the gods are much less predictable than mortals imagine. Aeneas gives credit to Zeus (who has nothing to do with it) for his potential success; he is almost led to his death by Apollo, a god on whom he and the Trojans consistently count; he is saved in the nick of time by Poseidon, one of his greatest divine nemeses. And he's a lucky one, since he will be one of the very few Trojan heroes to survive the war. Usually such theological miscalculations end in death. The events in life do not, as it turns out, depend upon the will of any predictable divine power. Aeneas errs in the same way most devout people have probably always erred, but this time the text is there to reveal the reality.

The real force behind life's vagaries in Homer is of course the Olympians' competing claims, overlapping realms of authority, all-too-human passions, and interminable rivalries. Homer wastes no time in pointing out the seriousness of this divine friction. Just halfway through the first book of the *Iliad*, Achilles reminds Thetis of why Zeus owes her a big favor:

> Often in the halls of my father I have heard you boasting, when you said that you alone among the immortals warded off disgraceful destruction from the son of Cronus of the dark clouds, when the other Olympians wanted to bind

him, Hera and Poseidon and Pallas Athena. But you went, goddess, undid
his bonds, swiftly calling to high Olympus the hundred-handed one, whom
the gods call Briareus, but all men call Aegaeon; for he in turn, stronger than
his father, sat down next to the son of Cronus, exulting in his glory. And the
blessed gods feared him and ceased their binding.

(1.396–406)

This tale of an attempted heavenly coup is known only from this passage; no
subsequent Greek author mentions it. The revolt looks like a Homeric invention
to give Thetis a claim on Zeus. The poet probably included these three particular
deities in the failed insurrection because of their subsequent opposition to Zeus's
efforts to aid the Trojans. In any case, Homer has no problem including a story
depicting Zeus as vulnerable, coming very close to being "bound" and potentially
losing his position as ruler of the gods.

Poseidon's role in the unsuccessful putsch is particularly interesting, since he
has the most difficulty in accepting Zeus's supreme position. Hera is proud and
willful and has a "predilection for authority" (Louden 2005:94–5), but her complaints are primarily with Zeus's policies. Poseidon considers his brothers to be
his equals, their authority distinguished merely by the luck of the draw. He concedes that Zeus is far stronger (8.210–11) but only reluctantly yields to his threats
of physical combat. He tells Hera that he would deal with the gods differently than
Zeus does, which suggests he has thought about what it would be like to be the
top god (13.351–60; 15.184–217; 20.133–5). For his part, Zeus is glad Poseidon
backed down, for if it had come to a physical struggle, "not without sweat would
the issue have been completed" (15.226–8). This sounds like a harder challenge
than Zeus's normal bluster about throwing gods from heaven and zapping them
with his thunderbolt. Poseidon, though inferior to Zeus, *is* a potential threat.

While non-Olympians like Calypso (*Od.* 5.118–36) and Thetis (1.514–16) note
with some frustration their inferior status to "those holding Olympus," there is
no strict hierarchy among the major deities themselves beyond Zeus's tenuous
authority. Unlike in Yahweh's regimented council, it's mostly a free-for-all. Hera
can't force Sleep to help her trap Zeus; she has to bribe him. He turns down the
offer of a throne and ottoman; he can't be bought with furniture. His resolve
withers, however, when she offers him "one of the younger Graces" as a bride
(14.233–76). Principle and fear only go so far when there's sex with a beautiful
goddess on the horizon.

Still, Homer clearly has his favorites and some gods consistently fare better than
others in the intra-Olympian rivalries. Athena and Apollo are usually presented in
a dignified fashion (by Homeric standards). Enemies on the battlefield (though
they never confront one another directly), at one point they even respectfully
agree to stop the fighting for the day (7.17–43). Athena claims her delay in helping Odysseus was out of respect for her uncle Poseidon (*Od.* 6.328–31; 13.341–3).
But given their disparate desires and general self-absorption, conflict constantly
arises among the gods and any sort of omnipotence is out of the question. We've

already seen what happens to Artemis when confronted by Hera, and how Athena sends both Ares and Aphrodite sprawling unconscious on the ground. At Zeus's insistence the gods supporting Troy line up, one-on-one, against those favoring the Greeks. Some of the gods have been going after each other indirectly throughout the entire epic, but this *theomachy* remains one of the more bizarre events in the *Iliad* (20.21–75; 21.342–513). The fiercest fight is the first, between Hephaestus and the Trojan river Scamander. Scamander attempts to drown the berserk Achilles, upset at the corpses dumped into his waters. Hera rouses Hephaestus to fight water with fire, and the boiling river soon retires (21.328–82), prefiguring the eventual burning of Troy itself.

The other "duels" in the theomachy are rather anticlimactic, either aborted or completely one-sided, hardly supporting Hades' initial fears that with the gods thundering and shaking the earth so loudly "Poseidon the Earth-Shaker would burst open the earth and his [Hades'] terribly dank house that even the gods hate would be made visible for mortals and immortals" (20.62–65). All in all, the entire theomachy can look like a rather silly affair and frequently became the target of theological criticism among later Greek intellectuals. Modern scholars don't much like it either, offended at its crude theology – an "undignified episode" (Dietrich 1979:132) – or disappointed on aesthetic grounds, "the least successful [episode] in the entire poem" (Fox 2008:330). Gods just shouldn't act that way. But the episode neatly contrasts divine immutability with the reality of human suffering, a distinction that is one of the most significant poetic functions of the divine. The poor performances of most of the Trojan supporters (Scamander, Ares, Artemis, Aphrodite) also point to Troy's doom. More significantly, this often-criticized installment of Olympian delinquency brings into focus the challenges – and advantages – of polytheism and anthropomorphism that permeate Homer's epics. With gods like these, of varying abilities, limited powers, individual agendas, and huge egos, the events of life influenced by them will necessarily appear random. To count on the divine to shape a rational, organized human existence would be the height of folly. "Fools!" Homer would simply grumble. Since when is human existence rational or organized?

Gods vs mortals: not as lopsided as you think

The Olympians are obviously far more powerful than the human characters. As Phoenix reminds Achilles, the gods surpass mortals in their excellence (*aretê*), status (*timê*), and strength (*biê*, 9.498). But that doesn't mean the gods always come out on top in conflicts with mere mortals. We've heard how Diomedes, with the aid of Athena, wounds Aphrodite and Ares, sending them both scampering back to Olympus. Ares histrionically claims that he barely escaped with his life. Both deities are healed immediately and easily, for, as Homer notes of the war-god, "he was in no way created mortal" (5.901).[5]

It's not the first time a human has gotten the better of a deity. Particularly impressive is the tale told by Dione to Aphrodite in an effort to console – and to inspire a bit of resilience in – her traumatized daughter. Other gods, she says, have suffered at the hands of mortals:

> Hera suffered too, when the powerful son of Amphitryon [Heracles] struck
> - her in the right breast with a three-barbed arrow; then unsoothable pain seized
> even her. Fearsome Hades among these also endured a swift arrow, when the
> same man, the son of Zeus who wields the aegis, struck him in Pylos among
> the corpses and offered him up to pain. But he went to the house of Zeus and
> to high Olympus, grieving in his heart, transfixed with pain, for the arrow had
> been driven in his firm shoulder, and troubled his mind. Paeëon, sprinkling
> painkilling drugs, healed him; for he was in no way created mortal.
>
> (5.392–402)

Dione emphasizes the genuine agony caused by the wounds: "Unsoothable pain," "suffered," "pain," "grieving in his heart," "transfixed with pains," "troubled his mind." Omnipotence and impassibility are out the window. Circe seems genuinely panicked when Odysseus draws his sword "as though to kill her" (*Od.* 10.294–6,321–4). Diomedes knows the story of Dionysus' flight from the mortal Lycurgus, the god "filled with fear" (6.130–141). The mortal Tityus "dragged off" Leto (*Od.* 11.576–81).

But the winners for Mortal Challenge to the Gods have to be the brother act of Otus and Ephialtes, whose nearly successful attacks on the gods are chronicled in both epics (5.385–91; *Od.* 11.305–320). The sons of Poseidon and a mortal Iphimedeia, they were the tallest mortals and extremely handsome. At nine years they were already over 50 feet in height. Dione tells Aphrodite about what must have been one of their first adventures, when they tied Ares "in strong bonds; he had been bound in a bronze jar for thirteen months. Ares, insatiable in war, would have perished right there, if [their stepmother] had not brought the news to Hermes; and he stole Ares away, who by then was hard pressed, for the harsh imprisonment was breaking him" (5.386–91). There are some by now familiar motifs: It's Ares, whom everybody picks on; a god is "hard pressed" from the assault of a mortal; Ares is "bound," the standard image of divine conquest.[6] The bronze jar is a nice detail from folklore. Somewhat startlingly, Ares was trapped in there (unmissed?) for over a year! Dione also adds the curious touch of a near-death experience – "he would have perished" – a "theological absurdity" (Kirk 1990:101) that we must assume is intentional hyperbole for effect.

Apparently the brothers are unpunished (and quite young), for they are alive and well enough to attempt to storm Olympus:

> They threatened the immortals on Olympus that they would rouse the din of
> impetuous war against them. They were eager to pile [Mt.] Ossa on Olympus,
> and Pelion, with its quivering leaves, on Ossa, so heaven could be scaled.
> And they certainly would have been successful if they had come to their
> prime. But the son of Zeus, whom fair-haired Leto bore, destroyed them both

before the first growth of their beards bloomed beneath their temples and covered their chins with a full beard.

(Od. 11.313–20)

The stacking of mountain on mountain to wage war against the gods became proverbial, but the details are odd, since Olympus would have been on the *bottom* of the pile. Perhaps Olympus and heaven are different places here; perhaps we're demanding too much consistency (again). But the stories reveal that not just Ares but many of the gods are open to a human attack.[7]

Consequences: You don't have a prayer

We began this chapter with a glance at the psychology of theistic prayer, and we can now conclude our review of the fallibility of Homeric gods by surveying the very similar faith of Homer's characters. The key difference, once again, is that the poet often reveals that this faith is misplaced. The gods are unreliable, a theological insight that matches our experience and that should serve all of us as a guide to making realistic choices.

Heroes pray and sacrifice (the two activities are often connected) to the gods, requesting all the kinds of aid one would expect. But do the gods thus have a strong sense of reciprocal obligation imposed on them, even if they "are sometimes unable to fulfill it," as has been argued (e.g., Seaford 2010:178)? Occasionally the gods are receptive – Homer says "they heard" the petitioner, although the human character is not privy to the divine response. Most of the time no divine response is indicated; the request may or may not be fulfilled in the subsequent action, and in neither case do we or the petitioner have a way of knowing if the gods were involved in the outcome. Still, an unanswered prayer is just that, and in retrospect heroes can observe that the god or gods failed to grant their appeal. After escaping from Polyphemus' cave, Odysseus sacrifices his "savior" ram to Zeus, clearly in the hopes that he and his men would make it home quickly and safely. Since this does not happen (rather the *opposite*), Odysseus later concludes that Zeus "did not care about my sacrifice, but was pondering how all my strong-decked ships and trusty comrades might be destroyed" (*Od.* 9.553–5). We, the audience, know by now that it is Poseidon who will be doing the "planning," although Zeus and Athena are as yet strangely unwilling to help Odysseus if it means annoying Poseidon. Similarly, Nestor tells Telemachus that the ships departing from Troy sacrificed to the gods, but "Zeus, a cruel god, was not yet contriving our return, but stirred up evil strife again a second time" (*Od.* 3.160–61). The characters don't know why Zeus was "stubborn," only in retrospect that their prayers and sacrifices were rejected. Homer, however, offers us no evidence that Zeus had any role in their struggles to return (cf. Peleus' futile ritual at 23.144–51). Sarah Hitch concludes her study of sacrifice in the *Iliad* by noting that despite what characters believe, "sacrifices do not succeed in changing the will of the gods. . . . The inadequacy of sacrifice, which is refuted throughout the poem as a potential support system, is one part of the wide-sweeping portrayal of mortal vulnerability pervasive in the poem" (Hitch 2009:134, 139).

Just as tragic – and fully human – as failed sacrifices are the prayers that we, the audience, know will not be fulfilled, although the characters (like modern theists) remain filled with hope of their accomplishment. "Gods usually hear, often react, and *sometimes* grant 'reported' Homeric prayers (*Il.* 18.328)" (Lateiner 1997:260, emphasis his).[8] The Trojan hero Glaucus begins a prayer to Apollo with typical confidence: "Hear me, lord, who are perhaps in the rich land of Lycia or in Troy, but on every side can hear a man in trouble . . ." (16.514–16) – and we are told that Apollo responds.

But the occasional successful appeal is just as likely to give wishful mortals false hope. Sometimes it's as simple as characters not being privy to the Trojan saga. Thus when all the Greek and Trojan troops pray to Zeus that the guilty duelist die – they don't care whether it's Menelaus or Paris – and that the rest of the warriors be bound by "friendship and oaths" (3.318–23), we don't have to wait for Zeus's response (there is none) to know that their prayers are pointless. We know that the Trojans wishing for "friendship" will all be killed by the (surviving) Greeks.

Even more tragically poignant is Hector's prayer for his infant son Astyanax, his last words (little did he realize) before his only child:

> Zeus and you other gods, grant that this child, my son, become distinguished among the Trojans, just as I am, and just as good in strength, and that he rule over Ilion with might. And one day may someone say of him as he returns from war, "This man is far better than his father." And having killed an enemy combatant, may he carry back the bloody spoils, and may his mother rejoice in her heart.
>
> (6.476–81)

Hector probably holds his son up to the heavens as he utters these sadly ironic words. As the audience well knows, Astyanax will be hurled from the walls of a burning Troy shortly before the Greeks set sail for home. And as for the child's mother "rejoicing," she instead will be assigned as a sex-slave to Neoptolemus, the slayer of Hector's father and the son of Achilles, the killer of her husband, father, and brothers. Hector's prayers will never be answered. His crushing ignorance of what we and the gods can see coming represents the Homeric view of the human condition.

As the Greek troops prepare for the first battle of the epic, "each sacrificed to the eternal gods, one to one god, one to another, praying to escape death and the tumult of war" (2.400–401). Polytheistic prayers are tricky in and of themselves. We the audience know that the gods may be at cross-purposes, but the petitioners usually do not. The prayer is hopeless – none of them will avoid the tumult of war. Agamemnon sacrifices a "fat five-year-old bull" to Zeus and prays that the sun not go down before he has burnt down Troy and "split Hector's tunic from his breast" with his sword (2.411–18). "So he spoke," Homer tells us, "but the son of Cronus did in no way bring this to fulfillment for him; he accepted the sacrifice, but he increased the dreadful struggle" (2.419–20). The fickle gods can accept the gift and reject the request. Or grant half a prayer and not the other. This happens when Achilles prepares an elaborate ritual libation and prays to Zeus that

Patroclus may successfully drive the Trojans away from the ships, "then may he come back to the swift ships unscathed with all his armor and his comrades who fight with him in close quarters" (16.220–48). But Zeus is thrifty in his response: "Zeus, the counselor, heard him – the father granted him one of his prayers, but the other he rejected" (16.249–50). No surprises are in store for the audience, but Achilles will be driven to near suicidal grief when the death of his closest friend is announced. Homeric deities simply "do not meet the expectations of the human characters" (Van erp Tallman Kip 2000:401).

And finally, there is the explicit and total rejection of a request. When a Trojan complains to Zeus about the course of battle, calling the supreme god a "lover of lies," Homer tells us that "he did not persuade the mind of Zeus by declaring these things" (12.164–74), since Zeus has other plans, a prior commitment (Pulleyn 1997:197). Gods have their own priorities. At the height of Diomedes' *aristeia*, the Trojans fear he may even sack Troy. The prophet Helenus tells his brother Hector to enter Troy and have Hecuba gather the older women at Athena's temple on the citadel. There they should offer a precious gift and vow a sacrifice in the hope that the goddess will hold back Diomedes. Hector does as requested, passing along the seer's suggestion to their mother. Hecuba takes the women to the temple where Athena's priestess, Theano, leads them in a ritual cry and prayer. Theano changes things up a bit, vowing a sacrifice on the more specific request that Diomedes "fall head-first in front of the Scaean gates." Homer, or Athena, or both, wastes no time in responding: "So she [Theano] spoke in prayer, but Pallas Athena refused" (6.311). Athena is one of the two major "guardian" deities of Troy (along with Apollo), but her loyalties are not evenly divided in this particular war. The Trojans don't know how doomed they are.

Conclusions

The power of the gods, never unlimited in itself, is frequently curtailed by the very nature of their number and personality, that is, by the polytheism and anthropomorphism inherent in the Homeric vision of the divine. Their consequent random potency and overall inefficacy have been interpreted by Western theologians as evidence of the inadequacy of the entire Homeric divine apparatus. The theologically transfigured God of the Bible has become the preferred model for the past 1500 years. But this bias is inverted. Homer's gods can't be "real" gods only if you approach the entire subject of the divine from the theological perspective of the Abrahamic religions: God must be omnipotent, omniscient, benevolent, etc. because, well, otherwise we would have a world without divinely organized *meaning*.

But why would any reasonable person freed from religious inculcation ever conclude that our world has any inherent meaning for humans? What evidence – and I mean even vaguely persuasive evidence – could possibly suggest that the world is guided by any sensible divine power? (Please don't answer "love," as a campus priest once responded to my query. You might as well say that proof of the Easter bunny resides in my passion for chocolate.) The anthropomorphic Homeric gods provide a *realistic* account of human experience, of the apparent randomness of events and unpredictability of life. The Olympians' multiplicity and very imperfect nature perfectly match with human experience. If there *are* gods, these (or something like them) would be they. We would be hard pressed to distinguish between life's completely random events and those influenced by these gods. Over the long haul the gods' existence would be superfluous.

This truth is one of the major themes of the *Iliad*. Achilles, consumed by his own pride and passion, loses everything that gave his world meaning. Honor, friendship, filial duty, trust in the gods – these have all evaporated by the end of the epic through the consequences of his own actions. As he takes responsibility, he also comes to see that life does not offer up meaning as conventional social, familial, and religious institutions fancy. As he stares into the face of the father of his greatest enemy, his compassion for the human condition emerges in a flash of insight about the relationship between the gods and human flourishing. The unhappy and parallel fates of his own father, now to perish alone without Achilles at his side, and King Priam, bereft of his heroic son(s) and forced to watch the inevitable destruction of his once prosperous city, drive the Greek warrior into his ultimate heroic act – facing the abyss with courage:

> For in such a way the gods have spun the threads of destiny for miserable mortals, that they should live sorrowing, but the gods themselves are free from care. For on Zeus's floor are set down two jars of gifts of the sort he gives, one of evil, the other of good. To whatever man Zeus, who delights in the thunderbolt, gives a mixed lot, that man now encounters evil, now good; but to whatever man he gives solely of the miserable, Zeus makes him an object of shame, and evil famine drives him across the bright earth, and he rambles honored neither by gods nor by mortals.
>
> (24.525–33)

The arbitrariness, or at least the inscrutability (as far as the mortal characters are usually concerned), of the gods renders them unhelpful if not completely pointless. The burden of making sense of it all, of finding a purpose to our existence, falls completely on our shoulders. It's a tremendous burden – freedom and responsibility are always onerous. Is Achilles up to the task now that he knows the game is fixed, that no one gets out alive and there is no supernatural kibitzing to count on? Are we? Homer wisely ends the epic on that question. Humans must mourn, commiserate, and summon the courage to move ahead. The *Iliad* closes with a short truce and the burial of Hector. What lies ahead besides more conflict and death? Here is the real challenge we all must face if we are honest and jettison contemporary mythologies.

The insistence by the major Western religions that the world itself is not merely under the control but is the *product* of a god with divine perfections has been an additional source of much unnecessary suffering and anxiety, not to mention inevitable confusion, smug denial, and just plain scientific illiteracy. So in the next two chapters we turn to tales of creation, myths embedded in Homer and the Tanakh that "explain" the nature of human existence. The creation tales that the contemporary faithful have turned to for solace and clarification in their search for meaning are inadequate once again, especially when contrasted with the turbulent cosmic history assumed in the Homeric epics.

Notes

1 Every skeptic knows Ambrose Bierce's piercing definition of the verb "to pray": "To ask that the laws of the universe be annulled in behalf of a single petitioner, confessedly unworthy."
2 Odysseus tells us that the Sirens claim to know "whatever happens upon the much-nourishing earth" (*Od.* 12.191), but no one vouches for them, and it turns out they aren't even aware that their own efforts to lure Odysseus to his death will fail.
3 On one occasion we learn that nothing "is revocable, or deceitful, or unfulfilled, to which I [Zeus] nod my head" (1.526–7; cf. 17.209). This gesture marks the most important decision in the *Iliad*, Zeus's granting of Thetis' request to aid the Trojans in order (ultimately) to give honor to Achilles. And Poseidon seems to confirm the irreversibility of the Jovian nod when he admits to his brother that "I did not altogether deprive him [Odysseus] of his return as soon as you promised it and gave your assent [nodded your head]" (*Od.* 13.132–3). But the implication is that at other times Zeus's word might be changed or unfulfilled, and indeed he is known to change his mind, and not everything he wishes comes to fruition.
4 Zeus is also jolted into prophylactic action when Helius threatens to "enter Hades and shine among the dead" (*Od.* 12.382). Apparently Zeus wouldn't be able (or doesn't want to be forced to try) to stop him.
5 The pain of the gods is genuine but temporary. When Hephaestus was thrown from heaven by Zeus, he landed on Lemnos with "little life still in me" and needed tending by the locals (1.592–4). "Pain reached" him due his ejection by Hera and subsequent fall as well (18.395–6).
6 Noriko Yasumura argues that these episodes of binding evoke the Succession Myth (2011:40–57; cf. Slatkin 1991:66–70). In post-Homeric literature and art, Hephaestus is said to have taken his revenge on Hera for tossing him out of Olympus by creating a magical throne for her. She sits in it and is "bound." Ares is sent to fetch Dionysus but is chased off. Dionysus manages to bring Hephaestus to Olympus by getting him drunk, and Hera is released.
7 In later Greek literature a challenge to Zeus crops up in the form of the Giants. There was a lengthy battle – a Gigantomachy often confused or conflated later with the battle against the Titans, the Titanomachy (which we will examine in the next chapter) – that was only brought to a successful conclusion when Heracles joined the side of the Olympians. Homer knows of Giants, but some commentators have concluded that "Homer doesn't know that the Giants fought against the gods" (scholion on *Od.* 7.59; cf. Hainsworth 1988:324). Other critics, however, have found "frequent allusions" to Zeus's near overthrow by the Giants (Janko 1992:169). Athena recalls the destruction of this "insolent" and "wild" people through their own recklessness (*Od.* 7.58–60; cf. 206), which sounds to me like a possible reference to the Gigantomachy. The monstrously cannibalistic Laestrygonians, at least one of whom is as "big as a peak of a mountain," are said to attack Odysseus' comrades "not like men, but like Giants" (*Od.* 10.112–124). Homer is content to conjure up the Giants only a couple times, but that is enough to remind a well-versed audience of their former threat to Zeus and the Olympians: "The mythological allusions . . . point to the contingency of Zeus's rule" (Friedman 2001:103).
8 One scholar, using what I think is an unrealistically strict definition of prayer, has calculated that 63 percent of all prayers get a positive response, although even he concludes the primary function of prayers, granted or not, is to prepare the audience for later episodes (Morrison 1991).

Section II
Creating meaning

9 Homeric creation

Cosmogonic myths – stories about the origins and structure of the universe – are designed to address social, political, historical, psychological, and religious issues of importance to those telling – and listening to – the tales. These narratives naturally reveal far more about the fears, hopes, and assumptions of the creators of the tale than about the actual origin of the cosmos, a topic that lies in the purview of science. Take this version from ancient Egypt:

> Atum created by his masturbation in Heliopolis. He put his phallus in his fist, to excite desire thereby. The twins were born, Shu and Tefnut.
> (Pyramid Text: Utterance 527, Mercer, tr.)

This, as they say in the theological biz, is creation by the hand of god. Each culture of the ancient Near East produced multiple, contradictory creation stories. From Egypt, for example, in addition to the "self-generating" variant provided above from Heliopolis, we have cosmogonies associated with many different places and various creator gods, some of which have a more familiar ring, with creation brought about by the word or breath of god or through the metaphor of a craftsman working with clay (Clifford 1994).

The Greeks possessed numerous creation tales as well. Homer does not focus on the origins of the universe or the Olympians, taking for granted a significant awareness of this material from his listeners. Although most scholars consider him to be our first extant Greek author (Rosen 1997:464–73), he was drawing on hundreds of years of oral tradition and often refers casually to events and figures outside of the narrative. Classicists have spent a good deal of effort trying to determine if Homer is alluding to one specific version of a tale or drawing from a shifting and multifaceted tradition or perhaps inventing his own versions as he goes along. All three answers are likely to be correct at different places in the poems. Because these references are often brief and elusive, to explore creation in the epics we will need to bring in other early texts, especially Hesiod's *Theogony*, a 1000-verse epic that most scholars believe was composed shortly after Homer's poems. Our knowledge will not be exact. Homer no doubt drew on numerous cosmogonic traditions, some of which are no longer extant, and most likely he was completely unaware of some of the myths that we encounter in later authors. But we can piece together a reasonable picture of the primeval history of the Homeric gods as the poet envisioned it.

In this chapter we will turn our attention to what is called the Succession Myth, the narrative common to Near Eastern and Indo-European mythologies of a sequence of intrafamily generational battles between gods for control of the universe. *Everybody* wants to be king of the cosmos. There are numerous allusions to the Olympians' struggles with their parents' generation (called the Titans) for power. This reconstruction of the "history" of the gods of the *Iliad* and *Odyssey* is another important step towards recovering Homer's accomplishment and its potential benefits for us today.

For most people, there is a direct connection, either explicit or unexpressed, between their views of the divine and their thoughts on the origins of the world. What is most important in the case of the Homeric variant of the creation story – similar to many other creation narratives but crucially different from Genesis, the formative myth of Western culture – is that the creator god is *not* the god who presently sits in power, and his authority is not unchallenged. Zeus did not create the universe and is not responsible for it; rather, he was born (Greek gods have beginnings), fought to take control of it, and continues to guard his throne with understandable zealotry. We will see that a similar myth is also hinted at throughout the Hebrew Bible, with Yahweh's battles against cosmic adversaries to establish or maintain his control, and thus we can appreciate his equally justified obsession with divine competition. But whereas Yahweh absorbs the diverse (and some would argue irreconcilable) roles of national deity, warrior, universal god and creator, Homer separates creation from the god who is currently on the throne.

Also critically important is what is *not* in the epics – an account of human creation. Humans are not at the center of the universe in early Greek thought, and in fact mythological reflection on the origins of our species remains a refreshingly minor concern for most of Greek history. Any meaning we find in life will not come from a debt we owe to our creator. No one granted us dominion. We are neither the culminating act of creation nor the eternally disappointing failures of a divine potter or orthopedic surgeon. Our existence didn't come built in with 613 regulations for pleasing the gods or avoiding their wrath, and we have no divine offering of a blessed eternity provided we confess faith in the Truth of a fabled biography. Meaning for our lives doesn't come from a fictional account of human origins in the mythical past but from the daily exploration of our humanity. The search by the major Western religions for the True origins of the universe in a religious myth bound to an omnipotent and benevolent creator has led to strained, bitter, and ultimately futile theological wrangling and a costly, pointless battle between myth and science. But the real price has been paid by those mortals who have been convinced that this creative act put them in the center of a meaningful cosmos with a divine blueprint for contemporary life spelled out in ancient mythological texts.

While Zeus's position in the cosmos is not original, absolute, or necessarily eternal, and human origins are of no consequence to Homer, the late editors of the Tanakh try very hard to position Yahweh as the primeval and timeless

CEO of the cosmos, with humans as his all-consuming product. Homer's vision of the divine eliminates the clumsy efforts necessitated in Abrahamic religions to account for the patently imperfect nature of God's creation under the eternal administration of a single just, omnipotent, loving, perfect (etc.) deity. In Homer's case, once we see how the gods got to be who and where they are, we can begin to understand how the world is constituted. This picture runs exactly counter to the traditional Judeo-Christian understanding of creation myths, which argues that "the polytheistic accounts of creation often present narratives of the gods' follies and misdeeds which the modern world cannot take seriously as a basis for personal belief" (Lambert 2008:16). But this "personal belief" is a matter of enculturation rather than any reasoned argument. Does the world really look or function like the product of a God of divine perfections? Besides, *which* biblical creation tale is to be taken so seriously?

The disjunction between God and human reality is so severe that we've needed 2500 years of textual and theological therapy to try to make it work. Not so with Homer's Olympians. As we saw in the last chapter, the gods' extremely imperfect actions – their competition, rivalries, favoritism, and reluctantly shared offices – affect humans unpredictably, both positively and adversely. That's just the way it is: "To ascribe the origin and fabric of the universe to these imperfect beings never enters into the imagination of any polytheist . . ." (Hume 1964:47). To Homeric polytheism and anthropomorphism we will now add divine "history" to account for the indifferent and mercurial universe we inhabit. Our energy then needs to be spent on discovering how to live meaningful lives within that reality, rather than on the impossible task of trying to reconcile the realities of existence with a 2500-year old myth of a "very good" (Gen 1:31) world created by a benevolent and all-powerful deity.

Growing up (a) god

The Olympians have beginnings. Beyond the ubiquitous patronymics (nicknames that refer to one's father), Homer's epics leave little room for background details. Still, a number of allusions suggest the audience was familiar with the gods' biographies. Ares makes a sly and disgruntled reference to Athena's birth from Zeus's head (5.880), and we can assume that Hephaestus was young when he was tossed from Olympus by his mother, "who wished to hide me because I was lame" (18.396–7).[1] The incident surely refers to her *initial* disgust at his deformity, since it's clear that she has come to accept him and perhaps even appreciate his talents (he built her house) by the time the *Iliad* begins. The one extended tale in the epics about Dionysus (6.130–40) refers to his attendant band of "nurses," the Greek word used elsewhere by Homer only to refer to the nurse of Hector's infant son Astyanax (6.132; cf. 6.389, 467; 22.503). It appears that Dionysus was once a child.[2]

Accounts of the Olympians' births and youthful exploits no doubt proliferated, and shortly after Homer's time, hymns in honor of the gods began to be codified into what eventually became a corpus known as the *Homeric Hymns*. The third hymn in this collection depicts the birth of Apollo, whose healthy diet of ambrosia and nectar causes him to burst out of his swaddling clothes. Dionysus is raised by nymphs (*HHymn* 26), Athena explodes from Zeus's head (*HHymn* 28), and Persephone is a nubile young teenager (*HHymn* 2). But by far the most spectacular tale of a god's birth and youth is that in the fourth hymn, which focuses entirely on the first 48 roguish hours in the life of Hermes, his celebrated "frauds and thefts" (Hobbes' *Leviathan* 1.10). It will be worth reviewing this amusing version of a god's birth to appreciate the thorough comfort Homer and his audience would have with the assumption of a deity's origins in time.

The poet of the *Hymn* begins by asking the Muse to sing of Hermes, "the son of Zeus and Maia, guardian of Cyllene and Arcadia rich in flocks . . ." (1–3). Within hours of his birth in a cave where "the son of Cronus unseen by deathless gods and mortal men used to have sex with the nymph of lovely hair in the middle of the night, as long as sweet sleep had a hold on white-armed Hera" (6–9), Hermes eviscerates a tortoise and invents the lyre. Forget about the lyre for a second and note the explicit reference to the adulterous affair Zeus was having with Maia. He apparently (and with some regularity) slipped out of his bed while his wife, Hera, was asleep, and snuck into a cave to have sex with Maia. Not only is the hymnist not embarrassed by this acknowledgment, he notes that Hermes himself proudly celebrates his parentage. For immediately after tuning his new invention, Hermes croons the first song ever crafted for the lyre, "about Zeus the son of Cronus and Maia of the beautiful sandals, how they used to chat intimately in close affection, Hermes thus announcing his own renowned ancestry" (57–9). The newborn's musical talent is amazing in its own right – imagine Moses breaking into a musical number (perhaps "Proud Mary"?) as his little reed raft heads down the Nile. But Hermes' song happily extolls the details of his parents' illicit affair. The form of the verbs that both the hymnist and Hermes use indicates that the relationship went on for some time – no one-nighter here. By the standards of Zeus (who was credited by ancient scholars with over 130 sexual partners), this was a serious relationship. Hermes, a god-in-the-making but of course not yet recognized as a major player, is establishing his own credentials. His parentage suggests that he has what it takes to become an Olympian.

A few hours (!) later Hermes steals 50 of Apollo's cattle, not to eat them (he doesn't – he's tempted, but gods don't eat human food, and he *so* wants to climb that divine ladder) but to draw attention to his existence. He's a god with a plan. A tiny god, to be sure – keep in mind that he may be divine, but he still has the size and appearance of a human infant. Myths involving cattle theft had a long Indo-European pedigree, and Hermes' actions may reflect rites of initiation into adulthood, or in his case, godhood. After creating the first fire stick in order to start a fire, he tosses two of the cattle onto their backs and slaughters them in a fully professional manner. He then sets aside 12 portions for the gods. It's not clear if this is for a sacrifice or a meal, but in either case one can only assume he's already counting himself an Olympian, even though the canonical number "12" is a comparatively late innovation (Long 1987; Rutherford 2010).

Not a bad first day. He tries to sneak back into the cave, but Maia spots him and warns him that Apollo will be angry. That, apparently, is exactly what Hermes has in mind. This is one ambitious baby. No more hanging out in a cave for this aspiring tyke – 24 hours of that is more than enough. He's going to get his mother and himself to Olympus. Even Jesus didn't bounce out of the cradle to announce to the three wise men that both he *and* his mom would be translated to heaven one day (which has been the official Catholic assumption since 1950). Moreover, Hermes insists that if Apollo tries to find him, he will break into the temple at Delphi and steal lots of "beautiful tripods and cauldrons and gold and plenty of flashing iron and many clothes" (179–81). Hermes has more confidence and self-esteem than a California public school student.

The next morning Apollo tracks his stolen cattle back to the cave and confronts the resourceful babe. Hermes denies everything:

> Son of Leto, what is this harsh word you declare? . . . What you are saying makes no sense. I was born yesterday, and my feet are delicate and the ground beneath is rough. But if you wish, I will swear a great oath by my father's head: I promise that neither I myself am guilty nor have I seen any other thief of your cows, whatever cows are; for I hear of them only through rumor.
>
> (261–77)

Hermes is so innocent that he has never even *seen* a cow. What *is* a cow? He's only a day old, for god's sake! But Apollo isn't buying it, and he grabs Hermes to carry him off. The infant immediately reveals his intestinal fortitude:

> But then the strong Argus-slayer [Hermes] at once devised a plan, and as he was being lifted up in the hands of Apollo he sent forth an omen, a reckless servant of the belly, a rash messenger, and he quickly sneezed afterwards. When Apollo heard it, he threw glorious Hermes from his hands onto the ground.
>
> (294–8)

Most scholars interpret the "reckless servant of the belly" as a fart. Scatological humor is pure comedy, as the Greek playwright Aristophanes (and any ten-year-old boy) can tell you. The Olympians can laugh and be laughed at under the right circumstances. In Aristophanes' *Frogs* – a comedy performed at a festival in honor of Dionysus – the god Dionysus is the lead character, and at one point shits in terror (479)! A character in Aristophanes' *Clouds* says that he believed rain was just Zeus pissing in a sieve.

Hermes is taken by Apollo to Olympus so Zeus can settle the matter in front of the "scales of judgment." Apollo lays out the charges against Hermes, who answers them with brazen denial:

> Believe me (for you claim to be my dear father), that I did not drive his cows to my home – so may I prosper! – or even cross over the threshold. I'm declaring this in all truth. I have much reverence for Helius and the other gods, and I love you, and I respect him. You yourself know that I am not

guilty. And I will give a great oath: by these well-adorned porches of the gods, there is no way I will ever pay for this ruthless theft, as strong as he [Apollo] may be; but come to the aid of us younger ones.

(378–86)

And how does Zeus respond to this bluster? He laughs aloud "seeing his evil-scheming child well and skillfully denying his guilt about the cattle" (389–90). Zeus bids them get along and tells Hermes to show Apollo where he has hidden the cattle. They obey him – not even Hermes will mess with Zeus at this point. He gives Apollo the lyre as a friendship gift, and then invents the reed pipe for himself.

There is more, but you get the picture. The Greeks had no problem considering the beginnings of their gods; and they had a sense of humor, something sadly missing in the gods of the major Western religions. Now it's time to turn to the generational struggle that takes place before Hermes' birth for control of the cosmos. Creation and the current Olympian regime are carefully separated in Homer, which goes a long way towards explaining the mess we're all in.

How did Zeus get on top?

Let's start with a couple of patronymics: *Kronidês* and *Kronion*. Both mean "son of Cronus" and are used with Zeus's name and as substitutes for his name over 100 times in the *Iliad* and *Odyssey*. Homer expects his audience to know about this relationship, and that it's an important one, since there are only a handful of extremely brief allusions to Cronus himself. The first thing to note – something we take for granted in Greek myth in general but is crucially significant – is that Zeus has a *history*. There was a time *before* Zeus, before he and the other Olympians who currently "rule" the cosmos existed, much less came into power. Unlike Yahweh, who in Genesis 1 must be assumed to have been around forever and unengendered (although there are hints elsewhere, as we have seen, that he was once viewed as a son and brother), Zeus has a father. And a mother, too, and siblings. As Hera reminds him, "my lineage is from the same origin as yours – crooked-counseling Cronus fathered me as the most venerable of his daughters, both by birth and because I am called your wife" (4.58–61). So who is this Cronus, and why is his most frequent epithet "crooked-counseling"?

The references to Cronus in Homer all focus on the uncomfortable relationship he has with Zeus: Cronus exists to be overthrown by his own son. Zeus "sent Cronus down under the earth and the restless sea" (14.203–4), where he and his brother Iapetus now "sit and take pleasure neither in the light of Helius Hyperion nor in the breezes, but deep Tartarus surrounds them" (8.479–81). Iapetus and Cronus are two of "all the gods dwelling below in Tartarus, who are called Titans" (14.278–9; cf. 274), those "gods who are down below, who are with Cronus" (15.225).

Homer is referring to the Titanomachy, the fight over succession to divine rule between Zeus, his siblings, and allies on one side and most of his parents' generation on the other. This myth forms the backbone to Hesiod's *Theogony*, the most influential cosmology for the Greeks (but by no means the only one), which in turn was highly influenced by similar succession myths found in Hurro-Hittite, Babylonian, and Syrian texts. Other references and allusions in the *Iliad* suggest that we will not be too far off if we imagine Homer had something similar to Hesiod's version in mind as the background to the Olympian ascendancy to power. A review of Hesiod's account of the generational battle for cosmic power will enable us to sketch a reasonably clear picture of Homer's own vision of the history of the cosmos. Once we have reviewed Hesiod's epic account – composed, most scholars believe, very close in time to Homer's poems – we will be able to turn Homer's scattered references into a fairly coherent picture. Hesiod had different thematic intentions in his poems and an independent vision of the meaning of Zeus's rise to power than we find in Homer. But for our purposes, we are using merely the bare bones of his tale – our best source for the relevant mythological tradition – to help tease out Homer's vision of creation.

Hesiod's *Theogony* and Homer

Hesiod's creation tale begins with the appearance (Hesiod does not specify *how* or *whence*) of four principal deities: Chaos, which is often translated as "Chasm" because the Greek root denotes a gap rather than disorder, although its exact nature remains cloudy; then Gaia, or Earth, described in her future role as "the firm seat of the immortals who inhabit the peaks of snowy Olympus"; Tartarus, the murky depths of the earth (some scholars interpret it as part of earth, but it has a distinct and separate existence later in the poem); and Eros, the power of sexual passion, a little cocktail to kick the party into high gear. The following chart should help keep the basic structure of the generational battles clear:[3]

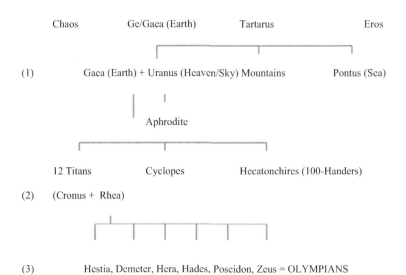

Chaos	Ge/Gaea (Earth)	Tartarus		Eros

(1)   Gaea (Earth) + Uranus (Heaven/Sky)   Mountains   Pontus (Sea)

Aphrodite

12 Titans	Cyclopes	Hecatonchires (100-Handers)

(2)   (Cronus + Rhea)

(3)   Hestia, Demeter, Hera, Hades, Poseidon, Zeus = OLYMPIANS

Hesiod enumerates multiple offspring of Chaos, but our focus can be on Earth, who parthenogenetically (without a mate) produces Uranus (Heaven or Sky) and several other deities. Gaea and Uranus, Earth and Sky, then form the first dynastic couple (row 1 above), a "sacred marriage" that results in three batches of children: Six sons and six daughters who will later be named "Titans" by their father; three Cyclopes who will eventually fashion Zeus's thunderbolts; and the "100-Handed Ones," a traditional if unwieldy (and un-Hesiodic) name for three brothers who have 100 arms, 50 heads, and "the mighty strength in their great figure was tremendous" (*Theogony* 153).

Now begins the fun of cosmic familial turmoil. For some unstated reason, Sky was not pleased with his children. In fact he *hated* them, never allowing them to see the light of day: "As soon as any of them was born, he hid them all away in a secret place of Earth and did not let them into the light, and Sky delighted in his evil deed" (156–8). This most likely means that Sky never ceased having intercourse with Earth, their children being crammed back in the womb or birth canal. "Earth groaned within" and formulated a "crafty, evil cunning." She fashioned a big, jagged-toothed, adamantine sickle.[4] Earth asked if any of her children would volunteer to ply her new creation to "avenge your father's evil outrage" (165–6). Only the youngest Titan, Cronus "of crooked counsel," has the courage. He is uniquely placed for the deed his mother has in mind, wedged within her reproductive tract as he is. Cronus "reached out with his left hand from his hiding place, and with his right hand he took hold of the monstrous sickle, long and jagged, and he swiftly reaped the genitals from his dear father and threw them behind to be carried away" (178–82). This trenchant tale is an example of a common folk motif explaining the separation of Earth and Sky (think Chicken Little, or better yet, Jack and the Beanstalk – you'll never view that severed stalk quite the same). We now know why the Sky stays up there and doesn't collapse upon the Earth.

Thus we have the first revolution, with Cronus (row 2) now running things after his bloody coup. His epithet "of crooked counsel" probably originally meant "of bent sickle," a reflection of his most infamous act, but the sense had changed by the time of Homer and Hesiod.[5] And there are some positive if unanticipated side effects. From the severed genitals of Sky, for example, tossed into the "great swelling sea," develops Aphrodite, who floats around the Mediterranean until she walks ashore on Cyprus, the grass sprouting beneath her lovely feet (188–206). This version of Aphrodite's origin is quite different from the one we find in Homer, whose Aphrodite is the pampered daughter of Zeus and Dione. Homer and Hesiod are drawing on different traditions or inventing variants to suit their own thematic purposes, which is why we must tread with some caution when using Hesiod's account to illuminate Homer's assumptions about creation.

Hesiod's gods are now propagating as fast as the poet can name them. Eventually he returns to the offspring of the Titans, as they match up to produce a variety of important deities. This initial catalogue culminates with the "marriage" of Cronus and Rhea, Titanic siblings who produce a group of "splendid children" that will form the core of the Olympian dynasty (row 3): Hestia, Demeter, Hera,

Hades, Poseidon, and Zeus (453–58). With children, though, comes the inevitable threat to kingship. Cronus learns from Earth and Sky that "although he was strong, it was destined for him to be overcome by his own child, through the plans of great Zeus" (463–5).[6] To abort the revolt, Cronus resorts to a variant of his father's strategy – he keeps his children from seeing the light of day by swallowing each one as he or she pops out of Rhea's womb, taking care that "no one else of Sky's illustrious children would hold royal office among the immortals" (461–2). Rhea is gripped with "unceasing grief," but it is not until the sixth child that she takes evasive action. Once again Earth and Sky provide crucial advice, telling Rhea to give birth to Zeus secretly on Crete. She subsequently hands a huge stone in swaddling clothes to Cronus in place of newly born Zeus. Cronus happily swallows the stone in one gulp, thinking he has preserved his kingship.

Zeus, however, is alive and well in a Cretan cave, and his strength and "glorious limbs" grow quickly. We don't want to miss a crucial point in the midst of this multilayered cosmology: Hesiod's Zeus was born as an infant, deposited on Crete, and there was nursed and reared. Later accounts provide all sorts of details about his raising by various nurses and guardians (including a goat and noisily dancing warriors), but the important observation is that gods have beginnings.

A year later Zeus somehow "by cunning devices and force" (and with help from Earth) manages to get Cronus to vomit up Zeus's siblings. Hesiod is thankfully sparing when it comes to the details. Zeus and his siblings must now fight for supremacy against their father's cosmic dynasty.[7] In preparation for the upcoming battle, Zeus frees the Cyclopes, who had remained trapped inside Earth when the Titans escaped. Hesiod tells us that these brothers in gratitude manufacture thunder, the thunderbolt, and lightning for Zeus. Hesiod concludes this section proleptically by noting that it is with these weapons that Zeus "rules over mortals and immortals" (506), nudging us slowly towards the inevitable generational conflict.

Bring 'em on

Hesiod picks up the Titanomachy, this time with Zeus and his siblings freeing the other three forgotten offspring of Sky still trapped "under the wide-pathed earth" (620), the 100-Handed Ones. Zeus and his siblings fight from Olympus, the war against the Titans raging "in mighty battles" for ten years with no advantage to either side. Zeus turns to the 100-Handed Ones and in the manner of a Homeric chieftain rouses them to fight, not hesitating to remind them that they owe him big time for deliverance from their "dank gloom" (653). Zeus heaves thunderbolts with newly inspired passion, the entire cosmos shaking, the earth blazing, the noise and shouting and screaming on both sides reminding Hesiod of the sound of Heaven mounting Earth during sex. And you know what *that's* like. The battle remains a stalemate until suddenly, within a little over four verses, the three 100-Handed Ones chuck a boulder from each hand (that would be 300 boulders for the math-challenged) and "covered over the Titans with their missiles" (713–17). They send the Titans down under the earth in chains to Tartarus, fenced in by a bronze barricade with gates built by Poseidon.

At this point, Zeus would appear to be securely in place. But wait! The Succession Myth can't just stop, or it wouldn't be a myth of succession. Zeus, like his father and grandfather, must immediately face a challenge to his kingship, this time from a monstrous creature called by Hesiod both Typhoeus and Typhon, from whose neck sprout 100 serpentine heads blazing fire. This "monster of hurricanes and winds" (845–6) is given a water-monster nature as well in later texts, thus connecting him with a common motif in Near Eastern creation myths, as we will see in the next chapter. He is "acosmia incarnate," disorder that "threatens to dismantle the articulated cosmos" (Clay 2003:26). Zeus uses his customary weapons and hurls Typhoeus "into wide Tartarus, causing him grief in his spirit" (867–8). Hesiod informs us that the Olympians then encouraged far-thundering Zeus to become king and to rule over the immortals, and "he distributed their honors well for them" (884–5).[8]

So Zeus is in his heaven, all's okay with the world, right? But there's still the potential for further problems, and Hesiod wants Zeus to put a stop to the revolving kingships. We've had sons castrating fathers and fathers ingesting sons, but no one has swallowed a spouse . . . yet. Zeus takes Mêtis (Cunning Intelligence) for his first wife, who "of the gods and mortal human beings knows the most" (887). But when she is about to give birth, Earth and Sky deliver another ominous prophecy: "She [Mêtis] would give birth first to a maiden, gleaming-eyed Tritogeneia [Athena], possessing strength equal to her father's and thoughtful counsel, but then to a son, a king of gods and of men, possessing an overly violent heart" (895–8). So Zeus puts his pregnant wife "into his belly," thereby gaining the double benefit of removing the chance that "some other one of the ever-living gods hold the royal honor instead of Zeus" (892–30) and also assuring that "the goddess would take counsel with him about good and evil" (900). Zeus thus manages (by the tortuous logic of myth) to gain cunning intelligence (one of his frequent epithets is *mêtieta*, "all-wise"), give birth to a daughter (Athena) who will be his closest divine companion, and stop the merry-go-round of cosmic succession.

Creation in Homer

That's Hesiod's account. How much of this material does Homer refer to or assume his audience knows? (We are not concerned with direction of influence here, that is, which composer drew from whom, but simply what elements of Hesiod's Succession Myth seem to stand in the background of Homer's understanding of the gods' origins.) Homer is aware of the union of Earth and Sky as found in Hesiod's *Theogony*, but he does not seem to subscribe to their primacy in the succession myth. Gaia and Uranus are twice invoked by Olympian deities when taking oaths in a formulaic pattern (15.36–8; *Od.* 5.184–6), a reflection of some sort of primordial importance. And both times they are linked with the river Styx, who is uniquely associated by Hesiod with the Succession Myth.[9]

For Homer, however, the first power par excellence is Oceanus, and the primeval pair may be Oceanus and his spouse Tethys (both relatively minor Titans in Hesiod) rather than Sky and Earth.[10] Homer insists that Oceanus is not just a deity "from whom flow all rivers and the entire sea and all the springs and deep wells" (21.196–7) but the "origin [*genesis*] of the gods" (14.201, 302) and even "the origin for everything" (14.246; Clay 1992:137). The important point of all this is that Homer, like Hesiod, clearly views the world progressively, with an earlier generation of gods, not the Olympians, as progenitors of the cosmos.

The Homeric poems make no direct reference to Cronus' ingestion of his children – Homer tends to avoid narrating the more bizarre aspects of myth (or puts them in mouths of his characters) – but there is some interesting indirect testimony based on the culturally crucial issue of primogeniture. Stay with me on this. Being the eldest brother is a good thing. While in myth and folklore it is often the *youngest* child – Cronus is a good example, or Jacob and David – who ends up doing something spectacular, it stinks to be a younger brother when it comes to inheritance. The Olympians' gastric genesis in Cronus' belly, however, makes for an entertaining argument (if you are really, really desperate): Who was actually born first? Hesiod's order is clear: Hestia, Demeter, Hera, Hades, Poseidon, and Zeus. Zeus thus is the youngest. But that is the exit alignment from Rhea's womb. The initial five gods never make it out into the world the first time around, instead heading right into Cronus' belly for an extended "gestation." So, you *could* argue that Zeus is the eldest sibling, since he's the first one actually out into the world (Heiden 2008:173). Thus in an early *Homeric Hymn* Hestia is said to have been born first and also be the youngest "by the plan of aegis-holding Zeus" (*HH* 5.22–4). Homer may take advantage of this ambiguity. If the poet needs Zeus to be older, as he does in the various familial conflicts (especially with Poseidon) in the *Iliad*, he is acknowledged as the senior sibling of the three males (13.354–5; 15.164–6, 181–2). In the *Odyssey*, however, Homer spares Zeus's reputation by giving him an excuse for not intervening sooner on Odysseus' behalf – he did not want to go against the wishes of what now turns out to be his *elder* brother (*Od.* 13.141–2). Thus Zeus can have it both ways: He is youngest (folklorically good) by WDT (Womb Departure Time) and simultaneously oldest (culturally excellent) by SMT (Swaddled by Mom Time). So it's possible to connect Homer's flip-flopping on the Poseidon-Zeus/Zeus-Poseidon birth order with Hesiod's account of their "double" births. Homer seems to be aware of this tradition of Cronus' voracious parenting. (Sadly, no one seems to care where Hades fits into any of this sibling rivalry, a neglected middle child stuck in the underworld.)

Homer knows about the Titanomachy, referring at separate moments to the relegation of Cronus to Tartarus, calling the Titans "gods who are in the world below with Cronus."[11] The vacillating birth order of the children of Cronus and Rhea, the close association of Styx with Earth, Sky, and the Titans, as well as the general agreement of genealogical material, all suggest that Homer was familiar with something like Hesiod's account. Homer also knows of the 100-Handed Ones, or at least one of them, as we saw in the previous chapter. Briareus (also called Obriareus in Hesiod) was the 100-handed savior of Zeus whom Thetis fetched to ward off the rebellious efforts of Poseidon, Hera, and Athena to bind him (1.396–406).[12]

Homer would seem to agree with Hesiod that Zeus gains his ascendancy to the top of the Olympian gang soon after the defeat of the Titans and solidifies his control with the defeat of the storm monster Typhoeus. Homer refers once to Typhoeus in a simile describing the force of the attacking Greek army: "And the earth groaned, as it does for an angry Zeus, delighting in the thunderbolt, when he lashes the land around Typhoeus in the land of the Arimi, where they say is the lair of Typhoeus" (2.781–3). As with the Titanomachy, Homer clearly expects his audience to be acquainted with the story (or stories) conjured up by a name alone (Nimis 1987:73–84).[13]

Consequences

Three obvious but crucial conclusions emerge from our efforts to uncover the background to Homer's Olympian pantheon:

1) Zeus and the Olympians are not responsible for creation of the cosmos but instead inherit whatever structure and rules were initially established. Don't turn to them for explanations – they were heirs to the same cosmos that you and I live in. The Olympians, the gods who currently influence human life, have historical origins *after* creation.[14]

2) Creation is not "good" or meant to be "good" in relation to humans. It's not bad either. The cosmos emerges in the form of deities. For Hesiod, there are four primal gods – he makes no effort to account for the nature of their "births." Homer mentions only in passing that Oceanus was the origin of gods and perhaps "all"; the question of where the "early" gods came from is simply not of interest, and the "quality" of creation is not an issue.

3) Homer is not concerned with the origin of humans as a species: "That myth which elsewhere is one of the most important of all is almost completely suppressed in Greek mythology: the creation of man by gods" (Burkert 1985:188; cf. Kirk 1990:7). In this lack of speculation the Greeks are actually quite distinct from almost all their Mediterranean neighbors. In a different text (*Works and Days*), Hesiod tells a myth about the gods' creation of different *ages* of mankind. The previous four ages have all been led to extinction, and the current Iron Age is the worst of all, fated to be destroyed by Zeus. Hesiod is so fascinated with – and annoyed by – the creation of *woman* that he relates the story of Pandora *twice* in two different poems, but the beginnings of humankind are not even a matter for conjecture. Homer is not interested in human origins either and has nothing to say on the issue.[15]

The Greeks in general were far more fascinated with cultural than physical anthropology or anthropogony (Heath 2005c:24–9). Just as the Homeric epics do not offer a world designed for humans, they never suggest humans were designed by god(s) for some specific purpose. Humans just are. Our lot is a limited and tragic one, not the zenith of a deity's workweek or the favored species or chosen nation of divine creation. The gods pity our existence and often regret dragging themselves into our affairs. As Hephaestus remarks to Hera after she quarrels with Zeus in the first book of the *Iliad*:

This will surely be destructive business and no longer endurable, if you two for the sake of mortals contend in this way and raise this wrangling among the gods. And there will be no enjoyment of our excellent feast, since the worse things prevail.

(1.573–6)

Human events are not worth disrupting the divine party. Similarly, as the gods face each other to do battle, Apollo addresses his potential opponent, Poseidon:

Earth-Shaker, you would not say that I was sound-minded if I should fight with you for the sake of miserable mortals, who are now like leaves full of the fire of life, eating the fruit of the field, but now waste away to death. But let us cease from the fight with all haste, and let them contend among themselves.

(21.462–7)

Even Zeus is forced to reflect upon human limitations when he sees the immortal horses of Achilles weeping in mourning for Patroclus, their dead charioteer:

Ah, miserable pair, why did we give you to lord Peleus, a mortal, but you are ageless and immortal? Was it so that you might have sorrows among unhappy men? For without doubt there is nothing more wretched than man of all the things that breathe and creep on earth.

(17.443–7)

The tragic, circumscribed nature of humanity is fully acknowledged by the heroes. We are all replaceable, and ultimately replaced:

Just as generations of leaves, such is that also of men. The wind scatters some leaves on the ground, but the dense forest produces others when the season of spring draws on; so with a generation of men – it comes into being, and passes away.

(6.146–9)

The threat of their potential (and likely) insignificance is the driving force behind the heroes' struggle to *do* something, to strive for honor, glory, and epic or monumental fame, their primary means to transcend mortal limitations.

There is no imagined "divine meaning" or heavenly "purpose-driven" life for mortals. Homer understands that. But he also sees that a life without some cosmic justification or explanation is not a source for depression or an excuse for sloth or a cause of hedonistic amorality, common criticisms from concerned theists. The exact opposite is the case – such a world demands heroic acceptance of the daunting responsibility to make a difference. We, of course, may (and should) search for meaning in other places than lethal duels on the battlefield or mere procreation, just as Achilles comes to realize at the end of the *Iliad*. But we also face an acute obligation to look beyond the "answers" supplied by an antediluvian mythology.

In the world of Homer's poems, the universe is not created as a benevolent *or* hostile environment to humans. The gods within it may certainly be either at various times, but those deities have not always been in charge and may not always have authority. Our existence is embedded in a world that was not created for us or the current divine regime. We are not the culminating act of creation, as in the Tanakh: "Yet you have made them [human beings] a little lower than God [or 'gods' or 'angels'], and crowned them with glory and honor" (Ps 8:5). For Homer, the universe just came to be and is currently determined by the violent and rather random consequences of intrafamilial power struggles and fallible deities.

There are no expectations that the world is fair or just or designed with us in mind or that there is some hidden divine meaning in it all just because we happen to have evolved to the point of self-reflection. The universe just *is*. We just *are*. Zeus and his siblings fought to take over dominion of the known universe, subduing the previous generation and using luck (the shaking out of lots) to divide up the conquered territory. On the other hand, the Olympians may be an improvement over the earlier ruling powers. Sky and Cronus seemed to rely on simple force alone, while Zeus is constantly driven into some sort of deal-making and even a bit of compromise. Scholar of Greek religion John Gould puts it well: "The Homeric image of divinity is an image of marvelous and compelling adequacy; it underwrites and explains the human sense of contradiction and conflict in experience, and yet contains contradiction within a more fundamental order. It enables divinity to be understood as the source of disorder in the world, and, in the extreme case, mirrored in the myth of war between gods and giants, as the ultimate defence of order against brute chaos. . . ." (1985:25).

Humans, too, seem to have emerged without much notice. The gods currently "in charge" inherited the same "rules" as humans – not even they will stop a favored hero or beloved mortal child from his or her inevitable end. Sometimes good things happen; sometimes bad things. It's tragic but not sad. There is no "oppressive miasma of fatalism and pessimism" pervading the *Iliad*, as some contemporary readers despair (Gottschall 2008:4). Rather, Homer's world demands that you make your own meaning, that you engage in order to find a life worth living, that you grow up. And yes, our efforts will most likely come up short. "Only the fact of death can make action heroic; heroism and tragedy are the peculiar province and privilege of mortal man" (Knox 1964:50). Its vision is honest, realistic, and compelling. Our task is to think and act, to make our brief and happily random appearance here count as much as possible. Nothing could be more different from the kind of docile life demanded by the writers of the first chapter of Genesis.

Notes

1 Yoav Rinon suggests that Hephaestus was not born lame but became crippled when Zeus threw him off of Olympus. Hera then tosses him off because his lameness reminds

her of her losing quarrel with her husband (2008:129). It's fun (if difficult) to imagine Hera hoisting her adult son onto her shoulders and heaving him into the ocean.

2 Or so I take it, but Christos Tsagalis (2008:6–7) argues that the word for nurse here has Dionysiac rather than nurturing connotations. Why not both?

3 Some scholars understand Hesiod to be saying that Earth, Tartarus, and Eros descend from Chaos rather than emerge from the same mysterious origin as Chaos – the Greek merely lists the four entities one after the other.

4 Adamant is a legendary material used by the gods to make unbreakable objects, like shields and sickles. Homer, shying away from most aspects of mythological magic, never mentions it. But it would be good to have around.

5 Confusion between Cronus and Chronus, "Time," has led to the figure of Father Time bearing a sickle. It gives a whole new thrill to New Year's Eve.

6 Earth is consistently associated with prophecy, reproduction, and succession, but why Sky would overlook his missing genitals to warn his son remains a mystery. Since the Greek only says that Cronus "had heard" from his parents about this threat, perhaps Sky was not so much warning his son about it as taunting him (cf. *Th.* 210 and West 1966:295).

7 Robert Mondi suggests that the poet has combined two separate traditions, one in which Zeus struggles successfully with Cronus one-on-one for the kingship, and another that spreads the conflict between groups of gods representing each generation (1984, 1986).

8 The more frequent account of this distribution of divine authority is the drawing of lots as we find in Homer (15.187–93; Burkert 2004:35–6; Kelly 2008:262–73). There is another version (known from later sources) in which Typhoeus is much more formidable, managing to cut out Zeus's sinews and render him powerless until Hermes steals them back. Either Hesiod did not know that variant or did not want to depict a powerless Zeus, eager as he is to celebrate Zeus's regency. In one other strange variant, from the *Homeric Hymn to Apollo* (2.305–55), it is *Hera* who gives birth to Typhaon parthenogenically in revenge for Zeus's self-production of Athena! Here the cosmic challenge to Zeus's reign is combined with the kind of Olympian machinations we examined in the previous chapter.

9 Styx, Hesiod tells us long before his narrative actually makes it to the Titanomachy, earned her famous role as the "great oath of the gods" by being the first non-Olympian (along with her children) to join Zeus's side in the upcoming battle (*Th.* 383–403). In the *Iliad* Hera swears by the "inviolable water of Styx" and also, for no apparent reason, "invoked all the gods below Tartarus, who are called Titans" (14.271–9). By linking Earth, Sky, Styx, and the Titans, Homer seems to be acknowledging his awareness of something very similar to a Hesiodic cosmogony. And once Homer uses a term (*Ouraniônes*) that usually means "Gods of the Sky," that is, the Olympians, instead to label the *Titans* as "children of Uranus" (5.898; Kirk 1990:153).

10 Richard Janko (1992:180–2) has suggested that Homer's version may be similar to an Orphic theogony and have Near Eastern origins. Tethys would be related to a Near Eastern primal deity of the sea who is supplanted in a succession myth that we will find reflected in the Bible. But Kelly (2008:275–80) argues that Oceanus and Tethys need not be seen in these passages as the original couple.

11 Iapetus is the only other named Titan said to be punished along with Cronus in the epics. It is worth remembering the centrality of Iapetus' son, Prometheus, in Hesiod's tale.

12 Scholars have suggested that Homer at times refers not just to the tradition borrowed and developed by Hesiod but to other Titanomachies as well, including one credited to the epic cycle (D'Alessio 2015:202–12).

13 Not that Zeus's rule is necessarily secure after defeating Typhoeus. We saw in the previous chapter that Zeus must constantly be on the lookout for challenges to his authority. There are other myths that feature threats to Zeus's kingship, the most famous of which is that found in Aeschylus' *Prometheus Bound* (it first appears in the lyric

poet Pindar): A prophecy reveals that some unnamed female is fated to give birth to a son greater than the father, but only Prometheus knows who it is (Thetis). Since Zeus spends a good deal of his time having sex with random females – and, one assumes, he can only swallow so many of them – he must now live an unprecedented and no doubt frustratingly monogamous life. When Zeus finally learns the fateful mother-to-be is Thetis, he marries her off to the mortal hero Peleus. Their son, Achilles, is indeed greater than his father. Homer may have been aware of this tale. Scholars frequently point to the strange and unnecessary remark that Briareus is "better in strength than his father" (1.404), which could allude to the story (Slatkin 1991:70–7). There are several references to the wedding of Peleus and Thetis in the *Iliad*, which the gods attended (e.g., 24.62). Thetis also makes it very clear that Zeus forced her against her will to marry a mortal (18.429–34). Moreover, Zeus's seemingly excessive concern about Hera's reaction should she learn of Thetis' visit at the beginning of the *Iliad* makes sense when seen in the light of this amatory history (Yasumura 2011:18).

14 The text of Hesiod's *Theogony* ends with a series of Zeus's marriages and offspring that symbolize his reign. If these lines are indeed by Hesiod (which they may not be; West 1966:48–50, 398–9), it would seem that Zeus shifts the nature of human experience after he takes the cosmic reins, even if the basics of creation have already been established. But here Homer diverges almost completely from Hesiod's account, both in the details and in general. Homer's Zeus does not organize human experience through the marriage and production of abstractions.

15 Zeus is metaphorically the "father of men and gods," although he does his share of actual begetting of both. In a curious extension of this metaphor, at one point Odysseus complains aloud to Zeus that "you do not have compassion for men when you yourself gave them birth" (*Od.* 20.202). It has been suggested that this is a Homeric echo of a proverbial Near Eastern address to a chief divinity, "Do not destroy what you have created" (Russo 1992:118). Job cries out to Yahweh, "Your hands fashioned and made me; and now you turn and destroy me" (10:8).

10 The failure of Genesis, the Genesis of failure

If my students know anything about the Tanakh, it's God's handiwork in the first chapter (plus the very beginning of the second chapter) of Genesis, how the universe was created ex nihilo, out of nothing, in six easy days. Through a series of indirect commands – "Let there be . . ." – God organizes the basic building blocks of the cosmos: Light, dark, sky, waters, land, vegetation, moon, sun, stars. On the fifth day he orders some of these elements to "bring forth" flying and aquatic animals. The sixth day begins with the appearance of terrestrial life, "wild animals of the earth of every kind, and the cattle of every kind, and everything that creeps upon the ground of every kind" (Gen 1:25). Then, later in the day, as the culminating act of his work, "God created humankind in his image, in the image of God he created them; male and female he created them" (Gen 1:27). God is proud: He "saw everything that he had made, and indeed, it was very good" (Gen 1:31). Then he rests (Gen 2:2–3). Creation is hard work.

My students also have a fuzzy knowledge of the Adam-and-Eve-in-Eden creation story that immediately follows in Genesis 2:4–3:24, although they are usually startled to learn that it's a completely separate tale. They are even more surprised when they realize that the second account of creation directly contradicts the first one. In this second creation tale, Yahweh creates man from the dust of the earth towards what appears to be the *beginning* of creation, "when no plant of the field was yet in the earth and no herb of the field had yet sprung up" (Gen 2:4–7). *After* Adam's creation the "Lord God planted a garden in Eden" and ineffectually commanded his new creation not to eat the fruit of the tree of the knowledge of good and evil (Gen 2:8–17). Yahweh finally noticed that man was alone and that "it is not good." He decided to "make him a helper as his partner" (Gen 2:18). At this point my students' knowledge generally evaporates, for they forget that Yahweh's first attempt to solve the problem resulted not in Eve but in "every animal of the field and every bird of the air" (Gen 2:19). Surprisingly for an omniscient and omnipotent deity, his efforts are a fiasco. Animals are not good partners for man, as it turns out. At least not *that* kind of partner. (Although at least one rabbi in the Babylonian Talmud suggested that Adam had sex with every animal but found no satisfaction until he had intercourse with Eve; Tractate Yebamoth Folio 63a.) So it is only then that Yahweh gives it another shot and uses one of man's ribs to create Eve (Gen 2:21–3). And the rest, as a surprising number of Americans still say, is history.[1]

The two creations raise questions. Was vegetation created *before* (Gen 1:11) or *after* (Gen 2:8–9) humans? Were animals created *before* humans (Gen 1:19–25) or *after* (Gen 2:19–20)? Were animals created for humans to have dominion over (Gen 1:28) or as a (failed) "partner"? Most problematically, were man and woman created together as the culmination of creation (Gen 1:26–8) or was man created first, then plants and animals, and finally woman through supernatural rib resection? The two accounts are incompatible. (You may recall the irrepressible Lilith from our earlier discussion.) As literature, the two tales together paint a complementary if schizophrenic picture of the character of God and his relationship to creation and of the nature of our tragic, human condition. But the two stories cannot be grafted into a coherent account of creation.

Since one (and perhaps the most) important purpose of creation tales is to clarify the nature of our existence in some fashion – something the second creation story attempts with anthropomorphic vitality – it is unfortunate that we have spent so much intellectual and emotional energy for over 2000 years trying to accommodate the first chapter of Genesis to a reality for which it is so manifestly unfit. The quixotic cosmology of Genesis 1 has reigned over Western culture, just as its late composers and biblical editors had hoped by placing it in its emphatic opening position. The God of Genesis 1 provides perhaps the dominant image of the biblical deity whose towering presence has dwarfed the Olympians' influence over our lives. Thus in this chapter we must contrast Yahweh's role of creator God with the early Greek vision of the relationship between the divine and creation.

We actually know a lot about the evolution of humans and the origins of the solar system, and quite a bit (but certainly not everything) about the beginnings of the universe. If you must supplement your scientific knowledge with one *myth* to guide your reflections on human existence, Homer's gods and their place in creation will take you a lot further. Genesis 1 is not historically or scientifically accurate – no news there – but neither it is particularly *helpful*. It's an unprofitable myth that has been made worse through theological abuse. If you are going to choose an ancient myth to give you some guidance, it shouldn't be one that cannot account for the most obvious elements of the human dilemma.

In this chapter, two charges are brought against Genesis 1. First, Genesis 1 does *not* address the puzzling issue of origins *even as a myth*. This needs to be demonstrated up front because this chapter of the Bible remains a cornerstone of theistic belief as a credible (if miraculous) explanation for the emergence of the universe. But this fictional tale answers no questions and resolves no riddles about "the beginning."

Secondly, and more crucially, the picture of the universe presented in Genesis 1 of an orderly world created by an all-powerful, benevolent deity simply does not line up with human reality. By trying to make Yahweh solely responsible for the world and unchallenged for authority, the authors unwittingly make him responsible for all natural evil, thereby condemning Western culture to millennia of failed efforts to find excuses for God's incompetence or cruelty. Penned by "intolerant monolatrists" who brooked no divine competition for Yahweh, the first creation account goes one step further than most of the rest of the Bible and wipes the slate completely clean of all contending forces. God is master of the cosmos. The roaming seas, dangerous monsters, and astral divinities that peek their polytheistic heads out here and there elsewhere, often in what can be taken as primordial and antagonistic contexts, have been completely eradicated or demythologized by the Priestly authors of Genesis 1. The editors placed this new "master" version in front of its competing narrative to make a strong theological statement: The Hebrew God (he is not called Yahweh in Genesis 1, although I will continue to use the name for convenience) gave order to the universe, an act we can call creation.[2] Unlike Zeus, he was in charge from its beginning, and remains in control with no serious challengers to his authority. His work was deemed good. Very good. By him.

But Yahweh's remarks on his week of work either make him a liar – his creation is and always has been seriously flawed by natural evil (as well as human weakness: "For the inclination of the human heart is evil from youth," he concedes) – or reveal a divinity of extremely low standards. (One recalls Woody Allen's line: "If it turns out that there is a God . . . the worst that you can say about him is that basically he's an underachiever.") Or perhaps God is simply sadistic. This picture of God's sole mastery of a good universe "conflicts with the reality principle" (Frymer-Kensky 1992:100), both that of the experience of ancient Israel and any sentient being's awareness of the facts of mortal existence. Genesis 1 fails to provide any insight into the mortal condition because it is at such odds with human experience. The Homeric understanding of creation – the universe created for no apparent purpose and now populated by competing, flawed gods with little concern for the consequences for humans – accounts far better for the chaotic nature of personal experience and human history, and makes far more meaningful demands on us all.

I. Genesis 1 and beginnings

I have several theistic friends whose last, tenacious grasp on God derives from their concern about origins. Something had to get the universe started, they think, and for lack of a better answer, they cling to the one handed down by their Christian tradition. They don't quote Aquinas, but they are ultimately following along the lines of what is known as the "cosmological argument," which posits in its most basic form that there must be an uncaused cause at some point in the historical regression, and they call this first cause, the unmoved mover, God. There is no need to repeat here the many philosophical arguments refuting this and the rest of Aquinas' "five proofs" of God's existence, even in its more sophisticated version known as the Kalam Cosmological Argument as offered by William Lane Craig (1979; Nowacki 2007; cf. Feser 2013; see Smith 1974:235–56; Martin 1990:96–124; Grayling 2013:72–106). Even the usually sanguine Karen Armstrong acknowledges that "these proofs do not hold water today" (1993:239).

Now I have to admit that there are subtleties in this debate that escape me, especially when quantum physics is invoked. (I'm always suspicious when humanists use physics, or physicists talk philosophy, or anyone starts talking about "quantum spirituality.") But I have encountered no cogent rebuttals to the most basic objections to the cosmological argument: Why is the first cause exempt from needing a cause? Why would the first cause be synonymous with the Abrahamic God, or *any* god who cares about what he's done? Why not the God of deists – a reticent deity who set the whole works in motion and then retired to Florida – an omnipotent and unchangeable creator God credited with "power, wisdom, and goodness" even by the radical deist Thomas Paine (Holmes 2006:39)? Why not Atum or Oceanus? What if time simply *started* with the Big Bang? What if the universe created itself and appeared spontaneously? Or what if the universe really has *always been around*? Or what if our universe is just one of many (Stenger 2012:165–97)? It's quite true that we have as yet no agreed-upon scientific theory for the origins of the universe (as opposed to viable theories of the origins of Homo sapiens or the solar system). But this should no longer mean that we turn to ancient myths for answers, one final "God of the gaps," the theological maneuver to make God the answer to questions that remain without scientific solutions.

The cosmological argument is more of a "gut" thing anyhow. Most believers are unaware of the philosophical and theological arguments pro and con. The psychological demand for an emotionally satisfying causal explanation for the universe can be overwhelming. Life can't all be a marvelous, purpose-free, and terrifying accident as all evidence suggests it is! As A.C. Grayling concludes, "most religious people do not, of course, subscribe to their religion because of arguments in favour of it, still less arguments establishing the existence of the deity central to it. The arguments examined here are without exception rationalisations of beliefs which are already accepted" (2013:68). Believers turn to Genesis 1 and find what is simply not there – it turns out that *even as a myth* Genesis fails to answer questions about origins.

Nix on the ex nihilo

The whole ex nihilo (creation "from nothing") reading of Genesis 1 is misguided. The opening verses of Genesis reveal that there was in fact much already in existence when God started his work. Take the RSV's (1952) translation with the conventional reading of the first verse:

> (1) In the beginning God created the heavens and the earth. (2) The earth was without form and void, and darkness was upon the face of the deep; and the Spirit of God was moving over the face of the waters. (3) And God said let there be light; and there was light.
>
> (Gen 1:1–3)

Creation does not start until the third verse; the first two verses are merely summarizing the *following* account, an introduction setting the scene or describing the state of things when God decided to step in: "In either case, the text does not describe creation out of nothing" (NOAB). God does not actually create the heavens until verse 7, or the earth until verse 9. The first two verses reveal that, preceding creation, the building blocks were *already in existence*, namely earth (a word which refers here to dry land, not the planet), darkness, and waters (the deep). And God, of course, or some manifestation of God as wind or breath or spirit.

The earth existed *before* Yahweh's intervention, a "formless void." The two words used here, *tohu wabohu*, do not denote nothingness but unproductive and unstructured waste without function (Tsumura 2005:9–35; Walton 2011:122). The verb used for creation, *bara*, always has God as an explicit or implicit subject, and in none of its 50 or so appearances is the divine act one of *creating* material (Walton 2011:38–46). Yahweh's actions give a function and role to the cosmic material by separating, differentiating, and ordering, not by manufacturing. Like other Near Eastern creation tales (Walton 2009:28–36), Genesis 1 is not about ultimate origins but the *process* by which the universe reached its present form.[3] God did not create the world out of nothing; he took what was already there and gave it a useful structure: "It needed some tidying up to become 'created'" (Lambert 1988:138).[4]

The ex nihilo concept doesn't exist in Genesis 1; in fact, it does not seem to have been invented until a half millennium after the composition of Genesis 1. The first vague reference is found in 2 Maccabees 7:28, a Jewish text influenced by Hellenistic Greek thought from the first century BCE. Despite hints of the doctrine in Rom 4:17 and Heb 11:3, there is no explicit reference to it in the New Testament (Gregory 2007:205–6). A majority of early Church fathers accepted the existence of matter before creation. The Christian doctrine of ex nihilo didn't fully emerge until the end of the second century CE (May 2004). In the Rabbinic tradition we find numerous lists of things that existed *before* Yahweh created the world. One text specifies seven different items (Kugel 1998:45). The Genesis Rabbah (1.1) – a collection of rabbinical interpretations (midrash) of Genesis from 1500 years ago – even tells us that Yahweh, like any architect, had to consult the preexisting Torah for the blueprints of creation!

So why do Christians insist on the most unlikely reading of the very first verses of their sacred text? As Karen Armstrong notes, "Today the doctrine of creation ex nihilo is regarded as the linchpin of Christianity, the truth on which theism stands or falls. So it is interesting to note how slowly and uncertainly this idea emerged" (2009:105; cf. Fergusson 2014). If creation falls apart, if the "Creator-Redeemer" did not create everything and independently ex nihilo, then what power has he to redeem? "In Christian theology, the doctrines of creation and redemption are inseparably linked" (Habgood 1983:129–30). Professor of early Christian theology (and priest of the Russian Orthodox Church) Andrew Louth acknowledges the nonbiblical status of ex nihilo while passionately articulating the linkage of the concept to Christian myth:

> The idea of God as Creator, fashioning the universe ex nihilo, was a new and revolutionary idea [in the second century CE, he admits], perhaps just as striking as the Gospel of Jesus Christ and, indeed, an integral part of it, for if one

did not grasp that the Father of the Lord Jesus Christ was the Creator of the universe, who had indeed created the universe through his Son, Jesus Christ, then one could never grasp the universal significance of Christ's death and resurrection.

(2009:42)

Some Christians have been willing to nod to the facts of *human* evolution, to let go of a literal Adam and Eve (that is, Genesis 2–3), as long as they can keep a divine hand in the ordering of a universe that would give rise to such a biological development (Genesis 1). If their God did not create the world, then there is no real place for him and certainly no need. In fact, he just gets in the way. Contemporary devotional scholars therefore feel compelled to repeat the mantra of ex nihilo. One commentary on Genesis by a Catholic monk, for example, begins – I mean, literally opens – with these confessional words: "God saves. God is always savior. The Bible begins with a story that recounts the creation out of nothing, by the one eternally existing God of all that exists" (Cotter 2003:3).

Genesis does not in fact answer my friends' cosmic quandary about the beginning of time or substance, and the questions remain: Where did all that "stuff" come from? And where did God come from? If God can be eternal, why not the stuff as well? What made God decide to act on that first day in verse 3? And how can a transcendent being affect matter in the first place? The myth simply wasn't designed to address these issues of origins any more than Hesiod's or Homer's myths. That is not the purpose of creation myths. The most honest critic I have run across on this topic is American Indologist Wendy Doniger, whose comments are worth quoting at length:

> And indeed, if you believe that time is infinite or eternal then there is no problem about finding its beginning. But the creation myths do not usually take this cowardly way out, preferring instead to wrestle with the problems of beginnings. Perhaps the mythological mind, unlike the philosophical, just can't deal with the mind-boggling concept of a time without beginning or end. . . . Yet many mythologies do tackle this paradox . . . [and] most of them fudge this fact by positing the unexplained sudden appearance of an original something – god, or a kind of chaotic primeval matter (as in Plato's *Timaeus*) – and moving quickly off this highly debatable point into a labyrinth of baroque elaboration. . . . This is a false trail that lures the listener or reader away from the opening point, the inevitable weak point, the question that cannot be answered. . . . For the ultimate moment of transition from pre-creation to post-creation is a moment that no one can actually know and that presents a logical dilemma that no argument can resolve. Instead, the texts devise indirect strategies to give the false impression that the basic question has been answered when it has not; they try to explain it by adopting various attitudes (ranging from dogmatic certainty to humble confession of ignorance) and various techniques of obfuscation, all designed to cover up

the unavoidable but inadmissible fact of (the origin of) life, the fact that you can't get here from there.

(Doniger 2008:88–9)

She goes on to celebrate the "charming humility" of an Indian hymn, the famous "There was not" hymn, earlier than both the Tanakh and Homer's epics, which begins "there was neither non-existence nor existence then" and ends with "Whence this creation has arisen – perhaps it formed itself, or perhaps it did not – the one who looks down on it, in the highest heaven, only he knows – or perhaps he does not know" (*Rg Veda* 10.129).

Genesis 1 is a "bad" myth, then, in the way it has been misused over the past 2000 years in an effort to offer psychotherapy to and provide redemption for our anxious species in the guise of answering a question about ultimate origins that the text itself does not pose. But that's not half the problem. The first creation story has so successfully scrubbed God of his Olympian origins – a nature revealed many times elsewhere in the Tanakh – that the tale cannot function in any helpful way even as fiction.

II. Yahweh alone: Not a good thing

Although we are programed to focus on the opening of Genesis, which is surely the most influential cosmology in Western mythology, there are actually many creation accounts in the Bible. This makes sense, since available evidence suggests that Yahweh was not at first primarily a creator deity. He originated as a storm deity, a warrior-god, and "above all a loner" (Gnuse 1997:196). Although a few references to his act of creation may antedate Israelite exile to Babylon (e.g., Jer 27:5–6), this aspect of his nature gains prominence primarily after Yahweh's failure as a national god and his subsequent postexilic promotion (Lang 1983:48; Thiel 2002:54–5; Smith 2010:200). Before turning directly to Genesis 1, we need to examine the nature of Yahweh's role in and his relationship to his creation(s) throughout the text. We will see that there are clear indications in the Hebrew Bible that Yahweh in earlier traditions faced similar challenges to those of Zeus and the Olympians, both from humans and other divinities. We first need to examine these bits of evidence of the earlier tradition of Yahweh's Olympian struggle for supremacy. Then we will be well positioned to see just how radical and polemical the first chapter of the Bible really is, even by the standards of the Tanakh. On full display suddenly will be the authors' efforts to "clean up" the story, to remove all hints of a challenge to Yahweh and present him as eternally in control of his creation – in other words, their attempt to excise his Olympian nature. Genesis 1 is an "anomaly," biblical scholar Lester Grabbe observes in his recent effort to accept the scientific model while simultaneously maintaining a belief that "God somehow – in his own way – is author of creation and all that exists." Genesis 1 is a chapter composed by a "capable polemicist" making a "sophisticated theological move" (2018:15, 22). Sophisticated, yes, but misconceived. By putting

Yahweh in complete and eternal control of the ordering of the cosmos, Genesis 1 presents a severe (if unintended) indictment of God and a meretricious picture of the universe.

Putting humans in their place

One early potential challenge to Yahweh must be quickly squashed before Genesis can even gather some momentum. I mean humans, of course. Yahweh's explicit reason for ejecting Adam and Eve from Eden and condemning them (and us) to difficult lives was not so much their initial disobedience in eating the fruit but his fear that they might *continue* to disobey. "The ferocity of the curses seems to betray the divine strength of feeling and the extent of the perceived threat posed by humanity acquiring knowledge" (Kraus 2011:31). God shares these concerns with his divine compatriots, the members of his divine cabinet: "'See, the man has become *like one of us*, knowing good and evil; and now, he might reach out his hand and take also from the tree of life, and eat, and live forever' – therefore the Lord God sent him forth from the garden of Eden, to till the ground from which he was taken" (Gen 3:22–3, my emphasis). God fears that humans will become gods, rivals to his authority. They are already "like" deities in their knowledge of good and evil. Whatever that may mean, it is clearly one of the defining characteristics of Yahweh and his council, and Yahweh wants to keep the barriers between the two species sealed shut. Death will do that.

At Babel, all humans share one language and are capable of working together, which they immediately do by planning a group project. "Come, let us build ourselves a city, and a tower with its top in the heavens, and let us make a name for ourselves; otherwise we shall be scattered abroad upon the face of the whole earth" (Gen 11:4). Mankind instinctively, heroically, tragically strives to leave its mark, to "make a name" just as the Homeric heroes' goal is to achieve fame and glory.

But from a god's perspective, to "reach for heaven" is a form of rebellion, a denial of our human limitations and a danger to the status of the divine (Whybray 1996:96). The unruly humans even use the divine hortatory "let us." We saw a similar version of this tale with the Homeric Otus and Ephialtes, who threatened to pile mountain upon mountain to scale heaven. In that case the threat was explicit – the human brothers wanted to bring war against the reigning deities – but their plan was discovered and stopped. Yahweh allows that humans just might be successful, so he encourages his divine council to join him in heading off the threat to his power: "Look, they are one people, and they have all one language; and this is only the beginning of what they will do; nothing that they propose to do will now be impossible for them. Come, let us go down and confuse their language there, so that they will not understand one another's speech" (Gen 11:6–7). His action, like that of Apollo against Otus and Ephialtes, is effective – humans are scattered "over the face of all the earth, and they left off building the city" (Gen 11:8). The story "explains" in mythological fashion human ethnic and linguistic diversity as well as our challenging life in a difficult world that an all-powerful god could have made otherwise. (And the episode is nicely spiced up with a healthy dash of anti-Babylonian xenophobia with all those nasty skyscraping shrines perched atop ziggurats.) But these stories also reveal Yahweh's fear of competition from his new creation. Humans were once a potential threat, just as they were to the Olympians; for most of the rest of the Tanakh they are just a constant disappointment.

We can capture the essence of the idea of creation in the Hebrew Bible with the word "mastery." Hesiod's devotion to Zeus pales in comparison to the zealotry for Yahweh felt by the Priestly composers of Genesis 1. "The creation narratives, whatever their length, form, or context, are best seen as dramatic visualizations of the uncompromised mastery of YHWH, God of Israel, over all else" (Levenson 1988:3). One editorial trick to this extolling of Yahweh's mastery by the late redactors of the text was to eliminate or smooth over the challenges he once faced. Like the *Iliad*, the culmination (but not the conclusion) of hundreds of years of Troy story variants, the Bible as it stands is a compilation of hundreds of years of different theological visions of God and his relation to Israel and humanity. We will now examine two much-discussed examples of this theological transformation as we catch brief glimpses of what was once there and how it has been shaped and repressed to reaffirm Yahweh's steady hand in creation, both initial and ongoing. It is this final effort that culminates with Genesis 1, a narrative that is hopelessly removed from human experience. Yahweh's "mastery" turns out to be a condemnation of his reign rather than a celebration of his glory.

The sea

Many mythologies of the ancient Near East depict a battle for power between a warrior deity and the sea (and monstrous representatives of the sea).[5] The Tanakh also offers numerous allusions to Yahweh's imposition of order and limits on what were once threatening waters. Like Zeus's battle against the natural forces represented by Typhoeus, Yahweh's combat against his *early* enemies is a struggle for power, which means the Hebrew God was not untested. He, too, had challenges to overcome to establish and maintain his rule.

Biblical scholar Debra Scoggins Ballentine's recent (2015) reexamination of all the evidence leads to her to conclude that these references to Yahweh's past victories over the sea and its monstrous manifestations exhibit six (often overlapping) rhetorical functions: to assert Yahweh's dominion; to claim that his dominion is universal; to endorse royal authority; to promote select groups of people; to portray present enemies as destined for defeat; and to invoke Yahweh to intervene against contemporary enemies. The authors of the Tanakh promoted Yahweh as an "incomparable deity, victorious divine warrior, divine king, and creator with universal dominion." But I would draw attention to the more obvious fact: Yahweh, like Zeus, once had what appears to be formidable competition for supremacy.

This combat imagery shows up slightly differently in various generic contexts, in petitionary prayers, prophetic petitions and promises, supernatural visions, oracles against foreign nations, and wisdom literature (Fishbane 2003:37–65). But the basic story behind the evocations of the battle motif remains consistent. We can start with a passage from Job. Yahweh begins speaking to Job out of the whirlwind, furious that a mere mortal has stood up to him:

> Where were you when I laid the foundation of the earth? Tell me, if you have understanding. Who determined its measurements – surely you know! Or who stretched the line upon it? On what were its bases sunk, or who laid its cornerstone when the morning stars sang together and all the heavenly beings [sons of God] shouted for joy? Or who shut in the sea with doors when it burst out from the womb? – when I made the clouds its garment, and thick darkness its swaddling band, and prescribed bounds for it, and set bars and doors, and said, "Thus far shall you come, and no farther, and here shall your proud waves be stopped"?
>
> (Job 38:4–11)

God recounts his shutting in the adversarial sea as the ultimate sign of his creational efforts. One of the primary shorthands for conjuring up Yahweh's sovereignty is to allude to his victory over water. "Do you not tremble before me? I placed the sand as a boundary for the sea, a perpetual barrier that it cannot pass; though the waves toss, they cannot prevail, though they roar, they cannot pass over it" (Jer 5:22). Yahweh's taming of the sea in what looks like a creation context (but need not be) stands for *everything* he has done and can do (Ps 93:1–4). "At your rebuke" the waters flee "to the place that you appointed for them. You set a boundary that they may not pass, so that they might not again cover the earth" (Ps 104:7–9; cf. Pss 33:6–9; 65:6–8; 69:13–15; Prov 8:24–31; Nah 1:4).

Mythologically, then, Yahweh's control over the cosmos is frequently represented by his suppression and constraining of the sea. The sea itself may not be as explicitly personified or deified in these passages as it is in the parallel Near Eastern texts, but then again it may be (this is a matter of some debate). In several passages it seems to be not just the sea but the Sea, or even a Sea Monster (e.g., Job 7:12; 9:8; Hab 3:15). There are dreadful figures in the Hebrew Bible associated with the sea who are obvious relatives of similar beasts in neighboring mythologies, including Typhoeus. The most familiar sea monster in the Bible is probably Leviathan, but closely associated (and perhaps eventually identified) with Leviathan is a creature known as Rahab. And *tannin* can refer to an ancient dragon, sometimes of the sea, but also serpents on land (Ex 7:12; cf. Deut 32:33), although it's not clear if and when it is used as a proper name, a mythical being or demythologized symbol (Heider 1999:835–6).

Leviathan is generally a serpentine creature who appears in numerous creational contexts.[6] Whatever he is (Day 1985:65–75), he and his fellow sea serpents exist for Yahweh to smack around. "Yet God my King is from of old, working salvation in the earth. You divided the sea by your might; your broke the heads of the dragons (*tannin*) in the waters. You crushed the heads of Leviathan . . ." (Ps 74:12–17).

"The biblical texts clearly consider Yahweh's mastering of Leviathan as an aspect of creational order" (Uehlinger 1999:513). Yahweh boasts of his unique ability to defeat this fire-breathing beast: ". . . were not even the gods overwhelmed at the sight of it? . . . When it raises itself up the gods are afraid; at the crashing they are beside themselves." No one "under the whole heaven" can confront it and be safe (Job-41; cf. Ps 104:26).

Job also cites Yahweh's suppression of Rahab as evidence of his power: "He [Yahweh] has described a circle on the face of the waters, at the boundary between light and darkness. The pillars of heaven tremble, and are astounded at his rebuke. By his power he stilled the Sea [note the editorial decision to capitalize]; by his understanding he struck down Rahab. By his wind the heavens were made fair; his hand pierced the fleeing serpent" (Job 26:10–13; cf. 9:13).

Some scholars see the great flood as a remnant of this cosmic battle. Bernard Batto (2013a:51), for example, notes that Yahweh hangs his bow in the sky (Gen 9:8–17) after the flood, just as Marduk does after his defeat of Tiamat and her allies: What did Yahweh need his bow for if not for battle? Seen in this light, "chaos is not destroyed but is only placed within bounds although if God so determines, these bounds may be removed, allowing the earth to return to chaos, as almost happened during the Great Flood . . ." (Anderson 1984).

The Hebrew God, for all his eternity, has three major triumphs on his résumé that form the heart of his biblical persona and his covenantal relationship with humanity – creation, exodus, and the conquest of Canaan. After that, to be honest, it's pretty much downhill. (Cyrus' defeat of the Babylonians and his return of the Israelites to Israel also feature on God's highlight reel in a few late texts.) So these three actions – by which the creation of the universe and the building of the nation of Israel are equated – are repeatedly celebrated in the Tanakh with water imagery.[7] It is used by extension to describe either Yahweh's punishment of Israel or its rescue from hostile nations (e.g., Assyria) and personal enemies (Pss 18:16; 46:1–3; 144:7; Isa 8:5–8; 17:12–13; Hab 3:8, 15). But Yahweh's defeat of the sea and its monstrous representatives is especially associated with the other two "historical" highlights on his CV. There are frequent celebrations of the Israelites' river-splitting exodus from Egypt (Ex 14:21–29) and entrance into Canaan (Josh 3:15–4:24) that draw on this imagery. These two defining moments in Israelite history are brought into symmetry in Psalm 114: "When Israel went out from Egypt, the house of Jacob from a people of strange language, Judah became God's sanctuary, Israel his dominion. The sea [the one Moses parted, as most commentators take it] looked and fled; Jordan [the river marking the boundary of the Promised Land] turned back. . . . Why is it, O sea, that you flee? O Jordan, that you turn back? . . . Tremble, O earth, at the presence of the Lord . . ." (cf. Ex 15:1–10; Pss 77:16–19; 106:7–9).[8]

Yahweh's past victory over the sea and its representatives are consistently used to illustrate his control over the cosmos in the present and future. But the history lying underneath his ultimate triumphs is that he once *did* face serious challenges to his sovereignty – and not just from the unruly waters.

The sky

Homer's Zeus is no longer concerned about his primordial challengers. The real threat comes from his fellow Olympians, who are the remaining source of problems and potential opposition. Cronus and the Titans are safely locked away; Typhoeus has been subdued; Otus and Ephialties lie stretched out in the underworld. The existing risks derive primarily from a possible rebellion within Zeus's own family and divine council, as when Athena, Hera, and Poseidon nearly overthrow him, or when Poseidon considers ignoring his ultimatums, or when Hera seduces him.

Yahweh, oddly enough, is in a similar situation. He has conquered, destroyed, or derailed his earlier rivals for power, both divine and human. He faces two remaining potential foes. The first group, all those competing deities associated with "foreign" nations, seems not to be considered a threat to his divine kingship as much as rivals for the hearts and minds of the Israelites. There is no suggestion that Yahweh's authority in the cosmos is at stake in this constant conflict over cultic loyalty. Even if all of Israel should abandon him, he'd still be *da man*. But the other possible source of conflict comes from the same group that threatens Zeus, namely those divine beings with whom he shares sacred space.

Scholars have detected hints of previous divine competition, perhaps even a heavenly revolt by a luminous solar deity, in Isaiah 14:4–21 (Mullen 1980:238; cf. Ezek 28). There the King of Babylon is compared to the "Day Star, son of Dawn," who once arrogantly claimed: "I will ascend to heaven; I will raise my throne above the stars of God; I will sit on the mount of Assembly on the heights of Zaphon; I will ascend to the tops of the clouds, I will make myself like the Most High." A similar story of an attempted coup by an astral deity has been found in earlier Canaanite sources (Fishbane 2003:74–5). And the rebellion doesn't stop there. Recall those "sons of god" who defied Yahweh by having sex with human women (Gen 6:1–8). These unsanctioned unions – a forbidden "intermingling of domains" – produced a race of heroes whom Yahweh wiped out in the ensuing flood. The tale in Genesis suggests that these offspring were punished rather than the miscreant sons of God, but later tradition focuses on the wicked divinities. The Book of Enoch (1 Enoch 6f.), a composition probably originating in the third century BCE (Reed 2005) that didn't make it into the official canon, provides extraordinary details about the motives and fates of the 200 "fallen" angels (called Watchers) and their illegitimate offspring who first eat mankind and then themselves! Another noncanonical text, the Book of Jubilees, links Satan for the first time with the rebel angel tradition (Forsyth 1987:182–91). No wonder, then, that we are already told in the Tanakh that "God puts no trust even in his holy ones, and the heavens are not clean in his sight" (Job 15:15). In addition to the charge of untrustworthiness, "his angels he charges with error" (Job 4:18). And most untrustworthy of all is the protean group known as "the host of heaven."

This heavenly host can be construed in numerous ways in the Tanakh, as Yahweh's court, the sons of gods, the sons of Elyon, even a son of Yahweh, or eventually as the gods of foreign nations (Halpern 2009:90–6). At the origin of the concept of the host of heaven – used approximately 200 times – probably stands the metaphor of Yahweh as warrior: The host formed his army (Niehr 1999:428). Perhaps from this image derives the frequent reference to Yahweh as "Lord of Hosts." But if true, not many traces remain of their martial character, although a divine being does stand at the head of Yahweh's army in Canaan (Josh 5:13–15) and at one unnerving moment "the stars fought from heaven" against the Canaan-ites (Judg 5:20). It must have been an impressive army, too, for Moses remarks, "The Lord came from Sinai, and dawned from Seir upon us; he shone forth from Mount Paran. With him were myriads of holy ones; at his right, a host of his own" (Deut 33:2). The "host of heaven" can also apply to the divine council members (e.g., 1 Kgs 22:19–23; Isa 6:3, 5). As Mark Smith observes, "with the sun, moon, and the hosts of heaven in attendance, the divine assembly of Yahweh is quite full" (2001:52).

The expression, however, most commonly refers to astral bodies – the sun, moon, stars, even everything in heaven or the stars alone, all of whom can be con-sidered celestial beings. It is significant, then, that we are repeatedly – one might say maniacally – reminded that it is Yahweh who "commands the sun, and it does not rise; who seals up the stars; who alone stretched out the heavens and trampled the waves of the Sea; who made the Bear and Orion, the Pleiades and the chambers of the south" (Job 9:7–9; cf. Job 38:31–3; Pss 19:2–6; 74:12–17; Hab 3:10–11; Amos 5:8). The Hebrew God created and thus controls the host: "It was my hands that stretched out the heavens, and I commanded all their host" (Isa 45:12; cf. 40:26; Ps 8:3). The host now exists, as do all of Yahweh's divine colleagues, to praise and "do his will." From the moment of creation, he himself insists, when he was laying the foundation of the earth, "the morning stars sang together and all the heavenly beings [sons of God] shouted for joy" (Job 38:4–7; cf. Pss 69:34; 89:5; 96:11; 103:21; 148:1–6; Isa 44:23). The sun and moon even stop their movement in the sky at Yahweh's command to provide more time for his people to slaughter the enemy (Josh 10:12–14).[9]

The focus and urgency of this insistence on the servility of the astral bodies, something entirely missing in Homer's world – remember how Helius' threat to shine into the world of the dead scared Zeus – seems out of place. Why is Yahweh so suspicious of *these* deities in particular? The host of heaven poses a more seri-ous challenge to Yahweh than gods like Baal and Asherah since they sit at the side of what is supposed to be the only authority in the universe. Yahweh must keep an eye on them just as Zeus does on his Olympian family.

There must have been a lot of astral worship in ancient Israel, as there was for the local Canaanites (Smith 2004:101–19). Solar symbols are found on many Isra-elite seals (Keel and Uehlinger 1998:282–309). Celestial or astral powers were surely popular among the Israelites, for the people are constantly warned *not* to worship them: "And when you look up to heavens and see the sun, moon, and stars, all the host of heaven, do not be led astray and bow down to them and serve them, things that the Lord your God has allotted to all the peoples everywhere under heaven" (Deut 4:19). They are not divine beings to be worshipped by the Israelites, we are assured by the anxious Moses, just "things." Yet even Moses can on occasion conjure up the once-legitimate polytheistic past, back when it was acceptable to turn to the sun and moon as divine witnesses. He calls on "heaven and earth" to validate Yahweh's threats (4:26), an expression that reveals "very old covenant (legal) terminology, originating in a polytheistic environment, and surviving in later times when particularly astral deities, like Helios in Homer, were called upon to witness an agreement" (NOAB and Deut 4:26). The expression jars so violently with the context that it is hard not to snicker. Moses tells his refractory wards that they must never be "led astray to bow down to other gods and serve them" or else they shall perish. And then, to punctuate his sincere monolatry, he calls on "heaven and earth to witness against you today . . ." (Deut 30:17–19).

Yahweh is *extremely* concerned about all this astral devotion. If at least two witnesses find someone doing "what is evil in the sight of the Lord your God . . . by going to serve other gods and worshiping them – whether the sun or the moon or any of the host of heaven, which I have forbidden . . . you shall stone the man or woman to death" (Deut 17:2–5). So much for a little howling at the moon. Worshipers of the host of heaven will be executed, and according to Jeremiah (in one of his blackly ironic moments) their bones eventually dug up and "spread before the sun and moon and all the host of heaven which they have loved and served" (Jer 8:1–2).

Nevertheless, "bad" kings like Manasseh continue to lead the Israelites in official worship of these deities: "He rebuilt the high places . . . erected altars for Baal, made a sacred pole [Asherah] . . . worshiped all the host of heaven, and served them. . . . He built altars for all the host of heaven in the two courts of the house of the Lord" (2 Kgs 21:2–5; cf. Job 31:26). Worshiping the host of heaven is said to be one of the religious crimes that led to Yahweh's destruction of both Israel and Judah by summoning the Assyrians to wipe out Samaria (2 Kgs 17:1–18) and the Babylonians to capture Jerusalem and carry the remaining Israelites into captivity (2 Kgs 17:19–20; Jer 19:13; Ezek 8:16–18).[10]

Good kings like Josiah, on the other hand, tear down all these non-Yahwistic cultic areas and implements, including the vessels inside the temple for worshiping Baal, Asherah, and "all the host of heaven" (2 Kgs 23:4). Note that they must have offered some serious competition for Yahweh, as altars to the host were built in the temple courtyards and some sort of veneration of them took place within the temple itself.

The control of the rowdy primeval waters and creational mastery of the potentially rebellious host of heaven form the heart of Yahweh's claims to cosmic authority. Biblical authors combine them with the Hebrew God's two most celebrated terrestrial acts, the exodus from Egypt and the appropriation of Canaan:

> O give thanks to the Lord, for he is good . . . who by understanding made the heavens, for his steadfast love endures forever; who spread out the earth on the waters . . . who made the great lights . . . the sun to rule over day . . . the moon and stars to rule over night . . . who struck Egypt through their firstborn . . . and brought Israel out from among them . . . who divided the

Red Sea in two . . . who struck down great kings . . . and gave their land as a heritage . . . a heritage to his servant Israel.

(Ps 136:1, 5–11, 13, 17, 21–2; Clifford 1992:65–6)

Yahweh does appear to have overcome quite pugnaciously a lot of challenges, and he remains suspicious of his celestial compadres. Overall, Yahweh is once again potentially quite Homeric throughout the text. Or is he? All his Olympian trials magically disappear in opening chapter of the Tanakh.

Demythologizing the threats

As we saw earlier, Yahweh and the basic material of the universe are simply there at the beginning, just as Oceanus in Homer and Chaos in Hesiod exist without explanation. One of these preexistent materials is "the deep," Hebrew *tehom* (Gen 1:2), which is etymologically related to the primeval oceanic "chaos" goddess/ monster Tiamat in the Babylonian creation account (and perhaps to Tethys, Oceanus' partner in Homer). But note the complete absence of any personification of *tehom* in Genesis 1 (Alster 1999:869). For the authors of Genesis 1, Yahweh has no competition, and many scholars have seen this use of the word as intentionally polemical. Unlike his Near Eastern counterparts, in Genesis 1 Yahweh is presented as unchallenged in his position as creator and ruler of the universe. *Tehom* is just the inert primeval sea pushed to the edges and bound in place. The troublesome, divinely adversarial waters of Near Eastern mythology that we find in other places of the Hebrew Bible are simply "gathered together," and "the waters that were gathered together he called Seas. And God saw that it was good" (Gen 1:9–10). Yahweh's complete control is signaled by his naming the waters. There is no conflict. Yahweh is unopposed. Elsewhere in the Tanakh we are reminded of Yahweh's efforts to crush his opponents; the authors of Genesis 1 have eliminated the competition altogether.

This pointed approach by the composers of Genesis 1 is on even brighter display when it comes to Yahweh's other traditional and more threatening competitors, the "host of heaven." The Priestly authors manage to spend five verses (14–18) on the creation of the sun and moon (the stars are almost an afterthought) without actually naming them. Each verse is carefully intended to limit these heavenly bodies and remove any possibility that they were associated with deities or were deities in their own right, as they are in much of the rest of the Tanakh and other near Near Eastern mythologies. They are called "lights," mere "signs" meant for measuring out the seasons, days, and years. "God made two great lights – the greater light to rule the day, the lesser light to rule the night – and the stars" (v. 16). They are not even called the "sun" and "moon" in Hebrew, common Semitic words which might associate them with divine powers in "heterodox" Israelite religious practice and other local cultures.

This depersonalization of former divine threats is typical of the monotheistic and monolatrous trends of the exile and postexile period. Deuteronomy likewise de-deifies other gods and avoids mentioning them by name, treating them as common nouns in order to stress their inferiority and to attempt to expunge their history (Hadley 2007). And you'll note how I did not bring up the ancient head-scratcher of the sun being created on day four – how, exactly, were the previous three days measured? Light is created (uniquely in Near Eastern creation tales) *before* the heavenly bodies, another uncomfortable detail included "to combat the idea that the heavenly bodies were divine signs, or symbols of divine beings, with an independent part to play in control of the cosmos" (Saggs 1978:53).

And what of all those sea creatures like Leviathan and Rahab and the *tannin* who represented some sort of challenge to Yahweh "long ago"? The Priestly authors have an answer to that as well. On the fifth day, "God created the great sea monsters and every living creature that moves, of every kind, with which the waters swarm, and every winged bird of every kind. And God saw that it was good. God blessed them saying 'Be fruitful and multiply and fill the waters in the seas, and let birds multiply on the earth'" (Gen 1:21–2). The potentially threatening, serpentine sea monsters (*tannin*) are now mere products of Yahweh's manufacture, the objects of the same divine verb of creation that has been used since the first verse (Frayne 2013:63–5). They are part of the created order now, items in a new bestiary so unthreatening that Yahweh blesses them and tells them to "fill the waters in the seas."

Finally, "let us" not forget the human competition. The fractious Adam and Eve of Genesis 2–3 apparently pose a serious threat to Yahweh – they prove God to be a liar and *almost* become like the gods before he can exile them. In Genesis 6, the sons of gods break down the barrier separating Yahweh from mortals, having children with the "daughters of men" and creating a race of heroes. Yahweh floods the entire earth to stop that sort of thing. The first heady actions of civilized humans at Babel (Genesis 11) are swiftly crushed by the paranoid deity. The creators of Genesis 1, however, have solved Yahweh's "mortal problem" by creating humans in God's own image and, crucially, with no personality whatsoever. This primordial couple – Stepford children – will be too busy multiplying and subduing the earth – their only tasks – to cause any problems. They say not one word, not even in thanks. Good little mortals.

Consequences

The result of this revised cosmic history in Genesis 1 is that Yahweh has no history, no origin, no life cycle that would imply limits. He is older than creation, if not its materials – the ordered universe never existed without him. Yahweh has total control over creation. He deserves all the credit – but also all the blame. We find ourselves plunged back into the familiar theological challenge – God is assumed to be a benevolent, omnipotent creator of a "very good" world. This "providentialist" vision of a caring God is even more of a chimaera than the deistic version of a reclusive creator God. The world we know is only rarely "very good." It is, overall, indifferent to human ambition, need, and desire, and there are many manifestations of natural (nonmoral) evil. Genesis 1 simply makes no sense of the world – it is in conflict with the obvious facts. It's a myth, and a bad one that thousands of expert defenders have only made worse. Yet theologians and scholars trapped in a Judeo-Christian perspective go on trying to justify Yahweh and denigrate the Greeks: "The role of Yahweh as creator gives the natural order a numinous character lacking in Hellas" (Brown 2003:11). If Brown means that the Bible tries to hide the harsh realities and genuine triumphs of life (the "natural order") behind the shimmer of a rationally indefensible portrait of the divine ("numinous character"), I completely agree. But I get the sense he's heading in the other direction. And I sense he hasn't really understood Homer or spent much time looking out his window at the "natural order" of a tsunami or Tay Sachs, much less at the "natural order" through the window of a pediatric cancer ward.

The myths lying behind Homer's gods make sense of our human experience. Zeus didn't create the world – he and his Olympians merely took over a preexisting world. He can't be blamed or celebrated for the nature of human experience – he inherited the "facts" of the universe just as we have. No appeals to the Olympians will be able to change the basic outline of life. The competition and bickering among those who have found themselves in charge accord far better with the randomness and moral neutrality of the natural world. Sometimes things work out for humans; sometimes they don't. Homer's vision of the divine doesn't provide the false sense of confidence and reassuring loopiness engendered by the Bible's insistent "very good" that has proved so counter-productive to a puzzled and suffering humanity. As noted biblical scholar Mark Smith (2010:113) confesses in a moment of personal revelation, "Genesis 1 is wildly optimistic, a vision of good that can be hard to accept in the face of real experience. Nonetheless, for Jews, Christians, and Muslims alike, this vision of goodness remains the bedrock and beginning of *our* traditions" (my emphasis, just so it doesn't slip by unnoticed). Hans-Jürgen Hermission similarly defends the "hopeless" advocacy of a fully benevolent creation that is also found in Psalms: "Such a radiant view of the created world as is presented in Psalm 104 is certainly not without problems in the face of reality. But one must not scold the poet for being a dreamer . . ." (1984:128). Scold, no, as long as we accept that these are humanly constructed dreams of a utopia (similar to Egyptian hymns to Atum) and not in any way allied with a description of reality. And especially provided that we don't swallow these Panglossian "poetic" fictions as a Truth by which to guide our lives.

Genesis 1 is a failure, especially gussied up in its theological cloak as it inevitably must be. Yahweh's sole mastery of his creation leaves no reasonable explanation for natural evil, no room for tragedy, no place for the reality of human life, for finding meaning in our struggles, failures, and victories. It has left its adherents either glibly cheerful, angrily judgmental, diffidently passive, and (for the more thoughtful) driven to nonsensical speculation. Many theological escape hatches have been devised, but even "free will" won't work in Genesis 1, since it's simply not an issue as it is in Genesis 2–3, a conflicting and far superior tale. After all these centuries, the theists still have no solution to all that "natural evil" that Yahweh must have created (since he is all-powerful and created "everything") or continues to tolerate or "permit" (although he is supposedly benevolent).

Nowhere is this confidence in unhelpful mythology more misplaced or more deleterious than in the wish fulfillment of a Christian afterlife. In the next section we will contrast the biblically based vision of immortality with Homer's acceptance of "pitiless death."

Notes

1 Nearly half of the people (42 percent) in the United States still believe Genesis 1 or 2 (or both!) to be the God's honest truth (Gallup June 2, 2014), while three quarters of Americans think God had at least a hand in human evolution. Eighty-two percent of Danes, on the other hand, accept the evidence for evolution, even though a majority still identify themselves as Christians (Zuckerman 2008:10). Ninety percent of both atheists and agnostics accept the evolutionary origins of humanity without divine intervention (Baker and Smith 2015:97).

2 Most scholars put the composition of Genesis 1 ("Priestly") long after that of Genesis 2–3, often in the sixth century, but it has also been argued that the second creation story was placed there by a redactor to "correct the optimism of the Priestly creation account" (Gertz 2012). Classical scholar Jan Bremmer has suggested that the creation in Genesis 1 may be a competitive Jewish reaction to similar claims made in the sixth century by the Persian King Darius I in his promotion of the "great god" Ahurmazda as creator deity (2008b:339–45).

3 This is true of early Greek philosophical speculation on creation as well: "That even a divine creator would, like any craftsman have to use preexisting materials is an assumption that the ancient Greeks apparently never questioned" (Sedley 2007:xvii).

4 There is also an important grammatical issue involved in the history of the ex nihilo interpretation. Many scholars argue that the "traditional" reading of Genesis 1:1 as given above by the RSV is a mistranslation of the ambiguous Hebrew. This debate about the meaning of the opening verse of the Tanakh was introduced by two scholars in the 11th century, but the traditional interpretation has persisted primarily because so much of Christian theology depends upon it (Fergusson 2014:15–35). The first verses of the Torah *could* say, "In the beginning God created . . ." etc., the famous rendition upon which so much theological dogmatizing has been based. But in fact there are at least four different ways to treat the first three verses of Genesis, and the one opted for by numerous contemporary scholars and many recent translations of the Bible (e.g., Anchor Bible, Study Bible; New American Bible, The New JPS, NRSV, Alter's 1996 version) makes it clear that God's creation did not begin at the beginning. The first verse – not unlike the first verse in the second creation story (2:4b–7) – is likely not an independent sentence but a temporal clause as found in several other Near Eastern creation accounts as well. The opening would then best be translated as "when at first God created" or "in the beginning of when God created" or "when God began to create" (Smith 2010:45–8). It is probably a subordinate clause either to verse 2 or to verse 3 (verse 2 would then be parenthetical and 3 the main clause; Arnold 2009:35). In either case, it is merely a reference to the state of things at the remote time when the creator decided (for some unstated reason, another theological conundrum) to begin to do something; it does not signify an absolute beginning. Smith translates: "When at first God created the heavens and the earth – the earth was void and vacuum, and darkness was over the deep, and the wind of God was sweeping over the face of the waters – (then) God said . . ." (2010:52; cf. Kugel 1998:61). Even scholars who opt for the traditional rendering of verse 1 often acknowledge that verse 2 describes the situation *prior* to the detailed creation that is spelled out in verse 3, this last being the first day of divine activity (e.g., Hamilton 1990:115–17). E.A. Speiser points out one further troubling consequence if the traditional interpretation of the first verse is retained: "If the first sentence states

that 'in the beginning God created heaven and earth,' what ensued was chaos (vs. 2) which needed immediate attention. In other words, the Creator would be charged with an inadequate initial performance, unless one takes the whole of vs. 1 as a general title, contrary to established biblical practice" (1964:12–13).

5 Scholars continue to debate whether this "Combat Myth" is necessarily a part of an account of creation, creation through *agon* (competition) rather than *logos* (the word) Fishbane (2003:34–5; cf. Wakeman 1973), as in the Babylonian creation tale *Enuma Elish*. For most of the 20th century the majority scholarly opinion considered this biblical combat as part of a creational struggle, with various creatures standing for "chaos" which Yahweh had to overcome to establish the order of the universe. In this century, however, there have been numerous arguments against both this "creational" battle and also the use of the term "chaos," with its conflicting Greek and modern associations. Many scholars, however, still find a link with creation in some of the biblical passages that allude to Yahweh's conflict with the sea (e.g., Ballentine 2015:87; Pitard 2013:201–2; Batto 2013b). At least one scholar has tried to uncover this "hero's battle with a water demon/divinity" in both the *Iliad* and the *Odyssey* (Mills 2002), and Neil Forsyth argues that the Zeus's battle with Typhon/Typhoeus is an adaptation of the combat myth (1987:83–5; cf. Bachvarova 2016:250–65).

6 One theological issue the sheer existence of these primeval elements of evil or disorder elicits is their relation to God's "good" creation: "If he has created them [Leviathan and Behemoth], then they originate from his dark side, the one that generates evil" (Brenner 1981:134).

7 The crucial symbolism of the temple comes to embrace all three acts, as well as many other facets of his authority and covenantal links to the Israelites, but the building of the temple itself is rarely mentioned as one of *Yahweh's* remarkable feats.

8 Rahab in particular became associated with Egypt, and thus the crossing of the Red Sea (Sea of Reeds) was seen as another stab at the poor sea monster (Isa 51:9–10; cf. Isa 30:7; Ps 87:4; perhaps Ps 89:9–15). *Tannin*, too, can stand in for Egypt and the Pharaoh (Ezek 29:3–6; 32:2) as well as Babylon (Jer 51:34–6). And Isaiah couches his hopes for a better future in eschatological applications of the same myth of the conquest of the sea: On some future day Yahweh will take on and defeat the oppressive Leviathans, dragons, and Rahabs (e.g., Isa 27:1; 43:16–21; cf. Ps 91:13; Dan 7:1–3; cf. Rev 13:1–10; Melvin 2013).

9 Patrick Miller (1973:123) suggests this famous passage reflects an episode in ancient epic poetry that tells how the celestial bodies participated in the battles that Yahweh fought for Israel.

10 The Hebrew God seems to hold the host of heaven personally accountable for the misbehavior of his own chosen people. One day "the Lord will punish the host of heaven in heaven, and on earth the kings of the earth. They will be gathered together like prisoners in a pit; they will be shut up in a prison, and after many days they will be punished. Then the moon will be abashed, and the sun ashamed . . ." (Isa 24:21–3). Yahweh will go after his heavenly competition, killing off all their worshipers until "all the host of heaven shall rot away, and the skies roll up like a scroll. All their host shall wither like a leaf withering on a vine, or fruit withering on a fig tree" (Isa 34:1–5). Solar devotion was tenacious. Early synagogues were often decorated with mosaics of the zodiac with Helius in the middle, either pulled in his chariot or even with his full face and form depicted (Schama 2013:196–8).

Section III
The demands of finitude

11 Cheating death, squandering life

Most of our first-world illusions are relatively harmless; in fact, they often reveal an endearing optimism: We can lose weight and keep it off by eating lots of steak; our children are all cute and gifted; penises can be "naturally enhanced." But some acts of self-deception are not so innocent, and perhaps none has caused more unnecessary turmoil and misdirected energy than the continued inability to accept our mortal natures. As Woody Allen admitted, "I don't want to achieve immortality through my work; I want to achieve immortality through not dying."

Our reluctance to deal honestly with the inevitable victory of time and the unlikelihood of postmortem bliss has frustrated our search for meaning as we frantically seek to reverse aging, stop death, and find eternal salvation. And who can blame us? Old age isn't nearly as fun as AARP commercials suggest. The loss of those we care about seems inexplicably cruel, and our own extinction is nearly inconceivable. The final gestures of life itself – thanks to diminishing health care options and religious scruples about euthanasia – are often protracted, painful, and grotesque. Life *must* offer us more than this, even if it's in the *after*life. Why *shouldn't* we gravitate to myths that promise paradise to the faithful and a reunion with our loved ones? To Homer, the expression "deathless and ageless for all days" was the very definition of the gods. It's only human, isn't it, to want to share in the divine, to taste a bit of ambrosia and sip some nectar, to sit by God himself in "a brighter mansion over there"?

It's human, perhaps, but also a fundamental obstacle to living a meaningful life. The great Homeric paradox is that the closer we get to a life of the gods, the more inconsequential our lives become. Just look at the Olympians. One of the primary functions of Homer's divinities is to act as foils, not models. Unlike Christianity's interpretation of Jesus, the Homeric gods are the embodiment of what humans cannot and should *not* strive to be, *especially* in their literal immortality. This unbridgeable gulf has many dimensions, but the critical distinction is extraordinarily straightforward: The gods don't die, and we do, and there is no rapturous afterlife awaiting even the most heroic. We remember that one of the most common Greek words for gods is a negative formation – *athanatoi*, the "deathless ones" (*im*mortals) – in contrast to us *thnêtoi*, "the dying ones" (mortals) – for whom death (*thanatos*) is inevitable. Homer also refers to the

Olympians as *ambrotoi* (related to "ambrosia"), which means "not mortal." The gods are defined primarily against our human limits.

Death and afterlife have various manifestations in the Tanakh, but overall the picture is similar to that of Homer in its rejection of human immortality. There is a diversity of views of Sheol, the destination of the dead, but in general it is a shadowy place underground where, with a very few exceptions, everyone seems to go and from which there is no escape (Job 16:22; Hess 2007:266). Like Homer's Hades, it has gates (Isa 38:10; Pss 9:13; 107:18; Job 38:17; cf. bars in Jonah 2:6), and the dead require burial to enter (Niditch 2010:20). Two religion scholars, even though they are coauthoring an effort to bring the parallels between Judaism and Christianity closer together, must acknowledge that overall Sheol is nothing like Christian heaven or hell: "The conclusion to which the data impel us is that for those ancient Israelites who produced the Hebrew Bible, Sheol seems in general to have remained as lifeless, as remote, and as inaccessible as the psalms of thanksgiving and of lament portray it. . . . Death is the prolongation of an unfulfilled life" (Madigan and Levenson 2008:65, 77). The afterlife does not seem to have been of much interest to the authors of the Tanakh, an "infrequent theme and an unwelcome fate" (Johnston 2002:85). The rarity of exceptions to death's finality – two individuals who seem not to die (Enoch and Elijah), ghostly influences such as necromancy, and a few late references to resurrection of some sort (Isa 26:19; Daniel 12:2; Lang (1988:154–5) would add Ezekiel 37:1–15) – also suggests that the focus was on the here and now and that death was seen as a separation from what mattered (family, society, and God). Postmortem survival in the Tanakh comes, as it often does in the Greek epics, not through a heavenly rebirth but indirectly from one's lineage. Ultimately, death is quietly tragic, with life as fragile as a flower or grass, transient as a shadow, and brief as breath, until we return to dust (Marlow 2016:299; van Uchelen 1994:79–84).

This vital disjunction between life and death that is found in both the Tanakh and Homer's epics is muddled in Christianity, however, and so we will turn to Christian visions of afterlife in this chapter. The central Christian myth tells how an immortal God becomes mortal (in some mystifyingly filial fashion) only to die, return to earth, and finally ascend to heaven so that mortals can become immortal provided they believe the story about an immortal God who becomes mortal. This tale is explicitly designed to palliate fear and grief and to corner the market on "the way and the truth and the life."

The 17th-century polymath and Christian apologist Blaise Pascal famously acknowledged the "incomprehensibility" of God and so, in defense of a deity's existence, came up with what is now known as "The Wager": Since we can't be certain, the reasonable choice is to believe in God. If we're right, we win eternal salvation, and if we're wrong and there is no God, nothing has been lost.

What are we to make of Pascal's strange suggestion that one can or should believe something merely because it would be great if it were true? As philosopher Marvin Belzer observes, Pascal's wager "presupposes that God is a complete moral idiot" (2007:100). (It may be, as Daniel Garber argues, that Pascal knew that belief is not a matter of decision or will, but it is no more flattering to Pascal – or God – to suggest that he recommends that we simply "act as a believer would"; 2007:36). And note Pascal's assumptions: If there is a God, it is the Christian God, and if there is a Christian God, then there is a heaven; and if there is a heaven, it lies open for those whose sole objective is to get an invitation.

But what if the god that exists is Zeus? There goes heaven. Or what if it's Allah? You will have messed up royally, ignored the "five pillars" while nibbling the wafer or speaking in tongues, and no paradise will be waiting. So it's hardly the 50/50 guess that Pascal proposes – even if there is a deity (or lots of deities), the chances of making yourself believe – or acting like you believe – in the right one are miniscule. There are numerous philosophical holes in this kind of "prudential argument" or "consequential justification" for belief (Everitt 2004:150–77; Cliteur 2010:59–63), but the real problem I rarely see mentioned is what seems to me to be the most important: There is in fact a *whole lot to lose* by jumping onto the posthumous bandwagon. The unfounded hope that the next life is the purpose of this life diminishes everything in this life. Every decision, every act, every chance event comes complete with an insurance policy against the potentially tragic consequences. It's not an easy life, but it's challenging for all the wrong reasons. It's exhausting to follow all the vacuous rules embedded in the mythology, aggravated by theologians, and cemented by tradition. It's a life on drugs, a reverie that evangelicals firmly embrace: "A proper Christian worldview is uniquely focused heavenward. Though some would deride this as 'escapism,' it is, after all, the very thing Scripture commands" (MacArthur 2013:68).

Besides, according to most experts on the Christian afterlife, the gates of heaven don't swing open just because one wants them to – you have to *earn* your ticket. The promised path to paradise is paved with scores of other unsupported beliefs, time-consuming performances, and debilitating assumptions. Since this earthly life is all we can be certain of, an existence founded upon a posthumous eternity is at best muted, at worst misspent. "If you choose to ignore this precautionary tale of a fleeting life without supernatural consequences," psychologist Jesse Bering concludes, "there will be no hell to pay. Only missed opportunities. And then you die" (2012:205).

Don't get me wrong – the Homeric heroes also raged "against the dying of the light." Epic mortals and immortals alike fear and loathe death. But it was essential that humans ultimately succumb and know that they must; human purpose is impossible without limitations. So it was crucial that there be no promises of Isles of the Blessed, Elysium, or golden mansions of the gods waiting for them after death. You've got one shot – don't blow it. (They often did, just like us.) Because the gods don't die and mortals do, the imperatives for and consequences of human action take on real meaning whereas those of the gods cannot. The adultery of Ares and Aphrodite ends in a laugh among the Olympians with no enduring repercussions (*Od.* 8.266–366); the adultery of Paris and Helen, and of Clytemnestra and Aegisthus – and the potential infidelity of Penelope – drives the human destruction in the two epics. The gods' quarrel at the end of the first book of the *Iliad* quickly morphs into a party, whereas the clash between Achilles and

Agamemnon in the same book leads to the deaths of Sarpedon, Patroclus, Hector, and eventually Achilles himself.

But before he meets his fate, Achilles will also gain a clarity of vision and offer a gesture of compassion unavailable to the immortals. The finality of death provides the very possibility and demand for discovering an authentic life, what some contemporary ethics scholars have called the "virtue of finitude." We as individuals are merely an ephemeral part of nature's eternal cycle:

> Just as generations of leaves, such is that also of men. The wind scatters some leaves on the ground, but the dense forest produces others when the season of spring draws on; so with a generation of men – it comes into being, and passes away.
>
> (6.146–9)

This temporality is not a cause of depression for the heroic but a call to meaningful thought and action and to a profound compassion for the human condition. As classicist Emily Vermeule concludes in her study of Greek ideas about death (1979:123):

> Whether life is simply unpredictable, as the common poetic theme has it, and all action leads to danger; or whether there is active malice from "the blessed ones," or indifference, the Greek consensus was that life was short, deceptive and painful. It is part of the Greek legacy to the West, and almost a definition of humanism, that the Greeks found grief, defect and mortality, when faced with gallantry of mind, to be better than unearthly states of blessed existence.

In these next two chapters we will learn that living under the Homeric banner – that is, without reliable help from the gods – demands accepting death as the limit beyond which there is no meaning. We can try to ignore the daily march towards the looming barrier, but ultimately we must acknowledge that boundary and dismiss the temptation to daydream about what may lie beyond. If we are to live heroically, we must see the wall and nevertheless put the pedal to the floor to discover – and create – what is important in *this* life, right here and now. It's an adventure that is impossible to complete successfully. The fix is in, but it's the only game in town. And in that hokey "it's the journey, not the destination" sense that on occasion poets can capture more profoundly – as in Cavafy's wonderful poem *Ithaka* – it's not a bad game all in all.

In this chapter, we summarize some of the fundamental weaknesses in Christian mythology about death and dying. But first, to distinguish the Homeric attitude from its modern American counterpart, let's begin with a different myth from contemporary culture, one of my favorite tales about death and dying. You may feel I have picked an extreme case, but I think it serves as a felicitous introduction to modern American attitudes. Besides, it's just one of those stories that gets better with each telling. So gather 'round the campfire, boys and girls, and listen to the strange and eerie tale of Ted Williams' head.

The ballad of Ted's head: A modern myth of death and immortality

Ted Williams, the last professional baseball player to end the season officially batting over .400, died of heart disease on July 5, 2002, but he remains a "neuropatient" in Arizona. To make sense of this apparent non sequitur, you have to decode the lingo of the Alcor Life Extension Foundation in Scottsdale, the self-proclaimed "world's largest and most advanced provider of cryonics technology." "Patient" means "dead client"; "neuro" is cryonic-speak for "head." Within 48 hours of his "deanimation" (death) at the age of 83, Williams underwent "cephalic isolation" (decapitation) and his head was "neuro-suspended" (plunged into a stainless-steel tank filled with liquid nitrogen). His body, along with those of several other "patients," floats in a separate tank, *sans* neuro. He awaits revival in the future when someone has figured out how to revive frozen heads and put his mind back into a body (either his old one or, preferably, a freshly cloned model). The Alcor Life Extension Foundation concedes that this could take centuries.

Ted's head has suffered, and not just as the butt of internet jokes and late-night comedic monologues. According to a report in *Sports Illustrated*, during the beheading, or as a result of poorly infused liquids, the skull was accidentally cracked in as many as ten different places. In addition to this fracturing, the head was intentionally shaved, drilled with holes, and saturated with "cryoprotectant," a sort of high-tech embalming fluid that is supposed to keep bad (even worse?) things from happening to the frozen brain cells. In a book by a former Alcor insider, we learn that the process for Ted's head seems "to have been especially gruesome, barbaric and utterly botched – even by Alcor's minimal standards" (Johnson and Baldyga 2009:176). They mistakenly severed the head – it was supposed to be a full-body "suspension" – and the primary process was overseen by a "perfusionist whose only medical training was as a dialysis machine technician" (196).

The story does not end here, for there ensued a two-year court battle between Mr. Williams' children over his fate. The will was explicit, according to Ted's elder daughter: Her father wanted to be cremated, his ashes scattered across one of his favorite fishing spots in the Florida Keys. But another daughter and Ted's only son produced an "oil-stained, handwritten note," signed by them and their dad in a Florida hospital, which stated that he wanted to be cryonically preserved. The first (pro-cremation) daughter eventually ran out of money to continue the legal maneuvers. Consequently, Ted's head is still suspended in "biostasis" (-320 degree slush).

No doubt at first glance it seems a bit unfair to use the bizarre story of Ted Williams' head as a paradigm for modern beliefs. The entire episode is rather sad and macabre, and to date only a few hundred people in the entire country are attempting their own super-chilled hibernation. There has long been a rumor that Walt Disney's body was cryonically entombed, but there is no truth to it. (While I was checking this out, at one point I cross-listed "Walt Disney" and "cryonics" on a search through Lexis/Nexis – I got referred to "*Snow* White.")

Despite the hopes of cryonicists and the extravagant claims of a handful of nanotechnicians, almost all medical experts believe that the "corpsicles" (as they have been happily, if privately, labeled by members of the industry) have a snow-ball's chance in hell of ever defrosting back into life. There is no reason to believe that science will ever be able to reverse the damage done by age, disease, death, mutilation, and freezing. Ted may have hit a home run in his last major league at bat, but one can't help feeling that he (or his son) took one more crazy swing for the fence and whiffed.

Most of us snicker or shake our heads (delighted we still have them) at such a self-indulgent and desperate faith in science. But Ted's head offers a revealing picture of our faith in the scientific effort to find a "cure" for aging and even death. Full cryonic suspension costs up to $200,000. The "Cryonics Insurance Page" suggests a policy of at least $155,000 to cover the long-term costs.[1] But the weird world of cryonics is merely the small (if coldest) tip of America's "longevity" ice-berg, our multibillion-dollar war against Father Time. Industry analysts estimate that the annual global market for "antiaging" skin care products alone will reach $154 billion by 2021. The amount we spend on the multifarious books, clinics, treatments, "lifestyles," and genetic research to extend our lives dwarfs that, not to mention the fringe theorists such as extropians, transhumanists, omega point theorists, singularians, "connectome preservationists," and foundations searching for "engineered negligible senescence" (Shermer 2018:131–58; Solomon et al. 2015:95). We do not go gentle into that good night, especially the aging Boomers, one of whom turns 65 every ten seconds.

It's easy to dismiss a few wealthy eccentrics as misguided suckers. A *vast majority* of Americans, however, have taken out an even more appealing, just as costly, and equally as credible policy against their obliteration, against the extreme probability that life is finally tragic and tragically final. A glance at sur-veys conducted over the past few years (2011–2017) in the U.S. suggests that we should tread carefully before scoffing too loudly at Ted and his children:

> 80% of Americans believe in God
> 80% of Americans believe in heaven
> 77% of Americans believe God or a higher power has protected them
> 75% of Americans believe in angels
> 72% of Americans believe in life after death (it's not clear how this lines up with "heaven")
> 67% (or 58% in another survey) of Americans believe in hell (61% in 2017 believed that God will judge all people. In a 2014 survey, 82 percent of respondents believed they were bound for heaven. Two percent anticipated an eternity in hell. A statistic I have not seen, but would like to, is the per-centage of *other* people we think will go to hell.)
> 67% of Americans believe that God has rewarded them
> 56% of Americans believe in God as described in the Bible
> 48% of Americans believe God or another power directly determines what happens in their lives most of the time
> 40% of Americans (including 44% of Catholics) believe in ghosts
> 40% of Americans believe that God has punished them

28% of Americans talk to God and say that God talks to them
21% of Americans believe we can contact the dead
18% of Americans believe in reincarnation

According to a 2014 survey, 32 percent of American *agnostics and atheists* believe in some sort of postmortem existence! Modern America is an interesting and in some ways spectacularly medieval place. Belief that science will progress to the point that it can bring the frozen dead back to life is seen as silly. Yet belief in a divine soul that survives death and moves on to eternal life is mainstream. In fact, it's mandatory if you want to be elected President. How strange is that! Ted's hope to see his children again on this earth – his son died of leukemia shortly after him and is also currently residing in one of Alcor's steel vats – is painted by the media as spookily perverse. Far more likely, we feel, is that dead family members will greet us in paradise.

The point of this invidious comparison between an irrational religious belief and an irrational faith in science is that most Americans – not just a few fringe oddballs – live in daily denial of the significance of the irrevocability of death. Death is *not* the end, they insist. For a more typical modern myth of life and death, I could have used any story in the media (they unfortunately appear almost daily) of a grieving parent's confidence that it was *their God* who took their child (through the inscrutable means of a drunken teenager in a Honda) for some ultimately meaningful purpose – and that they will all be together again one day.

Or I could have quoted from a bestseller like *Embraced by the Light*, the uplifting story of a woman who died, spent some time hanging out with Jesus in heaven, and then came back to tell us about it. (Plato relates a similar myth in the *Republic*, but for some reason few people believe that one.) This burgeoning "heaven tourism" genre – headlined by the 2004 bestselling book (6.5 million copies) and subsequent 2015 movie about a Baptist minister's *90 Minutes in Heaven* – took one on the chin when another bestselling account of a heavenly visit turned out to be a fraud. *The Boy Who Came Back From Heaven: A True Story* (made into a TV movie) was revealed to be not so true – by the author himself! A few years after writing the book (coauthored with his father), the "boy who came back" confessed that "I did not die. I did not go to Heaven. . . . I said I went to Heaven because I thought it would get me attention." Only six at the time of his accident, he now tells people to read the Bible, not his own "lies." Both he and his mother spent several guilt-ridden years trying to convince the publisher (a Christian publishing house with annual revenues close to $200 million) and the evangelical community that it was not a real-life story of "miracles, angels, and life beyond this world." Finally, five years after its publication and a million copies sold, the book was pulled from print by its publisher, and many Christian bookstores took it off the shelf. Lifeway Christian Resources, one of the biggest vendors of Christian paraphernalia, subsequently announced that it would cease selling *all* "experiential testimonies about heaven" in accordance with the Southern Baptist Convention resolution that scripture alone is sufficient "regarding the afterlife." After all, didn't Jesus say that "no one has ascended into heaven except the one who descended from heaven, the Son of Man" (John 3:13; cf. Prov 30:4)? Oh, and the family name of the father and son who coauthored the book? Malarkey. Really.

These tales of heavenly visitation annoy some hardened fundamentalists as well. John MacArthur, a pastor of a southern California megachurch and head of a minor evangelical empire, has nothing but contempt for Christians who turn to anything but scripture – and his own books – for *The Truth about Heaven, Angels, and Eternal Life*: "Given the rising tides of militant atheism, postmodern skepticism, biblical illiteracy, self-love, and gross immorality, what are we to make of the current interest in heaven? One thing is clear: it does not signal any significant upsurge of interest in what biblical revelation teaches about heaven. On the contrary, the data actually seem to indicate that lots of people are simply making up whatever concept of heaven pleases them" (2013:14). MacArthur's approach couldn't be more different, he insists, as he amplifies the nebulous sketch of heaven, angels, and eternal life provided by the New Testament into 200 pages of Christian certitude.

Christian hope?

Religions aren't all based on the fear of death and what happens afterwards, but Christianity certainly is, as the first great proselytizer of the religion insisted: "If there is no resurrection of the dead, then Christ has not been raised; and if Christ has not been raised, then our proclamation has been in vain and your faith has been in vain" (1 Cor 15:13–14). The second-century Christian apologist Tertullian stated simply that "the Christian's confidence is bound up with the resurrection of the dead. That makes us believers" (*On the Resurrection of the Dead* 1, cited in Daley 2004:493). As a leading Christian theologian recently concluded, "Christianity is a religion of hope, which focuses on the resurrection of Jesus as the ground for believing and trusting in a God who is able to triumph over death and to give hope to all those who suffer and die" (McGrath 2015:117). After all, as Paul commanded, "if you have been raised with Christ, seek the things that are above, where Christ is, seated at the right hand of God. Set your minds on things that are above, not on things that are on earth" (Col 3:1–2; cf. Cor 15:16–19).

One of America's best-known Christian apologists, William Craig Lane, spelled out the real concern in a speech entitled "The Absurdity of Life Without God" before the Academy of Christian Apologetics. The following quote captures the terror[2] that drives so many theists to demand an afterlife:

> Scientists tell us that everything in the universe is growing farther and farther apart. As it does so, the universe grows colder and colder, and its energy is used up. Eventually all the stars will burn out, and all matter will collapse into dead stars and black holes. There will be no light at all. There will be no heat. There will be no life, only the corpses of dead stars and galaxies, ever-expanding into the endless darkness and the cold recesses of space, a universe in ruins. The entire universe marches irreversibly toward its grave. So not only is each individual person doomed, the entire human race is doomed. The universe is plunging toward inevitable extinction. Death is written throughout

its structure. There is no escape. There is no hope. If there is no God, then man, and the universe, are doomed. Like prisoners condemned to death row, we stand and simply wait for our unavoidable execution. If there is no God, and there is no immortality, then what is the consequence of this? It means that life that we do have is ultimately absurd. It means that the life we live is without ultimate significance, ultimate value, ultimate purpose.

(quoted in Wielenberg 2005:14–18)[3]

My point is to reveal not the leaps of logic that Lane's argument involves but the reason that life after death remains so potent for those who simply can't imagine a significance, value, or purpose that is not guaranteed by a supernatural being. (Note that Craig's demand for immortality is a specific Christian vision. Homer's heroes live on in some form, as we shall see, and many cultures have believed in immortality through reincarnation. And then there's Ted's head.) Craig needs an afterlife that makes up for what he feels is clearly missing in *this* life, a life that is "absurd" without another, better one waiting.

But Craig's fears are not borne out by any data. Although death awareness can exaggerate some of the darker sides of human nature, it also motivates people to live more fulfilling, prosocial lives. Researchers have shown how the fact of our ultimate mortality can "foster loving relationships, encourage community involvement, and support intergroup peace-building; and foster certain self-enriching behaviors, such as creative expression or the exploration of novelty" (Vail and Juhl 2015:1036). And as we shall see in Chapter 14, theistic individuals and societies are not in any way more moral, happy, or successful.

Craig is not alone, however, in possessing a limited imagination about the positive aspects of human limitations. Most of the hymns, songs, prayers, and chants of the Christian faithful speak of sin and redemption, judgment day and salvation, Jesus' love, "crossing the Jordan," and loved ones waiting to greet each other in the paradise right after death. Christians sing about "flying away" on "some glad morning when this life is o'er . . . to a home on God's celestial shore." My own exposure to this rich tradition started with bluegrass gospel. From just one Flatt and Scruggs album (yes, I said "album" – that's how old I am), for example, I long ago learned the basic and traditional tenets of contemporary American Christianity. Choosing verses from just three songs:

They've joined the heavenly fold
They're walking the streets of pure gold
They left one by one as their work here was done
Gone home (they have gone home) gone home (they have).

("Gone Home")

And when this road is finished I wanna travel on
I can hear the angels singing up there around the throne
I want to see my mother and take her by the hand
Soon as I have finished the road to Gloryland.

("I'm Workin' On a Road")

> I wanna go to heaven when this life is over
> I wanna be with Jesus on eternity shore
> But if I've a crown coming when rewards go around
> Please blessed Jesus give mother my crown.
>   ("Give Mother My Crown")

It's a quick one-way ticket to the new heavenly home, streets of gold, angels singing, an enthroned Jesus, and Mom. Most American Christians cheerfully focus on their individual soul's immediate destiny after their demise, despite this doctrine not being "expressly taught in Scripture" (Hayes 1989:110–1). Sometimes the gospel songs talk about meeting up with a cherished spouse in the afterlife, but that's not going to happen, as least as they tend to envision it: Jesus himself was insistent that there is no marriage in heaven.

But as an academic, I was aware that American folk music could possibly be misleading as my primary source for Christian belief. So, to expand my horizons, I spent a sabbatical reading the New Testament in the original Greek and Christian theology that focused on ideas of the afterlife. And what I learned, in a nutshell, was this: The stuff that Christian theologians fret and write about *is not even on the radar* of most American Christians and in many cases is in direct conflict with what they actually believe, and very little of it can actually be found in the Bible.[4]

Since the one, prime, central, *crucial* element of Christianity is the tale of Jesus' crucifixion and resurrection and its significance for humanity, you would think that Jesus must have spent a good deal of time talking about posthumous existence, and that invested believers would have arrived at some sort of consensus on what it all means. But you would be wrong. It's all still a grand "mystery" with virtually no agreement on the nature of Christian immortality. This is primarily because Jesus actually doesn't have that much to say about it. "It is indeed ironic that our Christian faith provides so little information concerning life after death," notes William La Due in his introduction to over 20 different Christian theological approaches to the topic (2004:ix). The earliest parts of the New Testament seem especially indifferent to the subject. As scholar and retired Anglican bishop N.T. Wright states, "in none of the four gospels, nor in the first chapter of Acts, does Jesus' resurrection cause anyone to speculate about their own ultimate future" (2014:5). After all, why waste time in speculation when Jesus would be back in a few years to explain it all? Jesus himself is confident in the glories of heaven for the righteous and a "furnace of fire" for "all evildoers," but exactly who these folks are, what these terms mean, what happens and when, are not topics he explains clearly or at any length. Paul has a bit more to say, but the details remain vague and self-contradictory: "There is no consistent anthropology in the New Testament nor even in the writings of individual authors" (Badham 1983:145–6; cf. Evans 1983:502).

Thus we have the embarrassing chaos of a 2000-year dispute about "eschatology," a slightly abused term that now usually refers to theories of the final destination of both the individual soul and the cosmos itself.[5] History has seen its share of conflicting heresies, papal bulls, councils, creeds, catechisms, and schisms both within and between the many Christian traditions on these matters. For example, Jesus doesn't provide any details about corporeal resurrection, a vital Christian tenet that "plays little part in Jesus' teaching," although he does support it in arguing against the Sadducees (Evans 1983:501). Nevertheless, the early Christians were not body-soul dualists, but "expected the body to rise in a restored earthly paradise, whose arrival was imminent" (Bynum 1995:14). As hopes for the immediate *parousia* (Jesus' second coming) faded – and the corpses got moldier – Christians until the 13th century believed that there would be one Judgment Day *at some point* whereupon the bodies of the dead would be resurrected and the world would end. Belief in the bodily resurrection was mainstream Christian thought, even though, in the words of religion scholar Caroline Walker Bynum, "it seemed almost to require philosophical incoherence, theological equivocation, or aesthetic offensiveness." She adds that "it is clear that the resurrection of the body is a doctrine that causes acute embarrassment, even in mainstream Christianity" (1995:11, 14). Theologians still don't know what to do with the dead bodies. A contemporary Jesuit scholar must admit "how mysterious and unclear the content of bodily resurrection remains" (Daley 1991:222).[6]

The role of the human body in death and resurrection has never been sorted out. One theologian candidly concedes that "the world of professional New Testament scholarship remains deeply divided on this matter, with skepticism being more marked and extreme than previously" (Williams 2000:618). "Deeply divided on this matter" . . . and on just about every other one involving life after death. Here are some of the basic questions Christians raise, try to answer, and then can't agree on:

1) What's the relationship between the immortal soul and the bodily resurrection? Is there a "particular" judgment at death or a "general" judgment when Jesus gets the ball rolling a second time, or both? That is, do you go immediately to paradise or hell, as Jesus once implies (Luke 23:43), a "puzzling statement" that "sits uneasily with prevalent traditions that the dead rest in the earth until the last judgement and with the later tradition of Jesus' descent into hell between his death and Resurrection" (Pyper 2000d:514)? If the soul (or is it the body?) is put on hold until the resurrection of the flesh, is the soul asleep in the interim? Consciously waiting? Continuing to experience and "grow"? Or is it cleansed of the guilt of its sins in purgatory (an extratextual concept that is *de fide* for Catholics and completely rejected by Protestants)? If so, can this process be alleviated by the intercession of the faithful through prayers, sacraments, and cash? What about those who died BCE? What about unbaptized babies still covered in original sin? (Augustine said they went straight to hell, Aquinas focused on limbo, and the Catholic Church – as of 2017 – says there are "reasons to hope . . . that they may be saved and brought into eternal happiness.") Is the "reconstituted" body a material one, a spiritual one, or some combination thereof? Does God use the same particles to compose it or create particles identical to the original body? (It was only in 1997 that the Vatican granted permission for the "cremated remains of a body to be brought into

church for the liturgical rites of burial"; McGrath 2015:120.) Is the resurrected body clothed or is everyone running around naked? What's the "age" of the resurrected body? (Medieval theologians were pretty sure it was around 30, no matter the age of the person at death.)

2) What's heaven – is it literal or metaphorical, here and now or then and there, physical or relational? Do we experience it or is it merely God's eternal recollection of or perspective on us? If it's a place, are there subdivisions, say, between the "Overcomers" (those Christians who are spiritually prepared to take on Satan) and regular ole Sunday churchgoers? Is there an actual temple there? Or is the "new" world merely replacing the old? And who gets to go to heaven – just those who accept Jesus as savior and son of God (faith alone, *fide sola*); the faithful who have participated in the sacraments (the Eucharist was called the "medicine of immortality" by Ignatius, Bishop of Antioch, in his *To the Ephesians* 20, cited in Rowell 2014:63); everyone; a select number (144,000, according to Jehovah's Witnesses); just the predestined; all those who seek God with a sincere heart; or perhaps everyone who is a faithful adherent of *any* religious tradition ("anonymous Christians," as one Jesuit theologian famously put it)? Does judgment merely separate the saved from the condemned or put all of humankind on trial? Or is it just a matter of sexuality, as Jerome and Aquinas calculated: Virginal folks received 100 percent of the heavenly reward, widows and widowers 60 percent, and married people 30? (We all know what happens to homosexuals.)

3) Is there a hell? Is it a place of torment for the dead or a present or eternal existence separate from God? Does one stay there forever? Are the saved and the damned aware of each other? If so, how can the saved endure eternity when they find out some of their loved ones didn't make the cut? (Tertullian (*The Shows* 30) proclaimed that "one of the joys which the saved would experience would be watching the torments of the wicked in hell"; Laffine 2009:25. Ah, Christian love.) Or is immortality "conditional" and hell merely personal oblivion? Is hell a metaphor like everything else in the Bible?

4) What, exactly, happens when Jesus comes back? How many times does he come back – just once in a big bang or does he return in secret for seven years? Does he come before Armageddon to establish a millennial kingdom here on earth, or do the 1000 years come before Jesus' arrival? Is it a time of peace or suffering? Will worthy Christians have to endure the Tribulation or will they be plucked up to heaven before things hit the fan? Will the Anti-Christ launch a horrendous persecution of the Jews, slaughtering two thirds of them in a new Holocaust (Boyer 2003:539)? What's the postapocalyptic world look like? (Heaven-authority John MacArthur, using the figures in the book of Revelation, has determined that "New Jerusalem" will be a 1500-cubic-mile holy city with 2.25 million square miles of living space for up to 100 billion people; 2013:117–19.) Is the kingdom of God already started ("inaugurated"), realized, or in the future? Can we calculate when Jesus will return or is this a doomed effort, a humiliating series of Great Disappointments, better left alone? (The failed attempts are

legion, starting with Hippolytus of Rome's (c. 200 CE) suggestion of 500; Isichei 2000).

The list could go on, but you get the point. Learned New Testament scholars know the eschatological guesswork will always remain inconclusive. The author of a 600-page introduction to Christian theology acknowledges that "A central theme of Christian theology down the ages has been that unaided human attempts to discern fully the nature and purposes of God are ultimately unsuccessful" (McGrath 2015:152). But this inevitable failure doesn't stop them from trying to nail it down anyway (with God's help, as McGrath slyly suggests) and often attempting to impose their interpretations on others.

Actual believers, however, for the most part don't know or care about all this wheel-spinning. It turns out that the best evidence for American beliefs about the afterlife (70 percent of whom self-identified as Christian in 2014) is to be found not in theological writing but in the data gathered from the surveys (and bluegrass gospel). There are a lot of Christians in the U.S. (more than in any other country), and most believe their souls upon death will be immediately translated to heaven. There are also a lot of people waiting for the *parousia* (Jesus' encore): Nearly twice as many Americans believe in a forthcoming biblical rapture (55 percent – half think it will come in the next 30 years) as accept evolution without divine intervention. The relentless *Left Behind* Dispensationalist novels have sold over 70 million copies. (There's even a *Left Behind* video game that "puts players in command of an apocalyptic battle between the Tribulation Forces and the Global Community Peacekeepers during the End of Days raging in the streets of New York City.") Some conservative Christians and Orthodox Jews are encouraged by, rather than dismayed at, the conflict in the Middle East, interpreting the chaos as a necessary precursor to the arrival of the Messiah, although they are in strong disagreement about whether this will be his first or second layover on earth. And I need not emphasize the horrific consequences of the paradise promised to radicalized Muslims. Life after death has never been so popular.

And that is very unfortunate. If we want to base our lives on mythology, once again we would fare much better by adopting the wisdom of our earliest Hellenic blueprint. Heaven may cushion us psychologically from the nasty vicissitudes of existence, and hell may keep some from cheating on their spouses (or provide a few believers with smug visions of atheists and Jews sizzling for eternity). A concern about both postmortem destinations has no doubt been one source of charitable actions on behalf of the poor and powerless, as well as the torture and oppression of countless others. But to lead your life with heaven as your goal is like sitting on a couch for 60 years waiting to win the lottery. Well, not quite. The existence of the lottery is provable – we know some people really do win – and lotto-playing doesn't seem to lead to concomitant homophobia, racism, misogyny, anti-Semitism, and "unholy" violence as readily as a selective reading of the Bible regularly has (Lüdemann 1997; Thatcher 2008). But either way, a life spent waiting for a future "better time" is a sadly squandered opportunity.

Homeric heroes, on the other hand, have nothing to look forward to after death. They are not gods and share in no immortality. As Apollo reminds Diomedes with a "terrible cry": "Think about it, son of Tydeus, and give way – do not seek to think on equal terms with the gods, since at no time is the race of immortal gods and that of men who walk upon the earth the same" (5.440–2). The epics depict man's heroic struggle with a nature that in the long run will always win, of humanity's destined confrontation with its own limitations, after which there are no grand rewards or horrendous punishments. Robert Garland's study of Greek attitudes towards death concludes succinctly (2001:122–3):

> If Hades' very dreariness was the reverse image of a Greek *joie de vivre*, there was some compensation to be derived from the fact that the place was largely devoid of terrors. . . . The ordinary Greek dead were more to be pitied than to be feared. Sterile, deadlocked in time, conscious of loss, out of touch with the world above, lacking the sinews and strength of the living, yet preserving everlastingly their wounds, their rancour, their hatred – these are the "ghosts of worn out mortals" (*brotôn eidôla kamontôn*) as Homer represents them.

The central, determining facet of the tragic vision in Homer is that death awaits us all, that it is unavoidable, and that whatever looms afterwards is virtually meaningless. The early Greek emphasis on character, dignity, self-critique, empathy, and genuine compassion *for those living in the here and now* may present just the "spiritual path" so many people are seeking even today. To make it down that road, however, some pretty heavy baggage will have to be tossed aside. And some of it, to judge from the surveys, will be our favorite pieces of luggage. But most of us are way over-packed.

Notes

1 At one point there was even a Re-Life Asset Insurance Company that would pay you upon your return from cryogenic stasis, "providing assets to kick start your Re-life"! Alas, the company seems to have vanished, even with what I thought had to be a fool-proof business model.
2 Terror Management Theory (TMT) suggests that human awareness of mortality, coupled with our fundamental drive for self-preservation, produces an existential terror that we must learn to manage psychologically. We keep this paralyzing fear at bay by adopting worldviews – especially through religion – that help us transcend our mortality in some figurative or, in the case of some religions, literal fashion. Any challenge to our worldview threatens our fragile efforts, so we dig in even deeper when challenged. Various studies have revealed that "people indeed seek to find solace in the supernatural when faced with the existential meaningless elicited by reminder of mortality" (Greenberg et al. 2001; Newheiser et al. 2013:114–16; Burke et al. 2010). But religion scholars are hesitant to find the origins of religion in mechanisms to cope with death (e.g., Atran 2002:12), and social scientists are not all convinced (Shermer 2018:14–20). To me, the more TMT tries to account for *all* aspects of human activity (which its recent proponents seem to attempt, e.g., Solomon et al. 2015), the less convincing it appears. Other studies show that individuals with either high or low religiousness are least afraid of death; people who are moderately religious fear death most (Wink and Scott 2005). So it looks

like *ambivalence* regarding death and afterlife is most closely linked to anxiety. The lesson: Whether theist or atheist, commit.

3 See also the second chapter, "The Absurdity of Life Without God," in Craig's book on "reasonable faith" (2008:65–90). Craig, like many Christians, is obsessed with the concern that "if each individual person passes out of existence when he dies, then what ultimate meaning can be given to life?" (72). The terror of having to make sense of life on his own completely retards his ability to consider the logical and obvious alternatives to a God-given purpose. Sentimental variants of his general point can be found in many theological publications. I'll quote just one more. Christopher J.H. Wright cites Philip Pullman's stark vision of the underworld in *His Dark Materials* as a typical nontheistic interpretation of death (which it isn't – it's faintly Homeric, since the dead still exist in some fashion and have personalities at various stages): "As against the biblical vision of gloriously rich life in resurrection bodies in a renewed creation, what can Pullman offer? . . . I read that and I think, *Is that it? Is that the best that the atheist imagination can offer? Death as the popping cork of a champagne bottle, a little cursing bubble of happiness, and then . . . nothing. Nothing personal. Nothing gloriously human. Just the dissolution into the 'everything' of the rest of the universe.* And then I read 1 Corinthians 15 and the gospel narratives that provide the historical evidence for the resurrection of Jesus of Nazareth, and my heart leaps . . ." (2008:214–15). Catholics can be as terrified of autonomy as Protestants. In his Easter homily of 2011, Pope Benedict XVI warned that "if man were merely a random product of evolution in some place on the margins of the universe, then his life would make no sense and might even be a chance of nature" (quoted in Stenger 2012:110). *Might be?*

4 Not that every flavor of contemporary Christianity is fixated on the afterlife as Americans clearly are. While most Danes and Swedes identify themselves as Christians, only about 30 percent believe in life after death of any kind (Zuckerman 2008:10, 150).

5 The Greek term *eschata* means "final things," so eschatology is the study of or discourse about "the end," although the Greeks themselves never used the word in this religious sense. "Apocalyptic" is sometimes used in the same way, although it increasingly refers to a genre or literature in general that focuses on last things, like the books of Daniel and Revelation (McGrath 2011:444–5).

6 Almost as confusing was the nature of Jesus' body, which Christians believe disappeared from the tomb. It was certainly mortal enough at birth: Charlemagne received Jesus' foreskin (the "Holy Prepuce") from an angel (or perhaps Jesus himself) in Jerusalem and gave it to Pope Leo III in 800 when he was crowned Holy Roman Emperor. This sacred relic ended up in Calcata Vecchia in Italy, where it received authorized veneration. The Holy Prepuce of Calcata (one of the best titles of anything *ever*) disappeared in the 1980s – rumors abound that the Vatican, increasingly embarrassed by its unverified status (or worried that progressively sophisticated DNA tests could be administered with uncomfortable results), had it stolen. An alternate version has Charlemagne handing over a *fake* foreskin to the Pope and sending the real one to Conques, a small town in France, where it still resides. (There were more than a dozen of these divine foreskins in Europe in the Middle Ages.) Catholics celebrated the Feast of the Circumcision of Our Lord up to the middle of the 20th century.

12 We all have it coming

One of my favorite mythological characters is Sisyphus of Corinth, whom Odysseus spots as the third of an iniquitous triumvirate in his visit to Hades (*Od.* 11.593–600). You know him, or at least about his fate. Sisyphus is the one constantly trying to roll a stone up a hill, only to have it tumble back to the bottom each time he approaches the top. These "strong torments" raise enough sweat to run down Sisyphus' limbs – not something you might expect to find on a ghost. What did he do to deserve such punishment? Odysseus leaves that out of his account, but Homer reveals elsewhere that Sisyphus is one of the original trickster figures, the "slyest of men" as one of his descendants calls him (6.153). One post-Homeric tradition even postulates that the wily Odysseus was his illegitimate son. The poet Alcaeus labels him as "almost too clever to die," a phrase he means quite literally. According to later sources, after Sisyphus interrupts one of Zeus's illicit affairs, the king of gods hands him over to Thanatos (Death personified) for delivery to Hades. But Sisyphus manages to tie up Thanatos, with the consequence that *no one* can die!

Thanatos is finally freed from his shackles and pursues Sisyphus, but the sneaky Corinthian has another plan. He instructs his wife not to carry out the necessary funeral rites after his death. When Hades learns that these religious duties have not been performed, he sends Sisyphus back up to earth to chastise her. (You see where this is heading.) Once back on *terra firma*, Sisyphus "neglects" to return to the underworld and remains above ground until he dies (again) of old age. So when he is finally sent to Hades for good, the gods have a special punishment in store. Since he went up and down so many times before he died, he can spend eternity going up and down as well (Sourvinou-Inwood 1995:68–9). And the sheer monolithic heaviness of his task is likely to keep him from slipping away one more time.

None of these shenanigans are in Homer's account, merely the punishment. In the epics, once you're dead, you're dead. Even for a clever guy like Sisyphus, death is unavoidable, permanent, and tedious. As Clint Eastwood's tragic character in *The Unforgiven* observes, "We all have it coming." Or in Homeric terms, Achilles reminds Priam that "you will not raise him [Hector, his dead son] back to life; before that happens you will suffer still some other evil" (24.551). Such finality is essential if we are to focus on living now, on finding a genuine existence in our limited time on earth. We mortals must search for meaning not in a loophole around finitude but in the confrontation with our limits, a contest that reveals the depths of human character, the height of human dignity, and, if we're lucky, a triumph in the irrepressibility of the human spirit. Homer's tragic world is a far better cicerone for our journey than the fantastical threats and rewards so central to most theistic religions.

Homer's pitiless death

So, what happens when you die in Homer's world? Although we should expect no absolute consistency in these ancient, oral traditions, a fairly clear picture emerges. Homeric humans have numerous centers of mental, emotional, or psychological activity that we are told cease to function, or even flee from the body, upon death. These strange "organs" are hard to pin down, both in terms of their specific functions and their physical location. Homer often seems perfectly content to swap them around or leave them out altogether according to the needs of the context and meter. *Psychê, thumos, kardiê, phrenes*, and *noos* don't always (or even usually) correspond exactly with anything familiar to our modern physiological knowledge or metaphysical fancy. These terms are thus often difficult to translate and impossible to render in any one way consistently.

When it comes to matters of life, death, and Hades, the most important entity is the *psychê*.[1] The *psychê* is the life-breath that abandons the corpse upon death. In fact, the *psychê*'s *only* function in Homer is to bail on the dying (or, occasionally, on those entering a temporary deathlike unconsciousness, e.g., 5.696–7; 22.466–7) and fly off to reside in Hades. The *psychê* is never noticed by the poet or characters until that moment of crisis, which suggests that it is some essence that animates the living. While *psychê* is often rendered as "soul," this translation to a modern ear carries with it all sorts of inappropriate dualisms found only in later Greek, optimistic notions embedded in Christianity, or inapposite psychological/philosophical theories of "self" (although it will move this direction semantically in the post-Homeric period; Clarke 1999:287–319; Bremmer 2002:2). In a struggle to survive battle, a duel, or perilous adventures, it can often best be translated simply as "life" (Warden 1971:95). One can be said to risk his *psychê*. A Trojan waiting to meet Achilles in battle fortifies his courage by telling himself that "surely his [Achilles'] flesh is vulnerable to a sharp sword, and there is one *psychê* in him, and men say he is mortal" (21.568–70). Lose your *psychê*, lose your life, and vice versa.

Psychê is also the term most commonly used to describe the dead ("ghosts," "shades," "spirits") that are featured in several famous episodes in the epics we will be drawing on in this discussion. Although there are conceptual difficulties in linking these two senses of the word, classicist Michael Clarke suggests that they are connected because in both contexts the *psychê* is lifeless, cold, and vaporous. For the dead, it is "this lack of life, strength and substance, expressed in their flitting movement, that gives them the same name as is the cold breath of death" (1999:148).[2]

In Book 11 of the *Odyssey*, Odysseus recounts to his hosts, the Phaeacians, the story of his visit to Hades to consult the *psychê* of the dead seer Tiresias. The Greek hero also meets and talks with numerous other *psychai*, the ghosts of the dead, in one of the more famous parts of the epic often referred to as the Nekyia. At the beginning of the final book of the epic, Homer shows us the *psychai* of the dead suitors arriving in the underworld. Here, too, we meet notable ghosts and learn their stories.[3] We will be using both passages (as well as many passing comments) as evidence for Homer's concept(s) of death and its significance.

Our focus here is on the ultimate nature and fate of the *psychê* after the death of the Homeric mortal. (The body is cremated, and the remains placed in a marked grave, an important gesture for heroic commemoration.) The *psychê* of Anticleia, Odysseus' dead mother, sums up the process of dying when the hero encounters her at the edge of Hades:

> This is the inevitable way for mortals, when someone dies. For the sinews no longer hold the flesh and the bones together, but the powerful fury of blazing fire subdues them, as soon as the spirit (*thumos*) leaves the white bones, and the ghost (*psychê*) wings its way like a dream and flies off.
>
> (*Od.* 11.218–22)[4]

The *psychê* exits from the dead through the mouth (the "barrier of the teeth," 9.409), limbs (16.856; 22.362), or lethal wound (14.518; 16.505). The *psychê* is sometimes said merely to leave or fly off, but often the destination is spelled out: It heads off (down) to Hades (e.g., 7.330; *Od.* 10.560; 11.65), and the texts lead us to assume that all *psychai* end up there.

Hades

First off: Hades is not hell. Actually, it's not even technically a place. Hades is the name of the god, the brother of Zeus and Poseidon, who has control of the "gloomy darkness" and "rules over those below" (15.187–93). The phrase translated "to Hades" in Homer normally means "to (the house/hall/place of) Hades." Hades' realm is generally conceived as under the ground – the dead "pass beneath the earth" or "go down." It is one of the marks of great heroes that they confront their mortality, and this is often depicted in Greek mythology through their descent into and return from the underworld. Heracles, Theseus, Orpheus, and Aeneas all visit the world of the dead and return to tell the tale. The ultimate heroic deed, then, is to overcome death symbolically. (Christianity borrows the conceit by having Jesus literally triumph over death and ascend to heaven, thereby combining two separate events in Heracles' life.) These adventures are referred to as a *catabasis*, a "going down," although as the Sibyl tells Aeneas, it's getting back up that is the real challenge (*Aeneid* 6.128–9). For Heracles, this meant going to the underworld to fetch the three-headed dog, Cerberus, a task the hero's ghost tells Odysseus was his toughest labor (*Od.* 11.623–6; cf. *Il.* 8.364–9).

Hades himself is rarely featured in the main narrative of either poem. Not officially an Olympian, he stays in his own dreary world, although we are told that he once had to visit the emergency room on Olympus to have an arrow shot by Heracles removed from his shoulder (5.395–402). Hades is known for his horses, animals that have chthonic (earthy) associations in Greek religion, but the story of his violent abduction of his future wife (Persephone) in his chariot is absent from the epics. (In one disputed passage, Athena dons Hades' cap, which apparently makes her invisible (5.844–5) – his name etymologically may mean "unseen," a reference to the Stygian darkness of the underworld.)

Hades is not a diabolical figure. He does not bring death, snatch the dead, or torment the souls of mortals who look at someone with lust or did not accept the divine nature of Heracles, son of god. He is merely the ruler of the land of the dead, "king of those below" (20.61). He is feared, rarely mentioned (and when he is, often with a euphemism, e.g., "Zeus of the Underworld"), and even hated because he takes his job seriously: The dead are dead, we all end up there, and Hades does not let any *psychê* go once the body is buried. As Agamemnon bitterly observes, "Hades is without doubt inexorable and intractable, and therefore he is the most despicable of all the gods to mortals" (9.158–9). Hades' implacability becomes a cliché in Greek literature – he has no cult because it does no good to offer him sacrifices. But it's not personal; it's strictly business. Death is inevitable, nonnegotiable, and permanent, its grim ineluctability acknowledged by Achilles: "For not even the mighty Heracles escaped death, even though he was most dear to lord Zeus, the son of Cronus" (18.117–18).

Odysseus travels to the edges of the world to find an entrance to Hades. His visit with the dead weaves together necromancy – the conjuring up of the dead – with an actual descent. One of the few constants in Homer's hazy description of the topography of the underworld, like that of Sheol, is the "gates." Hades is called the "gate-keeper" (e.g., 8.367; 13.415; *Od.* 11.277). To "pass the gates of Hades" means to die, to leave the light of day and never return (e.g., 5.646). Both Achilles and Odysseus turn to this concrete image of death when they wish to emphasize the degree of their abhorrence of something: "For hateful to my mind as the gates of Hades, so is . . ." (9.312; *Od.* 14.156–7).

Even the other immortals hate what Hades represents. In his only semisignificant (five-verse) appearance in the epics, Hades worries that the fighting of the gods will split open the earth and "his terribly dank house – which [so Homer tells us] even the gods hate – would be made visible for both mortals and immortals" (20.61–5). Athena refers to "hateful" Hades (*stugeros*, 8.368), an epithet Hades shares with Ares. But what, exactly, is so detestable about the afterlife and Hades' realm? *Why* is death so forbidding if it is not the pit of fire and gnashing teeth that Jesus threatens us with or the dungeon of perpetual torture imagined by the medieval church and contemporary evangelicals? This is a crucial question, for the answer reveals a view of the afterlife that runs counter to the bipolar eschatological visions of many contemporary Abrahamic theists.

Death and the dead

In Book 23 of the *Iliad*, Patroclus' irritated *psychê* visits the sleeping Achilles. Achilles has taken vengeance on Hector, but the corpse of his best friend still lies unburied next to the ships. Achilles apparently assumes Patroclus now resides permanently in the halls of Hades (23.19), but the "ghost" arrives to remonstrate with the snoozing leader of the Myrmidons:

> The ghost [*psychê*] of miserable Patroclus came to him [Achilles], looking like him in every way, his stature, his handsome eyes, his voice, and also the clothes he wore on his body. The ghost stood above Achilles' head and addressed him: "You sleep, and have forgotten me, Achilles. . . . Bury me as quickly as possible; let me pass through the gates of Hades. The ghosts [*psychai*], the phantoms of the weary dead, keep me far away, and they do not yet let me come in contact with those beyond the river, but I wander point-lessly up and down the wide-gated house of Hades. And give me your hand, I beg you, for I will never again return from Hades, once you have honored me with the pyre."
>
> (23.65–76)

The speech continues for a bit, at the end of which Achilles promises to accomplish all that has been asked. He tries to embrace his friend one last time, reaching out his hands, "but he didn't take hold of him; but the ghost (*psychê*) departed beneath the earth like smoke, squeaking." Achilles, stunned, reaches a sudden conclusion: "Amazing! There is something, a ghost (*psychê*) and phantom (*eidolon*) – even in the house Hades, although there is no mind (*phrenes*) at all" (23.103–4).

The *psychê* looks exactly like the living Patroclus, down to his clothes. Similarly, in the Nekyia, the dead look like they appeared upon expiration – brides, old men, "frisking maidens," and men slain in battle "wearing their bloodied armor" (*Od.* 11.36–41). Yet despite their realistic appearance, in substance Patroclus and other spirits are "like smoke." The ghost of Agamemnon reaches his hands towards Odysseus but he "no longer had firm strength or any force" (*Od.* 11.392–4). Odysseus tries three times to embrace the *psychê* of his mother, and "three times she flew from my arms like a shadow or a dream" (*Od.* 11.204–8). The dead are frequently referred to as "phantoms/images" (*eidola*) as well as spir-its (*psychai*), although the two words are not always interchangeable. (*Eidola*, for example, don't exist in living beings, and so we don't hear of them except in reference to the dead.) Note also that Patroclus' spirit, perfectly capable of speak-ing in Homeric hexameters to Achilles and recognized in part by his "voice," then disappears into the earth "squeaking." The voices of the buried dead (and, appar-ently, the very-soon-to-be-buried) sound like the screech of bats to the living (e.g., *Od.* 24.5–9), although they chat perfectly coherently with each other. Once one is buried, the finality of death saps any vital strength, even enough to speak Greek. The dead must drink sacrificial blood in order to be able to converse with Odys-seus, as Tiresias reveals to Odysseus (*Od.* 11.147–9; Heath 2005b).

In Odysseus' account of his adventures in the underworld, we hear several times of the "mindless dead," as we see in Achilles' reference to the absence of a "mind" in Patroclus' departing *psychê*, yet in general the ghosts are aware of what is going on around them.[5] This apparent contradiction has puzzled scholars of Greek religion (including ancient Greek readers themselves), but both the "witless dead" and the "animated dead" contribute in important ways to the overall grim picture of Hades that Homer is emphasizing. "Witless dead" vividly intimates the end of any mind, memory, and personality – death is nothing to be desired. But that hardly supplies fodder for interesting narrative. Thus the poet ignores the ramifications of that picture of the dead when it suits his poetic purposes. And high on his thematic priority list is the meaninglessness that death signifies, a vision that requires the dead to act and have a point of view with or without Odysseus' presence and his hemoglobin energy drink.

The *psychai* of Agamemnon, Achilles, and Heracles are introduced as grieving or weeping. Life in the underworld is, shall we say, unfulfilling, a "joyless place," as Tiresias observes (*Od.* 11.94). Homer's Hades is not built upon "happy reunions." We don't see dead family members holding hands. Though Agamemnon and Achilles must have been in the underworld for some time, apparently they've never met before (*Od.* 24.24–34). The shades seem frozen, isolated amidst nameless crowds, locked in an eternal past. Agamemnon remains bitter about his fate, his cruel butchery at the hands of his wife and her lover on the day of his "triumphant" return from Troy. It's pretty much all he wants to talk about. Heracles, too, only comments on his difficult life: "I was the son of Zeus, son of Cronus, but I suffered boundless misery" (*Od.* 11.620–21). The hunter Orion spends his time chasing down the *very same* animals he killed when alive (*Od.* 11.572–5)!

A poignant exchange between Achilles and Odysseus is probably the most frequently quoted passage from the entire visit to Hades. Odysseus contrasts his own sufferings during his wanderings with the "happy" fate of Achilles:

> No man before this was, or hereafter ever will be, more blessed than you. For before, we Argives honored you when you were alive equally with the gods, and now, being here, you have great power over the dead. Therefore, do not give in to any grief, even if you are dead, Achilles.
>
> (*Od.* 11.482–6)

But Achilles, actually dead and aware of what this means, is not buying Odysseus' injudicious words of consolation:

> Don't speak consolingly to me about death, illustrious Odysseus. I would prefer being bound to the earth and forced to work for hire for another, some landless man who must scrape by, than to rule over all the dead who have perished.
>
> (*Od.* 11.488–91)

Achilles realizes the cost of death – he will not be able to support and defend his aged father, a Greek son's duty, for "I am not a helper (for him) beneath the rays of the sun, not the man I once was in wide Troy . . ." (*Od.* 11.498–9).

Achilles seems to reject the heroic ethos of the *Iliad* in which the risk of death is essential for making any significant mark in the world. We will return to his insights later in this chapter. But for now we can see that Homer needs his dead to keep their wits about them for the primary purpose of remarking on death as inevitably unenjoyable. What makes death gloomy is that it is *not* life. Those actions undertaken by the dead no longer make any difference to anyone – the few actions we see are hollow repetitions of previous activities. When Classicist Jan Bremmer (1994:101) states that the "idea of the dead, then, as an anonymous, countless group perfectly fits the early Greek concept of death as an unavoidable, natural process," he paints half the picture. Since death is the great equalizer, it is the antithesis of an authentic life. There can be no mortal "heroes" in Homer's underworld – there can be nothing of significance. It's the lack of meaning that crushes the dead, an eternal existence without change, without learning, without challenge, without glory. In this way, the dead are similar to the gods – and perhaps to Christians in their heaven, a place so often charged with unspeakable dullness that evangelicals have grown a bit sensitive: "This deep-seated suspicion that heaven may be an eternal bore reflects the sinful thinking of fallen minds" (MacArthur 2013:84). But perhaps that's why the "eternal abode of the redeemed" must have gates like Hades – a great, high wall with 12 gates guarded by angels (Rev 21:12) – to keep the restless residents from trying to bolt.

Odysseus does see three infamous criminals being punished for eternity, but their crimes and punishments underline the general emptiness of death for the rest of us: Most of us wouldn't even qualify to be tormented in Hades! The three criminals directly attacked the prerogatives – or actual bodies – of the gods, and they pay an appropriate penalty. We've already met Sisyphus and his rock. Odysseus also spots Tityus among the other dead, who "raped Leto, the honored consort of Zeus." He lies stretched out on the ground, two vultures tearing out his liver. His crime, a direct physical violation of a deity, is matched by the eternal assault on his own body. Odysseus does not mention the crime of Tantalus, just his notorious sentence. Later sources tell us that he killed and served his own son as dinner to test the gods and that he attempted in various ways to gain immortality. Tantalus ends up in the underworld, immortalized only in the legendary anguish Odysseus describes. The "old man" (*Od.* 11.585) stands in a river up to his chin, able neither to drink (the water recedes as he reaches for it) nor to eat (the ripe fruit dangling from branches just in front of him is blown out of reach whenever he moves towards it, "the wind kept pitching [the fruit] to the overshadowing clouds," *Od.* 11.582–92). Tantalized forever, Tantalus reaches eternally as punishment for reaching for eternity (or perhaps deprived of sustenance in return for cooking his own child). As another iconic Clint Eastwood character observes, "a man's got to know his limitations." These punishments – to which most mortals are not subject – are eternal repetitions, more painful but equally as dull as the perpetual monotony of the afterlife of everyone else.

Homeric hope? Giving death the slip

But perhaps there is a way out after all. We saw that in acknowledging his own precipitate death, Achilles remarked that even Heracles had to die. In fact, Heracles is an interesting case. In post-Homeric accounts the hero does *not* die in the usual, human fashion but becomes a god. As a reward for his labors on earth, his mortal parts are burned off while he is dying and he (or some part of him) is translated to Olympus. Such a proto-Christian fate is puzzling to a tragic poet like Homer, who is aware of that version of the tale but doesn't quite know what to make of it. In the *Iliad*, Heracles is simply dead, the ultimate paradigm for mortal limitations: *Even* Heracles had to die. When Odysseus visits the dead in the *Odyssey*, he sees and chats with Heracles in the underworld. So far so good. But Homer (or at least Odysseus, who is narrating the story at this point) then includes the other variant as well: "I noticed the mighty Heracles – his phantom (*eidolon*); for he himself delights in the festivities among the immortal gods and has fair-ankled Hebe for a wife" (*Od.* 11.601–3). Heracles somehow is in two places at the same time.

This brief passage has been the source of great confusion from antiquity onwards. Although many critics have considered it to be an interpolation, it may represent a sort of compromise between the Homeric norms of the afterlife and a separate tradition of Heracles' divine status (Heubeck 1988:114; Albinus 2000:81). Homer feels that even in his peculiar divinity something of Heracles must also abide in the shadows down below.

A few other Homeric figures also manage to miss death, or at least we are told they might. Like Heracles, Helen's brothers, Castor and Pollux, suffer different fates in the two epics. In the *Iliad*, Helen wonders where they are, "but the life-giving earth already held them there in Lacedaemon, in their dear native land" (3.236–44). Things again get a bit more complicated in the *Odyssey*, however, when Odysseus sees the shade of Leda, the mother of Castor and Pollux (and Helen): "The life-giving earth holds down these two, although they are still living, and even beneath the earth they have honor from Zeus; now they live in alternation, now they are dead, and they have received honor equal to the gods" (*Od.* 11.301–4). The brothers are somehow both dead and alive. Homer doesn't specify whether they alternate together or separately – they may take turns, never seeing each other (Stafford 2010).

Menelaus is told by Proteus that because he has Helen as a wife – and so Zeus as a father-in-law – he will be translated by the gods to the paradisical Elysian plain "where life is easiest for men" (*Od.* 4.561–9). The young Trojan prince and "the most handsome of mortal men," Ganymede, is swept up to Olympus to become the "cupbearer" of Zeus because of his beauty (*Il.* 20.232–5). Similarly, Homer tells us that "golden-throned Dawn (Eos) abducted Cleitus because of his beauty, so he might be among the immortals" (*Od.* 15.250–1). We also hear that Dawn "rose from her bed beside illustrious Tithonus" (11.2; *Od.* 5.1–2), the latter being the poor mortal who was traditionally granted immortality without eternal youth (although Homer specifically mentions neither divine "gift").

What are we to make of these exceptions to the Homeric insistence that everyone dies and suffers an unenviable posthumous existence? Scholars often suggest that we see in these references a hint of other options available to the bard that after his time become increasingly popular. Homer merely (carelessly?) slips in these alternatives to death on occasion or feels compelled to acknowledge them (as in the case of Heracles). We know that even in Homer's time there were other, less-tragic visions of afterlife available. Hesiod tells us that to the survivors of the heroic age – including those at Troy – Zeus "granted a means of life and abodes apart from mankind and settled them at the ends of the earth; and these live having untroubled hearts on the islands of the blessed beside deep-eddying Ocean. They are happy heroes, for whom the fruitful field bears honey-sweet fruit ripening three times a year" (*W&D* 167–73).[6] The non-Homeric epics in the Trojan cycle overflow with the divine gift of immortality and magical devices. From the *Aethiopis* (a poem of the epic cycle that continued the Troy story from the end of the *Iliad* through the burial of Achilles), for example, we learn that the Ethiopian Memnon comes to assist the Trojans after Hector's death but is killed by Achilles. "Dawn [Memnon's mother] confers immortality upon him after prevailing on Zeus" (2). In the same epic, when Achilles is killed by Paris and Apollo, "Thetis grabs her son from the pyre and carries him to the White Island" (4).

Scholars have convincingly argued that Achilles' immortality is likely to have been the dominant mythological tradition even in Homer's time; that is, Homer alters Achilles' fate to emphasize his tragic mortality (Slatkin 1991:21–8; Edwards 1985; Johnston 1999:13–14; Burgess 2009:106–10 sees the hero's two fates as not completely incompatible). Achilles' mortality would seem to be the poet's innovation. Homer wants nothing to do either with Achilles' potential invincibility (the heel-thing) or his escape from the common fate of mortals. *All* the warriors at Troy must risk their lives in battle, with no hope of Blessed Islands offering an option to the heroic code.

It thus appears that "heroic immortality is a theme that is deliberately minimized in the Homeric discourse," a "strategy of repression" not shared by the epic cycle (Albinus 2000:87). As classical scholar Jasper Griffin concludes, mortality is an essential characteristic of Homeric man: "In the *Iliad* an unkillable warrior would be an absurdity; every man must face death, and no magical armour can be allowed to exempt him from that terrible prospect. And that death must be real death, not one which is to be blurred or evaded by allowing the hero to be presented with immortality instead" (1980:167).

Since Homer's epics may regularly present a *starker* vision of the finality of death than the inherited tradition, how are we to account for this occasional "slippage"? Why do a handful of exceptions to human mortality sneak through? It's an important question, the answer to which will reveal just how central Homer considered human death and a cheerless afterlife to be.

First, let's review these (potential) violations of human mortality:

a) Tithonus (*Iliad/Odyssey*)
b) Ganymede (*Iliad*)
c) Menelaus (*Odyssey*)
d) Odysseus (*Odyssey*)
e) Ino/Leucothea (*Odyssey*)
f) Castor and Pollux (*Odyssey*)
g) Heracles (*Odyssey*)
h) Cleitus (*Odyssey*)

Critics often observe that most of these individuals appear in the less-tragic, folk-lorish, happy-ending *Odyssey*, where such things might be more tolerable. This distinction generally holds but doesn't really get us very far. It is also in the *Odyssey*, after all, that Homer presents his most extended and dramatically unpromising picture of death in the underworld. The first thing we should note is that with the exception of Ino/Leucothea, we are never actually shown in the epics any alternate postmortem existence. We *hear* briefly about these exceptions, but they take place in the future (c), or the past (a, b, e, f, g, h), or are skimmed over in the text (a, f,) without any explanation or explication, or are simply raised to be rejected: Odysseus (d) is bribed by Calypso with the offer of immortality to stay with her, but the hero dismisses her proposition (*Od.* 5.206–10; 23.336). Homer never shows us Ganymede, Menelaus, Castor, Pollux, Heracles, Odysseus, or Cleitus on Olympus or some paradisiacal oasis. We merely hear that Dawn leaves Tithonus' bed on two occasions. Homer doesn't want us to align ourselves with the destiny of any of these characters.

More to the point, what are the *reasons* for the special treatment of these few mortals? The answer is just what we'd expect from the epics – the gods play favorites, even with death and the afterlife. And their motives can be lumped into just two familiar divine proclivities: Lust and personal favoritism. Half of those on the list – Tithonus, Ganymede, Odysseus, and Cleitus – are spared (or offered the opportunity to skip) mortality because a deity wants to have sex with them and enjoy their "beauty" forever. Their potential immortality says little about human destiny but everything about the gods' eclectic and prodigious sexual appetites.

The others on the list have what we can understatedly call "good connections." Proteus says quite explicitly that the grounds for Menelaus' "get out of death" card are that his wife is Helen, who is the daughter of Zeus. The only other person Proteus mentions as existing on the "Elysian plane" is Rhadamanthys, whom we learn elsewhere is the son of Zeus (14.321–2). Classicist Jenny Clay (1983:151) also points out Homer's reluctance to state directly that Menelaus will not die. Rather, Proteus says that Menelaus will not die *in Argos* but instead will be whisked away to the Elysian plane, where, we *assume* by the similarity of the place to Olympus, he will live eternally.

No reason is given for the curious posthumous destiny of Castor and Pollux. In the *Odyssey* their father is the mortal Tyndareus, not Zeus, although early Greek tradition offers varying accounts of the parentage of these brothers, including that they are both the sons of Zeus (Hes fr 21 W = 24 M-W; *HomH* 17.2) or that Castor is the son of Tyndareus and Polydeuces of Zeus (Pindar *Nem.* 10.75–82; cf. *Cypria* 9 W). Their primary familial description in Homer is as the brothers of Helen. In fact, Helen fills up a slightly awkward verse emphasizing their consanguinity on their mother's side (3.238). If a nonblood relationship with Helen can get you out of Hades, then perhaps a fraternal connection can earn you enough "honor from Zeus" to spend half your death alive.

Heracles is one of Zeus's favorite offspring – "most dear to Zeus" (18.118), a son whom Zeus boasted prematurely would "rule over all those who dwell nearby, one of the race of the men who are from my blood" (19.104–5). We get no hints as to why Ino was "honored" with her transformation into a deity with a new name (Leucothea). Homer refers to her as if he expects us to know. Her story, however, is difficult to piece together from later references (Gantz 1993:176–9, 478). It is likely that she was driven mad by Hera and jumped into the sea with her son in her arms, at which point she received her metamorphosis (from Dionysus?). Her madness may be a punishment for her serving as Dionysus' nurse (Hera takes revenge for her husband's infidelities on *everyone*), but she also seems to have attempted to arrange the deaths of her stepchildren and rival. Her apotheosis seems to result from her connections as well, either with Dionysus or Zeus (who is closely connected to the fate of her family). Her "leap into the sea" has been called a "characteristically Dionysiac maneuver." Her apotheosis would seem to take place "under the sign of Dionysus" (Lyons 1997:122–3) and, given the insignificance of that god in Homer, may explain the lack of any details in her story.

Such exceptions to the "mortality" rule serve at least two important functions in the epics. First, they reinforce the limitations the rest of us face. *We* are not Zeus's son, or his son-in-law, or his, um, cupbearer. They are "exceptions that confirmed the rule, namely that heroes became mere shadows of themselves in the hereafter" (Albinus 2000:65). Eternal ineffectuality awaits us all. We must try to make sense of an indifferent world that offers us only a limited time to make a difference, after which nothing much matters.

But just as importantly, these exceptions reveal the kind of insignificant world that would result should the gods do whatever they wished whenever they wanted. Homer's tragic sense worries that the gods could bollix up the *very thing that makes a consequential human life possible*. What if a god could rescue a favorite from death at will for the most trivial reasons, reasons like sex or personal bonds?

So Homer plays his most controversial card: fate. The inherent conflict between fate and the will of the gods has troubled readers for centuries, and we are not going to disentangle the issues here. But I think one important aspect of fate's role in the epics has been undervalued that is crucial for our understanding of Homer's concept of death. Fate is the universe's (that is, Homer's) way of curbing the gods' irresponsibility when it comes to human mortality. Christianity celebrates as its central mystery Jesus' selective gift of immortality. Homer knows better, fearing the inevitable undermining of human endeavor should the gods' selfishness run completely free.

Fate

There are numerous words Homer uses for "fate" and its various manifestations, and as so often in Homeric Greek, they both overlap in meaning and can have their own nuances (Dietrich 1965:249–83; Clarke 1999:231–63). Most of these words derive from the concept of "share" or "allotment." Fate is a person's portion of life. Fate in Homer generally signifies the time allotted to a mortal's earthly existence or even that specific time appointed for death. Homerist Mark Edwards adds that "even divine foreknowledge usually means only foreknowledge of man's death" (1987:127). Although in the *Odyssey* it can allude to the hero's destined escape from his trials and his return home (e.g., *Od.* 5.41–2; 5.114–15, 288–9; 9.532–3; cf. 2.174–6), in both epics fate more often refers to the unfortunate elements in one's life, especially that most unfortunate limit, its termination: "The most universal aspect of one's lot is death, and so these words often connote death" (Janko 1992:5).

Moira and *aisa* are the most common words for fate, used virtually interchangeably, both often linked to *thanatos* (death). *Moros*, related to *moira*, is used in the same way and usually implies death. *Potmos* always refers to death – one frequently "meets" it. Hector's prophetic brother, Helenus, tells him that it is "not yet your *moira* to die and meet your *potmos*" (7.52). The only other term we need to mention here is *kêr*, which shares epithets with other terms but primarily means simply death, sometimes without the sense of necessity that accompanies the others. You can't escape your *moira*, but nearly a dozen times we hear of someone escaping or successfully fleeing *kêr*.[7]

There is an inherent tension in Homer's world in which both fate and meddlesome gods can circumscribe human options: "In fact the relationship between these two powers remains obscure, the poet seeming to refer to either according to the effect he wishes to produce rather than to theological doctrine" (Edwards 2005:311). In Book 3 of the *Odyssey*, Athena lays out for Telemachus what appears to be a great limitation to the power of the Olympians: "But certainly not even the gods can avert death, the great leveler, from a man even if they love him, whenever the destructive fate of mournful death takes him down" (*Od.* 3.236–8). No god in the epics prevents even a beloved offspring from a fated death. Zeus, Ares, and Poseidon all lose children. Other gods lose favorite mortals (5.49–68; 14.488–500). The "fate of mournful death" lies in store for Homeric characters – and all of us – no matter what the gods may wish. What, then, are we to make of incidents and expressions in the epics that suggest that Zeus (and perhaps all the Olympians) actually *do* have the power to change a man's final destiny?

The two most controversial incidents occur when Zeus contemplates saving a favored combatant *fated to die* in an imminent duel. The first episode of this sort comes when he sees his mortal son, Sarpedon, squaring off against Patroclus:

> And the son of crooked-counseling Cronus saw them and took pity, and addressed Hera, his sister and his wife: "How terrible! It is fate [*moira*] that Sarpedon, dearest of men to me, be overcome by Patroclus, son of Menoetius. And my heart is prompted two ways in my mind as I debate whether to grab him from tearful battle while he is still alive and set him in the rich land of Lycia, or whether to overwhelm him now by the hands of the son of Menoetius."
>
> (16.431–38)

Is he serious? First, we see that Zeus has knowledge of the future. Fate for the gods is usually just the movie of one's life that they have already seen. Except now Zeus proposes to rewrite the ending of the script! Besides undermining any reliable definition of fate, we have to wonder: Can he *do* that? Apparently he can, as an angry Hera concedes in her reply (he did ask her for her opinion, after all):

> Most dread son of Cronus, what a speech have you delivered! Do you wish to release a man who is mortal [*thnêton*], long ago doomed by fate [*aisa*], back from painful death [*thanatos*]? Do it. But be sure, all us other gods do not approve. And I'll tell you another thing, and store it in your mind: If you should send Sarpedon to his home alive, consider that in that case some other one of the gods also may wish to send his own dear son away from the power-ful battle. For many sons of the immortals are fighting around the great city of Priam; you will fill the gods with dreadful anger.
>
> (16.440–59)

It is clear, to Hera at least, that Zeus *can* change Sarpedon's fate and save the hero from his impending death. Moreover, she implies that the other Olympians have the same power. But what is fate if not what *must* take place?

Similarly, when Zeus sees Hector being pursued by Achilles, knowing that the Trojan prince is fated to die, he turns to his fellow gods for advice, asking them to "consider and deliberate whether we will save him from death, or now we will overcome him, although an excellent man, through Achilles, son of Peleus" (22.168–76). Athena responds with the same incensed words Hera had used (but stops short of suggesting the other gods will spare their own favorites).

There's no need to panic. Yet. Zeus decides in both of these cases to relent – he will allow fate to take its course. He backs down quickly to Athena, insisting that he hadn't really meant it (22.183–5). But to complicate this relationship between the gods and fate even more, Zeus then seems to appeal to an external "destiny" to confirm his own decision to allow Hector to meet his scheduled doom. When Hector (aided by Apollo) and Achilles run around the walls of Troy for the fourth time, Homer tells us that Zeus "poised his golden scales, and he put in them two fates [*kêr*] of long-painful death, one of Achilles, and one of horse-taming Hector; then he grasped the middle of the balance and raised it, and the fated [*aisimos*] day of Hector sank and departed to Hades, and Phoebus Apollo left him" (22.209–13). Who's in charge here, fate or Zeus?[8]

This strange but powerful scene is Homer's poetic way of dealing with multiple sources of human destiny. Zeus at times seems to have more authority than the impersonal concept of fate, but he is never allowed to exercise it. The poet is more interested in the thematic implications of this tension than in providing theological consistency or arriving at any philosophical clarity. (As critics have long pointed out, Homer does not raise the issue of free will in a world that seems to have so many external constraints.) In fact, to the poet and in the minds of Homeric mortals, fate, and the gods are interchangeable when it comes to accounting for life's limitations. They are both credited – and more often blamed – by characters for the way their lives have worked out. Examples are ubiquitous, but a glance at just one poetic trope reveals this flexibility, the idea that one's lot is determined at birth, often "spun out" (Dietrich 1965:289–94). But by whom?

Zeus sent heavy evil to us at our birth.

(10.70–1; cf. *Od.* 4.207–8)

... but he will later suffer whatever **fate** [*aisa*] spun for him with her thread at his birth when his mother bore him.

(20.127–8)

... whatever **fate** [*kêr*] that I obtained even from my birth.

(23.78–9)

Thus for him powerful **fate** [*moira*] spun with her thread at his birth when I myself bore him.

(24.209–10)

For in such a way the **gods** [*theoi*] have spun the threads of destiny for miserable mortals, that they live sorrowing, but they themselves are free from care.

(24.525–6; cf. *Od.* 3.208–9; 8.579–80; 11.139; 20.196)

But thereupon he will suffer whatever **fate** [*aisa*] and the grievous **Spinners** [*Klothes*] spun with their thread for him at his birth when his mother bore him.

(*Od.* 7.196–8)

For in this way **a god** [*daimôn*] has spun these things for him.

(*Od.* 16.64)

Responsibility for difficult lives or death is spread across a variety of possible agents: Zeus, the gods, a god, *kêr*, *moira*, and *aisa* (cf. *Od.* 1.16–18).[9] The gods and destiny generally work together in the epics. Nothing actually happens in the epics "beyond fate." The Sarpedon/Hector and scales scenes, in which it appears that something *could possibly* happen against or "beyond" fate, are expansions or dramatizations of a common poetic way of speaking, of marking a "crisis in the narrative" (Taplin 1992:141n20). At least 60 times in the epics we are told that "x would have happened if somebody had not done y" (Jong 1987:68–81; Lang 1989; Louden 1993). These "pivotal contrafactuals" bring up a possible plot development that would have become a reality if there had been no intervention. In over half these cases, it is a god who steps in to keep the events from going "astray." That is, the intervention preserves the plot and the mythical tradition which many scholars have ultimately identified with fate: "Fate, of course, is the will of the poet, limited by the major features of the traditional legends" (Edwards 1987:136). For example, Homer tells us that Patroclus would have led the Greeks to sack Troy, "if Phoebus Apollo had not stood on the well-built wall, having destruction in mind for him [Patroclus] and bringing aid to the Trojans" (16.698–701). Apollo flings him off the wall three times, and eventually tells Patroclus directly that it is not his fate (*aisa*) to sack Troy, nor that of Achilles, who is "much better than you" (16.707–9; cf. 18.454–6). Apollo thus secures the plot of the *Iliad* (fate) and saves the mythological tradition as well as Zeus's "plan."

At one point we are even told that Achilles "would have taken Aeneas' life with his sword" if Poseidon had not whisked Aeneas away. Poseidon tells

Aeneas to avoid confronting Achilles in battle in the future, "lest even beyond fate [*moira*] you go to the house of Hades" (20.336). "Beyond fate?" Don't let this expression cause your brain to explode. The poet uses the oxymoronic (at first sight) phrase "beyond fate" on occasion to highlight this kind of divine intervention. There is no implication that something will actually happen "beyond fate." Thus we hear that the Greeks would have fled home "beyond fate" (*hypermora*) in only the second book of the *Iliad* "had not Hera" stepped in (2.155; cf. 17.329–32; 20.30; 21.517). The possibility that "something would have happened (beyond fate) if someone had not . . ." is a poetic device to heighten the narrative, eulogize, and even editorialize (especially when someone is rescued), incite pathos, change the direction of the action, and perhaps confirm the reliability of the narrator who could have taken the narrative in the other direction (Jong 1987; Louden 1993).[10]

And here's a key point: Poseidon steps in to save Aeneas not just because the Trojan is "fated" to survive. The god steps in because Aeneas' ancestor was a favorite child of Zeus. That is, there is also a personal connection. Odysseus, too, would have perished "beyond fate" (*moira*) if his tutelary deity Athena had not aided him (*Od.* 5.436). Many of the gods enact rescues for similarly personal reasons. When Aphrodite snatches up Aeneas, who "would have perished" at the hands of Diomedes, the reason is simply that she is "his mother, who conceived him with Anchises as he pastured his cattle" (5.311–13). She is not working on behalf of fate – or justice, for that matter. Menelaus "would have dragged him [Paris] off and earned endless glory" had Aphrodite not carried the Trojan away for an afternoon tryst the prospect of which even Helen finds appalling (3.373–94; cf. 5.9–24; 11.750–2; 15.459–65). Homer sets up these interventions in a way that highlights or even critiques the god's motives.

The Homeric gods are clearly free to intervene in human affairs in order to protect a favorite facing death. But the Olympians never act in defiance of fate, even though they apparently are capable of it. When they rescue a favorite, Homer never informs us that the individual was *fated* to die at that time. In fact, we can safely assume that he was not. The gods merely postpone the death of a mortal, putting it off until his destined day. Hector would have been caught and slain running around the walls of Troy "if Apollo for the last and final time had not come close and roused his might and added speed to his knees" (22.202–4). Apollo merely buys him a few more minutes, until Hector arrives at his *moira*, his fatal duel with Achilles signaled by the scales of Zeus. The scales don't *create* his doom – they poetically confirm that, as Zeus knew, Hector has reached the end of his allotted time.

The divine interventions are often unwitting efforts by the gods in support of destiny. The gods are in this way "coauthors" of the poems. Like the poet they are aware of alternatives and capable of misleading the audience, but they never actually violate the "destined" action. In both epics the gods and fate are aligned (cf. Richardson 1990:138–9, 188–95). Paris is not destined to die *just yet* – the tradition tells us he must live in order to shoot Achilles. So Aphrodite can save him. But he *will* die before Troy falls, and no god, even Aphrodite, can prevent it. Aeneas and Odysseus will both die as well, but it is their fate to survive Troy. Ultimately, there is no escaping your destiny.

Fate: The "conscience" of the gods?

This rather lengthy excursus on fate in the Homeric poems reveals its crucial significance to the Homeric vision of death. Why does Homer bother with this double external motivation, especially, as we have seen, if the gods and fate (not to mention human character) work on parallel rather than contradictory paths? On a poetic level, the existence of fate allows for ominous predictions, foreshadowing, and tragic irony for great emotional effect. Hector's hopes for his own success (16.859–61) and his doomed son's future (6.476–81) gain their power from the audience's greater knowledge of their destinies.

But fate also functions crucially as a curb, a restraint on the selfish behavior of the gods. It can't stop them, but on occasion it makes them think of the consequences of their actions – and how often do the gods do that? Fate is something that can actually limit a god's whims. It almost functions as a conscience. Almost. The "exceptions" to human mortality found in the epics are all the products of the impulses of the gods. Homer lets us see that their motives are selfish rather than anything to do with maintaining cosmic order or enacting justice. Tithonus, Ganymede, and Cleitus (and potentially Odysseus) skip death because of the gods' sexual attraction to them. Menelaus, Heracles, and most likely Ino and Castor and Pollux all have personal connections with the gods. These are examples of what the gods would perhaps do *all the time* if given free rein, if they had *all* the power and took advantage of it. We have seen how often they intervene to save a favorite from death (for the moment) when fate doesn't oppose them. Without the obstacle of fate, Homer suggests that the gods would make personal and trivial – or at least idiosyncratic – decisions about life and death just as they often do about other matters. Hera directly declares that if Zeus saves his son, the other gods will start rescuing their own favorites from death.

It is the very *irresponsibility* of the gods that drives Homer's use of fate. Divine power is not accountable. Humans become heroic by facing their destiny head-on. The gods cannot be heroic, but on occasion fate helps them to act a little less capriciously than they could. It certainly gives Hera and Athena a bit of leverage to slow down Zeus, and it forces Poseidon in the end to accept the fact that Odysseus will make it home alive. Fate keeps the basic edifice that supports human significance from totally collapsing.

Homer had good reason to distrust the gods with their power. Even Yahweh lets at least one of his favorites get out of death. As we have seen, the Hebrew Bible (as well as myths from Babylonia and Ugarit) presents an afterlife as unpromising as Hades, but nevertheless the prophet Elijah "ascended in a whirlwind into heaven" (2 Kings 2:11; cf. Enoch in Gen 5:24). But for both Homer and the Tanakh, death remains an essential marker of all mortals.

Death is *the* defining criterion of human existence. The "exceptions" are not tales dangling the quixotic hope of immortality before us but cautionary anecdotes about the importance of accepting the inevitability of death and an inconsequential afterlife. Jasper Griffin beautifully summarizes the gravity of Homer's vision:

> . . . the poet insists on presenting death in its full significance as the end, unsoftened by any posthumous consolation or reward. . . . [He depicts] it dispassionately and fully in all its forms; and . . . [he shows] that even heroes fear and hate it. The hero is granted by the poet the single privilege of dying a hero's death not a random or undignified one, but that death haunts his thoughts in life and gives his existence at once its limitations and its definition.
>
> (1980:94)

Ramifications I: Weighing the gifts of the gods[11]

When Paris retreats from Menelaus like a man "who has stumbled upon a snake," Hector censures him as "pretty," "woman-mad," and destined to find neither the lyre nor the "gifts of Aphrodite" of any help when he is "coupled" with dust. Paris is shamed into dueling Menelaus, but he corrects his brother:

> Do not throw in my face the lovely gifts of golden Aphrodite. The glorious gifts of the gods are not to be cast aside, whatever they themselves might give – but one would not willingly choose them.
>
> (3.64–6)

Paris seems to suggest that all in all one may be better off without the gods' beneficence. The poet himself later refers to Paris' reward from Aphrodite as "difficult" or "grievous" (24.30), and he reminds us that "the glorious gifts of the gods are not easy for mortal men to tame or withdraw from" (20.265–6). These intangible gifts from the gods, whether referring to personal qualities (as in the case of Paris) such as intelligence, strength, and size, or to skills at various activities such as speech, poetry, warfare, dancing, singing, lyre-playing, seercraft, and metal-working, can be unreliable. Even more troublesome, however, are the tangible presents from the gods. The Trojan War traditionally both begins (Discord's apple and Aphrodite's winning bribe) and ends (the Trojan horse) with duplicitous divine gifts. Within the epics themselves, especially the *Iliad*, there is an irony connected with these divine "presents," as they are consistently enmeshed in human mortality. Only the bard Demodocus – never Homer himself – calls the gods "givers of good things" (*Od.* 8.325, 335). The most illustrious benefaction of all, Hephaestus' wondrous armor for Achilles, will not protect the hero from death, as its creator himself laments (18.464–7).

Nothing could be more different than the "gifts" credited to God in Christianity, gifts such as grace, salvation, and eternal life. Yet the promise of paradise is the more diabolical present. If death is not the end of any meaningful existence but in fact the necessary precursor to eternal bliss, then it does not create an incentive for living fully in any genuine sense. The definition of "a good life" is reduced to appeasing divine demands embedded in ancient mythological texts (and traditions constructed around those ancient texts) about which the religious experts themselves disagree. Christianity and Islam hand out fuzzy rules, and then their God punishes or rewards depending upon the interpretation *de jour*. Will suicide bombing get you into paradise? Will denying your children medical care earn you brownie points for your ticket to eternity? Will producing children you can't feed or educate prepare a quicker journey to heaven? Will polygamy and forced child-marriages appease your deity's demands to be fruitful and multiply? Can a wife really gain entry to the hereafter if she disagrees with her husband?

And then there is the huge waste of our energy and limited time on the planet on negotiating the correct cultic aspects underlying the promise of a smooth ride to the hereafter: How many times do you need to pray? When? Which direction? Should you ingest god literally or symbolically? How often? Do you need to be baptized? How many times? When? How much should you tithe? Should you give up sex? Forever? Or perhaps just chocolate for 40 days? What's the penalty for consuming alcohol, or tobacco, or a little caffeine? I don't even want to *hear* the word "masturbation." Do I really need to dance with *snakes*? Can I answer the phone on the sabbath? (How many sets of plates and dishwashers *do* I need?) These "extravagant displays" of commitment to the Big Gods may once in our evolutionary past have served to increase the trust of and cooperation among fellow believers that enabled the group to expand. Who would fake such costly (and, in the eyes of outsiders, ridiculous) displays? These rituals are the quaint product of thousands of years of an evolutionary arms race, the peacock feathers of human adaptation. But now, when linked to a promised passport to the afterlife, these prodigal activities obviate serious human reflection. The "get out of death" card is the great specious gift from heaven.

For Homer, the gifts of the gods hardly lighten the burden of existence or guide mortals to future bliss; in fact, they emphasize our mortal limitations and thus our genuine if limited potential in *this* life. The unavoidably ruinous collision between immortal gift and mortal recipient finds a particular symbolism in the gifts traditionally furnished by the gods to Peleus, Achilles' father, on his wedding day: A divine wife (Thetis), heavenly wrought armor, and deathless horses. Thetis is forced (unwillingly, she emphasizes) to marry a mortal man who is now "overcome with grievous old age." She gave birth to a mortal son whose race to an early death she can only assist (18.429–61) and then mourn *eternally*. "Through her the *Iliad* offers not the immortality of the *Aethiopis*, but a conception of heroic stature as inseparable from human limitation and of heroic experience as a metaphor for the condition of mortality, with all its contradictions. . . . Achilles' discovery of identity – of values, of morality – is inseparable from the apprehension of mortality" (Slatkin 1991:38–9).

Achilles inherits his father's armor "that the gods gave as splendid gifts to Peleus" (18.84). Yet we never see him don this gear. Rather, it is worn by Patroclus into battle, only to be stripped from his corpse by Hector. Zeus sadly watches the Trojan hero dress in turn, observing that the doomed Hector is vainly putting on immortal ("ambrosial") armor, never to return from battle (17.198–208). The divine gift may live forever, but those who come in contact with it grow old and die alone (Peleus) or grieve forever (Thetis) or perish young on the battlefield (Patroclus, Hector, Achilles).

No gift of the gods is more poignant than the immortal horses given to Peleus by Poseidon and then passed down to Achilles (16.380–1; 23.276–8). Their most famous appearance is when these horses prophesy his death (19.408–17). But the painful juxtaposition of divine immortality and human limitation is brought out most clearly when the horses mourn the death of Patroclus. They pour out "hot tears," befouling their manes in the dust, and even Zeus pities them:

> Ah, miserable pair, why did we give you to lord Peleus, a mortal, but you are ageless and immortal? Was it so that you might have sorrows among unhappy men? For without doubt there is nothing more wretched of all the things that breathe and creep on earth than man.
>
> (17.443–7)

The Homeric gods' gifts serve as a constant reminder of the mortality of the epic's major characters, especially Achilles. Like the Olympians themselves, divine presents reveal the limits of human existence in all its starkness. A meaningful life is only possible when its limits are fully understood and accepted. Achilles appears to be faring well in Hades, at least to Odysseus, but he realizes that this sort of existence is no life at all. Without death to frame one's life and achievements, without the quotidian struggle to make sense of it all, mere survival – even eternal survival – has no meaning. Achilles would rather have the humblest life on earth than *any* kind of postmortem existence.

Yet Homer is not obsessed with the dark side of fatalism. The inevitability of death is an incentive, not a depressant. Without mortality and an inconsequential afterlife, we would not be forced to deal so honestly with our own limitations and work within them and strive to do something memorable. While we might on bad days lament the absence of the divine paradise so facilely promised by Christianity and Islam in particular, Pandora's jar has been opened and there's no shoving death back inside. And perhaps that most infamous giver of divine gifts knew what she was doing when she opened the lid. Without the challenge of suffering, mortality, and the finality of death, our lives would be as trivial as those of the gods.

Ramifications II: Becoming a hero

The necessity of death and the meaningless existence of the dead (as well as of the immortals!) create a world that demands mortals *do* something with their lives. When Andromache tries to keep Hector from returning to battle, fearing (correctly, as it turns out) that he will be killed, he responds in heroic fashion:

> Dear woman, do not grieve excessively at heart in any way for me, for no man will hurl me to Hades beyond what is fated [*aisa*]; but I say no man escapes his fate [*moira*], not the coward, not the brave, after he is born.
>
> (6.486–9)

Hector's and Achilles' responses to the inevitable are not to give in, acquiesce, or become despondent. This is what Christian apologists often say would be the result of a Homeric world: Without God, without a promise of eternity, this life has no meaning and we would have nothing to live for – in essence, evil would win: "The suffering of the innocent makes no theological sense if this life is all there is" (Hebblethwaite 2000:320).

This stock religious response acknowledges the tragic limitations of human achievements and institutions (like justice) and then insists that this "senselessness" furnishes evidence for an afterlife that will "fix" it all. Basically, it's an admission that God and the promise of postmortem happiness are theological inventions so we can feel better about the patent messiness and inevitable terminus of life. In Homer's world, a meaningful life is not based on the promised payoff of posthumous joy but can result only from accomplishing something here and now. Calypso's offer of immortal lounging on the beach with a deity – not far from a Christian's vision of heaven (only with divine sex!) – would only "hide" (Greek *kalyptô*) Odysseus for eternity and prevent him from accomplishing anything in the future.

But I must emphasize that Homer – again, unlike the prescriptive Abrahamic religions – does not tell us *what* we are to do. Homer presents a complex set of cultural values only to expose the entire system as a fraud. The *Iliad* shows us a character who thought he had it all figured out and, through tragic events brought about primarily by his own heroic temper, discovers it was a lie. The things that his society had told him were important turn out to be immaterial.

One way that heroes in Homer's fictional world can leave a part of them behind is still familiar to many cultures in the 21st century – have a son. Achilles' joyful response to Odysseus' account of his son's valor at Troy is the only positive moment in the entire Nekyia. But Homer also points out that deriving meaning from the vicarious experiences and reputation of a child is problematic – sons, like Achilles and Hector, can die before fathers. While heroes count on their sons as their "legacy," the poet suggests there is no reason for confidence in such "genetic" immortality. Sons may not outlive their fathers, or on the other hand, if they live long enough, a son may even have to compete with his father for preeminence (as may be the case in Odysseus' family). A heroic son can extend his father's presence among the living (think of all the patronymics used in the epics), but that will only make a difference if the father is worth mentioning and the son distinguished, and even then usually for no more than one or two generations.

This intense search for making a mark that will last past death is most dramatically featured in the *Iliad*, where the daily risk of one's life in battle focuses and challenges mortal ambitions. The famous summary of the "heroic code" by Sarpedon, a Trojan ally, is worth presenting in full:

> Glaucus, why are we two most deemed worthy in Lycia of a seat of honor and meat and full cups, and all men behold us as gods? And we possess a great estate along the banks of Xanthus, a beautiful estate of orchards and wheat-bearing land. Therefore now we must take our stand among the foremost Lycians and take part in raging battle, so that any of the thick-armored Lycians

would say: "Truly not inglorious are they who rule over Lycia, our kings, and they feast on fat sheep and choice honey-sweet wine. But then their strength too is excellent, since they fight among the foremost Lycians." O friend, if we two escaped this battle and were meant to be ageless and immortal forever, I myself would neither fight among the foremost, nor would I make you ready for glorifying battle. But now, the fates of death stand near us, innumerable fates that no mortal can escape or evade. Let us go – we will either bestow glory on someone, or he on us.

(12.310–28)

Traditional heroic success is measured for the living by status, status is determined by how much stuff (material goods, which includes animals, food, land, stools, lumps of metal, and women) one possesses, and stuff primarily comes from the distribution of prizes after victory in battle. Honor (*timē*) comes not from war itself but fighting successfully, and if ultimately failing, at least going out big and bravely as Hector does. Posthumous "life" can come to warriors (when it does come) most immediately by commemoration through the fame and glory (*kleos*) provided by tombs and grave markers that are earned by greatness in life. Sarpedon's brothers and family will "bury him with a tomb and grave stone; for this is the privilege of the dead" (16.674–5; cf. Hector's remarks at 7.84–90). Even the naïve Telemachus raised by women understands the limited but crucial nature of this memorial. If Odysseus had died at Troy, then "all the Achaeans would have made a tomb for him, and he would have won great glory in the future for his son as well" (*Od.* 1.236–40; cf. *Od.* 14.369–70). This is a constant refrain throughout the epics, which refer to several monuments of earlier "heroes" (e.g., 2.603–4, 792–3, 813–4; 10.415; 11:166, 371–2; 23.326–32; 24.349). The shades of Patroclus and Elpenor both use their last ghostly words to request heroic internments (ironically in Elpenor's case). The funeral and burial of Patroclus prefigure those of Achilles. The ghost of Agamemnon describes in detail Achilles' majestic burial (*Od.* 24.36–94), "so you did not lose your name even when dead, but you will always have noble fame among all men, Achilles."

Although scholars debate the issue, there is little evidence of any cult honors (sacrifice and veneration) given to the dead heroes in the epics. If Homer knew about hero cult, he suppressed it (Currie 2005:55–7) – the poet never uses the term "hero" for a recipient of cult (Ekroth 2007). The tombs are primarily physical reminders of a man (Bremmer 2006; Grethlein 2008:28–32).[12] And even then, the tomb eventually covers many of the dead only in obscurity, defeating the primary purpose of the edifice. Homeric grave monuments were not inscribed, so they preserved the fame and glory of the interred individual only "for as long as the memory of the deceased lived on in the memory of the local community" (Sourvinou-Inwood 1995:117–18). The Trojans count off their allies on a place that "men call Bateia, but the immortals call it the gravesite of agile Myrine" (2.813–14). This is a tomb of a woman, perhaps an Amazon, but humans seem to have forgotten this association completely. When Nestor gives his son advice for the chariot race at Patroclus' funeral games, he points out an old tree stump and two white markers to be used as the turning post: "It is either the grave-marker of some man who died long ago, or was fashioned as a turning post in the time of men who came before us" (23.327–32). Critics have been puzzled by the lengthy description of this marker since it plays no important role in the race itself. But in a race that is to commemorate a dead hero and whose winner will earn "glory," it is surely intentional that the central landmark reveals the evanescence of human achievement. What may have been the memorial of a hero of old, a construction designed to defeat time, lies in anonymity – "what the hero fears most" (Zanker 1994:12) – like the dead themselves. But again, perhaps it's just an eroding turning post from a previous (and now long-forgotten) race. Jonas Grethlein concludes his survey of the commemorative function of tombs in the epics with a comment upon their ultimate *failure*: "The memory does not reach back very far; it spans up to three generations in one case, but it is usually only one generation" (2008:32).

If a hero is particularly lucky and remarkable enough – say, Achilles or Odysseus – he can be "wrested from oblivion" (Vernant 1981:286) through tales of his exploits, especially in epic song. Achilles himself sings of the "glorious deeds of men" to soothe his angry heart (9.189). This may sound far-fetched, but as I remind my skeptical students (who believe fame comes from going "viral"), they are still reading about Achilles nearly 3000 years later. But heroic glory (*kleos*) is complicated and filtered in the epics through Homer's tragic sense. Penelope objects to a bard's song of the Achaeans' "miserable return home" from Troy (a nice description of the very epic in which she resides) by asking him to sing one of the "many other things you know, charms for mortals, deeds of men and gods that singers make famous" (*Od.* 1.325–55; cf. *Il.* 6.357–8). A hero's commemoration in song under Homer's watchful eye will be the story of suffering, both his own and that which he causes: "The great theme of the *Iliad* is heroic life and death" (Griffin 1980:44). Achilles, whose name appears to mean something like "one who causes grief to and receives grief from the host of fighting men," is "pervasively associated with theme of grief" (Nagy 1979:69–83, 77).

Indeed, war itself, the source of so much of the heroic value system, is painted darkly by the poet. Even Sarpedon, whose celebration of the heroic code was quoted above, notes in an impossible wish that given the option – if he were a god – he would avoid battle. All in all, the troops at Troy would prefer not to fight (2.147–54; cf. 3.318–23). All the Greek heroes we meet in the *Odyssey* – including Odysseus – look back on the war and its aftermath with grief, despite their victory (*Od.* 3.103–19; 4.76–112; 8.83–92, 489–90, 521–31; 11.482–91, 24.27, 95–7; Griffin 1980:101; Jong 2001:75–6). The Trojan War is called an evil (*pêma, Od.* 8.81), a strongly emotional word. The poet seems to be revealing his own opinion "by calling the war/fighting 'unabating,' 'full of tears,' 'destructive,' 'bringing much woe,' 'violent,' 'forceful' and 'terrible'" (Jong 1987:61). Contrast this with the glorious extinction of the Canaanites in the Tanakh.

Although there is clearly honor and (with luck) glory to be had in fighting, Homer doesn't hesitate to paint the horrors of death in battle, both the physical agony and the tragedy of loss. We see this most clearly in the famous duels and foreboding of Achilles' looming fate, but a close reading reveals that many of the minor characters who function as fodder for the major heroes' success in battle are given miniature "obituaries." These short biographies, mentioning brief details of families, homes, professions, etc., often bring home the sorrow these seemingly insignificant deaths will evoke. Sometimes the nature of the loss is only implied, as with the death of Pedaeus. He is otherwise just a name, but the poet adds that "he was in fact a bastard, but noble Theano carefully raised him like her own children, as a favor to her husband" (5.69–71). We are left to feel the parents' grief in the distance.

At other times, however, Homer brings the pain directly home, to the surviving children, spouse, hometown, or parents:

> And he [Diomedes] went after Xanthus and Thoön, the two sons of Phaenops, both born to him late in life. Phaenops was worn out with miserable old age, and he produced no other son to be left for his possessions. There Diomedes slew them, and took away the dear life of both, but left lamentation and miserable sorrows for their father, since they did not return alive from battle for him to receive. And the surviving relatives divided his property.
>
> (5.152–8)

Now and again this background information even overshadows the actual fight (e.g., 11.218–30). Unlike modern action films in which scores of anonymous extras are gunned down every few minutes, Homer often wants us to see the victims as individuals, even if only for a moment. And when he doesn't – as in Achilles' relentless butchery of Trojans upon his reentry to battle – the absence of personal details emphasizes the hero's own war-crazed inhumanity. Death is meaningful, and tragic, for everyone, and the afterlife does nothing to mitigate its harshness.

As for the concatenation that supposedly makes meaning out of a warrior's life – fighting, stuff, status, glory – the heart of the *Iliad* for us now lies in Achilles' final disillusionment with this "code." He bitterly questions the value of not just material goods but also everything else his society has told him defines a hero and that thus makes sense of life – the gods, peers, "victory," and posthumous fame. Alone now – his best friend dead, his son never to be seen, his mother condemned to eternal grief, and he himself acutely aware that his successful slaughter has reduced the enemy to a childless state like that of his own abandoned father – he is left to figure it all out. No doubt he won't before he is killed. But he's not waiting for compensation in the afterlife. At least he can make one final genuine gesture of human compassion, sharing a meal – "the privileged sign of reconciliation" in the poems (Nimis 1987:38) – with Priam, during which each sees for the first time their shared humanity and weeps for his own losses. It is "only now that we can understand why all the earlier scenes of battlefield supplication ended with the refusal of pity and the slaying of the suppliant," observes Glenn W. Most. "They were designed to serve as a foil in order to increase our anxiety for Priam and as a contrasting measure of the change in Achilles' character" (2003:72).

This empathetic hosting of an enemy king in his tent violates the "rules" of his society (24.653–5, 686–8). But Achilles must *do* something, even when all the reasons his culture has given him for action no longer make sense. He's on his own now, and he makes a final, humane gesture of what Graham Zanker has aptly labeled "magnanimity," "unique in its intensity, in its sublimity, and in its centrality in the structure of the poem" (1994:149). For the hero, the reality of a world without divine meaning is not paralyzing but a call to action. "The friendship Achilles inaugurates with Priam," concludes classicist Kevin Crotty, "suggests that mortals are not simply confined to recognizing passively the indifference of the world. They can come to understand it and can find ways of responding and of expressing their response" (1994:83).

Courage, critical critique, empathy, and genuine compassion for the human condition are in the end all that's left. Achilles is confronted with a crisis in meaning, an existential Rubicon. Homer will not allow Achilles to dismiss the consequences of his own actions with an unthinking confidence that "everything happens for a reason." Homer asks him – and us – to figure out how to become human without giving us any divine footprints to follow and with no promise of a happy eternity strolling with the gods should we surrender our lives to a mythical construct. Achilles looks into that emptiness and stares it down. That is what, in the end, makes him heroic. We don't see what happens to him in his few remaining months of life. We know only that he dies shortly afterwards, and that what comes after that is not the answer.

One of the responses theists customarily have to this tragic vision of life is that it's unfair. Without moral gods or eternal reward and punishment, there can be no ultimate justice in this world, and that just can't be the case. It just *can't*: ". . . if God does not exist and there is no immortality, then all the evil acts of men go unpunished and all the sacrifices of good men go unrewarded. But who can live with such a view?" (Craig 2008:81). But "such a view" need not lead to despair but can instead inspire efforts to rectify *present* injustices.

As far as we can tell, there *is* no justice that we don't create, and our efforts – without which we truly will slip into chaos – will always remain imperfect. A glance at the world reveals that truth, one that Homer knows full well. His amoral Olympians' disinterest in cosmic justice compels us to search for a better world within our own lives. And so we now turn to the honest Homeric vision of a world without divine justice.

Notes

1 The *thumos*, which is the most frequently mentioned organ in the epics, is a protean element found in living humans and animals, a source of impulse or insight that provides a context for emotional motivation (Pelliccia 1995:55–6). Wherever it is and whatever it does in mortal beings (both humans and animals), upon their death the *thumos* is often said to "leave" or "fly away." It can be imagined as heading to the underworld (7.131), but we never actually see one depart for Hades and we don't encounter a *thumos* after the death of its possessor.

2 Only one animal is credited with a *psychê* (a boar, *Od.* 14.426), and the gods don't seem to have one.

3 Several aspects of this second Nekyia seem to contradict "rules" laid down in the first, discrepancies that from antiquity have suggested this passage represents a different tradition. For our purposes, these variations make little difference – they both present the same bleak view of the afterlife.

4 The *thumos* and *psychê* often seem to overlap in meaning at the moment of death or unconsciousness. Andromache, for example, faints and gasps out her *psychê* but regains her *thumos*. The *psychê* is never depicted as returning to those who faint and then recover, even though we must assume that it does.

5 Most of the *psychai* Odysseus encounters in his visit to the underworld display awareness and corporeality even without drinking the blood (e.g., *Od.* 11. 543–67, 568–71, 605–8). Scholars often try to disentangle these contradictions by appealing to different chronological layers, although which elements might be "Mycenaean" or "Dark Age" or "Archaic" is not settled (e.g., Morris 1989; Sourvinou-Inwood 1995; Tsagarakis 2000). Homer, like every other author who has described the world of the dead (Virgil and Dante spring to mind), is eclectic and necessarily creative. As Emily Vermeule observes, the underworld is "controlled not by Hades but by Greek poets" (1979:36).

6 Homer mentions a "race of demigods," but the one use of the term in the Homeric epics (12.23) deliberately rejects all associations with immortality. Rather, the phrase refers to the *dead* heroes who "fell in the dust" at Troy (Scodel 1982:34).

7 *Kêr* is sometimes called a "demon of death" by scholars, but I don't find this level of personification. There is a vivid and unique image of destructive *Kêr* on Achilles' shield (18.535–40), but this passage is unusual by Homeric standards, outside the narrative, and may be an interpolation (Edwards 1991:220–1).

8 These scales crop up elsewhere in the *Iliad* as well, both literally as here, 8.68–77, and more metaphorically, 16.658; 19.223–4, and seem to have been a traditional element in Greek myth. There was a famous weighing of fates for Memnon and Achilles in their post-Iliadic duel, and some scholars have argued that the *Iliad* scene is based on these scales found in the traditional material that eventually made its way into the *Aethiopis*.

9 Given their limited access to divine motives, the heroes often simultaneously credit (or accuse) *both* fate *and* the gods for their failures. The dying Patroclus rebukes Hector by telling him that "deadly fate and the son of Leto [Apollo]" were his real killers (16.849), just as Achilles' horses tell him that he will perish at the hands of "a great god and powerful fate" (19.410; cf. 18.117–19; 19.87–8; 22.297). Characters thus can use loose expressions like "the fate of god" (*Od.* 11.292), the "fate of Zeus" (9.608), and "the fate of the gods" (*Od.* 3.269). Homer refers to the "fate of Zeus" (17.321). "Whence *moira* comes, who allots it and who controls it, we do not learn from every single *moira*-utterance in Homer; not even from all *moira*-references put together" (Tsagarakis 1977:129).

10 These Greek words don't always translate best as "fate" but can signal "what is fitting, right, or reasonably to be expected" (S. West 1988:78); in other words, "one's share" or even "proper order." Paris can tell Hector that he rebuked him as was fitting (*aisa*) and not "beyond what was right" (*aisa*; 3.59; cf. 6.333; 16.367; *Od.* 2.251; 9.352). Some scholars see the phrase "beyond fate" as signaling an event that genuinely exceeded the destined boundaries on at least two occasions (especially 16.780; *Od.* 1.35). I agree, however, with other scholars who would translate the phrase in these passages as "beyond what was expected" or "beyond one's share"; cf. S. West 1988:78; Edwards 1991:93.

11 The first part of this section is adapted from Heath (1992).

12 There is one reference to sacrifices made to a dead Athenian (Erechtheus), but he resides in Athena's temple, not in a separate grave (2.546–51).

Section IV
Finding justice

13   Waiting for God. Oh. The myth of Iliadic justice

On December 6, 1947 – just a little over a year after the end of the Nuremberg trials – the Council of Ministers of the Oldenburg church in Germany sent a letter to its parishes regarding the "Jewish Question." Six million Jews had been killed under the watch of the church, a discomforting circumstance that prompted this reflection on the causes of the genocide:

> It is the understanding bestowed on the Christian Church from the begin-ning, and which is testified in the Holy Scriptures, that the people of Israel through the decree of God have a unique position in the history of salvation [*Heilsgeschichte*], [and] that the people of Israel, by rejecting their Mes-siah sent by God, became an example of divine judgment [*Gerichtes*] for all peoples . . .

Not to be outdone, a few months later (April 8, 1948) the Brother Council of the Evangelical Church in Darmstadt was given a lecture that came to a similar conclusion:

> By crucifying the Messiah, Israel has rejected its election and destiny. . . . Israel under [God's] judgment is the continuous confirmation of the truth, the truth of the divine word, and the continual warning of God to his church. That God can not be mocked is the silent lesson [literally "sermon," *Predigt*] of Jewish destiny, a lesson to us, to the Jews a warning, whether they would not become converts to him in whom alone their own salvation also rests.

Numerous Jewish leaders themselves arrived at an equally dreadful if religiously distinct verdict. One director of a Hasidic community in Ukraine inferred that the death of his son – burned alive by the Germans in a synagogue – was a "kindness of the Almighty that I also offered a personal sacrifice." Other Ultra-Orthodox Jewish leaders suggested that "Hitler was the new Nebuchadnezzar sent by God to chastise his people" and that the Final Solution was "just punishment for an act of blasphemy, that of initiating a return to Zion on their own, and, thereby, acting as substitutes for the awaited Messiah" (Watson 2014:373–4).

Historian Philip Jenkins makes an interesting if premature observation about this "providential" view of the world:

> The largest single mental marker separating the premodern or medieval world from our own was the belief that earthly error had cosmic implications. . . . If, as they believed, errors arose from sinful pride or diabolical subversion, then tolerating them attracted God's anger, as expressed through different forms of worldly catastrophe: famine, drought, plague, floods, and earthquakes, or defeat in war. . . . Suppressing these horrors meant prosperity and victory for the regime, and the people.
>
> (2010:127)

But we still regularly encounter this medieval response from fundamentalist theists in all Abrahamic religions when natural disasters, epidemics, and terrorists strike. (To be fair, these responses can be found from Hindu gurus and Buddhist monks as well; Sugirtharajah 2008:74.) Toleration of homosexuality, to take an easy example, has evidently so incensed God that he has summoned floods in the UK, earthquakes in Haiti, the tsunami in Japan, airplanes into the World Trade Center, and hurricanes almost everywhere. (Some Jewish and Evangelical Christian leaders even insisted that the benign and long-predicted solar eclipse in 2017 was a "judgment of sin" and a possible signal of the Final Judgment.) Televangelist Pat Robertson predicted that America's liberal attitudes towards homosexuality would result in hurricanes, earthquakes, tornadoes, and "possibly a meteor" (Kirsch 2006:232). Who knew? Well, a lot of Americans, apparently. In 2014, 14 percent of the country still believed that AIDS could be God's retribution for an "aberrant way of life" (PRRI 2/26/2014).

This answer to the questions surrounding the connection between unfathomable evil and God's justice – that suffering comes as punishment for disobedience, apostasy, sin, and unbelief – is the dominant version of theodicy in the Bible. This "idea is so prevalent that a thorough treatment would require an analysis of virtually all of the canon" (Crenshaw 2005:131). We will recall that this is exactly the "logic" applied by the Israelites themselves to the destruction of Jerusalem. And Christians have agreed, at least since Bishop Melito of Sardis preached a sermon one Easter in the second century CE in which he blamed the second destruction of Jerusalem on the Jews' murder of God (Ehrman 2009:241).

But even biblical authors were aware that this answer doesn't match reality very often. Why is God's punishment so indiscriminate? Why must the "good" suffer? Or the children and animals of the good? And shouldn't there be some reasonable degree of proportionality? Did God really need to kill six million Europeans to show his irritation at a few fellow Jews' "premature" interest in resettling in the Promised land? And what about the wicked? Many sinners clearly flourish – why doesn't God go after *them*? Morally repulsive individuals get rich, find spouses, have offspring, and sometimes even become president. Ethically thoughtful doctors dedicated to improving the health care system get trampled to death by elephants. (One of my lifelong friends actually met that peculiar fate a few years ago.) What's with that? As we have seen, even in Job, the Bible's most explicit exploration of this human dilemma, God's last words reject the simplistic equation between one's behavior and one's fate, while his final actions endorse it. The ambivalent conclusion matches the unsolvable mystery of a perfect deity's apparent indifference to issues of justice.

What are we to do, then, when the theory of "just gods" and "deserved punishment" fails to match the observable facts of life? Where is a just God amidst all this mortal misery? The various authors and genres of the Bible came up with numerous other possible solutions, including evil as an opportunity for redemption or atonement, the price of human freedom, a chance to build character, the necessary consequence of the divine balance of justice and mercy, a test, or just plain nastiness sent by a cosmic enemy (Crenshaw 2005; Ehrman 2008). One biblical maneuver to salvage a just god was the insistence that punishment will come to the *descendants* of the thriving culprit. Yahweh incorporates this threat into his commandments, promising that as a jealous God he will punish "children for the iniquity of parents, to the third and the fourth generation" (Ex 20:5; cf. 34:6–7; Num 14:18; Deut 5.9–10; Isa 14:20–1; 65:6–7; Jer 32:18). This cruelly unjust form of justice is both potent and foolproof: "If a man is unjust and prospers, his descendants are sure to suffer; if he does not prosper, it is only what he deserved; if he is just and prospers, he deserves to prosper; and if he is just and does not prosper, he is merely suffering for the misdeeds of some ancestors. Formally, this theory is flawless . . ." (Adkins 1960:68). This divine process can even explain the many days of suffering and death of a newborn baby (2 Sam 12:14–19) as punishment of the father's sins. (The father of one of my students recently told me that members of his parents' church informed him that the muscular dystrophy of his three-year-old child was God's punishment for the parents' (unspecified) sins.)

But the unfairness of cross-generational "justice" was apparent even to God, as Yahweh elsewhere in the Tanakh counters that he does *not* in fact visit punishment upon offspring (Deut 24:16 = 2 Chron 25:4; Deut 7:9–10; Jer 31:29–30; Ezek 18:1–4, 20). Yet many confessional scholars still feel compelled to defend their God: "It would be ironic if unjust cruelty were to be cited as evidence of God's covenant love. . . . We cannot, therefore, interpret the delaying of punishment stated in the pronouncement of the attributes as an injustice, and must regard deferral as essentially an act of divine kindness" (Levine 1993:381). *Must* we? Or you can skip the underlying injustice and instead insist that the "measurement of punishment is smaller than the measure of grace. God's anger lasts for four generations, while his grace extends for a thousand generations" (Weinfeld 1991:24). That must be of great comfort to those in the fourth generation whose innocent lives are ruined by a dogged God.

It is also revealing – and very human – that we don't seem to need to explain our present *success* as deriving from the *virtues* of our great-grandparents. We pretty much deserve our prosperity, no matter who we are. But this theory of inherited guilt is no longer prominent in Western culture beyond the basic sense of justice we sometimes feel when a personal rival meets with an unhappy fate. "Karma's a bitch," and a non-Western one at that.

The winning Western "solution" to the problem has of course been the belief that we get our just rewards for our behavior or beliefs only *after* death. This "deferred justice" is the Christian solution that culminates in the Final Judgment: "Apocalypticism is nothing so much as an ancient kind of theodicy, an explanation of why there can be so much pain and suffering in this world if a good and powerful God is in charge of it" (Ehrman 2008:256). Postmortem existence for Christians, then, provides not just an antidote to the fear of death but a necessary sense of justice, a chance that the apparently unfair upheavals in life actually *can* make sense of a just and immanent God's inaction. Or in the words of one scholar and believer:

> Without a clear hope (and it can be no more) of an afterlife in the eternal God, Paul's claim that through Christ death has lost its sting (1 Cor. 15:55) loses its force. There is no longer scope for resolution of the injustice and senselessness which are such features of human life on earth. . . . [if there is nothing after death, our] achievements in this life have no lasting meaning, and wickedness and injustices go for ever unrecompensed.
>
> (Sykes 2000:154, 153)

The Homeric epics reject *all* of this. The *Iliad* and *Odyssey* provide no indisputable example of inherited guilt (*pace* Gagné 2013:177–205), although the characters wish it upon their enemies, and the concept will become important in later Greek culture. The Homeric world, as we have seen, also lacks a conveniently invisible repository for everyday evildoers. Hades is not designed to rectify the injustices in this life. The underworld of the *Odyssey* has no place to make up for the trials and misfortunes of "good" people in general or to punish the generically "bad." It is not until roughly 250 years after Homer that we find unambiguous references to the punishment after death of ordinary mortals (Johnston 1999:12).

The Homeric gods – most obviously those in the *Iliad* – have no interest in justice as we would define it, in this life or the next, and that difference, once again, is all for the better. Let me pause here to define divine justice, because different concepts are often conflated or confused. On the one hand, we know that in some important ways concepts of justice in the ancient world were different from our modern version. We are often reminded that we shouldn't "impose our Western way of thinking" about justice (Koch 1983:74) onto our reading of ancient texts and that "we cannot equate it [an ancient concept of justice] with our understanding of the term" (Bellah 2011:222).

While this cultural and historical sensitivity is important to note, it is not relevant to our discussion. While each author, text, and culture can and often does renegotiate exactly how divine justice is manifested, nevertheless the basic concept as theists and classicists alike consider it in most of their discussions is relatively straightforward: **Divine justice is that interest the gods take in, and their actions taken in response to, *human behavior towards other humans*.** The italicized words are important, because we are not concerned with gods punishing and rewarding mortals solely for dishonoring or insulting divine prerogatives directly.

Yes, to try to rape Leto or work on Yahweh's day off is likely to meet with divine disfavor. And the penalty that follows could be labeled "divine justice." But that's not what the term has come to mean or why it's so central to theology and some branches of philosophy. The key to the concept is that people who act morally or immorally towards other members of their community by standards supposedly supported by the deities should encounter corresponding treatment at the hands of the gods. "Just" gods – deities that are somehow entwined in the judgment of human behavior – act to punish human agents of bad acts and reward agents who fulfill their obligations to other humans (within the community, however that is defined).

Classicists and theologians alike are not content with arguing that "Zeus was just by ancient Greek standards" or "Jesus was just by Jewish or Roman standards" or "Yahweh was just by ancient Near Eastern standards." Scholars and theologians – at least those with which I will take issue in this chapter – argue that these are deities who care about how humans treat humans and react to violations of morality. Thus I think Bruce Louden (2006:9) wrongly criticizes fellow classicist Van Erp Taalman Kip for using contemporary standards of divine justice in her examination of Iliadic gods: "In evaluating the Homeric gods she has no interest in placing them in an ancient context but analyzes them primarily according to late twentieth-century rhetoric. She seems unaware that the objection she raises could also be raised against Yahweh as he is depicted in OT myths." I'm not sure if she was aware of this or not, but I am: Yahweh *is* as unjust as the Homeric gods!

The Olympians and Yahweh are all amoral and often immoral deities who react egomaniacally to perceived wrongs, punishing anyone who damages *their* honor or challenges *them*. Homer knows what divine justice *should* look like. His gods just don't have that "justice" gene. Homer's deities don't punish or reward humans now or after death or unto the fourth generation on the basis of their morality, that is, for how mortals treat each other. *The gods don't care.* Once again these derelict Olympians provide a far more *useful* fiction than the construct of biblical theologians. Any justice the Homeric heroes and we are to find will be in this world – it's a wanton waste of a life to wait for death to straighten things out. The Olympians' selfishness and capriciousness turn out to be another strength in Homer's divine portrait, not a weakness for which classicists should apologize. We must determine how to live together, how to live *good* lives, without divine guidance from ancient mythology or fear of supernatural adjudication.

Justice and the Homeric gods

To any serious first-time reader of the *Iliad*, it might seem obvious that the gods' interactions with mortals are motivated by selfish interests such as genealogical connections, heroic favorites, military partisanship, personal grudges, and reciprocal favors. The Olympians are quick to work against anyone who even accidentally denigrates their honor. You would perhaps conclude, as familiar as we are by now with the mercurial nature of Homer's Olympians, that I could therefore simply state that these deities have no demonstrable interest in justice, and we could move on. But should I do so, I would bring down upon me a plague of protests from many of my fellow classicists, for I would be ignoring one of the more hotly contested issues in Homeric studies. The author of articles on "Justice" and "Theodicy" in a three-volume *Homer Encyclopedia* states categorically – that is, without fear of contradiction – that "the gods act as its [justice's] guardians and guarantors" (Friedrich 2011:2.427). How can this be? Given the patent amorality of the gods and divine indifference to most ethical concepts, how can they (especially Zeus) be not merely agents but "guardians and guarantors" of human justice? What evidence is there for a "complex system of norms and punishments in action" that embody a "consistent form of divine justice shared by both epics" (Allan 2006:2)?

If you will bear with me here for a minute – there is method to this particular academic madness – let me crudely outline some of the major scholarly approaches to the question of divine justice in the Homeric poems. There are, of course, all sorts of flavors available on this menu, and virtually every scholar writing on Homeric themes cooks up his or her own version of one of the following:

1) There was a development in ideas about the gods over time, a "moral progress" that took place between the composition of the *Iliad* and *Odyssey*. The gods of the *Iliad* are avowedly disinterested (or minimally interested) in justice, but the *Odyssey* contains gods (especially Zeus) who care about human conduct and invest themselves in righting human wrongs. This view of divine "improvement" over the time between the two poems has generally gone out of favor.

2) Another approach agrees that there is a strong difference between *Iliad* and *Odyssey*, but it does not rely on a model of chronological development. Instead, we find two very different attitudes about the gods' relation to justice, visions (or generic bases) so starkly at odds that a few scholars have even argued that this disparity provides proof that the epics cannot have been composed by the same individual. These studies often also suggest, as in my previous point, that the *Odyssey*'s moral gods are therefore "superior" (a more "mature" vision) to those of the *Iliad*.

3) A very common interpretation is that the *Odyssey* as a whole comprises a firm defense of just gods, a defense that may also be found underlying a few scenes in the *Iliad*. It's more a matter of emphasis and poetic purposes than complete theological differences. Again, the *Odyssey*'s gods are regularly said to be "more advanced" than those of the *Iliad*.

4) Several scholars have argued that the gods in both epics are concerned with justice in some serious respect. This usually requires that "divine justice" be defined by different criteria than I use here, such as something as vague as the "divinely appointed order of the universe."

5) Some scholars, who I think are right, find no compelling evidence of divine justice in either poem.

I am fairly convinced that the gods of the *Odyssey* are not appreciably different from those of the *Iliad* when it comes to their lack of concern for justice.

However, in that opinion I am distinctly in the minority.[1] For the purposes of my overall argument here, we can stick a bit less controversially with the gods of the *Iliad*. So in this chapter I will draw all my evidence from the *Iliad* alone. But it is important to be aware that a majority of experts think that the two epics reveal different visions of divine justice and that the version found in the *Odyssey* (i.e., gods who punish wrongdoers) is often considered to be fundamentally superior: "According to a widely held view, the *Odyssey* heralds a *more advanced ethical conception* of the gods and *more enlightened view of divine justice and human responsibility* than is to be found in the *Iliad*" (Clay 1983:215, my emphasis). The untested assumption is always that "a more advanced ethical conception of the gods" is one that insists the gods are intimately involved in enforcing justice. This presumption seems to me to be completely backwards, a combination of unchallenged religious preconceptions, the academic invention of a morally progressive "axial age," and wish fulfillment erroneously projected onto Homer's epics that ultimately derives from an evolutionarily engineered "punishing god." The Olympians' lack of interest in justice is not "primitive" or in need of development or a cause for concern. Homer can account for the realities of our existence; the Bible (and the traditions that derive from it) cannot. Which is more "advanced"? Which puts the greater demand on our maturing as individuals and a species?

Homer knows justice

Studies of the multiple meanings of the two words most commonly translated in the epics as "justice," *dikê* and *themis*, have shown that vocabulary alone is not of sufficient help for understanding divine justice. These words rarely (if ever) suggest any abstract notion of justice, much less divine justice. Naoko Yamagata concludes in her extensive study of these terms in the epics that there "is no indication, apart from a dubious example of Athena's support for Odysseus, of the gods' concern for men's administration of *themis* and *dike*" (1994:79). Homer does reveal – once, and once only in the *Iliad* – that he is aware of what divine justice *should* look like. Patroclus has entered the battle in Achilles' armor in order to drive the Trojans away from the Greek ships. His counterattack has proved successful, and he is now bent on chasing down Hector and the Trojans in their chariots:

> Just as the whole dark earth is weighed down under a tempest on a late summer day when Zeus pours down a torrential cloudburst, when in anger he rages at men who by force impose crooked judgments [*themistes*] in the place of assembly, and they drive away justice [or "the case," *dikê*] without concern for the vengeance [gaze] of the gods. And all their rivers swell full in the flood, and mountain torrents then cut away many of the hillsides, and they give a deafening roar as they stream headlong to the dark sea from the mountains, and the fields of men are eroded away; so the Trojan horses gave a deafening roar as they rushed on.
>
> (16.384–93)

Many decades ago this oft-discussed simile (we classicists still use phrases like "oft-discussed") was already called "one of the most controversial passages in the Homeric poems" (Moulton 1977:36), and it remains "one of the most problematic similes in the entire *Iliad*" (Tsagalis 2012:332). For here we find Zeus flooding a town in "vengeance" because some of its men have made crooked judgments and apparently forced them upon others. This is a Zeus who intervenes when humans "drive out justice." So, doesn't this mean that there is divine justice in the epic?

In fact, what makes this simile so "problematic" is that it is the *only* reference in the entire epic to divine justice – the poet never credits the gods within his actual tale of the Trojan War with any such effort to punish miscreants. Similes stand outside the narrative action. Not once in all the activity in and around Troy depicted in the *Iliad* do the gods actually intervene to punish humans who mistreat other humans as they seem to do in this one simile. Not a single violator of human morality in the *Iliad* meets with *divine* recompense, not those who break oaths or violate the guest-host relationship or lie or cheat or kill suppliants or give "crooked judgments" or engage in any other form of potential misconduct towards fellow mortals. Not once. Nor do the gods or the poet ever suggest that a malefactor will be punished in the future, whether in this life or in the underworld or through his or her descendants.[2] Several of the leading characters firmly *believe* that the gods involve themselves in human affairs as in the simile, but they are shown to be wrong every time. We hear about the unhappy fates of offenders in the past and present, but neither the poet nor the gods themselves ever suggest that this is the result of divine justice.

This singular simile is so at odds with the rest of the epic that some scholars have considered it an interpolation or "mistake," a piece of "Hesiodic" moralizing perhaps added by a later author. But Homeric similes often exhibit an originality in content and language that seems to be derived not from the heroic tradition of the past but from ordinary experiences of the poet and his audience. Homerist Mark Edwards concludes that "It is hard not to think that in these long similes one can see the personal eye and thought of the poet" (1987:103), noting this singular reference to just gods is only found in the "untraditional situation of a simile" (2005:311; cf. Coffey 1957:116; Mueller 1984:109; Fränkel 1997:106; Yamagata 1994:89–90 calls it a window into "the contemporary moral climate").

I am convinced that this simile is Homeric, a *deliberate exception* to the universal behavior of the gods throughout the epic that is designed to draw our attention to what is missing from these deities in the narrative itself. Like Menelaus' off-camera immortality in the *Odyssey*, this unique vision of a "just Zeus" provides the audience with a glimpse of an alternative world that is denied to the actual Homeric characters – and to Homer's audience, both then and now. The gods *could* involve themselves in human transgressions as Zeus does in the simile. They just don't.

When I claim that there is no evidence for divine justice in the *Iliad*, then, I do not mean that Homer doesn't know about the concept. It is clear from the simile that he expects his audience to be quite familiar with and perhaps even to have embraced the belief, just as his characters do, that gods punish men for unjust behavior. The poet quite intentionally – defiantly, even – ejects this sanguine vision of the gods from his narrative. By letting his characters demonstrate the same misplaced faith that his audience (including contemporary theists) has in the gods' just interventions, while simultaneously showing us over and over again the reality of the gods' indifference to justice, he slaps us in the face for our theological complacency.

Olympian "justice"

What Homeric deities care about is their own honor (*timê*) from mortals, which comes from obedience to the gods' demands and in ritual acknowledgment such as sacrifice. This is the system of reciprocity central to Homeric religion. Apollo's priest asks for the god's help "if I ever built for you a pleasing temple, or if I ever burned fat thigh pieces of bulls and goats in your honor" (1.39–41). Reciprocity forms the heart of the relations between gods and mortals (as well as between individual mortals), and sacrifice is thought to be the most efficacious act a hero can take to motivate the gods. In fact, simply reminding the gods of a history of pious sacrifices is sometimes enough to earn their attention. Agamemnon prays to Zeus, insisting that "not once did I sail by a beautiful altar of yours in my many-oared ship as I came here to my ruin, but on every one I burned the fat and thigh pieces of bulls" (8.238–40; cf. 15.372–4). One warrior even tells a parable about the power of Prayers, the "daughters of great Zeus," who can "bend" the gods since men can move them by praying, with "burnt offerings and kindly prayers and libation and the savor of sacrifice" (9.497–512).

Homer's gods are not shy about their attachment to ritual acknowledgment from mortals. Hera tries to convince Poseidon to ignore Zeus's order not to aid the Greeks by recalling that "for you they bring many pleasing offerings to Helice and Aegae, and you used to wish victory for them" (8.203–4). Poseidon turns the point back on Hera when he argues with her about saving Aeneas' life, asking "why does this guiltless man now suffer hardships for no purpose because of afflictions that belong to others, while he always gives pleasing gifts to the gods who hold broad heaven?" (20.297–9; cf. 4.48–9; 17.567–72).

But it turns out that this system of reciprocity frequently breaks down: "The Homeric gods can always say no without giving any reason" (Burkert 1985:189). Prayer and sacrifice (and the recollection of previous prayers and sacrifices) don't always work, as we saw in an earlier chapter. Despite what characters believe, sacrifices *never* change the will of the gods (Hitch 2009:134, 139). This difference between mortal expectation and divine reality is crucial to understanding the epics. In the disparity between the characters' beliefs and the gods' actions "we see the gap between the 'reality' of divine behavior and the belief of humble people who think that the gods behave in an intelligibly moral manner" (Yamagata 1994:126). Honor the gods and things *might* turn out in your favor. It's a pure crapshoot. On the other hand, forget to offer first fruits to Artemis (9.533–40) or skip a vow to Poseidon (7.446–53) and you absolutely *will* motivate the gods . . . *against* you. In one of the contests during Patroclus' funeral games, an archer forgets to vow a sacrifice to Apollo while his opponent remembers. Which one do you think wins (23.862–83; cf. 23.546–7, 770–2)? The important point here is the nature of divine motivation in the epics. The gods get involved not because of the way humans behave towards each other but in return for gifts or past favors or the promise of future benefactions or in response to personal slights. And even then, only if they feel like it at the moment.

But at least in these cases one can say the gods respond (as the spirit moves them) to what humans *do*, even if this has nothing to do with justice. All the other sources of divine interaction with humans in the epic are purely relational. Sometimes it's genealogical: Thetis races to aid her son; Aphrodite rescues Aeneas. The gods' nepotism is so familiar that Agamemnon can express his amazement at Hector's success by muttering that the Trojan "is the dear son of neither a goddess nor a god" (10.50) – Zeus must prefer Hector's sacrifices, Agamemnon naturally concludes. Given Zeus's numerous progeny, things can get complicated. At one point one of his grandsons faces off against one of his sons (5.627–62)! Or it can become a farcical battle of whose divine parent is more formidable. Apollo ill-advisedly encourages Aeneas to confront Achilles, "for she [Aeneas' mother] is the daughter of Zeus," but Achilles' mother is an "inferior goddess," her father merely the "old man of the sea" (20.104–7).

And of course the gods have their own familial, military, and political agendas, as well as their own favorites. Hera and Athena hate Troy and so support the Greek leaders; Apollo, on the other hand, preserves the Trojan leaders Polydamas and Hector and renders Patroclus easy pickings for the enemy. Hephaestus saves the son of his priest. Aphrodite protects Paris. Athena just plain *likes* Odysseus. Diomedes can even expect Athena to come to his support because she had formerly helped his father. Examples could be added *ad infinitum*. The point is that the gods in the narrative are never motivated by anything that we could reasonably call "justice." When it comes to humans dealing with humans, the Olympians remain morally disengaged "divine spectators."

Inventing justice

A vast majority of the deities and spirits in early religions did not have any considerable moral concern: "Religion's early roots did not have a wide moral scope" (Norenzayan 2013:7). But with the proliferation in more recent human history of "big" or "high" gods we have come to expect deities to be morally concerned, interventionalist "supernatural watchers." Religion scholar Pascal Boyer (2001:170–91) has shown that historically there are primarily three nonexclusive models of moral gods, three different ways to connect moral intuitions with supernatural agents: god-as-legislator (a god who commands – think Yahweh), god-as-exemplar (a god as role model – think Jesus), and god-as-onlooker (a god who cares about how mortals treat each other). The first two clearly won't work for Homer's Olympians, but some classicists have turned to the third model in their efforts to argue for divine justice in the *Iliad*. We'll take as our primary example of this interpretative (mis)step the argument that Paris is held accountable by the gods for his violation of the guest-host relationship (*xenia*). Paris' "punish-ment" is only one of several lines of argument taken by pro-justice scholars, but upon inspection these efforts all fail for similar reasons. For the suspicious reader (which will include many classicists), I have critiqued the other most commonly cited bits of support for Iliadic divine justice in Appendix 3.

Here's the deal with Paris: Wouldn't it be great if the gods punished the adul-terous weasel for his affair with Helen? Then perhaps all this suffering would be worthwhile, and some sort of justice would be served. Paris is certainly an adulterer guilty of violating the guest-host relationship, a central moral tenet of Homeric life that leading characters believe is overseen by Zeus Xenios, Zeus of Guests and Hosts. The *Trojans* don't even like Paris. The home troops would be happy if Paris lost his duel with Menelaus, provided that meant the end of the war (3.320–3). Paris "became hated by all of them like black death" (3.454). His own brother thinks the Trojans would have stoned him to death by now if they had any moxie (3.56–7; cf. 6.284–5). When things are looking bleak, one of the Trojan leaders argues that Helen should be returned, but he is rebuffed publicly by Paris (7.350–64). Paris is a very self-centered guy. Menelaus, as the cuckolded husband, thus understandably calls on Zeus to make an example of Paris as their duel begins: "Lord Zeus, grant me revenge on the one who first committed evils, godlike Alexander, and crush him beneath my hands; so anyone even of men yet to come would shudder to do harm to the host who offers friendship" (3.351–54).

Poor Menelaus. If there *were* divine justice we would see Paris suffer. The gods would grant Menelaus' prayer. But here we bump into the first key to understand-ing justice in the epics: We must always distinguish what mortals believe, say, hope, and do concerning the gods from what Homer reveals to us (but usually not to the heroes themselves) the gods are actually doing and saying. Homer creates a "pervasive dramatic irony in which the audience is repeatedly invited to note a gap between claims made and the reality of the situation as it unfolds" (Rose 1997:185). Unlike in *real* life, when we can pray without any evidence to support or deny the existence of the beseeched deity (beyond the general inefficacy our efforts), Homer *shows* us the complete lack of divine agency in remediating injus-tice among mortals. The narrative's account of the gods' favoritism, indifference, hostility, capriciousness, and limitations "pathetically contradicts human expres-sions of vain but touching confidence in divine anxiety for justice" (Lateiner 2004:21). Characters use the language of morality more than five times as often as the poet (Griffin 1986:39–40; Jong 1988).

Menelaus *thinks* the gods care, or at least *should* care; the truth, however – *what Homer shows us* – is that the gods do *not* answer his prayer. First, Menelaus' spear doesn't draw blood even though it pierces Paris' shield and corselet. Then his sword shatters as it hits Paris' helmet, prompting Menelaus to utter a "bitter cry" to heaven, censuring Zeus for moral delinquency (3.365–8). Homeric characters frequently both turn to the gods for support and fault them when they don't come through. It's refreshing, to be honest – Homeric characters don't tend to blame themselves and their inherent unworthiness for the gods' failures. They all seem to have a little bit of Job in them.

And it gets worse for the betrayed husband. What the gods actually do is *rescue* Paris from certain, merited death! Aphrodite saves him because he is one of her favorites, with not a word of objection from Zeus or any of the other gods. But Paris will *eventually* die, the proponents of divine justice hasten to add. *There's* your divine justice – the wheels of Homeric justice turn slowly, but Paris will be killed, and Troy will fall. And that slippery logic reveals the second key to judging fairly the presence or absence of divine justice: Evidence must come from the epics themselves, not from the traditional "story" of Troy. Paris will not die in the *Iliad*. We know from the mythological tradition and from bits of divine foreknowledge thrown our way in the text that *lots of people will die* in the next year at Troy, including virtually every Trojan male and many Greeks, including Achilles.[3] But we search the epic in vain even for an acknowledgment from the divine world that Paris will die, much less be punished.

This is a critical point. We can't take events in the later Troy-tradition as proof that the gods in the *Iliad* act with justice. Yes, Paris will be killed. Yes, Troy will fall. But are these acts of divine justice? Critics seem to have tried to wedge biblical "deferred justice" into a text where it doesn't exist. The Homeric gods can punish groups for *direct and personal insults* from their leaders. All the Greeks suffer from Apollo's plague sent because of Agamemnon's foolish rejection of the god's priest. But the king's actions are bad politics, not immoral – no one suggests Agamemnon should not have a woman as prize. Apollo acts because one of his favorites calls in a favor. Homer never connects the human mistreatment of other humans with divine punishment in the epic. The poet supplies no evidence that the adulterer's post-Iliadic death (which is never mentioned!) is any more an act of divine payback than the death of any other mortal associated with Troy. What we need is a simple statement – the Bible is filled with them – or even a hint, from a god or the poet, that Paris will eventually get what's coming to him from the gods. It doesn't happen. Some of the *Greeks* hope and even believe that Paris will pay, but the poet and the gods are silent on the issue. Instead, we are informed that Paris will get heroic credit for killing Achilles *with the help of the gods* (22.358–60; cf. 19.415–17)! There is not a single comment by any divinity in the *Iliad* in reference to Paris' guilt or possible punishment. It's not on their moral radar; *they don't have a moral radar*. To find justice here, one can only rely on the silence of the poet – he doesn't *not* say that Paris met divine retribution, so we can assume he does. As a noted Greek religion scholar concludes, "Many of the desperate attempts to detect 'justice' in Zeus' acts in the *Iliad* resort to such *e silentio* arguments" (Versnel 2011:167 n41).

Moreover, Paris is not the only guilty actor who would deserve divine punishment if the gods actually cared. Helen violates her husband's house and the expected role of a loyal wife in the guest-host relationship. And she is not shy about her own guilt (as Paris seems to be), repeatedly wishing she had died before she had abandoned her husband, daughter, and home (3.172–76, 240–2; 6.344–49; 24.762–75). She left willingly and with enough forethought to do some careful packing, since we hear a dozen times that Helen "and all her treasure" should be returned to the Greeks. Like Paris, she is "abhorred by all" and, with the exception of Priam and Hector, universally reproached (24.767–75; cf. 3.159–65, 241–42). Yet there is certainly no talk among the gods about her "just punishment." Helen is never explicitly censured by the poet or Zeus. Indeed, to follow the logic of proponents of divine justice in the epics, our "knowledge" of Helen's flourishing postwar life back in Sparta (as the *Odyssey* reveals) would be "proof" that there is no divine payback for illicit actions.

Neither Paris' death nor the fall of Troy occurs within the epic. These episodes are part of the tradition, to be sure, and both the audience and Zeus know that the city is fated to be destroyed. Homer counts on our knowledge of the tradition to create painful ironies. But it is surely a *post hoc ergo propter hoc* fallacy to suggest that the gods are depicted acting "justly" *in the text* solely because a year after the epic ends tradition has it that Paris is killed and the Greeks destroy Troy! We might as well say Troy will fall because Hecuba exposed her breast on the wall – who wants to see that? – or that Achilles will die because he mistreated animals (he slaughtered two innocent dogs on Patroclus' funeral pyre, after all). Pick any activity you don't like that is mentioned in the epic and point to the anticipated fall of Troy. All that's missing is any evidence of their interdependence. In fact, the text points the opposite direction: Troy is one Zeus's *favorite* cities and he regrets its inevitable end – and for just the selfish reasons we would expect:

> For of all the cities of men on earth under the sun and starry heaven that men inhabit, of these holy Ilion, along with Priam and the people of Priam of the good ash spear, has continuously been especially honored in my heart. For never was my altar lacking in a fair feast, the libation, and the savor of burnt offering; for we [gods] received this as our prerogative.
>
> (4.44–9)

"When this Zeus brings about the fall of Troy," Emily Kearns concludes, "it will be with sorrow and not with righteous indignation" (2004:69n14).

The Greeks attack and will eventually sack Troy for numerous reasons – to get Helen and her stuff back, to punish the Trojans for taking and keeping her and thus violating hospitality, to earn glory in a great war. It's about human lust, ambition, honor, status, outrage, and vengeance. Some gods are intimately concerned with the course of the war and no doubt think their cause is "just." Hera, for example, seems convinced that the obliteration of Troy is fair recompense for losing a beauty contest. But Homer's "theological" point is that their actions are not motivated by anything we would define as divine justice. The gods are driven by their own sense of honor and immortal passions and, on occasion, the thrust of fate. There is nothing that links the past misbehavior of a Trojan towards another human with any aspect of divine recompense as we might reasonably define it.

Moreover, a black-and-white morality is ill-suited for the epic and would undermine the careful balance Homer creates between the two sides of the war. If the Trojans are wicked and about to get their deserved punishment from just gods, the epic devolves into a simple tale of vengeance, a formulaic tale of triumph that one usually finds in Hollywood action films. Now it *could* be that the *Iliad* is such a story – my students often feel that way about it before I beat some sense into their heads. And it *could* be that the tradition that Homer received painted the Trojans as bad guys (Sale 1989; Heath 2005a). But that's not what the text now reveals. The Trojans are no more "evil" than the Greek leaders, and some of them receive far more sympathetic treatment: "By portraying amoral gods, Homer allows the audience to make up their own minds freely on moral issues in the *Iliad*" (Winterbottom 1989:33). "The poet needed these [amoral] gods to open the way for our pity and our awareness of the human condition," concludes Van Erp Tallman Kip (2000:402). "When we try to make them just and moralistic in spite of their creator, we dehumanize his poem."

If you are interested in other arguments often offered on behalf of Iliadic justice, go ahead and wade through Appendix 3. For now, though, my case for divine indifference to justice will be best served by looking at two examples of how the Greeks themselves read the *Iliad*.

Achilles reads the *Iliad*

The absence of divine justice is essential to the central theme of the *Iliad*—the wrath of Achilles and its consequences. James V. Morrison has shown how Homer uses misdirection, including the "epistemological gap" between the warriors and gods, to "draw the audience closer to the central problem faced by characters in the *Iliad*: mortal expectation and miscalculation" (1992). While Homer shows the heroic world futilely turning to the gods for justice, he sends his main character on such an intense emotional and introspective journey that in the final book Achilles comes to see through his culture's false expectations of the gods. Achilles' self-induced isolation, grief, and anger lead him to share Homer's own perspective on divine justice.

In this famous scene, Priam's supplication of Achilles for Hector's body has brought them both to tears, Priam for his dead son, Achilles for both his own father (for whom he is already as good as dead) and his beloved Patroclus. When they have had their "fill of weeping," Achilles helps the aged king to his feet and looks at him with pity. In an effort to console himself as much as Priam, he tells the king that they must try to allow their pain to rest. Achilles has come to see that there is no easy explanation for suffering, and that there is no divine justice:

> For in such a way the gods have spun the threads of destiny for miserable mortals, that they live sorrowing, but the gods themselves are free from care. For on Zeus's floor are set down two jars of gifts of the sort he gives, one of evil, the other of good. To whatever man Zeus, who delights in the thunderbolt, gives a mixed lot, that man now encounters evil, now good; but to whatever man he gives solely of the miserable, Zeus makes him an object of shame, and evil famine [poverty? Madness?] drives him across the bright earth, and he rambles honored neither by gods nor by mortals.
>
> (24.525–33)

In addition to Achilles' newly found compassion that we examined briefly at the end of the previous chapter, here we encounter the hero's sudden clarity of vision. Other Homeric heroes frequently blame the gods for evils or ask them for favors, but despite the apparent randomness of their success or failure, as far as we can tell they continue to believe in the "system." They are embedded religionists applying their identity-protective cognition – the incompatible evidence of life does not change their beliefs or alter their understanding. Achilles, on the other hand, has a revelation. He's not saying that humans are not responsible for the things they suffer (either good or bad). He takes full responsibility for the death of Patroclus and the misery he has caused Priam. And he is not claiming that the gods are evil; but he does accuse them of not caring enough to invest themselves in divine justice. They simply don't respond to human actions in any predictable fashion. Human morality doesn't affect them. A person's fate is unrelated to his or her character or behavior towards other mortals.

Critics raised in the Judeo-Christian tradition can fall into the either-or trap of its theology: Either God is good and there is justice and the good are rewarded and the wicked punished, or God is not good or doesn't exist or lacks omnipotence and therefore the world has no morality and no meaning. For example, Christian theologian Christopher J.H. Wright, admitting that polytheism has no trouble explaining evil, misleadingly states that this is because "some of the gods are evil all the time and most of the gods are evil some of the time" (2008:25–6; cf. biblical scholar Bob Becking's suggestion that polytheism is characterized by "good" and "bad" gods; 2001:194). This dualistic vision of the divine – completely irrelevant for Homer's gods – has dominated Western culture for millennia and is difficult to shed.

In one of the most famous works of classical scholarship – a book that has sparked a lively discussion of Homeric morality over the past 70 years – E.R. Dodds concluded that Achilles' tale of the urns means that "God's in his Heaven, all's wrong with the world" (1951:32). This is fundamentally a Judeo-Christian response, similar to that of the biblical commentators cited above. Similarly off the mark is Baruch Halpern, a professor of Jewish Studies, who refers to theodicy in all polytheistic cultures as an "adolescent genre" because it produces "that most pessimistic of relativist truths, 'Life is unfair'" (1987:106).

On the opposite side of this interpretive coin, Hugh Lloyd-Jones countered Dodds in his own highly influential study of divine justice by insisting that if "according to Achilles Zeus gives some men good and evil mixed and others unmixed evil, that is a mark not of his injustice but rather of his justice" (1971:27). Although they are both wrong, assuming as they do that a god must either be just or unjust, these influential opinions in turn make it into the general academic discussion. Distinguished sociologist of religion Robert Bellah, for example, cites both Lloyd-Jones and Dodds, and then states categorically that "the gods in general and Zeus in particular are indeed concerned with justice" (2011:326). If anything should be clear by now, it's that no such general statements can ever be made with any accuracy: *which* Greek gods, *which* version of Zeus, in what context? It's not true of the *Iliad*.

More convincing, but I think still not quite right, is Arthur W.H. Adkins' conclusion that the jars of Zeus presuppose "no qualities in the gods save malice or caprice" (1960:64). The results may strike us as malicious: Why can't the gods give us all good? Why don't they punish the iniquitous? Why can't we get only what we deserve? But what Achilles actually realizes is that the gods are on Olympus and *all in the world is as if they didn't exist at all*. The gods are *indifferent* to human flourishing in general and their "justice" is capricious, or what amounts to the same thing, inscrutable. There is no apparent link between a person's behavior and his fate, no easy system of reward for the good and punishment for the bad. The most one can hope for is a "mixed" lot, and no one, no matter what he does or how he acts, escapes random misfortune. The universe isn't unfair – it's insouciant.

This conclusion is exactly what a thoughtful individual would derive from the experiences presented in Homer's epic – and from *any* human life. Mortals, including even Achilles with his unique personal access to the divine, do not know what goes on among the gods. *It's as if the gods didn't exist.* There is no evidence for divine justice, so we are left on our own to figure out how to live a good life, a meaningful life, a moral life, to determine a better way to act – and to try to act that way. The existence or nonexistence of the gods is a pointless question when it comes to justice. In Achilles' case, he retains a belief in the gods. After all, his mother is a goddess. But the sudden awareness of the universe's indifference shatters his, and challenges the audience's, unthinking acceptance of what they have taken for granted about the gods' involvement in human behavior. This realization forms an important part of Achilles' great crisis at the end of the epic and, as we have seen, coincides with his virtual invention of "magnanimity" in Western culture, of tragic insight into and compassion for the human condition. Apollo, Hera, Athena, and Poseidon, "gods with rather less motive for their hatred than these two humans [Achilles and Priam]" (Davies 1981:60), are incapable of any such wisdom. They can only keep hating. In her study of tragedy and the Bible, J. Cherly Exum concludes that the "tragic vision isolates the hero over against an arbitrary and capricious world, a world in which – to get to the crux of the matter – the problem of evil is irreducible and unresolvable into some larger, harmonious whole" (1992:5). Achilles' confrontation with this truth makes him the great model of the tragic hero for all of Western literature.

The Greeks on Homer's amoral gods

There is no good evidence that the gods intervene for violations of human morality in the action of the epic. Achilles comes to see this with unusual clarity. The ancient Greeks saw it that way too, and they didn't distinguish between the *Iliad* and *Odyssey* in this respect.

Many later Greek authors, starting with Hesiod's *Works and Days* (but not his *Theogony*, as Clay (2016) has shown), suggest (or hope) that the gods punish offenders of human norms. The historian Herodotus, for example, who begins his history with a rationalization of stories of Io, Europa, Medea, and Helen, at the same time states at least seven times in his own authorial voice that the gods punish crime (as well as sacrilege; Fowler 2010:329). But they didn't read Homer that way. The earliest extant responses to Homer reveal a discomfort with these amoral gods who care nothing about human justice. I quoted in an earlier chapter some of the first impressions of Homer's gods, Xenophanes' famous complaints that "Homer and Hesiod have attributed to the gods everything that is shameful and disgraceful among men: Stealing, committing adultery, and deceiving each other" (Fr. 11). Though none of the fragments explicitly connects the gods' behavior to divine justice, it would be a remarkable stretch to find Xenophanes wishing to retain these gods as overseers of, say, the guest-host relationship, when he is rejecting them as adulterers.

Homer's gods were viewed by many Greek intellectuals as "unseemly" or "unfitting" or "improbable." What, then, was to be done with their greatest and most influential poet? In his famous treatise on justice, *The Republic*, Plato has Socrates reluctantly exile Homer from his ideal state partly because the gods are presented in the poems as immoral and patently unjust (2.376e-3.392c; 10.606e-608a). "Because it was inconceivable to him [Plato] that justice and the divine would not completely coincide, and because this is evidently not the case in Homer, he drew the radical consequence of banishing Homer from his Utopian commonwealth . . ." (Mueller 1984:146). Significantly, Plato, like a Judeo-Christian theologian, rejects Achilles' tale of the urns of Zeus because gods cannot – I mean, they just can*not* – be the cause of evil for humans (379c-e).

There was no public mechanism, however, "whereby stories of 'gods in sundry shapes, committing heady riots, incest, rapes' could be put under a ban as uncanonical" (Parker 2011:31). Far more frequently than abandoning these reprobate deities, the ancient Greek intellectuals tried to salvage Homer's gods through revisionist interpretations, just like the Judeo-Christian theologians have attempted to rehabilitate Yahweh. In rationalist readings like those of Euhemerus (c. 300 BCE), the gods were claimed to have been mortals of such remarkable achievements that they were treated as divine by their followers. Eventually their human origins were forgotten and people believed they had been gods (Hawes 2014:25–7). Thus they were not really divinities at all. Problem solved!

But to make Homer's gods morally acceptable, the most common critical program was allegory, the process of finding the ethical, theological, physical, and mystical truths that lay hidden in symbols and riddles under an otherwise offensive text (Lamberton 1986). Here we find precursors to the various hermeneutical approaches taken by rabbis and theologians to the stories of Yahweh's Olympian behavior. As one ancient critic noted, the divine elements in Homer, "if they are not taken allegorically, are entirely ungodly [*athea*], and do not preserve what is fitting" (Longinus 9.7). The results are the same as those of the rationalizers: Homer's gods were not gods after all. "If Apollo is actually the heat of the sun, we need not be bothered by his morals" (Van Erp Talman Kip 2000:385). The first writer on Homer we hear about (nothing remains of his writing), Theagenes of Rhegium, applied physical allegory to turn the dueling gods of the theomachy into an allegory of strife of the natural elements, dryness against humidity, heat against cold, etc. (Brisson 2004:35–6). A fifth-century author interpreted the gods as different parts of the body (Apollo was bile)! Allegorical reading of Homer was taken up by some Alexandrian critics and subsequent philosophical schools such as the Stoics and Neo-Platonists. Byzantine scholars were still using it to defend Homer from Christian attacks.

The important point here is that many Greek intellectuals viewed Homer's gods as amoral or immoral and unjust. There would have been no need for this creative and hopeless exercise if Homer's gods could be exonerated by the undisguised meaning of the text alone. The most substantial extant allegorical exegesis of Homer is Heraclitus' *Homeric Problems* (c. 100 CE), which begins with a direct comment on the necessity for the effort: "A great and difficult charge is declared by heaven against Homer concerning his contempt for the divine. For he acted completely impiously if he expressed nothing allegorically, and sacrilegious stories full of god-defying madness rage furiously through both poems" (1.1–2; note the reference to "both poems"). These critics are not merely complaining about how the gods behave towards each other but about their roles in human life. As classicist Peter Rose observes, these "critics" of Homer "implicitly recognize that their own efforts to construct a morally comprehensible universe are threatened by Homer" (1997:188). As silly as most of these efforts now appear (if no more reckless than the allegorical readings of the Bible many have forced on Yahweh or Jesus in a similar attempt to rescue their "divine" morality), they reveal that many Greeks themselves found Homer's gods embarrassingly unjust and morally unsound.[4]

The road to Hades is paved with good intentions

Classicists searching for justice in the *Iliad* are understandably reacting (if *over-responding*, I think) to flippant interpretations of Homer's gods. We may expect amateurs to make silly statements like "There is a whole soap opera of events that occurs on Mt. Olympus . . . that is irrelevant to what we can hope to retrieve from Homer's work" (Dreyfus and Kelly 2011:84). But there have been similarly disparaging remarks by well-respected classicists like Sir Cecil Maurice Bowra, who dismissed the Homeric deities with nothing more than a theistic wave of the hand: "This complete anthropomorphic system has of course no relation to real religion or to morality. These gods are a delightful, gay invention of poets" (1930:222). More particularly, some influential scholars in the past have banished Homer's gods explicitly *because* of their indifference to justice:

> The gods of the *Iliad* [in contrast to Hesiod's gods] are generally frivolous, unsteady creatures, whose friendship or enmity has little to do with human justice. They do not appear in the narrative as guarantors of human norms or as the sources of natural process. . . . They are in fact the chief source of comedy in the poem. We can, I think, explain this difference most easily by assuming that the gods of the *Iliad* belong to the conventional world of epic and were understood as such by the audience. Just as the epic tells, not of men, but of heroes, so also it tells stories, not of gods conceived as actual, but of literary gods.
>
> (Redfield 1975:76)

Scholars like Redfield – who rightly finds no divine justice in the *Iliad* – argue (alongside the ancient Greek critics and allegorists) that Homer's gods, because of their "deficiency" when it comes to justice, cannot be taken too seriously. In order for Homer's gods to have any thematic weight, the traditional Western thinking has it, they must be attached to justice in the same way (we have been told) Yahweh and Jesus are. As one great scholar of ancient religion revealingly wrote without hesitation, "since Homer and Hesiod there is an unshakable confidence in the justice of Zeus. God is no longer God if he does not join the attribute of justice to that of omnipotence" (Festugière 1952:27, cited in Versnel 2011:160 n27).

This reliance on the theistic myth of a just god can prevent readers from appreciating the brilliance of Homer's insight into the divine: His morally unresponsive gods make much *better* sense of our world. The *Olympians* are the more "advanced" portrait of the divine. The gods of the epics don't need a crafty lawyer inventing alibis for their behavior; they simply need to be seen for what they are without the distorted lens of Abrahamic theology. We Westerners, whether religious or not, are raised in a world that is dominated by a theistic vision that insists there must be an objective morality and ultimate justice embedded in the divine. Since Homer's scandalous gods cannot be the source of anything close to that vision, we must either abandon them or convert them. Hellenist David Cohen cuts right to the heart of the issue in discussing Aeschylean tragedy, although academic conventions encourage him to bury his insight in a footnote: "The problem is that few scholars like to face the intractability of the problem of evil; they would rather explain it away and believe that justice triumphs, that divinity is ultimately benevolent" (1986:140 n11). A. Maria van Erp Taalman Kip, on the other hand, boldly comments in an opening paragraph on what she suggests are often subconscious motives behind these renewed efforts to "rescue" Homer's gods: "Down through the ages Homer has been alternately attacked and defended on this point [the amorality of the gods], and I am convinced that the desire to justify the ways of the Homeric gods has not died out" (2000:385).

This theological bias is subtle, especially when compared with the depressing state of affairs in New Testament scholarship. In his dazzlingly comprehensive indictment of the academic study of the morality of Jesus, biblical scholar Hector Avalos rightly contrasts classicists with scholars in his field:

> Most New Testament scholars are affiliated with religious institutions and are part of what I have called an ecclesial-academic complex that has no counterpart in any other areas of the humanities. For example, most, if not all, scholars of Greek religion are not part of some Greek religious movement or organization. Despite biases that always exist in the study of the classics, it is fair to say that few have any personal stake in whether Zeus or Tiberius was good or bad because those entities don't constitute any sort of authority for their actions. That is not the case with Jesus, who is still viewed as the paradigmatic authority for most Christian scholars. . . .
>
> (2015:7; cf. 19)

While this statement is completely accurate – no classicist I have met or whose work I have read seems to shade his or her interpretation of Zeus because of a personal investment in the truth of the text or the reality of the Olympians – it doesn't mean that preconceptions about what a *consequential* god should look like are not read into the epics. As Michael D. Konaris concludes in his study of the links between scholars of Greek religion and their theistic background, "Greek religion and its gods may no longer serve as a proxy for the settling of confessional scores [as they did in the 19th and early 20th centuries], however, a lot appears still to be vested in their interpretation" (2016:288).

Homeric scholars frequently assume that for some (always unspecified) reason a serious deity *must* be one who punishes evildoers. Gods who invest themselves in human morality are just plain *better*, we are told, representing a more "advanced" state in the history of the human mind and civilization. Thus even those scholars who find no divine justice in the *Iliad* are often relieved to find it (mistakenly, I think) in the *Odyssey*. Here are a few such comments culled from important studies of the Homeric gods and justice (italics are my emphases):

> It was a misfortune for the Greeks that the idea of cosmic justice, which represented an *advance on the old notion of purely arbitrary divine Powers*, and provided a sanction for the new civic morality, should have been thus associated with a primitive conception of the family.
>
> (Dodds 1951:34)

> To consider the gods as moral, however, while clearly *an advance in thought*
> . . .
>
> (Adkins 1960:66)

> A god's wrath directed against a hapless mortal [as found in the *Iliad*] *is* something *relatively primitive*, and doubtless older than the concept of the gods as arbiters and overseers of justice on earth [as found in parts of the *Odyssey*].
>
> (Fenik 1974:218)

> The god's sense of justice was *underdeveloped* in the *Iliad*.
>
> (Dietrich 1979:141)

> The moral conception of the divine in the *Odyssey carries the evolution*, which has already reached an advanced stage in the anthropomorphism of the Iliadic gods, *a further step* beyond the primal notion of the gods as personifications of natural forces.
>
> (Friedrich 1991:18–19)

Charles Segal, who was one of our most highly decorated Ivy League classicists, managed to diss the gods of the *Iliad* five times in the first four pages of a frequently cited article (1992:489–92), referring to the "'*higher*' *morality* of Zeus articulated in the proem" [of the *Odyssey*]; the "*evolution of an increasingly moral* conception of the gods [in the *Odyssey*]"; the "*more evolved* notions of divinity [in the *Odyssey*]"; the *"less moral, more 'primitive'* divine behavior [in the *Iliad*]"; and concluding that "the *Odyssey* seems *more advanced morally* than the *Iliad.*"

This "advanced" or "evolved" morality is that of a punishing deity along the lines of biblical versions of God. Without any argument at all, scholars can insist that the relatively recent (in evolutionary terms) human invention of punishing gods is superior to the contrivance of gods who don't care. In other words, their assumptions about the nature of morality and divinity apparently do not differ from Christian scholars and theologians who insist that without a just God there can be no human justice and thus no meaningful life. Here are two typical examples from a dictionary of Christian theology:

> The suffering of the innocent makes no theological sense if this life is all there is.
>
> (Hebblethwaite 2000:320)

> Can men and women remain men and women in anything that can be called a human way without the meaning, the purpose, the values traditionally given and guaranteed by theism?
>
> (Thrower 2000:50)

These are not rhetorical questions: Thrower fully expects us to answer "of course not!" The "logic" of this theological presumption can be neatly summarized:

> This is the contention, taught by millions over the centuries, accepted by billions, and still expressed today by adherents of the theistic religions, that the only safeguard of morality is God, whose essence is goodness, whose will and purpose for his creatures have been made known, and to whom all people will ultimately be answerable. Without this divine sanction for morality, it is argued, the urge to "be good" will evaporate, the concept of goodness will vanish. . . .
>
> (Billington 2002:110)

Theologians often state the absolute necessity of a just and punishing deity quite emphatically. Stephen T. Davis' "exercise in Christian philosophical theology" offers little more on morality than *"the wrath of God is our only hope. . . .* The wrath of God is what keeps our world, at least most of the time, from deteriorating into something like Hobbes' state of nature" (2015:91, emphasis in original). This kind of morality, based solely on fear of punishment, is the ethical lowest common denominator. Freud pointed out that by limiting morality to obeying God for fear of his retribution, religion had made it impossible for humanity to grow up, to obtain an "education to reality":

> If the sole reason why you must not kill your neighbor is because God has forbidden it and will severely punish you for it in this or the next life – then,

when you learn that there is no God and that you need not fear His punishment, you will certainly kill your neighbor without hesitation, and you can only be prevented from doing so by mundane force.

(1961:50)

Fear of God's judgment has no doubt kept some believers in line over the centuries, even if it is "such a demeaning view of human nature" (Dennett 2006:279). A just and punishing God may temper our anxieties, and its invention may have once provided cultural advantages. But now it has become merely another unhelpful evolutionary concoction that gets in the way of living an honest and useful life and does not – despite what the theologians and devout theists believe – lead to a more ethical world or satisfying existence. The theistic critique of a naturalist view of the world – if there is no cosmic purpose, if each life and human life in general are finite, and if there is no divinely sponsored justice, then human existence is meaningless and absurd – doesn't hold up under philosophical scrutiny (Martin 2002:213–25). And practically, the evidence from Judeo-Christian history suggests that overall it doesn't seem to work very well, at least beyond advancing the procreative success of the original "in-group." It's not very effective in the *Iliad*, for that matter, even though the characters expect the gods to intervene to punish wrongdoers. Homer lets us see the mortal miscalculation, while presenting a far more beneficial depiction of the gods, one that meets reality head on: There is no divine justice in this world and no evidence of an afterlife of reward or punishment, so it's up to us to figure out how to live well with each other. This is the painful truth of human existence that the invention of postmortem judgment (and inherited guilt as well) is, at least in part, intended to suppress.

Abrahamic theists have been compelled to mislabel as "advanced" the intellectual contortions required to make a "just God" correspond with reality. Noted religious scholar Bart Ehrman (2008:121) sums up the tortuous efforts of "modern theodicists" succinctly: "Precise, philosophically nuanced, deeply thought out, filled with esoteric terminology and finely reasoned explanations for why suffering does not preclude the existence of a divine being of power and love. Frankly, to most of us these writings are not just obtuse, they are disconnected from real life, life as lived in the trenches . . ." Some religious philosophers have been just as guilty, relying on what Georges Rey calls the "philosophical fallacy," the idea that one needs powerful *philosophical theories* to address issues like this (2007:247–8). The modern propagation of a judging god is a wish fulfillment, a puerile projection of an outdated evolutionary tactic along the lines of giant antlers and our passion for salt, not a "higher" level of thought.

A fine example of these "extreme cognitive contortions performed in a desperate effort to avoid the only simple, obvious, and sensible answer to the argument from meaningless suffering" (Wathey 2016:41) comes from distinguished biblical scholar Robert Gnuse. He admits that monotheism "strangely enough" creates problems for itself with its one transcendent God when it comes to the question of evil, justice, and suffering. So how do theologians and scholars handle this intractable dilemma, attempting alchemic magic by turning leaden logic into theological gold?

> This demands sophisticated thinking, or what historians call the "second level" or the "second order" of intellectual reflection found in the Axial age. It involves the intellectual courage to use paradox extensively in the description of the divine, and it admits the deeper mystery of understanding the divine which transcends human knowledge.
>
> (1997:247–8)

Avoiding the obvious and justifying theological prestidigitation are "sophisticated intellectual reflection." Special pleading, selective reading, and wishful thinking are renamed "paradox," and confessing that the mysterious (i.e., nonexistent) answer "transcends human knowledge" is called "courage." Achilles' confrontation with the truth about divine justice is courageous; theistic daydreaming – the insistence on closing one's eyes to reality – is hobbling and, when allowed to run unchecked, dangerous. As philosopher Erik Wielenberg concludes in his study of *Value and Virtue in a Godless Universe* (2005:89): "Without God in the picture, the universe is only as just as we make it, and consequently there is a much greater urgency to pursue justice here on earth. In fact, the notion that there is a divine guarantee of perfect justice can lead not only to complacency, but to outright atrocity."

The good news here is that readers of the *Iliad* can stop laying an antediluvian Judeo-Christian template onto the epic in efforts to rescue Homer's gods. The Iliadic deities, who do not involve themselves in human justice, are not an embarrassment but provide a profound portrait of the way life actually works. We need not apologize for the Olympians, and we must certainly stop trying to turn them into pale copies of the theological invention of a just biblical deity. The ultimate irony of all is that, upon close inspection, the biblical Gods turn out to be no more models or enforcers of justice than Zeus and his family.[5] And to that happy thought we now must turn.

Notes

1 In Appendix 4 I have briefly outlined my reasons for doubting this *communis opinio doctorum* concerning the gods and justice in the *Odyssey*.

2 Scholars arguing for divine justice in the *Iliad* have occasionally turned to a second simile that compares the results of Achilles' destruction of Trojan warriors to a burning city, "and the anger of the gods incites it" (21.522–5). The argument is that since Achilles is attacking a *Trojan* army, and the angry gods are burning a *city*, this must imply that the gods in the narrative are also angry with a Trojan city (Troy) and will burn it (eventually). Besides the doubtful parallels – there is much debate about how Homeric similes align with their context – there is simply no hint of divine justice anywhere in simile. Yes, the gods are angry with some city, but why? The three gods who most want Troy destroyed are Hera, Athena, and Poseidon. Their "rationale" has nothing to do with divine justice, that is, with how humans treat each other, but stem from personal insults of the most pedestrian kind that would be dismissed out of hand or relegated to our

small claims courts, namely losing a beauty contest and getting stiffed on payment for construction work.

3 We are well informed that Achilles will perish, but it is hopeless to suggest that his inevitable, long-fated death is an act of divine justice for his quarrel with Agamemnon, as some scholars have maintained! Nowhere do the gods – or Homer – say that Achilles (or Agamemnon) is being punished for anything at all.

4 My favorite anecdote about ancient allegory is that found in several sources criticizing the Stoic philosopher Chrysippus for going too far. Apparently there was a famous image on the island of Samos of Hera providing oral sex to Zeus. The Christian apologist Origen gives the most complete rendition of the allegorical interpretation of Chrysippus, who, although "believed to have adorned the Stoic sect with many wise writings, explains a picture on Samos, in which Hera is depicted performing unspeakable acts. For this august philosopher says in his writings that matter, having received the spermatic words of the god, holds them within herself for the adornment of the universe. For in the picture at Samos, Hera is matter, and Zeus is the god" (*Cels.* 4.48).

5 Some readers, and all classicists, will have noted that I did not search for answers to the challenges posed by Homer's gods in the epic norms of human morality, that is, in the complex system that determines one's worth in the poems. This is a topic that has been much debated in classical scholarship, much more so even than the role of the gods. The discussion is important for understanding the themes of the epic and early Greek thought in general. But it is Achilles' *rejection* of the entire system at the end of the epic (including conventional belief in the justice of the gods) – however it is defined – that is far more consequential for our examination of justice. Homer's Olympians force Achilles – and us – to ask questions to which there are no easy answers supplied by the text.

14 Living without the gods

The myth of theistic justice

Richard Bentley was perhaps the greatest of the early English classicists, dubbed by a German scholar, no less, the "founder of historical philology." His first publication in 1690, when he was still in his 20s, explains or corrects in passing the texts of over 60 Greek and Latin authors (Jebb 1889:16). In his preliminary work on an edition of Homer that he never finished, he discovered that a lost letter of the early Greek alphabet (the digamma) still influenced the metrics of the Homeric hexameter, something all classicists now take for granted. Most famously, he demonstrated that a body of letters, the *Epistles of Phalaris*, supposedly written by a sixth-century Sicilian tyrant, was a forgery from at least a half a millennium later.

Bentley was also a deacon in the Anglican Church, and it is his celebrity in that role that plops him into the introduction to this chapter. In 1692 he was invited to deliver the first series of Boyle Lectures, funded by the estate of the recently deceased Robert Boyle. This is the Boyle of "Boyle's Law," one of founders of modern chemistry. A pious Anglican and something of a theologian as well, Boyle provided a stipend of £50 "for some divine, or preaching minister," who should "preach eight sermons in the year for proving the Christian religion against notorious infidels, viz. Atheists, Deists, Pagans, Jews, and Mahometans . . ." (Jebb 1889:20).

As the first to give the lectures, Bentley had his choice of notorious infidels. He selected atheists. In many ways an extended argument against Hobbes' *Leviathan*, the lectures were delivered from the pulpit of St. Martin's Church in London beginning on March 7, 1692. They were published a year later with the title of *The Folly and Unreasonableness of Atheism*. As you can imagine, Bentley had nothing good to say about atheists. Here is my favorite passage:

> This is the genuine spirit and the natural product of atheism. No man, that adheres to that narrow and selfish principle, can ever be just or generous or grateful; unless he be sometime overcome by good-nature and a happy constitution. No atheist, as such, can be a true friend, an affectionate relation, or a loyal subject. The appearance and show of mutual amity among them, is wholly owing to the smallness of their number, and to the obligations of a faction. 'Tis like the friendship of pick-pockets and high-way men, that are said

to observe justice among themselves, and never to defraud a comrade of his share of the booty. But if we could imagine a whole nation to be cut-purses and robbers; would there then be kept that square-dealing and equity in such a monstrous *den of thieves*? And if atheism should be supposed to become universal in this nation (which seems to be design'd and endeavour'd, though we know the gates of Hell shall not be able to prevail) farewell all ties of friendship and principles of honour; all love for our country and loyalty to our prince; nay farewell all government and society itself, all professions and arts, and conveniences of life, all that is laudable or valuable in the world.

(33–4, with some orthographical changes)

Ouch! And contemporary theists think the New Atheists are overly dramatic. But for the most part Bentley's beliefs about atheism were – and are – mainstream. He started a correspondence with Newton when preparing for his lectures, using Newton's mathematical ideas to "prove" God's existence, and Newton approved of this theological spin (Jebb 1889:24–30).

In this one minor historical anecdote we find the most eminent classicist, mathematician, and chemist of their time and place finding easy agreement on one key certainty: Without the biblical God and his justice, the world would collapse into complete anarchy. And we could throw in their contemporary John Locke, the "Father of Liberalism" and celebrator of religious tolerance, except when it came to Catholics and atheists. The world has a God, and the God must be good, and a good God must be just, and a good world must believe in that just God or all hell will break loose. Literally.

Many influential men have shared this opinion (Beit-Hallahmi 2010:113–19), especially here in the United States. Christians in the late 1700s forecasted that the United States wouldn't make it out of the century with the "godless" Constitution the founders had created. When those predictions failed, more were waiting: The election of the unreliably pious Jefferson as president would "destroy religion, introduce immorality, and loosen the bonds of society"; the War of 1812 was blamed on Madison's role in writing the nonreligious (and thus irreligious) Constitution; the Civil War was divine retribution for "America's 'speculative and infidel' ideas that government was not sanctified by God and divinely ordained" (Kramnick and Moore 1996:89, 105, 108). More recently, President George W. Bush climbed onto this wagon: "No, I don't know that atheists should be considered citizens, nor should they be considered patriots. This is one nation under God" (cited in Sinnott-Armstrong 2009:8). Well, at least since the phrase was added to the Pledge of Allegiance in 1954, under pressure from the threat of communism and a coalition of big business and even bigger religion (Kruse 2016).

This mistrust of atheists continues. In an article in which she brilliantly dismantles the arguments commonly used to support god-based morality, philosopher Elizabeth Anderson concludes that "people object to atheism because they think that without God, morality is impossible. In the famous words (mis)attributed to Dostoyevsky, 'If God is dead, then everything is permitted'" (2007:215–16). Atheism has been traditionally the "least trusted" quality of a candidate running for U.S. president. According to a 2015 Gallup poll, 42 percent of Americans said they would not vote for an atheist even if otherwise well-qualified and nominated by their party. That's down from 82 percent in the 1950s, and for the first time there's a characteristic that's worse than atheism – socialism. Thank you, Fox News! The word "secularist" was coined in the 19th century by George Jacob Holyoake to distinguish a godless worldview from an immoral one, since "atheist was often taken to denote one who is not only without God but without morality" (Buckley 1987:10–11). Holyoake had a point – he was the last person convicted for blasphemy in England.

In a set of psychological experiments, Americans intuitively judged a wide variety of immoral acts (e.g., serial murder, consensual incest, necrobestiality, cannibalism) as representative of atheists: "In sum, when reading a description of someone committing an immoral act, participants readily and intuitively assumed that the person was an atheist" (Gervais 2014). This is terribly unfair to most atheists. Personally, I may have had the urge to fool around with my siblings and then kill and eat them, but sex with my dead pets is way down my bucket list. The theistic conviction is that without belief in a punishing God of divine justice, a person has no reason to do what's right, and won't, and will instead just plain go berserk. This common but odd assumption seems to me to say a lot more about theists than atheists. Devout religionists worry about their own hidden passions and project them onto others, as we see so often in political sex scandals involving religious leaders and social conservatives. It appears that Christians require a reminder of a punishing God to behave. In several experiments, "Christians instructed to read and write about a forgiving God stole more money . . . and cheated more on a math assignment . . . than those who read and wrote about a punishing God" (Debono et al. 2017). It is the followers of Abrahamic religions, for example, rather than atheists, who seem to have trouble avoiding sex with animals. The Torah – that is, God – prohibits bestiality four different times (Ex 22:19; Lev 18:23; 20:15–16; Deut 27:21)! Clearly this was a problem that needed Yahweh's serious intercession. In contemporary Islam, the temptation was dealt with even more meticulously by Ayatollah Khomeini himself. In Azar Nafisi's wonderful memoir, *Reading Lolita in Tehran*, one of her students reflects on translating the *Political, Philosophical, Social and Religious Principles of Ayatollah Khomeini*:

> Did you know that one way to cure a man's sexual appetites is by having sex with animals? And then there's the problem of sex with chickens. You have to ask yourself if a man who has had sex with a chicken can then eat the chicken afterwards. Our leader [Khomeini] has provided us with an answer: *No*, neither he nor his immediate family or next-door neighbors can eat of that chicken's meat, but it's okay for a neighbor who lives two doors away.
> (Nafisi 2003:71)

Just the facts, ma'am

In this chapter we will survey some of the reasoning and historical evidence against the need to believe in any gods at all for humans to live a moral, meaningful life. This argument is necessary in order to free the Homeric gods from their theological chains. Like the fine golden net Hephaestus used to trap his wife and her lover *in flagrante delicto*, the bonds that often restrain readers' appreciation of Homer's gods are invisible but tenacious. It's *okay* if Homer's gods don't care about justice and provide little useful moral guidance to mortals; in this they are not substantially different from Yahweh or Jesus. As we will see, none of these mythological deities is coming to anyone's aid for morally acceptable reasons with any consistency. This puts the burden for determining the best way to live and the better things to do where it belongs – on us. We can only improve our world by accepting our responsibility for trying to discover what an ethical life entails. Any answers we may find as a moral community will be ours and ours alone.

Thousands of books and articles have been written on the difficulties of linking the Judeo-Christian God with human morality and justice. Most of the New Atheism books have chapters documenting the failed efforts to connect the two, and a majority of philosophers find it crucial to isolate ethics from any religious belief. As philosopher Daniel Dennett concludes, "there is no reason at all why a disbelief in the immateriality or immortality of the soul should make a person less caring, less moral, less committed to the well-being of everybody on earth than somebody who believes in 'the spirit'" (2006:305). There are many different approaches and sets of data in this ongoing discussion, and I can't hope to capture all of the arguments or do any of them "justice." Most of what follows is common knowledge to professionals in their respective fields, and I try to document each argument with references to far more complete studies of the topics. But my goal here is to bring together philosophical, theological, sociological, and historical evidence against the necessity of just gods. Homer's gods will serve us much better, as long as we take them for what they are.

First, let's search for some actual facts. Despite Americans' opinions about atheists and our dead pets, there is no evidence that people who don't believe in a just god act more unjustly or treat people more unfairly than theists. A study of 186 world cultures found that there was a correlation between belief in a punishing deity and cooperation that led to society *size*, but the results said little of the quality of those societies except that they were more likely than others also to experience internal warfare (Johnson 2005). Some studies that have been seized on by cultural conservatives have suggested that religious people are more likely to donate time and money. But a recent meta-examination of these studies finds them invalidated by "an array of methodological faults," such as reliance on self-reporting, counting tax deductions to churches, and fuzzy definitions of "religiosity" and "generosity" in the surveys. Using more objective methods to examine the data, "with a few exceptions, experiment studies put the size of the correlation of religiosity with generosity at zero" (Sablosky 2014:553). Religiosity often correlates with lower *self-reports* of dishonest behavior, but studies using behavioral measures typically show no effect of religiosity, and some have even found religious people actually cheat *more* (Debono et al. 2017).[1]

Religion has been linked to honesty and "an ability to resist temptation" (Gervais 2014), although its failures in this regard are also frequent and spectacular. Religiosity in the U.S. is also inversely related to a predisposition to cheat on taxes

(Beit-Hallahmi 2010:127). Some research (occasionally funded by conservative Christian organizations) suggests that religiosity may limit drug dependency and abuse or involvements with cults (assuming that we can adequately differentiate religion from cult), but these are not moral issues (Sparks 2016:109).

But beyond these few data points, the evidence for the long-term ethical benefits of religion runs almost dry. A recent cross-cultural study of children in Canada, China, Jordan, South Africa, Turkey, and the U.S. revealed that religion *negatively* influences children's altruism, regardless of the specific religious identification (Decety et al. 2015).[2] In Canada, surveys have shown that atheists score the *lowest* of all groups in hostility to homosexuals and in ethnic and racial prejudice, display more tolerance of other religious perspectives, and hold far less belief in a "dangerous and degenerate" world (Altemeyer 2010:11–13). On "moral sense" tests like the "runaway trolley" scenarios, there are "no statistically significant differences between research participants with or without religious backgrounds" (Singer and Hauser 2009:291). A meta-analysis of 55 separate studies found a small but statistically significant connection between some kinds of religiosity and racial prejudice (Hall et al. 2010). White evangelicals in the U.S. are the *most* likely people to object to neighbors of a different race (Wakefield 2006:58). A recent and thorough review of the search, both in the world and in the lab, for the correlation between morality and religious belief, found *no such link*: "Although it is often claimed that the moral ideas encoded in the world's religions have an important effect on our moral lives, there is little evidence for this popular view" (Bloom 2012:196).

Historically, many people living in societies without a single, punishing, creator deity or postmortem judgment have avoided self-extinction and lived good lives. Buddhists and Confucians are not notoriously less just than Jews, Christians, or Muslims. Members of these Eastern religions, like atheists, "have no problem being moral or finding meaning, purpose, or significance in human life" (Flanagan 2013:220). Fewer than one in three Danes and Swedes believes in a god of any kind, "yet these are perhaps the two most cooperative, peaceful, and stable large-scale societies in the history of humanity" (Gervais 2013:373, citing Zuckerman 2008).

J. Edgar Hoover penned a pamphlet (first delivered as a speech in 1945) entitled "Secularism – Breeder of Crime" (Baker and Smith 2015:119). You know you're in trouble when you have J. Edgar Hoover on your side. Atheists in fact are "grossly underrepresented in prisons" (Zuckerman 2014:22). Recent surveys show that .1 percent of inmates in Federal Prison self-identify as atheists, substantially less than the percentage of atheists (3 percent) in the overall population (Mehta 2015). Especially eye-opening here is criminologist Elicka Peterson Sparks' recent documentation – a startling as well as lively read – that fundamentalist Christian ideology is criminogenic. That is, contra Hoover, it is an absolutist, compassionless Christian perspective, not atheism, that actually promotes violent crimes (2016; cf. Topalli et al. 2013).

Overall, then, the belief of theists that nontheists must be unhappy and immoral is a prejudice supported by no evidence: Part visceral (it just sort of seems it should be that way), part cultural (they've heard this repeated many times), part scriptural (the Bible says nonbelievers should be killed or delivered to hell), part experiential (over 50 percent of the "actively religious" report they have no close friend who is secular; Baker and Smith 2015:165 – and studies show that the more atheists are perceived among individuals and communities, the less distrust people have of them; Gervais 2013:373), part a distrust of "critical thinking" and education (agnostics and atheists are nearly twice as likely to have a college degree as the actively and culturally religious – Baker and Smith 2015:116),[3] and all rooted in solid evolutionary traits such as out-group distrust and the creation of a punishing god to reinforce commitment to the in-group.

On the other hand, the list of immoral and unjust acts committed by "god-fearing" individuals, leaders, and nations is jaw-dropping. It has even been argued that religion was originally adaptive because its in-group cohesion led to a "xenophobic psychology" (Dunbar 2013) that promotes "exactly the kind of nasty behavior that aids survival in inter-group conflict and especially in times of war" (Johnson and Reeve 2013:71). I won't rehearse the wars, conflicts, genocides, atrocities, pogroms, crusades, ethnic cleansing, and general carnage inflicted on the world by followers of a "just god." In atrocitologist (that's right) Mathew White's compilation of the 30 deadliest religious killings in history, all but five involve Abrahamic religions (2012:108–11). Virtually every book in the New Atheistic camp contains a depressing inventory.

Even professional religionists are beginning to admit in public how biblical scripture supposedly depicting a "just god" has in practice endorsed and continues to fuel cruelty, hatred, murder, oppression, homophobia, racism, slavery, violence, child abuse, anti-Semitism, and misogyny (Lüdemann 1997; Spong 2005; Thatcher 2008). Pope John Paul II apologized for the persecution of Galileo (who, having dedicated his polemical work to one pope, was exonerated by another one 360 years later, nearly a quarter of a century after a human walked on the moon), the Catholic involvement in the slave trade, injustices committed against women, the crusade against Constantinople, and the Church's passive role during the holocaust. And this from a pope who himself fast-tracked the beatification of supporters of fascist regimes (including the Nazis) and set up sainthood for a previous pope who referred to Jews as dogs (Parenti 2010:95). Pope Francis has said that Christians should apologize to gays – although he hasn't mentioned changing church policy that condemns gay sex – and admitted that "the Church must say it is sorry for not having behaved as it should many times, many times."

Here's an interesting fact: There is an *inverse* relationship between the religiosity of a nation and its social progress. That is, belief in an all-just God actually does *not* correlate to most measures of prosperity or social justice but in fact is related to depressed economic and social conditions. Let me repeat and supplement some of the cross-cultural data I mentioned in the Introduction, back when you were young and innocent. The *least* religious nations in the world now have the *highest* standards of living, the best "quality of life," by virtually every measure – the healthiest democracies and per capita income, best educational systems, most affordable health care, longest life expectancies along with the lowest levels of corruption, incarceration, violent crime, alcohol consumption, and unemployment (Zuckerman 2008). There are high or significant correlations between secularity and societal gender equality, stronger rule of law, greater civil liberties, adult literacy rate, greater religious freedoms, and lower levels of income inequality (Baker and Smith 2015:203). Gregory Paul sums up his detailed examination of the connections between popular religiosity and societal dysfunction with eye-opening data:

> Of the 25 socioeconomic and environmental indicators the most theistic and procreationist western nation, the U.S. scores the worst in 14 and by a very large margin in 8, very poorly in 2, average in 4, well or very in 4, and the best in 1. Specifically, the U.S., scores the most dysfunctional in homicide, incarceration, juvenile mortality, gonorrhea and syphilis infections, abortions, adolescent pregnancies, marriage duration, income disparity, poverty, work hours, and resource exploitation base. The level of relative and absolute societal pathology in the U.S. is often so severe that it is repeatedly an outlier that strongly reinforces the correlation between high levels of poor societal conditions and popular religiosity.
>
> (2009a:416)

Although Paul's methodology in a previous paper (2005) has been challenged (e.g., Moreno-Riaño et al. 2006; Jensen 2006), this correlation between religiosity and dysfunction is evident *within* the United States as well, where the favored religion is overwhelmingly one that insists that God enacts his justice on all humanity: "When it comes to nearly all standard measures of society health, such as homicide rates, violent crime rates, poverty rates, domestic abuse rates, obesity rates, educational attainment, funding for schools and hospitals, teen pregnancy rates, rates of sexually transmitted diseases, unemployment rates, domestic violence, the correlation is robust: the least theistic states in American tend to fare much, much better than the most theistic" (Zuckerman 2014:50; cf. Eller 2010:329).

But theism needs the downtrodden. Political scientists Pippa Norris and Ronald Inglehart (2011) have demonstrated that worldwide religiosity is directly and inversely related to what they call "existential security": The most vulnerable populations in the world are the most religious. If you lack clean water, food, health care, education, financial resources, a responsive government, protection against natural evils such as disease and disasters – and face high infant mortality rates and a short life expectancy – where else can you turn? The poor have little else to look forward to than the promises held out for better world to come, and thus their "meaning in life" is far more likely to derive from their religiosity (Oishi and Diener 2014). This holds true even within postindustrial nations like the United States in which there are sharp socioeconomic disparities. The Lived Poverty Index reveals that "the most deprived segments of American society (lacking many essentials on the Lived Poverty Index) display both the strongest religious values and practices. . . . *Religious values* in America are strongest among the older generation, women, the less well-off, and less-educated, just as we have observed in other societies" (Norris and Inglehart 2011:261, 267). It is no coincidence that the U.S. is the most religious of developed nations as well as the country with the greatest economic inequality, and those at the bottom with the greatest declines in life expectancy are also the most devout (Harris 2010:146; Ezzati et al. 2008).

Religious belief in a just, punishing God is not necessary for a community to thrive, much less to live "justly." Nor is it required for a "happy" life, despite the "misery" that Christian apologists routinely insist accompanies atheism. For contemporary Americans, at least, there is "no statistically significant difference between atheists and the actively religious for predicting personal satisfaction when controlling for sociodemographic characteristics like age, gender, income, education, and marital status" (Baker and Smith 2015:94). Frank Pasquale's study of secularists concludes that they "overwhelmingly consider their lives worthwhile and find meaning, most of all, in family, friends, personally enriching experience, productive work, and positive contributions. Ironically, but for their secularist stances or naturalist worldviews, their values and lifestyles tend to be substantially similar to those of many (moderate or liberal) 'religious' neighbors in their communities" (2010:82).

You're my role model

But let's move past the facts to the logistical nightmares that arise if one insists that human morality is dependent upon a just, punishing divinity. How do we know what God wants, what "just" behavior entails? There are thousands of religions with differing visions of moral obligations – which one is right? (The 2001 edition of the *World Christian Encyclopedia* identified 33,820 Christian denominations alone!) As Homer Simpson observes with understandable concern, "Suppose we've chosen the wrong god. Every time we go to church we're just making him madder and madder!" And after we choose a god – which, of course, few people do – how do we know what that god wants us to do, what is divinely just? Do we model our behavior on the deity? Do we act justly by mimicking the deity – an *imitatio dei* – or, in novel situations, by pondering what the deity would do, as the bumper stickers proclaim?

I hope not. Our only "knowledge" of how gods act, at least as a model for our moral behavior, derives from scripture (do *not* listen to that voice in your ear telling you to kill), and the biblical gods do *not* act justly in any consistent fashion: "For those [Abrahamic] deities," concludes philosopher Michael Tooley, "not withstanding what the adherents of such religions claim, do not even make it to the starting blocks when it comes to a believable claim of moral perfection" (2009:311). Our survey of Yahweh's genocidal anthropomorphism has offered numerous examples of what any reasonable person would call immoral behavior. Yahweh's textual persona has been thoroughly documented by former minister Dan Barker (2016). Using over 1500 citations from the Bible, he demonstrates 27 (19 of which were listed by Richard Dawkins 2006:31) traits of this "most unpleasant character in all fiction." In short, Yahweh is jealous, petty, unjust, unforgiving, vindictive, bloodthirsty, misogynistic, homophobic, racist, infanticidal, genocidal, filicidal, pestilential, megalomaniacal, capriciously malevolent, angry, merciless, curse hurling, vaccicidal, aborticidal, cannibalistic, and a control freak, ethnic cleanser, bully, and slave monger. Even some biblical scholars have to agree: The Tanakh is a "parade of witnesss to this [Yahweh's] fiendish behavior" (Crenshaw 2005:178). Rabbi and Jewish theologian David R. Blumenthal concedes that in this post-Holocaust world we must "acknowledge the awful truth of God's abusing behavior" (1993:259; cf. Baumann 2003:234).

The logical consequences of Yahweh's nastiness have not escaped the notice of all theists over the past 2000 years. We saw the heretical efforts of Marcion to divorce the God of the Old Testament from the God of the New Testament. He insisted there were two separate Gods. Other early Fathers of the Church, like Origen, applied allegory to the troublesome passages and focused on the "spiritual" meaning of the text, whatever that needed to be. Eryl W. Davies has examined at length the various strategies used by biblical scholars to try to come to terms with the "ethically problematic" passages of scripture (2010). We don't need to survey them here at length, for the significant conclusion to be drawn from this analysis (though not one mentioned by Davies) is that all of these approaches but one admit that there is some external standard of morality beyond God's.[4] Reader-response approaches are likely to be openly critical of the text, to challenge its moral assumptions. All the other tactics (e.g., evolutionary, canonical, paradigmatic) also accept that Yahweh's actions frequently are despicable, but the theistic scholars then provide strategies for minimizing the horror of the specific incidents. That is, they all accept that there are moral standards outside of Yahweh's behavior by which he can be fairly judged, and he is found wanting in each – thus the need to find "strategies" to redeem his character. One critical school, the canon within a canon, even argues that one should sift through the Bible and retain only those sections that can be useful and relevant. We don't derive ethical standards from the text but apply them back onto the text. Ultimately, there is no need for Yahweh at all.

"Okay, fine. Yahweh is an occasionally unpleasant and wrathful God," some may concede. "But what about Jesus? Yahweh is a God of justice, but Jesus is a God of love." First, they're at least partially wrong to make this distinction. Jesus does sometimes draw a thin line between himself and God (e.g., Mark 13:32; John 14:28), and it may very well be that the historical Jesus made no claims to divinity. But throughout the Gospel of John, Jesus insists that he is God, the *same* God as the one named Yahweh in the Tanakh. "The Father and I are one" (John 10:30; cf. John 8:23; 10:36, 38; 14:9–11). He claims to be equal to the uncreated, eternal God: "Very truly, I tell you, before Abraham was, I am" (John 8:58; cf. Matt 5:17). This identity is now nearly universal Christian dogma. So, from a theological point of view, everything a Christian may concede about Yahweh bounces onto Jesus' head: "It follows that every single attribute Richard Dawkins used to describe the fictional God of the Old Testament applies equally to Jesus, because he claimed he was the God of the Old Testament" (Barker 2016:290.)

Secondly, that thing about "justice" versus "love"? "If you have heard this it was probably from a Christian, as there is in it an implicit, faintly anti-Semitic, criticism of Judaism . . ." (Teehan 2010:161). If not tainted with anti-Semitism, it's at least supersessionist, seeing the Hebrew Bible merely as a precursor to the superior principles eventually to be drawn from the teaching of Jesus: "The Old Testament was in many ways anticipatory of something far greater" (Copan 2011:220).

As for biblical love itself, in neither testament is divine love the kind of open, unadulterated love people seem to imagine – it as always connected with obedience. The first time the word "love" appears in the Bible is when God tells Abraham to slaughter his son Isaac, "whom you love" (Gen 22:2; Barker 2016:5). And as for Jesus' "love," Hector Avalos concludes, "Far from indicating mutuality or even lack of self-interest, *agapê* [love] has often become even more hierarchical, demanding and servile in the New Testament relative to that in the Hebrew Bible" (2015:41). New Testament scholar William Loader (2010:64) observes that while it was once conventional to see Jesus as setting aside Jewish law for the principle of love, scholars now more commonly see him observing the law with his own subtle tweaks (e.g., Matthew 5:21–48). The noun and verb for love appear only twice in the Mark, the earliest gospel. Universal love may not even have been part of Jesus' original message but was emphasized by Paul, who also ultimately limited it to believers (Wright 2009:257–83).

Jesus as depicted in the text has much to recommend him. Even a scholar who considers Jesus to be primarily mythical observes that the biblical character respects the dispossessed, shows compassion, heals lepers, feels pity, feeds the hungry, loves the sinner, encourages people to love each other, and forgives (Price 2016:39–51). But Jesus has many human failings as well – he is no perfect model of morality. In over 400 pages of carefully documented argument, Hector Avalos (2105) has demonstrated how New Testament scholars ignore the unethical (and very human) side of Jesus' behavior. Avalos' aim is not to discredit the Jesus of the New Testament (and we can't know if any of this applies to a "real" Jesus) but to reveal the uncritical lengths New Testament scholars and Christian theologians have gone to ignore, deny, and cover up the "bad" elements of Jesus' actions and statements.

Avalos focuses his study on the human side of Jesus, analyzing in detail a long list of unpleasant traits found in the textual Jesus, including Jesus as unloving, hateful, violent, imperialistic, anti-Jewish, an enemy of the poor, misogynistic, antidisabled, magically antimedical, and ecohostile. I encourage any incredulous readers to look for themselves at the evidence Avalos gathers. We'll take as one quick example Jesus' unethical attack on Jewish families, since so much current conservative Christian rhetoric concentrates on this institution.

Luke 14:26 sets the tone for Jesus' cult-like insistence that his followers completely reject their families: "Whoever comes to me and does not hate father and mother, wife and children, brothers and sisters, yes, and even life itself, cannot be my disciple." You can't imagine the lengths Christian apologists have gone to try to make this not mean what it does, including that the Greek verb used to mean "to hate" doesn't mean "to hate." Jesus' disruption of the family is actually emphasized in the gospels. He lures some of his disciples straight out of their fishing boat and away from their domestic duties (Mark 1:16–20).

What would we think of a cult leader who deprived families of their fathers, the primary breadwinners in a society always just one empty catch away from hunger or one failed harvest from starvation? Avalos wonders if "deadbeat dads" wouldn't be a better title for these "heroic" disciples (2015:201–3; Parenti 2010:44 refers to Jesus as a "home wrecker"). His followers have to give up everything from their previous lives (Matt 19:27–30; Mark 10:28–31; Luke 18:28–30). Jesus doesn't deny it; in fact, it's part of his primary message:

> Do not think that I have come to bring peace to earth; I have not come to bring peace, but a sword. For I have come to set a man against his father, and a daughter against her mother, and a daughter-in-law against her mother-in-law; and one's foes will be members of one's own household. Whoever loves father or mother more than me is not worthy of me; and whoever loves son or daughter more than me is not worthy of me. . . .
>
> (Matt 10:34–7)

Jesus appears to revel in the intrafamilial slaughter that will take place as part of the tribulations leading up to his (or the Son of Man's) (re)appearance:

> Brother will betray brother to death, and a father his child, and children will rise against parents and have them put to death; and you will be hated by all because of my name. But the one who endures to the end will be saved.
>
> (Mark 13:12–13)

All the familial destruction surfacing around his disciples will be worth it since they will win eternal life. As in most cults, the sect becomes the new family, his followers "my mother and my brothers" (Matt 12:48–50). And always with the same reward system in place: "And everyone who has left houses or brothers or sisters or father or mother or children or fields, for my name's sake, will receive a hundredfold, and will inherit eternal life" (Matt 19:29).

When one of the disciples asks Jesus for leave to bury his father – burial of kin was a sacred duty for Jews – he replied, "Follow me, and let the dead bury their own dead" (Matt 8:21–22 = Luke 9:59–60). And for someone who snarkily quotes the Tanakh to accuse the Pharisees of not obeying the commandment to "honor your father and your mother" (Matt 15:4–6; Mark 7:9–10; cf. Matt 19:19; Mark 10:19; Luke 18:20) – "whoever speaks evil of father or mother must surely die" – Jesus is on particularly thin ice when dealing rudely with his own mother (John 2:4).

Jesus' otherworldly callousness about the family is hardly characteristic of a just God, much less a model mortal. He's human after all and acts like one (except for the magic), sometimes well, sometimes not so well. The point is not that Jesus is a bad guy but that to use his actions as a guide to one's own behavior requires the same sifting through episodes as with Yahweh. Upon reflection, we can admire only certain parts of Jesus' behavior. To ignore the rest, we impose a previously determined ethical template onto the New Testament. Our morality precedes whatever Jesus does. It's not "what would Jesus do," but "what would a reasonable person on a good day want to do after giving it some thought," although I'm not sure that would fit on a bumper.

Written in stone

So let's say that a god doesn't need to be just to reinforce and "guarantee" human justice. Abrahamic apologists may insist it's not so much God's character – that may all be metaphorical anyway – as the laws and codes he promulgates in scripture that enable us to behave well. We have access to God's will, so this theory goes, either directly (a sort of mystic communion), through tradition and God's earthly representatives (the pope, for example), or most commonly, from the divinely authored text (Cliteur 2010:188–225). Human morality is only possible, mainstream theology insists, because there is an objective justice that emanates from God's prescriptions and instructions. In what is called Divine Command Theory – "the most widely accepted metaethics in Christian thought" (Martin 2002:121–55) – moral truths do not exist independently of God's will. As biblical scholar C.L. Crouch (2016:349) comments approvingly, "Ethics come from God and . . . human beings know about these moral norms because God has told humans about them. That is, human beings are able to distinguish between right and wrong behavior on the basis of explicit moral statements that are attributed to the deity." This is true for the Tanakh as well as the New Testament: "Obedience to the declared will of God is probably the strongest model for ethical obligation in most books of the Hebrew Scriptures" (Barton 2003:47).

But this won't do either. First, there is the famous Platonic challenge to Divine Command Theory's premise that morality means following god's laws. In the *Euthyphro*, Socrates asks his befuddled interlocutor if something is right (an act of piety, for example) because god commands it, or if god commands something because it is right. In the first case, applied to the Bible, if something is right only because God commands it, God could order anything at all. God's defenders insist that God would always be just "because they [some moral states of affairs] are incompatible with God's essential nature of moral impeccability" (Baggett and Walls 2011:200). As one confessional scholar concedes, "In fact, God's goodness and justice is so fundamental an axiom in Jewish and Christian faith that it is usually held to be indubitable" (Hofreiter 2012:241). But this is plainly nonsensical if we are to retain inerrant scripture: God ordered genocide and told men to abandon their families.

Neither can you argue (logically, at least) that God is just and therefore would only do what is just, since "just" has no meaning prior to God's command. There was no morality before God commanded it: "If the authority of morality depends on God's will, then, *in principle*, anything is permitted" (Anderson 2007:217). God is beyond questioning, as he himself insists in Job. God's moral perfection becomes meaningless, for "to say God is perfect will amount only to the tautology that God chooses what he chooses" (Everitt 2004:131–5).

On the other hand, if God commands something because it is right, then right and wrong are independent of and prior to God – he himself is responding to some external standard. We therefore do not need God's word for moral guidance. As philosopher Louise Antony concludes, "The objectivity of moral value is simply independent of God's existence. All that is lost, if there is no God, is a divine enforcer" (2007b:51). "In order to get from the premise that God is all-good to the conclusion that God could never command us to rape, we need to assume that rape is bad and wrong. That suppressed premise requires an independent standard that makes rape bad and wrong" (Sinnott-Armstrong 2009:105).

It should be noted at this point that none of this applies to many major religions. Eastern religions have only a very weak, and often nonexistent, link between how we should behave and God's will. Jainism and Theravada Buddhism, for example, do not require "monotheistic ethics." And both Taoism and Confucianism regularly ignore or reject the very idea of God as the Abrahamic exegetes have imagined him: "Eastern religions are quite indifferent to what has been termed in the West 'the morality of commands'" (Billington 2002:13).

But even more problematic are the divine rules themselves. It is obvious that only *some* of God's eternal laws as found in scripture can still reasonably apply, even if Yahweh threatens all sorts of terrible consequences if even a single rule is flouted (e.g., Deut 28:15–29:1). We have to start ignoring the anachronistic parts of the code, especially all those stonings, burnings, and strangulations for things even Texans don't believe should warrant capital punishment. Only the most ardent theists remain comfortable with capital punishment for someone picking up sticks on the Sabbath or lying about her virginity or trying to convert someone to a different religion (tough luck for all those Mormon boys!) or having sex while a woman is menstruating.[5] The necessity for this winnowing process again reveals that we don't really derive our morality from these texts. As philosopher James Rachels writes, "people's moral convictions are not so much derived from their religion as superimposed on it" (1986:51).

The Ten Commandments, for example, which some American politicians, state legislatures, and Christian nationalists (one of whom was Chief Justice of the Alabama Supreme Court and nearly governor of the state) unfamiliar with the Constitution or the commandments themselves (or that there are several different versions of them in the Tanakh) have wanted to post in courthouses, are mostly unworkable as moral guides.

Of the hundreds of laws found in the Torah, only the Decalogue (or parts of it) appears to be spoken directly by Yahweh. Nevertheless, scholars agree that the Ten Commandments "had a long history before reaching their final form" (Meyers and Rogerson 2008:92–3). The first commandment – using one of the traditional Jewish numberings rather than either the Protestant or Catholic enumeration, which don't agree with each other – is not really a commandment at all. Rather, it serves as a prologue to set the conditions: "I am the Lord [Yahweh] your God [deity], who brought you out of the land of Egypt, out of the house of slavery" (Ex 20:2). The motivation for obeying the commandments is thoroughly embedded in the acceptance of the mythic narrative of the Torah – there is nothing even vaguely secular about these injunctions (Duff 2004:166). The Decalogue was not *intended* to apply universally but is an in-group ethic, a contract between one God and one historical group (Coogan 2014:221–2).

The first four commandments have nothing directly to do with morality but are Yahweh's efforts to force the Israelites to pay attention to him alone. The first part of the second commandment, "you shall have no other gods before me," proscribes religious freedom and thus violates our first amendment, as well as Article 18 of the United Nations Universal Declaration of Human Rights. This rejection of religious freedom is at "the moral heart of the Old Testament," as we have seen, which demands the destruction of temples, the death of clergy, and the murder of anyone who tries to opt out (Avalos 2010:221).

Christians in general reject the second part of this commandment ("you shall not make for yourself an idol"). A less misleading translation than idol would be "image." Exactly what this means – it seems to be inclusive, with no divine (including the sun, moon, and stars), human or animal images allowed (Coogan 2014:56) – is still a matter of grave disagreement between the various branches of Abrahamic religions. This passage also contains the infamously unjust Yahwistic claim of a jealous God to punish "children for the iniquity of parents, to the third and fourth generation of those who reject me." As Thomas Paine observed, "this is contrary to every principle of moral justice." Moreover, the motivation for such a trivial act of piety is purely personal and not moral at all, namely the desire of a self-confessedly irrational deity to gain the "steadfast love to the thousandth generation of those who love me and keep my commandments" (Ex 20:6). Morality remains at its most base level in the Tanakh. The author of numerous books on biblical ethics concludes that the "possibility of good conduct unmotivated by the expectation of future benefit is in fact very rare in the Old Testament" (Barton 1998:87). The author can, in fact, think of only two examples in the entire text where good conduct is *not* motivated by the expectation of future benefits.

There is also quite a bit of debate about just what the third commandment about misusing the Lord's name entails (Miller 2009:63–115). Does it refer to use of the divine name period? Blasphemy? Lying or taking a false oath? Praying for the impossible? A vast majority of Christians and Jews conveniently ignore the fourth commandment as well ("remember the sabbath day, and keep it holy," Ex 20:8), no matter how they define the various terms (Greene-McCreight 2004). What "labor," exactly, is one to avoid on the penalty of death? The list kept growing over the centuries. (Jesus had little hesitation to do work or perform miracles on that day of rest; Matt 12:1–8 = Mark 2:23–8 = Luke 6:1–5; John 5:16–17.) In this commandment we also encounter one of scores of verses within the Tanakh that reveal Yahweh's approval of slavery: "You shall not do any work – you, your son or your daughter, your male or female slave, your livestock, or the alien resident in your towns" (Ex 20:10).

The fifth and seventh commandments, to honor your mother and father and avoid adultery, are solid bits of advice but hardly worth 20 percent of divine morality. Besides, sad to say, some parents are not worthy of honor, especially not with the kind of total obeisance expected in biblical times even of adult children. (Jesus did not consistently "honor" his mother, as we have seen.) And should the penalty for striking a parent, cursing one's father, or not listening to one's mother really be stoning (Ex 21:15, 17; Deut 21:18–21)? "Don't abuse indigenous people or those of different faiths or your wife or children . . . or the women who serve your God or the children of your parishioners" would have been more histori-cally profitable recommendations, if only God had possessed the foresight. And Yahweh again eliminates any independent moral quality to this commandment by providing an imperialistic motive: Treat mom and dad well "so that your days may be long *in the land that the Lord your God is giving you*" (Ex 20:12, empha-sis mine). As Christopher Hitchens asks in his deconstruction of the command-ments for *Vanity Fair* (Hitchens and del Conte 2010), "why not propose filial piety as a nice thing in itself?"

And if you define adultery as sex between a nonspouse and a married woman but not between a nonspouse and married man, or as sex between willing adults before marriage, or with a spouse in a second marriage, or if you allow men to marry more than one woman but not vice versa, or if you stone a woman on her father's doorstep if she is found not to be a virgin on her wedding night but have not a single word to say about a man's virginity (boys *will* be boys), or beat and pull out the hair of anyone who intermarries, we're clearly not talking about morality anymore. This commandment regurgitates the patriarchal and xenopho-bic structure of the antique society and nurtures dark fantasies about restoring one. Once you add the contemporary Catholic equation of divorce, premarital sex of any kind, masturbation, homosexual sex, coitus interruptus, contraception, and artificial insemination with adultery, the whole sexophobic apparatus has no use-ful ethical value whatsoever.

Number eight is a good one (not stealing – or, according to some scholars, not kidnaping), although it apparently does not apply to the land, houses, and livestock of the people inhabiting the land you would like to possess. As for num-ber nine (bearing false witness against a neighbor), biblical scholars have shown that "neighbor" in its context limits this moral concern only to fellow Israelites. Michael Shermer (2015:176–80) points out that the last commandment prohibit-ing the coveting of your neighbor's possessions – you know, like his slave or ox or donkey or his *wife* – is the "world's first thought crime," taking us into the dystopia of the movie *Minority Report*. Jesus one-ups Yahweh by making it a sin, "adultery with her in his heart," for a man just to look at a woman with lust (Matt 5:27–9).

I've left until the last what appears to be the most unembellished of the com-mandments: "You shall not kill" (number six), two Hebrew words that have a wholesome ring to them. But upon close inspection this seemingly essential com-mandment falls apart as well. First, we can't help noticing that Yahweh doesn't mean it. There are 36 capital offenses in Mosaic law calling for execution by stoning, burning, decapitation, or strangulation (Dulles 2003:132), and many of these are not for breaches of morality. Death to mediums and wizards (Lev 20:6,

27)? "Blaspheming" the name of Yahweh (Lev 24:10–16)? Sabbath violations (Num 15:32–6)? Five of the seven "new" capital laws found in the Revised Deuteronomic Code (Deut 12–19) involve false prophecy, apostasy, and inciting to allotheism, that is, to worshiping a god other than Yahweh (Hiers 2009:82–6). How much ethnic cleansing does Yahweh himself command? Steve Wells (2010) has catalogued 158 sets of killings committed, commanded, or countenanced by God in the Bible. Using the fanciful numbers supplied by the authors, Wells figures Yahweh must claim personal responsibility for the deaths of 2,821,346 people, many of them Israelites. And that's not counting the numerous massacres for which the text supplies no death toll. How many were killed in the flood, for example? How many firstborn children in Egypt? The point is not that an actual god committed these nightmarish atrocities, of course, but that by the Bible's own account "you shall not kill" can hardly stand as divine enlightenment.

But that's not half the problem with the sixth commandment. We all kill something, whether directly (a mosquito or bacterium) or passively (that Big Mac didn't grow on a burger-tree) or in defense of our country. The commandment may actually mean, "You shall not *murder*," as the NRSV and Jewish Study Bible render the verse (Ex 20:13). (Apparently the NRSV committee was "split down the middle on the matter"; Miller 2009:223.) The commandment thus addresses "illegitimate" killing only. But that doesn't help at all. Whether murder or killing, the term has to be defined *very* carefully. You can certainly attempt to exterminate the natives whose land you're confiscating. That's "legitimate." And you can slaughter fellow Israelites if they seem to be undermining group solidarity. That's "legitimate" as well. God's *very first thought* after handing Moses the two tablets inscribed with the Commandments is distinctly murderous. He wants to wipe out the entire Israelite camp because some of them have constructed a golden calf. Moses intercedes and God "changed his mind" – only 3000 Israelites – brothers, friends, and neighbors are specified – are killed (Ex 32:27–28)

Scripture taken in its entirety and directly from God's mouth is mostly pointless for moral guidance. There is an immediate need of legal counsel to spell out the numerous sub-clauses and exceptions to the basic precepts.[6] The Ten Commandments are much too vague to be of use without careful exegesis, the results of which must match our moral intuitions and reasoning to retain any validity. Even the Jews required the rabbinic production of the Mishnah to begin to convert the Bible into a moral code for daily living (Barton 2003:69). God is ultimately redundant, and the Decalogue fails as a moral guide. The Catholic catechism devotes nearly 100 of its 700 pages to explication of the Ten Commandments, and the results are strained and stultifying. Every significant statement the document has to make on human sexuality falls under the commandment about adultery. A recent attempt by two noted biblical scholars to reveal the applicability of the Tanakh to contemporary hot-button issues like homosexuality, abortion, women's rights, capital punishment, and the environment ultimately implodes on its own honesty. The Tanakh offers mixed messages on everything, they ultimately concede, so in the end we must sift through the text carefully, thoughtfully, with "humility and hesitation," remembering that this ancient, patriarchal scripture is only descriptive, not prescriptive (Friedman and Dolansky 2011). Their argument helps to counter those who cull the Bible for permission to treat others as if we lived in the Levant 3000 years ago, but the authors recognize that we must apply our own moral reasoning to derive any positive benefit from these ancient words.

Moral novelty in the New Testament? Well, there's always eternal damnation

Trying to uncover a single Christian morality is a Sisyphean task. Which interpretative strand should we turn to? What are we to do with the "literally hundreds of Christian creeds, and thousands of declarations in which one group or denomination anathematizes the creedal doctrines of another" (Fales 2005:472)? Or turning to the New Testament itself, we must first set aside reasonable skepticism about the likelihood that any particular statement was actually spoken by Jesus. Theologians have been scrambling for centuries to explain why early Christian writers say nothing about Jesus' ethical pronouncements (Martin 1991:11, 54, 162; 2002:158–9). Paul, for example, never cites Jesus in support of any of his moral assertions, including those that sound just like his savior, such as his statement about blessing those who persecute you (Rom 12:14). Three of the earliest and most important Christian creeds, the Apostles', Nicene, and Athanasian, say nothing about Jesus' ethical teachings. The simplest conclusion, and one that has been drawn by many scholars, is that the pronouncements now found in the gospels were probably not part of Jesus' message, or at least not part of the earliest strands of Christian doctrine.

Although the New Testament has of course been the source for a wide variety of interpretations of Jesus' moral message, it brings surprisingly little that is new to the world in its ethical program. Jesus refers to the Golden Rule (e.g., Matt 7:12), a moral rule of thumb found in other, earlier cultures. His wise words about the spiritual vacuity of wealth also have many pagan precursors, and the advice has generally gone ignored by Christians and non-Christians alike. How many give up *all* their possessions to the poor as Jesus insisted (Mark 10:21; Luke 12:33)? The Catholic Church is said to make $30 billion per year from real estate investments alone (Brain 2014:169), although much of its wealth has been used to buy off abuse victims and, more recently, to compensate them officially after court cases and to cover the costs of embezzlement (Berry 2011). There's a cultish acquisitiveness that accompanies Christian charity as soon as Jesus disappears. True believers are to sell off all their property and give all the proceeds to the "church." When a husband and wife retained for themselves some of the profit and brought "only a part and laid it at the apostles' feet," they were accused of colluding with Satan. God (that is, Jesus) killed them both, separately, within three hours (Acts 5:1–12). This was one of the "many signs and wonders" accomplished through the apostles.

The beatitudes offer numerous bits of solid ethical advice, to be sure, but they are not unique to Christianity. They "are a variant of widespread Jewish traditions that can be found in the Dead Sea Scrolls and also in other cultures" (Avalos 2015:211).

The various lists of virtues and vices found in the New Testament usually have "no explicit reference in our texts to a Christological connection," but "the abominations or the desired traits stand on their own, as self-evident marks of the wrong or right way to live" (Meeks 1993:67). That is, the ethical practices advocated by Jesus do not rely on his godhood or any monotheistic vision but are virtually "interchangeable with those of other [pagan] moralists of the time" (Meeks 1993:68). We don't need Jesus' wise words (when they *are* wise) to act well.

When you get right down to it, beyond his concern for the poor, Jesus has little to offer on any social question except divorce and adultery – he's against them. An act of adultery *mandated* divorce, no matter whether the spouses wanted to reconcile or not. Adultery was the *only* grounds for divorce – there was to be no escape from the wife beater in Jesus' ideal marriage. Actually, the New Testament offers a variety of conflicting statements about divorce. Paul differs from Jesus on the subject, and "Jesus' teachings in the Gospels do not agree" (Knust 2011:74–7). No wonder his current followers pay so little attention even to this primary ethical concern of their savior. Divorce rates among born-again and evangelical Christians are virtually identical to those of the general population (Sparks 2016:168), and the Catholic Church grants tens of thousands of annulments in the U.S. each year (24,000 in 2012, with an average of almost 60,000 per year since 1984).

Beyond his comments on marriage, Jesus "doesn't pronounce on war, capital punishment, gambling, justice, law, socialism, equality of income, equality of sex, equality of colour, opportunity, tyranny, freedom, slavery" (Robinson 1964:149) or any of the myriad of difficult issues that he should have seen coming like abortion, the environment, sexual harassment, euthanasia, genetic engineering, weapons of mass destruction, torture, etc. "Despite its moral focus, the Jesus tradition fails to supply guidance for changing political or social realities . . . Jesus' imperatives are not akin to the *Analects* of Confucius: they do not offer human solutions to concrete problems but rather look forward to God himself, through a miracle, setting all things right" (Allison 2003:148). In other words, the end of the world was coming right away, and there was no need for too many specifics on how to improve the soon-to-pass ills of the world.

Jesus says the second most important Christian commandment (after loving God) is "You shall love your neighbor as yourself" (Matt 19:19; 22:39; Mark 12:31). He is repeating one of Yahweh's commands (Lev 19:18, where "neighbor" means "fellow Israelite," Milgrom 2000a:1654). So what does it mean to love your neighbor? Theologians don't agree. Michael Martin's (1991:172–92) survey of Christian ethical theorists shows that besides having dissenting interpretations, many theologians sidestep Jesus' doomsday threats to end up with a Christian life that is no different from secular morality. That is, one can get to a reasonable morality only by ignoring Jesus' assignation of all nonbelievers to eternal damnation. To take one famous example, in Rudolf Bultmann's lengthy (648 pages in its current paperback version) and influential *Theology of the New Testament*, "hell and eternal damnation are simply ignored" (Kaufmann 1963:97).

But ultimately Jesus is not expanding the moral circle so much as changing it. It's hard to deny Robert Wright's conclusion that "Christianity replaced one kind of particularism with another" (2009:300). Rather than an in-group ("neighbor") defined by ethnic and religious identity (Israelites or Jews), his new morality creates an in-group based on belief. All others who do not accept his message are sentenced to an eternity in hell. Jesus may praise the "good Samaritan," but he also says things like "go nowhere among the Gentiles, and enter no town of the Samaritans" (Matt 10:5–6; cf. Jesus's initial refusal to help a Canaanite, Matt 15:21–8). Professor of the Old Testament John J. Collins aptly summarizes the problem:

> In the NT, identity is no longer tied to ethnicity or to possession of a particular land. What this literature shares with Deuteronomy, however, is the sharp antithesis with the Other, whether the Other is defined in moral terms, as sinners, or in political terms as the Roman Empire. Both Deuteronomy and the apocalypses fashion identity by constructing absolute, incompatible contrasts. . . . In both cases, the absoluteness of categories is guaranteed by divine revelation and is therefore not subject to negotiation or compromise. Herein lies the root of religious violence in the Jewish and Christian traditions.
>
> (2003:18)

And what about Jesus' "turn the other cheek" and "love your enemies" (e.g., Matt 5:38–44; 19:19; Luke 6:27–8), expressions Christians celebrate as examples of the "higher ethics" that derive from God? Again, we need to examine the fine print. Are we *never* to "resist an evil-doer" as Jesus commands? That's *terrible* moral advice! Are we not to defy the bully, the abusive spouse, the slave owner, the bloodthirsty tyrant? Once again, context is everything. These famous directives were not taken as a pacific imperative through much of Christian history, and Jesus himself didn't follow them. In his corporeal form he hasn't lost his Yahwistic anger. Although he cautions against the emotion (Matt 5:22) – he threatens eternal torment to anyone who grows angry or insults a sibling! – he gets irate at his mother, at the Pharisees who disapprove of his working on the Sabbath (Mark 3:5), and at folks in the temple (Matt 21:12–13; Luke 19:45–6; John 2:13–16). He even uses a whip to clear them out! He grows so furious at a fig tree (yes, a *fig tree*) because it had no snacks to offer when he hungrily passes by that he curses it (Matt 21:18–20; Mark 11:12–14).

For one who tells us to "love our enemies," Jesus seems perfectly happy to draw a line between friends and enemies: "Whoever is not with me is against me, and whoever does not gather with me scatters" (Matt 12:30; cf. Matt 11:20–4, and the vicious parable at Luke 19:26–7). In fact, a few chapters after his advice to love one's enemies he makes it clear that his theological opponents are weeds in the "field of the world," and "just as weeds are collected and burned up with fire," so will his enemies be thrown "into the furnace of fire, where there will be weeping and gnashing of teeth" (Matt 13:24–43). And as for universal love, Jesus condemns to hell "whoever speaks against the Holy Spirit" (Matt 12:31–2; Mark 3:28–9; Luke 12:10). This is not a moral issue, no matter what the Holy Spirit could possibly be. Jesus' supposed font of divine love runs completely dry when it comes to fellow Jews who haven't accepted his claim of divinity (again, this has nothing to do with ethics):

> Jesus said to them [the Jews], "If God were your Father, you would love me, for I came from God and now I am here. I did not come on my own, but he sent me. Why do you not understand what I say? It is because you cannot accept my word. You are from your father the devil, and you choose to do your father's desires."
>
> (John 8:42–4)

In any discussion about morality we can't forget motives. *Why*, according to Jesus, should we turn the other cheek and love our enemies? Because they are good things to do in and of themselves? Not at all. It's for the *reward*, "so that you may be children of your Father in heaven" (Matt 5:45; cf. Matt 5:12; Luke 6:35). Jesus' vision of eternal punishment in the flames of "Hades" has rightly been called "deferred" or "eschatological" violence (Avalos 2015:101–10). He doesn't describe hell in medieval detail, but he's sure it's not a picnic; it's a place "where their worm never dies, and the fire is never quenched" (Mark 9:48). The Son of Man "will send his angels, and they will collect out of his kingdom all causes of sin and all evildoers, and they will throw them into the furnace of fire, where there will be weeping and gnashing of teeth" (Matt 13:41–2; cf. Matt 8:12; 13:49–50; 22:13; 24:51; 25:30; Luke 12:46; 13:28).[7]

And who are these evildoers consigned to an eternity in hell? Occasionally they are folks who have acted badly – someone who grew angry at a brother without cause, for example (Matt 5:22). Still, the penalty hardly fits the crime. Or, more convincingly, the rich who don't take care of the poor (Luke 14:12–14; 16:19–31; cf. Matt 6:3–4; 25:31–46). Often it's left vague. "Sinners" – those who ignore or disobey Jesus in some (unspecified) way – will go to hell. Indeed, Jesus is certain that most people will end up there (Matt 7:13–14; 22:13–14; cf. Rev 20:15).

Much of the time, however, damnation has nothing at all to do with morality, but merely with belief. Only by accepting Jesus' theological claims will we avoid retribution and garner a ticket to heaven: "Those who believe in him are not condemned; but those who do not believe are condemned already, because they have not believed in the name of the only Son of God" (John 3:18; cf. 3:3–7, 36; 5:22–3; 6:40, 47, 51, 53–8; 11:25–6; 15:5–7; Mark 16:16). Jesus's message is as much about swallowing his messianic memorandum as tending the poor: "Everyone therefore who acknowledges me before others, I also will acknowledge before my Father in heaven; but whoever denies me before others, I also will deny before my Father in heaven" (Matt 10:32–3; cf. Mk 8:38; Luke 9:26; 12:8–9). Bart Ehrman aptly summarizes Jesus' message: "The reason to change your behavior was to gain entrance to the kingdom when it came. It was not in order to make society a happy place for the foreseeable future. The future was bleak – unless you sided with Jesus and did what he urged" (2009:162) .[8] The world was going to end very soon, within his audience's lifetime, Jesus (and Paul) wrongly insisted. There was just enough time to save yourself.

Jesus' moral vision is no improvement upon Yahweh's; in fact, it is a step back-wards. For Yahweh, apostasy and disobedience deserve *merely* death, a policy that we must condemn as immoral and unjust if we accept the freedom of religion established in the Bill of Rights and reject contemporary religious bullies like ISIS. (All 13 countries that currently inflict capital punishment for rejecting the established religion are Islamic; Coyne 2015:251–2.) One of our basic advanced moral intuitions is that the punishment should fit the crime, also a right guaran-teed by the Constitution. How much less just is Jesus who demands not *death* for "wickedness" by his curious standards (that is, for not being a true believer), but eternal postmortem torment!

Certainly such a severe verdict for creedal disagreement is "cruel and unusual" punishment for a Jewish civil rights activist, a Muslim protestor for women's equality, or a peace-loving Unitarian. What about a young Shinto child? Theo-logians wrestle with the problem, but Jesus didn't. He coyly says that "I do not judge anyone who hears my words and does not keep them, for I came not to judge the world, but to save the world" (John 12:47). But he's just messing with us, for in the very next verses he says it's "the Father" who will judge "on the last day," and we all know by now (having read the Nicene Creed) about the homoou-sion of the Father and Son. Besides, just a few chapters earlier, Jesus had insisted that "even if I do judge, my judgment is valid; for it is not I alone who judge, but I and the Father who sent me" (John 8:16). The primary act for which one is rewarded by Jesus with eternal paradise is not moral at all, but merely believing Jesus' message that the world is coming to a quick end and that he, or someone just like him,[9] will be leading the charge.

Jesus' insistence that all decisions – including skipping out on the wife and kids – be taken for the purpose of eternal life vitiates any serious moral motiva-tion: "The Beatitudes are all conditioned on some kind of reward and punishment" (Barker 2016:300). Even Jesus' charitable call to tend the poor – a mantra at my Jesuit university (and one found pervasively throughout the Tanakh) – becomes suspect. Are we to help the less fortunate because it embodies some intrinsically ethical position, because compassion is the heart of morality in general, because normal, psychologically healthy people feel *bad* when they see unnecessary suf-fering and have the resources to mitigate it? Or is it rather because a divine voice has suggested it, or, worse yet, as Jesus insists, because we get paid handsomely with a trip to paradise if we obey (Matt 19:16–26; Mark 10:17–27; Luke 18:18–26)? The poor themselves must ultimately be consoled with the assurance of postmor-tem existence. As atheist philosopher Richard Robinson notes, we must reject Jesus' reasons behind the precepts, promises, and threats. First, because they are likely to be false (there is no evidence for heaven and hell), "and anyhow they make his precepts precepts of prudence instead of precepts of morality. To obey rules because otherwise you will go to hell is prudence, not morality" (1964:152).

It may be true, as Matt Ridley argues, that ultimately "what matters to society is whether people are likely to be nice to each other, not their motives" (1996:21). But when trying to determine exactly *what* the best action is in a certain case, it does matter *why* one acts a certain way. There is crucial distinction between "actions which are in accordance with morality, and those which are done *because* they are moral" (Everitt 2004:134). If it's merely for the payoff in heaven – because that's what a 2000-year-old text suggests – then it may coincidentally be a good deed but it's not a morally motivated act. It's a gesture of devout obeisance of the kind that equally demands and sustains religious fanaticism and violence, beginning with Yahweh's dictate that Abraham slaughter his son and Jesus' call to abandon your family. To do something to gain eternal life after death is meaningless in and of itself – that "something" needs independent moral justification. The Crusaders welcomed martyrdom for God, having been promised by papal indulgences some ultimate relief for their sins. The leader of the Heaven's Gate cult convinced 38 followers to commit suicide in order to board a UFO trailing a comet that would take them to a higher postmortem level of existence. Many Islamic suicide bombers believe that virgins with pear-shaped breasts await them in paradise. The killer of three people at a Planned Parenthood clinic in Colorado no doubt thought his likely "martyrdom" (he in fact survived the eventual police stand-off) would lead to an eternal seat next to Jesus.[10]

Those who act under the conditions of eternal reward and torment are not giving a "morally relevant reason at all but are acting out of fear for their own hides" (Nielsen 1973:62). As Hector Avalos observes in a section mischievously titled "Jesus as Junk Bond Salesman," Jesus' promise of postmortem paradise "is worse than Wall Street because the returns and rewards promised can never be verified to exist, and historically they have never been fulfilled" (2015:219). Philosopher Bernard Williams argues that there must be more to morality than this either/or split between "moral" and "prudential" justifications for doing something. Morality is not simple, or as he says, "pure" in this way. But he also goes on to conclude that religious morality based on God is completely unworkable, for the "trouble with religious morality comes not from morality's being inescapably pure, but from religion's being incurably unintelligible" (1972:78).

Leading from behind

The history of shifting Christian dogma similarly reveals that morality is not derived from scriptural revelation. Instead, an underlying secular morality that eventually creates positive social change usually comes first, followed by the paradoxical effort of justifying radical shifts in interpretation of a just God's will in defiance of what the religious tradition has maintained and the holy text actually says. Biblical scholar Michael Coogan compares this process of change with that of legal policy: "For both the Bible and the Constitution, social change often precedes the reinterpretation of the foundational text. The text itself is not the principal catalyst for change, but once a change is under way, the text is invoked (or even emended) to support that change" (2010:192).

The Catholic Church – and I pick on Catholics here because of the importance they attach to their tradition of interpretation of God's will – has reversed its official position on a multitude of issues. Some of these are minor points, more a matter of marketing than dogma. For example, the Council of Trent in the 16th century insisted on the use of the Latin Vulgate. Anyone violating that command was anathema, that is, excommunicated. That didn't stop the struggling Church from giving up on the Vulgate and adopting the vernacular some 60 years ago.

But other Church backtracking is more startling, for it involves what should be core moral teachings, the kinds of things an eternal, omniscient, all-loving, and just God should have gotten right and made clear to his followers from the start. As the pope declared during the first Vatican Council, "Religion is immutable; not an idea, but the truth. Truth knows no change" (Kertzer 2018:341). Let's review some of the changes in unchangeable Church doctrine, with a focus on how long it took the Catholic magisterium to embrace even a moderately enlightened morality.

The Church rejected freedom of conscience until the end of the 19th century, and there was no official doctrine of religious freedom until the mid 1960s. The Church was openly antidemocratic until the 1940s. Pope Pius IX, who declared his opinions "infallible" and was beatified by Pope John Paul II in 2000, made it officially illegal for any Catholic to believe in freedom of speech, freedom of the press, or freedom of religion, while also insisting that all Catholics reject "progress, liberalism, and modern civilization" (Kertzer 2018:340). The Jews, thought of and treated as "Christ killers" since at least a sermon of Bishop Melito in the second century (Ehrman 2011:149), were officially "absolved" of deicide – in 1965. Torture was a standard, in fact, often mandated part of ecclesiastical justice for hundreds of years, and the right to silence of the accused in Church proceedings was not recognized until 1917, 200 years after the principle was ensconced in English law. Both Yahweh and Jesus approve of capital punishment – Jesus even affirms Yahweh's commandment to kill children who speak "evilly" of their parents (Matt 15:4; Mark 7:10, referring to Ex 21:17; cf. Lev 20:9). Church fathers were virtually unanimous for almost 2000 years in its support (Dulles 2003:136). The last 50 years have brought about some Catholic calls for the end of capital punishment, and Pope Francis has recently declared that the death penalty is an attack on human dignity and is wrong in *all* cases. Should his opinion prevail, this would mark another 180-degree shift in God's mandates.

As for issues of gender, there is perhaps no uglier tradition than the biblical attitudes towards women swallowed whole and amplified by the magisterium the past 1800 years. "Before Vatican II, popes assumed and explicitly taught women's inequality and subordination to men, as well as condemned advocates of both women's equality and public roles for women" (Gudorf 2003:270). The Church's official position now is for equal opportunity (its own hierarchy excluded) and rights (except for reproductive). Even beliefs in the soul and abortion have changed. Aquinas' amusing Aristotelian notion that the soul does not enter the fetus until several weeks into pregnancy was standard Catholic doctrine for half a millennium (Rachels 1986:51). Aquinas even adapted Aristotle's sexism, stating with certainty that a female fetus took twice as long (80 days) as a man's to acquire a soul after conception (Ranke-Heinemann 1990:74). It was only in 1869 that the official doctrine of the Church declared that the soul is infused at conception, a position equally poorly grounded in biology but at least metaphysically consistent with its position on the "beginning of life."

We often hear of the courageous efforts of Christians to overturn slavery in the U.S., but the Confederacy also declared itself a "Christian nation" and devoutly expected God to support its cause: "Lincoln puzzled over the fact that both sides prayed to the same God, read the same Bible, and claimed to do His will" (Kramnick and Moore 1996:65). After all, Southerners could (and did) cite excellent biblical evidence that slavery was ordained by God and mandated by scripture, and there was no Bible-based argument against it! Jesus has nothing to say directly on the matter but clearly took the institution for granted. He even uses slaves as characters in his parables. Oh, and he does have some recommendations on how hard to beat your slaves (Luke 12:47–8). Paul advises slaves to acquiesce in their fate and to "render service with enthusiasm" (Eph 6:5–8; cf. 1 Cor 7:21–4; 1 Tim 6:1–2; Avalos 2011:96–138). The Tanakh might be worse, accepting the institution of slavery as completely natural (Avalos 2011:62–95), offering three different and contradictory sets of laws for governing the Hebrew slave (Ex 21:2–11; Lev 25:39–46; Deut 15:12–18; Milgrom 2000b:2213–4). We learn in Exodus (21:7–9) that a man can sell his daughter into slavery (but he should not make her a prostitute, Lev 19:29, which implies that some fathers did! Larue 1983:111). It's not all bad news for the girl, however – should she fail to "please her master" (if you know what I mean), he can't turn around and sell her to a "foreign people."

Augustine, following good biblical precedent, saw slavery as part of God's punishment from the fall – any effort to resist it would be resisting God. Thus it took outlandish interpretive leaps to use the Bible as a tool against slavery:

> Antislavery and abolitionist crusaders ransacked Scripture for texts condemning slavery, but the New Testament proved a particularly thorny place for them to look. Two primary problems demanded detailed exegetical solution: first, the disturbing silence of Jesus Christ on slavery; and second, the perhaps more disturbing out-spokenness [in support of slavery] of the Apostle Paul.
>
> (Harrill 2000:150)

In one of the most execrable twists of biblical interpretation, 19th-century Americans – both Northerners and Southerners, blacks and whites – almost universally believed that blacks had their origins in the "curse of Ham" (Johnson 2004). In a bizarre tale told early in Genesis (9:20–7), for ill-defined reasons Noah curses Ham's son, Canaan, condemning him and thus his progeny to be slaves to his brothers. The etiological story is designed to justify the appropriation of the Promised Land (Canaan) by the Jews (descendants of Noah through one of his other sons). But Jewish, Christian, and Islamic exegetes converted the recipient of the curse to Ham (not in the Bible), made him black (not in the Bible), and eventually combined the predicted servitude with the dark skin and invented the cornerstone for the justification of black slavery (Goldenberg 2003:175). The year after the end of our Civil War the Holy Office in Rome pronounced that "Slavery itself . . . is not at all contrary to the natural and divine law." No wonder the Church favored the South. Slavery was not condemned by the Church until the end of the 19th century by Leo XIII, who could cite no convincing tradition or scriptural text in support of God's change of mind. But that's better than the Southern Baptists, who repudiated their traditional defense of slavery only in 1995. Some scholars still try to defend biblical slavery in a variety of perverse contortions (Avalos 2011:7–15).[11]

These moral U-turns in theistic teaching about "what God thinks is just" have not derived from scripture. Society had already started to change, way ahead of "enlightened" biblical exegesis and usually in stark contrast to scripture. Many theists have fought bravely for human rights of all sorts, but not because of a "just" God, no matter what they may have believed. Abolitionists could only use the Bible as support for their efforts by a radical reinterpretation of the text, another good example of "bad literary criticism" that Avalos rightly labels as "abandonment" of the original meaning of the Bible (2011:15, 29–37). Like the allegorists of Homer's epics, they tried to rescue the text by making it mean something completely different than what it clearly says.

The official reasons given for Catholic shifts in policy are theological post hoc rationalizations. We hear of the role played by the Holy Spirit, anthropological insights, "prophetic witness," "advances" in theological interpretation, change in historical circumstances, and limitations in the official moral teachings themselves (Curran 2003:ix). God reveals himself through time – progressive revelation, an historical "development of doctrine." For mysterious reasons he makes his will extremely hard to fathom even by the experts, thus allowing his followers to act unjustly for centuries before correcting the previous errant interpretation of his incremental self-revelations. And virtually none of it is based on scripture. Biblical scholar Joseph Blenkinsopp summarizes the situation with wry understatement: "In Catholic Christianity, tradition – understood with reference to a theory of the development of doctrine – is functionally on the same level as Scripture, though at times eventuating in positions whose relation to the biblical data is not easily perceived" (1990:149).

What this all really adds up to is that it has been moral intuition backed by emotion and promoted by reasoned argumentation derived from Enlightenment principles (some of which go directly back to the Greeks) and implemented through the flawed human processes of persuasion, protest, and legal maneuvering that first pushed for societal changes (Hanson and Heath 1998:21–81; Bernstein 2006:12–13; cf. Carrier 2010; Coyne 2015:212–17). Only later did the Church find it necessary to alter its position radically, to "perfect its doctrine." The leader of the opposition at Vatican II to the new policy of religious freedom – yes, there were traditionalists in the 1960s who fervently denied that people have a right to choose their own religion, much less reject all of them – correctly complained that the novel "liberal" policy derived not from Catholic tradition but from "Hobbes, Locke and Rousseau" (Noonan 2003:292–30). Positive changes in morality have come about not because of a textually "just" God but despite him and reluctant theists "after a shamefully protracted lag time" (Shermer 2015:151).

Goodness without god

Let's be clear. It's not necessarily religion itself that has slowed moral progress but the theologically engineered certainty one has about a just God and his necessarily just demands. In their cross-disciplinary study of the relationship between religion and intolerance, Russell Powell and Steve Clarke argue that "it is the way that people are religious, rather than religiosity per se or the content of religious belief, that disposes them toward prejudice and intolerance" (2013:16). Not surprisingly, the least tolerant are the fundamentalists who read the Bible as the literal biography of God. In those who maintain a critical, questioning attitude that considers doubt as positive and truth claims as invariably tentative rather than absolute, one finds a "strong and inverse correlation with prejudice and discrimination and intolerance" (cf. Batson 2013; Newheiser et al. 2013:110). A recent study with the catchy (if ungrammatical) title of "Christian Fundamentalists or Atheists: Who do Progressive Christians Like or Hate More?" reveals that liberal Christians feel more at home with atheists (Yancy 2017). Two book-length studies agree that "bad" religion, or religion that "becomes evil," is characterized by absolute truth claims, blind obedience, and the rejection of alternative viewpoints and open discussion of the meaning of texts (Vardy 2010; Kimball 2002).

The fact is, even most theists do not rely upon God, his actions, or his commands to make moral decisions. Although nearly 70 percent of Americans self-identify as actively religious, only a third of them believe that there is an absolute standard of right and wrong regardless of the situation (Pew 2014).[12] Even if there were an absolute morality and divine laws floating around out there – and we have seen that the Bible provides no windows into that ideal world – the insoluble philosophical objection is that "we should have no way of knowing whether we had found them" (Kaufmann 1963:295). For living a life of practical morality, there is no difference between believing in (and striving to uncover and act upon) a set of absolute standards or merely better ones. We have no need of a judging god, even if evolutionarily "the idea of a watchful, knowing, reactive God . . . uniquely helped our ancestors survive and reproduce" (Bering 2012:7). The development of a moral supernatural watcher as communities grew too large for individual oversight – a Super Nanny to encourage "norm compliance" that originally may have promoted high fertility and large-scale cooperation with co-believers (Gray and Wegner 2010; Norenzayan 2013:13–32; Johnson 2015; Norenzayan et al. 2016) – has outgrown its usefulness. Indeed, it has misdirected, and continues to impede, our efforts to improve ourselves and our world. Self-reflective moral philosophies and secular institutions now provide rational alternatives (Shariff 2016b), as the flourishing of contemporary secularized communities reveals. Numerous studies have linked intelligence with self-control and self-regulation, findings that suggest that there are innate nonreligious underpinnings to "good" behavior.[13] As philosopher Ronald Dworkin epigrammatically observes, "morality needs no miracles" (2011:85; cf. 340).

Notes

1 Reminding believers about a punishing God ("priming") does improve their moral behavior but only fleetingly and usually towards coreligionists only – the effect is real but "parochial, bounded, transient, situationally constrained, and often overstated" (Shariff 2016a). Without priming, there is "no difference in the behavior of the religious versus the non-religious."

2 Even an article challenging the interpretation of the data collected in this study concludes that "highly religious households do appear slightly less generous than those from moderately religious ones" (Shariff et al. 2016).

3 Some of the more traditional branches of Protestantism (e.g., Anglican, Episcopal, Presbyterian) and non-Christian religions (e.g., Jewish, Buddhist) in the U.S. have a higher percentage of college graduates as a group than do atheists and agnostics (PEW 2016). The two religions with the highest percentage of adults with college degrees are also the least monotheistic (Hindu and Unitarian). The bottom ten are all evangelical denominations (and Jehovah's Witness). Catholics are 20th of the 31 groups represented. But overall, the more education Americans have, the less they believe in God or a higher power (PEW 2018). More controversial but still well-documented is the negative association between intelligence and religiosity, which may derive from the lack of conformity among the intelligent, their analytic thinking style, or less need for the byproducts of religiosity (e.g., compensatory control, self-enhancement) (Zuckerman et al. 2013).

4 The one exception is the claim by cultural relativists that every culture must be judged by its own ethical standards. Sure, Yahweh's genocide *seems* wrong to *us* nowadays, but who are we to judge? Understandably, this is not a popular approach to biblical ethics, and as far as I can tell, no one takes it very seriously these days.

5 Gary North, cofounder of the theocratic movement called Christian Reconstructionism (or Theonomy or Dominion Theology), advocates stoning for blasphemers, children who curse their parents, adulterers, and homosexuals. After all, he observes, stones are "cheap and plentiful" (Wakefield 2006:26).

6 This eclecticism – that is, cherry picking what is an antiquated or personally distasteful divine mandate and what is an eternal rule – is standard theological practice in all areas of biblical "living," necessary for readers who imbue an ancient mythological text with the Truth. "In some cases, the rules are deemed historical artifacts to sidestep troublesome challenges. The Bible is the literal Word of God . . . but Christians see no problem in wearing clothing woven of two materials, wearing gold, pearls, and expensive clothing, cutting their hair and beards, and getting tattoos. Those commands are deemed no longer relevant, while, inexplicably, other very similar proscriptions are still thought to apply to modern life" (Sparks 2016:134–5).

7 It may be that Jesus didn't say these things, as some of his defenders argue, but that's true with just about everything reported in the New Testament. Christianity in general jumped on the concept right away with or without Jesus. Paul, our earliest witness, is very clear on the matter, contrasting the relatively lenient treatment of sinners in the Old Testament to the fate that awaits those who reject Christ: "Anyone who has violated the law of Moses dies without mercy 'on the testimony of two or three witnesses.' How much worse punishment do you think will be deserved by those who have spurned the Son of God . . .?" (Heb 10:28–9).

8 Ehrman argues in a later book (2014:108–9) that the historical Jesus probably *did* make behavior the key to eternal reward and punishment. The early Christian church, however, which determined the text of the New Testament, "taught that a person is rewarded with salvation by believing in the death and resurrection of Jesus." Unfortunately we're stuck with the textual rather than any "real" Jesus when it comes to finding scriptural authority for Christian morality.

9 Although Christians generally believe that his allusions to the cosmic judge known as the Son of Man are self-referential, it's not clear Jesus means it much of the time (Ehrman 2009:140). Some scholars now argue that the early Church, not Jesus, created the sayings about the coming of the Son of Man in the end times (Allison 2003:157–9).

10 Christian apologists, the first to criticize Islam for their extremists, go apoplectic at the suggestion that their own religion can still lead to medieval atrocities. Note the fury President Obama kindled when he referred to the delusional murderer as a "Christian terrorist," a fair description of a man who had written on an internet forum "Turn to JESUS or burn in hell."

11 To be Abrahamically comprehensive, it should be noted that Islam not only endorsed but managed the slave trade in the Mediterranean and North Africa, at least partially by capturing and selling crews and passengers sailing on the Strait of Gibraltar, as Christopher Hitchens reminds us; 2007:176–7, 181. White (2012:80–7) estimates that the Mideast slave trade resulted in over 18 million deaths, several million more than in Atlantic slave trade. One scholar of religion has famously argued that Christian theology was responsible for the end of slavery (Stark 2003:291–365), but his arguments have not withstood critical scrutiny (e.g., Avalos 2011:269–84).

12 Many conservative Christians have recently abandoned their traditional concern for morality, at least when it comes to politics. In a PRRI survey (10/19/16), "more than seven in ten (72%) white evangelical Protestants say an elected official can behave ethically even if they have committed transgressions in their personal life – a 42-point jump from 2011, when only 30% of white evangelical Protestants said the same." That way they could vote for a presidential candidate feigning Judeo-Christian convictions whose personal history was in fact notoriously Olympian (including Jovian boasts of sexual misconduct and Yahwistic antipathy to foreigners).

13 Many popular books over the past 40 years have laid out likely evolutionary accounts for the development of morality (human virtue, if you will). Those I have found especially illuminating include Wilson (1978), Wilson (1993), Midgley (1994), Wright (1994), Ridley (1996), Katz (2000), Shermer (2004), Hauser (2006), Teehan (2010), Harris (2010), Krebs (2011), Boehm (2012), Churchland (2013), and Liao (2016).

Section V
Heavenly sex

15 Divine *eros*, biblical celibacy, and God's little punching bag

A little over halfway through the *Iliad*, things are looking bleak for the Greeks. Achilles is still refusing to fight, many of their best warriors are wounded, the wall protecting their camp has been thrown down, Hector is on a rampage, and the Trojans are coming close to burning the Greek ships. Agamemnon even proposes that they sail home before it's too late. Poseidon mixes surreptitiously with the Greeks, trying to inspire their courage with a shout "as loud as nine or ten thousand men in battle" (14.147–9). Having forbidden any of the gods to take part in the fighting, Zeus monitors the battle from atop Ida, the loftiest mountain in Troy. Hera, desperate to aid her floundering Greeks, realizes she needs to distract "the mind of Zeus" so Poseidon can take a more active role:

> And this plan seemed best in her heart, to get herself nicely adorned and go to Ida, to see if perhaps Zeus might desire to lie by her body in love-making, and she might pour a harmless and gentle sleep on his eyelids and his sharp mind.
> (14.161–5)

Hera heads to her boudoir, where she carefully bathes and then puts on an ambrosial perfume whose fragrance "reached to earth and heaven" (14.170–4). Homer spares no detail in her "arming" scene as she prepares for "combat": Hera does her hair, puts on an ambrosial robe, and adorns herself with gold brooches, a 100-tasselled belt, and dangling earrings. Decked out from top (a veil) to bottom (sandals), she needs one more erotic accouterment to guarantee success. She calls aside Aphrodite to request the power of "love-making and desire" in the magical and tangible form of a strap the goddess of sexual passion wears around her breasts. This sash contains lovemaking, desire, and "fond beguilement" that "steals the wits even of the prudent." Aphrodite, no friend of the Greeks, nevertheless quickly hands it over, at least in part because Hera tells her an elaborate lie about desperately needing the talismanic belt to reconcile the quarreling Tethys and Oceanus by bringing "them back to bed to be united in making love" (14.188–223).

Hera enlists the god Sleep to help her, bribing him with the promise of a Grace for a wife. Then, ready for the seduction, she heads to the peak of Ida to tell Zeus – that is, *lie* to Zeus – that she is off to try to reunite Tethys and Oceanus. Zeus takes one look at her, "then desire encompassed his prudent mind, just as when they first mingled in love-making, hurrying off to bed behind the backs of their dear parents" (14.294–6). In the immortal words of Meat Loaf, "He couldn't take it any longer, Lord he was crazed, and when the feeling came upon him like a tidal wave" Zeus delivers one of the greatest (if least likely to be successful) "seduction" speeches in Western history:

> But come, let the two of us go to bed and take delight in making love. For never before has desire for a goddess or a mortal woman so flooded the heart in my chest and overwhelmed me: Not when I desired Ixion's wife, who bore Perithoüs, a counselor equal to the gods; nor when I desired fair-ankled Danaë, Acrisius' daughter, who bore Perseus, illustrious among all men; nor when I desired the daughter of far-famed Phoenix, who bore me both Minos and godlike Rhadamanthys; nor even when I desired Semele nor Alcmena in Thebes, who bore a stout-hearted son, Heracles, and Semele bore Dionysus, a source of joy for mortals; nor when I desired the lovely haired queen Demeter; nor when I desired glorious Leto; nor have I desired you yourself as much as I now want you – sweet desire holds me captive.
>
> (14.314–28)

Hera, unfazed by her husband's list of liaisons and their resulting progeny, pretends to be shocked at his suggestion – do it right *here*, right *now*? How embarrassing if one of the gods should see them! "Let's go to your bedroom," she suggests, trying to maneuver him out of sight of the earthly battles. But Zeus can't wait that long. He grabs his wife in his arms, "and beneath them the divine earth produced fresh-sprouting grass, and dewy clover, and crocus, and hyacinth so thick and soft it kept them up off the ground. They lay on this, and were enveloped in a beautiful golden cloud from which glistening dewdrops trickled down" (14.346–51).

The plan works. Zeus nods off after sex. Sleep (the personified version) then runs down to Poseidon and tells him to grant the Greeks glory, since "I have blanketed soft slumber around him [Zeus] – Hera has beguiled him to go to bed in love-making" (14.352–60). For us the important point is again the obvious one – all of the major Homeric gods (except Athena) and most of the minor ones have sex. Zeus and Hera even had a teenage dalliance! So central is sex to the Homeric concept of human nature that there is a goddess (Aphrodite) who represents desire and sexual passion (*eros*).

The Homeric gods are *fully* anthropomorphic; their sex lives are not substantially different in kind from those of mortals (although no Greek or Trojan warrior marries his sister). Zeus's flings spawn gods, heroes, nymphs, and the mortal representative of passion herself, Helen. Poseidon tends to produce monstrous offspring (e.g., the 100-handed Briareus, Polyphemus, Otus, and Ephialtes). Hermes and Ares have children; Apollo fights with a mortal over a woman. Even the personified Sleep, as we just saw, can be bought off with a Grace. Helius is the father of a king, several nymphs, and the goddess Circe, an enchantress who has sex with Odysseus in his year-long stay on her island. Yes, the goddesses are busy too. The most important mother goddess in Homer is Thetis, although Hera's off-spring are full-fledged divinities. Aphrodite is still watching over her son Aeneas. One of the few references to Demeter focuses on her ill-fated fling with a mortal named Iasion (Zeus killed him with his thunderbolt). Eos, the goddess of the dawn, pursues several different mortals as lovers. Calypso apparently has sex with Odysseus most nights for seven years. The quarrel between Zeus and Hera in the opening book of the *Iliad* ends when they climb into bed.

Divine *eros* is complicated in the epics, just as mortal sex usually is. As we see in this one humorous scene – known as the Deception of Zeus – sex can be mutually joyful, unitive, and fertile (note the imagery as well as the list of Zeus's offspring – "the beds of the gods are not fruitless," *Od.* 11.249–50). But *eros* can also be (as it is here) tainted with deception, irrationality, and destruction, convey-ing "fond beguilement" that "steals the wits even of the prudent." In fact, Poseidon takes advantage of Zeus's postcoital slumber to aid the Greeks, and as a result even Hector barely escapes the onslaught with his life. Sexual passion among the gods is powerful, wondrous, and potentially disastrous. How much more so is it for mortals. The entire Trojan War is the result of human lust engineered by Aph-rodite herself gone horribly awry. When sex messes up the gods, there are rarely any long-term ramifications (for them, at least); if the wrong passion is unleashed between mortals, an entire generation risks destruction.

The Greek gods were similar in their sexual natures to many Near Eastern pantheons but radically different from the God of the Tanakh. We have seen that for at least some Israelites Yahweh originally had a consort and was himself prob-ably a child of a god. Most of that history has been eliminated from the text, as Yahweh eventually became disassociated from death and sex. Just why this hap-pened remains a matter of speculation, although it's likely to have derived from the priestly ideal of purity: "Given the priestly insistence on the impurity of death and sexual relations, it is difficult to resist the suggestion that the presentation of Yahweh generally as sexless and unrelated to the realm of death was produced precisely by a priesthood whose central notions of holiness involved separa-tion from the realms of impurity, specifically sexual relations and death" (Smith 2002:205; cf. Frymer-Kensky 1992:190). This urge to "purify" Yahweh may also be the result of efforts to push back against the hypersexuality of neighboring gods (Christian theologians are more likely to call it something like "the sexual immorality linked to pagan fertility cults"; Davidson 2007:85–113). A Ugaritic poem glorifies the power of El – recall that Yahweh shares many characteristics with this deity – by insisting that "El's penis extends like the sea. . . . El's penis, like the flood" (CAT 1.23.33–4). And Baal was said to have had sex with a heifer, mounting her "sixty-six, seventy-seven times" (Smith 2001:84, 87).

Regardless of how he got that way, Yahweh as ultimately presented in the Tanakh has no direct sexual interests. (Although as Thomas Paine observed, according to the New Testament "the Almighty committed debauchery with a woman engaged to be married"; cf. Shermer 2015:179.) That absence can't be a good thing if he and his surrounding mythology are supposed to serve as any sort of help for mortals in living a fully human life. History shows how calamitous this sexless world of the divine has been for the human psyche. We don't have to document here Christianity's history of sexual repression and gender discrimination and the many crimes (both literal and psychological) committed in their pursuit – that's been done eloquently and thoroughly numerous times.[1] And that's not including the just plain bizarreness of many Christian responses to human sexuality, one of my most cherished of which is this practice noted by Bertrand Russell:

> I am sometimes shocked by the blasphemies of those who think themselves pious – for instance, the nuns who never take a bath without wearing a bathrobe all the time. When asked why, since no man can see them, they reply: "Oh, but you forget the good God." Apparently they conceive of the Deity as a Peeping Tom, whose omnipotence enables Him to see through bathroom walls, but who is foiled by bathrobes. This view strikes me as curious.
>
> (*Unpopular Essays:73*)

But we shouldn't forget that the problems start long before Christianity with the desexed Yahweh. The misadventure of Western attitudes about sex is rooted in part in the Tanakh's sex-free God. By offering nothing positive about divine *eros*, it left the interpretive alley wide open for later Judeo-Christian tradition, especially the repressed Church fathers (influenced, it must be admitted, by strains of anti-carnal Greek philosophy), to vilify sex in general. The authors of the New Testament "were creating new scripture by constructive abuse of the old" (Fox 1992:24). The starter myth for Christianity is that a neutered Father begat in some sexless fashion an abstinent Son through a virginal Mother (*The DaVinci Code* not withstanding). You can't remove *eros* much more thoroughly than that. To be sexless, the New Testament tells us, is to be more like God.

Skeptics about Jesus' miraculous engendering often point out the numerous similarities between his story and those told about Greco-Roman emperors and heroes. Heracles, for example, also has a mortal mother, divine father, and ends up a god. But it would never occur to Homer that this meant that Zeus didn't have actual sex or that Alcmena, Heracles' mother, remained a virgin. Christianity's "terror of semen" (Ranke-Heinemann 1990:171), fear of and disgust with female sexuality, and obsession with sex as sin begins with its first architects. Jesus himself said almost nothing about sex, other than his handful of comments on divorce and adultery and "looking at a woman with lust." But it didn't bode well for Western culture that his textual persona never married, didn't have or talk about sex, and insisted that *heaven* was sex-free as well. Paul's sexophobia and emphasis on celibacy, resting on his false belief that Jesus would return in the near future (1 Cor 7:25–6, 31), became a cornerstone of ruinous Church doctrine: "Paul left a fatal legacy to future ages" (Brown 1988:55). For Paul, marriage was for those Christians too weak for celibacy (1 Cor 7:9) – the only function of sex was to *extinguish* desire (Martin 2006:65–8).[2]

But there are also more immediate repercussions from a sexless Yahweh that are often overlooked. God's suppressed sexuality oozes out *metaphorically* – and catastrophically – in the Tanakh itself. And in religion, as we have seen, metaphors matter. In the Judeo-Christian tradition one learns about God through these "indirect" representations in a sacred text, and God provides a model for behavior. Unfortunately, Yahweh's sex life is particularly ugly. As the child molestation cases among Catholic priests have revealed – and the study of Greek texts like Euripides' *Hippolytus* have suggested for over two millennia – sex is a natural force and efforts to suppress it almost always backfire. *Eros* is the whack-a-mole of human psychology – you can try to smack it down, but it will materialize someplace else, usually arising as a bigger and more destructive beast. Bridling Yahweh's sexual nature only forced him to become the worst metaphorical partner ever.

Yahweh the battering husband

Yahweh's passionate but embittered relationship with the people of Israel is frequently described in the Tanakh in metaphorical terms of a marriage gone bad. The people of Israel (the unfaithful wife) are accused by Yahweh (the devoted but jealous husband) of "prostituting themselves" to foreign gods or "lusting for another" (e.g., Lev 17:7; 20:6; Num 15:38–40; Deut 31:16; Judg 2:16–17; 8:27, 33). Whether cavorting with locals (likely to be Baal-worshippers) or making foreign connections with Near Eastern powers like Egypt or Assyria, Israelites dishonor their God by (figuratively) hopping into bed with other gods. His people, Yahweh complains, are supposed to "worship no other god, because the Lord, whose name is Jealous, is a jealous God." God's jealousy is rooted in the marital metaphor (Davidson 2007:113–14). Yahweh adds that he is not only a jealous God but "a devouring fire" at Deuteronomy 4:24, but his implied threat doesn't work. When Israelite men take wives who worship another god, they are often unable to stick with Yahweh (Ex 34:12–16; cf. Num 25:1–3). Apostasy and foreign alliances (and occasionally judicial corruption) are thus intertwined in a single image of sexual infidelity and subsequent punishment. The Assyrian destruction of Israel and the Babylonian annihilation of Judah are portrayed as the righteous retribution of a possessive, dishonored, and angry husband on his adulterous bride. It's *her* fault that he had to teach her a lesson this way. She clearly had it coming.

Yahweh's "obsession with fidelity" reaches its first climax in Deuteronomy, where he "imposes the same kind of [oppressive] conditions on Israel that are described for a wife in Numbers 5" (Fewell and Gunn 1993:109–12). But the prophetic tradition is particularly fond of depicting the Hebrew God as a (loyal) spouse threatening and/or punishing a (cheating) wife. This "wife" is commonly an important city rather than Israel or Judah in their entirety. Jerusalem takes the most direct hits, but Samaria and Sodom are included; even foreign cities can be personified as derelict women (especially Nineveh and Babylon). This metaphor of the city as Yahweh's straying wife is a strange twist on a common Near Eastern understanding of a capital as a goddess married to the patron deity. But in the Tanakh, the city, especially Jerusalem, has been demoted to mortal status and painted in completely negative shades. In the Prophets, personified cities are always unfaithful wives who must be punished (Galambush 1992:20–43). "The marriage that results between these partners is intense and emotional; it [is] also a nightmare of domination in a punitive relationship" (Frymer-Kensky 1992:144). In the hands of the prophets who have seen (or fear they will see) the obliteration of Israel by foreign powers, this metaphor combines sexual prudery, misogynistic cruelty, physical and psychological abuse, religious authoritarianism, and xenophobia in a toxic elixir brewed up to scare and shame Israelites into a pristine monolatry that had as yet not emerged as the dominant ideology.

The earliest use of this extended metaphor is usually assigned to Hosea, where the prophet is compelled by Yahweh to marry a "wife of whoredom" – this is how he refers to his own spouse – so his life can provide a suitable parallel between his faithless human marriage and the divine metaphorical debacle (Hos 1–3; 4:12–19; 5:3–4; 6:10; 9:1). This "prostitute" or "whoring" city-country/wife is found scattered throughout other prophetic books as well: Isaiah (e.g., 1:21; 3:16–17; 54:1–10; 57:7–13; 62:3–5), Micah (1:7), Malachi (2:10–16), and especially in Jeremiah (e.g., 2:1–3, 16–25, 32–3; 3:1, 6–13; 4:30; 13:22–7; 22:20–2). Yahweh refers to the Assyrian destruction of "faithless" Israel and its dissolution as his "divorce" from one who "played the whore"; Israel was exterminated "for all the adulteries." The southern part of the country, however, did not take the warning to heart (Yahweh is apparently married to both "siblings"): "Yet her false sister Judah did not fear, but she too went and played the whore" (Jer 3:6–10). Judah will also perish for her infidelities. And the imagery grows more severe: "In Hosea the wife was an adulteress, but in Jeremiah she was a prostitute, a whore, a slut" (Weems 1995:55).

The general trend is horrific enough: Israel and Judah are slutty sisters who cheat on Yahweh with foreign alliances and alien gods. They are punished with godsent invasions, often expressed through humiliating images of "lifting up your skirts" to shame the women, stripping "her naked" to "expose her," "laying bear their secret parts." The exact import of these expressions of "uncovering nakedness" is debated, but many scholars see them as euphemisms for sexual assault. "The punishment [stripping naked and genital exposure] of the metaphorical adulteress describes the realities of war. When specifically visited upon the city, the actions represent siege warfare. The same actions visited upon the wife become gang rape, torture, and murder" (Bowen 2010:88). That is, Yahweh threatens Israel with gang rape (Coogan 2010:187), and in Jeremiah Yahweh "himself is depicted as a sexual abuser" (Baumann (2003:24; cf. 120): "God turns out to be a rapist" (Scholz 2010:185). The marriage imagery reaches its nadir in Ezekiel 16 and 23, where we learn of Yahweh's failed marriage with Jerusalem. Here the tale becomes so gruesomely detailed and the metaphor so elaborately expanded that it's easy to forget that he's talking about a *city*. The physical abuse feels personal and all-too-human.

Ezekiel 16 presents a graphic and disturbing picture of Jerusalem's maturation into a nubile young woman deflowered by Yahweh and then turned into a battered spouse. Abhorred and abandoned at birth by her wicked Canaanite parents, Jerusalem was saved by the word of God – "Live!" – and she developed into a beautiful young woman. Yahweh recalls his initial impressions with great fondness (and a touch of lechery):

You [Jerusalem] grew up and became tall and arrived at full womanhood; your breasts were formed, and your [pubic] hair had grown; yet you were naked and bare. I passed by you again and looked on you; you were at the age for love. I spread the edge of my cloak over you, and covered your nakedness [biblical euphemism for "they had sex"]; I pledged myself to you and entered into a covenant [marriage] with you, says the Lord God, and you became mine. Then I bathed you with water and washed off the blood from you, and anointed you with oil.

(Ezek 16:6–9)

Ah, the salad days of their relationship, as the marriage covenant blends with the one at Sinai (Bowen 2010:85–6). The wedding-night imagery is unusual: "But this husband-God does not kiss, embrace, fondle, or otherwise express physical affection for Israel, even within the poetic license of the metaphor" (Frymer-Kensky 1992:188). Yahweh is neither phallic nor affectionate. Sexually, at least, Yahweh is incorporeal. But metaphorically it's a good archaic, consummated marriage with proof of virginity in the bride's blood on display.[3] Yahweh is happy with his bride. He boasts of all the gifts he gave her – bracelets, necklaces, nose-rings and earrings, a crown, expensive clothes, food fit for a queen (the city was flourishing under God's attention).

But what did Jerusalem do in turn? You just have to feel some sort of archaic rap song coming on: "But you trusted in your beauty, and played the whore because of your fame, and you lavished your whorings on any passer-by" (v. 15). References to her "whoring" and "prostitution" are repeated almost hysterically to characterize Jerusalem's worship of other gods, performance of alien rites, and alliances with foreign powers. Jerusalem "played the whore" (vv. 16, 17, 26, 28, 34), "as if your whorings were not enough" (v. 20) "in all your abominations and your whorings" (v. 22), "prostituted your beauty" (v. 25), "multiplying your whoring" (vv. 25, 26, 29, 33, 34; cf. "brazen whore," v. 30). The NRSV uses a variant "whore" or "prostitute" over 20 times in this one chapter (with nearly a dozen "abominations" thrown in). The only instances in the Tanakh of one particular Hebrew word for "whoredom" are found in two chapters of Ezekiel nearly two dozen times (Baumann 2003:146, 20; Greenberg 1983:296)! The otherwise sexless Yahweh is now obsessed with sex and sexual fidelity. After all, as Ezekiel notes in a vision he has of God in the first chapter, Yahweh seems to have fire surrounding his loins (Ezek 1:27).

And how did the paranoid patriarch respond to his "wife's" infidelities? "*Therefore I stretched out my hand against you, reduced your rations, and gave you up to the will of your enemies*" (Ezek 15:27, my emphasis). Punishment is swift and physical, a violent spousal beating and starvation, the analogy apparently referring to the loss of Judean territory to the Philistines. Still, it's unsettling to find your benevolent and all-loving deity admitting that he beats and malnourishes his wife, even in an extended metaphor.

Midway through his rant Yahweh insists that "you were not like a whore, because you scorned payment. Adulterous wife, who receives strangers instead of her husband" (vv. 31–2). Jerusalem gave gifts to lovers (tribute to foreign powers) rather than soliciting them like "other women" in their "whorings." But Yahweh quickly reverts, as Ezekiel addresses God's straying spouse as "O whore," and God announces that because Jerusalem's "lust was poured out and your nakedness uncovered in your whoring with your lovers . . . I will bring blood upon you in wrath and jealousy. . . . I will stop you playing the whore . . ." (vv. 35–41). He will gather up Jerusalem's "lovers" (the foreign nations with which Israel has made alliances) to exact punishment for her adultery:

> I will uncover your nakedness to them, so that they may see all your nakedness. . . . They shall strip you of your clothes and take your beautiful objects and leave you naked and bare. They shall bring up a mob against you and they shall stone you and cut you to pieces with their swords. They shall burn your houses.
>
> (vv. 37–41)

Hmmm. Yahweh arranges for the gang rape, mutilation, and butchery of his wife. Thank goodness it's only a metaphor! Jerusalem survives, however, and Yahweh can be satisfied with his whorish wife's punishment and seek a reconciliation (lucky Jerusalem): "So I will satisfy my fury on you, and my jealousy shall turn away from you; I will be calm, and will be angry no longer" (v. 42). Although Jerusalem has broken her marriage vows (the covenant), Yahweh will forgive her. Sort of. It won't be a pretty rapprochement – she's done nothing to earn it: "Yet I will remember my covenant with you in the days of your youth, and I will establish with you an everlasting covenant. . . . I will establish my covenant with you, and you shall know that I am the Lord, in order that you may remember and be confounded, and never open your mouth again because of your shame, when I forgive you all that you have done, says the Lord God" (vv. 60–3). Yahweh will *force* Israel to return to him, a nonnegotiable repatriation.

As long as Jerusalem shuts up and behaves – Yahweh is the only character to speak in Ezekiel's tale – God will forgive and take her back. What does the future hold? We have no reason to believe that the cycle of abuse will stop, alas, since Yahweh has a history of sadistic behavior towards Jerusalem's "siblings." He admits to having brutalized Jerusalem's unfaithful "sisters" as he calls them, Samaria (the capital of the former northern kingdom) and Sodom, infamous for its sin and destruction (vv. 44–52). Yahweh doesn't specify that they were previous spouses, but it seems likely. He destroyed both of them for "their abominations" – infidelities not half as bad as those of Jerusalem, he insists – and he will restore their fortunes as well as hers. Apparently he's working his way through the whole Levantine family, striking them down for their unfaithfulness, shaming them into better behavior, and then inviting them back into his loving arms.

Ezekiel returns to the image of unfaithful sisters (now definitely sister-wives) in Chapter 23. Sisters Samaria and Jerusalem both "played the whore" in Egypt before they married Yahweh. Yahweh apparently has lost even the opportunity to deprive them of their virginity in this scenario. No good from their youth, the sisters continued to lust after others even after their polygamous union with God.

Samaria "defiled herself" with the Assyrians, so Yahweh delivered her "into the hands of her lovers." They "seized her sons and her daughters; and they killed her with the sword. Judgment was executed upon her, and she became a byword among women" (23:2–10).

Jerusalem, apparently paying no attention to the "byword" of her sibling, was even "more corrupt than she [Samaria] in her whorings," desiring not just the Assyrians but the Babylonians as well. She soon dumps the Babylonians, however, and turns with the same passion she had in her youth back to Egypt. She "lusted after her paramours there, whose members were like those of donkeys, and whose emission was like that of stallions. Thus you longed for the lewdness of your youth, when the Egyptians fondled your bosom and caressed your young breasts" (vv. 11–21). (Greenberg translates 16:26 as "Egyptians, your big-membered neighbors" 1983:283.) My guess is that most readers of the Bible are not aware that Yahweh worries about the size of his penis, jealous of the length of Egypt's member and the power of its ejaculation. Keep in mind that this is Ezekiel's preferred imagery to register his unhappiness with Israel's pro-Egyptian *political* policies, something every prophet at the time was wary about (Peterson 2013:311).

Yahweh responds in predictable fashion to Jerusalem's continued adultery, as he turns her lovers against her in what has been fairly labeled "graphic, even pornographic . . . massive sexual violence" (Bowen 2010:140):

> They shall cut off your nose and your ears, and your survivors shall fall by the sword. They shall seize your sons and your daughters, and your survivors shall be devoured by fire. They shall also strip you of your clothes and take away your fine jewels. . . . The assembly shall stone them and with their swords they shall cut them down; they shall kill their sons and their daughters, and burn up their houses. Thus will I put an end to lewdness in the land, so that all women may take warning and not commit lewdness as you have done.
>
> (23:25–6, 47–8)

The metaphor slips away to reveal the actual savagery of Yahweh's revenge on the city. But the analogous wife is mutilated and killed as well through orders given by the jealous deity. As scholar and ordained minister Renita Weems concludes in her book-length study of *Marriage, Sex, and Violence in the Hebrew Prophets*, "It is clear who the victim really is in this sordid drama: the husband. The husband's wounded honor is uppermost" (1995:97). Yahweh has had it this time – he makes no gesture of reconciliation. The sister cities are forever doomed.

Biblical scholars debate the lesson of verse 48, Yahweh's foreboding announcement that "all women may take warning and not commit lewdness as you have done" – is it aimed at cities or women? The primary lesson is political and religious. All Israelite cities (that is, Israelites) will suffer similarly should they stray from the covenant and ignore their commitment to Yahweh alone. But it is impossible to read Ezekiel and the other prophets without taking to heart the lessons implied by the metaphor itself: "The humiliation, mutilation, and death

of these adulteresses make them cautionary tales to frighten women into sub-
mission to their husbands, raising significant ethical issues" (Bowen 2010:143).
The brutality of the text has been subtly acknowledged by the religious traditions
themselves: "No portion of this chapter [16] appears in any Christian lectionary.
Jewish tradition also forbids the liturgical use of this chapter" (Bowen 2010:91;
cf. Scholz 2010:205), although the rabbis seem to have objected primarily to its
"explicit sexual language and its implication that Israel's roots were heathen"
(Kamionkowski 2003:6) rather than the abhorrent picture it paints of their God.

Many biblical experts, for the most part confident theists, remain remarkably
obtuse to the perversity of the marriage imagery. It was mostly ignored by *everyone* until the 1980s, when feminist scholars began drawing attention to Yahweh's
violence against women. Still, as Linda Day, a former editor of *The Catholic
Biblical Quarterly* concludes when analyzing five commentaries written by males
on Ezekiel, these commentators "speak overwhelmingly of the love and grace of
YHWH as the chief trait of his character. It is a recurring theme throughout these
discussions. YHWH is generous, amazingly gracious, and working for the best
for the woman: he is a husband whose love knows no bounds" (L Day 2000:226).
M.G. Swanepoel characteristically concludes that "the punishment fits the revolt-
ing deeds of the unfaithful wife," and so the "reader is moved by the kindness and
grace of Yahweh" (1993:90, 96). According to Paul M. Joyce, Ezekiel offers us a
"rich theology" with a "finely balanced dialectic between the presence of Yhwh
with his people wherever they are and his honouring of the particular location
of the revelation of his holiness" (2011:66). Eric M. Meyers and John Rogerson
label Ezekiel's thought and imagery in these "remarkable parables" in Chapter 16
as "daring in their application" (2008:211).

Feminist scholars have made the same observation about publications on other
prophets: The "standard interpretations of Hosea sympathize with the husband
who has put up with so much from this fickle woman" (Graetz 1995:129); "Many
of the commentators . . . displayed an almost prurient interest in Hosea's marital partner, and their outrage at her alleged behavior echoed Hosea's . . . which
ranges from erotic fantasy to moralistic condemnation" (Fontaine 1995:61);
"Many interpreters are caught in this prophetic perspective and endorse the prophetic position, which promotes a 'theology of the rapist'" (Scholz 2010:187).
Seventh-day Adventist scholar Richard Davidson, rejecting the "radical feminist
project" that finds offense in these old texts, concludes that "the characteristics of
the God-Israel relationship outlined in Hos 2 also by implication apply to human
husbands and wives: steadfast love, mutual compassion (suffering with the other),
intimacy, and ready response" (2007:367, 117). Corrine Patton, a female scholar
writing from what she calls "a commitment to Roman Catholicism," insists that
the text "does not substantiate domestic abuse" but instead offers a consoling
view of a "God for whom no experience, not even rape and mutilation in wartime,
is beyond hope for healing and redemption" (2000:227, 238). She seems to ignore
the inconvenient fact that the "rape and mutilation" are, according to Ezekiel,
Yahweh's vengeance upon his own people. And a female Protestant minister, in a
book on the marriage metaphors in Isaiah, Hosea, and Jeremiah revealingly (if not

intentionally kinkily) entitled *Bonds of Love*, concludes that this imagery demonstrates the "*revitalizing* power of the love and care of Yhwh for Zion," "implies that the covenant is perceived of as an affectionate relationship," and shows that Yahweh's love for Israel is characterized by "extensiveness in time, intimacy and pleasure." "The essence of the love of Yhwh," she decides, "seems to be that this love from the other side offers security and safety and a companionship from which one can never fall. The companionship with Yhwh, as every love relationship, provides Israel with a home and a future" (Abma 1999:257, 258, 259, emphasis in the original). A home and a future in intensive care, perhaps.

Yes, it's "just" a metaphor, and one that was rhetorically designed to be disturbing.[4] The picture is *supposed* to shock the (primarily male) audience, to shame them into better behavior and to explain the decimation of the population in war, the destruction of their major cities, and the loss of their temple: God didn't fail them or break the covenant, but used their enemies to punish them for their mistrust and apostasy. Scholars engaging in a strictly "historical-philological, searching for the primary, context-bound sense of Scripture," resist what they see as efforts to impose "expressions of the pain and outrage experienced by feminists searching Scripture for reflections of their constructions of reality" (Greenberg 1997:494). The focus, we are told, should be on "what the texts meant to those who composed and received them in their historical context." And of course it's true that "the violence in the text . . . can never be the *only* interpretative comment in relation to this text" (Abma 1999:29, emphasis in original).

But theists – and theologians – want the Bible to be more than a historical fiction embedded in a specific time and place, more than a "cultural artifact" like the *Iliad*. Ezekiel, they insist, says something about a *real living* god – it is not merely a metaphorical exploration of inauspicious political alliances and censured cultic practices and crushing military defeats 2600 years ago. So contemporary readers, most of whom consider the Bible to reveal some truths about their God, must deal with the fact that Yahweh's dominant display of sexuality in the Tanakh is as a figurative wife beater. Biblical scholar Katheryn Darr acknowledges the challenges of teaching these passages from Ezekiel to students:

> In our arguments about such figurative language, I must acknowledge that I become uneasy when Ezekiel employs female sexual imagery to depict the ostensible wickedness of sixth-century Judeans. This is not because I am squeamish, or because it offends my "southern sensibilities," but rather because imagery, especially biblical imagery, that details the degradation and public humiliation of women, that describes female sexuality as the object of male possession and control, that displays women being battered and murdered, and that suggests such violence is a means toward *healing* a broken relationship, can have serious repercussions.
>
> (1992:115)

Yahweh's behavior – and many commentators' responses – perfectly matches that of contemporary abusers. Psychologist Lenore Walker's work on the "battered woman's syndrome" over the past 40 years has yielded a definitive set of charac-teristics. Battered women accept responsibility for the batterer's actions, feel guilt, and "assign omnipotence to their batterer" (1979:31, 75). The abusive spouse dis-plays excessive possessiveness and/or jealousy accompanied by extreme verbal harassment and comments of a derogatory nature. He restricts her activity through physical or psychological means, using nonverbal and verbal threats of future punishment and/or deprivation. All this inevitably leads to actual physical attack (Walker 2009:46). There is a predictable cycle of violence, with three distinct and repeated phases: (1) tension-building accompanied by a rising sense of danger; (2) the acute battering incident; (3) loving-contrition, during which the batterer may apologize profusely, try to assist his victim, show kindness and remorse, and shower her with gifts and/or promises (Walker 2009:91). This cycle starts after the courtship period, a marriage "that often turns into stalking and surveillance that the battered woman discovers too late." Does this sound familiar? The profile of Yahweh's actions in Ezekiel "matches real-life batteries in significant ways" (L. Day 2000:216).

Looked at from the batteree's perspective, Yahweh becomes the jealous, stalker spouse who threatens, abuses, and often seeks reconciliation. In Hosea Yahweh explicitly tells Israel that he will reestablish his covenant and "take you for my wife forever" (Hos 2:14–20). "I am merciful," Yahweh insists through Jeremiah – "I will not be angry forever" (Jer 3:12; cf. Isa 54:4–8; Lam 4:22). This warped pattern is established at the very beginning of Yahweh's relationship with human-ity (e.g., after the flood, Gen 8:21–2, when he promises he will never do it again; cf. Isaiah 54:9–10), but it is most closely associated with his love/hate relationship with his chosen people that we have witnessed throughout this book: God will grow angry and punish the Israelites, but if they will return to him, "he will neither abandon you nor destroy you" (Deut 4:25–31). This, in case it slipped by, is one of the examples of God's "mercy" so often cited by the faithful. Christian apologists, eager to project a "God of love" onto the text, miss the entire cycle of brutality: "The promise that Yhwh will remarry Zion . . . [as in Isaiah 54:5] contributes to the comfort of Zion" (Abma 1999:257). Does it really?

A constant threat of destruction envelops this unhealthy relationship, a violence that Yahweh brings upon the Israelites over and over again for their disloyalty. It is perhaps understandable that he would threaten to "rape" a personified enemy like Nineveh (Nah 3:4–7) or Babylon (Isa 47:1–3), even if interpreters have often softened the translations or trivialized the context (Baumann 2003:195). But Jeru-salem is a special problem. Yahweh's masculine sense of honor has been threat-ened by his disloyal and independent spouse. God "re-established order of the gender chaos by putting his wife Jerusalem, the social body of the female, back in her place through public humiliation, gang-shame and stoning" (Kamionkowski 2003).

Given the constant abuse of his "wives," Yahweh's promise never to abandon them looks more like an ultimatum than a gesture of love. Robin Lane Fox calls Yahweh a "fond abuser" (1992:61), a gruesome oxymoron. Jack Miles suggests that "God is in the condition of a man who has beaten his wife and thrown her out of the house" but quickly discovers that he loves her, taking her back and chang-ing for the better with "an utterly new tone in his voice" (1995:243). It's not quite a "new" tone, however, but the same tone he had used in the honeymoon phase. The cycle merely starts anew. There is no final divorce from the Lord. The Israel-ites are going to need a restraining order.

But so does Hera, as we will remember. In the very first scene on Olympus in the *Iliad*, Zeus tells his spouse to "sit down in silence, and obey my word, or else the gods – as many as there are on Olympus – will be unable to keep me from coming over there when I lay my invincible hands on you" (1.565–7). Later, when Hera and Athena disobey his commands, Zeus threatens to blow them out of the sky, "and not in the revolution of ten years will they be fully healed of the wounds that my thunderbolt inflicts on them" (8.403–5). These are no idle threats – he's abused Hera before. Hephaestus, their son, tells his mother to stop quarreling with Zeus, "or I may see you, though you are dear to me, struck down before my eyes, and then, although it will grieve me, I will have no power to come to your aid" (1.587–9). When Hephaestus had tried to help Hera before, Zeus had thrown him off Olympus. Like Yahweh, Zeus uses the threat of physical punishment against his spouse and is perfectly willing to follow through. When he awakens after sex with Hera to find he has been tricked, Zeus threatens to whip her, and recalls when he bound her and hung her "among the clouds" with anvils on her feet (15.16–24).

Mythological abuse

Both Yahweh and Zeus, then, can be extremely unpleasant characters, insecure, and angry despots in the sky who mistreat their wives. Yahweh doesn't literally hit a woman or hang a goddess in chains, although his metaphorical abuse is intended to represent the hundreds of thousands of his own people – *real* men, women, and children – he sentences in fits of jealous rage to rape, slavery, or death. Mar-riage is the rhetorical vehicle for exploring the nature of the shattered covenant. The biblical authors use the imagery of spousal violence to describe the cycle of God's wrath, threats, punishment, and promises: ". . . The choice of a husband and wife metaphor to express covenant relationship is one that creates theological problems and legitimizes certain oppressive attitudes and actions that are unac-ceptable" (Dempsey 1998:7).

What is perhaps most disturbing is that this picture of a baleful God in the Tanakh is *officially* sanctioned. The image wasn't devised to insult or criticize or even invite a critique of God. Wife beating offers an analogy that the bib-lical writers thought *appropriate* for their deity. These are prophets delivering God's word – Yahweh *approves* of this characterization. It is, in essence, his self-portrait. Followers of the Bible who read these passages must conclude that this is what God is *actually like*. And the faithful are required to love, respect, obey – and model their own lives on the actions of – this deity.[5]

In stark contrast, Homer does not vouch for the gods' behavior. The Olym-pians are up for examination as much as Achilles or Odysseus or Helen. The poet often seems to portray the gods in a light designed to call their actions into question, just as Achilles comes to dismiss them as unreliable overseers of justice. Zeus looks like a bully when threatening Hera, and comes off as a dolt in his "comically self-aggrandizing attempt at seduction" (Lyons 1997:78) in the Deception Scene. His threats of physical punishment reveal his insecurities, the tenuousness of his hold on his fellow Olympians. Aphrodite and Ares are humiliated when caught having sex, naked, and trapped for all the other Olympians to see. Calypso whines like a child whose toy has been taken away when she is forced to let Odysseus leave. Apollo apparently *loses* the competition over a woman to a mortal. Circe's impressively wicked magical powers crumble and she quickly tumbles into bed with Odysseus when she is confronted by his sword (so to speak). These fallible deities are not models or guarantors of anything, as we have seen throughout this book. The poet's audience is free to laugh at Zeus's lasciviousness or endorse (at their own risk) Helen's attempted dismissal of Aphrodite. They are real gods, to be sure, but any single author's account of them provides thematic fodder and potential insights into the divine and what it represents, not inviolable truths.

It's interesting, then, to note that the *mortal* heroes (as opposed to the deities) in both the Hebrew Bible and Homer's epics are not that different when it comes to their sexual activities (although the Greeks are officially monogamous). The authors of the Tanakh are not shy about the personal lives of the patriarchs. The Israelites are certainly multiplying. (They need to keep begetting rather frantically if they are going to replenish their divinely orchestrated losses.) Abraham fathered children with three different women; he was over 137 years old when he married a teenager. Jacob wed two sisters and had a couple slave concubines to boot. David had at least seven different wives, one of them a half sister. And he infamously lusted after and committed adultery with Bathsheba, ordering her husband killed so he could marry her. Solomon, the son of David and Bathsheba, had 700 wives and 300 concubines, many from outside Israel. There is plenty of sex and sexual conflict – adulteries, false accusations, foreign liaisons, and jealousies abound. Rape texts are "common, if not ubiquitous" throughout both the prose and poetry of the Tanakh (Scholz 2010). And sex for itself is even celebrated on occasion in Near Eastern fashion. "Enjoy life with the woman you love," says Qohelet, "all the days of your vain life that are given you under the sun" (Eccl 9:9; cf. Prov 5:18–19; Deut 24:5). Thetis says something just like this to Achilles (24.128–31), and Gilgamesh receives similar advice (X.3). And then there is the Song of Songs, the most detailed exploration of human love and sexuality in the Tanakh (and one with good Near Eastern parallels). This imagistically rich poem gives voice to the passionate feelings of both a man and a woman, but – revealingly – there is no mention of God in the entire book.[6]

But sexuality in the Judeo-Christian tradition is entirely limited to the mortal world. *Eros* is something that *separates* us from the divine. Neither Yahweh nor Jesus has anything directly to do with sex. We are told Jesus ate and drank and slept and wept. He didn't laugh, he did die. Sort of. For a day or so. But the pervasive anthropomorphism in the Judeo-Christian world stops at sex.[7]

Consequences

So what are the ramifications of a sexless deity? What difference does having sexual deities ultimately make? There are at least four consequences that in total have had an immensely negative influence on Western culture.

1) With no divine sexuality, there is a complete divide between the world of the deity and ours. God's words and actions can make little direct comment on the nature of human sexuality. Seen in this light, the Tanakh is simply unhelpful in this challenging and central area of human experience.

2) Worse than being useless, if the divine is considered to be a perfect Other as well as sexless, the natural conclusion is that sex is *un*godlike. *Eros* becomes a marker of human weakness and defect that should be removed. While this antipathy is not spelled out explicitly in the Tanakh – God at least wants us to multiply – it is implied by the many taboos and impurities associated with it throughout the text. "Sexual activity brings people into a realm of experience which is *unlike* God; conversely, in order to approach God one has to leave the sexual realm" (Frymer-Kensky 1992:189, emphasis in text). Sex and God don't mix, and thus the Tanakh presents scores of purity injunctions – explicit periods of abstinence, bathing, delays, and behavior to be avoided before one can come near any arena of the sacred. (Some post-Homeric Greeks will have similar if less extensive taboos.)

This demarcation easily leads to a negative assessment of sex in general, one that blossoms in Christianity's long rejection of *eros*. In Homer's world, there is no denying the existence, the naturalness, the inherent delight, the potential danger, the power of sex. To repudiate passion would mean *spurning* the divine. The opposite is true in Christianity. Jesus has nothing to do with it, before, during, or after his birth. Paul thinks it's best if humans avoid it altogether. The Church fathers wrangled over sex, but their range of opinion was rather limited: Should sex be eliminated from human existence altogether (marriage to be forbidden) or should it be tolerated as a minor sin if performed solely for procreation, without passion, and only when absolutely necessary as a relief valve for "concupiscence"? The one good thing about marriage, the charitable ones argued, is that it produces more virgins.[8] And, of course, after 1000 years the Church cleared sex out of the priesthood. Or tried. (There was resistance and backsliding even then – it took 400 years of efforts to make it official in the 16th century.) More than just being unhelpful, sexless deities have led to an overwhelmingly pessimistic and damaging assessment of sex, one from which Western culture is still trying to emerge.

3) By limiting Yahweh's erotic energy to the ugly picture of a cuckolded and violent husband, the authors of the Tanakh not only seem to legitimize spousal violence but demonize women in general and female sexuality in particular. The metaphor "simultaneously shapes and distorts women's (sexual)

experience" (Dijk-Hemmes 1993:176). The only thing God's wife does in the Tanakh is cheat on her "loving" and "merciful" husband. A female acting independently can only be a slut like Jerusalem: "Even if an abuser does not read the Bible, he is significantly more likely than nonabusers to prefer a cultural system in which women hold a traditional, submissive role in the family, and the Bible goes far in providing the justification for this structure" (Sparks 2016:146).

We should not forget that these unfaithful cities in the Tanakh were often *divine* consorts in other Near Eastern mythologies, and that Yahweh himself once had a divine partner. The goddesses have been removed from the Bible, leaving no image of a female on the divine level, much less of an independently minded female, even much less of an independently minded female enjoying sex or playing an equal role in a sexual encounter. There are no Heras holding their own with Yahweh, no Circes or Calypsos exercising their autonomous sexuality, no Aphrodites representing the reality of human passion. True, these Homeric goddesses are constantly getting in the way of the ambitions of male gods and heroes – female sexuality has always been intimidating to males – but they are not consistently presented in an unsympathetic light. Their sheer existence as sexual goddesses – deities who cannot be ignored – is a crucial distinction.

4)   It could be that a sexless deity would just leave us mortals alone to figure it out. A useless deity is better than an obstructionist one. But Yahweh won't let us do anything on our own. He's got rules for us. Lots of rules. God without sex means that guidance on this sticky element of human nature is limited to the multitude of archaic "divine" laws and regulations in the Torah promulgated by old men in a desert over 2500 years ago. Or worse, we can rely on Christianity's distorted interpretations of these "old" tales and rules that are combined with the model of a sexless Jesus by psychologically twisted (e.g., Jerome), self-castrating (as Origen was said to be), or guilt-ridden (e.g., Augustine) authoritarians.

All archaic societies are going to have some strange ideas about sex. But the Tanakh's clueless deity is imagined to be an expert on sexual behavior! (It would be too easy to draw the parallel with Catholic priests giving marital advice, so I won't do that.) Homer's gods know better. With gods like Zeus, who would turn to the Olympians for sexual guidance of any kind? You will search the 48 books of the epics in vain to find a divinely sanctioned code of sexual behavior for mortals. But in the Judeo-Christian tradition, sexual behavior is monitored by what believers take to be a sexually inexperienced God's unalterable laws in the Tanakh and his subsequent manifestation as The (sexually inexperienced) Word in the New Testament. Consequently – and here's the real damage – the ability for society to grow, for attitudes to change, for sexuality itself to be examined and not just for sexual behavior (and women) to be severely regulated, for our sexual lives to *improve* over the centuries, is severely diminished. Cultural critique, must less change itself, becomes blasphemous, ungodly, and sinful. Satanic, if you will.

Want to consider divorce a two-way street (or a possibility at all for Christians)? You'll have to fight through God's word. Think women can have sex before marriage? The divine regulations won't budge. Understand that homosexuality is not a "lifestyle choice" and needn't be "fixed" by an LGBTQ "recovery" program? Oops – there are those biblical "proof" texts. Appreciate the tremendous benefits to *everyone* of family planning and contraception? Look what happened to Onan who "spilled his seed" (*coitus interruptus*) rather than impregnate his dead brother's wife as mandated by God. (Yahweh "put him to death," Gen 38:10.)[9] Consider sex between two (or more) consenting adults to be pretty much no one else's business? Don't be silly – violation of God's laws is punishable by stoning or, if you get away with it in this life, eternal damnation. The concepts of sexual choice, gender equality, and constructive erotic pleasure have not, and could not have, evolved from the biblical depiction of the divine or the various traditions that derive from it without flagrant misreading of the texts.

With Homer's fully sexual gods, sexuality itself is up for discussion. This doesn't mean that there aren't archaic gender roles and double standards in Homer's text (although they do not appear to be nearly as severe as they will become in the classical period). These epics also come from a patriarchal culture 3000 years ago. But the "norms" are understood to be cultural rather than divine statutes. The nature of passion and its manifestations remains open to examination and critique, as they will be in the rest of Greek and Roman literature, art, and philosophy until Christianity takes over. In the Homeric world, rules about sex, sexuality, and gender are not handed down by the gods, carved in stone in a fashion that conveniently matches the status quo. The gods are not superior to or completely disconnected from *eros* – they are as involved in and as overwhelmed by and messed up about it as we are. Even Aphrodite is engulfed by lust. The goddess of desire herself can't control her own passion. For Homer and most of the later Greeks, *eros* is a natural force represented by a deity who is just as unreliably answerable to prayers and sacrifices as any of the other gods. Try to ignore her, though, and you'll regret it. As a recalcitrant Helen learns when she tries to reject Aphrodite's strong recommendation that she have sex with Paris, you don't want to this goddess to turn on you.

In Homer's world, the erotic "rules" of the community that are designed to "control" sex – that is, to organize it so it can be as beneficial as possible and do the least amount of damage (marriage is a good example) – are understood to be just that – human conventions. There were no infallible *divine* codes in the epics making homosexuality a capital offense, no god-given laws that women everywhere *must* be subordinate (Arete, the Queen of the Phaeacians, seems at times to be as influential as her husband the king, and Penelope is more than a match for Odysseus, much less her suitors). There were community standards – in classical Athens sometimes as oppressive (if never as comprehensive) as those found in the Torah – but they could be challenged, mocked, scrutinized, and eventually – with difficulty – changed. Whatever improvement we in the West have made in gender equality and sexual openness have come from protocols first found in Homer, embedded in the Greek view of life, and reborn in the Enlightenment (Shermer 2015). We would have made progress a lot faster, and we would be a lot further down the road to a sensible understanding of gender and *eros*, if we had been living all these years with Zeus & Company rather than Yahweh & Son.

All of these detrimental products of a sexless deity still combine in today's warped and restricted views of sexuality and gender roles that are promoted by the "purity movement," especially in evangelical circles (but also found in strains of Catholicism, mainline Protestantism, Judaism, and Islam). In 1998 the Southern Baptist Convention added an Article on The Family (XVIII) to their Baptist Faith and Message that reinforced biblical tradition. This document insists that human marital relations be modeled on Jesus' figurative relationship with his church. In support of its official policy, the text cited 42 passages from the Bible – 28 of them from the Tanakh. The most deliberately atavistic thesis was the following: "The marriage relationship models the way God relates to His people. A husband is to love his wife as Christ loved the church. He has the God-given responsibility to provide for, to protect, and to lead his family. A wife is to submit herself graciously to the servant leadership of her husband even as the church willingly submits to the headship of Christ." It's not clear what "submit herself graciously" entails, but there is some evidence that the issue remains unsettled: "In one large sample of domestic violence victims, 85 percent identified themselves as 'Christian'" (Sparks 2016:146). And evangelical women are hesitant to report abuse, since they are taught from youth that whatever goes wrong in a marriage is the woman's fault. As one counselor at a Bible college advised, "If your husband beats you, you should thank Jesus for the opportunity to show your husband Christ's love by staying with him" (Klein 2018:126).

It is no coincidence that those in the West who still cling to the conviction of women's "natural" subordination, or marry off their underage daughters, or believe sex must be for procreation between a married man and woman (and often solely as the man's prerogative), are nearly always staunch followers of the Bible. And that's not counting the more mundane yet disfiguring and ubiquitous feelings of guilt, shame, distaste, and general discomfort with sex that emerged under the supervision of sexless gods and continue to haunt millions of adults. "Recovering" evangelicals (or "exvangelicals," as they also often call themselves) repeatedly decry the biblical rules, norms, and expectations of the "purity culture" that were drummed into them from birth: Women's bodies do not belong to them but to God, their father, and their husband; it is woman's job to be a submissive wife and please her husband, and become a mother (strong women "destroy" men); men cannot control themselves when it comes to sex, so women have no right to ask or expect men to try; having sex with your husband is a duty and a wife does not have the right to choose if or when; the primary job of an unmarried woman is to guard her "purity," and to fail to do so will separate her from God and ruin her chances of leading a fulfilling life. Evangelical daughters are kept in the dark about all practical details of sex. Premarital sex is shameful and a sin, they are told, but marital sex will be "pure" and "holy." (You can imagine the shock when it turns out to be messy and painful and mandatory and ultimately unsatisfying and even boring – the options for types of "appropriate" marital sex are limited.) Since this purity culture is reinforced through shame and guilt, the emotional and physical traumas deeply scar – and often permanently wound – the psyches even of those who escape the theological abuse. As Linda Kay Klein has recently documented, "evangelical Christianity's sexual purity movement is traumatizing many girls and maturing women haunted by sexual and gender-based anxiety, fear, and physical experiences that sometimes mimic the symptoms of post-traumatic stress disorder (PTSD)" (2018:8).[10] Men in this culture have equally deformed attitudes about sex and gender drilled into them as well, but they are rarely blamed when *eros* goes bad.

Tikva Frymer Krensky, writing on the disappearance of the Israelite goddesses from and its effect on the Hebrew Bible and subsequent history, is one of the few scholars to appreciate fully the long-term consequences of the depiction of sex and a sexless deity in the Tanakh, Yet even she skims over Yahweh's wife beating, as she tends to "exonerate" the Bible of the charge of patriarchy (Fuchs 2016:65–6):

> The biblical discussion of the force of sexual attraction (as opposed to sexual behavior) is inchoate and essentially inarticulate. There is no vocabulary in the Bible in which to discuss such matters, no divine image or symbolic system by which to mediate it. YHWH cannot model sex. Moreover, YHWH is not the patron of sexual behavior, and is not even recorded as the guarantor of potency; and there is no other divine figure who can serve to control or mediate this volatile, creative, and potentially chaotic force. The power of love and attraction serves as the basis for the powerful metaphor of Israel and God as wife and husband. But the Bible's lack of discussion of the dynamics and implications of sex creates a tension within the biblical system. There is a vacuum in an essential area of human concern. This vacuum was ultimately filled (in Hellenistic times) by the complex of antiwoman, anticarnal ideas that had such a large impact on the development of Western religion and civilization.
>
> (1992:197–8)

Yes, *eros* has the potential to be extremely destructive – Homer and the authors of the Tanakh agree on this. But the Tanakh and the New Testament offer nothing in their depiction of the divine that is beneficial to our continuing struggle to enjoy the benefits of desire while avoiding its pitfalls. Even as I write this concluding paragraph, the dominantly Judeo-Christian United States is swimming in a cesspool of sexual misconduct (harassment and assault) against women by men in power. Nearly two dozen women have accused the President of the United States of sexual misbehavior, a president for whom over 80 percent of white evangelicals voted. The biblical legacy of a neutered deity continues to stunt efforts to reach an enlightened attitude about *eros*. It is not and never has been *helpful* to pretend that sex is not an integral part of the cosmos or to claim that it is merely the problem of a "fallen" humanity. It is not and has never been *useful* to create a sexless deity who cares fanatically about sexual fidelity and smacks his "wife" around. It is not and never has been *constructive* to view sexuality through the cloudy lens of a "purity culture." (Roy Moore, a senatorial candidate in Alabama who in 2017 was accused of sexually harassing teenagers as young as 14, was defended by a southern pastor because Moore was merely "seeking the purity of a young woman.")[11] And nothing has been more detrimental to human psychological health and women's status than the promulgation of the divine myth of an abstinent son born from an eternally virginal mother.

Homer's rowdy, sexual gods *and goddesses* encourage us to acknowledge the reality of desire and to try to learn to deal honestly with human nature, something we paradoxically *share* with the Olympians. Flawed and hopelessly anthropomorphic, they provide a background and structure – and the space – for a frank discussion about the essential place of *eros* in a flourishing community. We certainly could have (and in sad truth have) done much worse.

Notes

1   The best example of this genre is Uta Ranke-Heinemann's *Eunuchs for the Kingdom of Heaven: Women, Sexuality, and the Catholic Church* (1990). I cannot recommend this book too highly just for the sheer amount of outrageous detail. Ranke-Heinemann, a Catholic convert, was the first woman to hold a chair of Catholic theology at a German university. In 1987 the Church withdrew her *missio canonica* (basically the official license to teach in the name of the Church).

2   The Tanakh often presents both the positive and negative sides of *human* sexual behavior in a realistic light. The debilitating Christian attitudes about *eros* frequently derive from the misogynistic *misreading* of the Hebrew text. The most influential example is the bizarre concept of original sin, the belief that the fall of the mythical Adam and Eve (often eroticized in some fashion by early Church fathers) and their "sin" have subsequently been passed on to all humanity through sexual intercourse itself. It's a powerfully magical and self-serving marketing ploy: If we're all born in sin (because our parents had sex), we are all in need of redemption. But *none of this* is in the Hebrew text of Genesis 2–3. It is not until the second century BCE at the earliest (if Sirach 25:24 refers to Eve) that the exegetical tradition finds the origin of sin in the tale of Eden – that is, at least half a millennium, if not twice that, *after* its composition – and Eve is not blamed for the "fall" before the first century CE (Fox 1992:24; Frymer-Kensky 1992:109). In fact, Eve is not mentioned at all in the rest of the Tanakh. The serpent is not Satan (much less the Devil). Eve is not sexually seduced but offered the opportunity to become like the gods. Yahweh's fear that humans may be successful is the reason, as we have seen, that he kicks them out of Eden. The forbidden fruit is not sex (or an aphrodisiac!) but wisdom (and it's not an apple either). God does not "curse" sex or sexuality or call *anything* a sin – the words for sin or sinfulness do not appear in the Hebrew text. The couple clearly has divinely approved sex – "therefore a man leaves his father and his mother and clings to his wife, and they become one flesh" (Gen 2:24) – despite the efforts of early theologians either to deny the obvious – the couple was sexless, they protest ("go forth and multiply" is . . . a *metaphor!*) – or insist that sex involved neither passion nor pleasure in paradise! Death does not enter the world with the "fall" – Adam and Eve were born mortal and were supposed to stay that way. (That's why Yahweh is so worried about their tasting the fruit of other tree, the one of *life*, although some scholars argue that the primal couple ate this fruit while in paradise and therefore were in fact immortal before they ate from the other tree. There

is no textual evidence to support this view, however.) The disobedience (the ingestion of the forbidden fruit) of Adam and Eve creates no "original sin," no taint on humanity's soul – humans in the Tanakh *do not have* souls that can be tainted. And finally, the argument of Augustine (the primary architect of this whole fiasco) that original sin originated with Adam may rest on a *mistranslation* of Paul's Greek into the faulty Latin that Augustine was working with (Fox 1992:25).

If you want to reach outside the text of the Bible for an interpretation of Genesis 2–3, how much better would Western culture have been served by adopting the humanist reading of the story as one in which Eve's actions enable us to grow up and live a human life with the potential of actually *doing* something with our existence – including having children, as I understand the text – rather than witlessly weeding God's garden. We *owe* Eve – big time.

3 Scholars argue, pointlessly it seems to me, that the blood is instead birth blood or menstrual blood (e.g., Greenberg 1983:278). Jerusalem is a teenager, a married girl with breasts and pubic hair, not a newborn baby. Both birthing and menstrual blood are notoriously unclean in the Tanakh (e.g., Lev 12:4, 5, 7; 15:19–24; 18:19; 20:18) – Yahweh's not going near that stuff. Though he mentions that he sees the abandoned baby Jerusalem "flailing about" in her blood (Ezek 16:6), he doesn't approach her physically, much less clean her up. The taboo against menstrual blood was even more fully developed by the Church fathers, terrified and repulsed as they were in general by both women and sex. Aquinas considered the mere attempt to have sex during a woman's period to be a mortal sin. Ranke-Heinemann (1990:22) quotes the following wisdom of the Franciscan Berthold of Regensburg (d. 1272): "You will have no joy from any children conceived during the menses. For they will either be afflicted by the devil, or lepers, or epileptics, or humpbacked, or blind, or crook-legged, or dumb, or idiots, or they will have heads like a mallet."

4 As S. Tamar Kamionkowski notes, the "metaphor is just a metaphor" excuse is a weak claim. Metaphors "create realities and shape our knowledge about" whatever is being compared (2003:55–6). Michael Coogan (2010:187) reminds us of the challenge of deciding what is metaphor and what isn't. Why not take Zeus's sex as merely figurative as did the allegorists? If all theology is taken as a metaphor, "and we read biblical descriptions of God's sexuality as merely metaphorical, then should we not do the same of mythological accounts of other gods as well?"

5 Scholars have invented a number of approaches for dealing with God the wife beater, in addition to simply ignoring the violence. Most of the feminist scholars who write on Yahweh's vicious treatment of his figurative wives have been theists struggling with what to do with these texts. Their occasional efforts to palliate Yahweh's savagery have been, for the most part, half-hearted. As David Carr, Professor of the Old Testament, notes, "Some [feminist scholars] have tried – unsuccessfully – to limit the damage" (2005:76). The actual solution to this "dilemma" is always just out of reach of the offended confessional scholar: This is a mythological deity constructed long ago, just like Zeus, in a brutal, patriarchal world. Should an educated modern reader base even part of his or her life on this (or any other) fictional characterization?

6 Jewish expositors, however, saw the Song of Songs as a poem celebrating the relationship not of two lovers but (metaphorically) between Israel and God, and Christians interpreted it allegorically as the love between Christ and, well, Christians: "The allegorical charade thus persisted for centuries with only sporadic protests" (Pope 1977:17). There are more Latin manuscripts of the Song of Songs extant than of any other biblical book. But when advanced scholarship in the 19th century demonstrated that the Songs of Songs is actually about the love and sexual attraction between two unmarried *humans* and not God and his people, its "great popularity plummeted" (Carr 2005:4, 119–151; cf. Pope's magisterial survey 1977:89–229).

7 Christianity knows a good metaphor when it sees one. It borrowed the marriage metaphor from the Tanakh, with the church becoming the bride of the bridegroom Christ

(Matt 9:15; Mark 2:19; Luke 5:34; John 3:29; 1 Cor 11:3; 2 Cor 11:2; Eph 5:22–33; Rev 19:7–9; 21:1–2, 8–9). Rome replaces Jerusalem and Samaria as the great "whore" committing "fornication" who will thus be made "desolate and naked"; other nations will be raised to "devour her flesh and burn her up with fire" (Rev 17:1–4, 15–18; Bowen 2010:92).

8 As has often been pointed out, over the centuries the Virgin Mary herself was periodically cleaned up and removed further and further from sex: Born immaculately (as of a papal bull in 1854 – it's not in the New Testament), impregnated virginally (a mistranslation of a prophecy in Isaiah), perpetually virginal (hymenally intact ever afterwards, even though she has several more children after Jesus who were not divinely engendered), and finally translated directly to heaven so as not be tainted by death (not in the New Testament, but made official in an "infallible" papal proclamation in 1950).

9 Onan did double duty for the Christians, as his "crime" was wrongly interpreted as masturbation and became the (only) biblical proof text against the act. The Bible says nothing about masturbation, but this didn't stop Pope Paul VI in 1975 from commenting on the "grave sin of onanism": The masturbator forfeits the love of God since it is a mortal sin, "even though," he admitted, "it is not possible to prove unequivocally that Holy Scripture expressly repudiates this sin as such" (Ranke-Heinemann 1990:313).

10 See also the 25 "lies the church told us about sex" (Carter 2017). Who else but sexually disoriented Christians could make a bestselling personal guidebook out of *I Kissed Dating Goodbye*, a fulmination by a 21-year-old, home-schooled virgin (who recently appears to have recanted)? On the other hand, Tim LaHaye (the coauthor of the *Left Behind* series) and his wife introduced a new genre, "evangelical sex guides," in 1976 with the *Act of Marriage*. And some evangelicals are now seeking sexual advice filtered through scripture on Christian sites on the internet (Burke's 2016).

11 Or to cite even more direct biblical precedent for Moore's assaulting teenage girls, the Alabama State Auditor Jim Zeigler brought up Jesus himself: "Take Joseph and Mary. Mary was a teenager and Joseph was an adult carpenter. They became parents of Jesus. There's just nothing immoral or illegal here. Maybe just a little bit unusual." Does he think Moore's dates were going to be inseminated by the Holy Spirit? More troubling is an elected official's apparent belief that Semitic social customs of 2000 years ago in the Middle East are the arbiters of what is "moral" or "legal" – if a "little bit unusual" – today in the U.S.

16 Conclusion

First, a quick review. We have seen that Yahweh in the Tanakh is often depicted very much like the Homeric gods. He's fallibly anthropomorphic (and generally disagreeable) in temperament and can be conceived of as having a physical nature. And like Zeus, he's CEO of a heavenly empire (that on occasion even includes his "sons" if no longer his wife). That seems well established and uncontroversial, except that much of Judeo-Christian commentary over the past two millennia has attempted to explain away his Olympian nature. Some of these efforts were already in full swing in the later traditions of the Tanakh itself (e.g., Genesis 1). Jewish and Christian exegetes advanced the cause by imposing divine perfections on the textually imperfect Yahweh, finally trying to suppress his fiery personality by smothering it with a blanket of metaphor. Western culture has been saddled with this theologically distorted divinity, leaving theists unable to accept, explain, or provide useful guidance for dealing with the basic realities of human existence.

And that's where Homer's delinquent deities shine through, their limited powers and polytheistic partisanship offering readers a more candid and healthy depiction of the universe. Fictional deities *can* be stimulants to helpful reflection – they just need to be the *right* fictional deities.

The universe depicted by Homer and populated by his gods is one that creates a unique and powerful responsibility for humans to discover ethical norms for themselves. Whatever justice we find on this earth will be our own creation.

Our mortality is not something that can or should be wished away with daydreams of a posthumous paradise, for it supplies a necessary limit that makes a meaningful life possible. We have one shot, a single opportunity to flourish – let's not waste it.

However the universe came into being, it was not created for us. Its patent indifference to our existence and the obvious imperfections in our "creation" reveal a randomness we must accept if we are to organize our lives in a way that is to make any difference at all.

Sex is an evolutionary, biological response, and how we deal with it makes a huge difference to our moral, psychological, and physical well-being. The myth of a sexless god (who produces a sexless son) has been an overall disaster for Western culture, especially for women. We need to jettison that entire mythology and deal directly and honestly with the delights and dangers of sex.

The heroic response to these realities is not despair but a compassion for our fellow living beings and a passion to *do* something with the years we have been given. Most of us will not have elaborate monuments erected by the community upon our deaths, and even fewer (I suspect) will be immortalized in epic poetry – so what *will* we do to etch a memory of our time here on earth?

That, in a nutshell, has been our journey. Let me conclude by addressing three obvious but as yet unstated assumptions that underlie my argument.

1) A life of self-examination, critical thought, thoughtful compassion, and joyous exploration within a community of relatively open-minded individuals is *by its very nature superior* to one that accepts the mandates concerning morality, mortality, gender roles, sex – and tales about the origins of humans and the solar system – from a 3000-year-old mythology and its myriad of interpretative traditions. (I told you these were obvious.)

2) The great unsolvable mystery for theists, answerable by most forms of polytheism, is unnecessary suffering. Theodicy – "the, or a, vindication of the divine attributes, esp. justice and holiness, in respect to the existence of evil" (*OED*) – is a fiasco. In short, we have the complete failure of explanations or justifications of the immeasurably unwarranted amount of natural evil, especially in the form of disease and disaster, in a world supposedly created as "very good" and governed by the Abrahamic God of divine perfections. It has been estimated that since humans appeared, "the number of infants and older children who died before maturity probably exceeds 50 billion, or at least half the total born" (Paul 2009b:128), most from horrendous diseases, billions from malaria alone. The various efforts at defending God have all been crushed by such philosophical refutations as the "evidential argument from evil" and "inductive arguments from evil" (Martin 1990:334–452; Martin and Monnier 2003:59–124; Tooley in Plantinga and Tooley 2008:97–146; Tooley 2015). Theists have been reduced to blaming "free will" (for your friend's Huntington's disease?) or arguing that God left evil in the world for some unfathomable "greater good" (the tornado was an omnipotent God's only way to make the world as good as it is?) or that anencephalic babies and animals dying in a drought are an essential part of God's plan to help *us* to improve. The tendentious arguments along the lines of theologians Richard Swinburne and John Hick – that a child's brain tumor is their God's way of developing character, of "soul-making" *for the rest of us* – I find to be morally disreputable. But at least these desperate conjectures are (unwittingly) consistent with the nasty and frequently immoral nature of the biblical deity.

In the end, the honest theist gives up, throwing a Hail Mary (or the Protestant equivalent) to the power of prayer (e.g., Fretheim 2010) or just admitting defeat: "The traditional speculative solution to this problem [suffering] by way of universal theodicy – that is, by way of some justification of God in the face of the evil of our world – transcends the limits of human reason" (Kaiser 2000:74). Most merely fall back into the comforts of myth: "The ultimate solution to the problem of evil must lie in the fact that the God who created the world is also the God who has redeemed it. . . . But only the Christian can know that Christ has explained evil in the act of defeating it" (Richardson 1983:193–6). This is no help at all, but at least it's ingenuous and not obfuscated by labored efforts to convince nonbelievers. Christian apologist Christopher J.H. Wright spends three chapters in his confessional book, *The God I Don't Understand,* hacking through the problem of natural evil, rejecting (as many fundamentalists do not) theories centered on God's curse or judgment. He comes up with three possible theistic solutions: (1) suffering in natural disasters is often greatly compounded by human sin; (2) there is a "mysteriousness about evil that we simply cannot understand (and it is good that we cannot)"; (3) the Bible (that is, Christianity) "allows us to lament, protest, and be angry." Of course, these answers would leave us all with an Olympian world where (1) we mess up, (2) it's usually unclear – although that's never really "good" – why terrible things happen, and (3) we respond in some authentically human fashion. Wright has no stomach for that possibility: "But if that were all, life would be bleak and depressing in the extreme, and faith would be nothing but gritting our teeth in the face of unexplained and unrelieved suffering" (2008:55). Rather than dealing frankly with these realities, or viewing life as a challenge to *address* the causes of suffering, he slides back down into the warm and sudsy pool of (non-Homeric) divine mythology: "Thankfully the Bible has a lot more to say to lift our hearts with hope and certainty." His final "answer" is that though life may indeed be filled with inexplicable suffering and we don't know why, it will *all become clear when Christ establishes his kingdom*: "The cross and resurrection of Christ accomplished it [redeemed reality and defeated all evil forever] in history and guarantee it for all eternity. In such hope we can rejoice with incomparable joy and total confidence" (2008:56–72). "Hope" and "certainty" and "guarantees" and "joy" and "total confidence" in the Truth of one carefully selected ancient myth – these are not arguments but a psychological panic room. I find all such suppositions not only unconvincing but irrelevant, a cosmic cop-out, a childish refusal or inability to accept life as it as rather than as one might wish it to be.

3) Ultimately, this book on ancient gods argues for the superiority of a non-theistic view of the world. Living in a world of Homer's Olympians, for all practical purposes, would be the same as living in a world with no gods at all. I view *all* gods I have run across so far as creative fictions. I am neither proud of nor embarrassed by this admission, although it does mean that I am prohibited from holding public office in seven southern states and Pennsylvania. With this public disclosure, I will now have to add "governor of Tennessee" to my ever-growing list of personal ambitions that will probably not come to fruition (the top two of which presently are to become a Supreme Court justice and the Dalai Lama).

Now what to call this nontheistic viewpoint? Agnosticism is a nebulous term, sort of "atheism lite" for the uncommitted. Agnosticism as I understand it is an epistemological opt-out rather than a true alternative to theism and atheism. An agnostic stakes his or her claim on the *impossibility of knowledge* about God (Smith 1974; cf. Cliteur 2010:60–3). As Bertrand Russell admitted in the midst of his explanation of why he considered himself to be an agnostic rather than an atheist, "an agnostic may think the Christian God as improbable as the Olympians; in that case he is, for practical purposes, at one with the atheists" (1992:577; cf. Grayling 2013:57–63). Amen.

Atheism has nearly as many different branches as theism, although these many alternatives have recently been organized into a culturally canonical "seven" types (Gray 2018). But there are two basic camps. Some atheists *believe* that there is no God, that God does not exist, and they have adduced "proofs" of God's nonexistence or extreme unlikelihood. (e.g., Stenger 2008; Martin and Monnier 2003). Other atheists, however, negate the verb – they *do not believe* that God exists, that there are any supernatural beings of any sort. Put this way, then, "atheism is the absence of theistic belief" (Smith 1974). The key here is *absence*. As many atheists have pointed out, they don't believe in trolls either because no one has ever produced any cogent evidence for trolls; that makes them atrollists. Thus to claim that atheism is a matter of "faith" or "religion" or "superstition," as theists often do (e.g., Hedges 2009), is to stretch the words beyond any useful definitions. As Paul Cliteur deftly notes, "atheism is no more a religion than not playing chess is a hobby" (2010:17). *A*theism does not have the burden of proof.

On the other hand, many recent critics of theism admit that the term "atheist" may now be too negative and easily misconstrued – and carry too much baggage – to be useful. It's a counter label, which is always a weak self-definition and immediately puts advocates on the defensive (like "pro-choice," which can never be as ear-catching as "pro-life"). "Secular humanist" embraces a positive and agreeable agenda, but it's slightly clunky and perhaps a bit overly confident. Michael Shermer's "skeptic" is opportune – a "skeptic simply does not believe a knowledge claim until sufficient evidence is presented to reject the null hypothesis (that a knowledge claim is not true until proven otherwise)" (2011:176) – but it may not be quite focused enough on the "god problem." "Freethinker" is redolent of a different century; "brights," a comparatively new coinage for someone holding naturalist worldviews, is counter-productive and, well, slightly (and no doubt intentionally) annoying. Zuckerman's "aweist" nicely emphasizes the positive side of a "godless" existence, but it's a bit too emotionally gleeful for me. So what *is* the best term for the modern consequences of living in Homer's world?

I don't have a better designation for individuals, but I think that "tragic vision" is a wonderfully rich expression for this view of life. (I use the term "tragic vision" without adopting all the political implications sometimes attached to it, e.g., Sowell 2007; Pinker 2002:287–96.) For me, the most powerful exploration of the human condition is to be found in the *Greek* tragic vision. I am grateful for an adult life spent with these Greeks, with Thucydides' unflinching gaze into human nature, Euripides' harsh critique both of the gods and of mortal efforts to rein in the chaos, and Sophocles' great-souled protagonists rising above their self-inflicted destinies with heroic dignity. And on top of that tragic vision pyramid sits Homer, especially his *Iliad*, for reasons I hope to have made clear in this book.

We inhabit an indifferent universe that constantly surprises me with what appears to be (but of course is not) a marvelously dark sense of humor. My relatively low expectations of my fellow humans are often happily tempered by the remarkable exceptions. My frequent delight in the wonders of this world is framed and sharpened by an awareness of the empty palette of mortal existence – what some philosophers call the "normative human predicament" (Taylor 2013) – and the responsibility that this undetermined, fragile, and one-time opportunity puts on us all. "Tragic" in the world of Homer is the antithesis of "depressing" or "oppressive"; instead, it demands a constant effort to push back against the universe, to insist to ourselves and each other that we *do* matter, that we *can* make a difference. It reveals our limits and challenges us to go down swinging. The Greek tragic vision signals a view of life that is honest and (on good days) inspiring – and yes, when we gain a temporary victory (and *every* victory is temporary), even ennobling. Homer's Olympians make such human endeavors possible – indeed, mandatory. What more could we want from our gods?

Appendices

Appendix 1

Short summaries of the *Iliad* and *Odyssey*

The *Iliad*. The epic begins in the tenth year of the Trojan War; that is, as the Roman poet Horace famously put it, Homer "snatches the listener into the middle of things [*in medias res*], just as though they were already known" (*A.P.* 148–9). Homer expects his audience to be familiar with the basic background to the conflict, alluding frequently but rarely at any length to earlier and later parts of the saga. The Greeks assumed that the Trojan War was a historical fact, the universal event that marked the last time gods and heroes mingled with any regularity and thus the beginning of their own "human" history. This "mythical" period lasted only a couple of generations, a brief moment when the gods participated openly in human affairs. We know of many variants and offshoots of the Trojan story, so we are often uncertain which traditions lie behind the action of the poem. But we won't go too far wrong if we assume the following events (not all mentioned explicitly in the epics).

The problems begin when the goddess Eris (Strife or Discord) stirs up, well, strife at the wedding of the Greek hero Peleus and his Nereid (immortal sea nymph) wife Thetis. Late accounts claim that Eris threw an apple inscribed "to the fairest" into the crowd. Three goddesses – Hera, Athena, and Aphrodite – claim the apple. Zeus is much too experienced to get personally involved in such a thorny matter – no good can result from unnecessarily aggravating (again) his wife, alienating Athena (his daughter and favorite), or turning the goddess of sexual passion against him. He announces that Paris, a shepherd and son of King Priam of Troy – a non-Greek (but, conveniently, Greek-speaking) city on the Hellespont (Dardanelles) in modern-day Turkey – would make the decision. Homer alludes to this Judgment of Paris a bit cryptically in the last book of the epic, and it probably explains the hatred Athena and Hera feel for Troy and Aphrodite. Each goddess bribes Paris in order to gain victory in the beauty contest, but the winning gift comes from Aphrodite – she promises Paris the most beautiful (that is, sexually attractive) woman in the world, Helen of Sparta.

Helen, unfortunately for Troy, is already married to Menelaus, King of Sparta. Paris sails to Greece and with Aphrodite's help seduces Helen and the two of them sail back to Troy. Menelaus turns to his brother, Agamemnon of Mycenae, the most powerful king in Greece, for help in restoring his wife and thus his honor. They gather a great fleet at Aulis to sail to Troy to reclaim Helen and the possessions she took with her. In some later accounts we hear that all the original suitors of Helen had vowed to come to the aid of her eventual husband should something like this occur, but Homer ignores this motivation. The poet wants his heroes risking their lives for fame and glory, not because they are duty-bound by a former oath. Before they sail from Aulis to Troy, Zeus sends a portent that is interpreted to mean that they will sack the city in the tenth year of war. Homer seems to leave out any direct reference to one infamous prewar act, Agamemnon's sacrifice of his daughter Iphigenia to soothe the anger of the goddess Artemis.

There are numerous other episodes involving the preparations for, journey to, and first nine years of the war, but the *Iliad* begins with a famous quarrel between two great Greek kings: Agamemnon, the nominal leader of the expedition because of his wealth and power, and Achilles, son of Peleus and Thetis (don't ask how he got to be old enough to fight so fast after the wedding), the greatest warrior in the world. After being compelled to stop an Apollo-sent plague by returning one of his war prizes, a female captive, Agamemnon dishonors and thus shames Achilles by taking away one of his "trophies," *his* favorite female captive. This is one of the many ways Homer replays the larger tale of Helen's abduction. Giving in to his anger – the first word of the epic and the driving force of Achilles' story – Achilles thinks of killing Agamemnon, but Hera and Athena (fervid supporters of the Greek side) intervene. Achilles withdraws from battle, pressing his divine mother to call in a favor from Zeus and aid the Trojan side so Agamemnon will come to see his great folly in dishonoring the "best of the Achaeans." Zeus reluctantly yields to Thetis' request, knowing that Hera and Athena will be even more difficult to deal with. But the first book ends with the gods partying on Olympus, after which Zeus and Hera retire to bed. The human quarrel that drives the entire plot will result in the deaths of nearly all the major characters including Achilles at some point shortly after the *Iliad* ends; the divine bickering doesn't change a thing.

The *Iliad*, a brilliantly tragic twist on the traditional tale of a hero's withdrawal, the destructive consequences, and his eventual victorious return, surprisingly presents only four days of actual battle, although the epic covers nearly two months of material. The major players for Troy are King Priam and his extensive family (he has numerous wives and many, many offspring) – his "primary" wife, Hecuba, sons Paris, Helenus, and Hector, Hector's wife Andomache, and various allies, especially Aeneas, a cousin of Hector, and the Lycian Sarpedon. In Achilles' absence (he does not enter battle until Book 21), other Greek heroes take their turns leading the fight, among the most prominent Diomedes, Ajax, Odysseus, Agamemnon, and Menelaus.

Many of the Olympians get involved in the action at some point. Athena and Hera break up a potential truce that could end the war before their hated Troy is leveled. Throughout the epic, they, along with Poseidon, do whatever they can to support the Greeks. Sometimes this is with Zeus's permission; more often, they give surreptitious aid. Apollo successfully sustains the Trojans until Hector is summoned to his fate, going so far as to rescue various Trojan warriors on the brink of death. Aphrodite, too, saves Paris from certain destruction and tries to rescue her son Aeneas as well. (She is wounded by Diomedes with Athena's help, as is the unpopular Ares.) Zeus bullies and blusters and threatens the other gods, struggling to bend them to his will so he can fulfill his promise to Thetis. He mostly succeeds, watching and controlling the action from up above.

As the Trojans under Hector's leadership and Zeus's (mostly) attentive eye become increasingly successful, capturing the plain for the first time in ten years and bringing the fight towards the Greek ships, Agamemnon relents and sends an embassy to Achilles to entice him back to war. Achilles refuses Agamemnon's generous offer of gifts – a turning point in the epic – but eventually allows his closest friend, Patroclus, to enter into battle to drive off the Trojans once they start to set fire to the Greek ships. Patroclus dons Achilles' armor and successfully pushes the Trojans away from the ships and back to the city, killing Sarpedon, the son of Zeus. But in his eagerness Patroclus ignores Achilles' warning to avoid attacking Troy, and he is knocked defenseless by Apollo, stabbed by a random Trojan, and finished off by Hector, who puts on Achilles' armor.

When Achilles learns of his friend's death, he goes berserk with guilt and anger. Gifted with new armor made by Hephaestus and brought to him by Thetis, he enters battle for the first time in the epic, slaughtering so many Trojans in his search for Hector that the Scamander river is clogged with corpses and tries to drown him. The inevitable duel between Hector and Achilles may strike the modern reader as rigged and a bit anticlimactic, since Athena tricks Hector into facing the rampaging Greek and gives Achilles material aid. Achilles kills Hector with a spear stab to the neck, and then ties the corpse to his chariot. He spends nearly two weeks dragging Hector's body around the Trojan plain whenever his anguished spirit moves him.

The highlight of the poem comes in the final book, after Patroclus' funeral, when King Priam is guided by the gods to Achilles' tent in order to ask for the release of his son's body in return for a handsome ransom. Achilles, warned by the gods, relents, and in his subsequent conversation with Priam over dinner reveals a new and profound awareness of the tragic nature of mortal existence. It is this moment of existential crisis, insight into the absence of divine justice, unanticipated compassion for the still-hated enemy, and glimpse into the limitations and potential dignity of the human condition that has formed the foundation of so many outstanding discussions of Homer's humanism over the past 50 years. It is a moment lost on most college freshmen, alas. The poem ends, just like the movie *Troy*, with the lamentation for and burial of Hector, "tamer of horses." Unlike in the movie, however, no coins are placed on Hector's eyes, as a system of coinage was not invented in the area for another 500 years.

The *Odyssey*. This romantic tale tends to be the more familiar epic, a favorite of high school AP classes and English professors (lots of gender issues, class distinctions, narratological subtleties, and general "otherness" here, as well as cool witches and monsters). Odysseus' wild adventures were also easily allegorized and thus made palatable to Christian intellectuals and educators over the centuries. There are obvious good guys and bad guys, and the plot is fairly straightforward, even if the structure of the poem is remarkably sophisticated. The Olympian gods play a much less important role than in the *Iliad*, however, so for our purposes the *Odyssey* is the less informative text. The epic recounts the ten-year struggle of Odysseus, a man noted for his speaking skills, endurance, adaptability, and "cunning intelligence," to return home from Troy and reestablish himself as a husband, father, son, and king on the island of Ithaca.

The opening scene takes place on Olympus, with Athena complaining to Zeus that a good and just hero, Odysseus, has been struggling for ten years to return home after the Trojan War. Zeus agrees to her immediate intervention, especially since Poseidon, who has been working hard to prevent Odysseus' homecoming, is away at a feast. Athena sets the wheels in motion, visiting Odysseus' home in disguise in order to spur his son, Telemachus, into some sort of maturing action. For at least the past three years the palace has been forced to entertain 108 suitors of Penelope (Odysseus' wife), local nobles who figure after a couple decades Penelope should move on and choose a new husband. They wouldn't mind becoming king, either, although exactly what the transfer of power on Ithaca has to do with Penelope (or Telemachus) has been the subject of debate. The suitors are illicitly camped out, eating up the palace's food and demonstrating they are villains by abusing the law of hospitality. The *Odyssey* is a moral epic, focusing on the rights and obligations of guests, strangers, and hosts. Good guys welcome guests and feed them; bad guys eat other people's food and detain their visitors . . . and some of them even eat their guests. Telemachus visits two of Odysseus' war buddies, the aged Nestor in Pylos and Menelaus (along with a seemingly contrite Helen) in Sparta, from whom he (and we) learns a bit about his long-absent father, and he thus begins his delayed journey to adulthood.

As for Odysseus himself, he doesn't appear in the poem directly until the fifth book of twenty-four. Zeus dispatches Hermes to Calypso's island, where the hero has been stuck for the past seven years, having sex with the goddess by night, pining for Penelope during the day while turning down Calypso's offer of immortality. Odysseus wants desperately to return home, and Hermes tells Calypso to let him go, which she reluctantly agrees to do. Odysseus builds a raft and sails across the sea before Poseidon returns from the feast, spots him, and shipwrecks him one last time. Washing up naked on the shores of the hospitable Phaeacians, Odysseus cleverly negotiates his way through the princess Nausicaä to the palace of her parents, King Alcinoüs and Queen Arete. Over a very, *very* long dinner he relates the celebrated "apologue," his fantastical adventures up to his arrival at Calypso's island. This is the part of Homer with which most people are familiar. Odysseus encounters such now-famous mythological characters and places as the Land of the Lotus Eaters (where ingestion of the lotus makes one forget home), Polyphemus the Cyclops (a cannibalistic son of Poseidon whose blinding provokes the sea-god's hostility), Circe the witch (who turns Odysseus' men into pigs), Hades (Odysseus visits the dead), the Sirens, Scylla, and Charybdis, and the cattle of Helius. It is during these adventures that he loses his 12 ships and all his men as result of bad luck and their own folly (and occasionally his).

With the help of the generous Phaeacians, Odysseus finally returns home unbeknownst to anyone but the gods. Athena meets him on the beach, and the two like-minded characters hatch a plot of revenge. Disguised as a beggar, Odysseus spends the next nine books scoping out the status of his palace and testing the loyalty of his family and slaves. He carefully maneuvers through a series of "recognition" scenes while dodging stools and chunks of animals hurled at him by the ruffian suitors. Telemachus, after finally meeting his father for the first time, proves worthy of his genealogy. A couple loyal servants join Team Odysseus. The disguised Odysseus strings his bow, and with Athena's aid they kill the suitors. Penelope has an intriguing meeting with the "beggar" before the slaughter – scholars still debate the degree to which, if any, she suspects that her husband has returned – and after the fight proves to be an appropriately clever match for her clever husband. By the end of the epic, the hero is successfully reunited with his wife, son, and father. His kingship is reaffirmed by both Athena and Zeus himself, and he seems to be ready to put his martial, Bronze Age life in the past after one more proposed adventure to appease Poseidon. Everything is looking good for Odysseus' future, even though his dog died the moment the aged, derelict hound spotted his long-absent master. It's heartrending; even Odysseus sheds a tear.

Appendix 2

Who are the Homeric gods?

As is to be expected in an ancient Near Eastern setting and with an Indo-European background, it all starts with the patriarchal **Zeus**. Forty percent of all references to Olympian gods in Homer are to Zeus (Dowden 2007:45). The son of the Titans Cronus and Rhea, he rules over his extended family, and the entire divine world, by force. Though "all-wise," a "counselor," "crafty," and with a generally accurate foreknowledge of what lies in store for some mortals, it is through his strength and threats of violence that he attempts to control his fractious kin. As a combination of a sky- and weather-god (his name bears the Indo-European root for "bright" or "shining"), he wields a weapon of the storm, the thunderbolt. He is also called the "aegis-holder" more than 50 times in the epics. His most common attributes are associated with his meteorological nature ("cloud-gathering," "loud-thundering," "of the dark clouds," "of the dazzling bolt," etc.). But he's happy to use his hands to get his point across as well, flinging refractory deities from Olympus and admitting that he has assaulted his wife and would be willing to do it again.

Zeus is often portrayed as king, sitting on a throne surrounded by an assembly of relatives. He can simply be called "The Olympian," a regal appellation, and both the political and juridical authority of kings is said to derive from him. Still, he needs his alone time and slips off to some mountainous height either on Olympus or near Troy to reflect and become an audience of the epic activity, most of which is in some fashion driven by his decisions. He never visits humans himself in Homer's poems, but watches events unfold from a distance and attempts to manipulate mortal business through intermediaries (messengers, dreams, oracles, omens, prophecies) and his own force of will. His relationship to fate is complicated and dealt with poetically rather than philosophically. He is sometimes called upon or claimed by humans to protect suppliants, to look after strangers (especially guests), and to oversee some sort of human justice. Whether he fulfills these roles is a question addressed in Chapter 13 and Appendices 3 and 4. Although not literally the "father of men and gods," it often seems that way. In Homer, he is the father or sibling of every other major Olympian. Zeus has also engendered numerous mortals (e.g., Heracles, Helen, Sarpedon, Dardanus).

Hera boasts that she is *both* sibling *and* spouse of Zeus, an Appalachian vaunt that can make a modern audience a bit queasy. But this is a common combination in Near Eastern mythology, one that Greek culture itself did not adopt. Hera's primary function in the *Iliad* is to oppose Zeus's improvised plan to aid the Trojans. She does not appear as an actor in the narrative of the *Odyssey*, mentioned only 7 times versus 121 in the *Iliad*. A rabid supporter of the Greeks, primarily, it seems, because of her pathological hatred of Troy after her loss in the apple-of-discord contest, she works on her own and with various allies (Athena and Poseidon in particular) to crush the Trojans. The depth of her animus towards Troy startles even Zeus. In fairness, her conflicts with her spouse may derive in part from his long history of infidelity.

Hera and Zeus have several children together. Ares and Hephaestus become "proper" Olympians, whereas their sister **Hebe**, the embodiment of immortal youth, is relegated to household tasks like pouring nectar, putting the wheels on Hera's chariot, and washing Ares. (Well, *someone* has to do it.) In the *Odyssey* she has been married off to Heracles in what looks like an effort to mark a reconciliation between the feuding parents. Hera is also the mother of the Eileithyiae, goddesses of childbirth, whom she directs to delay the birth of Heracles in one of her efforts to undermine Zeus and torment his heroic bastard (19.114–24). In later cult and worship Hera is a marriage goddess (although she is not usually associated directly with motherhood), but the *Iliad* leaves little room for this manifestation of her character – she's just too busy trying to wipe out Troy.

Hephaestus, the smith god, is called "little club foot" or "crooked-footed" and "lame." He was apparently born with deformed legs or weakness in some part of his lower limbs, for as he recalls with understandable bitterness, he was thrown off of Olympus "by the will of my shameless mother, who wished to hide me because I was lame" (18.395–7). He was saved by the sea nymph Thetis, Achilles' mother, and was reconciled with Hera long before the Trojan War begins. Hephaestus' father, Zeus, also tossed him to earth because he had attempted to intervene on his mother's behalf during one of their altercations (*Il.* 1.590–4; cf. 15.21–4). Childrearing on Olympus gives a whole new meaning to bickering parents "dropping off the kids." Hephaestus' primary task in the epics is to create marvelous and beautiful works like Achilles' shield, Agamemnon's scepter, and the golden urn in which the ashes of Achilles and Patroclus are to be buried. He is called "maker of famous works" and "renowned artificer," although on occasion he can be fire itself. One could argue that Hephaestus' weak legs must not detract too much from the Olympian sense of attractiveness, since in the *Iliad* he is married to "beautiful Charis of the gleaming veil." Aphrodite herself is his spouse in the *Odyssey*, although he catches her having sex with Ares.

Even his own father, Zeus, wants little to do with the bloodthirsty **Ares**. Ares is labeled "man-slaughtering," "blood-stained," "causing many tears," "insatiate of battle," and "hateful." His most common epithet – applied to him alone – is "man-destroying"; the root of his name probably means "to destroy." He is sometimes accompanied in battle by Terror, Rout, and Strife, personifications that reinforce Ares' negative characterization. Although often seemingly little more than personified abstractions, Terror and Rout also come to life as Ares' entourage on Olympus, where they yoke his horses. In one episode he is accompanied by a goddess of war, Enyo, "the sacker of cities" (5.333, 592). Zeus snarls that Ares is "the most hateful to me of the gods who hold Olympus," claiming that the war-god has inherited a violent personality, an "ungovernable, unyielding spirit," from his *mother* (5.890–3). Ares' lone close familial relationship appears to be with his half-sister Aphrodite, since they aid each other when they are injured in battle and are pinned together in Hephaestus' trap when caught having an illicit affair in the *Odyssey*. His name can be used metonymically for "battle"; there is no scene in which he is attractively portrayed. Ares is the only god personally to kill a human on the battlefield, to strip the dead for trophies, or to have switched sides. Homer doesn't seem to like this war-god, depicting him as wounded twice, once by the mortal Diomedes with Athena's help, Hera's approval, and Zeus's explicit permission. He's knocked out by Athena, much to his own mother's delight (21.391–414).

The wounded Ares complains to Zeus of his favoritism, wrongly (but not *that* wrongly) accusing his father of never opposing **Athena**, "for *you* brought forth this thoughtless maiden, destructive . . . since you yourself brought forth your destructive daughter" (5.875–80). This has long been seen as an allusion to the tale of Athena's birth directly out of Zeus's head, although the manner of her delivery is never spelled out in Homer. Athena is an ally of Hera in her staunch support of the Greek cause, probably for the same seedy reason. Athena nevertheless enjoys an especially close relationship with Zeus and has been the supporter of his favorite son and Hera's bête noire, Heracles. Known as Pallas Athena (the significance of Pallas is debated), she frequently carries her father's aegis. She is the sole deity to play a dominant role in the narrative action of both the *Iliad* and *Odyssey*. Odysseus is only slightly exaggerating when he tells Telemachus that Zeus and Athena rule both mankind and the immortal gods (*Od.* 16:264–5). Also a war deity who can be called "destructive," she is far more often associated with what the culture finds positive in war: A giver of "booty," "most glorious," "rouser of armies," "full of counsel," and "city-rescuing." Ironically—and unhappily for the Trojans, who have a temple for her on their citadel—both the Greeks and Trojans turn to her for help in the war.

Athena prides herself on her cleverness, claiming that she is renowned "among all the gods for cunning wisdom (*mêtis*) and shrewd counsel" (*Od.*13.298–9). She is the sponsor of those who have "civilizing" domestic skills such as weaving, metalwork, ship-building, and carpentry, although all of these activities can also be used in deceptive or destructive fashion (e.g., Penelope's weaving, a 1000-ship armada, the Trojan horse). Thus, while she is a famed supporter of many Greek heroes (e.g., Heracles, Achilles, Diomedes, Agamemnon), it is the wily Odysseus for whom she is particularly well suited. Her support of the Ithacan king begins in the *Iliad*, both on the battlefield and in counsel, and is on full display in the *Odyssey*. She instigates Odysseus' return home in two meetings with her father, and from the first scene through the last she sees to the safety of all the members of his family, as well as to the punishment of the suitors. Still, she has her limits. She will not work directly against Poseidon, waiting for his absence at a feast to get things rolling for Odysseus. (For that matter, Zeus doesn't want to anger his brother either.)

Artemis, Aphrodite, Apollo, and Hermes are all Olympians also acknowledged in the epics as the children of Zeus by various goddesses. **Artemis**, along with her brother Apollo, is the daughter of Leto, a cousin of Zeus's called the "wife" (or "bedmate") of Zeus (*Od.* 11.580). Artemis is a virginal archer-huntress who slays women, a petulant sister, and a feeble fighter verbally taunted and physically humiliated by Hera in her only major appearance in the Homeric narratives. Women's sudden deaths are attributed to the goddess's arrows. When the king of Calydon gave the first fruits to every deity *except* Artemis – "whether he forgot or did not notice" – she sends a wild boar to devastate his orchards (9.533–42). The *Odyssey* celebrates Artemis' beauty in several similes. The scene in which the Phaeacian princess Nausicaä is compared to Artemis as she joyfully hunts in the mountains with her nymphs, taller and more beautiful even than her comrades (*Od.* 6.102–9), became the model for depictions of Artemis in later literature and iconography.

Her brother **Apollo**, on the other hand, plays a major role in the *Iliad* as the only Olympian on the side of the Trojans to be treated consistently with dignity. He plays no role in the narrative of the *Odyssey*, but this archer god does have sacred groves in Thrace and outside Ithaca proper, where the people gather for a festival shortly before Odysseus shoots down the suitors. He is known by a wide variety of epithets and is connected with numerous aspects of life (and transitions in life). His most common epithet is Phoebus, a term of debated significance (it means "radiant") that is often used by itself in place of his name, probably for metrical convenience as much as anything. He is *not* a sun god in Homer. Most of his epithets refer to his talents with the bow, e.g., "of the silver bow," "working from afar," "far-darting," "famed for the bow." Within the first 50 verses of the *Iliad* his arrows are showering a plague down upon mules, dogs, and finally the Greeks themselves, a crisis precipitating the crucial confrontation between Achilles and Agamemnon that drives the plot of the entire epic. Archers receive their talents from him as a "gift," and he supports and punishes archers throughout the texts.

Although both Apollo and Poseidon were cheated of their pay when they were commanded by Zeus to serve the king of Troy for a year, Apollo remains by far the most prominent supporter of the Trojan side, both on the battlefield and in counsel. He saves Hector from Achilles and flies Aeneas out of battle, taking the injury-prone hero to his temple on the citadel of Troy to be healed. His slap on the back of Patroclus, Achilles' closest friend who is taking his place in battle, is so vicious that the borrowed armor flies completely off and Patroclus is left as easy pickings for the Trojans. Apollo does not appear in his traditional role as a healer in the poems, as there is an actual divine physician, Paean, who tends to some of the wounded gods such as Ares and Hades. Apollo preserves Hector's body from the abuse of time and Achilles' anger, and Achilles is told several times – once by the dying Hector and once by his horse(!) – that Apollo will play the key role in his death at Troy. Apollo strums his lyre and no doubt sings at the feast of the gods on Olympus in the first book of the *Iliad*. His famous oracular shrine at Delphi and sanctuary on Delos are familiar to the poet, although his control of prophecy, probably his most important function in later Greek religion, is virtually confined to his role as "giver of the gift of prophecy" to mortal seers.

Curiously, and perhaps a bit awkwardly, the polyamorous Zeus shares Olympus not just with Hera but with a few divine former lovers as well. Or perhaps even current lovers. We only hear about Ganymede, the "most handsome of mortal men," whom the gods took up to Olympus "so he might be among the immortals" and be "cupbearer" for Zeus (20.231–5). Zeus pays off his father with some horses, a good deal for everyone. The erotic overtones are subtle in Homer's account. Some would argue they are nonexistent, as Homer makes no overt references to homosexuality and we never see the youth in person. Hebe and Hephaestus, not Ganymede, pour nectar for the Olympians in the *Iliad*. (The Olympians drink, but they don't get drunk like some Near Eastern deities.)

Apollo and Artemis are the children of **Leto**, who is not an "official" Olympian but nevertheless makes a couple of odd appearances in the *Iliad*. She shows up in the infamous theomachy in which the gods are to duke it out amongst themselves. Leto faces Hermes, who graciously declines to fight (20.72; 21.497–501). She then picks up Artemis' bow and arrows that the archer goddess had dropped when slapped around in her own pathetic duel against Hera. Leto finally "went back" – but to where? The grammar is difficult here, and it could mean that she in fact went "after her daughter" to Olympus (Richardson 1993:96). The *Homeric Hymn to Apollo* tells us that Hera tried to prevent Leto from giving birth "out of jealousy" (3.100), a story that classicist Richard Janko argues was "surely familiar to Homer" (1992:204).

Dione, the mother by Zeus of Aphrodite (who has a more exotic birth tale in other authors), is definitely hanging out on Olympus. Her name is merely the feminine form of Zeus. She is rarely Zeus's consort in later mythology, although the two are closely linked historically at the prophetic shrine of Dodona, a site Homer mentions. When Aphrodite is wounded in battle, she races back to Olympus and flings herself into Dione's lap (5.370–417). Dione soothes her whining daughter and stops the pain with a simple swipe of the hand. As this scene reveals, Homer doesn't hesitate to point out that **Aphrodite**, the goddess of beauty and overpowering sexual passion, seems out of place in the martial epic. When she tries to rescue her wounded son Aeneas from battle she is pierced through the wrist by Diomedes' spear. Athena and Hera mock her pain, and Zeus smiles at his "golden" daughter and reminds her that "the works of war are not given to you, my child; instead, attend to the ardent works of marriage, and all these things [on the battlefield] will be of concern to swift Ares and Athena" (5.428–30). In the theomachy, when Aphrodite tries to help the semiconscious Ares leave the field of battle, Hera tells Athena to go after "the dog fly." Athena proceeds to smack Aphrodite on the breast so violently that the poor goddess is knocked to the "all-nourishing earth" (21.415–33). The animus is real, since Aphrodite is another love child of Zeus who not only supports Troy but was the winner of the apple of discord and aided Paris' seduction of Helen. Yet Hera turns to Aphrodite for sartorial assistance when it comes time to seduce Zeus. Aphrodite loans her some sort of decorated strap (an embroidered girdle?), a love charm that inspires sex, desire, love talk, and persuasion.

Aphrodite is said to anoint herself with "beauty" itself – a unique use of the word to indicate a divine facial scrub (*Od.* 18.192–4) – when she "goes to the lovely dance of the Graces." The **Graces** symbolize feminine beauty and we are told that they attend Aphrodite, bathing her and giving her perfumes at her sanctuary in Paphos on Cyprus and weaving a garment (*peplos*) for her. But they don't appear in this role in the narrative of the epics, and only one, the wife of Hephaestus in the *Iliad*, has anything to say (four verses). Hera promises one as a wife to Sleep as a bribe for supporting her plot against Zeus. Aphrodite's most impressive appearance is with her mortal doppelgänger, Helen, after the goddess saves Paris in his ill-conceived duel with Menelaus. It is Helen's sexual attractiveness that makes her a "prize" worth fighting for, a system of value Homer challenges by (among other things) basing the plot of the *Iliad* on the dispute between Achilles and Agamemnon over the former's favorite female trophy.

Zeus has one other significant offspring, **Hermes**, although his mother Maia (*Od.* 14.435) never appears in the epics. Hermes, a popular and multifaceted "trickster" god in the post-Homeric world, is provided limited opportunities to strut his stuff in the epics. A god of liminality – that is, a boundary- or threshold-crosser – his only significant task in the *Iliad* is to conduct Priam, the elderly king of Troy, safely through the Greek camp to Achilles' tent and then nudge him to leave. In addition to his flying sandals, he has a magic wand "with which he enchants to sleep the eyes of those whom he wishes, while on the other hand some he wakes even when they are sleeping" (24.343–4). Although ostensibly on the Greek side (15.214), his sole appearance on the battlefield is in the theomachy in which he artfully declines to fight Leto, apparently having little interest in traditional forms of glory. His notoriety as a god of thieves is downplayed in the *Iliad*, sneaking through only in a tale of the ancient past (5.390–1) and when some of the gods take pity on Hector's abused corpse and urge him to steal it away. He doesn't. Odysseus' maternal grandfather, Autolycus, "surpassed men in thievery and in the slippery oath," and it was "Hermes himself" who gave him this ability (*Od.* 19.394–97). Hermes' most popular epithet, Argeiphontes, *may* mean "dog-slayer" (if it does not refer to one of his non-Homeric myths). A protector of shepherds in both poems, he serves as Zeus's messenger god in the *Odyssey*. He shows up on the islands of both Circe and Calypso (to the latter's great annoyance) to facilitate Odysseus' safe return. In one passage Hermes fulfills his famous role as *psychopompos*, the deity who leads the dead down to Hades, the ultimate threshold. He and Apollo seem to have a fraternal (fraternity?) bond. In the tale of Hephaestus' snaring of his adulterous wife, the two share a joke about the delights of being "trapped" in bed with Aphrodite.

Zeus has another divine son, the fascinating Dionysus, whose mother is the mortal Semele. He does not appear *in propria persona* in the epics. There are a handful of references to him, which cumulatively indicate the poet's familiarity with many of the characteristics associated with the god in later cult and literature, e.g., his youth, "mania," cult-followers (a band of women brandishing improvised weapons), the rejection of his godhood and ultimate punishment of the offender. Homer made no room for this peculiar and nonaristocratic god of ecstasy, epiphany, and "otherness." The poet does not even associate Dionysus with his most familiar function as a god of wine despite the ubiquity of the beverage in the poems.

According to the epic poet Hesiod, Zeus had five full siblings, but besides Hera, **Poseidon** is the only other child of Cronus and Rhea to have an active role in the epics. Having been cheated out of his pay for building the walls of Troy, he bears a grudge almost as unyielding as those of Hera and Athena. And like Hera, in the *Iliad* he resents Zeus's tactless authority, working secretly and occasionally openly against Zeus's commands on behalf of the Greeks. Although his most frequent epithets probably refer in some fashion to his function as a god of earthquakes (and perhaps a sexual relationship with Earth, e.g., "Earth-shaker"), his control of the seas and association with horses are more central to his character in the epics. Richard Martin (2016:84) has recently argued that Poseidon is more accurately seen as the god of the *interaction between* the sea and land, representing the threat of collision. Despite a fervid antipathy toward Troy, Poseidon can sometimes see the bigger picture that the other divine combatants cannot. Once, much to Hera's disgust, he even rescues the Trojan Aeneas from certain death in order to ensure that "the lineage of Dardanus may not perish without offspring and leaving no trace" in accordance with fate (20.293–339). In the *Odyssey*, on the other hand, Poseidon behaves more like the Iliadic Hera. His unrelenting anger at Odysseus for blinding his son, the Cyclops Polyphemus, serves as the primary cause of the hero's inability to return home. Zeus and Athena both respect Poseidon and fear his reaction sufficiently to feel it necessary to wait a very long time for the sea-god's absence before bringing any aid. At Odysseus' successful return to Ithaca, Poseidon takes out his vengeance on his own favored community of seamen, the Phaeacians, whose hyperhospitality had led them to escort the wanderer home.

Hestia, traditionally one of the original six children of Cronus and Rhea, is never mentioned in the epics. Demeter, another of Zeus's sisters (and lovers), is also missing from the narrative, as are almost all the chthonic (earth) deities and references to hero cult, also associated with the ground. Perhaps they were not "aristocratic" enough; maybe Homer simply didn't need them for his story. It has been suggested that as benefactors of all humanity they couldn't easily be squeezed into the partisan lineup of deities in the Trojan War (Rutherford 2013:47), although Homer finds a place for the usually uninspiring Dione and Leto. At any rate, Demeter's role presiding over agriculture, especially grain, is acknowledged in a simile and in the expression "grain of Demeter" for bread, and she has a sacred precinct. We hear that Zeus once hurled a thunderbolt at her mortal lover as they were having sex (sympathetic fertility magic) in "a thrice-plowed fallow field" – the imagery is mind-boggling. She is no doubt the mother by Zeus of **Persephone**, the "dread" queen of the underworld. The famous story of Persephone's rape and forced marriage to Zeus's third brother, Hades – the cause of her traditional part-time residence in the underworld – is also left out of the poems, but she got her gig in the world of the dead *somehow*.

Hades himself is called "inexorable and intractable, and therefore he is the most despicable of all the gods to mortals" (9.158–9). Ruler of the underworld, he is rarely mentioned by humans for obvious reasons, but he is not diabolical.

Most of the references are instead to the "house of" Hades, the location generally under the earth where the ghosts of the dead reside. He is not a proper Olympian either, since he spends no appreciable time above ground and never appears in the action of the poems. We are told, however, that he was once shot in the shoulder by Heracles, and in order to be healed by Paean, he had to go "to the house of Zeus and high Olympus, grieving in his heart, transfixed with pain" (5.395–402). Even divine physicians don't make house calls to Hades.

There are other, less important deities scurrying about Olympus on business. The **Horae**, for example – usually translated as the "Seasons" or "Hours" – have the strange function of tending the gates of Olympus, which seem to open and shut on their own anyway. They also unyoke Hera's horses, tether them to their "ambrosial manger," and put away her chariot, apparently sharing the transportational duties with Hebe. Or maybe the task just falls to whoever happens to be around and suits the poet's needs. Even Poseidon unyokes Zeus's horses at one point, and Zeus himself is capable of both yoking and unyoking his own chariot. Their parentage goes unmentioned, but in Hesiod they are the children of Zeus and Themis. **Themis**, a sister of the Titans, is in fact also floating around Homer's Olympus, although there is no reference to her former sexual relationship with the king of the gods. Her singular task in the epics is to summon the gods to Zeus's assembly, the word *themis* – usually meaning "law" or "custom" – once referring to the human assembly itself (a "place of assembly," 11.807–8).

The **Muses**, more offspring of Zeus, are specifically labeled "Olympian" and "those holding dwellings on Olympus." They sing with a "sweet voice" at the festivities at the end of the first book of the *Iliad*, and, if you can trust a ghost, the dead Agamemnon tells us that "all nine" sang at Achilles' funeral (*Od.* 24.60–1). Despite this sole reference to "nine" – Homer supplies no names – the epics refer to the singular Muse or plural Muses indiscriminately. They "give" singers their ability and just as easily take it away when abused. Homer calls on the Muse at the beginning of both poems and at crucial other moments in the narrative, asking as much for information that validates the truth of his verse as for general inspiration. **Iris** is the messenger on Olympus in the *Iliad* (Hermes takes over this role in the *Odyssey*), carrying the words of Zeus and of other deities as the narrative requires to both gods and mortals. All of her major epithets refer to her function and speed. She retains a bit of the color her name ("rainbow") adumbrates, on several occasions supplementing and redirecting her message to fit a changing context. And she must have a will of her own, since she shows up unbidden several times pursuing what appears to be her own agenda.

By far the most important non-Olympian deity in the *Iliad* is **Thetis**, the Nereid mother of Achilles. A goddess married off to a mortal hero, Peleus, she embodies and propels many of the central themes of the epic. She is a cosmically important deity but also a non-Olympian lightweight who suffers immeasurably (Slatkin 1991). **Calypso** is another nymph, "immortal and ageless" like the Olympians (*Od.* 5.218). Her immortality, like that of Thetis, brings the stark division of gods and humans into tragic reality. She and the sorceress **Circe**, both labeled "a dread goddess of human speech," are part of the exotically divine and monstrous (and often female) "otherworld" – Sirens, Scylla, and Charybdis, etc. – that Odysseus must negotiate in his return to a fully human and mortal existence after the war.

Finally, there are the divine heavenly bodies and occasional personifications. **Helius**, the sun, has some cattle of which he is very fond, or was, before Odysseus' last surviving men foolishly ate some of them and so brought about their own destruction. The dawn (Eos) is famously "rosy-fingered" and sleeps beside a mortal lover, but she does not have a place in the epic narrative. The winds can be divine or nonpersonified storm-winds. The rivers attend an Olympian assembly, and the main Trojan river **Scamander** (known as Xanthus to the gods), another child of Zeus, actually goes toe to toe against Achilles and nearly drowns him. **Oceanus**, a river that is generally thought to flow around the edges of the earth, "from whom all rivers flow and the whole sea, and all the springs and deep wells" (21.196–7), is called the "origin of the gods" (14.201) and "the origin for all" (14.246 – for all *what* is a matter of debate). We have already met the personified abstractions Terror (Phobos), Rout (Deimos), Strife (Eris) and Sleep (Hypnos). Sleep's brother is Death (Thanatos) – the two of them transport Sarpedon's body to his home in Lycia for burial. Dream (Oneiros) has a brief but crucial role in delivering deceptive news from Zeus to Agamemnon to get the god's "plan" off the ground. And both Prayers (*Litai*) and Irrational Folly (*Atê*) come to life in allegorical fables.

There are numerous other gods, immortal monsters, and nymphs drifting through the epics. A nymph in the poems can refer to either a young mortal woman or a minor goddess. The divine sort is usually associated with a place or aspect of nature (rivers, meadows, springs, trees, caves, mountains, the sea). A *Homeric Hymn* tells us that mountain nymphs can have long lives and eat "ambrosial" food, but their souls depart with the death of their trees (*HHymn* 5.257–72); Homer's nymphs appear to be immortal, have altars, and receive regular cultic attention. Helius' cattle, however, are said to be immortal, and yet that apparently does not mean they can't be killed and eaten, even if their flesh continues to low. One senses that Homer makes these things up as he goes along. Achilles' immortal horses do not appear to be vulnerable, however, thus providing another tragic contrast to the hero's own looming death, a fate one of those very horses tells him about.

Appendix 3

Iliadic justice: Making sense of the Trojan War

To attempt to demonstrate the absence of something is almost pointless. The best we can do is address arguments that have been adduced to support a claim. If they don't hold up, it's fair to assume the case has not (yet) been made. Let's now turn to four strands of argument made by proponents of divine justice in the *Iliad*. (In this limited space, I have focused on what I consider to be the strongest claims for divine justice, but not every argument can be addressed here, including those that primarily redefine justice.)

(1) If, as we have seen in Chapter 13, Paris' adultery provides no support for the Olympian interest in justice, could it be that the Trojans as a whole deserve divine punishment because some of them have been morally slimy *in the past*? This is a very common argument found in arguments for Iliadic divine justice: The eventual (post-Iliadic) destruction of Troy is brought about by the gods (especially Zeus) because of a previous (pre-Iliadic) history of Trojan duplicity. It is undeniable that several Trojans in addition to Paris have acted unjustly. And it is also true that Troy will fall to the Greeks at some point in the future. As we have seen, critics can't resist drawing a line between these two events. But there is no textual support for this kind of "inherited guilt" anywhere in the epics. As common as it was in the Near East (witness the Tanakh and later Greek literature), neither the poet nor the gods in the Homeric epics ever state that someone is being punished for the crimes of his (or her) ancestors or community history. Heroes wish, pray, and hope that the children of their enemies will suffer for some personal injury, but the poet never draws a connection between that expectation and any subsequent action. Even that consolation – the good are suffering at least for *some* reason – is absent from Homer's world.

But let's get to the specifics. Paris, we learn, had bribed Antimachus, a Trojan leader, to reject Menelaus' initial request (before the war began) to return Helen. According to Agamemnon, Antimachus had even encouraged the Trojans to kill Menelaus on the spot (11.122–42). Aren't *all* Trojans therefore tarred by this brush?

Well, no, at least not as far as the gods are concerned. This episode tells us a lot about the nastiness of Antimachus but also something about the Trojans – they did *not* accept this outrageous advice. But perhaps all the Trojans pay the price for morally corrupt leadership? Communal punishment for an individual's crime is a common Near Eastern motif. As for the fate of the Trojans, however, there is no supporting evidence from the poem. There are no divine consequences as far as we are told to Antimachus' evil counsel. The gods didn't even notice. Homer is happy on other occasions to show us corporate punishment for a leader's direct violation of the *god's* prerogatives. The *Iliad* begins with a plague delivered to all the Greeks because of Agamemnon's unwise rejection of a suppliant priest of Apollo. There, too, the Greeks disagreed with a leader's actions, but they still paid for his actions. But the poet *shows us* the entire causal chain, putting in plain view Apollo attacking the Greeks. Homer says nothing about the consequences of Antimachus' bad behavior, however. If you want to find some sort of "poetic justice" in connection with Antimachus, it is purely on the human plane and has nothing to do with the gods. Agamemnon subsequently slaughters two of Antimachus' sons in battle, and a third is killed shortly later. If you are preconditioned to believe that evildoers will be punished by the gods, then of course you can see *any* human disaster as the work of the divine. That logic may satisfy the contemporary religionist as well – Christian commentators frequently claim that the wildfires that have ravaged California recently are punishments of our immoral state – but Homer shows the gods in action, so we can usually tell when he wants us to draw a connection, and none is made here.

Even further in the past are the dishonest deeds of Laomedon, former king of Troy and father of Priam. We learn that he cheated both the gods and Heracles out of hard-earned rewards, and so, proponents of divine justice suggest, Troy is about to get what it (implicitly) deserves under the firm hand of justice-seeking gods. But once again when we look at the details, there is no connection made in the text between these events and Troy's eventual fate. Laomedon's offense and its consequences were clearly known to Homer's audience. Various pieces of the story are related in three different books of the *Iliad* by three different characters and the poet. Poseidon reminds Apollo how they had been mistreated by Laomedon. Forced by Zeus to serve the king for a year "at a fixed wage," Poseidon built the city walls and Apollo herded the cattle. Yet when it came time to pay the gods, Laomedon defrauded them, refusing to pay and threatening to bind them, lop off their ears, and sell them abroad (21.441–60). In retribution, Poseidon sent a sea monster to wreak havoc on Troy (20.144–8). Laomedon is told the only way to appease the monster is to surrender his daughter to it. (This part is missing from Homer's account, but it is clear that something very much like this is to be supplied.) Heracles arrives and agrees to save Laomedon's daughter in return for the king's immortal horses. After Heracles defeats the monster, however, Laomedon once again reneges on his promise to pay. Heracles then "laid waste the city of Ilion and made desolate its streets" (5.638–52).

Some scholars insist that divine punishment for Laomedon's behavior will come (again) with a second sacking of Troy. Divine justice works on a different time scale, we are told, but there is justice nevertheless. Troy will be destroyed in the future because of a former king's unjust acts. After all, isn't Poseidon still a driving force behind the Greeks? First, let's just get this out there: At no point in the text does any character, much less Homer or the gods themselves, link the coming destruction of Troy with Laomedon. Laomedon was already punished – twice – for his acts. The second story of crime and punishment, that of refusing to pay Heracles and the resulting first sack of Troy, is a simple tale of heroic vengeance of a slight to a hero's honor. Heracles attacks Laomedon's city and takes the king's horses. Story over, as far as Homer reveals. (Later texts tell us that Laomedon was killed during the sack, and that Heracles gave the king's sister to his comrade, Telamon.) There is no need to evoke divine justice – the gods aren't even involved. Once again, humans have taken care of things directly.

And as far as the first story of Laomedon's crime and punishment is concerned, Poseidon has already brought a sea monster against Troy. True, he clearly continues to bear a grudge, encouraging Apollo to hate Troy as much as he does, but Apollo doesn't bite. In fact, Apollo famously *supports* Troy. There's no concept of justice at play here. It's a personal slight to Poseidon, *not* a form of abstract divine justice in which the god punishes the king for mistreating another human. Poseidon's honor has been challenged and he can't forgive Troy. (One could add that Poseidon has recently grown "enraged in his heart" with the Trojans because his grandson has been killed by Hector, 13.206–7.) The episode has nothing to do with how mortals behave towards each other, which is the crucial point about divine justice. Poseidon isn't upset with Troy because Laomedon defrauded his own people; he's out to make Troy pay for his personal dishonor, for defrauding *him*. We know that if you challenge or mistreat or ignore a god, you will pay, and pay quickly (e.g., 2.594–600; 6.130–40; 24.602–17).[1] And there is often collateral damage. Laomedon is a creep, and a really, really dumb one at that. But he (and his people) pay for it immediately, and it's ancient history. If the Homeric gods are upset, or care, they act. I can't think of any group less likely to choose the delayed gratification of inherited guilt or postmortem torment over immediate, satisfying reprisal. When that doesn't happen in the text, there is no reason to believe it happens later.

(2) If past misdemeanors don't warrant the destruction of Troy, what about the Trojan treachery in the action of the poem itself: Doesn't Zeus himself "implicitly" indicate his approval of the destruction of Troy for such behavior? This third variant of "the Trojans have it coming" at least focuses partly on action within the epic but falls victim to the same errors upon which the other arguments have rested, namely, failing to distinguish between what the characters say and what the poet reveals about the gods, and concluding that the eventual fall of Troy proves that the gods punish moral failure.

The key episode here is the breaking of an oath by the Trojan Pandarus, the only broken oath in the *Iliad*. The Greeks and Trojans have sworn a "great oath" by Zeus, the Sun, and various other deities that the winner of the duel between Menelaus and Paris will take Helen and "all her treasure." If Menelaus wins, the Trojans will also pay proper recompense; if Paris wins, the Greeks will depart (3.264–291). As they pray to the gods, both the Greeks and Trojans add:

> Zeus, most glorious, most great, and you other immortal gods, whichever side first violates their oaths, may their brains stream out on the ground just

like this wine, both their own and their children's, and may their wives be
mastered by other men.

(3.298–301)

The troops *hope* that Zeus Horkios, Zeus of the Oath, will bring divine oversight
to human pledges, but Homer warns us that they will be disappointed: "The son of
Cronus did in no way bring this to fulfillment for them" (3.302).[2] The duel com-
mences, and as we have seen, just as Menelaus is about to drag Paris off and win
"boundless glory," Aphrodite sweeps her favorite away to have sex with Helen.
Menelaus scours the field for his missing rival, whom, Homer tells us, the Trojans
would gladly have handed over. Finally Agamemnon declares Menelaus the victor, and "the rest of the Achaeans approved" (3.461).

Thereupon comes a crucial scene on Olympus, what classicist Pietro Pucci
has called the "dark comedy of mockery" (2002:29). Zeus first taunts Hera and
Athena for their lack of support of Menelaus. Then, to provoke Hera with even
more "mocking words," he suggests it is time to deliberate what to do next. Menelaus is the clear winner, so should the gods renew the battle or end the war, cast-
ing "friendship among both [armies]," so then "the city of king Priam might be
inhabited, and Menelaus might lead back home Argive Helen again" (4.1–19)?
Although Zeus's motives are a bit cloudy – is he merely annoying his willful
spouse, or is he manipulating her into doing what he wants her to do? – it is
clear that he can't really want the war to end if he is going to follow through on
his promise to Thetis to make the war go so badly for the Greeks that they come
crawling back to Achilles.

Athena and Hera are outraged at the possibility of even deliberating the question. In response to Hera's angry denunciation of the mere suggestion that Troy
be spared – all her sweat and toil in conjuring up "an evil for Priam and his sons"
would be in vain – Zeus yields and gives her what he himself probably wanted all
along, namely, more fighting. No divine justice has been spotted yet, and things
only get uglier. Zeus quickly agrees with Hera's suggestion that he "most quickly
command Athena to go into the dread din of battle of the Trojans and Achaeans,
and try to arrange it so that the Trojans first against their oaths begin to work harm
on the triumphant Achaeans" (4.64–72). He "speeds on Athena," who enters the
Trojan troops in disguise and persuades the Trojan archer Pandarus to shoot at
Menelaus in order to "win thanks and glory from all the Trojans" (4.95). Pandarus
vows a sacrifice to Apollo (who had given him his bow) and lets fly the arrow,
which Athena then nudges aside "as when a mother keeps a fly from her child
when he lies in sweet sleep." The arrow strikes Menelaus but only grazes him.
Agamemnon now provides the gospel for proponents of divine justice, complaining about the Trojan violation of their oaths:

Yet in no way is an oath fruitless, and the blood of lambs and the pure libations and pledges of faith which we trusted. For even if the Olympian does
not fulfill them immediately, he will fulfill them thoroughly if long after-
ward, and they will atone greatly with their own lives and those of their

wives and children. For I know this well in my mind and heart: a day will come at some point when holy Ilion is destroyed, and Priam, and the people of Priam of the good ash spear; and Zeus, son of Cronus, enthroned up high, dwelling in the heavens, will himself brandish against all of them his grim aegis in anger for this deception.

(4.158–68)

This is the faith of the pious, heroes trusting that Zeus is the protector of oaths and that he will punish those who violate them. Agamemnon repeats his claim a few minutes later (4.234–9), as does another Greek leader (4.269–71). Menelaus had similar misguided faith in Zeus as both the guardian of oaths (3.104–7) and the protector of the guest-host relationship. Later in battle he accuses the Trojans of lacking neither outrage nor insult, "with which you have done outrage to me, you treacherous bitches. And you did not fear at all in your heart the severe wrath of loud-thundering Zeus, the god of hospitality, who will some day utterly lay waste your high city" (13.622–5).

But as Irene de Jong observes with some understatement in her commentary on the *Odyssey*, "In the Homeric epics there is often a discrepancy between the faith which mortal characters have in the justice of the gods and the actual behavior of those gods" (2001:249). Agamemnon and Menelaus – and some classical scholars – so want to believe in divine justice that they find it exactly where we are shown it doesn't apply, in the gods' eventual destruction of Troy.[3] Even classicist Renaud Gagné, who argues that this mortal expectation that the breakers of the great oath "will atone greatly with their own lives and those of their wives and children" provides the "only explicit attestation of something like ancestral fault in Homer," must ultimately concede: "The theme of the generational oath plays little more than a minor role in the larger economy of the poem. . . . [It is] a latent theme. The fall of Troy in the *Iliad* ultimately remains a 'tragic' event beyond human understanding. Beyond rare hints of order, the world of the *Iliad* ultimately remains opaque" (2013:179–80, 198).[4]

Mortals look to Zeus, guardian of oaths, to punish the Trojans for violating the oath. After all, Homer tells us that the gods do care about oaths between themselves, with Hera swearing by Earth, Heaven, and the "down-flowing water of Styx, which is the greatest and most dreaded oath for the blessed gods" (15.36–8; cf. 2.755; 14.271). But Zeus is never presented to us as bothered in the slightest by the abrogation of the mortal oath. How could he be? *It is Zeus himself* who takes Hera's advice and commands Athena to see to it that the oath is broken! Heroes may *believe* in Zeus's concern for justice – the suppliants' plea is *felt* to impose a moral obligation, especially in the *Odyssey* (Crotty 1994:133–4) – but Homer goes out of his way to show us that Zeus is no more the guarantor of oaths than he is of the guest-host relationship. Or of suppliants (Zeus Hiketesios). In the *Iliad*, there are no successful supplications in the battle narrative. Every suppliant is butchered on the spot without any specified negative consequences for the killer. Characters keep making their final appeals, even if, as one classical scholar understatedly concludes, the "prevailing prospect for suppliants in the *Iliad* is gloomy"

(Pedrick 1982:132). (We do hear of several Trojans whom Achilles had spared in the past in return for ransom, but these stories are presented to contrast with current realities.) Yet we never hear of Zeus riding in to protect the suppliants; not once is the killer of a defenseless warrior punished for his act. Zeus never even makes a comment.

"Justice" in this case is once again limited to the human plane in the eventual death in battle of Pandarus, whose crime was advocated by Athena in disguise. By Homeric standards, he is still responsible for his actions, and he pays the ultimate price in the battle that his own actions renewed, but hardly as a piece of *divine* justice. He is slain by Diomedes shortly afterwards with a spear guided by . . . wait for it . . . Athena (5.290–96)! If this is divine justice, it is lusciously perverse! Pandarus is the gods' dupe, a Trojan chosen by Athena no doubt for his archery skills and eagerness to be a "hero." Neither the poet nor any character suggests that Pandarus' death has any connection with his breaking the truce.[5]

Yet proponents of divine justice insist that Zeus's moral approval of the destruction of Troy is implied since he is both aware of and intends to see through the city's ultimate fate. He lays out for Hera the major episodes of the war: Hector's *aristeia*, Patroclus' slaying of Sarpedon and his own death at the hands of Hector. And after that Zeus will "engineer a constant and unceasing rally of the Achaeans from the ships, to the point where the Achaeans capture steep Ilion through the plans of Athena" (15.49–75). It is impossible for me to see how this foreknowledge suggests that "Zeus's desire that Troy should fall (15.69–71) is predicated upon his belief that it is right" (Allan 2006:7). There is no indication here or anywhere in the epic that Zeus "desires" to see Troy fall, much less that he believes it is "right." Zeus hardly desires to see Troy fall at all. If anything, he is angry at its necessary fate. Yes, he knows Troy will fall – and this time we know his knowledge is accurate, although his predictions are not always correct (Morrison 1992). His plan to aid the Trojans fits into the story of Troy's demise over which he has a general control, but he never utters a single word that suggests he thinks Troy deserves that fate. When he acquiesces to Hera's hatred of Troy and agrees to renew the war, he suggests bitterly that perhaps only if she were to "enter inside the gates and the high walls and to devour Priam raw and the sons of Priam and all the Trojans besides, then perhaps you might heal your anger." *Hera* (with Athena and Poseidon) is the one who "desires" and works tirelessly for the demolition of Troy: "Hera's rage, arising, as we finally discover, from a trivial slight to her beauty, is a permanent, demonic imbalance with neither noble origin nor foreseeable end" (O'Brien 1993:83). Homer makes this distinction painfully clear in the scene. As for Zeus, he has yielded to his seething spouse "with an *unwilling* heart":

> For of all the cities of men on earth under the sun and starry heaven that men inhabit, of these holy Ilion, along with Priam and the people of Priam of the good ash spear, has continuously been especially honored in my heart. For never was my altar lacking in a fair feast, the libation, and the savor of burnt offering; for we [gods] receive this as our prerogative.

(4.44–9)

We again are missing any direct evidence (rather than the heroes' hopes) that Zeus is associated with justice and that he thinks Troy's destruction will be justly deserved.[6] All Homer gives us is a Zeus who knows that Troy is doomed and wishes otherwise because they have provided him with his due share of sacrifices, the "privilege" of the gods. Zeus's only direct comments about Troy are about its *piety* (as he defines it). He never mentions Paris, Laomedon, Antimachus, or even Pandarus. So upset is he at Troy's doom that he tells Hera that if he gives up Troy to her anger, then when he chooses to "lay waste a city myself" that happens to be dear to Hera, she should remember this and not get in his way. That sounds like a god who would much prefer that his dearest city – a city favored for its devotion rather than abandoned for its crimes – not be destroyed (4.31–56). Classicist Martin Mueller summarizes the issue nicely: "The poet of the *Iliad* does not justify the ways of God to men, but he shows the gods in their bewildering contradictions as guarantors of the logic of events. That is a theodicy of sorts, and by claiming less it may be truer to the facts of our experience" (1984:147).[7]

Looking to Zeus

(3) Some scholars argue that Zeus oversees human justice because of his connection with kings, who are said by several characters to "guard" or "fulfill" *themistes*, the long-established human laws or customs (1.238–9; 9.156 = 9.298). Achilles refers to "*themistes* from Zeus" when angrily announcing to Agamemnon that he is withdrawing from battle because of the king's selfish ruling. These few references to the expectations of rulers are an abstract vision of kingship at its best – note the context in which Achilles raises the issue, contrasting the ideal with the reality – but we don't see kings acting consistently in any way we would associate with justice. Sarpedon, a Trojan ally, is said by his cousin to have "protected Lycia with his judgments and strength" (16.542), but as we've observed, Zeus supports him not because of his "just" rule (which he never mentions) but because he is his son. Again, humans and gods look at the world differently. Most of the Greek warriors are kings, and *none* is described specifically as acting justly by the poet. Kings are associated with power and honor, not exemplary behavior. In fact, the two most "regal" individuals in the epic are *decidedly unkingly* if this is supposed to mean acting with justice in the best interest of their people. Agamemnon's rejection of Apollo's priest and dishonoring of Achilles are his most influential actions in the epic (although there has been a misguided trend in some recent scholarship to try to "rehabilitate" his reputation). And Priam never mentions Paris' role in his city's suffering (although Hector and other Trojans do), doesn't blame Helen – or himself – but the gods, allows Helen to remain even after the duel, and doesn't respond in any way when Pandarus breaks the oath and thus ends the truce. As Jasper Griffin observes, "But above all, it is in being irresponsible and arbitrary that kings resemble gods" (1980:88–9).

Laws and customs are ultimately human and under human control. For example, on Achilles' shield, Hephaestus depicts a vigorous arbitration between two men, the crowd cheering as they each speak in turn, with a prize of gold set out "to give to the one who among them declares the straightest judgment" (18.497–508;

exactly who is to get the award for what is unclear). It is the gods' unpredictability and *lack* of justice that will drive the Greek political world of man-made laws and philosophical ethics rather than divine commands.

There is no definitive connection in the epic between Zeus and humans, kings or otherwise, because of justice. There is one passage in which the poet tells us that Zeus turns his gaze from the battle at the ships to look over the land of the Thracian horsemen, Mysians, "and of the illustrious Hippemolgi who live on milk, and of the Abii, the most just men" (13.1–6). Occasionally a scholar will oddly conclude that Zeus's absorption with the Abii is *because* they are the "most just of men." This won't do. Classicist Van Erp Taalman Kip's rejoinder to this line of argument is unassailable: "If we infer from 13.4–7 that Zeus is interested in the Abioi because of their justice, we must, I am afraid, also infer that he is interested in the Hippemolgoi because of their milk drinking" (2000:395).

(4) Finally, a few scholars who are understandably impressed by some of the gods' concern for the burial of Hector in the final book wrongly conclude that this has something to do with divine justice. Achilles is madly dragging Hector's body around Patroclus' funeral mound three times each morning, trying to disfigure the corpse. Apollo, ever the defender of all things Trojan, protects the body from corruption, and eventually many of the other gods also begin to pity the dead hero. Some of them even propose having Hermes steal the body and return it to Troy, but Hera, Athena, and Poseidon resist. Apollo launches into a lengthy remonstration, pointing out that Achilles is acting savagely, without pity or shame: "Let him take care that we not grow justly angry with him, noble though he is; for he insults the dull earth in his anger" (24.53–4). Apollo's concern may go beyond his mere support of Troy – he is the god most closely associated with burial rites in the epic, as in his oversight of the burial of Sarpedon. His accusation feels like it has ethical overtones. What Achilles is doing is not *right* in some way. However, the god does not claim that Achilles is acting *unjustly* but rather that his anger has gone beyond mortal limits. Achilles is behaving not as a human but as an animal ("like a lion," Apollo says) – and a god. To draw this connection, Homer immediately depicts Hera's angry response to Apollo's speech – by no means do Achilles, "the child of a goddess," and Hector, a mere "mortal," deserve the same honor.

More significantly, Apollo's appeal to his fellow gods lands in quite familiar divine territory: "Did Hector then never burn for you the thighs of bulls and goats without blemish?" (24.33–4). And when Zeus steps in to settle the matter, his solution is based not upon some interest in human justice but on this same system of reciprocity:

> Hera, do not be so indignant at the gods, for their honor will not be the same; but Hector too was most dear to the gods of all mortals who are in Ilion. For so he was to me at least, since in no way did he fail to offer pleasing gifts. For never was my altar lacking a fair feast, neither a libation nor the savor of a sacrifice; for we gods received this as our prerogative.

> (24.65–70)

Thetis is summoned, and Zeus commands her to advise Achilles to release the body since the gods and especially Zeus are angry that the corpse has not been returned. Moreover, Achilles will receive gifts from Priam for the body. Once again, we find no reference at all to any kind of divine justice as we would understand it; instead, reciprocity forms the heart of the exchange. Iris is dispatched to convince Priam that it is safe for him to come ransom his son's body. The grieving father naturally expects Hector's body after all this time and abuse to have been completely ravaged, but when he learns that it has been preserved, he understands the gods' motives, as should we:

> Truly it is good to give proper gifts to the immortals, since my son (if he ever really existed) never forgot in his halls the gods who hold Olympus. They remembered him, even in the fate of death.
>
>   (24.425–8; cf. Hecuba's similar comments when the body enters Troy, 24.748–59)[8]

There is, then, no general "justice" revealed in this episode: "It seems to imply that they [the gods] do not protect all the dead, but only the ones from whom they have received a lot of gifts" (Yamagata 1994:16). The gods *may* tend to the corpse of someone who sacrifices to them, if they also happen to really like them or their cause.

Notes

1 It is possible to imagine (as did some ancient readers of Homer) that Apollo and Poseidon were disguised as mortals, "testing Laomedon," when he defrauded them; that is, Laomedon didn't know he was cheating gods and thought that he was merely scamming some fellow mortals. But for Poseidon's response to be associated with divine justice, we would still need evidence that the god was acting on some sort of principle rather than out of revenge for a personal slight. But he says nothing about Laomedon's behavior or his subsequent punishment to suggest this was anything but vengeance for a personal injury, whether aimed at a god or a human. And, of course, none of this scenario applies to the eventual fall of Troy a second time. Moreover, if Homer knew of the "theoxeny" variant, he has carefully excluded it. There is no "testing" of Laomedon in his version – the gods are serving him as a punishment; they are *not* traveling through the world trying to uncover human injustice.

2 There is an interesting issue here with the Greek. After Homer quotes the Greek and Trojan prayer, he says: "So they spoke; but never/not yet (*ou pô*) would the son of Cronus grant them fulfillment." There's a big difference between the two options, and both are legitimate translations. Pucci (2002:21–2 with n8) argues convincingly for "never" (or, as he phrases it, "not at all").

3 Agamemnon also has faith that an underworld deity or deities – Erinys or Erinyes – will punish anyone who violates an oath. When swearing an oath to Achilles, he calls on Zeus, Earth, Sun, and "the Erinyes, who under earth take vengeance on men, whoever has sworn a false oath" (19.258–60). It's not clear here whether he envisions the goddesses (the Furies) merely working their magic from under earth or if this punishment is inflicted on those under the earth, that is, the dead. But for the oath between the Greeks and the Trojans, he is more explicit, calling upon Zeus, Sun, rivers, Earth, and "you who in the world below take vengeance on men who are done with life, whoever has sworn

a false oath" (3.276–9). Since this is the only reference in the epics to an explicit punishment after death for a mortal who doesn't personally insult the gods, scholars have been puzzled. And in fact the manuscripts offer several other possibilities and critics have suggested different readings and interpretations, and not without reason: These same transgressors of Agamemnon's oath only 20 verses later will be envisaged having their brains (and those of their children) poured out on the ground and their wives made to serve other men (3.298–301; Kirk 1985:305–6). Punishment will come in typical Homeric fashion, in *this* life, not the next. As Walter Burkert notes, the reference to the Erinyes "does not presuppose a judgment of the dead: the Erinyes are simply an embodiment of the act of self-cursing contained in the oath" (1985:197–8). But it may also be the case that Agamemnon in particular believes in the power of the Furies – he famously claims that Zeus, Fate, and Erinys inflicted him with delusion, thus causing him to dishonor Achilles (19.87–9). In the *Iliad*, only Agamemnon links the Erinyes with oaths – even Menelaus calls upon only Zeus, Earth, and the Sun to take vengeance upon a violator of oaths (3.104–7), and the poet never connects the goddesses to punishment. The Erinyes are also said by both Phoenix (Achilles' old tutor) and Athena to have fulfilled familial curses (by a father to a son, 9.453–7 and a mother to a son, 9.568–72; 21.412–14). But the only duty assigned to these deities by the poet himself in the epic is the rather specific task of checking the voice of Achilles' horse (19.418).

4 Some pro-justice scholars have suggested that there is "guilt-by-association" in the epic. For example, Aeneas encourages truce-breaking Pandarus in the ensuing battle and, in the process of helping him, eventually loses his horses to the Greeks. Since (the argument goes) Pandarus is sort of a second Paris, Aeneas is like the Trojans who don't punish Paris: His loss of his horses is an "implicit" ethical judgment on his behavior (e.g., Taplin 1992:109). But not a single mortal, much less the poet or the gods, draws this parallel. Instead, Aeneas will be one of only a couple Trojan warriors to survive the end of the war – the gods favor him; they have nothing to do with lost horses. In other words, as far as the text is concerned, Aeneas commits no crime, receives no condemnation, encounters no punishment (by Iliadic standards, losing your horses is an inconvenience and humiliation), and is uniquely spared the fate of all those supposedly "bad" Trojans. Going earlier into the tradition, some scholars surmise that some of Laomedon's horses were stolen by Aeneas' father (which is how Aeneas obtained such fantastic horses himself, 5.268–72) as a just punishment for Laomedon's treatment of Apollo, Poseidon, and Heracles. Even if we could accept this connection – which is not made anywhere in the text – there is no evidence that this is the work of the gods.

5 Plato also reads the Pandarus episode as a tale of the gods' injustice rather than divine justice (and so he must discard it): "But as to the breaking of the oaths and the truce that Pandarus effected, if anyone says it to have been brought about through Athena and Zeus, we will not approve . . ." (*Rep.* 2.379e).

6 Some readers are confused that at one point Poseidon complains to Hera that Zeus "now hates the race of Priam" (20.306). But he only says this because he can't understand why Zeus has not stepped in to save Aeneas, a Trojan descendant of Dardanus "whom the son of Cronus loved most of all the children who were born to him with mortal women" (20.304–5) and who is fated to continue the seed of Dardanus in the future. It is solely with regard to Aeneas' fate that Poseidon makes this (erroneous) *complaint*. Otherwise he would be delighted if Zeus really did hate Troy, sworn enemy of the city that Poseidon is. But Zeus in fact *likes* Troy.

7 Naturally, the one simile that conjures up divine justice (16.384–93) is customarily adduced as supporting evidence that the gods within the narrative punish the Trojans. Just as Zeus sends a storm on a city where men expel justice, so Zeus sends Patroclus against the wicked Trojans. As I hope to have demonstrated, the simile is the *lone* hint of just gods in the entire epic. The simile stands outside the story of the fall of Troy and is included quite intentionally at a crucial juncture – we are about to witness the deaths of Sarpedon, Patroclus, and Hector in quick succession – to remind us that the gods are

sorely missing from any similar "just" action in the plot. See my discussion in Chapter 13. Troy will *not* fall in the epic, and when it does it will not be because the gods care about how humans relate to each other. Sarpedon, Patroclus, and Hector are not "punished by the gods" but are victims of the consequences of Achilles' anger. Other scholars who find no divine justice in the *Iliad* have handled the simile differently, besides those who reject it as an interpolation; Van Erp Talman Kip (2000:396–7), Yamagata (1994:61–92), and Scott (1974:155).

8 The gods' concern for Hector, which derives from his piety, sufficiently counters those scholars who have argued that Hector himself is "justly punished" for his "arrogance and recklessness" (which is not to deny that Hector can demonstrate both). Zeus may note Hector's donning of Achilles' armor with some dismissiveness, but – once again – when we actually have evidence from the gods or the poet, it turns out that there is no suggestion anywhere that Hector "has it coming." To the contrary: Hector is caught between duties to his city and family, and he is trapped in a system of honor that he, unlike Achilles, never confronts head on. Like so many other Homeric warriors, he dies fighting for glory in circumstances the poet carefully crafts to help the audience peer into the cracks of the "heroic" system. Hector is a victim of his own character, his own time and place within the epic. He is not "punished" by anyone, especially not by Zeus. Achilles is not a divine vehicle for justice. Achilles kills Hector out of a desire for brute personal vengeance, and he succeeds because he is the better warrior (and thus has divine aid throughout) and knows the weak spot on Hector's armor – it's *his*, after all!

Appendix 4
Divine justice in the *Odyssey*?

Unlike the *Iliad*, the *Odyssey* culminates in the triumph of its main character over a villainous enemy, a band of parasitic suitors who *do* have it coming ("baddies" as one scholar labels them; Jong 2001:28). Since Athena herself finds the actions of the suitors to be iniquitous and aids Odysseus and his son in their vengeance against the interlopers, it is easy to conclude that the epic reveals a firm vision of divine justice, a "knockdown proof of Olympian theodicy" (Benardete 1997:6). Entire books have been written defending this position, and a majority of publications on the subject agree. There are numerous arguments advanced in support of divine justice in the *Odyssey*, and space does not permit (nor does my argument about justice in the *Iliad* require) a complete response. But I owe the reader at least a brief outline of my reasons for doubting this conventional reading of the gods in the epic, a reading which since antiquity attests to the human impulse "to moralize an overtly amoral text" (Ford 1996). As in our examination of the *Iliad*, it is not a question here of what the mortal characters *believe* – the "good guys" all think that the gods care about oaths and suppliants and will support them in their quest for justice (even a few "bad guys" grow concerned that the gods will judge them) – but what the gods, poet, and text itself reveal.

Of the handful of important deities in the epic, the only one who can reasonably be associated with divine justice – that is, with caring about and becoming involved in the way humans treat other humans – is Athena. Not that scholars haven't tried to bring the other gods into the fold, but their efforts are unconvincing. Helius appeals to Zeus to punish Odysseus' one remaining ship because the men ate his cattle. They are not punished for breaking an oath or ignoring advice or generically failing to exercise self-restraint or mistreating each other or Odysseus, but specifically because they "insolently" killed and ate Helius' favorite animals, critters in which he "rejoiced." Helius is quite explicit about it: "If they do not pay me suitable requital for my cattle, I will enter Hades and shine among the dead" (12.382–3). This is the same kind of vengeance for a personal slight to a god's honor we find in the *Iliad*, not an act of divine justice. Neither Helius nor Zeus in this context is concerned with how the men treated each other.

Similarly Iliadic is Poseidon's pursuit of Odysseus. The text is again unequivocal: The sea-god hates Odysseus because he blinded Polyphemus, his son the Cyclops. Zeus knows that is the reason for Poseidon's anger (1.68–79); Athena knows it (13.341–3); and Odysseus ultimately knows it as well. Scholars wishing to find a consistent theodicy in the epic based on divine justice have performed all sorts of uncomfortable contortions in their efforts to convict Odysseus of a crime serious enough to warrant Poseidon's "just" response. Odysseus is no saint, to be sure. He's a bad guest (helping himself to Polyphemus' cheese), eternally suspicious (withholding important information from his crew – and even his father), arrogant (foolishly gloating over Polyphemus' blinding and thereby revealing his – and his crew's – identity), reckless on occasion (unnecessarily risking his men's lives), and he tells lies with consummate ease. But nowhere are we informed that Odysseus' character flaws or supposed "hubris" are the source of Poseidon's (or any other god's) animus. Polyphemus was *eating his men* – the hero did what heroes have to do. Virtually all of Odysseus' "mistakes" derive from his distrustful nature or are the residue of his Bronze Age warrior mentality that he struggles and fails to suppress right up to the very last verses of the final book of the epic. He has done nothing that could reasonably transform Poseidon's family-based vendetta into warranted divine justice. Like Helius, Poseidon is motivated by a personal grudge.

What has always surprised me the most about the "divine justice" argument is the frequent drafting of Zeus to the cause. As a character, in contrast to his ubiquity in the *Iliad*, Zeus plays a very minor role in the epic, despite some ingenious efforts to uncover his "subliminal" control of the plot (e.g., Marks 2008). His limited actions have nothing do to with anything we could call divine justice. Zeus responds favorably to Athena's plea on behalf of Odysseus for quite Iliadic reasons, namely as a favor to his daughter and because Odysseus is cultically pious. "Didn't Odysseus show favor to you by performing sacrifices next to the ships of the Argives in broad Troy?" she asks (1.60–2). Zeus responds that he could never forget a man with a mind like Odysseus', a hero who "over and beyond others offered sacrifices to the immortal gods" (1.65–7). In Zeus's eyes, Odysseus is particularly pious. Nevertheless, Zeus has done nothing previously to aid the hero because Poseidon has been so angry with the Ithacan. But, we have just learned, Poseidon has now gone off to that cone of silence known as the Ethiopians, so Zeus agrees that the time has come to plot Odysseus' return. The father and daughter can conspire in Poseidon's absence, and Poseidon will just have to deal with it when he returns. In a second council scene, Zeus tells his favorite Olympian that she is free to carry out her plan to protect Telemachus and bring Odysseus home to take vengeance upon the suitors. He then dispatches Hermes to command Calypso to release him, knowing as he does that it is Odysseus' fate to be carried back to Ithaca by the Phaeacians with a boatload of prizes (5.1–42).

There is nothing here that speaks directly to divine justice. Zeus put his family (his respect for Poseidon, or, more likely, his desire not to antagonize his brother) ahead of Odysseus' suffering. He steps into action – sort of – only when twice cajoled by his daughter and reminded of the hero's cultic devotion. Even the signs or portents said to be sent specifically by Zeus that signal Odysseus' return and revenge "serve first and foremost to foreshadow these events" and "to keep alive hopes of a happy ending for Odysseus and his family" – they "have no influence on the development of the action" (Saïd 2011:336). The king of the gods does nothing in the rest of the epic to support any "mistreated" individual. There is no evidence that Zeus cares about human rights or wrongs at all.

I agree with many scholars that the Zeus of the *Odyssey* is not exactly the same as the Zeus of the *Iliad*, but these differences in his nature do not involve his increased interest in justice. My reading of Zeus in the *Odyssey* suggests that his primary characteristic is, oddly enough, a fervent desire to avoid conflict. Scholars often acknowledge that in the *Odyssey* the gods are generally less involved in the human world – except as (many insist) "dispensers of justice" – that "the separation between gods and mortals is further advanced than in the *Iliad*" (Graziosi and Haubold 2005:77). But I would add that the issue is as personal as it is cosmic and has nothing to do with justice. Zeus didn't want to disrupt the family dynamics by upsetting Poseidon. He agrees with everything Athena says. Zeus may be concerned about the "preservation of world order" by keeping Helius in the heavens (Segal 1992:511) – Zeus does not like discord of any kind – but that is irrelevant to moral order on earth. At the end of the epic, he tells Athena that he would prefer that the angry relatives of the dead suitors and the family of Odysseus come together under the hero's kingship: "Let them conclude a treaty, and let him always be king, and let us inspire them to forget the bloodshed of their sons and brothers. And let them love each other as before, and let wealth and peace be in abundance" (24.483–6). Zeus is the Rodney King of the Olympians. This resolution is of course exactly what Athena wants: "It is typical of the relationship between Zeus and Athena that what is fitting to him is also what is most pleasing to her" (Murnaghan 1995:77). In the very last scene, when Odysseus ignores Athena's first warning shout to cease from war – he is still holding onto his martial (Iliadic) instincts – Zeus hurls a thunderbolt in support of Athena's call for a truce. Odysseus obeys, and the epic closes as Zeus wants it to, with everyone, right or wrong, just or unjust, oblivious to past injuries and compelled to get along.

Zeus's characterization also explains his initial "programmatic" speech in the epic. Supporters of divine justice usually place this statement at the center of their argument, one scholar even finding that "the Zeus who presides over the heavenly council in the *Odyssey* personifies a high philosophical conception of the world-conscience," whatever that may be (Jaeger 1945:24). But Zeus is no more anxious about divine justice here than anywhere else in the epics:

> It's terrible how much mortals blame the gods. For they say that evils come from us, but they themselves also have troubles beyond expectation from their own recklessness. As just now Aegisthus beyond what was fitting married the wedded wife of the son of Atreus [Agamemnon] and killed him after he returned home, even though he knew it would bring utter destruction, since we ourselves, sending Hermes, the sharp-seeing Argos-slayer, told him beforehand not to kill Agamemnon or court his wife. For vengeance for the son of Atreus would come from Orestes whenever he came into his prime and longed for his own land. So Hermes told him, but though he was

well-intentioned he did not persuade the mind of Aegisthus. And now Aegisthus has atoned for it in full.

(1.32–43)

Zeus is complaining that mortals blame the gods for their ills. He doesn't deny that some problems come from the gods (nor does he admit this possibility directly), but he adds that mortals *also* are responsible for their own problems. This speech provides a fitting introduction to the Zeus we see in the rest of the epic. He just wants folks to go about their business, but instead mortals are constantly blaming *him* for what are often problems they caused for themselves. It's so *annoying*. If humans were just more responsible. Zeus proffers an example of human obduracy and querulousness, *not* of divine justice. Having access to the movie of the future, he knew that if Aegisthus pursued his murderous adultery, he would be killed in turn by Orestes. It's not clear why Zeus intervenes on this occasion and not others, but nothing in the passage suggests it's about the particular injustice of Aegisthus' intended act or about justice in general. The point of the story is the suffering Aegisthus will bring on himself from another mortal for his own actions – it's not Zeus's fault! Zeus is ultimately doing little more here than absolving himself and his fellow gods of any responsibility for most of human suffering. "Rather than an authoritative pronouncement justifying the ways of the gods to men Zeus's words emerge from this scene as defensive and self-serving" (Crotty 1994:133). The speech provides an example of humans causing their own problems even when they know – in this case, Aegisthus is informed directly by the gods – the consequences of their bad decisions. Neither Zeus nor any other deity is involved in the punishment of Aegisthus. Agamemnon's son, Orestes, without any divine prompting as far as the text reveals (we can't read Aeschylus' *Oresteia* back into the text), fulfilled his predicted role. The story presents a paradigm of human obstinacy, of a mortal doing wicked things despite a warning from the gods that he would be sorry and who then is punished (as foretold) by a mortal. Divine justice isn't an issue. Zeus just wants people to take some responsibility for their own actions and stop dragging him and the other gods into it. His point isn't that "Aegisthus had it coming and so we gods punished him"; rather, it's that "Aegisthus has no grounds to blame the gods for what happened to him when Orestes returned for revenge."

The story of Agamemnon's ill-starred return from Troy is used five other times in the epic as a direct parallel to Odysseus' own efforts to get back to Ithaca. Will Telemachus become an Orestes and take vengeance on those trying to supplant his father? Will Odysseus face Agamemnon's fate and be betrayed by Penelope, an unfaithful wife like Clytemnestra yielding to her suitor(s)? Will the suitors meet Aegisthus' doom? The Olympian gods play no part in this paradigmatic tale of revenge. As told throughout the *Odyssey*, the story of Aegisthus is completely focused on decisions and actions taken by mortals. Neither Zeus nor Athena has a role in this analogous tale of the return of a Greek hero from Troy. If Zeus's speech is supposed to reveal his interest in human justice in the case of Aegisthus and imply by correspondence that he is equally involved in the punishment of the suitors, it fails on both counts. Zeus wants things to go frictionlessly everywhere, on earth and on Olympus. He displays no interest in investing himself in the messiness of acting on the principle of divine justice. By turning Zeus's opening speech into "a showcase of moral policy," scholars have unnecessarily sent themselves into a whirlwind of activity to make sense of Zeus's subsequent actions (or lack thereof). Pro-justice critics struggle awkwardly to explain their self-created "gap between the Zeus of the first divine assembly, the enlightened god who cares for human ethics and morality, and the seemingly vindictive, capricious Zeus of the Thrinacia episode" (Bakker 2013:114–34). There is no gap – Zeus is simply never interested in human ethics and morality.

Zeus is so eager for an untroubled existence that he is quick to patch things up with Poseidon. When the sea-god complains that mortals will no longer honor him since his own beloved Phaeacians have escorted the hated Odysseus home against his will, Zeus (who knew this would happen and gave his imprimatur to Athena's actions) quickly tells his brother to take whatever vengeance he desires on the entire race of the Phaeacians! Scholarly promoters of divine justice in the *Odyssey*, in order to defend Zeus and Poseidon, must now search for the hidden felony the Phaeacians have committed by being excellent hosts: *Excessive* hospitality? Excessive *pride* in their seamanship? Forgetting a prophecy? But there is nothing in the text to suggest the source of the Phaeacians' punishment is anything but Poseidon's personal, divine spite and Zeus's desire to smooth things over with his brother. Zeus even gives Poseidon a few tips on the best way to make his vengeance as visible and spectacular as possible (13.128–64). The two gods seem to bond over their fraternal (and deadly) pranks on the gracious Phaeacians. All is well among the Olympians again, and that is the last we hear from Poseidon or the Phaeacians. Zeus remains the same Odyssean Zeus he has always been.

So we really come down to one admittedly considerable source of hope for divine justice in the *Odyssey*, and that is in Athena's support of Odysseus and Telemachus in their punishment of the suitors. There can be no question that within the values of the epic, as a group (but not necessarily individually) the suitors deserve what they get. They violate all aspects of hospitality as signaled throughout the *Odyssey* (eating their host's food, sleeping with his maids, abusing his son, trying to marry his wife, mistreating his guests, including him(!), attempting to usurp his kingship); some of them try to kill Telemachus; they claim they would kill Odysseus should he return. And the narrative includes the deaths of all the suitors, so it is fair to read the epic as a romantic tale of a satisfying vengeance. All of the major characters, including Odysseus himself, believe the hero is also acting as an agent of divine justice in this revenge. But is he?

My major concern with this approach to the *Odyssey* is that Athena seems to act primarily out of a personal interest in Odysseus and his family rather than in the pursuit of justice itself. Odysseus has been wronged, to be sure, and the goddess witnesses and judges some of the wickedness of the suitors firsthand. Athena uses the rhetoric of justice on occasion, but her actions reveal that she is far more interested in building the glory of Odysseus and his son. She wants

Odysseus to kill every single suitor, even though according to Homer a couple of them are relatively innocent and even wanted to leave if the goddess had let them. She delays helping Odysseus and Telemachus during the fight with the suitors in order to prolong the "test of strength and valor of both Odysseus and his glorious son" (22.236–8). Her concern is more to promote Odysseus and his family than in justice, and "in the end it is his [Odysseus'] revenge, not that of the gods" (Winterbottom 1989:40). Odysseus is not even an "agent of the gods" but a human actor in a pseudotheoxeny – it is Odysseus in disguise, not a deity, who is abused and then punishes the criminals. Odysseus takes the place of the divine. The "whole apparatus of divine justice" is not behind the hero (*pace* Kearns 1982:8; cf. Reece 1993:181–7). It's merely Athena supporting her favorite, just as she did in the *Iliad*. Athena champions her chosen father-son teams in both texts, comparing Diomedes to his father just as she does Telemachus to his. The gods in the *Odyssey* "retain their typical characteristics, of which the most prominent are their loyalties to human favourites (Athena and Odysseus) or family (Poseidon and Polyphemus) and their ruthless punishment of those who anger or offend them . . ." (Allan 2006:17). But this is not divine justice (*pace* Allan); divine favoritism and wrath propel Homer's gods in both texts. Athena's "attitude is not morally advanced over that of Poseidon towards Odysseus," concludes Homeric scholar Jonathan S. Burgess: "The Homeric gods are, instead, capricious; their disinterest in ethics represents the uncertainty of the human condition" (2015a:39).

Neither Athena nor any other god responds in any other case in the epic to protect a victim of injustice. The gods in the *Odyssey* don't otherwise punish murderers, adulterers, or those who violate oaths or hospitality, no matter how much the characters may wish that were true. Polyphemus kills and eats six of his guests, but the gods don't punish him. *Odysseus* punishes him, without any divine aid. Poseidon quickly *answers* the prayers of the despicable Cyclops! Athena explains to Odysseus that she couldn't intervene because she was concerned about offending her uncle Poseidon. But Odysseus doesn't buy that excuse: Athena was conspicuously absent *even before he and his men encountered the Cyclops*! The goddess was AWOL, Odysseus later complains, from the time he left Troy until he arrived among the Phaeacians: "I did not see you after that [the departure from Troy], daughter of Zeus, nor did I perceive you coming on board my ship to defend me from some hardship" (13.316–19).[1] Athena doesn't punish inhospitality per se; she helps Odysseus in the last stage of his return home because he is her favorite and Poseidon takes a vacation.[2]

No gods step in to punish Heracles for his outrageous mistreatment of guests. Heracles, in his own house, kills a guest who has come to reclaim his stolen "strong-hoofed" mares. Homer labels Heracles "savage" and adds that the hero "had respect for neither the anger of the gods nor the very table he had set before his guest." As far as Homer tells us, the gods do absolutely nothing in response – there is *no* anger of the gods to be seen (21.22–30). (Zeus and Athena, as well as Hermes, we may recall, are staunch allies of that much-suffering but inhospitable hero in the epics.)

The *characters* in the *Odyssey* see the working of the gods everywhere, in both positive and negative results, equally blaming and praising the mostly unseen powers. Odysseus wrongly thinks (or at least claims that) "Zeus and the other gods" have punished Polyphemus (9.475–9), while equally errantly believing that it was already Zeus who plotted the destruction of his ships and comrades (9.553–5). Academic promoters of Odyssean justice, when not arguing for uniformly just gods in the epic, have often found a solution to the apparent inconsistency between what they call "justice-oriented deities" (Zeus and Athena) and vengeful deities (Poseidon and Helius, whose anger we are told disturbs the *Odyssey*'s "ethical uniformity," Fenik 1974:219). Two historical "layers" have been embedded in the text, the argument runs, an older, "archaic" or "primitive" version of capricious gods and a more "evolved" vision of divine justice. Or some scholars find here a "transition" from a primitive to a more advanced stage of religion, or dual, incompatible conceptions of divine justice revealing a morally complicated world. As in the case of the *Iliad*, however, we search the text in vain for persuasive evidence for the existence of the supposed "advanced" vision of causality, the "evolved vision" of divine justice. And we must continue to reject this pejorative interpretation of Homer's mercurial gods whose amoral nature so acutely accounts for the realities of human existence. *Which* is really the more incisive view of the reality of divine justice in the world?

More helpfully, Jenny Strauss Clay has suggested that the *Odyssey* offers a *thematically* significant "double theodicy," with the gods presented sometimes as involved in justice and other times as pursuing their own personal agendas: "The occasional fulfillment of justice in an exemplary fashion by gods fundamentally indifferent to men but jealous of their prerogatives – perhaps that would be Homer's answer and the message of our *Odyssey*" (1983:238–9; cf. Thalman 1992:32–4). Perhaps. I don't want to repeat the theologians' error of finding only what I would like to find in the text. But even this "occasional fulfillment of justice" still strikes me as a coincidence rather than "exemplary" evidence for divine justice. On one occasion two gods aid a favorite who *happens* to be suffering some injustice – he's *already* a favorite for some *other* reason, after all. Athena loves Odysseus because they are both known for their slippery resourcefulness, not for being "just." (She may also appreciate his cultic piety, but she seems to emphasize this aspect of Odysseus only when trying to get Zeus to step in.) Sometimes the gods advise a nefarious character like Aegisthus that human vengeance is on the horizon. A more advantageous act would have been to warn Agamemnon! The gods don't support a hero *because* he is acting justly towards his fellow man, and they don't punish an individual, either in this life or the next, *because* he treated innocent mortals unjustly. Athena eventually aids Odysseus' return and destruction of the suitors because she is emotionally invested in Odysseus. "Justice" is *always* personal for Homeric deities.

It may be true that "the fact that they [Homeric gods] are not swayed by considerations of morality alone does not show that they are never swayed by consideration of morality at all" (Cairns 2011:3.922). But where do we find a divine action clearly based on morality? And are we satisfied defining "divine justice" as an action taken by the gods that is sort of kind of partially based on morality but is just as much or more dependent upon loyalties and perceived personal slights? In the narrative action of neither epic do I find the gods at any point acting on principle, out of a concern for how humans treat each other, rewarding the "good" or punishing the "bad" solely on the basis of their behavior. Maybe that's too much to ask, even of gods.

Notes

1 Odysseus and some of his men blind Polyphemus with a large stake of "green olive-wood" (9.319–20, 378). The olive is closely associated with Athena. A believer in Odyssean justice might see this as a proxy for divine action, but it strikes me as a stunning marker of the goddess's disappearing act during the hero's wanderings.

2 The epic never spells out just why Athena doesn't step in to help Odysseus before Poseidon and his anger enter the picture. Perhaps she had confidence that he was fated to get home no matter what happened, as she suggests at one point; or, as Jenny Strauss Clay has argued (1983), Athena may have been angry at Odysseus. If so, then once again a deity is acting purely on human emotions. But in any case, Athena hardly can be said to act in the epic on any *principle* of divine justice.

Bibliography

Aaron, David H. 2002. *Biblical Ambiguities: Metaphor, Semantics, and Divine Imagery*. Boston.

Abma, Richsje. 1999. *Bonds of Love: Methodic Studies of Prophetic Texts with Marriage Imagery*. Assen, The Netherlands.

Adams, Lisa and John Heath. 2007. *Why We Read What We Read: A Delightfully Opinionated Journey Through Bestselling Books*. New York.

Adkins, Arthur W.H. 1960. *Merit and Responsibility: A Study of Greek Values*. Chicago.

Ahrensdorf, Peter J. 2014. *Homer on the Gods and Human Virtue: Creating the Foundations of Classical Civilization*. Cambridge.

Albertz, Rainer. 2003. *Israel in Exile: The History and Literature of the Sixth Century B.C.E.* D. Green, tr. Atlanta.

Albinus, Lars. 2000. *The House of Hades: Studies in Ancient Greek Eschatology*. Aarhus.

Albright, William F. 1957. *From the Stone Age to Christianity: Monotheism and the Historical Process*. Baltimore.

Allan, William. 2006. "Divine Justice and Cosmic Order in Early Greek Epic." *JHS* 126:1–35.

———. 2008. "Performing the Will of Zeus: The Διὸς βουλή and the Scope of Early Greek Epic," in *Performance, Iconography, Reception: Studies in Honour of Oliver Taplin*, M. Revermann and P.J. Wilson, eds. Oxford:201–16.

Allison, Dale C. 2003. "The Eschatology of Jesus," in McGinn et al. (2003) 139–65.

Alster, Baruch. 1999. "Tiamat," in Van der Toorn et al. (1999) 867–69.

Altemeyer, Bob. 2010. "Atheism and Secularity in North America," in Zuckerman (2010b) 1–21.

Anderson, Bernhard W., ed. 1984. *Creation in the Old Testament*. Philadelphia.

Anderson, Elizabeth. 2007. "If God Is Dead, Is Everything Permitted?," in Antony (2007a) 215–30.

Antony, Louise M., ed. 2007a. *Philosophers without Gods: Meditations on Atheism and the Secular Life*. Oxford.

———. 2007b. "For the Love of Reason," in Antony (2007a) 41–58.

Archer, Gleason L. 1985. *A Survey of Old Testament Introduction*. Chicago.

Armstrong, Karen. 1993. *A History of God: The 4000-Year Quest of Judaism, Christianity and Islam*. New York.

———. 2009. *The Case for God: What Religion Really Means*. London.

———. 2014. *Fields of Blood: Religion and the History of Violence*. New York.

Arnold, Bill T. 2009. *Genesis*. Cambridge.

Asen, Bernhard A. 2012. "Annihilate Amalek! Christian Perspectives on 1 Samuel," in Renard (2012) 55–74.

Aslan, Reza. 2017. *God: A Human History*. New York.

Assmann, Jan. 1997. *Moses the Egyptian: The Memory of Egypt in Western Monotheism*. Cambridge, MA.

———. 2010. *The Price of Monotheism*. Stanford.

Athanassiadi, Polymnia and Michael Frede, eds. 1999. *Pagan Monotheism in Late Antiquity*. Oxford.

Atran, Scott. 2002. *In Gods We Trust: The Evolutionary Landscape of Religion*. Oxford.

Auerbach, Eric. 1953. *Mimesis: The Representation of Reality in Western Literature*. W.R. Trask, tr. Princeton.

Avalos, Hector. 2005. *The Origins of Religious Violence*. Amherst.

———. 2007. *The End of Biblical Studies*. Amherst.

———. 2010. "Yahweh Is a Moral Monster," in Loftus (2010a) 209–36.

———. 2011. *Slavery, Abolitionism, and the Ethics of Biblical Scholarship*. Sheffield.

———. 2015. *The Bad Jesus: The Ethics of New Testament Ethics*. Sheffield.

Bachvarova, Mary R. 2016. *From Hittite to Homer: The Anatolian Background of Ancient Greek Epic*. Cambridge.

Badham, Paul. 1983. "Death," in Richardson and Bowden (1983) 145–6.

Baggett, David and Jerry L. Walls. 2011. *Good God: The Theistic Foundations of Morality*. Oxford.

Baines, John. 2011. "Presenting and Discussing Deities in New Kingdom and Third Intermediate Period Egypt," in Pongratz-Leisten (2011a) 41–89.

Baker, Joseph O. and Buster G. Smith. 2015. *American Secularism: Cultural Contours of Nonreligious Belief Systems*. New York.

Bakker, Egbert J. 2013. *The Meaning of Meat and the Structure of the Odyssey*. Cambridge.

Ballentine, Debra Scoggins. 2015. *The Conflict Myth and the Biblical Tradition*. New York.

Bar-Ilan, Meir. 1993. "The Hand of God: A Chapter in Rabbinic Anthropomorphism," in *Rashi 1040–1990: Hommage à Ephraïm E. Urbach*, Gabrielle Sed-Rajna, ed. Paris:321–35.

Barker, Dan. 2016. *God: The Most Unpleasant Character in All Fiction*. New York.

Barker, Margaret. 1992. *The Great Angel: A Study of Israel's Second God*. London.

Barrett, Justin L. 2004. *Why Would Anyone Believe in God?* Walnut Creek, CA.

Barton, Carlin A. and Daniel Boyarin. 2016. *Imagine No Religion: How Modern Abstractions Hide Ancient Realities*. New York.

Barton, John. 1998. *Ethics and the Old Testament*. Harrisburg, PA.

———. 2003. *Understanding Old Testament Ethics: Approaches and Explorations*. Louisville.

———. 2007. "Imitation of God in the Old Testament," in Gordon (2007) 35–46.

———, ed. 2016a. *The Hebrew Bible: A Critical Companion*. Princeton.

———. 2016b. "The Hebrew Bible and the Old Testament," in Barton (2016a) 3–23.

Barton, Stephen C. and David Wilkinson, eds. 2009. *Reading Genesis after Darwin*. Oxford.

Batson, C. Daniel. 2013. "Individual Religion, Tolerance, and Universal Compassion," in Clarke et al. (2013) 88–106.

Batto, Bernard F. 1992. "Creation Theology in Genesis," in Clifford and Collins (1992) 16–38.

———. 2013a. *In the Beginning: Essays on Creation Motifs in the Ancient Near East and the Bible*. Winona Lake.

———. 2013b. "The Combat Myth in Israelite Tradition Revisited," in Scurlock and Beal (2013) 217–36.

Baumann, Gerlinde. 2003. *Love and Violence: Marriage as Metaphor for the Relationship between YHWH and Israel in the Prophetic Books*. L.M. Maloney, tr. Collegeville, MN.

Becking, Bob. 1997. "Assyrian Evidence for Iconic Polytheism in Ancient Israel?," in Van Der Toorn (1997) 157–71.

———. 2001. "Only One God: On Possible Implications for Biblical Theology," in Becking et al. (2001) 189–201.

———. 2011. "David at the Threshold of History: A Review of Steven L. McKenzie, *King David: A Biography* (2000), and Baruch Halpern, *David's Secret Demons: Messiah, Murderer, Traitor, King* (2001)," in Grabbe (2011a) 197–209.

Becking, Bob, Meindert Dijkstra, Marjo C.A. Korpel, and Karel J.H. Vriezen. 2001. *Only One God? Monotheism in Ancient Israel and the Veneration of the Goddess Asherah*. London.

Beit-Hallahmi, Benjamin. 2010. "Morality and Immorality among the Irreligious," in Zuckerman (2010a) 113–48.

Bellah, Robert N. 2011. *Religion in Human Evolution: From the Paleolithic to the Axial Age*. Cambridge, MA.

Bellinzoni, Arthur J. 2009. *The Old Testament: An Introduction to Biblical Scholarship*. Amherst.

Belzer, Marvin. 2007. "Mere Stranger," in Antony (2007a) 90–103.

Bembry, Jason. 2011. *Yahweh's Coming of Age*. Winona Lake.

Benardete, Seth. 1997. *The Bow and the Lyre: A Platonic Reading of the Odyssey*. Lanham.

Benjamins, Hendrick S. 1998. "Noah, the Ark, and the Flood in Early Christian Theology: The Ship of the Church in the Making," in Martínez and Luttikhuizen (1998) 134–49.

Bering, Jesse. 2012. *The Belief Instinct: The Psychology of Souls, Destiny, and the Meaning of Life*. New York.

Berlejung, Angelika. 2017. "The Origins and Beginnings of the Worship of YHWH: The Iconographic Evidence," in Oorschot and Witte (2017) 67–91.

Berlin, Adele, Marc Zvi Brettler, Michael A. Fishbane, and Jewish Publication Society, eds. 2004. *The Jewish Study Bible*. Oxford.

Berlinerblau, Jacques. 2005. *The Secular Bible: Why Nonbelievers Must Take Religion Seriously*. Cambridge.

Berner, Christoph. 2017. "'I Am YHWH Your God, Who Brought You Out of the Land of Egypt' (Exod 20:2): Reflections on the Status of the Exodus Creed in the History of Israel and the Literary History of the Hebrew Bible," in Oorschot and Witte (2017) 181–206.

Bernstein, Andrew. 2006. "The Tragedy of Theology: How Religion Caused and Extended the Dark Ages: A Critique of Rodney Stark's *The Victory of Reason*." *Objective Standard* 1:11–37.

Berry, Jason. 2011. *Render Unto Rome: The Secret Life of Money in the Catholic Church*. New York.

Besançon, Alain. 2000. *The Forbidden Image: An Intellectual History of Iconoclasm*. Chicago.

Bettini, Maurizio. 2016. *Éloge du polythéisme: Ce que peuvent nous apprendre les religions antiques*. V. Pirenne-Delforge, tr. Paris.

———. 2017. "Visibilité, invisibilité et identité des dieux," in Pironti and Bonnet (2017) 21–42.

Bevan, Edwyn. 1940. *Holy Images: An Inquiry into Idolatry and Image Worship in Ancient Paganism and in Christianity*. New York.

Billington, Ray. 2002. *Religion without God*. London.

Blackford, Russell and Udo Schülenk, eds. 2009. *50 Voices of Disbelief: Why We Are Atheists*. West Sussex.

Blair, Judith M. 2009. *De-Demonising the Old Testament: An Investigation of Azazel, Lilith, Deber, Qeteb and Reshef in the Hebrew Bible*. Tübingen.

Blenkinsopp, Joseph. 1990. "Theological Honesty Through History," in *Hebrew Bible or Old Testament? Studying the Bible in Judaism and Christianity*, Roger Brooks and John J. Collins, eds. Notre Dame:147–52.

Block, Daniel L. 2000. *The Gods of the Nation: Studies in Ancient Near Eastern National Theology*. 2nd ed. Grand Rapids.

Bloom, Paul. 2010. "Religious Belief as an Evolutionary Accident," in Schloss and Murray (2010) 118–27.

———. 2012. "Religion, Morality, Evolution." *Annual Review of Psychology* 63:179–99.

Blumenthal, David R. 1993. *Facing the Abusing God: A Theology of Protest*. Louisville.

Boda, Mark J. and Lissa M. Wray Beal, eds. 2013. *Prophets, Prophecy, and Ancient Israelite Historiography*. Winona Lake.

Boehm, Chrisopher. 2012. *Moral Origins: The Evolution of Virtue, Altruism, and Shame*. New York.

Bonnet, Corrine. 2017. "Les dieux en assemblée," in Pironti and Bonnet (2017) 87–112.

Borgman, Erik, Maria C.L. Bingemer, and Andrés T. Queiruga, eds. 2009. *Monotheism: Divinity and Unity Reconsidered*. London.

Bowen, Nancy R. 1995. "Can God Be Trusted? Confronting the Deceptive God," in Brenner (1995) 354–65.

———. 2010. *Ezekiel*. Nashville.

Bowie, Fiona. 2000. *The Anthropology of Religion: An Introduction*. Malden.

Bowra, Cecil M. 1930. *Tradition and Design in the Iliad*. Oxford.

Boyer, Pascal. 2001. *Religion Explained: The Evolutionary Origins of Religious Thought*. New York.

———. 2003. "The Growth of Fundamentalist Apocalyptic in the United States," in McGinn et al. (2003) 516–44.

Brain, Marshall. 2014. *How "God" Works: A Logical Inquiry on Faith*. New York.

Bremer, Jan Maarten, Theo P.J. van den Hout, and Rudolph Peters, eds. 1994. *Hidden Futures: Death and Immortality in Ancient Egypt, Anatolia, the Classical, Biblical and Arabic-Islamic World*. Amsterdam.

Bremmer, Jan N. 1994. "The Soul, Death and the Afterlife in Early and Classical Greece," in Bremer et al. (1994) 91–106.

———. 2002. *The Rise and Fall of the Afterlife*. London.

———. 2006. "The Rise of the Hero Cult and the New Simonides." *ZPE* 158:15–26.

———. 2007. "Greek Normative Animal Sacrifice," in Ogden (2007) 132–44.

———. 2008a. "Atheism in Antiquity," in Martin (2008) 11–26.

———. 2008b. *Greek Religion and Culture, the Bible and the Ancient Near East*. Leiden.

———. 2010. "Introduction: The Greek Gods in the Twentieth Century," in Bremmer and Erskine (2010) 1–18.

——— and A. Erskine, eds. 2010. *The Gods of Ancient Greece: Identities and Transformations*. Edinburgh.

Brenner, Athalya. 1981. "God's Answer to Job." *Vetus Testamentum* 31:129.

———, ed. 1995. *A Feminist Companion to the Latter Prophets*. Sheffield.

———, ed. 2001a. *A Feminist Companion to Exodus to Deuteronomy*. Sheffield.

———. 2001b. "An Afterworld: The Decalogue: Am I an Addressee?," in Brenner (2001a) 255–8.

Brettler, Marc Zvi. 1989. *God Is King: Understanding an Israelite Metaphor*. Sheffield.

Breytenbach, Cilliers and Peggy L. Day. 1999. "Satan," in van der Toorn et al. (1999) 726–32.

Brisson, Luc. 2004. *How Philosophers Saved Myths: Allegorical Interpretation and Classical Mythology*. Chicago.

Bröcker, Walter. 1975. *Theologie der Ilias*. Frankfurt.

Brown, John Pairman. 1995. *Israel and Hellas*. Vol. 1. Berlin.

———. 2000. *Israel and Hellas: Sacred Institutions with Roman Counterparts*. Vol. 2. Berlin.

———. 2001. *Israel and Hellas: The Legacy of Iranian Imperialism and the Individual*. Vol. 3. Berlin.

———. 2003. *Ancient Israel and Ancient Greece: Religion, Politics, and Culture*. Minneapolis.

Brown, Peter. 1988. *The Body and Society: Men, Women, and Sexual Renunciation in Early Christianity*. New York.

Brown, Raymond E. 1977. *The Birth of the Messiah: A Commentary on the Infancy Narratives in Matthew and Luke*. Garden City, NY.

Brown, William P., ed. 2004. *The Ten Commandments: The Reciprocity of Faithfulness*. Louisville.

Brueggemann, Walter. 1982. *Genesis: Interpretation. A Bible Commentary for Teaching and Preaching*. Atlanta.

———. 2008. *Old Testament Theology: An Introduction*. Nashville, TN.

Buckley, Michael J. 1987. *At the Origins of Modern Atheism*. New Haven.

Buckman, Robert. 2002. *Can We Be Good without God?: Biology, Behavior, and the Need to Believe*. Amherst.

Burgess, Jonathan S. 2009. *The Death and Afterlife of Achilles*. Baltimore.

———. 2015a. *Homer*. London.

———. 2015b. "Coming Adrift: The Limits of Reconstruction of the Cyclic Poems," in Fantuzzi and Tsagalis (2015) 43–58.

Burke, Brian L., Andy Martens, and Erik H. Faucher. 2010. "Two Decades of Terror Management Theory: A Meta-Analysis of Mortality Salience Research." *Personality and Social Psychology Review* 14:155–95.

Burke, Kelsy. 2016. *Christians Under Covers: Evangelicals and Sexual Pleasure on the Internet*. Oakland, CA.

Burkert, Walter. 1985. *Greek Religion*. J. Raffan, tr. Cambridge, MA.

———. 1992. *The Orientalizing Revolution: Near Eastern Influence on Greek Culture in the Early Archaic Age*. M.E. Pinder and W. Burkert, trs. Cambridge, MA.

———. 2004. *Babylon, Memphis, Persepolis: Eastern Contexts of Greek Culture*. Cambridge, MA.

Burton, Robert A. 2008. *On Being Certain: Believing You Are Right Even When You're Not*. New York.

Buxton, Richard. 2010. "Metamorphoses of Gods into Animals and Humans," in Bremmer and Erskine (2010) 81–91.

Bynum, Caroline Walker. 1995. *The Resurrection of the Body in Western Christianity, 200–1336*. New York.

———. 2007. *Wonderful Blood: Theology and Practice in Late Medieval Northern Germany and beyond*. Philadelphia.

Cairns, Douglas. 2011. "Values," in Finkelberg (2011) Vol. 3:919–22.

Callahan, Tim. 1997. *Bible Prophecy: Failure or Fulfillment?* Altadena.

Campbell, Antony, S.J. 2014. *Opening the Bible: Selected Writings of Antony Campbell, S.J.* Hindmarsh, South Australia.

Carr, David M. 1989. "Introduction to Genesis," in *The New Oxford Annotated Bible*. 4th ed. M.D. Coogan, ed. Oxford:7–11.

———. 1996. *Reading the Fractures of Genesis: Historical and Literary Approaches*. Louisville.

———. 2005. *The Erotic Word: Sexuality, Spirituality, and the Bible*. Oxford.

———. 2014. *Holy Resilience: The Bible's Traumatic Origins*. New Haven.

——— and Colleen M. Conway. 2010. *An Introduction to the Bible: Sacred Texts and Imperial Contexts*. West Sussex.

Carrier, Richard. 2010. "Christianity Was Not Responsible for Modern Science," in Loftus (2010a) 396–419.

Carter, Neil. 2017. "Lies the Church Told Us about Sex." Blog article in "Removing the Fig Leaf" December 26, accessed at Patheos.com.

Caspi, Mishael and Sascha Benjamin Cohen. 1995. *The Binding (Aqedah) and Its Trans-formations in Judaism and Islam: The Lambs of God*. Lewiston.

Cavanaugh, William T. 2009. *The Myth of Religious Violence: Secular Ideology and the Roots of Modern Conflict*. Oxford.

Caws, Peter and Stefani Jones. 2010. *Religious Upbringing and Costs of Freedom: Personal and Philosophical Essays*. University Park, PA.

Chapman, Stephen B. 2003. "How the Biblical Canon Began: Working Models and Open Questions," in Finkelberg and Strousma (2003) 28–51.

———. 2016. "Collections, Canons, and Communities," in Chapman and Sweeney (2016) 28–54.

——— and Marvin A. Sweeney, eds. 2016. *The Cambridge Companion to the Hebrew Bible/Old Testament*. Cambridge.

Cherbonnier, E. La B. 1962. "The Logic of Biblical Anthropomorphism." *The Harvard Theological Review* 55:187–206.

Childs, Brevard S. 1985. *Old Testament Theology in a Canonical Context*. Philadelphia.

Choksy, Jamseed K. 2012. "Justifiable Force and Holy War in Zorastrianism," in Renard (2012) 158–76.

Churchland, Patricia. 2013. *Touching a Nerve*. New York.

Cimino, Richard and Christopher Smith. 2010. "The New Atheism and the Empowerment of American Freethinkers," in *Religion and the New Atheism: A Critical Appraisal*, Amarnath Amarasingam, ed. Leiden:139–56.

Clark, Elizabeth A. 1992. *The Origenist Controversy: The Cultural Construction of an Early Christian Debate*. Princeton.

Clarke, Michael. 1999. *Flesh and Spirit in the Songs of Homer: A Study of Words and Myths*. Oxford.

Clarke, Steve, Russell Powell, and Julian Savulescu, eds. 2013. *Religion, Intolerance, and Conflict: A Scientific and Conceptual Investigation*. Oxford.

Clauss, James. J., Martine Cuypers, and Ahuvia Kahane, eds. 2016. *The Gods of Greek Hexameter Poetry: From the Archaic Age to Late Antiquity and Beyond*. Stuttgart.

Clay, Diskin. 1992. "The World of Hesiod." *Ramus* 21:131–55.

Clay, Jenny Strauss. 1974. "Demas and Aude: The Nature of Divine Transformation in Homer." *Hermes* 102:129–36.

———. 1981–2. "Immortal and Ageless Forever." *CJ* 77:112–17.

———. 1983. *The Wrath of Athena: Gods and Men in the Odyssey*. Lanham.

———. 1989. *The Politics of Olympus: Form and Meaning in the Major Homeric Hymns*. Princeton.

———. 2003. *Hesiod's Cosmos*. Cambridge.

———. 2011. *Homer's Trojan Theater*. Cambridge.

———. 2016. "The Justice of Zeus in the *Theogony*," in Clauss, Cuypers, and Kahane (2016) 21–31.

Clements, Ronald E. 2000. "Achan's Sin: Warfare and Holiness," in Penchansky and Reddit (2000) 113–26.

———. 2007. "Monotheism and the God of Many Names," in Gordon (2007) 47–59.

Clifford, Richard S.J. 1992. "Creation in the Psalms," in Clifford and Collins (1992) 57–69.

———. 1994. *Creation Accounts in the Ancient Near East and in the Bible*. Washington, DC.

——— and John J. Collins, eds. 1992. *Creation in the Biblical Traditions*. Washington, DC.

Clines, David J.A. 1989. *Job 1–20*. (World Biblical Commentary Vol. 17). Dallas.

———. 2011. *Job 38–42*. (World Biblical Commentary Vol. 18b). Dallas.

Cliteur, Paul. 2010. *The Secular Outlook: In Defense of Moral and Political Secularism*. West Sussex.

Coffey, Michael. 1957. "The Function of the Homeric Simile." *AJP* 78:113–132.

Cohen, David. 1986. "The Theodicy of Aeschylus: Justice and Tyranny in the *Oresteia*." *Greece and Rome* 33:129–41.

Collins, Derek. 2002. "Reading the Birds: Oionomanteia in Early Epic." *Colby Quarterly* 38:17–41.

Collins, John J. 2003. "The Zeal of Phinehas: The Bible and the Legitimation of Violence." *JBL* 122:3–21.

Coogan, Michael David. 1987. "Canaanite Origins and Lineage: Reflections on the Religion of Ancient Israel," in Miller, Hanson, and McBride (1987) 115–24.

———. 2010. *God and Sex: What the Bible Really Says*. New York.

———. 2014. *The Ten Commandments: A Short History of an Ancient Text*. New Haven.

Cook, Irwin F. 1995. *The Odyssey in Athens: Myths of Cultural Origins*. Ithaca.

Cooper, Alan. 1990. "Reading and Misreading the Prologue to Job." *JSOT* 46:67–79.

Coote, Robert B., and David Robert Ord. 1991. *In the Beginning: Creation and the Priestly History*. Minneapolis.

Copan, Paul. 2011. *Is God a Moral Monster? Making Sense of the Old Testament God*. Grand Rapids.

——— and William Lane Craig. 2004. *Creation Out of Nothing: A Biblical, Philosophical, and Scientific Exploration*. Leicester.

Cotter, David W. 2003. *Genesis*. Collegeville.

Coyne, Jerry A. 2015. *Faith versus Fact: Why Science and Religion Are Incompatible*. New York.

Craig, William Lane. 1979. *The Kalâm Cosmological Argument*. London.

———. 2008. *Reasonable Faith: Christian Truth and Apologetics*. 3rd ed. Wheaton, IL.

Crenshaw, James L. 1984. *A Whirlpool of Torment: Israelite Traditions of God as an Oppressive Presence*. Philadelphia.

———. 1992. "When Form and Content Clash: The Theology of Job 38:1–40:5," in Clifford and Collins (1992) 70–84.

———. 2005. *Defending God: Biblical Responses to the Problems of Evil*. Oxford.

Cross, Frank Moore. 1973. *Canaanite Myth and Hebrew Epic: Essays in the History of the Religion of Israel*. Cambridge.

Crotty, Kevin. 1994. *The Poetics of Supplication: Homer's Iliad and Odyssey*. Ithaca.

Crouch, Carly L. 2009. *War and Ethics in the Ancient Near East: Military Violence in Light of Cosmology and History*. Berlin.

———. 2016. "Ethics," in Barton (2016a) 338–55.

Curley, Edwin. 2007. "On Becoming a Heretic," in Antony (2007a) 80–9.

Curran, Charles E., ed. 2003. *Change in Official Catholic Moral Teachings*. New York.

Currie, Bruno. 2005. *Pindar and the Cult of Heroes*. Oxford.

Dacey, Austin. 2009. "The Accidental Exorcist," in Blackford and Schülenk (2009) 182–6.

Dahood, Mitchel S.J. 1966. *Psalms I 1–50: Introduction, Translation, and Notes*. (Anchor Bible Vol. 16). Garden City, NY.

———. 1968. *Psalms II 51–100: Introduction, Translation, and Notes*. (Anchor Bible Vol. 17). Garden City, NY.

D'Alessio, Giambattista. 2015. "*Theogony* and *Titanomachy*," in Fantuzzi and Tsagalis (2015) 199–212.

Daley, Brian E. 1991. *The Hope of the Early Church: A Handbook of Patristic Eschatology*. Cambridge.

———. 2004. "Death, Afterlife, and Other Last Things: Christianity," in Johnston (2004) 493–5.

Darr, Katheryn Pfisterer. 1992. "Ezekiel's Justifications of God: Teaching Troubling Texts." *JSOT*:97–117.

Davidson, Richard M. 2007. *Flame of Yahweh: Sexuality in the Old Testament*. Peabody, MA.

Davies, Eryl W. 2010. *The Immoral Bible: Approaches to Biblical Ethics*. London.

Davies, Malcolm. 1981. "The Judgement of Paris and *Iliad* Book XXIV." *JHS* 101:56–62.

Davies, Philip R. 1995. *Whose Bible Is It Anyway?* Sheffield.

———. 2015. *The History of Ancient Israel: A Guide for the Perplexed*. London.

Davis, Stephen T. 2015. *After We Die: Theology, Philosophy, and the Question of Life after Death*. Waco.

Dawkins, Richard. 2006. *The God Delusion*. Boston.

Day, John. 1985. *God's Conflict with the Dragon and the Sea: Echoes of a Canaanite Myth in the Old Testament*. Cambridge.

———. 2000. *Yahweh and the Gods and Goddesses of Canaan*. Sheffield.

Day, Linda. 2000. "Rhetoric and Domestic Violence in Ezekiel 16." *Biblical Interpretation* 8:205–30.

Debono, Amber, Sarah Poole, Azim F. Shariff, and Mark Muraven. 2017. "Forgive Us Our Trespasses: Priming a Forgiving (But Not a Punishing) God Increases Unethical Behavior." *Psychology of Religion and Spirituality* 9.Suppl. 1:Sa-S10.

Decety, Jean, Jason M. Cowell, Kang Lee, Randa Mahasneh, Susan Malcolm-Smith, Bilge Selcuk, and Xinyue Zhou. 2015. "The Negative Association between Religiousness and Children's Altruism across the World." *Current Biology* 25:2951–55.

De Hamel, Christopher. 2001. *The Book: A History of the Bible*. London.

de Moor, Johannes C. 1997. *The Rise of Yahwism: The Roots of Israelite Monotheism*. Leuven.

Delaney, Carol. 1998. *Abraham on Trial: The Social Legacy of Biblical Myth*. Princeton.

Dempsey, Carole J. 1998. "The 'Whore' Ezekiel 16: The Impact and Ramifications of Gender-Specific Metaphors in Light of Biblical Law and Divine Judgment," in *Gender and Law in the Hebrew Bible and the Ancient Near East*, Victor H. Matthews, Bernard M. Levinson, and Titkva Frymer-Kensky, eds. Sheffield:57–78.

Dennett, Daniel C. 2006. *Breaking the Spell: Religion as a Natural Phenomenon*. New York.

Dever, William G. 2005. *Did God Have a Wife? Archaeology and Folk Religion in Ancient Israel*. Grand Rapids.

————. 2017. *Beyond the Texts: An Archaeological Portrait of Ancient Israel and Judah.* Atlanta.

Dietrich, Bernard C. 1965. *Death, Fate and the Gods: The Development of a Religious Idea in Greek Popular Belief and in Homer.* London.

————. 1979. "Views of Homeric Gods and Religion." *Numen* 26:129–51.

————. 1997. "From Knossos to Homer," in *What Is a God? Studies in the Nature of Greek Divinity*, Alan B. Lloyd, ed. London:1–13.

Dietrich, Wendell S., Theodore Vial, and Mark A. Hadley, eds. 2001. *Ethical Monotheism, Past and Present: Essays in Honor of Wendell S. Dietrich.* Providence, RI.

Dijk-Hemmes, Fokkelien van. 1993. "The Metaphorization of Woman in Prophetic Speech: An Analysis of Ezekiel 23," in *On Gendering Texts: Female and Male Voices in the Hebrew Bible*, Athalya Brenner and Fokkelien van Dijk-Hemmes, eds. Leiden:167–76.

Dijkstra, Meindert. 2001a. "I Have Blessed You By YHWH of Samaria and His Asherah: Texts with Religious Elements from the Soil Archive of Ancient Israel," in Becking et al. (2001) 17–43.

————. 2001b. "El, the God of Israel: Israel, the People of YHWH: On the Origins of Ancient Israelite Yahwism," in Becking et al. (2001) 81–126.

Di Vito, Robert A. 1992. "The Demarcation of Divine and Human Realms in Genesis 2–11," in Clifford and Collins (1992) 39–56.

Dodds, Eric R. 1951. *The Greeks and the Irrational.* Berkeley.

Doniger, Wendy. 2008. "You Can't Get Here from There: The Logical Paradox of Ancient Indian Creation Myths," in Geller and Schipper (2008) 87–102.

Dowden, Ken. 2007. "Olympian Gods, Olympian Pantheon," in Ogden (2007) 41–55.

Dozeman, Thomas B. 2015. *Joshua 1–2: A New Translation with Introduction and Commentary.* (The Anchor Yale Bible Vol. 6B.). New Haven.

———— and Konrad Schmid, eds. 2006. *A Farewell to the Yahwist? The Composition of the Pentateuch in Recent European Interpretation.* Atlanta.

Drange, Theodore M. 1998. *Nonbelief & Evil: Two Arguments for the Nonexistence of God.* Amherst.

Dreyfus, Hubert L. and Sean Kelly. 2011. *All Things Shining: Reading the Western Classics to Find Meaning in a Secular Age.* New York.

DuBois, Page. 2014. *A Million and One Gods: The Persistence of Polytheism.* Cambridge, MA.

Duff, Nancy J. 2004. "Should the Ten Commandments Be Posted in the Public Realm? Why the Bible and the Constitution Say, 'No'," in Brown (2004) 159–70.

Dulles, Avery. 2003. "Catholicism and Capital Punishment," in Curran (2003) 132–44.

Dunbar, Robin I.M. 2013. "The Origin of Religion as a Small-Scale Phenomenon," in Clarke et al. (2013) 48–66.

Durant, William. 1992. *The Age of Faith.* Norwalk, CT.

Dworkin, Ronald. 2011. *Justice for Hedgehogs.* Cambridge.

————. 2013. *Religion without God.* Cambridge.

Edelman, Diana V., ed. 1996. *The Triumph of Elohim: From Yahwisms to Judaisms.* Grand Rapids.

————. 2010. "Cultic Sites and Complexes beyond the Jerusalem Temple," in Stavrakopoulou and Barton (2010a) 82–103.

Edwards, Anthony T. 1985. "Achilles in the Underworld: *Iliad, Odyssey*, and *Aethiopis.*" *GRBS* 26:215–27.

Edwards, Mark W. 1987. *Homer: Poet of the Iliad.* Baltimore.

————. 1991. *The Iliad: A Commentary. Vol. V: Books 17–20.* Cambridge.

————. 2005. "Homer's *Iliad*," in Foley (2005) 302–14.

Edwards, Paul. 1967. "Atheism," in *The Encyclopedia of Philosophy*. Vol. 1. New York:174–89.

Ehnmark, Erland. 1935. *The Idea of God in Homer*. Uppsala.

Ehrman, Bart D. 2008. *God's Problem: How the Bible Fails to Answer Our Most Important Question: Why We Suffer*. New York.

————. 2009. *Jesus, Interrupted: Revealing the Hidden Contradictions in the Bible (and Why We Don't Know about Them)*. New York.

————. 2011. *Forged: Writing in the Name of God: Why the Bible's Authors Are Not Who We Think They Are*. New York.

————. 2014. *How Jesus Became God: The Exaltation of a Jewish Preacher from Galilee*. New York.

Eilberg-Schwartz, Howard. 1994. *God's Phallus and Other Problems for Men and Monotheism*. Boston.

Ekroth, Gunnel. 2007. "Heroes and Hero-Cults," in Ogden (2007) 100–14.

————. 2011. "Meat for the Gods," in *'Nourrir les dieux?' Sacrifice et representation du divin*, Vinciane Pirenne-Delforge and Francesca Prescendi, eds. Liège:15–41.

Eller, Jack David. 2010. *Cruel Creeds, Virtuous Violence: Religious Violence across Culture and History*. Amherst.

Ellwood, Gracia Fay. 1988. *Batter My Heart*. Wallingford.

Elmer, David F. 2013. *The Poetics of Consent: Collective Decision Making and the Iliad*. Baltimore.

Emerton, John A., ed. 1988. *Congress Volume: Jerusalem 1986*. Leiden.

Emlyn-Jones, Chris. 1992. "The Homeric Gods: Poetry, Belief and Authority," in *Homer: Readings and Images*, C. Emlyn-Jones, L. Hardwick, and J. Purkis, eds. London:91–103.

Evans, Christopher F. 1983. "Resurrection," in Richardson and Bowden (1983) 501–3.

Everitt, Nicholas. 2004. *The Non-Existence of God*. New York.

Exum, J. Cheryl. 1992. *Tragedy and Biblical Narrative: Arrows of the Almighty*. Cambridge.

Ezzati, Majid, Ari B. Friedman, Sandeep C. Kulkarni, and Christopher J.L. Murray. 2008. "The Reversal of Fortunes: Trends in County Mortality and Cross-County Mortality Disparities in the United States." *PLoS Medicine* April 5.4:0057-0568.

Fales, Evan. 2005. "Reformed Epistemology and Biblical Hermeneutics," in Price and Lowder (2005) 469–89.

Fantuzzi, Marco and Christos Tsagalis, eds. 2015. *The Greek Epic Cycle and Its Ancient Reception: A Companion*. Cambridge.

Feeney, Denis C. 1991. *The Gods in Epic*. Oxford.

Fenik, Bernard. 1974. *Studies in the Odyssey*. Wiesbaden.

Fergusson, David. 2014. *Creation*. Grand Rapids.

Ferré, Frederick and R. Ferré. 1984. "In Praise of Anthropomorphism." *International Journal for Philosophy of Religion* 16:203–212.

Feser, Edward. 2013. "The New Atheists and the Cosmological Argument," in *The New Atheism and Its Critics*. (Midwest Studies in Philosophy, Vol. 37). P.A. French and H.K. Wettstein, eds. Boston:154–77.

Festugière, Andre-Jean. 1952. *Personal Religion among the Greeks*. Berkeley.

Fewell, Danna Nolan, and David M. Gunn. 1993. *Gender, Power, and Promise: The Subject of the Bible's First Story*. Nashville.

Finkelberg, Margalit. 2005. *Greeks and Pre-Greeks: Aegean Prehistory and Greek Heroic Tradition*. Cambridge.

————, ed. 2011. *The Homer Encyclopedia*. 3 Vols. West Sussex.

———. 2015. "Meta-Cyclic Epic and Homeric Poetry," in Fantuzzi and Tsagalis (2015) 126–38.

——— and Guy G. Stroumsa, eds. 2003. *Homer, the Bible, and beyond: Literary and Religious Canons in the Ancient World*. Leiden.

Firestone, Reuven. 2012. "A Brief History of War in the Hebrew Bible and the Jewish Interpretive Tradition," in Renard (2012) 29–54.

Fishbane, Michael. 2003. *Biblical Myth and Rabbinic Mythmaking*. Oxford.

Flanagan, Owen. 2013. "The View from the East Pole: Buddhist and Confucian Tolerance," in Clarke et al. (2013) 201–20.

Flew, Antony. 1987. *The Logic of Mortality*. Oxford.

Flower, Michael A. 2008. *The Seer in Ancient Greece*. Berkeley.

Foley, Johns Miles, ed. 2005. *A Companion to Ancient Epic*. Malden, MA.

Fontaine, Carole R. 1995. "A Response to 'Hosea'," in Brenner (1995) 60–9.

Ford, Andrew. 1992. *Homer: The Poetry of the Past*. Ithaca.

———. 1996. "Review of Irwin Cook's *The Odyssey in Athens: Myths of Cultural Origins*." *BMCR* 96.04:27.

Ford, David. 2007. *Christian Wisdom: Desiring God and Learning in Love*. Cambridge.

Forsyth, Neil. 1987. *The Old Enemy: Satan and the Combat Myth*. Princeton.

Fortner, Barry V. and Robert A. Neimeyer. 1999. "Death Anxiety in Older Adults: A Quantitative Review." *Death Studies* 23:387–411.

Fowler, Robert L, ed. 2004. *The Cambridge Companion to Homer*. Cambridge.

———. 2010. "Gods in Early Greek Historiography," in Bremmer and Erskine (2010) 318–34.

Fox, Robin Lane. 1992. *The Unauthorized Version: Truth and Fiction in the Bible*. New York.

———. 2008. *Travelling Heroes: Greeks and Their Myths in the Epic Age of Homer*. New York.

Fränkel, Hermann. 1997. "Essence and Nature of the Homeric Similes," in *Homer: German Scholarship in Translation*, G.M Wright and P.V. Jones, eds. and trs. Oxford:103–23.

Frayne, Douglas. 2013. "The Fifth Day of Creation in Ancient Syrian and Neo-Hittite Art," in Scurlock and Beal (2013) 63–97.

French, Peter A. and Howard K. Wettstein, eds. 2013. *The New Atheism and Its Critics*. (Midwest Studies in Philosophy, Vol. 37). Malden, MA.

Frendo, Anthony J. 2011. *Pre-Exilic Israel, the Hebrew Bible, and Archaeology: Integrating Text and Artefact*. New York.

Fretheim, Terence C. 1984. *The Suffering of God: An Old Testament Perspective*. Philadelphia.

———. 2002. "Theological Reflections on the Wrath of God in the Old Testament." *Horizons in Biblical Theology* 24:1–26.

———. 2004. "God and Violence in the Old Testament." *Word & World* 24:18–28.

———. 2010. *Creation Untamed: The Bible, God, and Natural Disasters*. Grand Rapids.

Freud, Sigmund. 1961. *The Future of an Illusion*. J. Strachey, tr. New York.

Friedman, Richard Elliott. 1997. *The Hidden Face of God*. San Francisco.

———. 2001. "Divine Dissension in the Narrative of the *Iliad*." *Helios* 28:99–118.

——— and Shawna Dolansky. 2011. *The Bible Now*. Oxford.

Friedrich, Rainer. 1991. "The Hybris of Odysseus." *JHS* 111:16–28.

———. 2011. "Justice," in Finkelberg (2011) Vol. 2:427–8.

Frymer-Kensky, Tikva. 1992. *In the Wake of the Goddesses: Women, Culture, and the Biblical Transformation of Pagan Myth*. New York.

Fuchs, Esther. 2016. *Feminist Theory and the Bible: Interrogating the Sources*. Lanham.

Gagné, Renaud. 2013. *Ancestral Fault in Ancient Greece*. Cambridge.

Gaifman, Milette. 2012. *Aniconism in Greek Antiquity*. Oxford.

Galambush, Julie. 1992. *Jerusalem in the Book of Ezekiel: The City as Yahweh's Wife*. Atlanta.

Gantz, Timothy. 1993. *Early Greek Myth: A Guide to Literary and Artistic Sources*. Baltimore.

Garber, Daniel. 2007. "Religio Philosophi," in Antony (2007a) 32–40.

Garcia, Hector A. 2015. *Alpha God: The Psychology of Religious Violence and Oppression*. Amherst.

Gardiner, Martin. 2000. *Did Adam Have a Navel? Debunking Pseudoscience*. New York.

Garland, Robert. 2001. *The Greek Way of Death*. 2nd ed. Ithaca.

Garr, W. Randall. 2003. *In His Own Image and Likeness: Humanity, Divinity, and Monotheism*. Leiden.

Geller, Markham J. and Mineke Schipper, eds. 2008. *Imagining Creation*. Leiden.

Geller, Stephen A. 2000. "The God of the Covenant," in Porter (2000a) 273–319.

Gerhards, Meik. 2015. *Homer und die Bibel: Studien zur Interpretation der Ilias und ausgewählter alttestamentlicher Texte*. Göttingen.

Gerstenberger, Erhard S. 1996. *Yahweh the Patriarch: Ancient Images of God and Feminist Theology*. F.J. Gaiser, tr. Minneapolis.

Gertz, Jan Christian. 2012. "The Formation of the Primeval History," in *The Book of Genesis: Composition, Reception, and Interpretation*, Craig A. Evans, Joel N. Lohr, and David L. Petersen, eds. Leiden:107–35.

Gervais, Will M. 2013. "In Godlessness We Distrust: Using Social Psychology to Solve the Puzzle of Anti-Atheist Prejudice." *Social and Personal Psychology* 7:366–77.

———. 2014. "Everything Is Permitted? People Intuitively Judge Immorality as Representative of Atheists." *PloS One* April 9.9:e92302.

——— and Ara Noranzayan. 2013. "Religion and the Origins of Anti-Atheist Prejudice," in Clarke (2103) 126–45.

Gibson, Jeffrey C.L. 1998. *Language and Imagery in the Old Testament*. Peabody, MA.

Gnuse, Robert Karl. 1997. *No Other Gods: Emergent Monotheism in Israel*. Sheffield.

Goldenberg, David M. 2003. *The Curse of Ham: Race and Slavery in Early Judaism, Christianity, and Islam*. Princeton.

Goldenberg, Robert. 1998. *The Nations That Know Thee Not: Ancient Jewish Attitudes towards Other Religions*. New York.

Goldingjay, John. 2016. "The Theology of the Hebrew Bible/Old Testament," in Chapman and Sweeney (2016) 466–82.

Gomes, Peter J. 1996. *The Good Book: Reading the Bible with Mind and Heart*. New York.

Goodblatt, David M. 2006. *Elements of Ancient Jewish Nationalism*. Cambridge.

Gordon, Cyrus H. 1955. *Homer and Bible: The Origin and Character of Eastern Mediterranean Literature*. Ventnor, NJ.

Gordon, Robert P., ed. 2007a. *The God of Israel*. Cambridge.

———. 2007b. "Introducing the God of Israel," in Gordon (2007a) 3–19.

Gottschall, Jonathan. 2008. *The Rape of Troy: Evolution, Violence, and the World of Homer*. Cambridge.

Gottstein, Alon Goshen. 1994. "The Body as Image of God in Rabbinic Literature." *The Harvard Theological Review* 87:171–95.

Gould, John. 1985. "On Making Sense of Greek Religion," in *Greek Religion and Society*. P.E. Easterling and J.V. Muir, eds. Cambridge:1–33.

Grabbe, Lester L. 2007. *Ancient Israel: What Do We Know and How Do We Know It?* London.

———, ed. 2011a. *Enquire of the Former Age: Ancient Historiography and Writing the History of Israel.* New York.

———. 2011b. "The Big Max: Review of *A Biblical History of Israel,* by Iain Provan, V. Philips Long, and Tremper Longman, III," in Grabbe (2011a) 215–34.

———. 2018. *Faith & Fossils: The Bible, Creation, & Evolution.* Grand Rapids.

Graetz, Naomi. 1995. "God Is To Israel as Husband Is to Wife: The Metaphoric Battering of Hosea's Wife," in Brenner (1995) 126–45.

Gray, John. 2018. *Seven Types of Atheism.* New York.

Gray, Kurt and Daniel M. Wegner. 2010. "Blaming God for Our Pain: Human Suffering and the Divine Mind." *Personality and Social Psychology Review* 14:7–16.

Grayling, Anthony Clifford. 2010. *Against All Gods: Six Polemics on Religion and an Essay on Kindness.* London.

———. 2013. *The God Argument: The Case Against Religion and for Humanism.* New York.

Graziosi, Barbara and Johannes Haubold. 2005. *Homer: Resonance of Epic.* London.

Green, Alberto Ravinell Whitney. 2003. *The Storm-God in the Ancient Near East.* Winona Lake.

Greenberg, Jeff, Jamie Arndt, Jeff Schimel, Tom Pyszczynski, and Sheldon Solomon. 2001. "Clarifying the Function of Mortality Salience-Induced Worldview Defense: Renewed Suppression or Reduced Accessibility of Death-Related Thoughts?" *Journal of Experimental Social Psychology* 37:70–76.

Greenberg, Moshe. 1983. *Ezekiel 1–20.* (The Anchor Bible Vol. 22). New York.

———. 1997. *Ezekiel 21–37.* (The Anchor Bible Vol. 22A). New York.

Greene-McCreight, Kathryn. 2004. "Restless Until We Rest in God: The Fourth Commandment as Test Case in Christian 'Plain Sense' Interpretation," in Brown (2004) 223–36.

Greenspahn, Frederick E. 2016. "The Hebrew Bible in Judaism," in Chapman and Sweeney (2016) 375–87.

Gregory, Andrew. 2007. *Ancient Greek Cosmogony.* London.

Grenz, Stanley J. 2001. *The Social God and the Relational Self: A Trinitarian Theology of the Imago Dei.* Louisville.

Grethlein, Jonas. 2008. "Memory and Material Objects in the *Iliad* and the *Odyssey.*" *JHS* 128:27–51.

Griffin, Carl W., and David L. Paulsen. 2002. "Augustine and the Corporeality of God." *The Harvard Theological Review* 95:97–118.

Griffin, Jasper. 1980. *Homer on Life and Death.* Oxford.

———. 1986. "Homeric Words and Speakers." *JHS* 106:36–57.

Griffiths, J. Gwyn. 1991. *The Divine Verdict: A Study of Divine Judgement in the Ancient Religions.* Leiden.

Gudorf, Christine E. 2003. "Encountering the Other: The Modern Papacy on Women," in Curran (2003) 269–84.

Guthrie, Stewart. 1993. *Faces in the Clouds: A New Theory of Religion.* Oxford.

Gutteridge, Richard. 1976. *Open Thy Mouth for the Dumb!: The German Evangelical Church and the Jews, 1879–1950.* Oxford.

Gutting, Gary. 2013. "Religious Agnosticism," in French and Wettsetin (2013) 51–67.

Habgood, John. 1983. "Creation," in Richardson and Bowden (1983) 129–30.

Hackett, Jo Ann. 1987. "Religious Traditions in Israelite Transjordan," in Miller, Hanson, and McBride (1987) 128–36.

Hadley, Judith M. 2000. *The Cult of Asherah in Ancient Israel and Judah: Evidence for a Hebrew Goddess.* Cambridge.

———. 2007. "The De-Deification of Deities in Deuteronomy," in Gordon (2007) 157–74.

Haft, Adele J. 1992. "'tà Dè Nûn Pánta Teleîtai': Prophecy and Recollection in the Assemblies of *Iliad* 2 and *Odyssey* 2." *Arethusa* 25.2:223–40.

Haidt, Jonathan. 2012. *The Righteous Mind: Why Good People Are Divided by Politics and Religion.* New York.

Hainsworth, Bryan. 1988. *A Commentary on Homer's Odyssey. Vol. I. Introduction and Books I–VIII.* Oxford.

———. 1993. *The Iliad: A Commentary. Vol. III: Books 9–12.* Cambridge.

Hall, Deborah L., David C. Matz, and Wendy Wood. 2010. "Why Don't We Practice What We Preach? A Meta-Analytic Review of Religious Racism." *Personality and Social Psychology Review* 14:126–39.

Hall, Douglas John. 1986. *Imaging God: Dominion as Stewardship.* Grand Rapids.

Halpern, Baruch. 1983. *The Emergence of Israel in Canaan.* Chico.

———. 1987. "'Brisker Pipes Than Poetry': The Development of Israelite Monotheism," in *Judaic Perspectives on Ancient Israel.* Jacob Neusner, B.A. Levine, and E.S. Frerichs, eds. Philadelphia:77–115.

———. 2009. *From Gods to God: The Dynamics of Iron Age Cosmologies.* Matthew J. Adams, ed. Tübingen.

Hamilton, Victor P. 1990. *The Book of Genesis Chapters 1–17.* Grand Rapids, MI.

Hammes, Erico. 2009. "The Triune God versus Authoritarianism," in Borgman et al. (2009) 79–89.

Hamori, Esther J. 2008. *When Gods Were Men: The Embodied God in Biblical and Near Eastern Literature.* Berlin.

Handy, Lowell K. 1994. *Among the Host of Heaven: The Syro-Palestinian Pantheon as Bureaucracy.* Winona Lake.

———. 1996. "The Appearance of Pantheon in Judah," in Edelman (1996) 27–43.

Hanson, Victor Davis and John Heath. 1998. *Who Killed Homer? The Demise of Classical Education and the Recovery of Greek Wisdom.* New York.

Harrill, J. Albert. 2000. "The Use of the New Testament in the American Slave Controversy: A Case History in the Hermeneutical Tension between Biblical Criticism and Christian Moral Debate." *Religion and American Culture: A Journal of Interpretation* 10:149–86.

Harris, Sam. 2005. *The End of Faith: Religion, Terror, and the Future of Reason.* New York.

———. 2010. *The Moral Landscape: How Science Can Determine Human Values.* New York.

Hartung, John. 1995. "Love Thy Neighbor: The Evolution of In-Group Morality." *Skeptic* 3:86–99.

Hastings, Adrian, Alistair Mason, and Hugh S. Pyper, eds. 2000. *The Oxford Companion to Christian Thought.* Oxford.

Haubold, Johannes. 2013. *Greece and Mesopotamia: Dialogues in Literature.* Cambridge.

Hauser, Marc D. 2006. *Moral Minds: How Nature Designed Our Universal Sense of Right and Wrong.* New York.

Havelock, Eric Alfred. 1978. *The Greek Concept of Justice: From Its Shadow in Homer to Its Substance in Plato.* Cambridge.

Hawes, Greta. 2014. *Rationalizing Myth in Antiquity.* Oxford.

Hayes, Zachary. 1989. *Visions of a Future: A Study of Christian Eschatology.* Wilmington.

Haynes, Stephen R. 2002. *Noah's Curse: The Biblical Justification of American Slavery.* Oxford.

Heath, John. 1992. "The Legacy of Peleus: Death and Divine Gifts in the *Iliad*." *Hermes* 120:387–400.

———. 2005a. "Are Homer's Trojans 'Hyper'?" *Mnemosyne* 58:531–39.

———. 2005b. "Blood for the Dead: Homeric Ghosts Speak Up." *Hermes* 133:389–400.

———. 2005c. *The Talking Greeks: Speech, Animals, and the Other in Homer, Aeschylus, and Plato*. Cambridge.

Hebblethwaite, Brian. 2000. "Immortality," in Hastings et al. (2000) 320–1.

Hedges, Christ. 2009. *When Atheism Becomes Religion*. New York.

Heiden, Bruce. 2008. *Homer's Cosmic Fabrication: Choice and Design in the Iliad*. Oxford.

Heider, George C. 1999. "Tannin," in Van der Toorn et al. (1999) 834–36.

Hendel, Ronald S. 1997. "Aniconism and Anthropomorphism in Ancient Israel," in Van der Toorn (1997) 205–28.

———. 1998. *The Text of Genesis 1–11: Textual Studies and Critical Edition*. New York.

———. 1999. "Serpent," in Van der Toorn et al. (1999) 744–7.

———. 2017. "God and Gods in the Tetrateuch," in Oorschot and Witte (2017) 239–66.

Henrichs, Albert. 2010. "What Is a Greek God?," in Bremmer and Erskine (2010) 19–39.

Hermission, Hans-Jürgen. 1984. "Observations on the Creation Theology in Wisdom," in Anderson (1984) 118–34.

Herrmann, Wolfram. 1999. "Rider Upon the Clouds," in Van der Toorn et al. (1999) 703–5.

Hess, Richard S. 2007. *Israelite Religions: An Archaeological and Biblical Survey*. Grand Rapids.

Heubeck, Alfred. 1988. *A Commentary on Homer's Odyssey. Vol. II: Books IX–XVI*. Oxford.

Hick, John. 1976. *Death and Eternal Life*. New York.

———. 1978. *Evil and the God of Love*. New York.

Hiers, Richard H. 2009. *Justice and Compassion in Biblical Law*. New York.

Hitch, Sarah. 2009. *King of Sacrifice: Ritual and Royal Authority in the Iliad*. Cambridge, MA.

Hitchens, Christopher. 2007. *God Is Not Great: How Religion Poisons Everything*. New York.

——— and Jacques del Conte. 2010. "The New Commandments." *Vanity Fair*. March 4, accessed at www.vanityfair.com/news/2010/04/hitchens-201004

Hofreiter, Christian. 2012. "Genocide in Deuteronomy and Christian Interpretation," in *Interpreting Deuteronomy: Issues and Approaches*, David G. Firth and Philip S. Johnston, eds. Downers Grove, IL:240–62.

Holmes, David L. 2006. *The Faiths of the Founding Fathers*. Oxford.

Hopkins, Keith. 2000. *A World Full of Gods: The Strange Triumph of Christianity*. New York.

Howard-Snyder, Daniel, ed. 1996. *The Evidential Argument from Evil*. Bloomington.

Hume, David. 1964. *Hume on Religion*. Richard Wollheim, ed. Cleveland.

Humphreys, W. Lee. 1985. *The Tragic Vision and the Hebrew Tradition*. Philadelphia.

———. 2001. *The Character of God in the Book of Genesis: A Narrative Appraisal*. Louisville.

Hutton, Jeremy H. 2010. "Southern, Northern and Transjordanian Perspectives," in Stavrakopoulou and Barton (2010a) 149–74.

Isichei, Elizabeth. 2000. "Millenarianism," in Hastings et al. (2000) 435–6.

Jaeger, Werner. 1945. *Paedeia: The Ideals of Greek Culture. Vol. I: Archaic Greece: The Mind of Athens*. 2nd ed. Gilbert Highet, tr. New York.

Janko, Richard. 1992. *The Iliad: A Commentary. Vol. IV: Books 13–16*. Cambridge.

Jebb, Richard C. 1889. *Bentley*. London.

Jenkins, Everett. 2003. *The Creation: Secular, Jewish, Catholic, Protestant, and Muslim Perspectives Analyzed.* Jefferson.

Jenkins, Philip. 2010. *Jesus Wars: How Four Patriarchs, Three Queens, and Two Emperors Decided What Christians Would Believe for the Next 1,500 Years.* New York.

Jensen, Gary F. 2006. "Religious Cosmologies and Homicide Rates among Nations: A Closer Look." *JR&S* 8:1–14.

Jerryson, Michael. 2013. "Buddhist Traditions and Violence," in *The Oxford Handbook of Religion and Violence*, Mark Juergensmeyer, Margo Kitts, and Michael Jerryson, eds. Oxford:41–66.

Johnson, Dominic D.P. 2005. "Public Goods: A Test of the Supernatural Punishment Hypothesis in 186 World Cultures." *Human Nature* 16:410–46.

———. 2015. *God Is Watching You: How the Fear of God Makes Us Human.* Oxford.

——— and Zoey Reeve. 2013. "The Virtues of Intolerance: Is Religion an Adaptation for War?," in Clarke et al. (2013) 67–87.

Johnson, Larry, and Scott Baldyga. 2009. *Frozen: My Journey into the World of Cryonics, Deception, and Death.* New York.

Johnson, Sylvester A. 2004. *The Myth of Ham in Nineteenth-Century American Christianity: Race, Heathens, and the People of God.* New York.

Johnston, Philip S. 2002. *Shades of Sheol: Death and Afterlife in the Old Testament.* Downers Grove, IL.

Johnston, Sarah Iles. 1999. *The Restless Dead: Encounters between the Living and the Dead in Ancient Greece.* Berkeley.

———, ed. 2004. *Religions of the Ancient World: A Guide.* Cambridge.

Jong, Irene J.F. de. 1987. *Narrators and Focalizers: The Presentation of the Story in the Iliad.* Amsterdam.

———. 1988. "Homeric Words and Speakers: An Addendum." *JHS* 108:188–9.

———. 1997. "Narrator Language versus Character Language: Some Further Explorations," in *Hommage À Milman Parry: Le Style Formulaire de L'épopée Homérique et La Théorie de L'oralité Poétique*, Francoise Létoublon, ed. Amsterdam:293–302.

———. 2001. *A Narratological Commentary on the Odyssey.* Cambridge.

Jonsson, Gunnlaugur. 1988. *The Image of God: Genesis 1:26–28 in a Century of Old Testament Research.* Stockholm.

Joyce, Paul M. 2011. "Ezekiel," in Lieb, Mason, and Roberts (2011) 64–76.

Kahan, Dan M. 2017. "Misconceptions, Misinformation, and the Logic of Identity-Protective Cognition." *The Cultural Cognition Project.* Working Paper No. 164.

Kahneman, Daniel. 2011. *Thinking, Fast and Slow.* New York.

Kaiser, Otto. 2000. "Deus Absconditus and Deus Revelatus: Three Difficult Narratives in the Pentateuch," in Penchansky and Reddit (2000) 73–88.

Kamionkowski, S. Tamar. 2003. *Gender Reversal and Cosmic Chaos: A Study in the Book of Ezekiel.* Sheffield.

Kang, Sa-Moon. 1989. *Divine War in the Old Testament and in the Ancient Near East.* Berlin.

Katz, Leonard D., ed. 2000. *Evolutionary Origins of Morality: Cross-Disciplinary Perspectives.* Bowling Green, OH.

Kaufmann, Walter. 1963. *The Faith of a Heretic: What Can I Believe? How Should I Live? What Do I Hope?* Garden City, NY.

Kearns, Emily. 1982. "The Return of Odysseus: A Homeric Theoxeny." *CQ* 32:2–8.

———. 2004. "The Gods in the Homeric Epics," in Fowler (2004) 59–73.

———— and Simon R.F. Price, eds. 2003. *The Oxford Dictionary of Classical Myth and Religion*. Oxford.

Keel, Othmar and Christoph Uehlinger. 1998. *Gods, Goddesses, and Images of God in Ancient Israel*. A.W. Mahnke, tr. Minneapolis.

Kekes, John. 1990. *Facing Evil*. Princeton.

Kelemen, Deborah and Evelyn Rosset. 2009. "The Human Function Compunction: Teleological Explanation in Adults." *Cognition* 111:138–43.

Kelly, Adrian. 2008. "The Babylonian Captivity of Homer: The Case of the ΔΙΟΣ ΑΠΑΤΗ." *Rheinisches Museum für Philologie* 151:259–304.

Kelly, Henry A. 2006. *Satan*. Cambridge.

Kelly, John N.D. 1972. *Early Christian Creeds*. New York.

Kertzer, David I. 2018. *The Pope Who Would Be King: The Exile of Pius IX and the Emergence of Modern Europe*. New York.

Kessels, Antonius H.M. 1978. *Studies on the Dream in Greek Literature*. Utrecht.

Kimball, Charles. 2002. *When Religion Becomes Evil*. San Francisco.

Kirk, G.S. 1985. *The Iliad: A Commentary. Vol. I: Books 1–4*. Cambridge.

————. 1990. *The Iliad: A Commentary. Vol. II: Books 5–8*. Cambridge.

Kirsch, Jonathan. 2005. *God against the Gods: The History of the War between Monotheism and Polytheism*. New York.

————. 2006. *A History of the End of the World: How the Most Controversial Book in the Bible Changed the Course of Western Civilization*. San Francisco.

Kitts, Margo. 1994. "Two Expressions for Human Mortality in the Epics of Homer." *History of Religions* 34:132–51.

————. 2005. *Sanctified Violence in Homeric Society: Oath-Making Rituals and Narratives in the Iliad*. New York.

Klein, Linda Kay. 2018. *Pure: Inside the Evangelical Movement That Shamed a Generation of Young Women and How I Broke Free*. New York.

Kloos, Carola. 1986. *Yhwh's Combat with the Sea: A Canaanite Tradition in the Religion of Ancient Israel*. Leiden.

Knafl, Anne K. 2014. *Forming God: Divine Anthropomorphism in the Pentateuch*. Winona Lake.

Knox, Bernard M.W. 1964. *The Heroic Temper: Studies in Sophoclean Tragedy*. Berkeley.

Knust, Jennifer Wright. 2006. *Abandoned to Lust: Sexual Slander and Ancient Christianity*. New York.

————. 2011. *Unprotected Texts: The Bible's Surprising Contradictions about Sex and Desire*. New York.

Koch, Klaus. 1983. "Is There a Doctrine of Retribution in the Old Testament?," in *Theodicy in the Old Testament*, James L. Crenshaw, ed. Philadelphia:57–87.

————. 2007. "Ugaritic Polytheism and Hebrew Monotheism in Isaiah 40–55," in Gordon (2007) 205–28.

Koenen, Ludwig. 1994. "Greece, the Near East, and Egypt: Cyclic Destruction in Hesiod and the Catalogue of Women." *TAPA* 124:1–34.

Kofoed, Jeans Bruun. 2005. *Text and History: Historiography and the Study of the Biblical Text*. Winona Lake, IN.

Konaris, Michael D. 2016. *The Greek Gods in Modern Scholarship: Interpretation and Belief in Nineteenth and Early Twentieth Century Germany and Britain*. Oxford.

Korpel, Marjo Christina Annette. 1990. *A Rift in the Clouds: Ugaritic and Hebrew Descriptions of the Divine*. Münster.

Kramnick, Isaac and R. Laurence Moore. 1996. *The Godless Constitution: The Case against Religious Correctness*. New York.

Kratz, Reinhard G. 2016. "The Prophetic Language," in Barton (2016a) 133–59.

Kraus, Helen. 2011. *Gender Issues in Ancient and Reformation Translations of Genesis 1–4*. Oxford.

Krebernik, Manfred. 2017. "The Beginnings of Yahwism from an Assyriological Perspective," in Oorschot and Witte (2017) 45–65.

Krebs, Dennis. 2011. *The Origins of Morality: An Evolutionary Account*. Oxford.

Kruse, Kevin M. 2016. *One Nation under God: How Corporate America Invented Christian America*. New York.

Kugel, James L. 1998. *Traditions of the Bible: A Guide to the Bible as It Was at the Start of the Common Era*. Cambridge.

———. 2004. *The God of Old: Inside the Lost World of the Bible*. New York.

Kullman, Wolfgang. 1956. *Das Wirken der Götter in der Ilias. Untersuchungen zur Frage der Entstehung des homerischen 'Götterapparats'*. Berlin.

———. 1985. "Gods and Men in the *Iliad* and the *Odyssey*." *HSCPh* 89:1–23.

Laato, Antti and Johannes Cornelis de Moor, eds. 2003. *Theodicy in the World of the Bible*. Leiden.

La Due, William J. 2004. *The Trinity Guide to Eschatology*. New York.

Laffine, Josephine. 2009. "What Happened to the Last Judgment in the Early Church?," in *The Church, the Afterlife and the Fate of the Soul*, Peter Clarke and Tony Claydon, eds. Rochester:20–30.

Lambert, Wilfred G. 1988. "Old Testament Mythology in Its Ancient Near Eastern Context," in Emerton (1988) 124–43.

———. 2008. "Mesopotamian Creation Stories," in Geller and Schipper (2008) 14–59.

Lamberton, Robert. 1986. *Homer the Theologian: Neoplatonist Allegorical Reading and the Growth of the Epic Tradition*. Berkeley.

Lang, Bernhard. 1983. *Monotheism and the Prophetic Minority: An Essay in Biblical History and Sociology*. Sheffield.

———. 1988. "Life after Death in the Prophetic Promise," in Emerton (1988) 144–56.

———. 2002. *The Hebrew God: Portrait of an Ancient Deity*. New Haven.

Lang, Mabel. 1989. "Unreal Conditions in Homeric Narrative." *GRBS* 30:5–26.

Lanzillotta, F. Lautaro Roig. 2010. "Christian Apologists and Greek Gods," in Bremmer and Erskine (2010) 442–64.

Larson, Jennifer. 2007. "A Land Full of Gods: Nature Deities in Greek Religion," in Ogden (2007) 57–70.

Larue, Gerald A. 1983. *Sex and the Bible*. Buffalo.

Lateiner, Donald. 1997. "Homeric Prayer." *Arethusa* 30:242–72.

———. 2004. "The *Iliad*: An Unpredictable Classic," in Fowler (2004) 11–30.

Lee, Dionys J.N. 1964. *The Similes of the Iliad and the Odyssey Compared*. Parkville.

Leeming, David Adams. 2010. *Creation Myths of the World: An Encyclopedia*. Santa Barbara.

Lefkowitz, Mary R. 2003. *Greek Gods, Human Lives: What We Can Learn from Myths*, New Haven.

Lemaire, André. 1998. *The Israelites in History and Tradition*. Louisville.

———. 2007. *The Birth of Monotheism: The Rise and Disappearance of Yahwism*. Washington, DC.

Lemche, Niels Peter. 1998. *The Israelites in History and Tradition*. Louisville.

———. 1999. *The Canaanites and Their Land: The Tradition of the Canaanites*. Sheffield.

Lemos, Tracy M. 2015. "Dispossessing Nations: Population Growth, Scarcity, and Genocide in Ancient Israel and Twentieth-Century Rwanda," in *Ritual Violence in the Hebrew Bible*, Saul M. Olyan, ed. Oxford:27–65.

Lenowitz, Harris and Charles Doria, eds. 1976. *Origins: Creation Texts from the Ancient Mediterranean: A Chrestomathy*. Garden City, NY.

Leonard, Kathleen C., Kaye V. Cook, Chris J. Boyatzis, Cynthia Neal Kimball, and Kelly S. Flanagan. 2013. "Parent-Child Dynamics and Emerging Adult Religiosity: Attachment, Parental Beliefs, and Faith Support." *Psychology of Religion and Spirituality* 5:5–14.

Leonard, Miriam. 2012. *Socrates and the Jews: Hellenism and Hebraism from Moses Mendelssohn to Sigmund Freud*. Chicago.

Leuenberger, Martin. 2017. "YHWH's Provenance from the South: A New Evaluation of the Arguments Pro and Contra," in Oorschot and Witte (2017) 145–79.

Levaniouk, Olga. 2008. "Penelope and the Pandareids." *Phoenix* 62:5–38.

Levenson, Jon. 1988. *Creation and the Persistence of Evil: The Jewish Drama of Divine Omnipotence*. San Francisco.

———. 1993. *The Death and Resurrection of the Beloved Son: The Transformation of Child Sacrifice in Judaism and Christianity*. New Haven.

Levine, Baruch A. 1993. *Numbers 1–20: A New Translation with Introduction and Commentary*. (Anchor Bible Doubleday Vol. 4). New York.

———. 2000. *Numbers 21–36: A New Translation with Introduction and Commentary*. (Anchor Bible Doubleday Vol. 4A). New York.

Lewis, Theodore J. 1999. "Teraphim," in Van der Toorn et al. (1999) 844–50.

Liao, S. Matthew, ed. 2016. *Moral Brains: The Neuroscience of Morality*. New York.

Lieb, Michael, Emma Mason, and Jonathan Roberts, eds. 2011. *The Oxford Handbook of the Reception History of the Bible*. Oxford.

Lietzmann, Hans. 1953. *A History of the Early Church*. B.L. Woolf, tr. New York.

Linafelt, Tod. 2016. *The Hebrew Bible as Literature: A Very Short Introduction*. Oxford.

Lindholm, Jennifer A., Helen S. Astin, and Alexander W. Astin. 2006. *Spirituality and the Professoriate*. Los Angeles.

Lipton, Diana. 2007. "By Royal Appointment: God's Influence on Influencing God," in Gordon (2007) 73–93.

Liverani, Mario. 2003. *Israel's History and the History of Israel*. London.

Lloyd, Alan B., ed. 1997. *What Is a God? Studies in the Nature of Greek Divinity*. London.

Lloyd-Jones, Hugh. 1971. *The Justice of Zeus*. Berkeley.

Loader, William. 2010. *Sexuality in the New Testament: Understanding the Key Texts*. London.

Loewen, James W. 2007. *Lies My Teacher Told Me: Everything Your American History Textbook Got Wrong*. New York.

Loftus, John W., ed. 2010a. *The Christian Delusion: Why Faith Fails*. Amherst, NY.

———. 2010b. "What We've Got Here Is a Failure to Communicate," in Loftus (2010a) 181–206.

———. 2012. *Why I Became an Atheist: A Former Preacher Rejects Christianity*. Amherst.

———. 2013. *The Outsider Test for Faith: How To Know Which Religion is True*. Amherst.

Long, Charlotte R. 1987. *The Twelve Gods of Greece and Rome*. Leiden.

López-Ruiz, Carolina. 2010. *When the Gods Were Born: Greek Cosmogonies and the Near East*. Cambridge.

Loraux, Nicole. 1994. "What Is a Goddess?," in *History of Women in the West, Volume I: From Ancient Goddesses to Christian Saints*, Pauline Schmitt Pantel, ed. Cambridge:11–44.

Louden, Bruce. 1993. "Pivotal Contrafactuals in Homeric Epic." *Classical Antiquity* 12:181–98.

———. 2005. "The Gods in Epic, or the Divine Economy," in Foley (2005) 90–104.

———. 2006. *The Iliad: Structure, Myth, and Meaning.* Baltimore.

———. 2011. *Homer's Odyssey and the Near East.* Cambridge.

Louth, Andrew. 2009. "The Six Days of Creation According to the Greek Fathers," in Barton and Wilkinson (2009) 39–55.

Lowe, Nicholas J. 2000. *The Classical Plot and the Invention of Western Narrative.* Cambridge.

Lüdemann, Gerd. 1997. *The Unholy in Holy Scripture: The Dark Side of the Bible.* John Bowden, tr. Louisville.

Lynn-George, Michael. 1996. "Structures of Care in the *Iliad.*" *CQ* 46:1–26.

Lyons, Deborah. 1997. *Gender and Immortality: Heroines in Ancient Greek Myth and Cult.* Princeton.

MacArthur, John. 2013. *The Glory of Heaven: The Truth about Heaven, Angels, and Eternal Life.* 2nd ed. Wheaton, IL.

MacDonald, Dennis Ronald. 2000. *The Homeric Epics and the Gospel of Mark.* New Haven.

MacDonald, Nathan. 2012. *Deuteronomy and the Meaning of 'Monotheism'.* 2nd ed. Tübingen.

Machinist, Peter. 2011. "How Gods Die, Biblically and Otherwise: A Problem of Cosmic Restructuring," in Pongratz-Leisten (2011a) 189–240.

MacLeod, Colin W. 1982. *Homer: Iliad Book XXIV.* Cambridge.

Madigan, Kevin and Jon Douglas Levenson. 2008. *Resurrection: The Power of God for Christians and Jews.* New Haven.

Marks, Jim. 2008. *Zeus in the Odyssey.* Cambridge, MA.

Marlow, Hilary. 2016. "The Human Condition," in Barton (2016a) 293–312.

Marshall, David and Lucinda Mosher, eds. 2014. *Death, Resurrection, and Human Destiny: Christian and Muslim Perspectives.* Washington, DC.

Martin, Dale B. 2006. *Sex and the Single Savior: Gender and Sexuality in Biblical Interpretation.* Louisville.

Martin, Michael. 1990. *Atheism: A Philosophical Justification.* Philadelphia.

———. 1991. *The Case against Christianity.* Philadelphia.

———. 2002. *Atheism, Morality, and Meaning.* Amherst.

———, ed. 2008. *The Cambridge Companion to Atheism.* New York.

——— and Ricki Monnier, eds. 2003. *The Impossibility of God.* Amherst.

Martin, Richard P. 2016. "Poseidon in the *Odyssey,*" in Clauss, Cuypers, and Kahane (2016) 76–94.

Martínez, Florentin Garcia and Gerard P. Luttkhiuzen, eds. 1998. *Interpretations of the Flood.* Leiden.

May, Gerhard. 2004. *Creatio Ex Nihilo: The Doctrine of 'Creation out of Nothing' in Early Christian Thought.* A.S. Worrall, tr. London.

McCarter, P. Kyle, Jr. 1984. *II Samuel: A New Translation with Introduciton, Notes and Commentary.* (Anchor Bible Doubleday Vol. 9). Garden City, New York.

———. 1987. "Aspects of Religion of the Israelite Monarchy: Biblical and Epigraphic Data," in Miller, Hanson, and McBride (1987) 137–55.

McClain-Jacobson, Colleen, Barry Rosenfeld, Anne Kosinski, Hayley Pessin, James E. Cimino, and William Breitbart. 2004. "Belief in an Afterlife, Spiritual Well-Being and End-of-Life Despair in Patients with Advanced Cancer." *General Hospital Psychiatry* 26:484–6.

McDannell, Colleen and Bernhard Lang. 1988. *Heaven: A History*. New Haven.

McGinn, Bernard, John J. Collins, and Stephen J. Stein, eds. 2003. *The Continuum History of Apocalypticism*. New York.

McGrath, Alister E. 2011. *Christian Theology: An Introduction*. 5th ed. West Sussex.

———. 2015. *Christianity: An Introduction*. 3rd ed. Chichester.

McInerney, Peter K. 1992. *Introduction to Philosophy*. New York.

McKeown, James. 2008. *Genesis*. Grand Rapids.

McKinsey, Claud Dennis. 1995. *The Encyclopedia of Biblical Errancy*. Amherst, NY.

Meeks, Wayne. 1993. *The Origins of Christian Morality: The First Two Centuries*. Yale.

Mehta, Hermant. 2015. Friendly Atheist Blog, accessed at http://2015/08/21/atheists-now-make-up-0-1-of-the-federal-prison-population/

Meier, Samuel A. 1999. "Angel of Yahweh," in Van der Toorn et al. (1999) 53–9.

Melanchthon, Monica J. 2001. *Rejection by God: The History and Significance of the Rejection Motif in the Hebrew Bible*. New York.

Melvin, David. 2013. "Making All Things New (Again): Zephaniah's Eschatological Vision of a Return to Primeval Time," in Scurlock and Beal (2013) 269–81.

Mermelstein, Ari and Shalom E. Holtz, eds. 2014. *The Divine Courtroom in Comparative Perspective*. Leiden.

Mettinger, Tryggve N.D. 1995. *No Graven Image? Israelite Aniconism in Its Ancient Near Eastern Context*. Stockholm.

———. 1997. "Israelite Aniconism: Developments and Origins," in Van der Toorn (1997) 173–204.

———. 1999. "Cherubim," in Van der Toorn et al. (1999) 189–92.

Meyers, Carol L. 1988. *Discovering Eve: Ancient Israelite Women in Context*. New York.

Meyers, Eric M. and John Rogerson. 2008. "The World of the Hebrew Bible," in *The Cambridge Companion to the Bible*, Bruce Chilton, H.C. Kee, A.-J. Levine, E.M. Meyers, J. Rogerson, and A.J. Saldarini, eds. Cambridge:39–325.

Middleton, J. Richard. 2004. "Violent God? The Ethical Problem of the Conquest of Chaos in Biblical Creation Texts." *Interpretation* 58:341–55.

———. 2005. *The Liberating Image: The Imago Dei in Genesis 1*. Grand Rapids.

Midgley, Mary. 1994. *The Ethical Primate: Humans, Freedom, and Morality*. London.

Mielczarek, Eugenie V. and Brian D. Engler. 2012. "Measuring Mythology: Startling Concepts in NCAAM Grants." *Skeptical Inquirer* 36:35–43.

Mikalson, Jon D. 2005. *Ancient Greek Religion*. Malden, MA.

Miles, Jack. 1995. *God: A Biography*. New York.

Milgrom, Jacob. 1991. *Leviticus 1–16: A New Translation with Introduction and Commentary*. (Anchor Bible Doubleday Vol. 3). New York.

———. 2000a. *Leviticus 17–22: A New Translation with Introduction and Commentary*. (Anchor Bible Doubleday Vol. 3A). New York.

———. 2000b. *Leviticus 23–27: A New Translation with Introduction and Commentary*. (Anchor Bible Doubleday Vol. 3B). New York.

Miller, Patrick D. 1973. *The Divine Warrior in Early Israel*. Cambridge, MA.

———. 2000. *The Religion of Ancient Israel*. London.

———. 2009. *The Ten Commandments*. Louisville.

———, Paul D. Hanson, and S. Dean McBride, eds. 1987. *Ancient Israelite Religion: Essays in Honor of Frank Moore Cross*. Philadelphia.

Mills, Donald H. 2002. *The Hero and the Sea: Patterns of Chaos in Ancient Myth*. Wauconda.

Minchin, Elizabeth. 2011. "The Words of Gods: Divine Discourse in Homer's *Iliad*," in *Sacred Words: Orality, Literacy and Religion*, M.G.M. Poel, André Lardinois, and Josine Blok, eds. Leiden:15–36.

Mirto, Maria Serana. 2012. *Death in the Greek World: From Homer to the Classical Age.* Norman.

Mitchell, Stephen and Peter van Nuffelen, eds. 2010. *One God: Pagan Monotheism in the Roman Empire.* Cambridge.

Moberly, R. Walter L. 2007. "Is Monotheism Bad for You? Some Reflections on God, the Bible, and Life in the Light of Regina Schwartz's *The Curse of Cain*," in Gordon (2007) 94–112.

———. 2016. "Theological Approaches to the Old Testament," in Barton (2016a) 480–506.

Mollenkott, Virginia R. 1983. *The Divine Feminine: The Biblical Imagery of God as Female.* New York.

Mondi, Robert. 1984. "The Ascension of Zeus and the Composition of Hesiod's *Theogony*." *GRBS* 25:325–44.

———. 1986. "Tradition and Innovation in the Hesiodic Titanomachy." *TAPA* 116:25–48.

Montefiore, Claude G., J. Edwin Odgers, and Solomon Schechter. 1890. "The Doctrine of Divine Retribution in the Old Testament, the New Testament, and the Rabbinical Literature." *The Jewish Quarterly Review* 3:1–51.

Moreno-Riaño, Gerson, Mark Caleb Smith, and Thomas Mach. 2006. "Religiosity, Secularism, and Social Health: A Research Note." *JR&S* 8:1–10.

Morris, Ian. 1989. "Attitudes toward Death in Archaic Greece." *CA* 8:296–320.

———. 2001. "The Use and Abuse of Homer," in *Oxford Readings in Homer's Iliad*, Douglas L. Cairns, ed. Oxford:57–91.

——— and Barry Powell, eds. 1997. *A New Companion to Homer.* Leiden.

Morrison, James V. 1991. "The Function and Context of Homeric Prayers: A Narrative Perspective." *Hermes* 119:145–57.

———. 1992. *Homeric Misdirection: False Predictions in the Iliad.* Ann Arbor.

Morrow, William. 2004. "Post-Traumatic Stress Disorder and Vicarious Atonement in the Second Isaiah," in *Psychology and the Bible, Vol. 1: From Freud to Kohut*, J. Harold Ellens and Wayne G. Rollins, eds. Westport. Vol. 1:167–85.

Most, Glenn W. 2003. "Anger and Pity in Homer's *Iliad*," in *Ancient Anger: Perspectives from Homer to Galen*. (Yale Classical Studies Volume XXXII), Susanna Braund and Glenn W. Most, eds. Cambridge:50–75.

Moulton, Carroll. 1977. *Similes in the Homeric Poems.* Göttingen.

Mueller, Martin. 1984. *The Iliad.* London.

Muffs, Yochanan. 2005. *The Personhood of God: Biblical Theology, Human Faith, and the Divine Image.* Woodstock.

Mullen, E. Theodore. 1980. *The Divine Council in Canaanite and Early Hebrew Literature.* Chico.

Müller, Reinhard. 2017. "The Origins of YHWH in Light of the Earliest Psalms," in Oorschot and Witte (2017) 207–38.

Murnaghan, Sheila. 1987. *Disguise and Recognition in the Odyssey.* Princeton.

———. 1995. "The Plan of Athena," in *The Distaff Side: Representing the Female in Homer's Odyssey*, Beth Cohen, ed. New York:41–80.

Mussies, Gerard. 1999. "Giants," in Van der Toorn (1999) 343–5.

Nafisi, Azar. 2003. *Reading Lolita in Tehran: A Memoir in Books.* New York.

Nagy, Gregory. 1979. *The Best of the Achaeans: Concepts of the Hero in Early Greek Poetry*. Baltimore.

———. 1994. *Pindar's Homer: The Lyric Possession of an Epic Past*. 1982. Baltimore.

Neusner, Jacob. 1992. *The Incarnation of God: The Character of Divinity in Formative Judaism*. Atlanta.

Newheiser, Anna-Kaisa, Miles Hewstone, Alberto Voci, Katharian Schmid, Andreas Zick, and Beate Küpper. 2013. "Social-Psychological Aspects of Religion and Prejudice: Evidence from Survey and Experimental Research," in Clarke et al. (2013) 107–25.

Newsom, Carole A., Sharon H. Ringe, and Jacqueline E. Lapsley, eds. 2012. *Women's Bible Commentary*. 3rd ed. Louisville.

Niditch, Susan. 1985. *Chaos to Cosmos: Studies in Biblical Patterns of Creation*. Chico.

———. 1993. *War in the Hebrew Bible: A Study in the Ethics of Violence*. New York.

———. 2010. "Experiencing the Divine: Heavenly Visits, Earthly Encounters and the Land of the Dead," in Stavrakopoulou and Barton (2010a) 11–22.

Niehr, Herbert. 1996. "The Rise of YHWH in Judahite and Israelite Religion: Methodological and Religio-Historical Aspects," in Edelman (1996) 45–72.

———. 1997. "In Search of YHWH's Cult Statue in the First Temple," in Van der Toorn (1997) 73–95.

———. 1999. "Host of Heaven," in Van der Toorn et al. (1999) 428–30.

———. 2010. "'Israelite' Religion and 'Canaanite' Religion," in Stavrakopoulou and Barton (2010a) 23–36.

Nielsen, Kai. 1973. *Ethics without God*. Buffalo, NY.

Nimis, Stephen A. 1987. *Narrative Semiotics in the Epic Tradition: The Simile*. Bloomington.

Noegel, Scott B. 2007. *Nocturnal Ciphers: The Allusive Language of Dreams in the Ancient Near East*. New Haven.

Nogales, José Luis Sánchez. 2009. "The Unity of Revealed Law: The Torah and the Koran," in Borgman et al. (2009) 34–42.

Noll, Kurt L. 2013. "Presumptuous Prophets Participating in a Deuteronomic Debate," in Boda and Beal (2013) 125–42.

Noonan, John T., Jr. 2003. "Development in Moral Doctrine," in Curran (2003) 287–305.

Noort, Ed. 1998. "The Stories of the Great Flood: Notes on Gen 6:5–9:17 in Its Context of the Ancient Near East," in Martínez and Luttikhuizen (1998) 1–38.

———. 2005. "Balaam the Villain: The History of Reception of the Balaam Narrative in the Pentateuch and the Former Prophets," in van Kooten and van Ruiten (2005) 3–23.

Norenzayan, Ara. 2013. *Big Gods: How Religion Transformed Cooperation and Conflict*. Princeton.

———, Azim F. Shariff, Will M. Gervais, Aiyana K. Willard, Rita A McNamara, Edward Slingerland, and Joseph Henrich. 2016. "The Cultural Evolution of Prosocial Religions." *Behavioral and Brain Sciences* 39:1–65.

Norris, Pippa and Ronald Inglehart. 2011. *Sacred and Secular: Religion and Politics Worldwide*. 2nd ed. Cambridge.

Nowacki, Mark R. 2007. *The Kalam Cosmological Argument for God*. Amherst.

O'Brien, Joan V. 1993. *The Transformation of Hera: A Study of Ritual, Hero, and the Goddess in the Iliad*. (Greek Studies). Lanham.

——— and Wilfred Major. 1982. *In the Beginning: Creation Myths from Ancient Mesopotamia, Israel, and Greece*. Chico.

Odell, Margaret S. and John T. Strong, eds. 2000. *The Book of Ezekiel: Theological and Anthropological Perspectives*. Atlanta.

Ogden, Daniel, ed. 2007. *A Companion to Greek Religion*. Malden, MA.

Oishi, Shigehiro, and Ed Diener. 2014. "Residents of Poor Nations Have a Greater Sense of Meaning in Life Than Residents of Wealthy Nations." *Psychological Science* 25:422–30.

Olson, S. Douglas. 1995. *Blood and Iron: Stories and Storytelling in Homer's Odyssey*. Leiden.

O'Neill, John C. 1983. "Wrath of God," in Richardson and Bowden (1983) 606–7.

Oorschot, Jürgen van and Markus Witte, eds. 2017. *The Origins of Yahwism*. Berlin.

Otto, Walter F. 1964. *The Homeric Gods: The Spiritual Significance of Greek Religion*. Moses Hadas, tr. New York.

Pagels, Elaine. 1996. *The Origin of Satan*. New York.

Paine, Thomas. 1794. *The Age of Reason*. Paris.

Pakkala, Juha. 1999. *Intolerant Monolatry in the Deuteronomistic History*. Helsinki.

———. 2017. "The Origins of Yahwism from the Perspective of Deuteronomism," in Oorschot and Witte (2017) 267–81.

Paper, Jordan D. 2005. *The Deities Are Many: A Polytheistic Theology*. Albany.

Parenti, Michael. 2010. *God and His Demons*. Amherst.

Parker, Robert. 2005. *Polytheism and Society at Athens*. Oxford.

———. 2011. *On Greek Religion*. Ithaca.

———. 2017. *Greek Gods Abroad: Names, Natures, and Transformations*. Berkeley.

Parker, Simon B. 1999a. "Council," in Van der Toorn et al. (1999) 204–8.

———. 1999b. "Sons of (the) God(s)," in Van der Toorn et al. (1999) 794–800.

Pasquale, Frank L. 2010. "A Portrait of Secular Group Affiliates," in Zuckerman (2010a) 43–87.

Patai, Raphael. 1990. *The Hebrew Goddess*. 3rd ed. Detroit.

Patton, Corinne. 1996. "'I Myself Gave Them Laws That Were Not Good': Exekiel 20 and the Exodus Traditions." *JSOT* 69:73–90.

———. 2000. "'Should Our Sister Be Treated Like a Whore?' A Response to Feminist Critiques of Ezekiel 23," in Odell and Strong (2000) 221–38.

Patton, Laurie L. 2012. "The Failure of Allegory: Notes on Textual Violence and the Bhagavad Gita," in Renard (2012) 177–99.

Paul, Gregory S. 2005. "Cross-National Correlations of Quantifiable Societal Health with Popular Religiosity and Secularism in the Prosperous Democracies: A First Look." *Journal of Religion & Society* 7:1–17.

———. 2009a. "The Chronic Dependence of Popular Religiosity Upon Dysfunctional Psychosociological Conditions." *Evolutionary Psychology* 7:398–41.

———. 2009b. "Theodicy's Problem: A Statistical Look at the Holocaust of the Children, and the Implications of Natural Evil for the Free Will and Best of All Worlds Hypotheses." *Philosophy & Theology* 19:125–49.

Paulsen, David L. 1990. "Early Christian Belief in a Corporeal Deity: Origen and Augustine as Reluctant Witnesses." *The Harvard Theological Review* 83:105–16.

Peckham, Brian. 1987. "Phoenicia and the Religion of Israel: The Epigraphic Evidence," in Miller, Hanson, and McBride (1987) 79–99.

Pedrick, Victoria. 1982. "Supplication in the *Iliad* and *Odyssey*." *TAPA* 112:125–40.

Pelliccia, Hayden. 1995. *Mind, Body, and Speech in Homer and Pindar*. Göttingen.

Penchansky, David. 2005. *Twilight of the Gods: Polytheism in the Hebrew Bible*. Louisville.

——— and Paul L. Reddit, eds. 2000. *Shall Not the Judge of All the Earth Do What Is Right? Studies on the Nature of God in Tribute to James L. Crenshaw*. Windona Lake.

Penglase, Charles. 1994. *Greek Myths and Mesopotamia: Parallels and Influence in the Homeric Hymns and Hesiod*. London.

Penner, Hans H. 1989. *Impasse and Resolution: A Critique of the Study of Religion*. New York.

Perdue, Leo G. 1994. *Wisdom & Creation: The Theology of Wisdom Literature*. Nashville.

Peterson, Brian. 2013. "Ezekiel's Perspective of Israel's History: Selective Revisionism?," in Boda and Beal (2013) 295–315.

Petrovic, Ivana. 2010. "Transforming Artemis: From the Goddess of the Outdoors to City Goddess," in Bremmer and Erskine (2010) 209–27.

PEW. 2014. http://www.pewforum.org/religious-landscape-study/compare/belief-in-absolute-standards-for-right-and-wrong/by/religious-tradition/

PEW. 2016. http://www.pewresearch.org/fact-tank/2016/11/04/the-most-and-least-educated-u-s-religious-groups/ft_16-10-06_educationreligiousgroups/

PEW. 2018. http://www.pewforum.org/2018/04/25/when-americans-say-they-believe-in-god-what-do-they-mean/

Pfeiffer, Henrik. 2017. "The Origin of YHWH and Its Attestation," in Oorschot and Witte (2017) 115–44.

Pinker, Steven. 2002. *The Blank Slate: The Modern Denial of Human Nature*. New York.

———. 2011. *The Better Angels of Our Nature: Why Violence Has Declined*. New York.

Pironti, Gabriella and Corinne Bonnet, eds. 2017. *Les dieux d'Homère: Polythéisme et poésie en Grèce ancienne*. Liège.

Pitard, Wayne T. 2013. "The Combat Myth as a Succession Story at Ugarit," in Scurlock and Beal (2013) 199–205.

Plantinga, Alvin and Michael Tooley. 2008. *Knowledge of God*. Malden, MA.

Pleins, J. David. 2003. *When the Great Abyss Opened: Classic and Contemporary Readings of Noah's Flood*. Oxford.

Podlecki, Anthony J. 1967. "Omens in the 'Odyssey'." *Greece & Rome* 14:12–23.

Pongratz-Leisten, Beate, ed. 2011a. *Reconsidering the Concept of Revolutionary Monotheism*. Winona Lake.

———. 2011b. "A New Agenda for the Study of the Rise of Monotheism," in Pongratz-Leisten (2011a) 1–40.

———. 2011c. "Divine Agency and Astralization of the Gods in Ancient Mesopotamia," in Pongratz-Leisten (2011a) 137–87.

Pope, Marvin H. 1965. *Job: Introduction, Translation, and Notes*. (Anchor Bible Vol. 15). Garden City, NY.

———. 1977. *Song of Songs: A New Translation with Introduction and Commentary*. (Anchor Bible Vol. 7C). Garden City, NY.

Porter, Barbara N., ed. 2000a. *One God or Many? Concepts of Divinity in the Ancient World*. Chebeague, ME.

———. 2000b. "The Anxiety of Multiplicity: Concepts of Divinity as One and Many in Ancient Assyria," in Porter (2000a) 211–17.

Powell, Russell and Steve Clarke. 2013. "Religion, Tolerance, and Intolerance: Views from Across the Disciplines," in Clarke (2013) 1–35.

Pressler, Carolyn. 2001. "Sexual Violence in Deuteronomic Law," in Brenner (2001a) 102–12.

Price, Robert M. 2000. *Deconstructing Jesus*. Amherst.

———. 2005. "Introduction: The Second Life of Jesus," in Price and Lowder (2005) 9–18.

———. 2016. *Blaming Jesus for Jehovah: Rethinking the Righteousness of Christianity*. Valley, WA.

——— and Jeffery Jay Lowder, eds. 2005. *The Empty Tomb: Jesus beyond the Grave*. Amherst.

Propp, William H.C. 1998. *Exodus 1–18: A New Translation with Introduction and Commentary.* (The Anchor Bible Doubleday Vol. 2). New York.

———. 2006. *Exodus 19–40: A New Translation with Introduction and Commentary.* (The Anchor Bible Doubleday Vol. 2A). New York.

Prothero, Stephen R. 2007. *Religious Literacy: What Every American Needs to Know – and Doesn't.* New York.

Provan, Iain W. 2014. *Seriously Dangerous Religion: What the Old Testament Really Says and Why It Matters.* Waco.

———, V. Philips Long, and Tremper Longman III. 2003. *A Biblical History of Israel.* Louisville, KY.

Pucci, Pietro. 1998. *The Song of the Sirens.* Lanham, MD.

———. 2002. "Theology and Poetics in the *Iliad.*" *Arethusa* 35:17–34.

Puech, Émile. 2005. "Bala'am and Deir 'Alla'," in van Kooten and van Ruiten (2005) 25–47.

Pulleyn, Simon. 1997. *Prayer in Greek Religion.* Oxford.

Pyper, Hugh S. 2000a. "Israel," in Hastings et al. (2000) 332–3.

———. 2000b. "Myth," in Hastings et al. (2000) 462–3.

———. 2000c. "Old Testament," in Hastings et al. (2000) 493–7.

———. 2000d. "Paradise," in Hastings et al. (2000) 514–5.

Queiruga, Andrés Torres. 2009. "Monotheism and Violence versus Monotheism and Universal Brother-/Sisterhood," in Borgman et al. (2009) 67–78.

Raaflaub, Kurt A. 1997. "Homeric Society," in Morris and Powell (1997) 624–48.

Rachels, James. 1971. "God and Human Attitudes." *Religious Studies* 7:325–37.

———. 1986. *The Elements of Moral Philosophy.* Philadelphia.

Ranke-Heinemann, Uta. 1990. *Eunuchs for the Kingdom of Heaven: Women, Sexuality, and the Catholic Church.* P. Heinegg, tr. New York.

———. 1994. *Putting Away Childish Things: The Virgin Birth, the Empty Tomb, and Other Fairy Tales You Don't Need to Believe to Have a Living Faith.* San Francisco.

Ratsch, Del. 2010. "Humanness in Their Hearts: Where Science and Religion Fuse," in Schloss and Murray (2010) 215–45.

Ratzinger, Joseph Cardinal. 2003. *Truth and Tolerance: Christian Belief and World Religions.* H. Taylor, tr. San Francisco.

Ready, Jonathan L. 2011. *Character, Narrator, and Simile in the Iliad.* Cambridge.

Redfield, James M. 1975. *Nature and Culture in the Iliad: The Tragedy of Hector.* Chicago.

Reece, Steve. 1993. *The Stranger's Welcome: Oral Theory and the Aesthetics of the Homeric Hospitality Scene.* Ann Arbor.

Reed, Annette Yoshiko. 2005. *Fallen Angels and the History of Judaism and Christianity: The Reception of Enochic Literature.* Cambridge.

Renard, John, ed. 2012. *Fighting Words: Religion, Violence, and the Interpretation of Sacred Texts.* Berkeley.

Rey, Georges. 2007. "Meta-Atheism: Religious Avowal as Self-Deception," in Antony (2007a) 243–65.

Richardson, Alan. 1983. "Evil," in Richardson and Bowden (1983) 193–6.

——— and John Bowden, eds. 1983. *A New Dictionary of Christian Theology.* London.

Richardson, Nicholas. 1993. *The Iliad: A Commentary, Vol. VI: Books 21–24.* Cambridge.

———, ed. 2010. *Three Homeric Hymns.* Cambridge.

Richardson, Scott Douglas. 1990. *The Homeric Narrator.* Nashville.

Ridley, Matt, ed. 1996. *The Origins of Virtue: Human Instincts and the Evolution of Cooperation.* London.

Rinon, Yoav. 2008. *Homer and the Dual Model of the Tragic*. Ann Arbor.

Roberts, Jimmy J.M. 1988. "Does God Lie? Divine Deceit as a Theological Problem in Israelite Prophetic Literature," in Emerton (1988) 211–220.

Robinson, Richard. 1964. *An Atheist's Values*. Oxford.

Rochberg, Francesca. 2011. "The Heavens and the Gods in Ancient Mesopotamia," in Pongratz-Leisten (2011a) 117–36.

Römer, Thomas. 2006. "The Elusive Yahwist: A Short History of Research," in Dozeman and Schmid (2006) 9–27.

————. 2013. *Dark God: Cruelty, Sex, and Violence in the Old Testament*. New York.

————. 2015. *The Invention of God*. Cambridge.

————. 2016. "The Narrative Books of the Hebrew Bible," in Barton (2106a) 109–32.

Rose, Peter W. 1997. "Ideology in the *Iliad*: Polis, Basileus, Theoi." *Arethusa* 31:151–99.

Rosen, Ralph M. 1997. "Homer and Hesiod," in Morris and Powell (1997) 463–88.

Rowell, Geoffrey. 2014. "Death, Resurrection, and Human Destiny in the Christian Tradition," in Marshall and Mosher (2014) 61–71.

Rubenstein, Richard E. 1999. *When Jesus Became God: The Epic Fight over Christ's Divinity in the Last Days of Rome*. New York.

Ruse, Michael. 2013. "Making Room for Faith: Does Science Exclude Religion?," in French and Wettsetin (2013) 11–27.

Russell, Bertrand. 1992. *The Basic Writings of Bertrand Russell: 1903–1959*. Robert E. Egner and Lester E. Denonn, eds. London.

Russo, Joseph. 1992. *A Commentary on Homer's Odyssey, Vol. III: Books XVII–XXIV*. Oxford.

Rutherford, Richard B. 1982. "Tragic Form and Feeling in the *Iliad*." *JHS* 102: 145–60.

————. 2010. "Canonizing the Pantheon: The Dodekatheon in Greek Religion and Its Origins," in Bremmer and Erskine (2010) 43–54.

————. 2013. *Homer*. 2nd ed. Cambridge.

Sablosky, Roy. 2014. "Does Religion Foster Generosity?" *The Social Science Journal* 51:545–55.

Saggs, Henry W.F. 1978. *The Encounter with the Divine in Mesopotamia and Israel*. London.

Saïd, Suzanne. 2011. *Homer and the Odyssey*. Oxford.

Sale, William M. 1989. "The Trojans, Statistics, and Milman Parry." *GRBS* 30:341–410.

Sasson, Jack M. 2014. *Judges 1–12: A New Translation with Introduction and Commentary*. (The Anchor Yale Bible Vol. 6D). New Haven.

Savran, George W. 2005. *Encountering the Divine: Theophany in Biblical Narrative*. London.

Sawyer, John F. 2011. "Job," in Lieb, Mason, and Roberts (2011) 25–36.

Schäfer, Melsene. 1990. *Der Götterstreit in Der Ilias*. Stuttgart.

Schama, Simon. 2013. *The Story of the Jews: Finding the Words 1000 BC–1492 AD*. New York.

Scheid, John. 1987. "Polytheism Impossible: Or, the Empty Gods: Reasons behind a Void in the History of Roman Religion," in Schmidt (1987b) 303–25.

Schein, Seth L. 1984. *The Mortal Hero*. Berkeley.

Schloss, Jeffrey and Michael J. Murray, eds. 2010. *The Believing Primate: Scientific, Philosophical, and Theological Reflections on the Origin of Religion*. Oxford.

Schmid, Konrad. 2011. "The Quest for 'God': Monotheistic Arguments in the Priestly Texts of the Hebrew Bible," in Pongratz-Leisten (2011a) 271–89.

Schmidt, Francis, ed. 1987a. *The Inconceivable Polytheism: History and Anthropology*. Vol. 3. London.

―――. 1987b. "Polytheisms: Degeneration or Progress?," in Schmidt (1987a) 9–60.

Schneider, Laurel C. 2008. *Beyond Monotheism: A Theology of Multiplicity*. London.

Schniedewind, William M. 2004. *How the Bible Became a Book: The Textualization of Ancient Israel*. Cambridge.

Schoen, Edward L. 1990. "Anthropomorphic Concepts of God." *Religious Studies* 26:123–39.

Scholz, Susanne. 2010. *Sacred Witness: Rape in the Hebrew Bible*. Minneapolis.

―――. 2012. "Judges," in Newsom, Ringe, and Lapsley (2012) 113–27.

Schwager, Raymund S.J. 1987. *Must There Be Scapegoats? Violence and Redemption in the Bible*. M.L. Assad, tr. Cambridge.

Schwartz, Baruch J. 2000. "Ezekiel's Dim View of Israel's Restoration," in Odell and Strong (2000) 43–67.

Schwartz, Regina M. 1997. *The Curse of Cain: The Violent Legacy of Monotheism*. Chicago.

Scodel, Ruth. 1982. "The Achaean Wall and the Myth of Destruction." *HSCPh* 86:33–50.

Scott, William C. 1974. *The Oral Nature of the Homeric Simile*. Leiden.

Scurlock, Jo Ann and Richard Henry Beal, eds. 2013. *Creation and Chaos: A Reconsideration of Hermann Gunkel's Chaoskampf Hypothesis*. Winona Lake.

Seaford, Richard. 2010. "Zeus in Aeschylus: The Factor of Monetization," in Bremmer and Erskine (2010) 178–92.

Sedley, David. 2007. *Creationism and Its Critics in Antiquity*. Berkeley.

Segal, Alan F. 1977. *Two Powers in Heaven: Early Rabbinic Reports about Christianity and Gnosticism*. Leiden.

Segal, Charles. 1992. "Divine Justice in the *Odyssey*: Poseidon, Cyclops, and Helios." *AJP* 113:489–518.

Seow, Choon L. 2013. *Job 1–21: Interpretation and Commentary*. Grand Rapids.

Shariff, Azim F. 2016a. "Does Religion Increase Moral Behavior?" *Current Opinion in Psychology* 6:108–13.

―――. 2016b. "Are Wrathful Gods the Killer App of Religion? Two Nits to Pick with Johnson's God Is Watching You." *Religion and Brain Behavior* 8. doi: 10.1080/2153599X.2017.1302985.

―――, Aiyana K. Willard, Teresa Andersen, and Ara Norenzayan. 2015. "Religious Priming: A Meta-Analysis with a Focus on Prosociality." *Personality and Social Psychology Review* 20:27–48.

―――, Aiyana K. Willard, Michael Muthukrishna, Stephanie R. Kramter, and Joseph Henrich. 2016. "What Is the Association between Religious Affiliation and Children's Altruism?" *Current Biology Magazine* 26:R699–700.

Sharot, Tali. 2017. *The Influential Mind: What the Brain Reveals about Our Power to Change Others*. New York.

Shermer, Michael. 2000. *How We Believe: Science, Skepticism, and the Search For God*. 2nd ed. New York.

―――. 2004. *The Science of Good and Evil: Why People Cheat, Gossip, Care, Share, and Follow the Golden Rule*. New York.

―――. 2011. *The Believing Brain: From Ghosts and Gods to Politics and Conspiracies: How We Construct Beliefs and Reinforce Them as Truths*. New York.

―――. 2015. *The Moral Arc: How Science and Reason Lead Humanity toward Truth, Justice, and Freedom*. New York.

―――. 2018. *Heavens on Earth: The Scientific Search for the Afterlife, Immortality, and Utopia*. New York.

Shinan, Avigdor and Yair Zakovitch. 2012. *From Gods to God: How the Bible Debunked, Suppressed, or Changed Ancient Myths and Legends*. V. Zakovitch, tr. Lincoln, NB.

Singer, Peter and Marc Hauser. 2009. "Why Morality Does Not Need Religion," in Blackford and Schülenk (2009) 288–93.

Sinnott-Armstrong, Walter. 2009. *Morality without God?* Oxford.

Skjærvø, Prods Oktor. 2011. "Zarathustra: A Revolutionary Monotheist?," in Pongratz-Leisten (2011a) 317–50.

Slatkin, Laura. 1991. *The Power of Thetis: Allusion and Interpretation in the Iliad.* Berkeley.

———. 2011. "Gods," in Finkelberg (2011) Vol. 1:317–21.

Smith, Daniel L. 1989. *The Religion of the Landless: The Social Context of the Babylonian Exile.* Bloomington.

Smith, George. 1974. *Atheism: The Case against God.* Los Angeles.

Smith, Mark S. 2001. *The Origins of Biblical Monotheism: Israel's Polytheistic Background and the Ugaritic Texts.* Oxford.

———. 2002. *The Early History of God: Yahweh and the Other Deities in Ancient Israel.* 2nd ed. Grand Rapids.

———. 2004. *The Memoirs of God: History, Memory, and the Experience of the Divine in Ancient Israel.* Minneapolis.

———. 2008. *God in Translation: Deities in Cross-Cultural Discourse in the Biblical World.* Tübingen.

———. 2010. *The Priestly Vision of Genesis 1.* Minneapolis.

———. 2011. "God in Translation: Cross-Cultural Recognition of Divinity in Ancient Israel," in Pongratz-Leisten (2011a) 241–70.

———. 2014. *Poetic Heroes: Literary Commemorations of Warriors and Warrior Culture in the Early Biblical World.* Grand Rapids.

———. 2017. "YHWH's Original Character: Questions about an Unknown God," in Oorschot and Witte (2017) 23–43.

Smith, Morton. 1968. "On the Shape of God and the Humanity of Gentiles," in *Religions in Antiquity: Essays in Memory of Erwin Ramsdell Goodenough,* J. Neusner, ed. Leiden:315–26.

Solomon, Sheldon, Jeff Greenberg, and Tom Pyszczynski. 2015. *The Worm at the Core: On the Role of Death.* New York.

Sommer, Benjamin D. 2009. *The Bodies of God and the World of Ancient Israel.* Cambridge.

———. 2016. "Monotheism," in *Barton:*239–70.

Sourvinou-Inwood, Christiane. 1995. *Reading Greek Death: To the End of the Classical Period.* Oxford.

Sowell, Thomas. 2007. *A Conflict of Visions.* New York.

Sparks, Elicka Peterson. 2016. *The Devil You Know: The Surprising Link between Conservative Christianity and Crime.* Amherst.

Speiser, Ephraim A. 1964. *Genesis: Introduction, Translation, and Notes.* (Anchor Bible Vol. 1). Garden City, NY.

Sperling, S. David. 2014. "God: God in the Hebrew Scriptures," in *Encyclopedia of Religion.* 2nd ed. Vol. 5, Lindsay Jones, ed. Detroit:3527–43.

Spong, John Shelby. 2005. *The Sins of Scripture: Exposing the Bible's Texts of Hate to Reveal the God of Love.* San Francisco.

Stafford, Emma. 2010. "Herakles Between Gods and Heroes," in Bremmer and Erskine (2010) 228–44.

Stark, Rodney. 2001. *One True God: Historical Consequences of Monotheism.* Princeton.

———. 2003. *For the Glory of God: How Monotheism Led to Reformations, Science, Witch-Hunts, and the End of Slavery.* Princeton.

Stavrakopoulou, Francesca. 2004. *King Manasseh and Child Sacrifice: Biblical Distortions of Historical Realities*. Berlin.

———. 2010. "'Popular' Religion and 'Official' Religion: Practice, Perception, Portrayal," in Stavrakopoulou and Barton (2010a) 37–58.

———. 2016. "The Historical Framework," in Barton (2016a) 24–53.

——— and John Barton, eds. 2010a. *Religious Diversity in Ancient Israel and Judah*. London.

———. 2010b. "Introduction: Religious Diversity in Ancient Israel and Judah," in Stavrakopoulou and Barton (2010a) 1–10.

Stenger, Victor J. 2008. *God: The Failed Hypothesis: How Science Shows That God Does Not Exist*. Amherst.

———. 2012. *God and the Folly of Faith: The Incompatibility of Science and Religion*. Amherst.

Stern, David. 1992. "Imitatio Hominis: Anthropomorphism and the Character(s) of God in Rabbinic Literature." *Prooftexts* 12:151–74.

Stern, Ephraim. 2010. "From Many Gods to the One God: The Archaeological Evidence," in *One God-One Culture-One Nation*, Reinhard G. Kratz and H. Spiekermann, eds. Berlin:395–403.

Stern, Philip D. 1991. *The Biblical Herem: A Window on Israel's Religious Experience*. Atlanta.

Steward, Anne W. 2012. "Jephthah's Daughter and her Interpreters," in Newsom, Ringe, and Lapsley (2012) 133–7.

Stuart, Elizabeth and Adrian Thatcher. 1997. *People of Passion: What the Churches Teach about Sex*. London.

Suggs, M. Jack, Katharine Doob Sakenfeld, and James R. Mueller, eds. 1992. *The Oxford Study Bible: Revised English Bible with the Apocrypha*. New York.

Sugirtharajah, Rasiah S. 2008. *Troublesome Texts: The Bible in Colonial and Contemporary Culture*. Sheffield.

Surin, Kenneth. 1986. *Theology and the Problem of Evil*. Oxford.

Swanepoel, Michael G. 1993. "Ezekiel 16: Abandoned Child, Bride or Adorned or Unfaithful Wife?," in *Among the Prophets: Language, Image and Structure in the Prophetic Writings*, Philip R. Davies and David J.A. Clines, eds. Sheffield:84–104.

Sweeney, Marvin A. 2012. *Tanak: A Theological and Critical Introduction to the Jewish Bible*. Minneapolis.

Sykes, Nygel. 2000. "Death," in Hastings et al. (2000) 153–5.

Synodinou, Katerina. 1987. "The Threats of Physical Abuse of Hera by Zeus in the *Iliad*." *Wiener Studien* 100:13–22.

Taplin, Oliver. 1992. *Homeric Soundings: The Shaping of the Iliad*. Oxford.

Taylor, Charles. 2007. *A Secular Age*. Cambridge, MA.

Taylor, John. 2007. *Classics and the Bible: Hospitality and Recognition*. London.

Taylor, Kenneth A. 2013. "How to Vanquish the Lingering Shadow of the Long-Dead God," in French and Wettstein (2013) 68–86.

Teehan, John. 2010. *In the Name of God: The Evolutionary Origins of Religious Ethics and Violence*. Malden.

Thalmann, William G. 1992. *The Odyssey: An Epic of Return*. New York.

Thatcher, Adrian. 2008. *The Savage Text: The Use and Abuse of the Bible*. Chichester.

Thiel, Winfried. 2002. "God as Creator and Lord of Nature in the Deuteronmistic Literature," in *Creation in Jewish and Christian Tradition*, H.G. Reventlow and Y. Hoffman, eds. London:54–71.

Thrower, James. 2000. "Atheism," in Hastings et al. (2000) 49–51.

Tillich, Paul. 1948. *Shaking of the Foundations*. New York.

Timmer, Daniel. 2013. "Is Monotheism Particularly Prone to Violence? A Historical Critique." *JR&S* 15:1–15.

Tobin, Paul. 2009. *The Rejection of Pascal's Wager: A Skeptic's Guide to the Bible and the Historical Jesus*. Befordshire.

Tooley, Michael. 2009. "Helping People to Think Critically about Their Religious Beliefs," in Blackford and Schülenk (2009) 310–22.

———. 2015. "The Problem of Evil," in *The Stanford Encyclopedia of Philosophy*. Fall 2015 ed., Edward N. Zalta, ed., accessed at https://plato.stanford.edu/archives/fall2015/entries/evil/

Topalli, Volkan, Timothy Brezina, and Mindy Bernhardt. 2013. "With God on My Side: The Paradoxical Relationship between Religious Belief and Criminality among Hardcore Street Offenders." *Theoretical Criminology* 17:49–69.

Towner, W. Sibley. 2005. "Clones of God: Genesis 1:26–8 and the Image of God in the Hebrew Bible." *Interpretation* 59:341–56.

Trampedach, Kai. 2008. "Authority Disputed: The Seer in Homeric Epic," in *Practitioners of the Divine: Greek Priests and Religious Officials from Homer to Heliodorus*, Beate Dignas and Kai Trampedach, eds. Washington, DC:207–30.

Travis, Stephen H. 2009. *Christ and the Judgement of God: The Limits of Divine Retribution in New Testament Thought*. Milton Keynes, UK.

Trépanier, Simon. 2010. "Early Greek Theology: God as Nature and Natural Gods," in Bremmer and Erskine (2010) 273–317.

Trible, Phyllis. 1978. *God and the Rhetoric of Sexuality*. Philadelphia.

———. 1984. *Texts of Terror: Literary-Feminist Readings of Biblical Narratives*. Philadelphia.

Tropper, Josef. 2017. "The Divine Name *Yahwa," in Oorschot and Witte (2017) 1–21.

Tsagalis, Christos. 2008. *The Oral Palimpsest: Exploring Intertextuality in the Homeric Epics*. Washington, DC.

———. 2012. *From Listeners to Viewers: Space in the Iliad*. Washington, DC.

———. 2016. "The Gods in Cyclic Epic," in Clauss, Cuypers, and Kahane (2016) 95–117.

Tsagarakis, Odysseus. 1977. *Nature and Background of Major Concepts of Divine Power in Homer*. Amsterdam.

———. 2000. *Studies in Odyssey 11*. Stuttgart.

Tsumura, David Toshio. 2005. *Creation and Destruction: A Reappraisal of the Chaoskampf Theory in the Old Testament*. Winona Lake.

Turkeltaub, Daniel. 2007. "Perceiving Iliadic Gods." *CP* 103:51–81.

Turner, Frank M. 1997. "The Homeric Question," in Morris and Powell (1997) 123–45.

Uehlinger, Christoph. 1997. "Anthropomorphic Cult Statuary in Iron Age Palestine and the Search for Yahweh's Cult Images," in Van der Toorn (1997) 97–155.

———. 1999. "Leviathan," in Van der Toorn et al. (1999) 511–15.

Vail, Kenneth E., III and Jacob Juhl. 2015. "An Appreciate View of the Brighter Side of Terror Management Processes." *Social Sciences* 4:1020–45.

Van der Toorn, Karel, ed. 1997. *The Image and the Book: Iconic Cults, Aniconism, and the Rise of Book Religion in Israel and the Ancient Near East*. Leuven.

———, Bob Pecking, and Pieter W. van der Horst, eds. 1999. *Dictionary of Deities and Demons in the Bible*. 2nd ed. Leiden.

Van erp Tallman Kip, Anna M. 2000. "The Gods of the *Iliad* and the Fate of Troy." *Mnemosyne* 53:385–402.

Van Kooten, George H. and Jacques van Ruiten, eds. 2005. *The Prestige of the Pagan Prophet Balaam in Judaism, Early Christianity and Islam*. Leiden.

Van Seters, John. 2006. "The Report of the Yahwist's Demise Has Been Greatly Exaggerated," in Dozeman and Schmid (2006) 143–57.

Van Uchelen, Nico. 1994. "Death and the After-Life in the Hebrew Bible of Ancient Israel," in Bremer et al. (1994) 77–90.

Van Wees, Hans. 2010. "Genocide in the Ancient World," in *The Oxford Handbook of Genocide Studies*, Donald Bloxham and A. Dirk Moses, eds. Oxford:239–58.

Vardy, Peter. 2010. *Good and Bad Religion*. London.

Vergados, Athanassios. 2013. *The Homeric Hymn to Hermes: Introduction, Text and Commentary*. Berlin.

Vermeule, Emily. 1979. *Aspects of Death in Early Greek Art and Poetry*. Berkeley.

Vernant, Jean-Pierre. 1981. "Death with Two Faces," in *Mortality and Immortality: The Anthropology and Archaeology of Death*. S.C. Humphreys and Helen King, eds. London:285–91.

———. 1991. *Mortals and Immortals: Collected Essays*. F.I. Zeitlin, ed. Princeton.

Versnel, Henk S. 2000. "Thrice Three: Three Greek Experiments in Oneness," in Porter (2000a) 79–104.

———. 2011. *Coping with the Gods: Wayward Reading in Greek Theology*. Leiden.

Vriezen, Karel J.H. 2001. "Archaeological Traces of Cult in Ancient Israel," in Becking et al. (2001) 45–80.

Wakefield, Dan. 2006. *The Hijacking of Jesus: How the Religious Right Distorts Christianity and Promotes Prejudice and Hate*. New York.

Wakeman, Mary Katherine. 1973. *God's Battle with the Monster: A Study in Biblical Imagery*. Waltham.

Walker, Lenore E. 1979. *The Battered Woman*. New York.

———. 2009. *The Battered Woman Syndrome*. New York.

Walls, Neal H., ed. 2005. *Cult Image and Divine Representation in the Ancient Near East*. Boston, MA.

Walton, John H. 2009. *The Lost World of Genesis One: Ancient Cosmology and the Origins Debate*. Downers Grove.

———. 2011. *Genesis 1 as Ancient Cosmology*. Winona Lake.

Warden, John. 1971. "*Psyche* in Homeric Death-Descriptions." *Phoenix* 25:95–103.

Warrior, Robert. 1989. "Canaanites, Cowboys and Indians." *Christianity and Crisis* 49:261–5.

Wathey, John C. 2016. *The Illusion of God's Presence: The Biological Origins of Spiritual Longing*. Amherst.

Watson, Peter. 2014. *The Age of Atheists: How We Have Sought to Live Since the Death of God*. New York.

Watson, Rebecca Sally. 2005. *Chaos Uncreated: A Reassessment of the Theme of 'Chaos' in the Hebrew Bible*. Berlin.

Weeks, Stuart. 2007. "Man-Made Gods? Idolatry in the Old Testament," in *Idolatry: False Worship in the Bible, Early Judaism and Christianity*, Stephen C. Barton, ed. New York:7–22.

Weems, Renita J. 1995. *Battered Love: Marriage, Sex, and Violence in the Hebrew Prophets*. Minneapolis.

Weinfeld, Moshe. 1991. *Deuteronomy 1–11: A New Translation with Introduction and Commentary*. (Anchor Bible Doubleday Vol. 5). New York.

Wells, Steve. 2010. *Drunk with Blood: God's Killings in the Bible*. United States.

Werblowsky, Raphael J. Zwi. 1987. "Anthropomorphism," in *Encyclopedia of Religions*, M. Eliade, ed. New York.

West, Martin L. 1966. *Hesiod: Theogony*. Oxford.

———. 1988. "The Rise of Greek Epic." *JHS* 108:151–72.

———. 1997. *The East Face of Helicon: West Asiatic Elements in Greek Poetry and Myth.* Oxford.

———. 2007. *Indo-European Poetry and Myth*. Oxford.

West, Stephanie. 1988. *A Commentary on Homer's Odyssey, Vol. I: Introduction and Books I-VIII*. Oxford.

White, Ellen. 2014. *Yahweh's Council: Its Structure and Membership*. Tübingen.

White, Matthew. 2012. *The Great Big Book of Horrible Things: The Definitive Chronicle of History's 100 Worst Atrocities*. New York.

Whitman, Cedric H. 1958. *Homer and the Heroic Tradition*. Cambridge, MA.

Whitmarsh, Tim. 2015. *Battling the Gods: Atheism in the Ancient World*. New York.

Whybray, Roger N. 1996. "The Immorality of God: Reflections on Some Passages in Genesis, Job, Exodus and Numbers." *Journal for the Study of the Old Testament* 72:89–120.

———. 2000. "'Shall Not the Judge of All the Earth Do What Is Just?' God's Oppression of the Innocent in the Old Testament," in Penchansky and Reddit (2000) 1–19.

Wiebe, Donald. 1999. *The Politics of Religious Studies*. New York.

Wielenberg, Erik J. 2005. *Value and Virtue in a Godless Universe*. Cambridge.

Wiggins, Steve A. 2007. *A Reassessment of Asherah: With Further Considerations of the Goddess*. Piscataway, NJ.

Wilkinson, David. 2009. "Reading Genesis 1–3 in the Light of Modern Science," in Barton and Wilkinson (2009) 127–44.

Williams, Bernard. 1972. *Morality: An Introduction to Ethics*. New York.

———. 1985. *Ethics and the Limits of Philosophy*. Cambridge.

Williams, Peter J. 2007. "Is God Moral? On the Saul Narratives as Tragedy," in Gordon (2007) 175–89.

Williams, Rowan. 2000. "Resurrection," in Hastings et al. (2000) 616–18.

Wilson, Andrew N. 1999. *God's Funeral*. New York.

Wilson, Edward O. 1978. *On Human Nature*. Cambridge, MA.

Wilson, James Q. 1993. *The Moral Sense*. New York.

Wilson, John. 2000. *Sense and Nonsense in Homer: A Consideration of the Inconsistencies and Incoherencies in the Texts of the Iliad and the Odyssey*. Oxford.

Wink, Paul and Julia Scott. 2005. "Does Religiousness Buffer against the Fear of Death and Dying in Late Adulthood? Findings from a Longitudinal Study." *The Journals of Gerontology: Series B, Psychological Sciences and Social Sciences* 60:207–14.

Winterbottom, Michael. 1989. "Speaking of the Gods." *Greece & Rome* 36:33–41.

Wright, Christopher J.H. 2008. *The God I Don't Understand: Reflections on Tough Questions of Faith*. Grand Rapids, MI.

Wright, J. Edward. 2001. "W.F. Albright's Vision of Israelite Religion." *Near Eastern Archaeology* 65:63–8.

Wright, Nicholas T. 2014. "Death, Resurrection, and Human Destiny: Christian and Muslim Perspectives," in Marshall and Mosher (2014) 3–22.

Wright, Robert. 1994. *The Moral Animal: Why We Are the Way We Are: The New Science of Evolutionary Psychology*. New York.

———. 2009. *The Evolution of God*. New York.

Xella, Paolo. 1999. "Resheph," in Van der Toorn et al. (1999) 700–3.

Yamagata, Naoko. 1994. *Homeric Morality*. Leiden.

Yancy, George. 2017. "Christian Fundamentalists or Atheists: Who Do Progressive Christians Like or Hate More?" *JR&S* 19:1–25.

Yasumura, Noriko. 2011. *Challenges to the Power of Zeus in Early Greek Poetry*. London.

York, Michael. 2003. *Pagan Theology: Paganism as a World Religion*. New York.

Zaidman, Louise Bruit and Pauline Schmitt Pantel. 1992. *Religion in the Ancient Greek City*. P. Cartledge, tr. Cambridge.

Zanker, Graham. 1994. *The Heart of Achilles: Characterization of Personal Ethics in the Iliad*. Ann Arbor.

Zevit, Ziony. 2001. *The Religions of Ancient Israel: A Synthesis of Parallactic Approaches*. London.

Zuckerman, Miron, Jordan Silberman, and Judith A. Hall. 2013. "The Relation between Intelligence and Religiosity: A Meta-Analysis and Some Proposed Explanations." *Personality and Social Psychology Review* 17:325–54.

Zuckerman, Phil. 2008. *Society without God: What the Least Religious Nations Can Tell Use about Contentment*. New York.

———, ed. 2010a. *Atheism and Secularity, Volume 1: Issues, Concepts, and Definitions*. Santa Barbara.

———, ed. 2010b. *Atheism and Secularity, Volume 2: Global Expressions*. Santa Barbara.

———. 2014. *Living the Secular Life: New Answers to Old Questions*. New York.

Zvi, Ehud Ben. 2011. "General Observations on Ancient Israelite Histories in Their Ancient Contexts," in Grabbe (2011a) 21–39.

Index

Made in the USA
Monee, IL
22 May 2023

34251983R00236